T0297068

Federal Cloud Computing

Federal Cloud Computing

The Definitive Guide for Cloud Service Providers

Second Edition

Matthew Metheny

Technical Editor

Waylon Krush

SYNGRESS®

elsevier.com

British Library Cataloguing-in-Publication Data
A catalogue record for this book is available from the British Library

Library of Congress Cataloging-in-Publication Data
A catalog record for this book is available from the Library of Congress

ISBN: 978-0-12-809710-6

For Information on all Syngress publications
visit our website at https://www.elsevier.com

Working together
to grow libraries in
developing countries

www.elsevier.com • www.bookaid.org

Publisher: Todd Green
Acquisition Editor: Chris Katsaropoulos
Editorial Project Manager: Anna Valutkevich
Production Project Manager: Priya Kumaraguruparan
Designer: Mark Rogers

Typeset by MPS Limited, Chennai, India

This book is dedicated to my beautiful wife and amazing son.

To my dear, loving wife Erin, you make me complete.

Thank you for tirelessly standing by my side and supporting me every step of the way. There are many times in one's life where the task may seem too difficult, but having someone like you there as a guiding arm to encourage and to consult has been a blessing.

You have always been there when the times were challenging. It is with great honor to share this accomplishment with you.

To my wife, with love.

To my dear, baby boy Greyson, you are my greatest accomplishment.

Your daily smiles inspire me.

Although you are too young to read this book, I hope one day to share this with you.

To my son, I love you.

Contents

About the Author

Matthew Metheny, PMP, CISSP, CAP, CISA, CSSLP, CRISC, CCSK, is an Information Security Executive and Professional with twenty years of experience in the areas of finance management, information technology, information security, risk management, compliance programs, security operations and capabilities, secure software development, security assessment and auditing, security architectures, information security policies/processes, incident response and forensics, and application security and penetration testing.

Mr. Metheny is the Chief Information Security Officer and Director of Cyber Security Operations at the Court Services and Offender Supervision Agency (CSOSA), and is responsible for managing CSOSA's enterprise-wide information security and risk management program, and cyber security operations. Prior to joining CSOSA, Mr. Metheny was employed at the US Government Publishing Office (GPO), where he led the Agency Governance, Risk Management, and Compliance (GRC) Program and served as the Agency subject matter expert for cloud security, responsible for evaluating service provider solutions against federal and industry security standards and integrating Agency and service provider security services. Mr. Metheny was the founder and instructor at CloudSecurityTraining.com, a business unit of One Enterprise Consulting Group, LLC, which was an approved training partner with the Cloud Security Alliance (CSA). He was also the Co-Chair for the CSA CloudTrust Protocol (CTP) Working Group, a Founding Member and Member of the Board of Director for the CSA-DC Chapter which was CSA's Federal Cloud Center of Excellence, and a Founding Member of the OpenStack DC user group focused on expanding the knowledge of OpenStack within the Washington, DC metro area. Mr. Metheny received a Bachelor's degree in Computer and Information Science from the University of Maryland University College and a Master's degree in Information Assurance from University of Maryland University College. He also holds the Certified Information Systems Security Professional (CISSP), Certified in Risk and Information Systems Controls (CRISC), Certified Secure Software Lifecycle Professional (CSSLP), Certified Information Systems Auditor (CISA), Certified Authorization Professional (CAP), Project Management Professional (PMP) and Certificate in Cloud Security Knowledge (CCSK) Certifications.

About the Technical Editor

Waylon Krush is the Co-Founder and Chief Executive Officer (CEO) of Lunarline, Inc. and helped to create and serves on the Board of Directors for Warrior to Cyber Warrior (W2CW.org). Lunarline, Inc. is a successful privately held Cyber Security and Privacy Company that provide secure solutions for the Federal Government, Department of Defense (DoD), Intelligence Community (IC), and commercial corporations world-wide.

Waylon Krush has over twenty years' experience working on various projects in the management, strategy, design, architecture, collection, exploitation, monitoring, and training of telecommunications, networks, systems, and data. Mr. Krush has been a co-author of "The Definitive Guide to the C&A Transformation", the National Institutes of Standards and Technology (NIST) Special Publication (SP) 800-53A, and the CIO Council's Federal Enterprise Architecture Security and Privacy Profile (FEA-SPP) version 3.0. Mr. Krush has been featured as a cyber security SME on CNBC, Fox News, AP, NPR, and William Shatner's Moving America Forward. Mr. Krush has also been called to testify as a Subject Matter Expert (SME) on topics of cyber security before the Committee on Homeland Security U.S. House of Representatives and the Committee on Science, Space and Technology.

Foreword by William Corrington

In recent years, "cloud computing" has emerged as a model for providing information technology (IT) infrastructure, resources, and services that have the potential to drive significant value to organizations through increased IT efficiency, agility, and innovation. However, federal agencies who were early adopters of cloud computing have learned that there are many challenges and risks that must be addressed in order to realize these benefits.

These early adopters have learned that the use of a Cloud Service Provider (CSP) represents a fundamental shift in how IT assets are deployed and delivered on a day-to-day basis. Successful adoption of cloud computing requires a change in approach to (among other things) security, privacy, end-user support, operations, acquisition, and contract management. Challenges exist for CSPs as well. Many players in this emerging marketplace are new to doing business with the federal government. As a result, they not only need to learn the nuances of the federal acquisition processes, they must also address a myriad of security, privacy, and certification requirements that are specific to federal customers.

In order to mitigate these challenges and to catalyze the adoption of cloud computing within the federal government, the Federal Cloud Computing Strategy was released on February 8, 2011.

The National Institute of Standards and Technology (NIST) and the General Services Administration (GSA) have key roles in the implementation of this "Cloud First" strategy. NIST has developed a number of Special Publications that provide definitions, architectural standards, and roadmaps for cloud computing. GSA has developed the Federal Risk and Authorization Management Program (FedRAMP) to define security, auditing, continuous monitoring, and other operational requirements for federal agency use of cloud computing.

I admire the groundbreaking initiatives that have been spearheaded by NIST and GSA. And yet, these efforts have created a new landscape with its own set of twists and turns that must be navigated by both federal agencies and CSPs wishing to serve the federal marketplace. What has been missing so far is a definitive reference guide that will allow anyone with a stake in federal IT to quickly ascend the learning curve associated with the goals, objectives, implementation, and operational aspects of the Federal Cloud Computing Strategy. Mr. Metheny's book fills this gap by providing a comprehensive view of how and where cloud computing fits in the federal government and how the critical components of the Cloud First strategy will work together in a complementary fashion.

I believe that this book will prove to be an invaluable resource to anyone who needs to successfully navigate the brave new world of federal cloud computing.

CSPs will gain an understanding of the security and operational requirements that must be met in order to provide cloud-based services to federal agencies. Cloud auditors who wish to provide services to federal agencies or CSPs will learn the detailed requirements for becoming a Third Party Assessment

Organization (3PAO). Federal agency Chief Information Officers (CIOs), Chief Technology Officers (CTOs), and Chief Information Security Officers (CISOs) will benefit from greater clarity regarding the impacts that the move to cloud computing will have on their existing IT strategy and operations.

The Cloud First strategy is a critical component of broader efforts that are underway to transform federal IT in the 21st century. This book will provide excellent guidance to everyone who wishes to undertake that journey.

William Corrington

Founder and Chief Cloud Strategist, Stony Point Enterprises
(Former Chief Technology Officer at the US Department of Interior)

Foreword by Jim Reavis

Cloud computing is an epochal change in the use of technology by mankind. Broadly considered, it represents the transition toward the use of computer as a utility, with profound implications. Just as when nations became electrified, the dawn of new industries, reorganization of societies, and other unexpected outcomes are surely at our doorstep. Access to supercomputer capabilities, previously only available to small groups of people with millions of dollars, is now available to all.

The ability for individuals, small businesses, and large enterprises to have "on demand" access to a virtually unlimited supply of computer power and storage challenges our ability to innovate. From discovering new drugs to unlocking the mysteries of the universe to finding better solutions for the human condition, we are only limited by our imagination.

Governments are no different than any other organization in their propensity to be impacted by, and leverage the cloud. The very largest problems that governments face have the potential to be solved, in large part, by the cloud. Cloud will also force government agencies to be more transparent and collaborative with the information that forms the backbone of their services. At the same time, a rush to adopt cloud computing without a sound understanding of its potential and risks could prove a devastating setback. This book, "Federal Cloud Computing: The Definitive Guide for Cloud Service Providers" is a timely addition to our shared knowledge of what cloud computing is, the inherent risks, regulatory requirements, and the ecosystem of standards and best practices.

Cloud Security Alliance (CSA) is a not-for-profit organization that is the leading global force in building trust within cloud computing. We congratulate author and CSA member Matthew Metheny for his excellent contribution to the topic of cloud computing within the US federal government. We feel that this book is a must-read for anyone interested in information technology within our government. Both government consumers and providers must understand the regulatory requirements, the processes for making cloud services available, and best practices to mitigate risks and operate cloud systems securely.

Cloud computing is not only our future, but is also here today. Whatever role you play in this topic, you have a mandate to find strategies to securely adopt cloud in an agile manner. "Federal Cloud Computing: The Definitive Guide for Cloud Service Providers" is an excellent coach to help define those strategies.

Best,

Jim Reavis

Chief Executive Officer, Cloud Security Alliance

Introduction to the federal cloud computing strategy

1

INFORMATION IN THIS CHAPTER:

- Introduction
- A Historical View of Federal IT
- Cloud Computing: Drivers in Federal IT Transformation
- Decision Framework for Cloud Migration

INTRODUCTION

In February 2011, the former US Chief Information Officer (CIO), Vivek Kundra, published the *Federal Cloud Computing Strategy*, herein referred to as the "*Cloud Strategy.*"[1]

The Cloud Strategy, as illustrated in Fig. 1.1, was one of six major components of the *25 Point Implementation Plan to Reform Federal Information Technology Management*, the US CIO's roadmap to the cloud. The roadmap focused on shifting to cloud services, which can be deployed rapidly, and shared solutions that will result in substantial cost savings, allowing federal agencies to optimize spending and to reinvest in their most critical mission needs [1].

In the 25 Point Implementation Plan to Reform Federal Information Technology Management, the *Cloud First* policy, also referred to as "Cloud First," requires federal agencies to implement cloud-based solutions whenever a secure, reliable, and cost-effective cloud option existed. The publication of the *Cloud Strategy* facilitates the implementation of the Cloud First policy by initiating a program[2] to "accelerate the safe and secure adoption of cloud computing across the government" [2]. Additionally, the Cloud Strategy directs the National

---

[1]*Federal Cloud Computing Strategy.* Available from: https://www.whitehouse.gov/sites/default/files/omb/assets/egov_docs/federal-cloud-computing-strategy.pdf.

[2]From McClure D. Statement of Dr. David McClure, Associate Administrator, Office of Citizen Services and Innovative Technologies, US General Services Administration, Before the House Committee on Oversight and Government Reform Subcommittee on Government Management, Organization, and Procurement. Washington: US House of Representatives [cited December 13, 2015]. Available from: http://www.gsa.gov/portal/content/159101. *"To assist in fostering cloud computing adoption, the Federal Cloud Computing Program Management Office (PMO) was created in April 2009 at GSA."*

Federal Cloud Computing. DOI: http://dx.doi.org/10.1016/B978-0-12-809710-6.00001-9

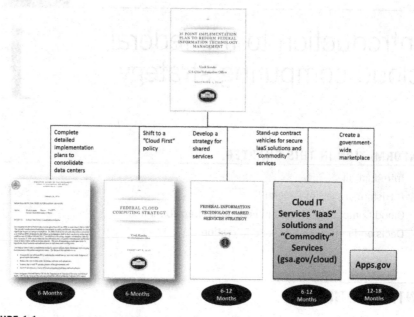

FIGURE 1.1

25 Point implementation IT reform plan—"Roadmap to the Cloud."

Institute of Standards and Technology (NIST) to lead the standards development[3] related to security, interoperability, and portability, to reduce barriers to cloud adoption by federal agencies.

In the Cloud Strategy, the US federal government's strategic approach for the adoption of cloud computing technologies was described, including the potential benefits, considerations, and trade-offs [2]. The strategy also provided a decision framework[4] for federal agencies to use in outlining their plan for using cloud computing services. The migration plans and government-wide initiatives help identify candidate cloud services to improve their efficient use of IT investments to support their missions by leveraging shared infrastructures and economies of scale. The decision framework focused on changing how federal agencies approached the acquisition and use of IT[5] and how they could effectively integrate cloud services into their IT portfolio.

---

[3]The NIST Cloud Computing Standards Working Group is discussed in detail in Chapter 2, Cloud Computing Standards.

[4]From Powner, D. *"Progress Made but Future of Cloud Computing Efforts Should Be Better Planned."* Washington, DC: US Government Accountability Office; 2012. *"The decision framework, among other things, identifies several key areas for determining the readiness for moving to a cloud environment, including the ability of the cloud service provider to address government security requirements."*

[5]From Kundra, V. *Federal Cloud Computing Strategy.* Washington, DC: Executive Office of the President, Office of Management and Budget; 2011. *"Organizations that previously thought of IT as an investment in locally owned and operated applications, servers, and networks will now need to think of IT in terms of services, commoditized computing resources, agile provisioning tools, and their enabling effect for American citizens."*

The Cloud Strategy also established a set of basic principles and guidelines through which decision-makers within federal agencies could use it to accelerate their secure adoption of cloud services. Through the strategy, federal agencies were empowered with the responsibility for making their own decision on "what" and "how" to migrate to the cloud in support of the government-wide Cloud First policy. The Cloud First policy creates the momentum for federal agencies to proactively adopt cloud computing services by requiring them to begin with the selection of three[6] "cloud-ready"[7] IT services.[8] To assist federal agencies in acquiring (procuring)[9] cloud services to meet the Cloud First policy, the US General Services Administration (GSA) through the Cloud Computing Services (CCS) Program Management Office (PMO), established contracts that federal agencies could leverage for purchasing commodity cloud services. As depicted in Fig. 1.2, Email as a Server (EaaS)[10] a commodity cloud service, was one of the most common types of IT systems migrated to the cloud.

In the section, the *Decision Framework for Cloud Migration*, a three-step framework described the foundational elements that were identified as being necessary for building a successful cloud migration plan.[11] In addition, the Cloud First policy gave federal agencies the opportunity to exercise their migration plans[12] and develop and share "lessons learned" from their experiences.

---

[6]*Agencies Have Identified 78 Systems Migrating to the Cloud.* Available from: https://cio.gov/wp-content/uploads/downloads/2012/09/IT_Reform_Agency_Cloud_Migrations_FINAL.pdf

[7]Cloud readiness was one dimension for making risk-based decisions when determining which IT service to migrate to the cloud. Readiness included factors such as security, service characteristics, market characteristics, network infrastructure, application, and data readiness, government readiness, and technology lifecycle.

[8]From Powner, D. *Progress Made but Future of Cloud Computing Efforts Should Be Better Planned.* Washington, DC: US Government Accountability Office; 2012. *"To accelerate the shift, OMB required agencies, by February 2011, to identify three IT services to be migrated to a cloud solution and develop a plan for each of the three services, migrate one of the services to a cloud-based solution by December 2011, and migrate the remaining services by June 2012."*

[9]From Federal Acquisition Regulation (FAR), Definition of Words and Terms [Internet]. Washington, DC: US General Services Administration (GSA) [cited August 27, 2012]. Available from: https://www.acquisition.gov/?q = /browse/far/2. *"'Acquisition' means the acquiring by contract with appropriated funds of supplies or services (including construction) by and for the use of the Federal Government through purchase or lease, whether the supplies or services are already in existence or must be created, developed, demonstrated, and evaluated. Acquisition begins at the point when agency needs are established and includes the description of requirements to satisfy agency needs, solicitation and selection of sources, award of contracts, contract financing, contract performance, contract administration, and those technical and management functions directly related to the process of fulfilling agency needs by contract."*

[10]*GSA Cloud IT Services.* Available from: http://www.gsa.gov/portal/content/190333.

[11]From Kundra, V. *Federal Cloud Computing Strategy.* Washington, DC: Executive Office of the President, Office of Management and Budget; 2011. *"Each migration plan includes major milestones, execution risks, adoption targets, resource requirements, and retirement plans for legacy services after the cloud service is online."*

[12]From Kundra, V. *25 Point Implementation Plan to Reform Federal Information Technology Management.* Washington, DC: Executive Office of the President, Office of Management and Budget; 2010. *"The three-party strategy on cloud computing technology will evolve around using commercial cloud technologies where feasible, launching government clouds, and utilizing regional clouds with state and local government where appropriate."*

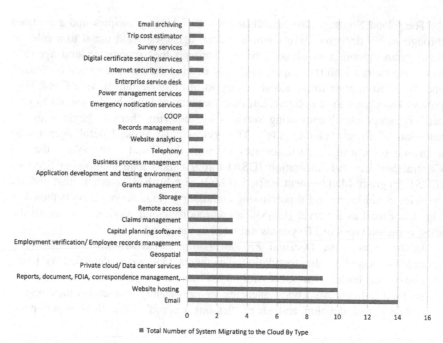

FIGURE 1.2

Total number of systems migrating to the cloud by type.

The Cloud First policy also established the requirement for a program[13] to be developed that would encourage Cloud Service Providers (CSPs) to meet federal security and privacy requirements through the development of "government-ready" (or FedRAMP compliant[14]) cloud services.[15]

The federal government has started the shift, from a traditional, asset-based model focused on acquiring IT, to a service (or utility[16])-based model, focused on

---

[13]The Federal Risk and Authorization Management Program (FedRAMP) is discussed in detail in Chapter 8, FedRAMP Primer, and Chapter 9, The FedRAMP Cloud Computing Security Requirements.

[14]*FedRAMP Compliant Systems*. Available from: http://www.fedramp.gov/marketplace/compliant-systems/.

[15]"Government-ready" cloud services refer to those that can satisfy a broad range of federal security and privacy requirements to include statutory compliance, data security, protection of privacy-related information, integrity, access controls, and governance and security management.

[16]Federal CIO Council and Chief Acquisition Officers Council. Creating effective cloud computing contracts for the federal government. Washington, DC: Executive Office of the President, Office of Management and Budget; 2012. *"Cloud computing presents the Federal Government with an opportunity to transform its IT portfolio by giving agencies the ability to purchase a broad range of IT services in a utility-based model. This allows agencies to refocus their efforts on IT operational expenditures and only pay for IT services consumed instead of buying IT with a focus on capacity. Procuring IT services in a cloud computing model can help the Federal Government to increase operational efficiencies, resource utilization, and innovation across its IT portfolio, delivering a higher return on our investments to the American taxpayer."*

consuming IT services. Cloud computing was not only a change in the technology used by federal agencies, but also a cultural change.[17] The "shift" towards cloud services required federal agencies to change the people and processes that are needed for procuring and provisioning cloud services. Cloud computing places an increased importance on how technology is planned, selected, and integrated.[18] The new service-based approach to IT required federal agencies to learn how to manage services rather than assets. To effectively provision cloud services so that there can be an achieved optimization of resources, federal agencies had to link the benefits of cloud computing to their IT strategic plans.[19] In addition, federal agencies also had to establish new IT governance processes and practices to ensure the adoption of secure cloud services adhered to the federal information security and privacy requirements.

NOTE

Importance of Federal IT Strategic Planning in the Adoption of Cloud Computing

Government-wide IT strategic planning for information and IT management has been highlighted as a systematic challenge almost since federal agencies began using IT. As early as 1960,[20] the US General Accounting Office (GAO)[21] " ... call(ed) attention to the need for more positive central planning of a long-range nature within the executive branch of the government to promote the maximum degree of efficiency, economy, and effectiveness in the administration and management of costly automatic data processing facilities" [3].

However, it was not until 1980[22] that the management of federal IT authority was centralized within the federal government. The Office of Management and Budget (OMB) was given government-wide responsibility to "oversee the use of information resources to improve the efficiency and effectiveness of governmental operations to serve agency missions" [4]. Federal agencies were also required to designate a senior agency official (also known as the Agency CIO) to be responsible for information resource management (IRM)[23] at the department and agency level. As the government-wide IRM activities evolved, Agency CIOs were also given additional

(Continued)

---

[17]From Powner, D. Cloud Computing: Additional Opportunities and Savings Need to Be Pursued. Washington, DC: US Government Accountability Office; 2014. *"Overcoming cultural barriers was identified as one of seven common challenges in moving services to cloud computing."*

[18]Office of Management and Budget (OMB) Circular A-11, Part 7—*"Planning, Budgeting, Acquisition, and Management of Capital Assets."* Available from: http://www.whitehouse.gov/omb/circulars_a11_current_year_a11_toc.

[19]Office of Management and Budget (OMB) Circular A-11, Part 6—*"Preparation and Submission of Strategic Plans, Annual Performance Plans, and Annual Program Performance Reports."* Available from: http://www.whitehouse.gov/omb/circulars_a11_current_year_a11_toc.

[20]Review of Automatic Data Processing Developments in the Federal Government.

[21]The GAO was established under the Budget and Accounting Act of 1921. In July 7, 2007, the General Accounting Office was changed to the Government Accountability Office.

[22]*Paperwork Reduction Act of 1980.* Available from: http://www.gpo.gov/fdsys/pkg/PLAW-104publ13/html/PLAW-104publ13.htm.

[23]From Melvin, V. Federal Chief Information Officers: Opportunities Exist to Improve Role in Information Technology Management. Washington, DC: US Government Accountability Office; 2011. *"IRM is the process of managing information resources to accomplish agency missions and to improve agency performance."*

NOTE (CONTINUED)

responsibilities in developing "strategic plans[24] for all [departmental and agency] information and information technology management functions" [5].

IT Strategic Plans[25] play an important role in the adoption of cloud computing specifically when planning the expected improvements in productivity, efficiency, and effectiveness. Agency CIOs will need to be more effective in aligning IT Strategic Plans with Agency Strategic Plans[26] that enable the development and monitoring of performance metrics used to evaluate the business value of cloud services. Therefore, the IT strategic planning process used by Agency CIOs will need to emphasize the establishment of criteria that are more focused on objectively and quantitatively measuring the benefits of the investment of cloud computing technologies across the department and agency.

A HISTORICAL VIEW OF FEDERAL IT

In the Cloud Strategy, the federal IT environment was characterized as having "low asset utilization, a fragmented demand for resources, duplicative systems, environments which are difficult to manage, and long procurement lead times" [2]. This characterization was the result of an accumulation of issues stemming from years of mismanagement and the overcapitalization of IT.

In this section, we will focus on introducing several key historical points within the federal government where the adoption of IT produced trends that led to the growth in the federal IT budget. As illustrated in Fig. 1.3, a high-level timeline is provided that depicts how the federal government's IT budget and portfolio changed with the transition to newer technologies.

---

[24]From Office of Management and Budget (OMB). Revision of OMB Circular No. A-130, Transmittal No. 4 [Internet]. Washington, DC: Executive Office of the President, Office of Management and Budget [cited August 27, 2012]. Available from: http://www.whitehouse.gov/omb/fedreg_a130notice. *"The IRM Strategic Plan is the agency's IT vision or roadmap that will align its information resources with its business strategies and investment decisions."*

[25]From Office of Management and Budget (OMB). Revision of OMB Circular No. A-130, Transmittal No. 4 [Internet]. Washington, DC: Executive Office of the President, Office of Management and Budget [cited August 27, 2012]. Available from: http://www.whitehouse.gov/omb/fedreg_a130notice. *"The Clinger-Cohen Act directs agencies to work together towards the common goal of using information technology to improve the productivity, effectiveness, and efficiency of Federal programs and to promote an interoperable, secure, and shared government-wide information resources infrastructure."*

[26]From Office of Management and Budget (OMB). Revision of OMB Circular No. A-130, Transmittal No. 4 [Internet]. Washington, DC: Executive Office of the President, Office of Management and Budget [cited August 27, 2012]. Available from: http://www.whitehouse.gov/omb/fedreg_a130notice. *"IRM Strategic Plans should support the Agency Strategic Plans, describing how information resources will help accomplish agency missions and ensuring that IRM decisions are integrated with organizational planning, budget, financial management, procurement, human resources management, and program decisions."*

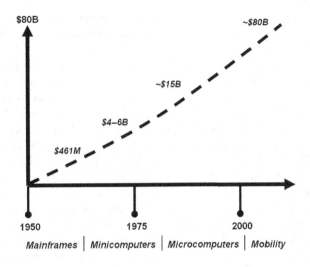

FIGURE 1.3

History of federal IT portfolio.

Our review will begin with mainframe computing (a highly centralized environment) and end with the federal government's transition to mobility (a highly decentralized environment). For completeness, the review will also include a brief discussion of the evolution of federal IT laws and policies developed over time to manage IT related issues across the federal government such as program management, acquisition, governance, privacy, and information security.

THE EARLY YEARS AND THE MAINFRAME ERA

The origins of modern computing[27] can be directly linked to the federal government. As the first significant[28] user of computers, the federal government consequently became one of the primary sources for most of the funding for the innovation and research in computing technology. In the early years, computers were very expensive, slow, inefficient, and took up a sizeable footprint,[29] making them impractical for use outside of the US government or research facilities. Despite limitations, the US government continued to finance the development and advancement of computer technologies. Originally, computers were only used for

[27]*University of Pennsylvania. John W. Mauchly and the Development of the ENIAC Computer. April 23, 2003.* Available from: http://www.library.upenn.edu/exhibits/rbm/mauchly/jwmintro.html.
[28]*Project Whirlwind Reports.* Available from: http://dome.mit.edu/handle/1721.3/37456.
[29]From Margherio, L., Henry, D., Cooke, S., and Montes, S. *The Emerging Digital Economy.* Washington, DC: US Department of Commerce, Economics and Statistics Administration; 1998. *"In 1946, the world's first programmable computer, the Electronic Numerical Integrator and Computer (ENIAC), stood 10 ft tall, stretched 150 ft wide, cost millions of dollars, and could only execute up to 5000 operations per second."*

military applications.[30] However, this initial investment would serve to establish the beginnings of an industry that would shape how the federal government would use and operate computers today.

The first digital computers[31] used by the federal government before the 1950s were primarily used for scientific and defense purposes,[32] although from the late 1940s to early 1950s the federal government's interest began to change their focus on using computers to address broader business challenges. In 1951, the emergence of the UNIVersal Automatic Computer (UNIVAC) I[33] created opportunities to use computers for applications outside of the US Department of Defense (DoD). The UNIVAC became the first business computer purchased by the Bureau of the Census[34] to be used for the population and economic censuses. During the remainder of the 1950s, several other civilian federal agencies also began to acquire[35] and use mainframes to supplement and support mission-specific operations. Federal agencies saw these computers as a useful tool for improving the productivity of more resource-intensive business support functions. For example, mainframes were used to more efficiently and accurately calculate tax returns (Internal Revenue Service), to calculate social security benefits (Social Security Administration), and to generate labor statistics (US Department of Labor).

The federal government's acquisition activity for computers began to increase significantly as the shift changed from using mainframes for basic business support functions to more complex mission-specific applications.[36] As a result, the federal government increased its purchasing of computers from 531 computers (or $464 million) in 1960 to over 5277 computers (or an estimated $4 to $6 billion[37]

---

[30]US Army Research Laboratory (ARL) Computing History. Available from http://www.arl.army.mil/www/default.cfm?page = 148.

[31]*US Census Bureau. History: Univac I. Census History Staff. June 30, 2011.* Available from: http://www.census.gov/history/www/innovations/technology/univac_i.html.

[32]*Problems Found With Government Acquisition And Use of Computer From November 1965 to December 1976.* Available from: http://www.gao.gov/assets/120/116645.pdf.

[33]Fay, F. X. The engineers get together … Look back at the future. The Norwalk Hour. October 25, 1996. Available from: http://rowaytonhistoricalsociety.org/index.php/rowayton-history/first-business-computer.

[34]*US Census Bureau. History: Univac I. Census History Staff. June 30, 2011.* Available from: http://www.census.gov/history/www/innovations/technology/univac_i.html.

[35]From Comptroller General of the United States. Problems Found With Government Acquisition And Use of Computer From November 1965 to December 1976. Washington, DC: US General Accounting Office; 1977. *Between 1955 and 1960, the number of computers in the federal government increased from 45 to 531.*

[36]From Comptroller General of the United States. Problems Found With Government Acquisition and Use of Computers From November 1965 to December 1976. Washington, DC: US General Accounting Office; 1977. *Example applications included: automating clinical laboratory processing (US Department of Veteran Affairs); managing housing grants (US Department of Housing and Urban Development); storing and retrieving criminal data (US Department of Justice); and predicting crop level (US Department of Agriculture).*

[37]$2 billion was being spent annually on software.

in capital expenditures) in 1970 [6]. The significant increase in the computer inventory was primarily the result of federal agencies having the purchasing power to procure resources needed to support their own individual needs and requirements.

As the federal government's mainframe inventory grew, federal agencies began to face challenges associated with vendor and technology lock-in.[38] As was customary in industry pricing practices at that time, software and engineering support services were bundled with the hardware [6]. This bundling resulted in federal agencies being locked into their mainframe vendors, making the migration between technologies a challenge because the manufacturer had full control over the entire stack, from the proprietary mainframe hardware platform to the software applications. In the 1980s, after the pricing practices began to change as major mainframe manufacturers started to unbundle the hardware, software, and engineering support services, the federal government was faced with a limited number of companies in the mainframe market.[39] This made it even more difficult for federal agencies to modernize their legacy applications.[40]

SHIFTING TO MINICOMPUTER

The advancement in hardware technology introduced the integrated circuit and the market evolved to midsized computers. Throughout the 1970s and 1980s, the federal government also began to shift away from using mainframes and began acquiring minicomputers. For the federal government, minicomputers provided a more efficient improvement in central processing and "time sharing" capabilities offering a much lower cost and size, thereby enabling them to be more broadly available across the federal government. By 1974, as illustrated in Fig. 1.3, more than 50% of the computers in the federal government cost less than $50,000 and the inventory exceeded 8600. Fig. 1.4.

Minicomputers offered the federal government greater opportunities to use technology to increase productivity through the use of automation to lower economic costs in areas where repetitive activities were being performed manually. As an example, minicomputers were used by the National Weather Service to automate forecast offices [7], the Internal Revenue Service for electronically

---

[38]Brown, K., Adler, S. M., Irvine, R. L., Resnikoff, D. A., Simmons, I., Tierney, J. J. United States memorandum on the 1969 case. Washington, DC: US Department of Justice; 1995. Available from: http://www.justice.gov/atr/cases/f0800/0810.htm.

[39]From US General Accounting Office (GAO). Mainframe Procurements: Statistics Showing How and What the Government Is Acquiring. Washington, DC: US General Accounting Office; 1990. The top vendor of IBM-compatible procurements was IBM with 65% of the total obligated federal dollars.

[40]From US General Accounting Office (GAO). Mainframe Procurements: Statistics Showing How and What the Government Is Acquiring. Washington, DC: US General Accounting Office; 1990. "35 federal agencies had 3,255 procurements and obligated $1,943.1 million for mainframe computers and mainframe peripherals during the 3 ½ fiscal years ending in March 1989."

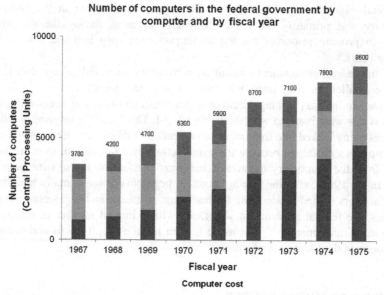

Number of computers in the federal government by computer and by fiscal year

FIGURE 1.4

Comparison of computers purchased between 1967 and 1975 [7].

preparing individual tax returns [8], the Federal Aviation Administration to automate air traffic control functions, and the US Department of Justice to automate legal information and retrieval [9].

DECENTRALIZATION: THE MICROCOMPUTER ("PERSONAL COMPUTER")

By the mid-1970s, the emergence of the microcomputer decentralized computing and empowered end-users within the federal government. The significantly lower cost gave federal agencies the ability to extend microcomputers to a broader workforce with hopes of improving productivity across the federal government. For example, in 1983, the US GSA began opening Office of Technology Plus (OTP) stores ("GSA microcomputer stores") to make it easier for federal agencies to procure microcomputers by streamlining the buying process.

Microcomputer adoption continued to gain significant momentum in the mid-1980s. By 1986, the federal government had amassed the largest inventory of computer equipment in the world, with a cumulative IT budget of over $60 billion between fiscal years (FY) 1982 and 1986.[41] As illustrated in Fig. 1.5,

---

[41]The federal government 2011 IT budget was approximately $80 billion a year.

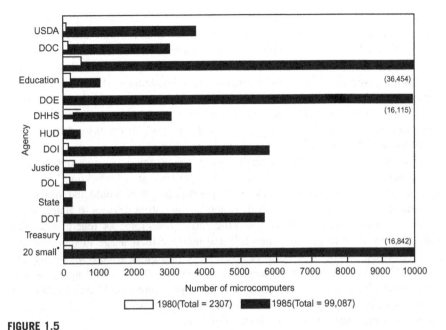

FIGURE 1.5

Comparison of microcomputers purchased between 1980 and 1985 [3].

the government-wide microcomputer inventory increased from 2307 in 1980 to 99,087 in 1985.

The accelerated growth in the IT inventory was also challenged with an under-developed IRM practice[42] that began to impact the overall value and performance of the federal government's return on its IT investment. The federal government saw impacts in areas such as the efficiency in delivering citizen services; maintaining the security and privacy of information stored in computerized form; and the quality of government IT management [3].

TRANSITIONING TO MOBILITY

Fastforwarding to today, the federal government operates in a more complex world that includes a mix of technologies. The emergence of different, even smaller types of platforms (i.e., smartphone, phablet, and tablet computers) and digital services offers the federal government new opportunities to improve its

---

[42]From US Congress, Office of Technology Assessment (OTA). Federal government information technology: Management, security, and congressional oversight. Washington, DC: US Government Printing Office; 1986. *IRM brings together under one management structure previously disparate functions and reorients the focus of information systems management from hardware and procedures to the information itself.*

efficiency, while at the same time it faces the challenge of ensuring the security and privacy of vast amounts of digital information. With a broad array of mobile devices available, the federal government has started to embrace the investment[43] in mobility. The expansive adoption of technologies that enable mobility required the federal government to confront potential new challenges relating to the management of these different devices, the supporting infrastructures, and the software applications. In addition, federal agencies are learning to manage the continued growth in mobile applications[44] and services[45] to optimize the efficient use of these technologies.

Many federal agencies have already become accustomed to using mobile computing devices (e.g., laptops) through their experience in teleworking.[46] Federal agencies are also continuing to explore opportunities that would maximize the benefits gained through the use of other mobile computing devices to enable them to operate more cost-effectively and efficiently. Therefore, as federal agencies make the transition to be more mobile[47] and increase their usage of mobile computing devices, they will be required to be more proficient at both managing and securing[48] different types of devices. This also means that federal agencies will need to learn how to *select*, *provision*, and *manage* secure cloud services that will be leveraged as more information is moved into digital services,[49] so they can be accessed by endpoint devices anytime, anywhere.

---

[43]From Cha, C. Agencies Need Better Controls to Achieve Significant Savings on Mobile Devices and Services. Washington, DC: US Government Accountability Office; 2015. *"According to OMB, as of May 2012 the federal government was spending approximately $1.2 billion annually on mobile devices and services and had an inventory of about 1.5 million devices."*

[44]*Making Mobile Gov Project.* Available from: http://www.gsa.gov/portal/category/101571.

[45]From Federal Chief Information Officers Council. Federal Mobility Strategy [Internet]. Washington, DC: Office of Management and Budget [cited April 30, 2011]. Available from: http://mobility-strategy.ideascale.com/a/pages/draft-outline. *In January 11, 2012, the Federal CIO [Steven VanRoekel] launched the Federal Mobility Strategy development to focus on accelerating the Federal government's adoption of mobile technologies and services.*

[46]In December 9, 2010, the Telework Enhancement Act of 2010 (P. L. 111−192) was signed into law requiring federal agencies to include as part of their telework programs an assurance of adequate information and security protection. OMB 11−27, *"Implementing the Telework Enhancement Act of 2010: Security Guidelines"* established the guidelines on security requirements.

[47]From Office of Management and Budget (OMB). Digital Government: Building a 21st Century Platform to Better Serve the American People. Washington, DC: Executive Office of the President, Office of Management and Budget; 2012. *"The Digital Government Strategy incorporates a broad range of input from government practitioners, the public, and private-sector experts. Two cross-governmental working groups—the Mobility Strategy and Web Reform Task Forces—provided guidance and recommendations for building a digital government."*

[48]*Creating a Foundation for Mobile Security.* Available from: https://cio.gov/creating-a-foundation-for-mobile-security/.

[49]*Digital Government: Building a 21st Century Platform to Better Serve the American People.* Available from: https://www.whitehouse.gov/sites/default/files/omb/egov/digital-government/digital-government.html.

EVOLUTION OF FEDERAL IT POLICY

In the previous section, we briefly explored the history of IT adoption within the federal government from *mainframes* to *mobility*. In this section, the focus will include highlights of key federal IT laws and policies. Many of the laws and IT policies were developed to govern the general practices for using IT within the federal government; others addressed more specific topics such as security and privacy. Tables 1.1 and 1.2 provide a chronological timeline of how the current IT policy framework evolved over time to address government-wide oversight and the management of IT-related issues and challenges. However, the policy framework established by Congress and the executive branch to control, oversee, and encourage the effective management and efficient use of IT was overtaken by the rapid pace at which new technology applications, issues, and opportunities were being generated or were not envisioned at the time of enactment or development of the policies [3].

The early adoption of IT was a significantly small portion of the annual budget in the 1960s. Therefore, purchasing power was performed in an isolated, decentralized manner, where each federal agency was given the flexibility to make its own buying decisions, including determining the types of technologies that were needed to meet its requirements. It was not until the mid-1960s that Congress took actions to improve the efficiency and effective use of IT across the federal government.

The enactment of the Brooks Act of 1965[50] was the first significant legislation focusing specifically on federal IT issues by establishing an oversight and management structure. The Brooks Act[51] outlined the major roles and responsibilities for the government-wide management of IT, which mostly operate under the same functions today (with an exception (*) noted):

- The US GSA* was given the authority and responsibility over the purchase, lease, maintenance, operation, and utilization of ADP equipment;
- OMB was given the fiscal and policy control; and
- The Secretary of Commerce, through the National Bureau of Standards (NBS), now known as the NIST, was directed with setting technical standards and guidelines.

The Brooks Act was established to reform federal IT by addressing three main issues: (1) competitiveness and "best value" through centralized government purchasing; (2) acquisition and IT management; and (3) common computing standards that would enable federal agencies to share information. In 1996, the enactment of the Information Technology Management Reform Act (ITMRA) of 1996 (now known as the Clinger–Cohen Act) repealed the Brooks Act, effectively eliminating GSA's role as the primary federal agency for setting policy and

---

[50]*Brooks Act.* Available from: www.itl.nist.gov/History%20Documents/Brooks%20Act.pdf.
[51]89th Congress. Public Law 89–306, Brooks Act of 1965. Washington, DC: US Congress; 1965.

Table 1.1 Timeline of Major Federal IT Legislation

1949—*Federal Property and Administrative Services Act of 1949*—Established the US GSA.

1950—*Federal Records Act of 1950 (P.L. 81–754)*—Established the framework for records management programs in federal agencies.

1965—*Brooks Act of 1965 (P.L. 89–306)*—Designated GSA with the authority and responsibility for automated data processing (ADP) equipment, OMB with fiscal and policy control, and NIST the responsibility for standards and guidelines development.

1974—*Privacy Act of 1974 (P.L. 93–579)*—Governed the collection, maintenance, use, and dissemination of information about individuals that is maintained in systems of records by federal agencies.

1980—*Paperwork Reduction Act of 1980 (P.L. 96–511)*—Established the OMB, Office of Information Regulator Affairs (OIRA), and gave authority to regulate federal information collection from the public and to establish information policies.

1984—*Competition in Contracting Act of 1984 (P.L. 98–369)*—Established a policy to encourage competition resulting in savings to the federal government through competitive pricing.

1987—*Computer Security Act of 1987 (P.L. 100–235)*—Established minimum acceptable security practices for federal computer systems and reaffirmed the responsibility of NIST for standards and guidelines development.

1988—*Computer Matching and Privacy Protection Act of 1988 (P.L. 100–503)*—Established new provisions regulating use of Privacy Act records in performing certain types of computer matching.

1993—*Government Performance and Results Act of 1993 (P.L. 103–62)*—Required federal agencies to develop multi-year strategic plans, annual performance plans, and evaluate and report on the results annually.

1994—*Federal Acquisition Streamlining Act of 1994 (P.L. 103–355)*—Enhanced simplified procurement procedures for small purchases, facilitated acquisition of commercial off-the-shelf (COTS) technologies, and promoted the use of fixed-price performance based contracting.

1998—*Government Paperwork Elimination Act of 1998 (P.L. 105–277)*—Established new provisions regulating use of Privacy Act records in performing certain types of computer matching.

2000—*Government Information Security Reform Act of 2000 (P.L. 106–398)*—Required federal agencies having control over unclassified and national security programs establish an information security management program.

2002—*E-Government Act of 2002 (P.L. 107–347)*—Enhanced the management and promotion of electronic government services and processes by establishing the Federal Chief Information Officer within OMB. Additionally, the Federal Information Security Management Act (FISMA) was enacted as part of the E-Government Act.

2010—*GPRA Modernization Act of 2010 (P.L. 111–352)*—Created a more defined performance framework by prescribing a governance structure and improved the connection between plans, programs, and performance information by requiring federal agencies to set clear performance goals that they can accurately measure and publicly report in a more transparent way.

2014—*Cybersecurity Enhancement Act of 2014 (P.L. 113–274)*—Provided for an ongoing, voluntary public–private partnership to improve cybersecurity, and to strengthen cybersecurity research and development, workforce development and education, and public awareness and preparedness, and for other purposes.

(Continued)

Table 1.1 Timeline of Major Federal IT Legislation *Continued*

2014—*National Cybersecurity Protection Act of 2014 (P.L. 113–282)*—Codified existing operations center for cybersecurity.

2014—*Federal Information Security Modernization Act of 2014 (P.L. 113–283)*—Amended chapter 35 of title 44, United States Code, to provide for reform to federal information security.

2014—*National Defense Authorization Act for Fiscal Year 2015 Subtitle D—Federal Information Technology Acquisition Reform*

- Enhanced the authorities for CIOs;
- Enhanced transparency and improved risk management in IT investments;
- Required portfolio review of IT investments;
- Required the consolidation of federal data centers;
- Required the development, strengthening, and deployment of IT acquisition personnel;
- Required regulations be established for the use of Federal Strategic Sourcing Initiative and requirements when using sources outside the initiative; and
- Required a strategic sourcing initiative to enhance government-wide acquisitions, shared use, and dissemination of software, as well as compliance with end-user license agreements.

regulations for federal IT procurements. Instead, the Clinger–Cohen Act delegated this authority to the newly created role of the Agency CIO.[52] In addition to the decisions of IT procurement, the Agency CIO was required to establish goals and report on efforts to reduce costs and increase efficiency through improved information management [10]. In 2011,[53] the role of the Agency CIO was further expanded to include four additional areas: governance (IT investment review and portfolio management), commodity IT (IT infrastructure, enterprise-wide IT systems, and business support systems), program management (IT program management resource identification, and hiring), and information security (direct or delegated authority and primary responsibility). The Federal CIO Council[54] was

---

[52]From Seifert, J. Government Information Technology (IT) Management: The Clinger-Cohen Act and the Homeland Security Act of 2002. Washington, DC: The Library of Congress, Congressional Research Service (CRS) Office; 2005. *"The duties of the CIO as described in the act are to provide information management advice and policy to the agency head; develop, maintain, and facilitate information systems; and evaluate, assess, and report to the agency head on the progress made developing agency information technology systems."*

[53]Office of Management and Budget (OMB) Memorandum 11–29, *Chief Information Officer Authorities* was designed to enable Agency CIO to have a direct authority to effectively implement the 25 Point Implementation Plan to Reform Federal IT Management.

[54]From Federal Chief Information Officers Council. About the Council [Internet]. Washington, DC: Office of Management and Budget [cited September 22, 2011]. Available from: https://cio.gov/wp-content/uploads/downloads/2013/02/CIOCCharterNov2012Approved.pdf. *"The CIO Council is one element of an interagency support structure established to achieve information resource management objectives delineated in legislation including the E-Government Act of 2002, Government Paperwork Elimination Act, Government Performance and Results Act, and the Information Technology Management Reform Act of 1996."*

Table 1.2 Timeline of Major Federal IT Policy

1961—*Policies on Selection and Acquisition of Automatic Data Processing Equipment (OMB Circular A-54)*: Outlined policies on selecting ADP equipment to replace and upgrade equipment and acquiring on hand and provides that federal agencies revalidate the workload and data processing requirements to determine if a reduction can be effected, and determine the possibility of improving the performance of existing facilities through program modifications, rescheduling, or the selective replacement of software or peripheral devices that offer greater efficiency or lower cost.

1979—*Security of Federal Automated Information Systems (OMB Circular A-71)*: Required federal executive departments and agencies to establish automated security programs and develop security plans that would be reviewed by OMB.

1996—*Implementation of the Information Technology Management Reform Act (OMB Memorandum 96-20)*: Designated the CIO and the role of the General Services Board of Contract Appeals (GSBCA) in IT protests.

1996—*Funding Information System Investments (OMB Memorandum 97–02)*: Directed the OMB to establish clear and concise direction regarding investments in major information systems, and to enforce that direction through the budget process.

1997—*Local Telecommunication Services Policy (OMB Memorandum 97–15)*: Provided federal agencies the flexibility and responsibility to acquire, operate, manage, and maintain telecommunications resources while taking advantage of the economies of scale and management efficiencies that aggregation of service and acquisitions can produce.

1997 – *Information Technology Architecture (OMB Memorandum 97–16)*: Provided guidance for federal agencies in the development and implementation of Information Technology Architectures.

1999 – *Instructions for complying with President's Memorandum of May 14, 1998, "Privacy and Personal Information in Federal Records" (OMB Memorandum 99–05)*: Provided instructions to federal agencies orf complying with the President's Memorandum of May 14, 1998, "Privacy and Personal Information in Federal Records."

1999 – *Privacy Policies for Federal Web Sites (OMB Memorandum 99–18)*: Directed federal agencies to provide guidance and post clear privacy policies on their websites.

1999 – *Security of Federal Automated Information Resources (OMB Memorandum 99–20)*: Reminded federal agencies that they must assess the risk to their computer systems and maintain adequate security commensurate with that risk.

2000—*Management of Federal Information Resources (OMB Circular A-130)*: Established a policy for the management of federal information resources. OMB includes procedural and analytic guidelines for implementing specific aspects of these policies as appendices.

2000—*Incorporating and Funding Security in Information Systems (OMB Memorandum 00–07)*: Reminded federal agencies of the principles for incorporating and funding security as part of IT systems and architectures and decision criteria for evaluating security for information systems investments.

2000—*Implementation of the Government Paperwork Elimination Act (OMB Memorandum 00–10)*: Provided procedures and guidance to implement the Government Paperwork Elimination Act.

2000—*Privacy Policies and Data Collection on Federal Web Sites (OMB Memorandum 00–13)*: Reminded federal agencies of their requirement by law and policy to establish clear privacy policies for web activities.

(Continued)

Table 1.2 Timeline of Major Federal IT Policy *Continued*

2001—*Guidance On Implementing the Government Information Security Reform Act (OMB Memorandum 01–08)*: Provided guidance on the implementation of the Government Information Security Reform Act, primarily addressing program management and evaluation aspects of security. It covers unclassified and national security systems and creates the same management framework for each. At the policy level, the two types of systems remain separate.

2001—*Guidance for Preparing and Submitting Security Plans of Action and Milestones (OMB Memorandum 02–01)*: Provided guidance on a standard format for information federal agencies should include in their plan of action and milestones (POA&Ms).

2003—*Implementation Guidance for the E-Government Act of 2002 (OMB Memorandum 03–18)*: Explained how the E-Government Act fits within existing IT policy, such as OMB Circulars A-11 (Preparation, Submission, and Execution of the Budget) and A-130 (Management of Federal Information Resources).

2003—*Reporting Instructions for the Federal Information Security Management Act and Updated Guidance on Quarterly IT Security Reporting (OMB Memorandum 03–19)*: Provided direction to federal agencies on implementing FISMA.

2003—*OMB Guidance for Implementing the Privacy Provisions of the E-Government Act of 2002 (OMB Memorandum 03–22)*: Provided information to federal agencies on implementing the privacy provisions of the E-Government Act of 2002.

2003—*E-Authentication Guidance for Federal Agencies (OMB Memorandum 04-04)*: Required agencies to review new and existing electronic transactions to ensure that authentication processes provide the appropriate level of assurance. It establishes and describes four levels of identity assurance for electronic transactions requiring authentication.

2004—*Maximizing Use of SmartBuy and Avoiding Duplication of Agency Activities with the President's 24 E-Gov Initiatives (OMB Memorandum 04–08)*: Enhanced the ability of federal agencies to manage software and to maximize the federal government's buying power.

2004—*Development of Homeland Security Presidential Directive (HSPD)—7 Critical Infrastructure Protection Plans to Protect Federal Critical Infrastructures and Key Resources (OMB Memorandum 04–15)*: Provided the required format for federal agenices to use when submitting internal critical infrastructure protection (CIP) plans.

2004—*Software Acquisition (OMB Memorandum 04–16)*: Reminded federal agencies of policies and procedures covering acquisition of software to support agency operations.

2004—*FY 2004 Reporting Instructions for the Federal Information Security Management Act (OMB Memorandum 04–25)*: Provided direction to agencies for meeting FY 2004 FISMA reporting requirements.

2004—*Personal Use Policies and "File Sharing" Technology (OMB Memorandum 04–26)*: Provided specific actions that federal agencies must take to ensure appropriate use of certain technologies used for file sharing across networks.

2004—*Policies for Federal Agency Public Websites (OMB Memorandum 05–04)*: Provided direction for federal agencies in fulfilling the requirements of section 207(f) of the E-Government Act of 2002.

2005—*Designation of Senior Agency Officials for Privacy (OMB Memorandum 05–08)*: Required agencies to designate a senior official who has the overall agency-wide responsibility for information privacy issues.

2005—*FY 2005 Reporting Instructions for the Federal Information Security Management Act and Agency Privacy Management (OMB Memorandum 05–15)*: Provided direction to agencies for meeting FY 2005 FISMA reporting requirements.

(Continued)

Table 1.2 Timeline of Major Federal IT Policy *Continued*

2005—*Improving Information Technology (IT) Project Planning and Execution (OMB Memorandum 05–23)*: Provided guidance to assist federal agencies in monitoring and improving project planning and execution and fully implementing Earned Value Management Systems (EVMS) for IT projects.

2005—*Implementation of Homeland Security Presidential Directive (HSPD) 12—Policy for a Common Identification Standard for Federal Employees and Contractors (OMB Memorandum 05–24)*: Provided instructions for the implementation of HSPD-12 and FIPS 201.

2006—*Safeguarding Personally Identifiable Information (OMB Memorandum 06–15)*: Reemphasized federal agency responsibilities under law and policy to appropriately safeguard sensitive personally identifiable information and train employees on their responsibilities in this area.

2006—*Protection of Sensitive Agency Information (OMB Memorandum 06–16)*: Provided recommendations for federal agencies to properly safeguard information assets while using IT.

2006—*Acquisition of Products and Services for Implementing HSPD-12 (OMB Memorandum 06–18)*: Provided direction for the acquisition of products and services for the implementation of HSPD-12.

2006—*Reporting Incidents Involving Personally Identifiable Information and Incorporating the Cost for Security in Agency Information Technology Investments (OMB Memorandum 06–19)*: Provided updated guidance on the reporting of security incidents involving personally identifiable information.

2006—*FY 2006 E-Government Act Reporting Instructions (OMB Memorandum 06–25)*: Provided for federal agencies annual E-Government reports required under the E-Government Act of 2002.

2006—*FY 2006 Reporting Instructions for the Federal Information Security Management Act and Agency Privacy Management (OMB Memorandum 06–20)*: Provided direction to federal agencies for meeting FY 2006 FISMA reporting requirements.

2007—*Safeguarding Against and Responding to the Breach of Personally Identifiable Information (OMB Memorandum 07–16)*: Required federal agenices to develop and implement a breach notification policy.

2007—*Ensuring New Acquisitions Include Common Security Configurations (OMB Memorandum 07–18)*: Provided recommended language for federal agencies to use in solicitations to ensure that new acquisitions include common security configuration and IT providers certify that their products operate effectively using these configurations.

2007—*FY 2007 Reporting Instructions for the Federal Information Security Management Act and Agency Privacy Management (OMB Memorandum 07–19)*: Provided direction to federal agencies for meeting FY 2007 FISMA reporting requirements.

2008—*Implementation of Trusted Internet Connections (TIC) (OMB Memorandum 08–05)*: Initiated the Trusted Internet Connections (TIC) initiative to optimize individual federal agency network services into a common solution for the federal government.

2008—*FY 2008 Reporting Instructions for the Federal Information Security Management Act and Agency Privacy Management (OMB Memorandum 08–21)*: Provided direction to federal agencies for meeting FY 2008 FISMA reporting requirements.

2008—*Guidance on the Federal Desktop Core Configuration (FDCC) (OMB Memorandum 08–22)*: Required industry and the federal government to use Security Content Automation Protocol (SCAP) validated tools with FDCC scanner capabilities to certify product operate correctly with the FDCC configurations.

(Continued)

Table 1.2 Timeline of Major Federal IT Policy *Continued*

2008—*Guidance for Trusted Internet Connection (TIC) Compliance (OMB Memorandum 08–27)*: Provided guidance and clarification on coordination with the Department of Homeland Security's (DHS's) National Cyber Security Division (NCSD).

2008—*Information Technology Management Structure and Governance Framework (OMB Memorandum 09–02)*: Reaffirmed and clarified the organizational, functional, and operational governance framework required within the executive branch for managing and optimizing the effective use of IT.

2009—*FY 2009 Reporting Instructions for the Federal Information Security Management Act and Agency Privacy Management (OMB Memorandum 09–29)*: Provided direction to federal agencies for meeting FY 2009 FISMA reporting requirements.

2009—*Update on the Trusted Internet Connections Initiative (OMB Memorandum 09–32)*: Provided an overview of the TIC initiative and to request updates to federal agencies POA&Ms for meeting TIC requirements.

2010—*Open Government Directive (OMB Memorandum 10–06)*: Directs executive departments and federal agencies to take specific action to implement the principles of transparency, participation, and collaboration set forth in the President's Memorandum on Transparency and Open Government.

2010—*FY 2010 Reporting Instructions for the Federal Information Security Management Act and Agency Privacy Management (OMB Memorandum 10–15)*: Provided direction to federal agencies for meeting FY 2010 FISMA reporting requirements.

2010—*Guidance for Agency Use of Third-Party Websites and Applications (OMB Memorandum 10–23)*: Required federal agencies to take steps to protect individual privacy whenever using third-party websites and application to engage with the public.

2010—*Reforming the Federal Government's Effort to Management Information Technology Projects (OMB Memorandum 10–25)*: Directed the Federal CIO to review high-risk IT projects, executive departments, and federal agencies to refrain from awarding task orders or contracts for financial system modernization projects, and OMB's Deputy Director Management to develop recommendations for improving the federal government's IT procurement and management practices.

2010—*Information Technology Investment Baseline Management Policy (OMB Memorandum 10–27)*: Provided policy direction regarding the development of agency IT investment baseline management policies and defined a common structure for IT investment baseline management policy with the goal of improving transparency, performance management, and effective investment oversight.

2010—*Clarifying Cybersecurity Responsibilities and Activities of the Executive Office of the President and the Department of Homeland Security (DHS) (OMB Memorandum 10–28)*: Outlined and clarified the respective responsibilities and activities of the OMB, the Cybersecurity Coordinator, and DHS, in particular with respect to the federal government's implementation of the 2002 FISMA (44 U.S.C. §§ 3541–3549).

2010—*NARA Bulletin 2010–05—Guidance on Managing Records in Cloud Computing Environments*: Addressed records management considerations in cloud computing environments and is a formal articulation of National Archives and Records Administration's (NARA's) view of federal agencies' records management responsibilities.

2011—*Sharing Data While Protecting Privacy (OMB Memorandum 11–02)*: Encouraged federal agencies to share high-value data, while at the same time reinforcing their responsibility for protecting individual privacy.

(Continued)

Table 1.2 Timeline of Major Federal IT Policy *Continued*

2011—*Continued Implementation of Homeland Security Presidential Directive (HSPD) 12— Policy for a Common Identification Standard for Federal Employees and Contractors (OMB Memorandum 11–11)*: Outlined DHS's plan of action for federal agencies that will expedite the executive branch's full use of the personal identity verification (PIV) credentials for access to federal facilities and information systems.

2011—*Presidential Memorandum Managing Government Records*: Executive branch-wide effort to reform records management policies and practices to develop a 21st-century framework for the management of Government records.

2011—*Delivering on the Accountable Government Initiative and Implementing the GPRA Modernization Act of 2010 (OMB Memorandum 11–17)*: Provided interim guidance on implementing the Government Performance and Results Act (GPRA) Modernization Act of 2010 (GPRAMA).

2011—*Implementing the Telework Enhancement Act of 2010 IT Purchasing Requirements (OMB Memorandum 11–20)*: Provided guidance to ensure the adequacy of information and security protections for information and information system used while teleworking.

2011—*Implementing the Telework Enhancement Act of 2010: Security Guidelines (OMB Memorandum 11–27)*: Provided guidance on security requirements for implementing the Telework Enhancement Act of 2010.

2011—*Chief Information Officer Authorities (OMB Memorandum 11–29)*: Clarified the primary area of responsibility for Agency CIOs.

2011—*FY 2011 Reporting Instructions for the Federal Information Security Management Act and Agency Privacy Management (OMB Memorandum 11–33)*: Provided direction to federal agencies for meeting FY 2011 FISMA reporting requirements.

2011—*Security Authorization of Information Systems in Cloud Computing Environments*: Established a federal policy for the protection of federal information in cloud services.

2012—*Principles for Federal Engagement in Standards Activities to Address National Priorities (OMB Memorandum 12–08)*: Provided principles and direction to federal agencies in a convening or active engagement with private sector standardization organizations to address national priorities.

2012—*Implementing PortfolioStat (OMB Memorandum 12–10)*: Provided federal agencies with instructions on implementing PortfolioStat reviews.

2012—*FY 2012 Reporting Instructions for the Federal Information Security Management Act and Agency Privacy Management (DHS FISM 12–02)*: Provided direction to federal agencies for meeting FY 2012 FISMA reporting requirements.

2012—*Managing Government Records Directive (OMB Memorandum 12–18)*: Created a robust records management framework that complies with statutes and regulations to achieve the benefits outlined in the Presidential Memorandum to reform records management policies and practices to develop a 21st-century framework for the management of Government records.

2012—*FY 2012 Reporting Instructions for the Federal Information Security Management Act and Agency Privacy Management (OMB Memorandum 12–20)*: Provided direction to federal agencies for meeting FY 2012 FISMA reporting requirements.

2012—*Improving Acquisition through Strategic Sourcing (OMB Memorandum 13–02)*: Built on the Administration's successful efforts and establishes a broad strategic sourcing initiative to ensure that all federal agencies manage their acquisitions effectively and that, wherever possible, agencies join together to negotiate the best deal for the taxpayer.

(Continued)

Table 1.2 Timeline of Major Federal IT Policy *Continued*

2013—*Improving Financial Systems Through Shared Service (OMB Memorandum 13–08)*: Directed all executive agencies to use, with limited exceptions, a shared service solution for future modernizations of core accounting or mixed systems.

2013—*Fiscal Year 2013 PortfolioStat Guidance: Strengthening Federal IT Portfolio Management (OMB Memorandum 13–09)*: Built upon the successes of Portfolio Stat to date by highlighting lessons learned, integrating PortfolioStat, and the Federal Data Center Consolidation Initiative (FDCCI), streamlining agency reporting requirements, and establishing guidance for the conduct of PortfolioStat sessions in FY 2013.

2013—*Open Data Policy-Managing Information as an Asset (OMB Memorandum 13–13)*: Required federal agencies to collect or create information in a way that supports downstream information processing and dissemination activities.

2013—Appendix D *to Circular No. A-123, Compliance with the Federal Financial Management Improvement Act of l996 (OMB Memorandum 13–23)*: Provided guidance in determining compliance with the Financial Management Improvement Act of l996 (FFMIA) for agencies subject to the Chief Financial Officers Act of 1990 (CFO Act).

2013—*Enhancing the Security of Federal Information and Information Systems (OMB Memorandum 14–03)*: Provided federal agencies with guidance for managing information security risk on a continuous basis and builds upon efforts toward achieving the cybersecurity cross-agency priority (CAP) goal.

2013—*Fiscal Year 2013 Reporting Instructions for the Federal Information Security Management Act and Agency Privacy Management (OMB Memorandum 14–04)*: Provided instructions for meeting your agency's FY 2013 reporting requirements under the 2002 FISMA. It also includes reporting instructions on your agency's privacy management program.

2014—*Guidance on Managing Email (OMB Memorandum 14–16)*: Reaffirmed the importance of recordkeeping and is a reminder that agencies, and employees, are responsible for properly managing and retaining email records.

2014—*Fiscal Year 2014–2015 Guidance on Improving Federal Information Security and Privacy Management Practices (OMB Memorandum 15–01)*: Identified current administration information security priorities, provided agencies with FY 2014–2015 FISMA and Privacy Management reporting guidance and deadlines, as required by the 2002 FISMA, and established new policy guidelines to improve federal information security posture.

2015—*Promoting Private Sector Cybersecurity Information Sharing (Executive Order)*: Encouraged the voluntary formation of such organizations, to establish mechanisms to continually improve the capabilities and functions of these organizations, and to better allow these organizations to partner with the federal government on a voluntary basis.

2015—*Policy to Require Secure Connections across Federal Websites and Web Services (OMB Memorandum 15–13)*: Required that all publicly accessible federal websites and web services only provide service through a secure connection. The strongest privacy and integrity protection currently available for public web connections is Hypertext Transfer Protocol Secure (HTTPS).

2015—*Management and Oversight of Federal Information Technology (OMB Memorandum 15–14)*: Provided implementation guidance for the Federal Information Technology Acquisition Reform Act (FITARA) and related IT management practices.

2015—*Category Management Policy 15–1: Improving the Acquisition and Management of Common Information Technology: Laptops and Desktops (OMB Memorandum 16–02)*: Directed federal agencies to take new steps to improve the acquisition and management of office laptop and desktop computers to drive us to greater performance, efficiencies, and savings.

(Continued)

Table 1.2 Timeline of Major Federal IT Policy *Continued*

2015—*Fiscal Year 2015–2016 Guidance on Federal Information Security and Privacy Management Requirements (OMB Memorandum 16–03)*: Established current administration information security priorities and provided agencies with FY 2016 FISMA) and Privacy Management reporting guidance and deadlines, as required by the 2014 FISMA.

2015—*Cybersecurity Strategy and Implementation Plan (CSIP) for Federal Civilian Government OMB Memorandum 16–04)*: Directed a series of actions to improve capabilities for identifying and detecting vulnerabilities and threats, enhance protections of government assets and information, and further develop robust response and recovery capabilities to ensure readiness and resilience when incidents inevitably occur.

2016—*Category Management Policy 16–1: Improving the Acquisition and Management of Common Information Technology: Software Licensing (OMB Memorandum 16–12)*: Addressed challenges in IT commodity management, specifically software licensing, in order to help agencies improve the acquisition and management of common IT goods and services.

2016—*Category Management Policy 16–2: Providing Comprehensive Identity Protection Services, Identity Monitoring, and Data Breach Response (OMB Memorandum 16–14)*: Required, with limited exceptions, that when federal agencies need identity protection services, agencies address their requirements by using the government-wide blanket purchase agreements (BPAs) for Identity Monitoring Data Breach Response and Protection Services awarded by the GSA.

2016—*Federal Cybersecurity Workforce Strategy (OMB Memorandum 16–15)*: Detailed government-wide actions to identify, expand, recruit, develop, retain, and sustain a capable and competent workforce in key functional areas to address complex and ever-evolving cyber threats.

2016—*2016 Agency Open Government Plans (OMB Memorandum 16–16)*: Included supplemental best practices and information to assist agencies in updating their Open Government Plans.

2016—*OMB Circular No. A-123, Management's Responsibility for Enterprise Risk Management and Internal Control (OMB Memorandum 16–17)*: Modernized Circular No. A-123 existing efforts by requiring agencies to implement an Enterprise Risk Management (ERM) capability coordinated with the strategic planning and strategic review process established by the GPRAMA, and the internal control processes required by Federal Managers Financial Integrity Act (FMFIA) and Government Accountability Office (GAO)'s Green Book.

2016—*Data Center Optimization Initiative (DCOI) (OMB Memorandum 16–19)*: Defined a framework for achieving the data center consolidation and optimization requirements of FITARA, the criteria for successful agency data center strategies, and the metrics OMB Office of the Federal Chief Information Officer (OFCIO) will use to evaluate the success of those strategies.

2016—*Category Management Policy 16–3: Improving the Acquisition and Management of Common Information Technology: Mobile Devices and Services (OMB Memorandum 16–20)*: Required federal agencies to take new steps to improve the acquisition and management of mobile devices and services.

2016—*Managing Information as a Strategic Resource (Updated OMB Circular A-130)*: Established the general policy for the planning, budgeting, governance, acquisition, and management of personnel, equipment, funds, and IT resources that support the quality, integrity, design, collection, processing, editing, compilation, storage, transmission, analysis, release, dissemination, accessibility, maintenance, security, cataloguing, sharing, and disposition of federal information and supporting infrastructure and services.

2016—*Federal Source Code Policy: Achieving Efficiency, Transparency, and Innovation through Reusable and Open Source Software (OMB Memorandum 16–21)*: Seeked to address challenges by ensuring that new custom-developed federal source code be made broadly available for reuse across the federal government.

also established in 1996[55] to provide a central focal point for coordinating issues across the federal government and to make recommendations for IT management policies. Finally, in December 2014, the Federal Information Technology Acquisition Reform Act (FITARA) was enacted within the National Defense Authorization Act for Fiscal Year 2015. The FITARA not only addressed IT reform through government-wide programs and initiatives, but also enhanced the authorities and responsibilities of the CIO for covered federal agencies, by requiring their involvement in the planning, programming, budgeting, and execution process related to IT.

Today, a combination of federal laws and government-wide policies provide the foundation for the federal IT policy framework used to manage and control IT issues within the federal government. The IT policy framework consists primarily of four main sources:

1. Federal statutes, written and enacted by Congress to address major IT issues;
2. Government-wide executive directives and mandates issued by the OMB to guide implementation of federal statutes;
3. Department or agency IT-level policies that address department or agency-specific needs and requirements; and
4. IT policies that reflect the requirements of a specific community of interest (COI).[56]

Through this policy framework the government-wide governance manages IT-related issues such as information security, capital planning and investment management, IT strategic planning, enterprise architecture, privacy, records management and retention, and information use (e.g., dissemination, collection, and disclosure).

CLOUD COMPUTING: DRIVERS IN FEDERAL IT TRANSFORMATION

The federal IT environment is undergoing a transformation. As discussed previously, the Cloud Strategy set forth the strategic direction for approaching the adoption of cloud services. However, for this cloud transformation to be successful and long-lasting, cultural changes[57] will need to occur. The cultural

---

[55]Executive Order 13011, *"Federal Information Technology,"* which became law through the E-Government Act of 2002. Available from: http://www.gpo.gov/fdsys/pkg/FR-1996-07-19/pdf/96-18555.pdf.

[56]For example, the Committee on National Security Systems (CNSS) establishes policies and directives for the National Security Community (https://www.cnss.gov/cnss/).

[57]Figliola, P., Fischer, E. Overview and Issues for Implementation of the Federal Cloud Computing Initiative: Implications for Federal Information Technology Reform Management. Washington: The Library of Congress, Congressional Research Service (CRS) Office. *"... there are challenges facing agencies as they make this shift. For example, some agency CIOs have stated that in spite of the stated security advantages of cloud computing, they are, in fact, concerned about moving their data from their data centers, which they manage and control, to outsourced cloud services. This and other concerns must be addressed to build an agency culture that trusts the cloud."*

changes will need to focus on overcoming potential challenges of cloud adoption.[58] Solutions need to be established and embraced that address security and privacy concerns, and other challenges impeding[59] the realization of the benefits of cloud computing. The institution of the federal government's culture toward IT needs to be oriented to consuming IT as a service, which requires moving data and other resources to be housed off-site and placed under the control of the CSPs (commercial or federal).

Through a continued and close collaborative partnership between federal agencies and industry, the investment in transitioning individual federal agency business processes to cloud services will serve as an accelerator in the transformational drivers to improve federal IT. In addition to a change in mindset, Agency CIOs responsible for developing IT strategic plans need to be cultivated to think of cloud services as increasing the efficiency and effectiveness that enable them to address their strategic objectives, goals, and performance measures.

WARNING

One can easily justify how cloud services, if appropriately planned and integrated, could present potential benefits for cost-savings and improve federal IT by maximizing efficiency, improving agility, and enabling innovation. Through the right mixture of cloud computing services, the federal government's IT investment portfolios can achieve better optimization. However, the adoption of cloud computing technologies will likely face ongoing impediments[60] as "there continues to be a need for a more thorough understanding of the cloud's deployment models, unique security implications, and data management challenges" [11]. Example impediments could include:

- Cultural resistance.
- Security and privacy concerns.
- Network access, availability, and resiliency limitations.
- Data portability and standardization.
- Liability and regulations.

Therefore, federal agencies will continue to carefully navigate these challenges to ensure that there is a limited impact to their mission and business.

---

[58]Figliola, P., Fischer, E. Overview and Issues for Implementation of the Federal Cloud Computing Initiative: Implications for Federal Information Technology Reform Management. Washington: The Library of Congress, Congressional Research Service (CRS) Office. *"In its 2014 study, GSA found five challenges in implementing cloud services. Two, meeting federal security requirements and overcoming cultural barriers within agencies, remained from the 2012 study, and three new challenges also emerged: meeting new network infrastructure requirements; having appropriate expertise for acquisition processes; and funding for implementation."*
[59]From Badger, L., Bernstein, D., Bohn, R., de Vaulx, F., Hogan, M., Mao, J., et al. NIST Special Publication (SP) 500–293 (Draft) US Government Cloud Computing Technology Roadmap, Volume I Release 1.0. Maryland: National Institute of Standards and Technology; 2011. *The US Government Cloud Computing Technology Roadmap was developed to foster adoption of cloud computing, improving information made available to decision-makers, and facilitate development in the cloud computing model.*
[60]*"Challenging Security Requirements for USG Cloud Computing Adoption."* Available from: http://collaborate.nist.gov/twiki-cloud-computing/pub/CloudComputing/CloudSecurity/Challenging_Security_Requirements_for_US_Government_Cloud_Computing_Adoption_v6-WERB-Approved-Novt2012.pdf.

DRIVERS FOR ADOPTION

Before proceeding with a discussion of the potential benefits offered to the federal government through the use of cloud computing, it is essential that we gain some basic understanding of some of the possible drivers[61] for cloud adoption. As previously highlighted, the *Cloud Strategy* characterized the federal government's IT environment as: *low asset utilization, fragmented demand, and duplicative systems, environments that are difficult to manage*, and *long procurement lead times* [2]. This characterization was largely the result of the way the federal government has acquired and operated IT over the years in independent silos.[62] "Federal IT change efforts are typically managed in isolation from business operations, so those working on long-term solutions are too often not concerned with, or even aware of, the evolution of day-to-day business considerations" [12]. These silos have led to the continued decentralization of the federal IT environment, mostly because the federal agencies have developed overlapping, duplicative, and, in many instances, fragmented programs that are not always shared across the federal government or community boundaries. However, these are not necessarily new issues. The scope of federal IT may have changed (i.e., size and complexity of programs, services, and systems), but the lack of strategic alignment and functional integration[63] between federal agencies has existed long before the *Cloud Strategy*. This misalignment has led to expensive and overly redundant development and maintenance costs. Across the federal government, multiple instances of similar shared services[64] have been developed, IT modernization efforts have been independently executed, and information security programs have been operated with little or no intra- and inter-agency coordination.

---

[61]Figliola, P., Fischer, E. Overview and Issues for Implementation of the Federal Cloud Computing Initiative: Implications for Federal Information Technology Reform Management. Washington: The Library of Congress, Congressional Research Service (CRS) Office. *"The two main drivers of cloud adoption by federal agencies continue to be budget concerns and data center consolidation."*

[62]A self-contained organizational structure that can operate independent of others within the larger organization.

[63]From Office of Management and Budget (OMB). The Common Approach to Federal Enterprise Architecture. Washington, DC: Executive Office of the President, Office of Management and Budget; 2012. *"Functional integration means interoperability between programs, systems, and services, which requires a meta-context and standards to be successful."*

[64]From VanRoekel, S. Federal Information Technology Shared Services Strategy. Washington, DC: Executive Office of the President, Office of Management and Budget; 2012. *"The Federal Information Technology Shared Services Strategy provides organizations in the Executive Branch of the United States Federal Government (Federal Agencies) with policy guidance on the full range and lifecycle of intra- and inter-agency information technology (IT) shared services, which enable mission, administrative, and infrastructure-related IT functions."*

> **NOTE**
>
> - In May 2002, OMB identified 10 potentially redundant systems across the federal government that related to the rule-making process.[65] As a result, OMB focused on "consolidating redundant IT systems relating to the President's on-line rulemaking initiative" [13].
> - The GAO reported in May 2004, "the duplicative and stovepiped nature of DOD's [US Department of Defense] systems environment is illustrated by the numerous systems it has in the same functional areas. For example, DOD reported that it has over 200 inventory systems. These systems are not integrated and thus have multiple points of data entry, which can result in data integrity problems" [14].
> - In a March 2011 GAO report, *"Opportunities to Reduce Potential Duplication in Government Programs, Save Tax Dollars, and Enhance Revenue,"* the GAO "identified 81 areas for consideration—34 areas of potential duplication, overlap, or fragmentation as well as 47 additional cost-saving and revenue-enhancing areas" [15]. Although not all specifically related to the duplication of IT resources, since IT plays a critical role in supporting most government programs and mission-specific operations, many areas of duplication would include the underlying IT capabilities.

The duplication, coupled with the low utilization of IT resources, has continued to increase federal IT costs. Federal agencies (and even program management offices) have worked independently to procure new hardware to satisfy their need for additional capacity, rather than optimizing the existing IT resources, either across an agency or between multiple agencies (for multiagency programs). As an example, in 2010, as an output of the initial findings of the FDCCI,[66] average server utilization rates were noted as low as 7% [16]. The absence of an effective IT management structure within the federal government has led to this underutilization of computing and storage resources. In the course of the initial phases of the FDCCI project, metrics similar to those included in Fig. 1.6 were established to assist federal agencies in making more informed IT management decisions for improving utilization within their consolidation plans.[67]

---

[65]Executive Office of the President, Office of Management and Budget. Regulation Information Frequently Asked Questions [cited July 27, 2011]. Available from: http://www.reginfo.gov/public/jsp/Utilities/faq.jsp. *Federal regulations are created through a process known as "rulemaking," which is governed by the Administrative Procedure Act (APA) (5 U.S.C.Chapter 5).*

[66]From Kundra, V. The Federal Data Center Consolidation Initiative. Washington, DC: Executive Office of the President, Office of Management and Budget; 2011. *"The FDCCI seeks to curb this unsustainable increase in the number of data centers by reducing the cost of data center hardware, software, and operations; shifting IT investments to more efficient computing platforms; promoting the use of Green IT by reducing the overall energy and real estate footprint of government data centers; and increasing the IT security posture of the government."*

[67]*FDCCI Data Center Consolidation Plans.* Available from: https://cio.gov/fdcci-public-plan-links/.

Utilization metrics	Typical results	Typical results
Average virtualization (%)	0–10%	30–40%
Average virtual OS per Host (#)	5–10	15–20
Average server utilization (%)	7–15%	60–70% (application dependent)
Average rack space utilization (%)	50–60%	80–90%
Average power density usage equivalent (W/sq.ft.)	50–100 W/Sq Ft	150–250 W/Sq Ft
Power usage efficiency (PUE)	3–2	1.6–1.3

FIGURE 1.6

Example of FDCCI utilization metrics [16].

NOTE

On January 14, 2010, the White House held *"The Forum on Modernizing Government"* where the forum noted the following conclusion:

The Federal Government has difficulty managing large-scale technology efforts. The Forum made it clear that there are best practices in industry for the design and ongoing review of these types of technology efforts that increase their likelihood of success. By comparison to these industry best practices, most Federal Government IT projects are too large and not sufficiently integrated into business unit operations. Multi-year Federal IT efforts are typically driven by technology managers—who often turn over during the life of the project— rather than agency business leaders. Agency business leaders are not held accountable for project success, and in turn do not adequately invest in IT project management. As a result, in comparison to industry best practices, Federal IT projects are too often marked by milestones spaced too far apart and deliverables that fail to deliver tangible end-user value. [17]

Another potential driver that is related to adoption of cloud computing includes issues associated with the IT acquisition process. Federal IT acquisition has been stagnant and largely unchanged for years. For example, in 1995, the GAO conducted a statistical analysis of the time taken to complete an IT acquisition, and noted that the time can vary depending on the dollar value, procurement type, and whether a bid protest was filed [18]. These same challenges still exist today.

The continued delays in streamlining the acquisition process have limited the potential benefits in the investment of IT. However, streamlining the acquisition process is not enough. Federal agencies will need to make improvements in their federal IT management practices to learn how to effectively leverage the cost-savings provided by technologies such as virtualization and cloud computing and make changes to their practices to accommodate acquiring IT as a service.[68]

---

[68]In February 2012, the Federal CIO Council and the Chief Acquisition Officers Council in coordination with the Federal Cloud Compliance Committee published the best practices to assist federal agencies in acquiring cloud services. Available from: https://cio.gov/wp-content/uploads/downloads/2012/09/cloudbestpractices.pdf.

> **NOTE**
>
> It is important to note, the challenges within the federal IT were not created overnight. GAO, OMB, and other organizations within the federal government have repeatedly highlighted weaknesses in required federal IT processes and controls to address IT reform challenges, and the ineffective government-wide and federal agency-specific IT oversight and management. As early as 2000, the GAO highlighted OMB's role as being "responsible for providing direction on government-wide information resources and technology management and overseeing agency activities in these areas, including analyzing major agency information technology investments" [19]. Although not limiting the governance over IT investments within each federal agency, a central focal point was noted as lacking to serve as this catalyst, working in conjunction with other executive officials to ensure that information resources and technology management issues were addressed within the context of the government's highest priorities and not in isolation from them [19].

CLOUD BENEFITS

The Cloud Strategy offered the following key benefits to improved operational efficiency, agility, and innovation through the use of cloud computing.

- *Efficiency*—better use of existing resources through a service-based model with a focus on improving utilization and to use technologies that would reduce duplicative services across the federal government.
- *Agility*—ability to deliver service faster and provision new resources based on the federal agencies' prioritization. For example, existing services that require long lead times to upgrade or increase/decrease capacity would receive high priority over services that are easier to upgrade, not sensitive to demand fluctuations, or unlikely to need upgrade in the longer term [1].
- *Innovation*—more access to innovation delivered through private sector services.

A summarization of the benefits provided in Table 1.3 describes how different characteristics of the federal IT environment can be improved through cloud adoption. Through these improvements, the *Cloud Strategy* suggested that federal agencies could benefit because they could redirect their "focus on mission-critical tasks instead of purchasing, configuring and maintaining redundant infrastructure" [1].

The 25 Point Implementation Plan to Reform Federal Information Technology Management highlighted similar benefits offered through the adoption of cloud computing, through a service-based model as:

- *Economical:* Pay-as-you-go approach to IT offers a lower initial investment, while allowing the ability to add investments as system usage increases [1].
- *Flexible:* Fluctuations in user demand and capacity can be added or subtracted without acquiring additional hardware and software [1].
- *Fast:* Long procurement times can be eliminated, while also enabling access to a continuously growing selection of services [1].

Table 1.3 Cloud Benefits: Efficiency, Agility, Innovation [1]

Cloud Benefits	Current Environment
Efficiency	
• Improved asset utilization (server utilization > 60–70%) • Aggregated demand and accelerated system consolidation (e.g., FDCCI) • Improved productivity in application development, application management, network, and end-user	• Low asset utilization (server utilization < 30% typical) • Fragmented demand and duplicative systems • Difficult-to-manage systems
Agility	
• Purchase "as-a-service" from trusted cloud providers • Near-instantaneous increases and reductions in capacity • More responsive to urgent agency needs	• Years required to build data centers for new services • Months required to increase capacity of existing services
Innovation	
• Shift focus from asset ownership to service management • Tap into private-sector innovation • Encourages entrepreneurial culture • Better linked to emerging technologies (e.g., devices)	• Burdened by asset management • De-coupled from private-sector innovation engines • Risk-adverse culture

However, to achieve sustainable benefits, the federal government will require more than just adopting new services and technologies. Federal stakeholders will need to commit to long-term transformational change in both the federal IT environment and culture.

Cloud computing reinvents the federal government's IT business acquisition model,[69] from capital expenditures (CAPEX) to operational expenditures (OPEX). With any significant change in business operations, there is an upfront cost required to support IT transformation. Federal agencies will need to understand that these costs may not be recaptured immediately, and will likely have to wait months, if not years, before savings are fully realized. Therefore, the benefits previously described will need to be weighed against the maturity of current federal IT processes and practices already established to determine if changes need

---

[69]Federal CIO Council and Chief Acquisition Officers Council. Creating effective cloud computing contracts for the federal government. Washington, DC: Executive Office of the President, Office of Management and Budget; 2012. *"By moving from purchasing IT in a way that requires capital expenditures and overhead, and instead purchasing IT 'on-demand' as an agency consumes services, unique requirements have arisen that Federal agencies need to address when contracting with cloud service providers (CSPs)."*

to be made. Federal agencies will need to ensure that the transformation benefits match their expectation of improved operational efficiency, resource optimization (e.g., data center real estate, compute, storage, etc.), and increased security through the delivery of IT as a service, something that will require change in the way the federal government plans for IT.

Improving efficiency

The transition to cloud services is more than a change in technology delivery models. It is also a shift in the focus from a federal government driven by IT asset ownership to service management. By exploiting the benefits of on-demand resource provisioning, federal agencies can learn to better understand their capacity requirements by scaling their usage, thereby improving overall utilization. Compared to fragmented and duplicative IT environments created by the investment in heterogeneous infrastructures in data centers across the country and around the world, the federal government can leverage cloud computing capability as a means to enable them to efficiently consolidate, transitioning the total cost of ownership (TCO) of data centers, and offering the ability to repurpose the savings to support their mission and business.

Improving agility

Agility in cloud computing provides federal agencies with the capability to rapidly provision/de-provision resources (e.g., compute, storage) as changes occur in their business requirements, making them more responsive and provides an opportunity to focus on identifying sources for improving their overall agency performance.[70]

Improving innovation

Federal agencies have operated in a mode that has focused on avoidance of risk, rather than managing risk. This has largely kept the federal government from innovating at a pace similar to the private sector. Cloud adoption will enable federal agencies to become more innovative through better service delivery by leveraging existing cloud services and emerging technologies that would increase their operational effectiveness.

DECISION FRAMEWORK FOR CLOUD MIGRATION

The *Cloud Strategy* presented a three-step structured framework. As depicted in Table 1.4, federal agencies can use the tool for assisting them when considering the migration to cloud services. As previously discussed, cloud transformation requires a shift in mindset. Federal agencies have been cultured to manage assets

---

[70]The Government Performance and Results Act (GPRA) Modernization Act of 2010 (GPRAMA) focuses improving performance and management to include information technology. Available from: http://www.gpo.gov/fdsys/pkg/PLAW-111publ352/pdf/PLAW-111publ352.pdf.

Table 1.4 Decision Framework for Cloud Migration [2]

Select	Provision	Manage
• Identify which IT services to move and when • Identify sources of value for cloud migrations: efficiency, agility, innovation • Determine cloud readiness: security, market availability, government readiness, and technology lifecycle	• Aggregate demand at department level where possible • Ensure interoperability and integration with IT portfolio • Contract effectively to ensure agency needs are met • Realize value by repurposing or decommissioning legacy assets and redeploying freed resources	• Shift IT mindset from assets to services • Build new skill sets as required • Actively monitor SLAs to ensure compliance and continuous improvement • Re-evaluate vendor and service models periodically to maximize benefits and minimize risks

Framework is flexible and can be adjusted to meet individual agency needs.

because it enables them to have more control over their IT infrastructure. The shift in mindset to managing IT as a service will require federal agencies to rely more on CSPs, a significant first challenge to overcome in cloud transformation.

Throughout the remainder of this section, we will briefly discuss each of the steps in the decision framework to demonstrate how they can be applied to a "Federal Agency" (a generic reference to a federal agency cloud service customer).[71]

SELECTING SERVICES TO MOVE TO THE CLOUD

First the "Federal Agency" needs to decide if it is ready to migrate to the cloud. In addition to the "Federal Agency" readiness, the Cloud Strategy identified several factors when performing a risk-based[72] evaluation of the readiness of CSPs as a preliminary activity to considering cloud services such as security requirements, service characteristics, market characteristics, network infrastructure, application and data, government readiness, and technology lifecycle [2]. After the "Federal Agency" has decided that it is ready to migrate some of its services to the cloud, the next important question is: "What services to move?" This determination calls for a full understanding of its IT investment portfolio and risk tolerance, among other things. Preliminary activities may include the "Federal Agency"

[71]As an example, in May 2012, the Federal Aviation Administration (FAA) released the FAA Cloud Computing Strategy. Available from: https://www.faa.gov/nextgen/programs/swim/documentation/media/cloud_computing/FAA%20Cloud%20Computing%20Strategy%20v1.0.pdf.
[72]The European Network and Information Security Agency (ENISA) published the *Security and Resilience in Government Clouds* that provides decision-making model for the identification of cloud solutions that meet the organization requirements. Available from: http://www.enisa.europa.eu/activities/risk-management/emerging-and-future-risk/deliverables/security-and-resilience-in-governmental-clouds.

CIO in collaboration with other key stakeholders to establish a clear set of criteria that will be used as a part of evaluating CSPs. Part of this process may include "identifying security, privacy, or other requirements for cloud services to meet, as a criterion for the selection of a cloud provider" [20].

Next, the "Federal Agency" can conduct a full evaluation of the current IT portfolio for potential services that are candidates to be included in its cloud adoption roadmap and plans. The services might be prioritized based on the "expected values" and "cloud readiness." Since the federal government tends to operate with a predominately risk-adverse mindset, the "Federal Agency" may need to develop additional metrics. These metrics could be used to measure the expected value by the "Federal Agency," and the readiness of both the "Federal Agency" and CSPs (commercial or federal). By evaluating short- and long-term benefits (i.e., efficiency, agility, and innovation) the "Federal Agency" can seek to properly align its migration planning with its governance and risk management functions that place an emphasis on identifying mitigations that would assist the "Federal Agency" in minimizing potential risks during the migration process.

PROVISIONING CLOUD SERVICES EFFECTIVELY

The federal government has had a history of "IT outsourcing." However, most IT outsourcing has been conducted by a "single" federal agency or multiple federal agencies through a joint program management office (PMO) using traditional procurement methods to contract services from providers to build and host services, applications, and information. In these types of outsourcing arrangements, the federal government mostly maintained control over IT assets and their information. By purchasing IT "on-demand," unique requirements may arise that federal agencies will need to address when contracting with CSPs [21]. Therefore, provisioning cloud services will require a change in the "Federal Agency" acquisition processes and practices. This new model of provisioning IT service will also enable the "Federal Agency" to be more cost-effective by pooling together the purchasing power through an aggregation of demand to the greatest extent possible before migrating services to the cloud [2].

Additionally, the Cloud Strategy outlined several other considerations [2] the "Federal Agency" should consider to reduce the risk associated with migrating to the cloud and to maximize efficiency such as:

- Integration of the IT service into the IT portfolio and functions that support business processes.
- Effective implementation of contract provisions that ensure portability and encourage competition (limit vendor lock-in); explicitly include service level agreements (SLAs) for security, continuity of operations, and service quality based on specific agency needs; and specific metrics that clearly state how and when they will be collected.
- Realizing the value through the appropriate use of cloud services through the decommissioning and release of assets used to support legacy applications and servers.

MANAGING SERVICES RATHER THAN ASSETS

When the "Federal Agency" has successfully migrated to the cloud, differences may exist in the relationship between the "Federal Agency" and the CSP, which will require adopting new governance processes. The "Federal Agency" will need to ensure that it can effectively manage SLAs based on the metrics defined previously as part of cloud service selection activity. "SLAs should clearly define how performance is guaranteed (such as response time resolution/mitigation time, availability, etc.) and require CSPs to monitor their service levels, provide timely notification of a failure to meet the SLAs, and evidence that problems have been resolved or mitigated" [21]. SLA monitoring will also require the "Federal Agency" to actively evaluate the metrics to ensure that they are enforced and usage charges are accurate. Since portability, interoperability, and security are key requirements for cloud service selection, the "Federal Agency" can periodically re-evaluate the market to identify opportunities that maximize capabilities offered by changes in technologies, new cloud services, and private-sector innovations.

SUMMARY

In this chapter, a brief overview of the Cloud Strategy was presented to highlight the key drivers for the federal government's adoption of cloud computing. In addition, the introduction provides CSPs with a basic understanding of how the strategy may be used by federal agencies considering cloud services as an extension of their IT portfolio. We briefly reviewed the history of federal IT with the purpose of understanding the potential challenges that may be a force behind the cloud adoption. We also discussed the key drivers for federal IT transformation and the expected benefits received through cloud computing. Lastly, a brief examination of the three-step decision framework offered insight into its application for cloud migration.

REFERENCES

[1] Kundra V. 25 Point implementation plan to reform federal information technology management. Washington, DC: Executive Office of the President, Office of Management and Budget, Washington, DC; 2010.
[2] Kundra V. Federal cloud computing strategy. Washington, DC: Executive Office of the President, Office of Management and Budget, Washington, DC; 2011.
[3] Congress US. Office of Technology Assessment (OTA). Federal government information technology: management, security, and congressional oversight. Washington, DC: US Government Printing Office; 1986.
[4] Paperwork Reduction Act [Internet]. Washington, DC: US National Archives and Records Administration [cited July 7, 2012]. <http://www.gpo.gov/fdsys/pkg/PLAW-104publ13/html/PLAW-104publ13.htm>.

[5] Melvin V. Federal chief information officers: opportunities exist to improve role in information technology management. Washington, DC: US Government Accountability Office; 2011.

[6] Comptroller General of the United States. Acquisition and use of software products for automated data processing systems in the federal government. Washington, DC: US General Accounting Office; 1971.

[7] Staats EB. Uses of minicomputers in the federal government: trends, benefits, and problems. Washington, DC: US General Accounting Office; 1976.

[8] Finch JC. Use of Minicomputers for Internal Revenue Service Tax Return Preparation. Washington, DC: US General Accounting Office; 1978.

[9] Comptroller General of the United States. Problems found with government acquisition and use of computers from November 1965 to December 1976. Washington, DC: US General Accounting Office; 1977.

[10] Seifert J. Government information technology management: past and future issues (The Clinger-Cohen Act). Washington, DC: The Library of Congress, Congressional Research Service (CRS) Office; 2002.

[11] McClure D. Statement of Dr. David McClure, Associate Administrator, Office of Citizen Services and Innovative Technologies, US General Services Administration, Before the House Science, Space and Technology Committee, Subcommittee on Technology and Innovation. Washington, DC: US House of Representatives; 2011.

[12] Office of Management and Budget (OMB). White House forum on modernizing government: overview and next steps. Washington, DC: Executive Office of the President, Office of Management and Budget; 2010.

[13] Daniels ME. Office of Management and Budget (OMB) Memorandum 02-08, Redundant Information Systems Relating to On-Line Rulemaking Initiative. Washington, DC: Executive Office of the President, Office of Management and Budget; 2002.

[14] Katz GD, Rhodes KA. DOD business systems modernization: billions continue to be invested with inadequate management oversight and accountability. Washington, DC: US General Accounting Office; 2004.

[15] Dodaro GL. Opportunities to Reduce Potential Duplication in Government programs, Save Tax Dollars, and Enhance Revenue. Washington, DC: US Government Accountability Office; 2011.

[16] Federal Data Center Consolidation Initiative (FDCCI). Workshop III: Final data center consolidation plan [Internet]. Washington: US General Services Administration [cited July 18, 2011]. <https://cio.gov/wp-content/uploads/downloads/2012/09/FDCCI-Workshop-III-Aug-10th-2010.pdf>.

[17] White House. White House forum on modernizing government: overview and next steps. Washington, DC: Executive Office of the President, Office of Management and Budget; 2010.

[18] Brock JL. Information Technology: A Statistical Study of Acquisition Time. Washington, DC: US General Accounting Office; 1995.

[19] McClure DL. Leadership Needed to Confront Serious Challenges and Emerging Issues. Washington, DC: US General Accounting Office; 2000.

[20] Jansen W, Grance T. NIST Special Publication (SP) 800-144, Guidelines on Security and Privacy in Public Cloud Computing. Maryland: National Institute of Standards and Technology; 2011.

[21] Federal CIO. Council and Chief Acquisition Officers Council. Creating effective cloud computing contracts for the federal government. Washington, DC: Executive Office of the President, Office of Management and Budget; 2012.

Cloud computing standards

2

INFORMATION IN THIS CHAPTER:

- Introduction
- Standards Development Primer
- Cloud Computing Standardization Drivers
- Identifying Standards for Federal Cloud Computing Adoption

INTRODUCTION

Standards play a critical role for cloud adoption, both by the federal government,[1] and the private sector. As we will discuss later in this chapter, the federal government has a responsibility to ensure voluntary consensus standards[2] are adopted in lieu of government-unique standards.[3] However, first it is important to obtain a basic understanding of what is meant by "standard" and the relationship to the federal government's adoption of cloud computing. Standardization can be characterized as the process by which new standards are developed or new products are brought to market implementing standards. A standard (or more specifically a

---

[1]From Kundra, V. Federal Cloud Computing Strategy. Washington, DC: Executive Office of the President, Office of Management and Budget; 2011. "*Standards encourage competition by making applications portable across providers, allowing Federal agencies to shift services between providers to take advantage of cost efficiency improvements or innovative new product functionality.*"

[2]Office of Management and Budget (OMB) Federal Participation in the Development and Use of Voluntary Consensus Standards and in Conformity Assessment Activities [Internet]. Washington, DC: Executive Office of the President, Office of Management and Budget [cited August 25, 2011]. <http://www.whitehouse.gov/omb/circulars_a119>. "*Standards developed or adopted by voluntary consensus standards bodies, both domestic and international. These standards include provisions requiring that owners of relevant intellectual property have agreed to make that intellectual property available on a non-discriminatory, royalty-free or reasonable royalty basis to all interested parties.*"

[3]From Office of Management and Budget (OMB) Federal Participation in the Development and Use of Voluntary Consensus Standards and in Conformity Assessment Activities [Internet]. Washington, DC: Executive Office of the President, Office of Management and Budget [cited August 25, 2011]. <http://www.whitehouse.gov/omb/circulars_a119>. Standards "*developed by the government for its own uses.*"

Federal Cloud Computing. DOI: http://dx.doi.org/10.1016/B978-0-12-809710-6.00002-0

Table 2.1 Sources of the US Government Definition of Standard

Source	Definition
National Institute of Standards and Technology (NIST) Cloud Computing Standards Roadmap	"A document, established by consensus and approved by a recognized body that provides for common and repeated use, rules, guidelines or characteristics for activities or their results, aimed at the achievement of the optimum degree of order in a given context" [1]
Office of Management and Budget (OMB) Circular No. A-119, Federal Participation in the Development and Use of Voluntary Consensus Standards and in Conformity Assessment Activities (Revised on January 27, 2016) and codified in National Technology Transfer and Advancement Act (NTTAA)	"Common and repeated use of rules, conditions, guidelines or characteristics for products or related processes and production methods, and related management systems practices" [2] "the definition of terms; classification of components; delineation of procedures; specification of dimensions, materials, performance, designs, or operations; measurement of quality and quantity in describing materials, processes, products, systems, services, or practices; test methods and sampling procedures; or descriptions of fit and measurements of size or strength" [2]

technical standard) can be classified[4] and published by many different organizations.[5] In Table 2.1, the generally accepted definitions are provided for what constitutes a standard for use by the federal government.

The *Federal Cloud Computing Strategy* identified the importance of standards development to ensure that the federal government's adoption and effective use of cloud computing and related technologies is supported by broad standardization. For federal agencies to leverage the capabilities and achieve the benefits offered by cloud computing, as described in Chapter 1, the development of standards focus on three major areas[6]: *interoperability*,[7] *portability*,[8] and *security*.[9] For example, standards "ensure clouds have an interoperable platform so that services provided by different providers can work together, regardless of whether they are provided using public, private, community, or a hybrid delivery model" [3].

---

[4]For example, the International Organization for Standardization (ISO) uses the convention in the International Classification for Standards (ISC). Available from: http://www.iso.org/iso/international_classification_for_standards.pdf.

[5]A list of some organizations involved in creating standards for cloud computing can be found at: http://cloud-standards.org.

[6]The first edition of the NIST Cloud Computing Standards identified expanded consideration in other areas such as maintainability, usability, reliability, and resiliency.

[7]Examples include functional and management service interfaces.

[8]Examples include workloads, storage, and data.

[9]Examples include authentication, data security, identity and access management, encryption and key management, governance, and compliance.

NOTE

Although there is no industry standard for the definition of cloud computing, the following National Institute of Standards and Technology (NIST[10]) [4] Cloud Computing definition has been widely accepted as the standard:

Cloud computing is a model for enabling ubiquitous, convenient, on-demand network access to a shared pool of configurable computing resources (e.g., networks, servers, storage, applications, and services) that can be rapidly provisioned and released with minimal management effort or service provider interaction. This cloud model is composed of five essential characteristics, three service models, and four deployment models.

Essential Characteristics

- *On-demand self-service*—a consumer can unilaterally provision computing capabilities, such as server time and network storage, as needed automatically without requiring human interaction with each service provider.
- *Broad network access*—capabilities are available over the network and accessed through standard mechanisms that promote use by heterogeneous thin or thick client platforms (e.g., mobile phones, tablets, laptops, and workstations).
- *Resource pooling*—the provider's computing resources are pooled to serve multiple consumers using a multitenant model, with different physical and virtual resources dynamically assigned and reassigned according to consumer demand. There is a sense of location independence in that the customer generally has no control or knowledge over the exact location of the provided resources but may be able to specify location at a higher level of abstraction (e.g., country, state, or datacenter). Examples of resources include storage, processing, memory, and network bandwidth.
- *Rapid elasticity*—capabilities can be elastically provisioned and released, in some cases automatically, to scale rapidly outward and inward commensurate with demand. To the consumer, the capabilities available for provisioning often appear to be unlimited and can be appropriated in any quantity at any time.
- *Measured service*—cloud systems automatically control and optimize resource use by leveraging a metering capability at some level of abstraction appropriate to the type of service (e.g., storage, processing, bandwidth, and active user accounts). Resource usage can be monitored, controlled, and reported, providing transparency for both the provider and consumer of the utilized service.

Service Models

- *Software as a Service (SaaS)*—the capability provided to the consumer is to use the provider's applications running on a cloud infrastructure. The applications are accessible from various client devices through either a thin client interface, such as a web browser (e.g., web-based email), or a program interface. The consumer does not manage or control the underlying cloud infrastructure including network, servers, operating systems, storage, or even individual application capabilities, with the possible exception of limited user-specific application configuration settings.

(Continued)

---

[10]From Office of Management and Budget (OMB) Federal Participation in the Development and Use of Voluntary Consensus Standards and in Conformity Assessment Activities [Internet]. Washington, DC: Executive Office of the President, Office of Management and Budget [cited August 25, 2011]. <http://www.whitehouse.gov/omb/circulars_a119>. "*A national science, engineering, and technology laboratory which provides measurement methods, standards, and associated technologies and which aids United States companies in using new technologies to improve products and manufacturing processes.*"

NOTE (CONTINUED)

- *Platform as a Service (PaaS)*—the capability provided to the consumer is to deploy onto the cloud infrastructure consumer-created or acquired applications created using programming languages, libraries, services, and tools supported by the provider. The consumer does not manage or control the underlying cloud infrastructure including network, servers, operating systems, or storage, but has control over the deployed applications and possibly configuration settings for the application-hosting environment.
- *Infrastructure as a Service (IaaS)*—the capability provided to the consumer is to provision processing, storage, networks, and other fundamental computing resources where the consumer is able to deploy and run arbitrary software, which can include operating systems and applications. The consumer does not manage or control the underlying cloud infrastructure but has control over operating systems, storage, and deployed applications; and possibly limited control of select networking components (e.g., host firewalls).

Deployment Models

- *Private cloud*—the cloud infrastructure is provisioned for exclusive use by a single organization comprising multiple consumers (e.g., business units). It may be owned, managed, and operated by the organization, a third party, or some combination of them, and it may exist on or off premises.
- *Community cloud*—the cloud infrastructure is provisioned for exclusive use by a specific community of consumers from organizations that have shared concerns (e.g., mission, security requirements, policy, and compliance considerations). It may be owned, managed, and operated by one or more of the organizations in the community, a third party, or some combination of them, and it may exist on or off premises.
- *Public cloud*—the cloud infrastructure is provisioned for open use by the general public. It may be owned, managed, and operated by a business, academic, or government organization, or some combination of them. It exists on the premises of the cloud provider.
- *Hybrid cloud*—the cloud infrastructure is a composition of two or more distinct cloud infrastructures (private, community, or public) that remain unique entities, but are bound together by standardized or proprietary technology that enables data and application portability (e.g., cloud bursting for load balancing between clouds).

To support the interests of the federal government, NIST was charged with providing technical guidance and support in the standards development efforts relating to cloud computing. The NIST Cloud Computing Program,[11] through the Cloud Computing Standards Roadmap Working Group,[12] developed the Cloud Computing Standards Roadmap[13] that focused on bolstering the federal government's ability to adopt cloud services. In addition, NIST was given the responsibility for directing and managing the strategic and tactical programs to ensure standards that already

---

[11]In 2010, the NIST Cloud Computing Program was launched at the direction of Vivek Kundra, the former US Federal Chief Information Officer (CIO). *NIST Cloud Computing Program.* Available from: http://www.nist.gov/itl/cloud/

[12]NIST Cloud Computing Standards Roadmap Working Group. *"This roadmap will define and prioritize USG requirements for interoperability, portability, and security for cloud computing in order to support secure and effective USG adoption of Cloud Computing."* Available from: http://collaborate.nist.gov/twiki-cloud-computing/bin/view/CloudComputing/StandardsRoadmap

[13]*NIST Cloud Computing Standards Roadmap.* Available from: http://www.nist.gov/itl/cloud/upload/NIST_SP-500-291_Version-2_2013_June18_FINAL.pdf

existed or are in development can be integrated into the US Government's Cloud Computing Technology Roadmap.[14] For the roadmap to be successful, NIST's participation was important to ensure that standards development supported acceleration by the private sector that would implement those new standards in products and services that could be procured by federal agencies.

Cloud computing is supported by many existing and emerging standards. Although not all of them were specifically developed with cloud computing in mind, many of them do directly support cloud services delivery. NIST and many leading industry groups and associations[15] have focused on identifying the technology standards gaps for the development of cloud-specific standards, including broad standardization. When a significant gap within standards exists, standards organizations, industry groups, and the cloud communities are faced with the challenge of coordinating their efforts to ensure interoperability between standards and to limit the impact associated with too many standards.[16] Overlapping and duplicative standards efforts attempting to solve the same problem may inadvertently cause competition for the "best" standard to fill the gaps. Therefore, standards convergence is important to ensure that standards are developed to address the need for compatibility.

STANDARDS DEVELOPMENT PRIMER

Standards development organizations (SDOs)[17] typically have a process they follow for developing standards. As an example, the International Organization for Standardization (ISO) follows a six-step process[18] that includes: *proposal,*

---

[14]*US Government (USG) Cloud Computing Technology Roadmap High-Priority Requirements to Further USG Agency Cloud Computing Adoption:* International Voluntary Consensus-Based Standards; Solutions for High-Priority Security Requirements which are Technically De-coupled from Organizational Policy Decisions; Technical Specifications to Enable development of Service-Level Agreements; Clear and Consistently Categorized Cloud Services; Frameworks to Support Federal Community Clouds; Updated Organization Policy that Reflects the Cloud Computing Business and Technology Model; Defined Unique Government Requirements and Solutions; Collaborative Parallel "Future Cloud" Development Initiative; Defined and Implemented Reliability Design Goals; *and* Defined and Implemented Cloud Service Metrics. Available from: http://nvlpubs.nist.gov/nistpubs/SpecialPublications/NIST.SP.500-293.pdf

[15]For example, Distributed Management Task Force, Inc. (DMTF), Open Grid Forum (OGF), and Storage Networking Industry Association (SNIA).

[16]*Cloud Computing Standards: Too Many Cooks in the Kitchen?* Available from: http://collaborate. nist.gov/twiki-cloud-computing/bin/view/CloudComputing/ForumVAgenda.

[17]From National Institute of Standards and Technology (NIST). NIST Cloud Computing Standards Roadmap Working Group, Hogan H, Liu F, Sokol A, Tong J. NIST Special Publication (SP) 500–291, Version 2, NIST cloud computing standards roadmap. Maryland: National Institute of Standards and Technology; 2013. "*Any organization that develops and approves standards using various methods to establish consensus among its participants.*"

[18]*Developing ISO standards.* Available from: http://www.iso.org/iso/home/standards_development/ resources-for-technical-work/support-for-developing-standards.htm.

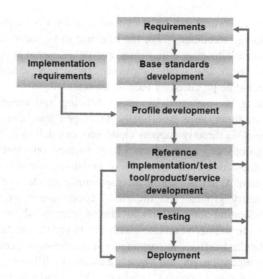

FIGURE 2.1

IT standards life cycle [1].

preparatory, committee, inquiry, approval, and *publication.* In Fig. 2.1, the NIST Cloud Computing Standards Roadmap included a "high-level conceptualization of ways in which IT standards are developed and methods by which standards-based IT products, processes, and services are deployed" [1]. Although only exemplary, the life cycle provides a good illustration of the relationship between the IT standards development process and the process by which IT standards are integrated, tested, and deployed in products and services that would be procured from the federal marketplace.[19]

The challenge faced with standardization using the conventional SDO-based standards development process in cloud computing exist in the length of time from standardization to product availability. The standards development process needs to be as agile and align with the maturing cloud service product development life cycle to address unique federal government requirements that support high priority[20] government-wide or federal agency projects. Therefore, the standards

---

[19]*Apps.gov* is a example storefront for cloud services. Available from: https://apps.gov/.

[20]From Chopra, A., Sapiro, M., Sustein, C. Office of Management and Budget Memorandum 12—08, Principles for Federal Engagement in Standards Activates to Address National Priorities. Washington, DC: Executive Office of the President, Office of Management and Budget; 2012. "...*national priority has been identified in statute, regulation, or Administration policy, active engagement or a convening role by the Federal Government may be needed to accelerate standards development and implementation to help spur technological advances and broaden technology adoption.*"

development model need to be accelerated,[21] while taking into consideration of the need for a voluntary consensus-based process. This new standards development model would reduce the technical uncertainty faced by federal agencies concerned with interoperability, portability, and security when adopting cloud service during the interim, while at the same time ensuring that Cloud Computing Standards are formalized and broadly available within the marketplace.

The US standardization system[22] is based on a set of globally accepted principles for standards development. Voluntary consensus is a critical part of this standardization system. A consensus-based process ensures standards meet the needs of both public and private sector[23] stakeholders before being finalized. The federal government's adoption of standards needs to be consistent with the objectives of the Technical Barrier to Trade (TBT)[24] Committee. By leveraging an "international" focused set of principles such as transparency,[25] openness,[26] and consensus,[27] the federal government can ensure that standards development increases the likelihood of standardization in cloud computing products and services.

---

[21]From NIST Cloud Computing Standards Acceleration to Jumpstart Adoption of Cloud Computing (SAJACC) Working Group. NIST Internal Group Report, SAJACC Working Group Recommendation to NIST. Maryland: National Institute of Standards and Technology; 2013. *"The Standards Acceleration to Jumpstart Adoption of Cloud Computing (SAJACC) project at the National Institute of Standards and Technology (NIST) seeks to generate concrete data about how different kinds of cloud system interfaces can support portability, interoperability, and security. By showing worked examples, the SAJACC project seeks to facilitate Standards Development Organizations in their efforts to develop high-quality standards that address these important needs."*

[22]The American National Standards Institute (ANSI) facilitates the development of American National Standards (ANS) by accrediting the procedures of standards developing organizations (SDOs). Overview of the U.S. Standardization System is available from: http://trade.gov/td/standards/United%20States/Overview%20of%20U.S.%20Standards%20System-%20Pamphlet.pdf.

[23]The terms *"public sector"* and *"private sector"* are used to identify the difference between government and nongovernment entities.

[24]From World Trade Organization (WTO) Technical barriers to trade [Internet]. Geneva: World Trade Organization Technical; [cited September 28, 2011]. Available from: http://www.wto.org/english/tratop_e/tbt_e/tbt_e.htm. *"The Agreement on Technical Barriers to Trade tries to ensure that regulations, standards, testing, and certification procedures do not create unnecessary obstacles."*

[25]From Breitenberg, M. NIST InterAgency Report (NISTIR) 7614, The ABC's of Standards National Institute of Standards and Technology, Maryland; 2009. *"Transparency means: (a) providing advance public notice of a proposed standards development activity; (b) identifying the scope of work to be undertaken; (c) providing information on conditions for participation; (d) and providing an opportunity for all interested parties to comment prior to final approval and adoption."*

[26]From Breitenberg, M. NIST InterAgency Report (NISTIR) 7614, The ABC's of Standards National Institute of Standards and Technology, Maryland; 2009. *"The standards development process should be to open to participation by all materially affected interests."*

[27]From Breitenberg, M. NIST InterAgency Report (NISTIR) 7614, The ABC's of Standards National Institute of Standards and Technology, Maryland; 2009. *"Consensus means that all views are heard and the resultant standard is generally agreed to by those involved."*

> **TIP**
>
> Standards adoption is an evolutionary process. Throughout the process, standards grow in both acceptance and maturity, and it could take years for standards to mature. Most standards can be generally classified as one (or more) of the following types at some point within the standards development lifecycle.[28]
>
> - *Open* standards are open to anyone to participate in developing and implementing (e.g., royalty-free).
> - *Proprietary* specifications are privately developed and are usually licensed for implementation. Sometimes, although not always, once they receive enough industry acceptance, they evolve into de facto standards.
> - *De facto* standards are considered industry norms through broad adoption and "in practice" application. They have gained acceptance and are therefore expected rather than required to be part of a product roadmap.
> - *De jure* standards are formalized through a standards body, thereby making them widely approved because of their formal acceptance.

As standards mature and broader market acceptance begins to see more participants, it is important for the federal government to ensure cloud-based products and services are conforming to the standards and requirements for implementation. Therefore, standardization requires using a process known as conformity assessment, to demonstrate "whether directly or indirectly, that specified requirements relating to a product, process, system, person, or body are fulfilled. Conformity assessment includes sampling and testing, inspection, supplier's declaration of conformity, certification, and management system assessment and registration. Conformity assessment also includes accreditation of the competence of those activities" [12].

The conformity assessment process provides both the federal government and industry with the confidence that a Cloud Service Provider (CSP) has implemented standards that meet the interoperability, portability, and security requirements necessary to maximize the benefit offered by cloud computing. It also provides a framework for CSPs to use when assessing their own products and services against standards, potentially making them more competitive within industry based on federal agency requirements for specific standards.

CLOUD COMPUTING STANDARDIZATION DRIVERS

The key driver for the federal government in supporting the standardization of cloud solutions is to address security,[29] portability, and interoperability

---

[28]Sometimes standards maintain their status as either "*de facto*" or "*de jure*" throughout their entire lifetime.

[29]From Federal CIO Council and Chief Acquisition Officers Council. Creating effective cloud computing contracts for the federal government. Washington, DC: Executive Office of the President, Office of Management and Budget; 2012. "*Agencies must clearly detail the requirements for CSPs to maintain the security and integrity of data existing in a cloud environment.*"

requirements. For example, without commonly implemented standards addressing interoperability and portability, federal agencies may be required to make significant changes to their existing software or adapt their code to work within a specific cloud service environment using proprietary Application Programming Interfaces (APIs).[30] This potentially could increase the cost of migrating between CSPs, creating a scenario that may become a barrier for a particular federal agency that has a concern about being locked into a specific cloud service.

Many standards used in cloud computing are a convergence of existing standards. As cloud computing technologies mature, consensus within the industry will begin to establish new standards specifically developed for cloud environments. The NIST Standards Acceleration to Jumpstart Adoption of Cloud Computing (SAJACC)[31] initiative was established to support the acceleration of adopting these new standards by developing tests that show the extent to which specific use cases can be supported by cloud systems through a set of documented and public cloud system specifications [5].

FEDERAL LAWS AND POLICY

The federal government is directly concerned with setting and implementing standards through legislation, regulation, or contractual obligations for sales to government purchasers [6]. In its roles, supporting standards development accelerates the broader adoption of cloud computing within the federal government and also assists federal agencies in satisfying their responsibility under federal laws and policies. This responsibility requires them to use voluntary consensus standards, where practical, in their procurement activities.

Trade Agreements Act (TAA)

The Trade Agreements Act of 1979 (TAA)[32] governs trade agreements negotiated with other countries. Under the TAA, federal agencies are prohibited from engaging "in any standards-related activity that creates unnecessary obstacles to the foreign commerce of the United States" [7] and are required to consider international standards. However, the TAA also could prohibit data housed in cloud computing servers and storage devices reside within the countries[33] not covered under the Act.[34] NIST supports the implementation of the TAA, including

---

[30]Apache LibCloud (http://libcloud.apache.org/) is an initiative providing API abstractions from incompatible or difference in multiple cloud provider's proprietary APIs.

[31]*Standards Acceleration to Jumpstart Adoption of Cloud Computing (SAJACC)*. Available from: http://www.nist.gov/itl/cloud/sajacc.cfm.

[32]*Trade Agreements Act of 1979*. Available from: https://www.gpo.gov/fdsys/pkg/USCODE-2011-title19/html/USCODE-2011-title19-chap13.htm.

[33]*FAR Subpart 25.4—Trade Agreements*. Available from: https://www.acquisition.gov/far/current/html/Subpart%2025_4.html#wp1086589.

[34]*Data Center Location Requirement—Protest*. Available from: http://www.gao.gov/decisions/bid-pro/405296.pdf.

educating federal, state, and local governments on the fundamentals of standards, conformity assessment, and technical regulations.

National Technology Transfer and Advancement Act (NTTAA)

The National Technology Transfer and Advancement Act of 1995 (NTTAA) established a requirement that federal agencies use technical standards that are developed or adopted by voluntary consensus standards bodies and participate with such bodies in the development of technical standards[35] [2]. NIST,[36] through the Standards Coordination Office (SCO),[37] directly supported the requirement of the NTTAA by coordinating within the federal government, and state and local governments, the adoption of voluntarily developed standards.

Office of Management and Budget (OMB) Circular A-119

The Office of Management and Budget (OMB) Circular A-119 "directs agencies to use standards developed or adopted by voluntary consensus standards bodies rather than government-unique standards" [8]. The circular focused on minimizing the reliance on unique government standards. Consistent with the requirements of OMB Circular A-119, the Federal Cloud Computing Strategy established requirements for a cooperative effort between public and private sector organizations for the development of standards that would enable the federal government to securely adopt cloud computing technologies.

ADOPTION BARRIERS

Cloud computing as defined by NIST is "a model for enabling ubiquitous, convenient, on-demand network access to a shared pool of configurable computing resources (e.g., networks, servers, storage, applications, and services) that can be rapidly provisioned and released with minimal management effort or service provider interaction" [9]. With different cloud deployment and service models available (including derivatives classifications), standards development is an essential part of ensuring the federal agencies' adoption of cloud

---

[35]NIST ITL Participation in Voluntary Consensus Standards Organizations—Technical Groups. Available from: http://www.nist.gov/itl/upload/ITLVolStdsList.pdf.

[36]From the National Institute of Standards and Technology (NIST). About Our ANSI Accreditation [Internet]. Maryland: National Institute of Standards and Technology [cited August 25, 2011]. <http://www.nist.gov/itl/ansi/>. *"NIST ITL (and its predecessor organizations) has been accredited by ANSI as a standards developer since October 5, 1984."*

[37]*NIST Standards Coordination Office (SCO).* Available from: http://www.nist.gov/director/sco/.

computing technologies is not hindered by potential barriers such as poorly defined, or a lack of market acceptance of, standards. These barriers limit federal agencies from maximizing their cost-savings through the use of cloud services, impacting their ability to deliver results and produce opportunities for value creation.

As cloud computing matures, open and proprietary standards will coexist within the cloud computing ecosystem. As illustrated in Fig. 2.2, usage scenarios driving Cloud Computing Standards development will be different at each of the service layers (i.e., data portability at the Software as a Service layer and VM portability at the Infrastructure as a Service layer).

The requirements for each of the usage scenarios will need to support well-defined and documented standards or specifications to ensure the federal government's interoperability, portability, and security requirements can be satisfied.

> **TIP**
>
> The Federal Cloud Computing Strategy highlighted the need for federal agencies to consider the market characteristic (i.e., the competitiveness and maturity) for selecting services as part of their decision process for moving to the cloud. The strategy stated that "agencies should consider the availability of technical standards for cloud interfaces which reduce the risk of vendor lock-in" [3]. It also highlighted the importance of considering, in addition to security, the interoperability and portability requirements as an aspect to address in the development of contracts to procure cloud services.

IDENTIFYING STANDARDS FOR FEDERAL CLOUD COMPUTING ADOPTION

The NIST Cloud Computing Reference Architecture Working Group generated a consensus conceptual reference model. The conceptual reference model, illustrated in Fig. 2.3, provides a "high-level" model to assist in understanding, discussing, categorizing, and comparing cloud services to communicate and analyze security,[38] interoperability,[39] and portability[40] candidate standards and reference implementations [10].

---

[38]Examples include authentication and authorization, confidentiality, integrity, and identity and access management.
[39]Examples include the interoperability of services through the service management (consumer APIs) and functional interfaces.
[40]Examples include data and workload portability.

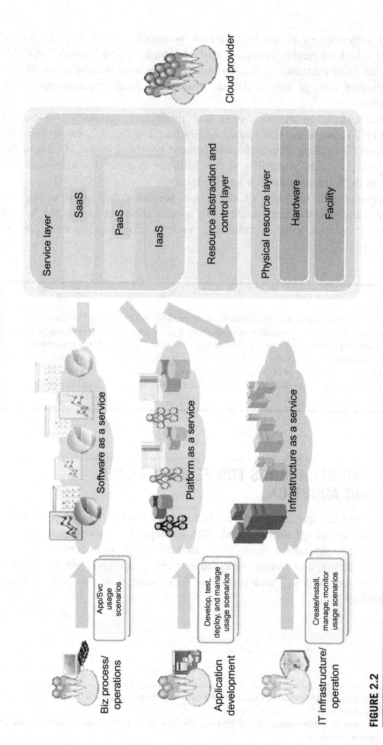

FIGURE 2.2

Cloud usage scenarios and cloud service layers [1].

TIP

As discussed in the reference "Creating Effective Cloud Computing Contracts for the Federal Government" jointly published by the Federal Chief Information Office (CIO) Council and Chief Acquisition Officers (CAO) Council [11]:

When procuring cloud solutions, it is important for federal agencies to understand:

1. How vendor solutions and agency roles map to the NIST Reference Architecture[41]; and
2. The role of federal agencies in the use of Cloud Computing Standards.

Reference Architecture

The NIST Reference Architecture describes five major actors with their roles and responsibilities using the newly developed Cloud Computing Taxonomy. The five major participating actors are: (1) *Cloud Consumer*; (2) *Cloud Provider*; (3) *Cloud Broker*; (4) *Cloud Auditor*; and (5) *Cloud Carrier*.

In order to fully delineate the roles and responsibilities of all parties in a cloud computing contract, federal agencies should align all actors with the NIST Reference Architecture.

Agency Roles in the Use of Cloud Computing Standards

There are several means by which federal agencies can ensure the availability of technically sound and timely standards to support their missions.

1. *Standards specification*: In accordance with the OMB Circular A-119, Federal Participation in the Development and Use of Voluntary Consensus Standards and in Conformity Assessment Activities, federal agencies should specify relevant voluntary consensus standards in their procurements. The NIST Standards.gov website includes a useful list of questions that agencies should consider before selecting standards for agency use.
2. *Standards requirements*: Federal agencies should contribute clear and comprehensive mission requirements to help support the definition of performance-based Cloud Computing Standards by the private sector.

In addition, the Conceptual Reference Model provides a useful tool for mapping and a common frame of reference for identifying the standards that will be required to facilitate adoption. By understanding the underlying business or technical use cases,[42] specific emphasis can be placed on those areas where gaps in standards exist based on the cross-cutting requirements. Federal agencies, as a cloud computing actor,[43] are the most likely sources for usage scenarios and for identifying requirements. Federal agencies' participation in the standards development process helps in the acceleration of the development and use of Cloud Computing Standards and standards-based products, processes, and services [11].

---

[41]*NIST Special Publication (SP) 500-292, NIST Cloud Computing Reference Architecture.* Available from: http://www.nist.gov/customcf/get_pdf.cfm?pub_id = 909505.

[42]*NIST Cloud Computing Business Use Cases Working Group.* Available from: http://collaborate. nist.gov/twiki-cloud-computing/bin/view/CloudComputing/ BusinessUseCases#Federal_Business_Use_Cases.

[43]*Five actors were identified in the NIST Cloud Computing Reference Architecture:* Consumer, Provider, Auditor, Broker, *and* Carrier.

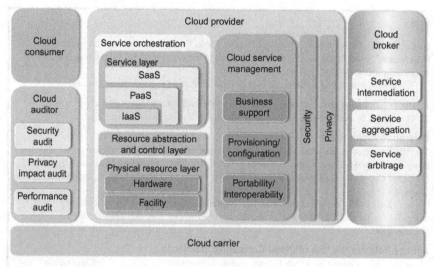

FIGURE 2.3

NIST conceptual reference model [10].

STANDARDS DEVELOPMENT ORGANIZATIONS (SDOs) AND OTHER COMMUNITY-DRIVEN ORGANIZATIONS

Standards development for cloud computing requires the active involvement of multiple standards bodies. Standards bodies are standards setting organizations that usually consist of stakeholders such as organizations or companies that produce technical standards to address the market's needs for standardization. Table 2.2 lists some of the international and national standards bodies involved in developing Cloud Computing Standards.

STANDARDS INVENTORY

Standards for cloud computing will continue to evolve, mature, and gain acceptance. This chapter does not attempt to provide a comprehensive catalog of standards supporting cloud computing, as harmonization of standards could take many years. Instead, it attempts to address the importance for cloud standards to promote openness and flexibility of choice by the federal government, while also supporting the minimum requirements of *interoperability*, *portability*, and *security*. This requires a focus on continued development of cloud computing use cases to anticipate where cloud technologies will be used, so that standards organizations, industry groups, and associations can coordinate their efforts to define existing standards, and identify where new standards will need to be developed.

Table 2.2 SDOs and Other Community-Driven Organizations

Name	Acronym	Website
American National Standard Institute	ANSI	www.ansi.org
Distributed Management Task Force	DMTF	www.dmtf.org
International Telecommunication Union	ITU	www.itu.int
Institute of Electrical and Electronic Engineers	IEEE	standards.ieee.org
		www.ieee.org
International Organization for Standardization	ISO	www.iso.org
Electronic Industries Alliance/ Telecommunications Industry Association	EIA/TIA	www.eia. orgwww.tiaonline.org
Internet Engineering Task Force	IETF	www.ietf.org
Internet Assigned Numbers Authority	IANA	www.iana.org
National Institute of Standards and Technology	NIST	www.nist.gov
Object Management Group	OMG	www.omg.org
Open Grid Forum	OGF	www.ogf.org
OpenID Foundation	OpenID Foundation	openid.net
Organization for the Advancement of Structured Information Standards	OASIS	www.oasis-open.org
Storage Network Industry Association	SNIA	www.snia.org
TeleManagement Forum	TM Forum	www.tmforum.org
World Wide Web Consortium	W3C	www.w3.org

The US Government Cloud Computing Technology Roadmap[44] required the development of a Cloud Computing Standards Roadmap for prioritizing standards developed to support the federal government's interoperability, portability, and security requirements. As part of the Cloud Computing Standards Roadmap development, the NIST Cloud Computing Standards Roadmap Working Group conducted a survey to identify existing industry standards, similar to those included in Tables 2.3−2.5, related to service interoperability, service performance agreements and monitoring, data and system portability, security, and accessibility.

The results included an inventory of standards that provides a starting point for mapping to applicable business and technical use cases. As previously discussed, this mapping activity is an important part in determining standards gaps and support prioritization with the standards community.

---

[44]From the National Institute of Standards and Technology (NIST). NIST Cloud Computing Standards Roadmap Working Group [Internet]. Maryland: National Institute of Standards and Technology; [cited August 16, 2011]. Available from: http://collaborate.nist.gov/twiki-cloud-computing/bin/view/CloudComputing/StandardsRoadmap. *"NIST is leading the development of a USG (US Government) Cloud Computing Technology Roadmap. This roadmap will define and prioritize USG requirements for interoperability, portability, and security for cloud computing in order to support secure and effective USG adoption of Cloud Computing."*

Table 2.3 Internet-Related Standards

Name	Organization	Document Reference (Publication Date)
Domain Name System (DNS)	IETF	RFC 1034 (11/1987)[a] RFC 1035 (11/1987)[b]
eXtensible Access Control Markup Language (XACML)	OASIS	XACML v3.0 (01/2013)[c]
Extensible Markup Language (XML)	W3C	XML v1.1 2nd Edition (08/2006)[d]
File Transfer Protocol (FTP)	IETF	RFC 959 (10/1985)[e]
Hypertext Transfer Protocol (HTTP)	IETF	HTTP v1.1, RFC 2616 (06/1999)[f] HTTP v2.0, RFC 7540 (05/2015)[g]
HyperText Markup Language (HTML)	W3C	HTML v4.01 (12/2009)[h] HTML v5 (10/2014)[i] HTML v5.1 (Draft) (05/2011)[j]
JavaScript Object Notation (JSON)	IETF (Douglas Crockford)	RFC 7159 (03/2014)[k]
Key Management Interoperability Protocol (KMIP)	OASIS KMIP TC	KMIP 1.1 (01/2013)[l]
OAuth (Open Authorization Protocol)	IETF, OAuth Working Group	OAuth 2.0, RFC 6749 (10/2012)[m]
OpenID Authentication	OpenID Foundation	OpenID Connect (02/2014)[n]
REpresentational State Transfer (REST)	University of California, Irvine (Roy Fielding)	Architectural Styles and the Design of Network-based Software Architectures (2000)[o]
Transmission Control Protocol/Internet Protocol (TCP/IP)	IETF	RFC 675 (12/1974)[p] RFC 791 (09/1981)[q] RFC 1180 (01/1991)[r]
Secure Sockets Layer (SSL)/Transport Layer Security (TLS)	Netscape Corporation (SSL Specification), IETF (TLS)	SSL v3.0 (1996)[s] TLS v1.2, RFC 5246 (08/2008)[t] TLS v1.3 (Draft), RFC 4492 (12/2014)[u]
Security Assertion Markup Language (SAML)	OASIS Security Service TC	SAML 1.1 (09/2003)[v] SAML 2.0 (03/2005)[w]
Service Provisioning Markup Language (SPML)	OASIS Provisioning Services TC	SPML v2.0 (04/2006)[x]
Simple Object Access Protocol (SOAP)	W3C, XML Protocol Working Group	SOAP v1.2 (06/2003)[y]
Simple Mail Transfer Protocol (SMTP)	IETF	SMTP RFC 5321 (10/2008)[z]
Web Services Addressing (WS-Addressing)	W3C	Web Services Addressing (WS-Addressing) (08/2004)[aa] Web Services Addressing 1.0—SOAP Binding (05/2006)[ab] Web Services Addressing 1.0—Metadata (09/2007)[ac]

Specification	Organization	Standard
Web Services Agreement Specification (WS-Agreement)	OGF	GFD.107: WS-Agreement 1.0 (03/2007)[ad]
Web Services Description Language (WSDL)	W3C	WSDL 1.1 (03/2001)[ae] WSDL 2.0 (06/2007)[af]
Web Services Federation (WSFED)	OASIS WSFED TC	WS-Federation 1.2 (03/2009)[ag]
Web Services Basic Reliable and Secure Profiles (WS-BRSP)	OASIS WS-BRSP TC	Basic Profile 1.2 (6/2014)[ah] Basic Security Profile 1.1 (10/2014)[ai]
Web Services Policy (WS-Policy)	W3C	Web Services Policy 1.5—Framework (09/2007)[aj] Web Services Policy 1.5—Attachment (09/2007)[ak]
Web Services Reliable Exchange (WS-RX)	OASIS WS-RX TC	Web Services Reliable Messaging Policy Assertion (WSRM Policy) (06/2007)[al] Web Services Reliable Messaging (WS-ReliableMessaging)1.2 (02/2009)[am] Web Services Make Connection (WS-MakeConnection) Version 1.1 (02/2009)[an]
Web Services Resource Access (WS-RA)	W3C	Web Services Event Descriptions (WS-EventDescriptions) (12/2011)[ao] WS-Eventing (12/2011)[ap] Web Services Fragment (WS-Fragment) (12/2011)[aq] Web Services Metadata Exchange (WS-MetadataExchange) (12/2011)[ar] Web Services Transfer (WS-Transfer) (12/2011)[as] Web Services Enumeration (WS-Enumeration) (12/2011)[at] Web Services SOAP Assertions (WS-SOPAAssertions) (12/2011)[au]
Web Services Resource 1.2 (ES-Resource)	OASIS WSRF TC	WSRF 1.2 (04/2006)[av]
WS-Secure Conversation	OASIS WS-SX TC	WS-SecureConversation 1.3 (03/2007)[aw]
Web Services Security (WSS)	OASIS WSS TC	Web Services Kerberos Token Profile 1.1.1 (05/2012)[ax] Web Services Rights Expression Language (REL) Token Profile 1.1 (05/2012)[ay] Web Services SAML Token Profile 1.1.1 (05/2012)[az] Web Services SOAP with Attachments (SWA) Profile 1.1.1 (05/2012)[ba] Web Services Username Token Profile 1.1.1 (05/2012)[bb] Web Services Security SOAP Message Security 1.1.1 (05/2012)[bc] Web Services X.509 Token Profile 1.1.1 (05/2012)[bd]

(Continued)

Table 2.3 Internet-Related Standards *Continued*

Name	Organization	Document Reference (Publication Date)
Web Services Transaction (WS-TX)	OASIS WS-TX TC	Web Services Atomic Transaction (WS-AtomicTransaction) 1.2 (02/2009)[be]; Web Services Business Activity. (WS-BusinessActivity) (10/2008)[bf]; Web Services Coordination (WS-Coordination) 1.2 (02/2009)[bg]
Web Services Trust (WS-Trust)	OASIS WS-SX TC	WS-Trust 1.4 (04/2012)[bh]
XML Encryption Syntax and Processing	W3C	XML Encryption Syntax and Processing (12/2002)[bi]
XML Path Language (XPath) v1.0 and v2.0	W3C	XPath 1.0 (11/1999)[bj]; XPath 2.0 (12/2010)[bk]
X.509 Public Key Infrastructure (PKI) Proxy Certificate Profile	IETF	RFC 3820[bl]
Internet X.509 Public Key Infrastructure Certificate and Certificate Revocation List (CRL) Profile	IETF	RFC 3280 (06/2004)[bm]
XML Signature Syntax and Processing (XMLSig)	W3C	XMLSig 1.1 (03/2011),[bn] XMLSig 2.0 (Draft) (07/2015)[bo]

[a]Domain Names—Concepts and Facilities. Available from: http://www.ietf.org/rfc/rfc1034.txt.

[b]Domain Names—Implementation Specification. Available from: http://www.ietf.org/rfc/rfc1035.txt.

[c]Extensible Access Control Markup Language Version 3.0. Available from http://docs.oasis-open.org/xacml/3.0/xacml-3.0-core-spec-os-en.pdf.

[d]Extensible Markup Language (XML) 1.1. Available from: http://www.w3.org/TR/xml11/.

[e]File Transfer Protocol. Available from: http://www.ietf.org/rfc/rfc959.txt.

[f]Hypertext Transfer Protocol 1.1. Available from http://www.ietf.org/rfc/rfc2616.txt.

[g]HyperText Transfer Protocol 2.0. https://httpwg.github.io/specs/rfc7540.html.

[h]HyperText Markup Language 4.0.1. Available from: http://www.w3.org/TR/html401/.

[i]HyperText Markup Language 5. Available from: http://www.w3.org/TR/html5/.

[j]HyperText Markup Language 5.1. Available from: https://www.w3.org/TR/html51/.

[k]JavaScript Object Notation. Available from: https://tools.ietf.org/html/rfc7159.

[l]Key Management Interoperability Protocol Specification Version 1.0. Available from: http://docs.oasis-open.org/kmip/spec/v1.1/os/kmip-spec-v1.1-os.html.

[m]The OAuth 2.0 Authorization Framework. Available from: http://tools.ietf.org/html/rfc6749.

[n]OpenID Connect. Available from: http://openid.net/connect/.

[o]Architectural Styles and the Design of Network-based Software Architectures. Available from: http://www.ics.uci.edu/~fielding/pubs/dissertation/top.htm.

[p]Specification of Internet Transmission Control Program. Available from: http://tools.ietf.org/html/rfc675.

[q]Internet Protocol. Available from: http://www.ietf.org/rfc/rfc791.txt.

[r]A TCP/IP Tutorial. Available from http://tools.ietf.org/html/rfc1180.

[s]The SSL Protocol Version 3.0. Available from: http://www.mozilla.org/projects/security/pki/nss/ssl/draft302.txt.

[t]The Transport Layer Security (TLS) Protocol Version 1.2. Available from: http://tools.ietf.org/html/rfc5246.

[u]Security Assertion Markup Language v1.1. Available from: http://www.oasis-open.org/standards#samlv1.1.

[v]Security Assertion Markup Language v2.0. Available from: http://www.oasis-open.org/standards#samlv2.0.

[w]Service Provisioning Markup Language Version 2. Available from: http://www.oasis-open.org/committees/download.php/17708/pstc-spml-2.0-os.zip.

[x]SOAP Version 1.2 Part 1: Messaging Framework. Available from: http://www.w3.org/TR/soap12-part1/.

[y]Service Provision Markup Language Version 2. Available from: http://www.oasis-open.org/committees/download.php/17708/pstc-spml-2.0-os.zip

[z]Simple Mail Transfer Protocol. Available from http://tools.ietf.org/html/rfc5321.

[aa]Web Services Addressing. Available from: http://www.w3.org/Submission/ws-addressing/.

[ab]Web Services Addressing 1.0—SOAP Binding. Available from: http://www.w3.org/TR/ws-addr-soap/.

[ac]Web Services Addressing 1.0—Metadata. Available from: http://www.w3.org/TR/ws-addr-metadata/.

[ad]Web Services Agreement Specification. Available from: http://www.ogf.org/documents/GFD.107.pdf.

[ae]Web Services Description Language 1.1. Available from: http://www.w3.org/TR/wsdl.

[af]Web Services Description Language 2.0. Available from: http://www.w3.org/TR/wsdl20/.

[ag]Web Services Federation Language Version 1.2. Available from: http://www.oasis-open.org/committees/download.php/31658/ws-federation-1.2-spec-cs-01.doc.

[ah]Basic Profile Version 1.2. Available from http://docs.oasis-open.org/ws-brsp/BasicProfile/v1.2/BasicProfile-v1.2.html.

[ai]Basic Security Profile Version 1.1. Available from http://docs.oasis-open.org/ws-brsp/BasicSecurityProfile/v1.1/cs01/BasicSecurityProfile-v1.1-cs01.html.

[aj]Web Services Policy 1.5—Framework. Available from: http://www.w3.org/TR/ws-policy/.

[ak]Web Services Policy 1.5—Attachment. Available from: http://www.w3.org/TR/ws-policy-attach/.

[al]Web Services Reliability Messaging Policy Assertion Version 1.2. Available from: http://docs.oasis-open.org/ws-rx/wsrmp/200702/wsrmp-1.2-spec-os.html.

[am]Web Services Reliable Messaging Version 1.2. Available from: http://docs.oasis-open.org/ws-rx/wsrm/200702/wsrm-1.2-spec-os.html.

[an]Web Services Make Connection Version 1.1. Available from: http://docs.oasis-open.org/ws-rx/wsmc/200702/wsmc-1.1-spec-os.html.

[ao]Web Services Event Descriptions. Available from: https://www.w3.org/TR/ws-event-descriptions/.

[ap]Web Services Eventing. Available from: https://www.w3.org/TR/ws-eventing/

[aq]Web Services Fragment. Available from: https://www.w3.org/TR/ws-transfer/.

[ar]Web Services Metadata Exchange. Available from: https://www.w3.org/TR/ws-metadata-exchange/.

[as]Web Services Transfer. Available from: http://www.w3.org/Submission/WS-Transfer/.

[at]Web Services Enumeration. Available from: https://www.w3.org/TR/ws-enumeration/.

[au]Web Services SOAP Assertions. Available from: https://www.w3.org/TR/ws-soap-assertions/.

[av]Web Services Resource 1.2. Available from: http://docs.oasis-open.org/wsrf/wsrf-ws_resource-1.2-spec-os.pdf.

[aw]WS-SecureConversation 1.3. Available from: http://docs.oasis-open.org/ws-sx/ws-secureconversation/v1.3/ws-secureconversation.html.

[ax]Web Services Security Kerberos Token Profile 1.1.1. Available from: http://docs.oasis-open.org/wss-m/wss/v1.1.1/wss-KerberosTokenProfile-v1.1.1.html.

[ay]Web Services Security Rights Expression Language Token Profile 1.1. Available from:http://www.oasis-open.org/committees/download.php/16687/oasis-wss-rel-token-profile-1.1.pdf.

[az]Web Services Security: SAML Token Profile 1.1.1. Available from: http://docs.oasis-open.org/wss-m/wss/v1.1.1/wss-SAMLTokenProfile-v1.1.1.html.

[ba]Web Services Security SOAP Messages with Attachments Profile 1.1.1. Available from: http://docs.oasis-open.org/wss-m/wss/v1.1.1/wss-SwAProfile-v1.1.1.html.

[bb]Web Services Security Username Token Profile 1.1.1. Available from: http://docs.oasis-open.org/wss-m/wss/v1.1.1/wss-UsernameTokenProfile-v1.1.1.html.

[bc]Web Services Security SOAP Message Security 1.1.1. Available from: http://docs.oasis-open.org/wss-m/wss/v1.1.1/wss-SOAPMessageSecurity-v1.1.1.html.

[bd]Web Services Security X.509 Certificate Token Profile 1.1.1. Available from: http://docs.oasis-open.org/wss-m/wss/v1.1.1/wss-x509TokenProfile-v1.1.1.html.

[be]Web Services Atomic Transaction Version 1.2. Available from: http://docs.oasis-open.org/ws-tx/wstx-wsat-1.2-spec.html.

[bf]Web Services Business Activity Version 1.2. Available from: http://docs.oasis-open.org/ws-tx/wstx-wsba-1.2-spec.html.

[bg]Web Services Coordination Version 1.2. Available from: http://docs.oasis-open.org/ws-tx/wstx-wscoor-1.2-spec.html

[bh]WS-Trust 1.4. Available from: http://docs.oasis-open.org/ws-sx/ws-trust/v1.4/errata01/ws-trust-1.4-errata01-complete.html.

[bi]XML Encryption Syntax and Processing. Available from: https://www.w3.org/TR/xmlenc-core/.

[bj]XML Path Language Version 1.0. Available from: https://www.w3.org/TR/xpath/.

[bk]XML Path Language Version 2.0. Available from: https://www.w3.org/TR/xpath20/.

[bl]Internet X.509 Public Key Infrastructure Proxy Certificate Profile. Available from: https://www.ietf.org/rfc/rfc3820.txt.

[bm]Internet X.509 Public Key Infrastructure Certificate and Certificate Revocation List Profile. Available from: http://www.ietf.org/rfc/rfc3280.txt.

[bn]XML Signature Syntax and Processing Version 1.1. Available from: http://www.w3.org/TR/xmldsig-core1/.

[bo]XML Signature Syntax and Processing Version 2.0. Available from: https://www.w3.org/TR/xmldsig-core2/.

Table 2.4 US Federal Government and International-Related Standards

Name	Organization	Document Reference (Publication Date)
Advanced Encryption Standard (AES)	NIST	Federal Information Processing Standard (FIPS) 197 (11/2001)[a]
Common vulnerabilities and exposures	NIST/MITRE	National Vulnerability Database (NVD) 2.2[b]
	ITU-T Study Group 17, Question 4 (SG17/Q4)	Recommendation X.1520 (04/2011)[c]
Common vulnerability scoring system	First.org, Inc.	CVSS 3.0 (06/2015)[d]
	ITU-T Study Group 17, Question 4 (SG17/Q4)	Recommendation X.1521 (04/2011)[e]
Computer Security Incident Handling Guide	NIST	NIST Special Publication (SP) 800-61, Rev. 2 (08/2012)[f]
Cyber Observable eXpression (CybOX)	DHS/OASIS/MITRE	CybOX 2.1[g] CybOX 3.x[h]
Digital Signature Standard (DSS)	NIST	FIPS 186-4 (07/2013)[i]
Escrowed Encryption Standard (EES)	NIST	FIPS 185 (02/1994)[j]
Guideline for incident preparedness and operational continuity management	ISO	ISO/PAS 22399:2007[k]
Minimum Security Requirements for Federal Information and Information Systems	NIST	FIPS 200 (03/2006)[l]
Overview of Cybersecurity information exchange (CYBEX)	ITU-T Study Group 17, Question 4 (SG17/Q4)	Recommendation X.1520 (04/2011)[m]
Personal Identity Verification (PIV) of Federal Employees and Contractors	NIST	FIPS 201-2 (08/2013)[n]
Security Content Automation Protocol (SCAP)	NIST	NIST Special Publication (SP) 800-126, 1.0 (11/2009)[o], NIST SP 800-126, 1.1 (02/2011)[p] NIST SP 800-126, 1.2 (09/2011)[q]
Secure Hash Standard (SHS)	NIST	FIPS, 180-4 (03/2012)[r]
Security Requirements for Cryptographic Modules	NIST	FIPS 140-2 (05/2001)[s]

Standard	Organization	Version (date)
Standards for Security Categorization of Federal Information and Information System	NIST	FIPS 199 (02/2004)[t]
Structured Threat Information eXpression (STIX)	DHS/OASIS/MITRE	STIX 1.2.1 (10/2015)[u] STIX 2.x[v]
Trusted Automated eXchange of Indicator Information (TAXII)	DHS/OASIS/MITRE	TAXII 1.1 (01/2014)[w] TAXII 2.x[x]
The Key-Hash Message Authentication Code (HMAC)	NIST	FIPS 198-1 (07/2008)[y]

[a]Advanced Encryption Standard. Available from: http://csrc.nist.gov/publications/fips/fips197/fips-197.pdf.

[b]National Vulnerability Database. Available from: http://nvd.nist.gov/.

[c]Cybersecurity information exchange—Vulnerability/state exchange: Common vulnerabilities and exposures. Available from: https://www.itu.int/rec/T-REC-X.1520-201401-I/en.

[d]A Complete Guide to the Common Vulnerability Scoring System Version 3.0. Available from: http://www.first.org/cvss/cvss-v30-specification-v1.7.pdf.

[e]Cybersecurity information exchange—Vulnerability/state exchange: Common vulnerability scoring system. Available from: http://www.itu.int/rec/T-REC-X.1521-201104-I.

[f]Computer Security Incident Handling Guide. Available from: http://nvlpubs.nist.gov/nistpubs/SpecialPublications/NIST.SP.800-61r2.pdf.

[g]Cyber Observable eXpression (CybOX), Version 1.1. Available from: http://cyboxproject.github.io/releases/2.1.

[h]Cyber Observable eXpression (CybOX) 3.X. Available from: https://www.oasis-open.org/committees/documents.php?wg_abbrev = cti-cybox.

[i]Digital Signature Standard (DSS). Available from: http://nvlpubs.nist.gov/nistpubs/FIPS/NIST.FIPS.186-4.pdf.

[j]Escrowed Encryption Standards. Available from: http://www.itl.nist.gov/fipspubs/fip185.htm.

[k]Societal security—Guidelines for incident preparedness and operational continuity management. Available from: http://www.iso.org/iso/catalogue_detail?csnumber = 50295.

[l]Minimum Security Requirements for Federal Information and Information Systems. Available from: http://csrc.nist.gov/publications/fips/fips200/FIPS-200-final-march.pdf.

[m]Cybersecurity information exchange—Overview of cybersecurity: Overview of cybersecurity information exchange. Available from: http://www.itu.int/rec/T-REC-X.1500-201104-I/en.

[n]Personal Identity Verification (PIV) of Federal Employees and Contractors Version 2. Available from: http://nvlpubs.nist.gov/nistpubs/FIPS/NIST.FIPS.201-2.pdf.

[o]The Technical Specification for the Security Content Automation Protocol (SCAP); SCAP Version 1.0. Available from: http://nvlpubs.nist.gov/nistpubs/Legacy/SP/nistspecialpublication800-126.pdf.

[p]The Technical Specification for the Security Content Automation Protocol (SCAP); SCAP Version 1.1. Available from: http://nvlpubs.nist.gov/nistpubs/Legacy/SP/nistspecialpublication800-126r1.pdf.

[q]The Technical Specification for the Security Content Automation Protocol (SCAP); SCAP Version 2.0. Available from: http://nvlpubs.nist.gov/nistpubs/Legacy/SP/nistspecialpublication800-126r2.pdf.

[r]Secure Hash Standard (SHS) Available from: http://nvlpubs.nist.gov/nistpubs/FIPS/NIST.FIPS.180-4.pdf.

[s]Security Requirements for Cryptographic Modules. Available from: http://csrc.nist.gov/publications/fips/fips140-2/fips1402.pdf.

[t]Standards for Security Categorization of Federal Information and Information Systems. Available from: http://csrc.nist.gov/publications/fips/fips199/FIPS-PUB-199-final.pdf.

[u]Structure Threat Information eXpression (STIX) 1.2.1. Available from: https://github.com/STIXProject/specifications/wiki/Work-Product:-STIX-1.2.1-Specification.

[v]Structure Threat Information eXpression (STIX) 2.X. Available from: https://www.oasis-open.org/committees/documents.php?wg_abbrev = cti-stix.

[w]Trusted Automated eXchange of Indicator Information (TAXI) 1.1. Available from: https://taxiiproject.github.io/releases/1.1/TAXII_Services_Specification.pdf.

[x]Trusted Automated eXchange of Indicator Information (TAXI) 2.X. Available from: https://www.oasis-open.org/committees/documents.php?wg_abbrev = cti-taxii.

[y]The Keyed-Hash Message Authentication code (HMAC). Available from: http://csrc.nist.gov/publications/fips/fips198-1/FIPS-198-1_final.pdf.

Table 2.5 Cloud Computing-Related Standards

Name	Organization	Document Reference (Publication Date)
Cloud Data Management Interface (CDMI)	SNIA	CDMI 1.0 (04/2010)[a] CDMI 1.0.1 (09/2011)[b] CDMI 1.0.2 (06/2012)[c]
Cloud Infrastructure Management Interface (CIMI) Model and RESTful HTTP-based Protocol	DMTF	DSP0263 (08/2012)[d]
Guide for Cloud Portability and Interoperability Profiles (CPIP)	IEEE, Cloud Profiles WG (CPWG) Working Group	IEEE P2301 (Draft)[e]
Job Submission Definition Language (JSDL) Specification, Version 1.0	OGF	GFD-R.136 (07/2008)[f]
Open Cloud Computing Interface (OCCI)	OGF	GFD.P-R.183: OCCI−Core (06/2011)[g] GFD.P-R.184: OCCI-Infrastructure (06/2011)[h] GFD.P-R.185: RESTful HTTP Rendering (01/2011)[i]
Open Virtualization Format (OVF)	DMTF ISO/IEC	OVF v2.0.0 (12/2012)[j] ISO/IEC 17203: 2011[k]
Requirement of IdM in cloud computing	ITU-T Study Group 17, Question 4 (SG17/Q4)	XX.idmcc (Draft) (4/2011)[l]
Standard for Intercloud Interoperability and Federation (SIIF)	IEEE, Intercloud WG (ICWG) Working Group	IEEE P2302 (Draft)[m]
Topology and Orchestration Specification for Cloud Applications (TOSCA) Simple Profile for Network Functions Virtualization (NFV) Version 1.0	OASIS TOSCA	TOSCA Simple Profile for NFV 1.0[n]
Usage Record (UR)	OGF	GFD-R. 098: Usage Record (9/2006). 98.[o]

[a]*Cloud Data Management Interface Version 1.0. Available from: http://snia.org/sites/default/files/CDMI_SNIA_Architecture_v1.0.pdf.*
[b]*Cloud Data Management Interface Version 1.0.1. Available from: http://snia.org/sites/default/files/CDMI_SNIA_Architecture_v1.0.1.pdf.*
[c]*Cloud Data Management Interface Version 1.0.2. Available from: http://snia.org/sites/default/files/CDMI/20v1.0.2.pdf.*
[d]*Cloud Infrastructure Management Interface (CIMI) Model and RESTful HTTP-based Protocol. Available from: http://dmtf.org/sites/default/files/standards/documents/DSP0263_1.0.0.pdf.*
[e]*Guide for Cloud Portability and Interoperability Profiles. Available from: http://standards.ieee.org/develop/project/2301.html.*
[f]*Job Submissions Definition Language (JSDL) Specification, Version 1.0. Available from: https://www.ogf.org/documents/GFD.136.pdf.*
[g]*Open Cloud Computing Interface−Core. Available from: http://www.ogf.org/documents/GFD.183.pdf.*
[h]*Open Cloud Computing Interface−Infrastructure. Available from: http://www.ogf.org/documents/GFD.184.pdf.*
[i]*Open Cloud Computing Interface−RESTful HTTP Rendering. Available from: https://www.ogf.org/documents/GFD.185.pdf.*
[j]*Open Virtualization Format Specification. Available from: http://www.dmtf.org/sites/default/files/standards/documents/DSP0243_2.0.0.pdf.*
[k]*Information technology−Open Virtualization Format (OVF) specification. Available from: http://www.iso.org/iso/catalogue_detail.htm?csnumber = 59388.*
[l]*Requirements of IdM in cloud computing. Available from: http://www.itu.int/md/T09-SG17-110411-TD-PLEN-1675.*
[m]*Standard for Intercloud Interoperability and Federation. Available from: http://standards.ieee.org/develop/project/2302.html.*
[n]*Topology and Orchestration Specification for Cloud Applications (TOSCA) Simple Profile for Network Functions Virtualization (NFV) Version 1.0. Available from: http://docs.oasis-open.org/tosca/tosca-nfv/v1.0/tosca-nfv-v1.0.htm.*
[o]*Usage Record−Format Recommendation. Available from: https://www.ogf.org/documents/GFD.98.pdf.*

SUMMARY

This chapter provided an overview of the standards activities and the importance of standards development to the adoption of cloud computing within the federal government. By briefly reviewing the standards development process, we can begin to characterize standards supporting cloud computing and their maturity based on the evolutionary standards life cycle. We then discussed the federal legislative and policy drivers that address the federal government's role in supporting standards activities and the drivers affecting cloud computing adoption. We concluded our discussion by looking at the NIST Conceptual Reference Model and how the reference architecture can be used to facilitate the identification of standards that would meet specific usage scenarios.

REFERENCES

[1] National Institute of Standards and Technology (NIST). NIST Cloud Computing Standards Roadmap Working Group, Hogan H, Liu F, Sokol A, Tong J. NIST Special Publication (SP) 500-291, Version 2, NIST cloud computing standards roadmap. Maryland: National Institute of Standards and Technology; 2013.
[2] National Institute of Standards and Technology (NIST). National Technology Transfer and Advancement Act (NTTAA) [Internet]. Maryland: National Institute of Standards and Technology [cited August 15, 2011]. <http://standards.gov/nttaa.cfm>.
[3] Kundra V. Federal cloud computing strategy. Washington, DC: Executive Office of the President, Office of Management and Budget; 2011.
[4] Mell P, Grance T. NIST Special Publication (SP) 800-145, The NIST definition of cloud computing. Maryland: National Institute of Standards and Technology; 2011.
[5] National Institute of Standards and Technology (NIST). NIST Standards acceleration to jumpstart adoption of cloud computing (SAJACC) [Internet]. Maryland: National Institute of Standards and Technology [cited August 22, 2011]. <http://www.nist.gov/itl/cloud/sajacc.cfm>.
[6] DeVaux C. NIST Interagency Report (IR) IR 6802, A guide to documenting standards. Maryland: National Institute of Standards and Technology; 2001.
[7] US House of Representatives Trade Agreements Act of 1979 [Internet]. Washington, DC: US House of Representatives [cited August 23, 2011]. <http://uscode.house.gov/download/pls/19C13.txt>.
[8] Office of Management and Budget (OMB) Federal Participation in the Development and Use of Voluntary Consensus Standards and in Conformity Assessment Activities [Internet]. Washington, DC: Executive Office of the President, Office of Management and Budget [cited March 15, 2016]. <https://www.whitehouse.gov/sites/default/files/omb/inforeg/revised_circular_a-119_as_of_1_22.pdf>.
[9] Mell P, Grance T. NIST Special Publication (SP) 800-145, The NIST definition of cloud computing. Maryland: National Institute of Standards and Technology; 2011.
[10] Fang L, Tong J, Mao J, Bohn R, Messina J, Badger L. NIST Special Publication (SP) 500-292, NIST cloud computing reference architecture. Maryland: National Institute of Standards and Technology; 2011.

[11] Federal CIO. Council and Chief Acquisition Officers Council. Creating effective cloud computing contracts for the federal government. Washington, DC: Executive Office of the President, Office of Management and Budget; 2012.

[12] National Institute of Standards and Technology (NIST). Conformity Assessment [Internet]. Maryland: National Institute of Standards and Technology [cited March 15, 2016]. <http://gsi.nist.gov/global/index.cfm/L1-5/L2-45>.

A case for open source

3

INFORMATION IN THIS CHAPTER:

- Introduction
- Open Source Software and the Federal Government
- Open Source Software Adoption Challenges: Acquisition and Security
- Open Source Software and Federal Cloud Computing

INTRODUCTION

Open source software (OSS)[1] and cloud computing are distinctly different concepts that have independently grown in use, both in the public and private sectors, but have each faced adoption challenges by federal agencies. Both OSS[2] and cloud computing individually offer potential benefits for federal agencies to improve their efficiency, agility, and innovation, by enabling them to be more responsive to new or changing requirements in their missions and business operations. OSS improves the way the federal government develops and also distributes software[3] and provides an opportunity to reduce costs through the

---

[1]From Wennergren, D. Clarifying Guidance Regarding Open Source Software (OSS). Washington: US Department of Defense; 2009. *"Open software is software for which the human-readable source code is available for use, study, reuse, modification, enhancement, and redistribution by the users of that software."*

[2]Some examples include operating systems (*Linux, Solaris*), web/middlewares (*Apache, JBoss Glassfish*), databases (*MySQLP, PostgreSQL*), applications (*Firefox, Thunderbird*), and programming languages (*Perl, Python, PHP*).

[3]From the Office of Management and Budget (OMB). OMB Memorandum 16–21, Federal Source Code Policy: Achieving Efficiency, Transparency, and Innovation through Reusable and Open Source Software. Washington, DC: Executive Office of the President, Office of Management and Budget; 2016. *"Accessible, buildable, version-controlled repositories for the storage, discussion, and modification of custom-developed code are critical to both the Government-wide reuse."*

Federal Cloud Computing. DOI: http://dx.doi.org/10.1016/B978-0-12-809710-6.00003-2

reuse of existing source code,[4] whereas cloud computing improves the utilization of resources and enables a faster service delivery.

In this chapter, issues faced by OSS in the federal government will be discussed, in addition to the relationship of the federal government's adoption of cloud computing technologies.[5] However, this chapter does not present a differentiation of OSS from proprietary software,[6] rather focuses on highlighting the importance of the federal government's experience with OSS in the adoption of cloud computing.

Over the years, the private sector[7] has encouraged the federal government to consider OSS by making a case that it offers an acceptable alternative to proprietary commercial off-the-shelf (COTS) software. Regardless of the potential cost-saving benefits of OSS, federal agencies have historically approached it with cautious interest. Although, there are other potential issues in transitioning from an existing proprietary software, beyond cost. These issues include, a limited in-house skillset for OSS developers within the federal workforce, a lack of knowledge regarding procurement or licensing, and the misinterpretation of acquisition and security policies and guidance. Although some of the challenges and concerns have limited or slowed a broader-scale adoption of OSS, federal agencies have become more familiar with OSS and the marketplace expansion of available products and services, having made considerations for OSS as a viable alternative to enterprise-wide COTS software. This renewed shift to move toward OSS is also being driven by initiatives such as the 18F[8] and the US Digital Service,[9] and the publication of the guidance such as the Digital Services Playbook, which urges federal agencies to "consider using open source, cloud based, and commodity solutions across the technology stack" [1].

---

[4]From the Office of Management and Budget (OMB). OMB Memorandum 16–21, Federal Source Code Policy: Achieving Efficiency, Transparency, and Innovation through Reusable and Open Source Software. Washington, DC: Executive Office of the President, Office of Management and Budget; 2016. *"Enhanced reuse of custom-developed code across the Federal Government can have significant benefits for American taxpayers, including decreasing duplicative costs for the same code and reducing Federal vendor lock-in."*

[5]*NASA Nebula Cloud Computing Platform*. Available from: https://open.nasa.gov/blog/nebula-nasa-and-openstack/.

[6]From the Office of Management and Budget (OMB). OMB Memorandum 16–21, Federal Source Code Policy: Achieving Efficiency, Transparency, and Innovation through Reusable and Open Source Software. Washington, DC: Executive Office of the President, Office of Management and Budget; 2016. *"Software with intellectual property rights that are retained exclusively by a rights holder (e.g., an individual or a company)."*

[7]For example, the Open Source for America (OSfA) is an effort to raise awareness in the federal government about the benefits of open source software. Available from: http://opensourceforamerica.org/.

[8]18F is a digital services delivery team within the General Services Administration that develops in-house digital solutions to help agencies meet the needs of the citizens and businesses it serves. Available from: https://github.com/18F/open-source-policy/blob/master/policy.md.

[9]*The US Digital Service*. Available from: https://www.whitehouse.gov/digital/united-states-digital-service.

> **NOTE**
>
> Example cases where OSS was identified as a viable option to support federal government programs:
>
> - In May 2011, the US Department of Veterans Affair (VA) CIO stated to avoid costs, and to find a way to involve the private sector in modernizing Veterans Integrated System Technology Architecture (VistA; *electronic medical records system*), the VA turned to open source [2]. In response, the VA launched the Open Source Electronic Health Record Alliance (OSEHRA) in August 2012 "as a central governing body of a new open source Electronic Health Record (EHR) community" [3].
> - In January 2012, the National Aeronautics and Space Administration (NASA) launched a new website, the NASA Open Government Initiative,[10] to expand the agency's OSS development. The NASA Open Government co-lead stated: "We believe tomorrow's space and science systems will be built in the open, and that code.nasa.gov will play a big part in getting us there" [4].

Interoperability, portability, and security standards[11] have already been identified[12] as critical barriers for cloud adoption within the federal government. OSS facilitates overcoming standards obstacles through the development and implementation of open standards.[13] OSS communities support standards development through the "shared" development and industry implementation of open standards.[14] In some instances, the federal government's experience with standards development has enabled the acceptance and use of open standards-based, open source technologies and platforms.

---

[10]*NASA Open Government Initiative. Available from*: http://www.nasa.gov/open/.

[11]Standards were discussed in detail in Chapter 2, Cloud Computing Standards.

[12]From Kundra, V. Federal Cloud Computing Strategy. Washington, DC: Executive Office of the President, Office of Management and Budget; 2011. *Standards will be critical for the successful adoption and delivery of cloud computing, both within the public sector and more broadly. Standards are also critical to ensure clouds have an interoperable platform so that services provided by different providers can work together, regardless of whether they are provided using public, private, community, or a hybrid delivery model.*

[13]From the Office of Management and Budget (OMB). OMB Memorandum 16−21, Federal Source Code Policy: Achieving Efficiency, Transparency, and Innovation through Reusable and Open Source Software. Washington, DC: Executive Office of the President, Office of Management and Budget; 2016. *"Regardless of the specific solution selected, all software procurements and Government software development projects should consider utilizing open standards whenever practicable in order to increase the interoperability of all Government software solutions. Open standards enable software to be used by anyone at any time, and can spur innovation and growth regardless of the technology used for implementation—be it proprietary, mixed source, or OSS in nature."*

[14]Open standards, in general terms, is a technical specification that is developed openly (participation and publication) and is vendor neutral with limited cost (or free availability) to implementers.

> **TIP**
>
> OSS also enables agile software development[15] where the federal agencies can more rapidly deploy technologies and capabilities; however, for agile software development to be viable across the government, supporting government-wide agile acquisition guidance needs to be established. The *TechFAR Handbook*,[16] consistent with the Federal Acquisition Regulation (FAR),[17] was published to guide federal agencies by explicitly encouraging the use of agile software development and procure development services of modern software development techniques used in the private sector through modular contracting practices.[18]
>
> Many modernization projects have identified the use of OSS as a more economical value for the federal government. Through the use of smaller, agile procurements, federal agencies are achieving a higher yield and greater return on investment (ROI) compared to slower, inefficient long-term investments that use traditional procurement methods that tend to be outpaced by private sector innovations due to lengthy development cycles. Additionally, federal agencies are required to consider multiple factors when defining the overall business case[19] for an Information Technology (IT) investment.[20] Some factors that must be considered as part of the IT investment decision-making process[21] includes the total cost of ownership (TCO) and lifecycle maintenance costs, the costs associated with mitigating security risks, and the security and privacy of data [5]. OSS also requires transitioning to a subscription-based model, thereby reducing the burden for federal agencies to invest in upfront costs, which lock them into capital expenses that may be unrecoverable if the requirements change or a program is canceled or rescoped.

---

[15]From TechFAR Handbook for Procuring Digital Services for Using Agile Processes [Internet]. Washington, DC: The White House [cited January 26, 2016]. Available from: https://playbook.cio.gov/assets/TechFAR%20Handbook_2014-08-07.pdf. *"Agile software development is a method of software development that is based on iterative and incremental processes and collaboration among a team."*

[16]From TechFAR Handbook for Procuring Digital Services for Using Agile Processes [Internet]. Washington, DC: The White House [cited January 26, 2016]. <https://playbook.cio.gov/assets/TechFAR%20Handbook_2014-08-07.pdf>. TechFAR Handbook *"highlights the flexibilities in the Federal Acquisition Regulation (FAR) that can help agencies implement 'plays' from the Digital Services Playbook that would be accomplished with acquisition support—with a particular focus on how to use contractors to support an iterative, customer-driven software development process, as is routinely done in the private sector."*

[17]From TechFAR Handbook for Procuring Digital Services for Using Agile Processes [Internet]. Washington, DC: The White House [cited January 26, 2016]. <https://playbook.cio.gov/assets/TechFAR%20Handbook_2014-08-07.pdf>. *"The FAR and each agency's supplement to the FAR, set forth Government-wide overarching Federal procurement principles, policies, processes and procedures on procuring goods and services, including IT and digital services."*

[18]*Contracting Guidance to Support Modular Development.* Available from: https://www.whitehouse.gov/sites/default/files/omb/procurement/guidance/modular-approaches-for-information-technology.pdf.

[19]Guidance on exhibit 300A (business cases). Available from: http://www.whitehouse.gov/sites/default/files/omb/assets/egov_docs/fy13_guidance_for_exhibit_300_a-b_20110715.pdf.

[20]From the Office of Management and Budget (OMB). OMB Circular A-11, Planning, Budgeting, and Acquisition of Capital Assets. Washington, DC: Executive Office of the President, Office of Management and Budget; 2011. *"Agencies should make security's role explicit in information technology investments and capital programming."*

[21]The Capital Planning and Investment Control Process (CPIC) includes a requirement to integrate IT security into the IT investment evaluation criteria. Available from: http://nvlpubs.nist.gov/nistpubs/Legacy/SP/nistspecialpublication800-65.pdf.

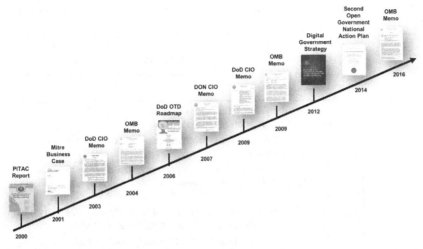

FIGURE 3.1

US Government OSS Policy Framework.

OPEN SOURCE SOFTWARE AND THE FEDERAL GOVERNMENT

The federal government's use of OSS has its beginning in the 1990s.[22] During this period, OSS was used primarily within the research and scientific community where collaboration and information sharing was a cultural norm. However, it was not until 2000 that federal agencies began to seriously consider the use of OSS as a model for accelerating innovation within the federal government. As illustrated in Fig. 3.1, the federal government has developed a list of OSS-related studies, policies, and guidelines that have formed the basis for the policy framework that has guided the adoption of OSS. This framework tackles critical issues that have inhibited the federal government from attaining the full benefits offered by OSS. Although gaps[23] still exist in specific guidelines relating to the evaluation, contribution, and sharing of OSS, the policy framework serves as a foundation for guiding federal agencies in the use of OSS. In this section, we will explore the policy framework with the objective of describing how the current policy framework has led to the broader use of OSS across the federal government, and more importantly how this framework has enabled the federal government's adoption of cloud computing by overcoming the challenges with acquisition and security that will be discussed in detail in the next section.

---

[22]*Timeline: A History of Open Source in Government.* Available from: http://gov-oss.org/.
[23]Lessons Learned: Roadblocks and Opportunities for Open Source Software (OSS) in US Government.

Table 3.1 Advantages and Challenges Highlighted in the PITAC Report [6]

Advantages	• Potentially improved security because programmers have developed access to source code that allows them to examine it for potential embedded trap doors and/or Trojan horses. • Increase in the number of programmers searching for software bugs and developing fixes.
Challenges	• Limitation in the project management and funding models to support "fiscal flexibility" for open source development. • Lack of policies or guidance governing export control and national security considerations. • Potentially incompatible licensing agreements used within the open source community may cause delays due to the lack of education of how to use them. • Poorly defined procurement[a] rules do not explicitly authorize competition between open source alternatives and proprietary software. • Lack of clear guidance regarding the decision-making authority and/or responsibility of the federal agency to use OSS. • Lack of a single repository for warehousing open source projects.

[a]From US Department of Homeland Security, Science and Technology. Open Source Software in Government: Challenges and Opportunities. Washington, DC: US Department of Homeland Security; 2013. *"Incentivize government program offices and contractors to build collaborative communities and to share code. Request for proposal developers should not presume that respondents have a particular business model and should not impose unnecessary paperwork burdens. The government should require sharing software and release software as OSS by default if it was developed with public funds; this may require changes to contracting strategies."*

The President's Information Technology Advisory Committee (PITAC),[24] which examined OSS, was given the goal [6] of:

• Charting a vision of how the federal government can support developing OSS;
• Defining a policy framework;
• Identifying policy, legal, and administrative barriers to the widespread adoption of OSS; and
• Identifying potential roles for public institutions in OSS economics model.

The PITAC published a report[25] concluding that the use of the open source development model (also known as the Bazaar model[26]) was a viable strategy for producing high-quality software through a mixture of public, private, and academic partnerships [7]. In addition, as presented in Table 3.1, the report also

---

[24]Co-Chaired by Raj Reddy of Carnegie Mellon University (http://www.rr.cs.cmu.edu/) and Irving Wladawsky-Berger of MIT (https://esd.mit.edu/people/scholars/wladawsky-berger/wladawsky-berger.htm).

[25]*Developing Open Source Software to Advance High End Computing.* Available from: http://www.nitrd.gov/pitac/report/index.html.

[26]*The Cathedral and the Bazaar.* Available from: http://www.catb.org/esr/writings/cathedral-bazaar/.

highlighted several advantages and challenges. Some of these key issues have been at the forefront of the federal government's adoption of OSS.

Over the years since the PITAC report, the federal government has gained significant experience in both sponsoring and contributing to OSS projects. For example, one of the most widely recognized contributions by the federal government specifically related to security is the Security Enhanced Linux (SELinux) project.[27] The SELinux project focused on improving the Linux kernel through the development of a reference implementation of the Flask security architecture[28] for flexible mandatory access control (MAC). In 2000, the National Security Agency (NSA)[29] made the SELinux available to the Linux community under the terms of the GNU's Not Unix (GNU) General Public License (GPL).[30]

NOTE

The Open Source Definition (OSD)[31] had its beginning as free software[32] in the early 1980s during the free software movement[33] starting with the GNU[34] project[35] that implemented the GPL. Although the early uses of the terms "open source" and "free software" had been used interchangeably during that period, it was not until 1998 that Netscape Communications Corporation released[36] their Netscape Navigator Web browser source code as Mozilla. At this time, the distinction of the "open source"[37] concept became more mainstream within the broader commercial software industry. The Free Software Foundation[38] and Open Source Initiative (OSI)[39] have similar goals, but there was a notable difference in respect to their philosophies[40] and approved licenses.[41]

---

[27]SELinux Frequently Asked Questions (FAQ). Available from: https://www.nsa.gov/what-we-do/research/selinux/faqs.shtml.

[28]*Flask security architecture*. Available from: http://www.cs.utah.edu/flux/fluke/html/flask.html.

[29]Raising the Bar in Operating System Security: SELinux and OpenSolaris FMAC. Available from: https://www.nsa.gov/resources/everyone/digital-media-center/publications/the-next-wave/assets/files/TNW-18-2.pdf.

[30]*GNU General Public License*. Available from: http://www.gnu.org/copyleft/gpl.html.

[31]Based loosely on the *Debian Software Guidelines (DFSG)*. Available from: http://www.debian.org/social_contract#guidelines.

[32]*The Free Software Definition*. Available from: http://www.gnu.org/philosophy/free-sw.html.

[33]*Why Software Should Not Have Owners*. Available from: http://www.gnu.org/philosophy/why-free.html.

[34]*GNU Not For Unix*. Available from: http://www.gnu.org/gnu/manifesto.html.

[35]The Free Software Foundation was a sponsoring organization of GNU.

[36]*The Beginning of Mozilla*. Available from: http://blog.lizardwrangler.com/2008/01/22/january-22-1998-the-beginning-of-mozilla/.

[37]*The Cathedral and the Bazaar*. Available from: http://www.catb.org/esr/writings/cathedral-bazaar/.

[38]*Free Software Foundation (FSF)*. Available from: http://www.fsf.org/.

[39]*Open Source Initiative (OSI)*. Available from: http://www.opensource.org/.

[40]*Why Open Source missed the point of Free Software*. Available from: http://www.gnu.org/philosophy/open-source-misses-the-point.html.

[41]*OSI Approved Licenses*. Available from: http://www.opensource.org/licenses/alphabetical and *Free Software Foundation Licenses*. Available from: http://en.wikipedia.org/wiki/List_of_FSF_approved_software_licenses.

Starting in 2001, the MITRE Corporation, for the US Department of Defense (DoD), published a report[42] that built a business case for the DoD's use of OSS. The business case discussed both the benefits and risks for considering OSS. In MITRE's conclusion, OSS offered significant benefits to the federal government, such as improved interoperability, increased support for open standards and quality, lower costs, and agility through reduced development time. In addition, MITRE highlighted issues and risks, recommending any consideration of OSS should be carefully reviewed.

Shortly after the MITRE report, the federal government began to establish specific policies and guidance to help clarify issues around OSS. The DoD Chief Information Officer (CIO) published the Department's first official DoD-wide memorandum to reiterate existing policy and to provide clarifying guidance on the acquisition, development, and the use of OSS within the DoD community [8]. Soon after the DoD policy, the Office of Management and Budget (OMB) established a memorandum to provide government-wide policy[43] regarding acquisition[44] and licensing issues.

Since 2003, there were multiple misconceptions, specifically within the DoD, regarding the use of OSS. Therefore, in 2007, the US Department of the Navy (DON) CIO released a memorandum[45] that clarified the classification of OSS and directed the Department to identify areas where OSS can be used within the DON's IT portfolio. This was followed by another DoD-wide memorandum in 2009, which provided DoD-wide guidance and clarified the use and development of OSS, including explaining the potential advantages of the DoD reducing the development time for new software, anticipating threats, and response to continual changes in requirements [9].

In 2009, OMB released the Open Government Directive,[46] which required federal agencies to develop and publish an Open Government Plan on their websites.

---

[42]*A Business Case Study of Open Source Software*. Available from: http://www.mitre.org/sites/default/files/pdf/kenwood_software.pdf.

[43]Office of Management and Budget (OMB) Memorandum 04–16, Software Acquisition. Available from: http://www.whitehouse.gov/omb/memoranda_fy04_m04-16.

[44]From Evans, K., Burton, R. Office of Management and Budget (OMB) Memorandum 04–16, Software Acquisition. Washington, DC: Executive Office of the President, Office of Management and Budget; 2004. *The Office of Management and Budget (OMB) Circulars A-11 and A-130 and the Federal Acquisition Regulation (FAR), guide agency information technology (IT) investment decisions and are intentionally technology and vendor neutral.*

[45]*Department of the Navy Open Source Software Guidance*. Available from: http://www.doncio.navy.mil/ContentView.aspx?ID = 312.

[46]From Transparency and Open Government [Internet]. Washington, DC: The White House [cited June 2, 2012]. <http://www.whitehouse.gov/the_press_office/Transparency_and_Open_Government>. *In 2009, a Presidential Memoranda was issued titled "Transparency and Open Government," which directed the OMB Director to issue an Open Government Directive to instruct federal agencies to take specific action in implementing the Open Government Initiative.*

The Open Government Plan[47] provided a description on how federal agencies would improve transparency and integrate public participation and collaboration [10]. As an example response to the directive support for openness, the National Aeronautics and Space Administration (NASA), in furtherance of its Open Government Plan, released the "open. NASA"[48] site that was built completely using OSS, such as the LAMP stack[49] and the Wordpress content management system (CMS).

On May 23, 2012, the White House released the *Digital Government Strategy* that complements[50] other initiatives and established principles for transforming the federal government. More specifically, the strategy outlined the need for a "Shared Platform" approach. In this approach, the federal government would need to leverage "sharing" of resources such as the "use of open source technologies that enable more sharing of data and make content more accessible" [11].

The Second Open Government Action Plan established an action to develop an OSS policy to improve access by federal agencies to custom software to "fuel innovation, lower costs, and benefit the public" [12]. In August 2016, the White House published the Federal Source Code Policy, which is consistent with the "Shared Platform" approach in the Digital Government's Strategy, by requiring federal agencies make available custom code as OSS.[51] Further, the policy also made "custom-developed code available for Government-wide reuse and make their code inventories discoverable at https://www.code.gov ('Code.gov')" [12].

In this section, we discussed key milestones that have impacted the federal government's cultural acceptance of OSS. It also discussed the current policy framework that has been developed through a series of policies and guidelines to support federal agencies in the adoption of OSS and the establishment of processes and policies to encourage and support the development of OSS. The remainder of this chapter will examine the key issues that have impacted OSS adoption and briefly examine the role of OSS in the adoption of cloud computing within the federal government.

---

[47]NASA released its original Open Government Plan 1.0 in April 2010 and in accordance with the requirement to review/update every two years under the Open Government Directive, NASA's current Open Government Plan was released in April 2012. Available from: http://www.nasa.gov/open/plan/.

[48]*open.NASA*. Available from: http://open.nasa.gov.

[49]Linux, Apache, MySQL, and Perl/PHP (LAMP).

[50]From the White House. Digital Government: Building a 21st Century Platform to Better Serve the American People. Washington, DC: Executive Office of the President, Office of Management and Budget; 2012. *"The Digital Government Strategy complements several initiatives aimed at building a 21st century government that works better for the American people. These include Executive Order 13571 (Streamlining Service Delivery and Improving Customer Service), Executive Order 13576 (Delivering an Efficient, Effective, and Accountable Government), the President's Memorandum on Transparency and Open Government, OMB Memorandum M-10-06 (Open Government Directive), the National Strategy for Trusted Identities in Cyberspace (NSTIC), and the 25-Point Implementation Plan to Reform Federal Information Technology Management (IT Reform)."*

[51]From the Office of Management and Budget (OMB). OMB Memorandum 16–21, Federal Source Code Policy: Achieving Efficiency, Transparency, and Innovation through Reusable and Open Source Software. Washington, DC: Executive Office of the President, Office of Management and Budget; 2016. *"Contracts for the custom development of software shall—at a minimum—acquire and enforce rights sufficient to enable Government-wide reuse of custom-developed code."*

OPEN SOURCE SOFTWARE ADOPTION CHALLENGES: ACQUISITION AND SECURITY

The adoption of OSS as previously mentioned, has faced a number of roadblocks within the federal government. In this section, we will focus our examination specifically on the acquisition and security challenges that have been key inhibitors in the broad adoption of OSS. In addition, through our review we will obtain a better understanding of how the federal government's relationship with OSS has changed over time and gain some insight into how this experience has eased the path to cloud computing.

> **NOTE**
>
> In a blog post titled "Streaming at 1:00: In the Cloud" [13], former US CIO Vivek Kundra noted three critical challenges facing the federal government in deploying new IT services and products:
>
> - Procurement processes can be confusing and time-consuming.
> - Security procedures are complex, costly, lengthy, and duplicative across agencies.
> - Our (federal government) policies lag behind new trends, causing unnecessary restrictions on the use of new technology.

ACQUISITION CHALLENGES

In the past, federal agencies have relied upon limited acquisition policy guidance[52] when considering the procurement and the use of OSS. In the PITAC report [14] discussed previously, two specific acquisition-related findings were highlighted:

- *Licensing agreements*—numerous licensing agreements, incompatible licensing requirements, and educating federal managers on open source licenses[53] and conditions.[54]
- *Federal procurement rules*—no explicit authorization of competition between open source alternatives and proprietary software, and lack of guidance on applicability and usage of OSS.

---

[52]From Federal Acquisition Regulation (FAR). Washington, DC: US General Services Administration; 2011. The Federal Acquisition Regulation (FAR) classifies open source software as commercial computer software (or "commercial item means")—"*(1) customarily used by the general public or by non-governmental entities and (1)(i) sold, leased, or licensed to the general public; or (1)(ii) offered for sale, lease, or license to the general public*".

[53]From Office of Management and Budget (OMB). OMB Memorandum 16-21, Federal Source Code Policy: Achieving Efficiency, Transparency, and Innovation through Reusable and Open Source Software. Washington, DC: Executive Office of the President, Office of Management and Budget; 2016. "*Licensing is a critical component of OSS and can affect how the source code can be used and modified.*"

[54]MITRE study conducted in 2003, "Use of Free and Open Source Software (FOSS) in the US Department of Defense." Available from: http://dodcio.defense.gov/Portals/0/Documents/FOSS/dodfoss_pdf.pdf.

Table 3.2 Federal Laws and Regulations

Federal Laws	• 41 U.S.C. § 430[a]—Definitions (defines *"commercial item"*)
	• 41 U.S.C. § 431[b]—Commercially available off-the-shelf item acquisitions: lists of inapplicable laws in FAR (defines *"Commercially available off-the-shelf (COTS) item"*)
	• 41 U.S.C. § 264B[c] and 10 USC § 2377[d]—Preference for acquisition of commercial items
Regulations	• FAR 2.101(b)[e], 12.000, 12.101(c)[f]—Acquisition of Commercial Items
	• FAR 10.001[g]—Market Research

[a]Available from: *http://www.gpo.gov/fdsys/pkg/USCODE-2009-title41/html/USCODE-2009-title41-chap7-sec403.htm.*
[b]Available from: *http://www.gpo.gov/fdsys/pkg/USCODE-2009-title41/html/USCODE-2009-title41-chap7-sec431.htm.*
[c]Available from: *http://www.gpo.gov/fdsys/pkg/USCODE-2009-title41/html/USCODE-2009-title41-chap4-subchapIV-sec264b.htm.*
[d]Available from: *http://www.gpo.gov/fdsys/pkg/USCODE-2006-title10/html/USCODE-2006-title10-subtitleA-partIV-chap140-sec2377.htm.*
[e]Available from: *https://www.acquisition.gov/far/html/Subpart%202_1.html.*
[f]Available from: *https://www.acquisition.gov/far/html/Subpart%2012_1.html.*
[g]Available from: *https://www.acquisition.gov/far/html/Subpart%202_1.html.*

Even with the limited policies guidance, federal agencies were required to understand how federal laws and regulations applied to the acquisition of OSS. Table 3.2 provides several references within federal laws and regulations that must be considered by federal agencies when procuring OSS (and other proprietary) COTS products.

In addition, federal agencies are also required to understand how to select and apply the various types of software licenses, specifically "where future modifications by the US government may be necessary" [15]. Guidelines in developing license criteria [16] used in determining which OSS license to use could include:

- Using an existing OSS license; not creating a new OSS license.
- Making sure it is actually OSS.
- Using a GPL-compatible license.
- Choosing a license that meets the expected uses of the OSS.
- Using a common OSS license.

In order to dispel concerns over these license issues, several policy documents were issued to govern acquisition and provide guidance on the use of OSS within the federal government. The OSS acquisition policy framework, outlined in Table 3.3, consists primarily of the existing OMB and DoD policies; however, some federal agencies have issued additional guidance[55] to provide specific direction on how OSS could be used to support their specific mission and business

[55]For example, Internal Revenue Service (http://www.irs.gov/pub/irs-utl/fti-in-opensourcesoftware. doc), the Consumer Financial Protection Bureau (http://www.consumerfinance.gov/developers/source-codepolicy/), and NASA (http://nodis3.gsfc.nasa.gov/displayDir.cfm?t = NPR&c = 2210&s = 1C).

Table 3.3 OSS Acquisition Policy Framework

Policy	Description
OMB Memorandum 04–16, Software Acquisition (2004)[a]	• Clarified the equal treatment of OSS and proprietary software in acquisition decision • Recommended caution when using OSS to understand the type of OSS license associated with software and obligations to make original source available • Employee education of licensing restrictions
Clarifying Guidance Regarding Open Source Software (2009)[b]	• Clarified the applicability of OSS in meeting the definition of "commercial software" in accordance with 10 U.S.C 2377 • Requirement for conducting market research when preparing for procurement of property or services, including OSS • Clarified DoD Instruction 8500.2,[c]Information Assurance (IA) Implementation—DCPD-1 Public Domain Software Controls, does not forbid usage of OSS • All software, including OSS, should include maintenance and support • Clarified misconceptions of requirements to distribute modified OSS to public and emphasized importance of understanding which licenses allow users to modify *for internal use only* • Required the usage of a DoD-wide collaborative software development environment to distribute software source code and design documents[d] • Distribution of OSS, including code fixes and enhancement, to the public when it is determined it is in the government's interest; the government has rights to reproduce and release, and public release of item is not restricted by other law or regulations (e.g., Export Administration Regulations (EAR)[e] or International Traffic in Arms Regulation (ITAR)[f])
Federal Source Code Policy: Achieving Efficiency, Transparency, and Innovation through Reusable and Open Source Software (2016)	• Provided a policy to agencies on considerations that must be made prior to acquiring any custom-developed code • Required agencies to obtain appropriate Government data rights to custom-developed code, including at a minimum, rights to Government-wide reuse and rights to modify the code • Required agencies to consider the value of publishing custom code as OSS • Established requirements for releasing custom-developed source code, including securing the rights necessary to make some custom-developed code releasable to the public as OSS under this policy's new pilot program

[a]From Evans, K., Burton, A. Office of Management and Budget (OMB) Memorandum 0416. Software Acquisition. Washington, DC: Executive Office of the President, Office of Management and Budget; 2004. "The Office of Management and Budget (OMB) Circulars A-11 and A-130 and the Federal Acquisition Regulation (FAR), guide agency information technology (IT) investment decisions."

[b]*DoD Instruction 8510.01*. Available from: *http://dodcio.defense.gov/Portals/0/Documents/FOSS/2009OSS.pdf*.

[c]From Stenbit, J. DoD Instruction 8500.2 Information Assurance (IA) Implementation. Washington: US Department of Defense; 2003. *The DoD memo also dispelled the misconceptions that OSS is classified as "freeware or shareware," which is prohibited from being "used in DoD information systems unless they are necessary for mission accomplishment and there are no alternative IT solutions available."*

[d]From DISA. Forg.mil [Internet]. Maryland: Defense Information Systems Agency [cited March 18, 2016]. *"Forge.mil is a DISA-led activity designed to improve the ability of the U.S. Department of Defense to rapidly deliver dependable software, services and systems in support of net-centric operations and warfare."*

[e]DoD Instruction 8510.01. Available from: *http://www.bis.doc.gov/policiesandregulations/index.htm*.

[f]International Traffic in Arms Regulation (ITAR). Available from: *http://pmddtc.state.gov/regulations_laws/itar.html*.

Table 3.4 Federal Government OSS FAQs

Frequently asked questions regarding OSS and the US DoD (2009)	"An educational resource for government employees and government contractors to understand the policies and legal issues relating to the use of OSS in the DoD" [15]
Frequently asked questions about copyright and computer software: issues affecting the US Government with Special Emphasis on OSS (2010)	"Provides general guidance on a special category of copyright works—computer software—and includes a details discussion of open source software" [17]

requirements. In addition to the policy documents, several frequently asked questions (FAQs) have been developed to facilitate understanding key acquisition-related issues (see Table 3.4).

SECURITY CHALLENGES

OSS has previously been characterized as offering a number of potential security advantages. The security advantages[56] include the ability for developers to access the source code, allowing for a more thorough examination and identification of security vulnerabilities, and an increased number of availability of programmers searching for bugs and subsequently developing fixes [14]. However, some of the same advantages have also been overshadowed by hindrances such as uncertainty of the trustworthiness of code repositories and the availability of source code to allow malicious attackers the ability to identify security vulnerabilities.

Challenges associated with security in OSS have also existed because there has been a lack of clarification and education of the processes and certifications required to ensure that software is validated for use within the federal government. Some of the commonly used processes[57] and certification methodologies that are required for verifying that software and applications meet federal security requirements include, but are not limited to:

- NIST Risk Management Framework (RMF).[58]
- DoD Information Assurance Security Certification and Accreditation Process (DIACAP).[59]

---

[56]From Wennergren, D. Clarifying guidance regarding OSS. Washington, DC: Department of Defense; 2009. *"The continuous and broad peer-review enabled by publicly available source code supports software reliability and security efforts through the identification and elimination of defects that might otherwise go unrecognized by a more limited core development team."*

[57]Certification and accreditation processes are discussed in detail in Chapter 7, Comparison of Federal and International Security Certification Standards.

[58]*NIST SP 800-37 Revision 1, Guide for Applying the Risk Management Framework (RMF) to Federal Information Systems.* Available from:<http://csrc.nist.gov/publications/nistpubs/800-37-rev1/sp800-37-rev1-final.pdf>.

[59]*DoD Instruction 8510.01, RMF for DoD Information Technology.* <http://www.dtic.mil/whs/directives/corres/pdf/851001_2014.pdf>.

- Risk Management Framework (RMF) for DoD Information Technology *(previously known as the DoD Assurance Certification and Accreditation Process (DIACAP))*.[60]
- National Information Assurance Partnership (NIAP), Common Criteria (CC).[61]

In addressing the challenges with OSS security, the federal government initiated a number of programs "to investigate open security methods, models and technologies and identify viable and sustainable approaches that support national cyber security objectives" [18]. For example, the US Department of Homeland Security (DHS), Science and Technology (S&T), and Directorate Cyber Security Research and Development Center (CSRDC) manages the Homeland Open Security Technology (HOST)[62] program, which is an information portal for open-source security tools and applications. In addition, the DHS also initiated the Open Source Hardening Project to maintain a database of analyzed OSS using the coverity scan.[63] The scan website offers qualified project developers of OSS with a portal where they can retrieve defects identified by Coverity[64] analyses [19].

OPEN SOURCE SOFTWARE AND FEDERAL CLOUD COMPUTING

Open source technologies have played a significant role in the federal government's adoption of cloud computing. From the inception of the *25-Point Implementation Plan to Reform Federal Information Technology Management*, which introduced the key components of the federal government's adoption of "light technologies" and "shared solutions," the federal government has initiated the shift toward more openness and shared platforms. Openness and shared platforms support the ability of the federal government to deliver agility and innovation. OSS has served as the enabler, spawning incubations[65] in technologies across the industry and public sector that have formed the foundation of many of the cloud computing platforms.

---

[60]NSTISSI-1000, National Information Assurance Certification and Accreditation Process (NIACAP).

[61]*National Informational Assurance Partnership (NIAP) Common Criteria Evaluation and Validation Scheme (CCEVS)*. Available from: http://www.niap-ccevs.org/.

[62]*Homeland Open Security Technology (HOST)*. Available from: / http://www.dhs.gov/science-and-technology/csd-host.

[63]List of open source software scanned by the Coverity Scan. Available from: https://scan.coverity.com/projects.

[64]Coverity provides the results of its static-analysis code inspection tool for free to open source community.

[65]Examples include python (http://www.python.org/), Java (http://www.java.com), Springsource (http://spring.io/), Apache Software Foundation (https://projects.apache.org/projects.html), and Linux (http://kernel.org/).

> **NOTE**
>
> In 2003, NASA began "assessing the formal barriers to distributing software they developed as open source and began reviewing the state of open source licenses"[66] [20]. Open source[67] directly addressed NASA's needs of the rapid and wide dissemination of software with minimal overhead and cost, supporting its functions under the National Aeronautics and Space Act.[68] However, it was not until September 15, 2009, when the former US CIO Vivek Kundra announced the launch of Apps.gov[69] at the NASA Ames Research Center (ARC),[70] did it set the stage for the next phase in the federal government's adoption of public cloud computing services. During this time, NASA ARC had already begun an effort in the development of a cloud environment through the Nebula project.[71] NASA Nebula, "which started out as a Web consolidation exercise" [21], succeeded primarily because of the experience obtained through NASA's involvement in OSS.[72] Following experimentation with both commercial and open source cloud computing solutions, the Nebula project initiated an effort to begin building the first open source Infrastructure as a Service (IaaS) cloud software platform.[73] Nebula provided a case study for demonstrating the value OSS brought to the federal government.

The Federal Data Center Consolidation Initiative (FDCCI) is a federal consolidation effort focused on reducing physical space by shifting IT investments to more efficient computing platforms and technologies [22]. These computing platforms and technologies leverage virtualization to support the ability to consolidate and improve government-wide IT utilization through shared infrastructures. The Cloud First and Shared First policies were established to increase the return on investment (ROI) associated with the federal government's use of its IT investment. The optimization of IT investment requires the use of the economies of scale offered by cloud

---

[66]NASA Open Source Agreement (NOSA), which became the only government agency to receive OSI Certification. Available from: http://www.opensource.org/licenses/nasa1.3.

[67]Instead of using an existing licensing model, NASA chose to produce the NOSA, which became an OSI-approved software license.

[68]From NASA, The National Aeronautics Space Act [Internet]. Washington, DC: NASA [cited May 21, 2012]. <http://www.nasa.gov/offices/ogc/about/space_act1.html>. *"Provide for the widest practicable and appropriate dissemination of information concerning its activities and the results thereof."*

[69]A storefront portal hosted by GSA for federal agencies to find cloud computing applications to include business applications, productivity applications, cloud IT services, and social media apps.

[70]NASA Ames Research Center (ARC). Available from: http://www.nasa.gov/centers/ames/.

[71]From NASA, Nebula Cloud Computing Platform [Internet]. California: NASA Ames Research Center [cited November 11, 2011]. <http://www.nasa.gov/open/nebula.html>. *"Nebula is an open-source cloud computing project and service developed to provide an alternative to the costly construction of additional data centers."*

[72]From Cureton, L., Braun, B. NPR 22101C, Requirement Waiver in Support of Open Source Software Development. Washington, DC: NASA; 2010. *"For example, in November 2010, the NASA Chief Information Officer (CIO) issued a request for a waiver to support the release of the Nebula software for development in a publicly accessible repository to accelerate development and leverage community expertise to produce higher quality software."*

[73]The NASA Nebula cloud fabric became the Nova fabric controller as the Compute component of the OpenStack cloud software. Available from: http://www.openstack.org.

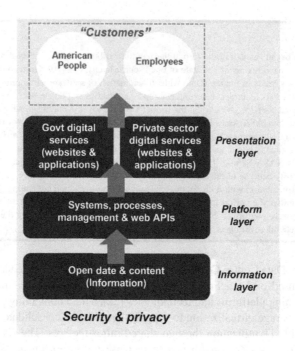

FIGURE 3.2

Conceptual layers of digital services [23].

commuting and other shared service[74] platforms. By leveraging reuse offered by OSS and the consolidation of redundant missions, through cross-organizational cloud services, efficiency can be delivered through more "economical" and "shared" delivery service models. The Digital Government Strategy, as illustrated in Fig. 3.2, reiterated the need to deliver more efficient customer-centric services at a lower cost point through technologies that support the *information*,[75] *platform*,[76] and *presentations*[77] layers. In addition, cloud computing and related technologies offer a shared

---

[74]From VanRoekel, V. Federal Information Technology Shared Services Strategy. Washington, DC: Executive Office of the President, Office of Management and Budget; 2012. "*An information technology function that is provided for consumption by multiple organizations within or between Federal Agencies.*"

[75]From the Office of Management and Budget (OMB). Digital Government: Building a 21st Century Platform to Better Serve the American People. Washington, DC: Executive Office of the President, Office of Management and Budget; 2012. "*The information layer contains digital information.*"

[76]From the Office of Management and Budget (OMB). Digital Government: Building a 21st Century Platform to Better Serve the American People. Washington, DC: Executive Office of the President, Office of Management and Budget; 2012. The platform layer includes all the systems and process to manage digital information.

[77]From the Office of Management and Budget (OMB). Digital Government: Building a 21st Century Platform to Better Serve the American People. Washington, DC: Executive Office of the President, Office of Management and Budget; 2012. "*The presentation layer defines the manager in which information is organized and provided to customers.*"

platform to support the federal government's ability to manage information[78] in an organized manner and deliver the information using multiple accessibility modes (e.g., websites and mobile applications). A shared platform approach also provides an efficient and low-cost mechanism to develop and deliver services and information that support the strategy through three strategic objectives:

- Securely architect for interoperability and openness.
- Develop governance structure for digital services[79] (e.g., procurement and security policies and processes).
- Spur innovation by providing the federal government's data in open and machine-readable formats.

OSS, as an enabler for cloud computing and other shared platforms, has accelerated the shift in technology delivery models, both in the public and private sectors. OSS has also produced many of the key technology innovations that are built into the foundation of this technology shift, such as different virtualization[80] technologies and cloud computing[81] platforms. These technologies and platforms can be leveraged to support the federal government's digital strategy through an open, standards-based approach that provides a more efficient use of rapidly evolving technologies. In addition, many OSS projects utilize a shared development methodology. This methodology promotes agility by bringing together a community of developers that can deliver innovative solutions faster and with fewer dedicated resources.

SUMMARY

In this chapter, a case for open source was presented with a focus on understanding how the accelerated pathway to the cloud was, in part, contributed to by the broader government-wide acceptance of OSS. Challenges faced by the federal government in addressing acquisition were examined, which included licensing

---

[78]From the Office of Management and Budget (OMB). Digital Government: Building a 21st Century Platform to Better Serve the American People. Washington, DC: Executive Office of the President, Office of Management and Budget; 2012. *"Information, as defined in OMB Circular A-130, is any communication or representation of knowledge such as facts, data, or opinions in any medium or form, including textual, numerical, graphic, cartographic, narrative, or audiovisual forms."*

[79]From the Office of Management and Budget (OMB). Digital Government: Building a 21st Century Platform to Better Serve the American People. Washington, DC: Executive Office of the President, Office of Management and Budget; 2012. "Digital services include the delivery of digital information (i.e., data or content) and transactional services (e.g., online forms, benefits applications) across a variety of platforms, devices and delivery mechanisms (e.g., websites, mobile applications, and social media)."

[80]Examples include Kernel-based Virtual Machine (http://www.linux-kvm.org/page/Main_Page) and Xen Hypervisor (http://www.xenproject.org/developers/teams/hypervisor.html).

[81]Examples include OpenStack cloud software (http://www.openstack.org), CloudStack (http://cloudstack.apache.org/), and Cloud Foundry (https://www.cloudfoundry.org/).

and federal procurement policies. Security was also discussed with specific focus on the processes and certification methods that provide risk-based approaches to verify OSS as part of the system development life cycle (SDLC). Finally, the chapter concluded with a brief discussion on how OSS is an enabler that supports the federal government's objectives of embracing technologies to promote efficiency and improved service delivery in a secure, standards-based approach.

REFERENCES

[1] The U.S. Digital Service. Digital Services Playbook [Internet]. Washington, DC: Executive Office of the President [cited January 28, 2016]. <https://playbook.cio.gov/>.

[2] US House of Representatives. Subcommittee on oversight and investigation of the committee on Veteran's affairs [Internet]. Washington, DC: US Government Printing Office [cited May 22, 2012]. <http://veterans.house.gov/sites/republicans.veterans. house.gov/files/documents/112-12transcripto-i5-11-11.html>.

[3] US Department of Veterans Affairs. VA launches open source custodian: open source electronics health record agent begins operations [Internet]. Washington, DC: US Department of Veterans Affairs [cited May 22, 2012]. <http://www.va.gov/opa/ pressrel/pressrelease.cfm?id=2153>.

[4] NASA. NASA clears the runway for open source software [Internet]. Washington, DC: National Aeronautics and Space Administration [cited May 24, 2012]. <http:// www.nasa.gov/home/hqnews/2012/jan/HQ_12-021_Open_Source_Software.html>.

[5] Evans K, Burton A. Office of Management and Budget (OMB) memorandum 04-16, software acquisition. Washington, DC: Executive Office of the President, Office of Management and Budget; 2004.

[6] President's Information Technology Advisory Committee. Developing open source software to advance high end computing. Washington, DC: National Coordination Office for Networking and Information Technology Research and Development; 2000.

[7] President's Information Technology Advisory Committee Letter [Internet]. Washington, DC: National Coordination Office for Networking and Information Technology Research and Development [cited October 20, 2011]. <http://www. nitrd.gov/Pitac/letters/pitac_ltr_sep11.html>.

[8] Stenbit DJ. Open source software (OSS) in the Department of Defense (DoD). Washington, DC: Department of Defense; 2003.

[9] Wennergren D. Clarifying guidance regarding open source software (OSS). Washington, DC: Department of Defense; 2009.

[10] Orszag P. Office of Management and Budget (OMB) Memorandum 10-06, Open Government Directive. Washington, DC: Executive Office of the President, Office of Management and Budget; 2009.

[11] The White House. Digital government: building a 21st century platform to better serve the American people. Washington, DC: Executive Office of the President, Office of Management and Budget; 2012.

[12] Office of Management and Budget (OMB). The Open Government Partnership, Announcing New Open Government Initiatives, Second Open Government National Action Plan. Washington, DC: Executive Office of the President, Office of Management and Budget; 2014.

[13] Streaming at 1:00 in the cloud [Internet]. Washington, DC: Office of Social Innovation and Civic Participation [cited November 2, 2011]. <http://www.white-house.gov/blog/Streaming-at-100-In-the-Cloud>.

[14] President's Information Technology Advisory Committee. Developing open source software to advance high end computing. Washington, DC: National Coordination Office for Networking and Information Technology Research and Development; 2000.

[15] US Department of Defense (DoD), Chief Information Officer (CIO). DoD open source software (OSS) FAQ. [Internet]. Washington, DC: US Department of Defense [cited October 31, 2011]. <http://dodcio.defense.gov/OpenSourceSoftwareFAQ.aspx>.

[16] US Department of Defense (DoD), Chief Information Officer (CIO). What license should the government or contractor choose/select when releasing open source software? [Internet]. Washington: US Department of Defense [cited June 2012]. <http://dodcio.defense.gov/OpenSourceSoftwareFAQ.aspx#Q:_What_license_should_the_government_or_contractor_choose.2Fselect_when_releasing_open_source_software.3F>.

[17] CENDI Copyright Working Group. Frequently asked questions about copyright and computer software: issues affecting the US government with special emphasis on open source software. Tennessee: CENDI Secretariat; 2010.

[18] DHS Homeland Open Security Technology (HOST) [Internet]. Washington, DC: US Department of Homeland Security [cited November 5, 2011]. <http://www.dhs.gov/science-and-technology/csd-host>.

[19] Stanford University. AFRL-RI-RS-TR-2009-192, Final technical report: the open source hardening project. New York: Air Force Research Laboratory; 2009.

[20] Moran P. Developing an open source option for NASA software. California: NASA Ames Research Center; 2003.

[21] Williams J. NASA Nebula in action: cloud computing case examples. California: NASA Ames Research Center; 2009.

[22] Kundra V. Federal cloud computing strategy. Washington, DC: Executive Office of the President, Office of Management and Budget; 2010.

[23] Office of Management and Budget (OMB). Digital government: building a 21st century platform to better serve the american people. Washington, DC: Executive Office of the President, Office of Management and Budget; 2012.

Security and privacy in public cloud computing

4

INFORMATION IN THIS CHAPTER:

- Introduction
- Security and Privacy in the Context of the Public Cloud
- Federal Privacy Laws and Policies
- Safeguarding Privacy Information
- Security and Privacy Issues

INTRODUCTION

In Chapter 1, Introduction to the federal cloud computing strategy, we already learned that public cloud computing presents the federal government with significant opportunities for reduced cost and improved operational efficiency. In this chapter, the discussion will focus specifically on security and privacy within the context of public cloud computing.

Public cloud services can provide benefits for improved information security, and even enhance privacy practices. But the benefits of public cloud computing can be outweighed by potential security and privacy issues, concerns, or risks[1] if there is not a comprehensive "due diligence" process. The due diligence process outlined in Chapter 1, helps ensure the issues, concerns, or risks are integrated into the preliminary cloud service selection and assessment activities.

---

[1]The European Network and Information Security Agency (ENISA), *Cloud Computing: Benefits, risks and recommendation for information security* provides a list of 35 risks that cover areas such as policy and organizational, technical, legal, and traditional IT. Available from: http://www.enisa.europa.eu/activities/risk-management/files/deliverables/cloud-computing-risk-assessment/at_download/fullReport.

Federal Cloud Computing. DOI: http://dx.doi.org/10.1016/B978-0-12-809710-6.00004-4

The Federal Cloud Computing Strategy [1] highlighted several potential security benefits that can be achieved through the use of cloud services, to include:

- *Staff specialization*—the ability to focus resources on areas of high concern as more general security services are assumed by the cloud provider.
- *Platform strength*—potential platform strength resulting from greater uniformity and homogeneity, and resulting improved information assurance, security response, system management, reliability, and maintainability.
- *Resource availability*—improved resource availability through scalability, redundancy, and disaster recovery capabilities; improved resilience to unanticipated service demands.
- *Backup and recovery*—improved backup and recovery capabilities, policies, procedures, and consistency.
- *Data concentration*—ability to leverage alternate cloud service to improve the overall security posture than that of traditional data centers.

Security and privacy are distinct and independent disciplines in which aspects of privacy, as will be discussed later in this chapter, include specific principles and considerations that do not necessarily overlap with security. But foundational security practices are required for privacy to be effective in a public cloud computing environment. Therefore, the information that will be hosted within a public cloud service needs to be designed and operate to meet the same security and privacy requirements as traditional federal information systems. Federal agencies will likely base their analysis in the context of their own use cases[2] for a public cloud service to ensure the Cloud Service Provider (CSP) has addressed all applicable laws, regulations, and policies. Their analysis could leverage existing practices when considering general security and privacy issues (e.g., data location, data ownership, risk, visibility, etc.) for privacy-related information that will be stored, processed, or transmitted through the use of public cloud services.

The transition to a public cloud service requires federal agencies and CSPs to review their governance practices (i.e., policies, procedures, and processes) to ensure, from an organizational perspective, that the existing roles and responsibilities can operate effectively in the context of privacy. Federal agencies may also have to introduce new risk management[3] processes. Risk assessments performed in a traditional computing environment where the federal agency has more control over the risks mitigations may not be possible to achieve within a public cloud service, and will instead require a close coordination with the CSP to ensure that

---

[2]From the National Institute of Standards and Technology (NIST). Cloud Computing Business Use Cases Working Group [Internet]. Maryland: National Institute of Standards and Technology [cited August 22, 2011]. Available from: http://collaborate.nist.gov/twiki-cloud-computing/bin/view/CloudComputing/BusinessUseCases. *The NIST CC Business Use Cases Working Group consists of federal agencies and industry to define target USG Cloud Computing business use cases (set of candidate deployments to be used as examples) for Cloud Computing model options, to identify specific risks, concerns, and constraints.*

[3]From Kundra, V. Federal Cloud Computing Strategy. Washington, DC: Executive Office of the President, Office of Management and Budget; 2011. "Risk management entails identifying and assessing risk, and taking the steps to reduce it to an acceptable level."

mitigations are appropriately integrated and managed. Therefore, the consistency between the federal agencies' and the CSPs' risk management process is essential to ensure that risks identified are adequately prioritized and mitigated through the selection and implementation of security controls that minimize the "significant privacy concerns associated with the [public] cloud computing environment" [2].

The Federal Risk and Authorization Management Program (FedRAMP),[4] which will be discussed in more detail in later chapters, provides a common framework that uses existing processes and practices already used by federal agencies to verify the security and privacy requirements.[5] For example, a Privacy Impact Assessment (PIA)[6] is a tool already required by federal agencies[7] and is used to determine the type of privacy-related information stored, processed, or transmitted through the use of the target public cloud computing environment. In addition, the PIA helps to guide the determination of the types of protections that are required for selecting appropriate security and privacy controls that need to be implemented by CSPs to adequately mitigate identified risks to privacy information. In addition, the Federal Enterprise Architecture Security and Privacy Profile (FEA-SPP)[8] can be used by federal agencies (and CSPs) in the context of public cloud computing to address the identification of information security and data privacy requirements [3].

SECURITY AND PRIVACY IN THE CONTEXT OF THE PUBLIC CLOUD

Public cloud computing by definition is a service that is owned, managed, and operated by a service provider (e.g., private company, federal or state government, etc.) on its premises and is consumed by the general public [4]. Cloud computing delivery models are comparably different from what is commonly used by many federal agencies where their information systems are hosted within traditional, dedicated infrastructures located within a federal data center or in a

---

[4]The Federal Risk and Authorization Management Program (FedRAMP) is discussed in detail in Chapter 8, FedRAMP Primer, and Chapter 9, The FedRAMP Cloud Computing Security Requirements.

[5]FedRAMP Privacy Threshold Analysis (PTA) and Privacy Impact Assessment (PIA) Template. Available from: https://www.fedramp.gov/files/2016/04/A04-FedRAMP-PIA-Template-2016-09-30-V01-01.docx.

[6]From McCallister, E., Grance, T., Scarfone, K. NIST Special Publication 800122, Guide to Protecting the Confidentiality of Personally Identifiable Information (PII). Maryland: National Institute of Standards and Technology; 2010. *"A structured process for identifying and mitigating privacy risks."*

[7]Office of Management and Budget (OMB) Memorandum 03–22 (M-03–22), *OMB Guidance for Implementing the Privacy Provisions of the E-Government Act of 2002.* Available from: http://www.whitehouse.gov/omb/memoranda_m03-22.

[8]The Federal Enterprise Architecture Security and Privacy Profile (FEA-SPP) is a common language that can be used when discussing security and privacy in the context of the organization's mission and integration into business processes.

contractor's data center. New types of technologies and delivery models will likely introduce new definitions of public cloud services, making it important to have a common context[9] for federal agencies to use when determining how the public cloud service will be used to store, process, or transmit sensitive data collected to support their mission and business requirements.

For the purpose of this chapter, the NIST definition provides a good starting point for discussing security and privacy issues in public cloud computing. The basic characterization by NIST of public cloud computing only intended to serve as a means for a broad comparison [5]. This definition is supported by a conceptual reference architecture, depicted in Fig. 4.1, (and taxonomy) that provides a high-level illustration of security and privacy as cross-cutting and existing across all architectural layers.

In addition, the conceptual reference architecture provides a useful tool for focusing on the security and privacy requirements for what CSPs need to provide rather than describing a specific solution that needs to be designed and implemented [4]. When federal agencies begin to plan for security and privacy considerations in public cloud services, the generalization of the NIST definition can be further

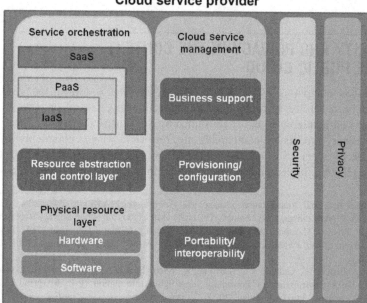

FIGURE 4.1

Conceptual reference model—cross-cutting security and privacy.

---

[9]Conditions (or facts) about the environment (i.e., public cloud) in which something (i.e., privacy information) exists (or resides).

expanded to include a definition of specific security and privacy security requirements. This elaboration of the basic NIST definition enables the selection of a common group of public cloud services based on an examination of the context given
by the federal agency's requirements. In contrast, the CSP can perform a similar
activity by identifying a target group of federal agencies, and reflect their requirements in the context of their cloud service to determine if any additional security
and privacy controls need to be applied to make it acceptable for use.

TIP

The Federal Cloud Computing Strategy [1] identified several key security considerations to guide
federal agencies in assessing the risk in the context of the public cloud computing environment
and improve confidence in the use of cloud services:

- carefully define security and privacy requirements during the initial planning stage at the start
  of the systems development life cycle;
- determine the extent to which negotiated service agreements are required to satisfy security
  requirements; and the alternatives of using negotiated service agreements or cloud computing
  deployment models that offer greater oversight and control over security and privacy;
- assess the extent to which the server and client-side computing environment meets
  organizational security and privacy requirements; and
- continue to maintain security management practices, controls, and accountability over the
  privacy and security of data and applications.

WARNING

Federal agencies are obligated through the Federal Information Security Modernization Act (FISMA)
with a number of requirements that include, although not specifically limited to, Office of Management
and Budget (OMB) policies, Federal Information Processing Standards (FIPS), federal agency-specific
policy requirements and authorization, and continuous monitoring requirements. Therefore, when
federal agencies make the decision to choose a public cloud service for their agencies' outsourcing
needs, they have been encouraged to carefully consider the following types of factors:

- *statutory compliance* (laws, regulations, and agency requirements);
- *data characteristics* (fundamental protections an application's data set requires);
- *privacy and confidentiality* (protect against accidental and nefarious access to information);
- *integrity* (ensure that data is authorized, complete, and accurate);
- *data controls and access policies* (where data can be stored and who can access physical
  locations); and
- *governance* (ensure that cloud computing service providers are sufficiently transparent, have
  adequate security and management controls, and provide the information necessary for the
  agency to appropriately and independently assess and monitor the efficacy of those controls) [1].

FEDERAL PRIVACY LAWS AND POLICIES

Privacy is a core value of American society. The importance of protecting privacy
information is already a part of many industries in which US federal privacy laws

Table 4.1 Coverage of Existing US Federal Privacy Laws [6]

Industry	Regulatory and Legislative Frameworks
Healthcare	Health Insurance, Portability and Accountability Act (HIPAA) and the associated Health Information Technology for Economic and Clinical Health (HITECH) Act
Financial	Gramm-Leach-Bliley (GLBA), the Fair and Accurate Credit Transaction Act (FACTA), and the Red Flags Rule
Education	Family Education Rights and Privacy Act (FERPA) and the Children's Internet Protection Act (CIPA)
Communications	First Amendment to the US Constitution, the Electronic Communications Privacy Act (ECPA), and the Telephone Consumer Protection Act (TCPA)
Government	Privacy Act of 1974, the Computer Security Act of 1987, and the E-Government Act of 2002
Employee and Labor Laws	Americans with Disability Act (ADA) and the Equal Employment Opportunity (EEO) Act

span. Table 4.1 provides an example of some of the types of regulatory and legislative frameworks that exist that might be relevant when considering the collection and storage of privacy-related information in a public cloud service.

In 1972, the Secretary of Health, Education, and Welfare (HW) formed the *Advisory Committee on Automated Personal Data Systems*, "to analyze the consequences of using computers to keep records about people" [7]. The committee produced a report[10] in which it was concluded that "safeguards for personal privacy based on our concept of mutuality in record-keeping would require adherence by record-keeping organizations to certain fundamental principles of fair information practice" [7]. The report recommended the adoption of a federal code of Fair Information Practices (FIPs)[11] for the protection of information within computers (referred to as automated personal data systems). In 1980, the Organization for Economic Cooperation and Development (OECD) revised and adopted the original FIPs and extended them to create a set of eight Fair Information Practice Principles (FIPPs)[12] listed in Table 4.2.

Many of the US privacy laws are based on the FIPPs as an industry recognized a set of practices for protecting data and privacy.

---

[10]*Records Computers and the Rights of Citizens*. Report of the Secretary's Advisory Committee on Automated Personal Data Systems, U.S. Department of Health, Education & Welfare.

[11]Privacy Online: Report to Congress. Available from: https://www.ftc.gov/sites/default/files/documents/reports/privacy-online-report-congress/priv-23a.pdf.

[12]*OECD Guidelines on the Protection of Privacy and Transborder Flows of Personal Data*. Available from: http://www.oecd.org/internet/interneteconomy/oecdguidelinesontheprotectionofprivacyandtransborderflowsofpersonaldata.htm.

Table 4.2 Fair Information Practice Principles (FIPPs) [8]

FIPPs	Description
Collection limitation	There should be limits to the collection of personal data and any such data should be obtained by lawful and fair means and, where appropriate, with the knowledge or consent of the data subject.
Data quality	Personal data should be relevant to the purposes for which they are to be used, and, to the extent necessary for those purposes, should be accurate, complete, and kept up-to-date.
Purpose specification	The purposes for which personal data are collected should be specified not later than at the time of data collection and the subsequent use limited to the fulfillment of those purposes or such others as are not incompatible with those purposes and as are specified on each occasion of change of purpose.
Use limitation	Personal data should not be disclosed, made available, or otherwise used for purposes other than those specified, except with the consent of the data subject or by the authority of law.
Security safeguards	Personal data should be protected by reasonable security safeguards against such risks as loss or unauthorized access, destruction, use, modification, or disclosure of data.
Openness	There should be a general policy of openness about developments, practices, and policies with respect to personal data. Means should be readily available of establishing the existence and nature of personal data, and the main purposes of their use, as well as the identity and usual residence of the data controller.
Individual participation	An individual should have the right: (a) to obtain from a data controller, or otherwise, confirmation of whether or not the data controller has data relating to him; (b) to have communicated to him, data relating to him within a reasonable time; at a charge, if any, that is not excessive; in a reasonable manner; and in a form that is readily intelligible to him; (c) to be given reasons if a request made under subparagraphs (a) and (b) is denied, and to be able to challenge such denial; and (d) to challenge data relating to him and, if the challenge is successful, to have the data erased, rectified, completed, or amended.
Accountability	A data controller should be accountable for complying with measures that give effect to the principles stated above.

The federal government has the legal responsibility to ensure governance and accountability of PII.[13] Safeguarding PII in the possession of the federal government and preventing its breach are essential to ensure the trust of the American public [9]. Therefore, before we can effectively discuss potential security and privacy issues, a basic understanding is required of some of the significant privacy

---

[13]From McCallister, E., Grance, T., Scarfone, K. NIST Special Publication (SP) 800—122, Guide to Protecting the Confidentiality of Personally Identifiable Information (PII). Maryland: National Institute of Standards and Technology; 2010. *"Treatment of PII is distinct from other types of data because it needs to be not only protected, but also collected, maintained, and disseminated in accordance with Federal law."*

laws and policies developed for the protection and preservation of privacy rights of individuals by federal agencies.

PRIVACY ACT OF 1974

The Privacy Act of 1974[14] was established as a statutory framework to govern the federal government's collection and use of personal information. This statutory framework balances the federal government's need to maintain information about individuals with the rights of individuals to be protected against unwarranted invasions of their privacy stemming from the collection, maintenance, use, and disclosure of personal information about them [10].

The Privacy Act is based on the internationally recognized FIPPs previously discussed. The Act protects certain federal government records[15] pertaining to individuals,[16] collected, maintained, used, and disseminated by federal agencies. The records containing PII are stored in a system of records (SOR) which is "a group of any records under the control of any agency from which information is retrieved by the name of the individual or by some identifying number, symbol, or other identifying particular assigned to the individual" [11].

In accordance with the Privacy Act,[17] federal agencies are required to give public notice through a Systems of Records Notice (SORN) in the Federal Registrar,[18] that includes information about the SOR such as:

- System name.
- Security classification.
- System location(s).[19]
- Categories of individual covered by the system.

---

[14]*The Pivacy Act of 1974 (Public Law 93–579)*. Available from: http://www.justice.gov/opcl/privstat.htm.

[15]From the Office of Management and Budget (OMB). Privacy Act Implementation: Guidelines and Responsibilities. Washington, DC: Executive Office of the President, Office of Management and Budget; 1975. *"The term 'record' means any item, collection, or grouping of information about an individual that is maintained by an agency."*

[16]From the Office of Management and Budget (OMB). Privacy Act Implementation: Guidelines and Responsibilities. Washington, DC: Executive Office of the President, Office of Management and Budget; 1975. *"The term 'individual' means a citizen of the United States or an alien lawfully admitted for permanent residence."*

[17]U.S.C. section 552a—Records maintained individuals.

[18]From the Federal Register [Internet]. Washington, US: Government Printing Office [cited September 31, 2011]. Available from: http://www.gpo.gov/help/about_federal_register.htm. *"The Federal Register is the official daily publication for rules, proposed rules, and notices of Federal agencies and organizations, as well as executive orders and other presidential documents."*

[19]From Federal CIO Council and Chief Acquisition Officers Council. Creating Effective Cloud Computing Contracts for the Federal Government. Washington, DC: Executive Office of the President, Office of Management and Budget; 2012. "Under the Privacy Act, Federal agencies must be able to inform individuals, in the applicable SORN, where their data is being maintained, which can be complicated in a CSP environment."

- Categories of records covered by the system.
- Authority for maintenance of the system.
- Disclosure to consumer reporting agencies.
- Routine use of records maintained in the system, including categories of users and the purpose of such uses.
- Policies and practices for storing, retrieving, access, retaining, and disposal of records in the system.
- Exceptions claimed for the system.

TIP

Under Section (m) of the Privacy Act, a government contractor's information system is subject to the requirements of the Act, if under contract, the federal agency contracts for the operation by or on behalf of the agency, a SOR to accomplish an agency function [11]. Since CSPs may store records covered under the Privacy Act, the CSPs' cloud service could be considered a SOR and be subject to the same requirements[20] as federal agencies. In addition, a cloud service operated by a CSP that is covered by the Privacy Act could be subject to civil and criminal implications if the CSP knowingly and willfully acts or fails to act as described in the Privacy Act [12].

NOTE

The Privacy Act Issuances[21]

According to the Privacy Act, the Office of the Federal Register (OFR) must biennially compile and publish (1) descriptions of system of records maintained on individuals by federal agencies, which were published in the Federal Register; and (2) rules of each agency, which set out the procedures that agencies will follow in helping individuals who request information about their records. In addition, the Privacy Act requires OFR to publish the compilation in a form available to the public at a low cost [13].

The extension of Privacy Act requirements for the collection and storage of PII to a public cloud service will likely need to be carefully evaluated by the CSP and the federal agency for a cloud service operating as the federal agencies' SOR. "Once an agency chooses a cloud computing provider to collect and store information, the individual is no longer providing information solely to the government, but also to a third party who is not necessarily bound by the same laws and regulations" [14]. Since federal agencies are "ultimately accountable for the security and privacy of data held by a cloud provider on their behalf" [4], the requirements of the Privacy Act and the responsibility for the implementation of privacy controls will be discussed later in this chapter. Therefore, assistance or requirements by the CSP to support the federal agency meeting requirements under the

---

[20]Government contractors fall under subsection (m) of the Privacy Act of 1974.
[21]*Privacy Act Issuances*. Available from: http://www.ofr.gov/privacy/AGENCIES.aspx.

Privacy Act will need to be clearly addressed through a contractual obligation (e.g., protecting privacy information, and reporting breaches or disclosures).

FEDERAL INFORMATION SECURITY MODERNIZATION ACT (FISMA)

The FISMA provides federal agencies with a recommended set of security control requirements[22] necessary to protect information contained within an information system.[23] In addition, federal agencies are required to identify and assess the risk to their PII, and to ensure security controls are implemented to provide adequate safeguards. Therefore, CSPs that collect, store, or process PII on behalf of the federal government may have a responsibility to meet specific security requirements. These security requirements are based on the confidentiality,[24] integrity, and available objectives for the information identified as a result of a security categorization conducted by the CSP or the federal agency.

NIST was given the responsibility for developing standards and guidelines for information systems. These standards and guidelines include providing federal agencies with guidance[25] on categorizing PII. The Privacy Act requires federal agencies to establish administrative, technical, and physical safeguards to insure the security and confidentiality of records and to protect against any anticipated threats or hazards to their security or integrity, which could result in substantial harm, embarrassment, inconvenient, or unfairness on whom information is obtained [9]. Harm is the adverse effect that would be experienced by an individual whose PII was the subject of a loss of confidentiality, as well as any adverse effects experienced by the organization that maintains the PII [15]. Therefore, the loss (or breach) of confidentiality would likely need to be evaluated against the unauthorized disclosure of the PII and the "effect on the organizational

---

[22]From the Federal Information Security Modernization Act of 2014 [Internet]. Washington, DC: US Government Printing Office [cited February 17, 2016]. Available from: https://www.congress.gov/113/plaws/publ283/PLAW-113publ283.pdf. *Comprehensive framework for ensuring the effectiveness of information security controls over information resources that support Federal operations and assets.*

[23]From the Office of Management and Budget (OMB), OMB Circular No. A-130 Revised (Transmittal Memorandum No. 4), Management of Federal Information Resources. Washington, DC: Executive Office of the President, Office of Management and Budget; 2000. "*A discrete set of information resources organized for the collection, processing, maintenance, transmission, and dissemination of information, in accordance with defined procedures, whether automated or manual.*"

[24]US Congress. 44 U.S. Code Chapter 35, Subchapter II—Information Security. Washington, DC: US Congress; 2002. "*Preserving authorized restrictions on access and disclosure, including means for protecting personal privacy and proprietary information.*"

[25]*Federal Information Processing Standards (FIPS) 199, Standards for Security Categorization of Federal Information and Information Systems.* Available from: http://csrc.nist.gov/publications/fips/fips199/FIPS-PUB-199-final.pdf.

Table 4.3 FIPS 199 Impact Level—Confidentiality [16]

Potential Impact	Potential Impact
Low	The unauthorized disclosure of information could be expected to have a *limited* adverse effect on organizational operations, organizational assets, or individuals
Moderate	The unauthorized disclosure of information could be expected to have a *serious* adverse effect on organizational operations, organizational assets, or individuals
High	The unauthorized disclosure of information could be expected to have a *severe or catastrophic* adverse effect on organizational operations, organizational assets, or individuals

operations, organizational assets, or individual" [16] based on the different confidentiality impact levels (see Table 4.3).

FISMA also required federal agencies to establish procedures for the detection, reporting, and response of security incidents. In addition, OMB requires federal agencies to report incidents involving PII to the US Department of Homeland Security (DHS), US Computer Emergency Readiness Team (US-CERT).[26] Incidents that involve breaches to PII are categorized by the US-CERT as a Category 1 and require reporting within one hour of the discovery/detection. The CSPs' incident response plan[27] will need to reflect any new requirements for notification and reporting[28] by ensuring service agreements address the requirements and responsibility for notification, reporting, and any costs associated with an incident involving the compromise of PII.

OMB MEMORANDUM POLICIES

PII refers to information that can be used to distinguish[29] or trace[30] an individual's identity, such as their name, Social Security number, biometric records,

[26]*US-CERT Incident Reporting System. Available from: https://forms.us-cert.gov/report/.*
[27]NIST Special Publication (SP) 800-61 Revision 2, Computer Security Incident Handling Guide. Available from http://csrc.nist.gov/publications/nistpubs/SP800-61rev2/SP800-61rev2.pdf.
[28]US-CERT Federal Incident Notification Guidelines—https://www.us-cert.gov/incident-notification-guidelines.
[29]From McCallister, E., Grance, T., Scarfone, K. NIST Special Publication (SP) 800–122, Guide to Protecting the Confidentiality of Personally Identifiable Information (PII). Maryland: National Institute of Standards and Technology; 2010. *"To identify an individual."*
[30]From McCallister, E., Grance, T., Scarfone, K. NIST Special Publication (SP) 800–122, Guide to Protecting the Confidentiality of Personally Identifiable Information (PII). Maryland: National Institute of Standards and Technology; 2010. *"Process sufficient information to make a determination about a specific aspect of an individual's activities or status."*

and so on, alone, or when combined with other personal or identifying information that is linked[31] or linkable[32] to a specific individual, such as date and place of birth, mother's maiden name, and so on [9].

- PII can include the following types of information:
- Name.
- Social Security number.
- Date and place of birth.
- Mother's maiden name.
- Biometric records.
- Education.
- Financial transactions.
- Medical history.
- Criminal or employment history and information, which can be used to distinguish or trace an individual's identity.

OMB has established a number of governing policies for federal agencies relating to PII over the years. Table 4.4 provides a list of applicable privacy-related policies that must be adhered to by federal agencies.

SAFEGUARDING PRIVACY INFORMATION

Privacy and security can mean different things to different people because they are identified as distinct disciplines. Privacy and security do overlap in many aspects. Privacy is more than security, however, and includes the principles of transparency, notice, and choice [17]. Although, it is widely agreed upon that some aspects of privacy require a sound security practice (e.g., accountability, integrity, confidentiality, and data destruction). Therefore, it is important to recognize that "organizations cannot have effective privacy without a solid foundation of information security" [17].

Privacy can be summarized as the need to protect certain information about individuals and organizations and "involves the right to control when, where, how, to whom, and to what extent an individual shares their own personal information, as well as the right to access personal information given to others, to correct it, and to ensure it is safeguarded and disposed of appropriately" [6]. Security, on the other hand, provides the safeguards (e.g., administrative,

---

[31]From McCallister, E., Grance, T., Scarfone, K. NIST Special Publication (SP) 800—122, Guide to Protecting the Confidentiality of Personally Identifiable Information (PII). Maryland: National Institute of Standards and Technology; 2010. *"Information about or related to an individual that is logically associated with other information about the individual."*

[32]From McCallister, E., Grance, T., Scarfone, K. NIST Special Publication 800—122, Guide to Protecting the Confidentiality of Personally Identifiable Information (PII). Maryland: National Institute of Standards and Technology; 2010. *"Information about or related to an individual that is logically associated with other information about the individual."*

Table 4.4 Federal Privacy-Related Policies

Government-wide Policy	Description
OMB Circular A-130, Managing Information as a Strategic Resource	This Circular establishes general policy for the planning, budgeting, governance, acquisition, and management of federal information, personnel, equipment, funds, IT resources, and supporting infrastructure and services. The appendices to this Circular also include responsibilities for protecting federal information resources and managing PII.
OMB Circular A-130, Managing Information as a Strategic Resource, Appendix I, Responsibilities for Protecting and Managing Federal Information Resources	This Appendix establishes minimum requirements for federal information security programs, assigns federal agency responsibilities for the security of information and information systems, and links agency information security programs and agency management control systems established in accordance with OMB Circular A-123, *Management's Responsibility for Enterprise Risk Management and Internal Controls.*[a]
OMB Circular A-130, Managing Information as a Strategic Resource, Appendix II, Responsibilities for Managing Personally Identifiable Information	This Appendix outlines some of the general responsibilities for federal agencies managing information resources that involve PII and summarizes the key privacy requirements included in other sections of this Circular. The requirements included in this Appendix apply to PII in any form or medium, including paper and electronic media.
OMB Memorandum 99−18, Privacy Policies on Federal Web Sites	This memorandum directs departments and agencies to post clear privacy policies on World Wide Web sites, and provides guidance for doing so.
OMB Memorandum 03−22, OMB Guidance for Implementing the Privacy Provisions	The memorandum provides guidance to federal agencies on implementing the privacy provisions of the E-Government Act of 2002.
OMB Memorandum 016−19, Reporting Incidents Involving Personally Identifiable Information and Incorporating the Cost for Security in Agency Information Technology Investments	This memorandum provides updated guidance on the reporting of security incidents involving personally identifiable information and to remind federal agencies of existing requirements, and explain new requirements federal agencies will need to provide addressing security and privacy.
OMB Memorandum 07−16, Safeguarding Against and Responding to the Breach of PII	The memorandum reemphasizes federal agency responsibilities under existing law, executive orders, regulations, and policy to appropriately safeguard personally identifiable information and train federal agency employees on responsibilities in this area. It also establishes additional privacy and security requirements.

(Continued)

Table 4.4 Federal Privacy-Related Policies *Continued*

Government-wide Policy	Description
OMB Memorandum 10–23, Guidance for Agency Use of Third-Party Websites	This memorandum requires federal agencies to take specific steps to protect individual privacy whenever they use third-party websites and applications to engage with the public.
OMB Memorandum 15–01, Fiscal Year 2014–2015 Guidance on Improving Federal Information Security and Privacy Management Practices	This memorandum included updates and expands the scope of M-06–19 and M-07–16 and requires Federal agencies to notify DHS US-CERT of all cyber related (electronic) incidents with confirmed loss of confidentiality, integrity or availability within one hour of reaching the agency's top-level Computer Security Incident Response Team (CSIRT), Security Operations Center (SOC), or IT department.
OMB Memorandum 16–03, Fiscal Year 2015–2016 Guidance on Federal Information Security and Privacy Management Requirements	This memorandum included a definition and framework for assessing whether an incident is "major" required by the Federal Information Security Modernization Act of 2014.
	FISMA 2014 requires OMB to define a major incident and directs agencies to report incidents designated as "major" to Congress within seven (7) days. This reporting should follow a process that takes into account the sensitivity of breach details and the classification level of the notification.

[a]OMB Memorandum 16–17, OMB Circular No. A-123, Management's Responsibility for Enterprise Risk Management and Internal Control.

technical, and physical) for achieving the confidentiality, integrity, and availability objectives for protecting the privacy information.

Confidentiality refers to what data may be disclosed and to whom the data may be disclosed, thereby ensuring that only legally authorized and appropriate disclosures are made. Integrity is the assurance that information and information systems are protected against improper or accidental modification. Availability is the assurance of timely and reliable access to information and information systems by authorized persons [18]. Fig. 4.2 provides an illustration that depicts the relationship that exists between privacy (FIPPs) and security (Safeguards)[33] and which might require implementation within a public cloud computing environment to prevent the unauthorized access, use, disclosure, modification, and destruction of PII.

---

[33]From Privacy Engineering at NIST [Internet]. Washington, DC: US Government Printing Office [cited February 22, 2016]. Available from: http://csrc.nist.gov/projects/privacy_engineering/. *"NIST's work on Privacy Engineering focuses on providing guidance that can be used to decrease privacy risks, and enable organizations to make purposeful decisions about resource allocation and effective implementation of controls in information systems."*

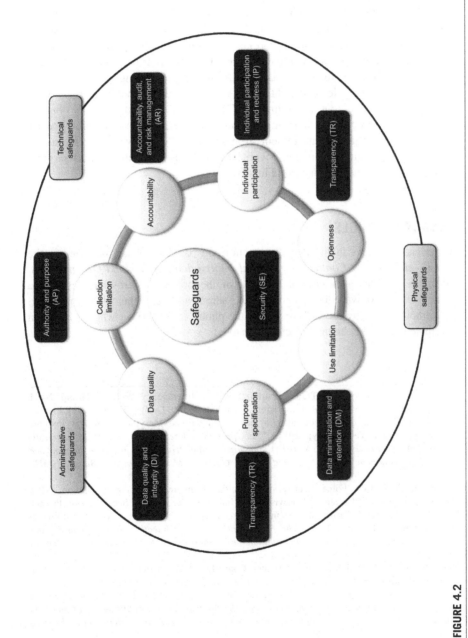

FIGURE 4.2

Relationship between FIPPs and safeguards.

As we already discussed, FIPPs provide an internationally accepted framework, reflected in many US laws for addressing privacy requirements. FIPPs also serve as the basis for analyzing privacy risks and determining appropriate mitigation strategies [17].

NIST and the Federal CIO Council's Privacy Committee developed a comprehensive set of privacy controls[34] for federal agencies to use for ensuring they develop and implement appropriate privacy protections and practices to achieve the organization's privacy objectives. Privacy controls[35] provide "a roadmap for organizations to use in identifying and implementing privacy controls concerning the life cycle of PII" [17] and when to "address potential risks when moving to a cloud computing environment" [19]. In addition, the privacy controls can be used within existing federal government frameworks[36] such as the Federal Risk and Authorization Management Program (FedRAMP) when specifying the federal privacy requirements for government-wide use of public cloud services when privacy-related information is involved.

PRIVACY CONTROLS

The privacy controls included in this section are based on those identified in the *Security and Privacy Controls for Federal Information Systems and Organizations*. Table 4.5 provides a description of each of the privacy control families. These privacy controls provide the safeguards (i.e., administrative, technical, and physical) to be implemented by the CSP or within the public cloud service when it has been determined that PII is being collected and stored.

---

[34]From the Joint Task Force Transformation Initiative Interagency Working Group. NIST Special Publication (SP) 800—53 Revision 4 (Initial Public Draft), Security and Privacy Controls for Federal Information System and Organizations. Maryland: National Institute of Standards and Technology; 2011. *"The privacy controls are based on the Fair Information Practice Principles (FIPPs) embodied in the Privacy Act of 1974, Section 208 of the E- Government Act of 2002 and related Office of Management and Budget (OMB) guidance."*

[35]From the Joint Task Force Transformation Initiative Interagency Working Group. NIST Special Publication (SP) 800—53 Revision 4 (Initial Public Draft), Security and Privacy Controls for Federal Information System and Organizations. Maryland: National Institute of Standards and Technology; 2012. *"The Federal Enterprise Architecture Security and Privacy Profile (FEA-SPP) also provided information and materials in development of the privacy controls."*

[36]From Federal Chief Information Officers Council, Privacy Committee, Web 2.0/Cloud Computing Subcommittee. Privacy Recommendations for the Use of Cloud Computing by Federal Departments and Agencies. Washington, DC: Executive Office of the President, Office of Management and Budget; 2010. *In August of 2010, the Federal CIO published as a framework that addresses privacy considerations posed by moving computer systems that contain PII to a Cloud Computing Provider (CCP).*

Table 4.5 Summary of Privacy Control Families [17]

Control Family	Description
Authority and Purpose (AP)	This family ensures that organizations: (i) identify the legal bases that authorize a particular PII collection or activity that impacts privacy; and (ii) specify in their notices the purpose(s) for which PII is collected.
Accountability, Audit, and Risk Management (AR)	This family enhances public confidence through effective controls for governance, monitoring, risk management, and assessment to demonstrate that organizations are complying with applicable privacy protection requirements and minimizing overall privacy risk.
Data Quality and Integrity (DI)	This family enhances public confidence that any PII collected and maintained by organizations is accurate, relevant, timely, and complete for the purpose for which it is to be used, as specified in public notices.
Data Minimization and Retention (DM)	This family helps organizations implement the data minimization and retention requirements to collect, use, and retain only PII that is relevant and necessary for the purpose for which it was originally collected. Organizations retain PII for only as long as necessary to fulfill the purpose(s) specified in public notices and in accordance with a National Archives and Records Administration (NARA)-approved record retention schedule.
Individual Participation and Redress (IP)	This family addresses the need to make individuals active participants in the decision-making process regarding the collection and use of their PII. By providing individuals with access to PII and the ability to have their PII corrected or amended, as appropriate, the controls in this family enhance public confidence in organizational decisions made based on the PII.
Security (SE)	This family supplements the security controls to ensure that technical, physical, and administrative safeguards are in place to protect PII collected or maintained by organizations against loss, unauthorized access, or disclosure, and to ensure that planning and responses to privacy incidents comply with OMB policies and guidance. The controls in this family are implemented in coordination with information security personnel and in accordance with the existing NIST Risk Management Framework.
Transparency (TR)	This family ensures that organizations provide public notice of their information practices and the privacy impact of their programs and activities.
Use Limitation (UL)	This family ensures that organizations only use PII either as specified in their public notices, in a manner compatible with those specified purposes, or as otherwise permitted by law. Implementation of the controls in this family will ensure that the scope of PII use is limited accordingly.

(Continued)

Table 4.5 Summary of Privacy Control Families [17] *Continued*

Authority and Purpose (AP)	
AP-1	**Authority to Collect**
Control requirement:	The organization determines and documents the legal authority that permits the collection, use, maintenance, and sharing of PII, either generally or in support of a specific program or information system need.
References:	• The Privacy Act of 1974, 5 U.S.C. § 552a (e). • Section 208(c), E-Government Act of 2002 (P.L. 107–347). • OMB Circular A-130, Appendix I, *Federal Agency Responsibilities for Maintaining Records About Individuals*.
AP-2	**Purpose Specification**
Control requirement:	The organization describes the purpose(s) for which PII is collected, used, maintained, and shared in its privacy notices.
References:	• The Privacy Act of 1974, 5 U.S.C. § 552a (e)(3)(A)–(B). • Sections 208(b), (c), E-Government Act of 2002 (P.L. 107–347).
Accountability, Audit, and Risk Management (AR)	
AR-1	**Governance and Privacy Program**
Control requirement:	The organization: a. Appoints a Senior Agency Official for Privacy (SAOP)/Chief Privacy Officer (CPO) accountable for developing, implementing, and maintaining an organization-wide governance and privacy program to ensure compliance with all applicable laws and regulations regarding the collection, use, maintenance, sharing, and disposal of PII by programs and information systems; b. Monitors federal privacy laws and policy for changes that affect the privacy program; c. Allocates [*Assignment: organization-defined allocation of budget and staffing*] sufficient resources to implement and operate the organization-wide privacy program; d. Develops a strategic organizational privacy plan for implementing applicable privacy controls, policies, and procedures; e. Develops, disseminates, and implements operational privacy policies and procedures that govern the appropriate privacy and security controls for programs, information systems, or technologies involving PII; and f. Updates privacy plan, policies, and procedures [*Assignment: organization-defined frequency, at least biennially*].
References:	• The Privacy Act of 1974, 5 U.S.C. § 552a. • E-Government Act of 2002 (P.L. 107–347). • Federal Information Security Modernization Act of 2014 (FISMA) Public Law No. 113–293.

(Continued)

Table 4.5 Summary of Privacy Control Families [17] *Continued*

Accountability, Audit, and Risk Management (AR)	
AR-1	**Governance and Privacy Program**
	• OMB Memorandum 03–22, *Guidance for Implementing the Privacy Provisions of the E-Government Act of 2002.* • OMB Memorandum 05–08, *Designation of Senior Agency Officials for Privacy.* • OMB Memorandum 07–16, *Safeguarding Against and Responding to the Breach of Personally Identifiable Information.* • OMB Memorandum 15–01, *Fiscal Year 2014–2015 Guidance on Improving Federal Information Security and Privacy Management Practices.* • OMB Circular A-130, *Management of Federal Information Resources.* • Federal Enterprise Architecture Security and Privacy Profile (FEA-SPP).
AR-2	**Privacy Impact and Risk Assessment**
Control requirement:	The organization: a. Documents and implements a privacy risk management process that assesses privacy risk to individuals resulting from the collection, sharing, storing, transmitting, use, and disposal of PII; and b. Conducts PIAs for information systems, programs, or other activities that pose a privacy risk in accordance with applicable law, OMB policy, or any existing organizational policies and procedures.
References:	• Section 208, E-Government Act of 2002 (P.L. 107–347). • Federal Information Security Modernization Act of 2014 (FISMA) Public Law No. 113–293. • OMB Memorandum 03–22, *Guidance for Implementing the Privacy Provisions of the E-Government Act of 2002.* • OMB Memorandum 05–08, *Designation of Senior Agency Officials for Privacy.* • OMB Memorandum 10–23, *Guidance for Agency Use of Third-Party Websites and Applications.*
AR-3	**Privacy Requirements for Contractors and Service Providers**
Control requirement:	The organization: a. Establishes privacy roles and responsibilities for contractors and service providers; and b. Includes privacy requirements in contracts and other acquisition-related documents.
References:	• The Privacy Act of 1974, 5 U.S.C. § 552a(m). • Federal Acquisition Regulation, 48 C.F.R. Part 24. • OMB Circular A-130, *Management of Federal Information Resources.*

(Continued)

Table 4.5 Summary of Privacy Control Families [17] *Continued*

AR-4	Privacy Monitoring and Auditing
Control requirement:	The organization monitors and audits privacy controls and internal privacy policy [*Assignment: organization-defined frequency*] to ensure effective implementation.
References:	• The Privacy Act of 1974, 5 U.S.C. § 552a.
	• Federal Information Security Modernization Act of 2014 (FISMA) Public Law No. 113–293.
	• Section 208, E-Government Act of 2002 (P.L. 107–347).
	• OMB Memorandum 03–22, Guidance for Implementing the Privacy Provisions of the E-Government Act of 2002.
	• OMB Memorandum 05–08, Designation of Senior Agency Officials for Privacy.
	• OMB Memorandum 06–16, *Protection of Sensitive Agency Information.*
	• OMB Memorandum 07–16, *Safeguarding Against and Responding to the Breach of Personally Identifiable Information.*
	• OMB Memorandum 15–01, *Fiscal Year 2014–2015 Guidance on Improving Federal Information Security and Privacy Management Practices.*
	• OMB Circular A-130, *Management of Federal Information Resources.*
AR-5	**Privacy Awareness and Training**
Control requirement:	The organization: a. Develops, implements, and updates a comprehensive training and awareness strategy aimed at ensuring that personnel understand privacy responsibilities and procedures; b. Administers basic privacy training [*Assignment: organization-defined frequency, at least annually*] and targeted, role-based privacy training for personnel having responsibility for PII or for activities that involve PII [*Assignment: organization-defined frequency, at least annually*]; and c. Ensures that personnel certify (manually or electronically) acceptance of responsibilities for privacy requirements [*Assignment: organization-defined frequency, at least annually*].
References:	• The Privacy Act of 1974, 5 U.S.C. § 552a(e).
	• Section 208, E-Government Act of 2002 (P.L. 107–347).
	• OMB Memorandum 03–22, *Guidance for Implementing the Privacy Provisions of the E-Government Act of 2002.*
	• OMB Memorandum 07–16, *Safeguarding Against and Responding to the Breach of Personally Identifiable Information.*
	• OMB Memorandum 15–01, *Fiscal Year 2014–2015 Guidance on Improving Federal Information Security and Privacy Management Practices.*

(Continued)

Table 4.5 Summary of Privacy Control Families [17] *Continued*

AR-6	Privacy Reporting
Control requirement:	The organization develops, disseminates, and updates reports to the OMB, Congress, and other oversight bodies, as appropriate, to demonstrate accountability with specific statutory and regulatory privacy program mandates, and to senior management and other personnel with responsibility for monitoring privacy program progress and compliance.
References:	• The Privacy Act of 1974, 5 U.S.C. § 552a. • Section 208, E-Government Act of 2002 (P.L. 107–347). • Federal Information Security Modernization Act of 2014 (FISMA) Public Law No. 113–293. • Section 803, 9/11 Commission Act, 42 U.S.C. § 2000ee-1. • Section 804, 9/11 Commission Act, 42 U.S.C. § 2000ee-3; • Section 522, Consolidated Appropriations Act of 2005 (P.L. 108–447). • OMB Memorandum 03–22, *Guidance for Implementing the Privacy Provisions of the E-Government Act of 2002.* • OMB Circular A-130, *Managing Information as a Strategic Resource.*
AR-7	**Privacy-Enhanced System Design and Development**
Control requirement:	The organization designs information systems to support privacy by automating privacy controls.
References:	• The Privacy Act of 1974, 5 U.S.C. § 552a(e)(10); • Section 208 (b) and (c), E-Government Act of 2002 (P.L. 107–347). • OMB Memorandum 03–22, *Guidance for Implementing the Privacy Provisions of the E-Government Act of 2002.*
AR-8	**Accounting of Disclosures**

Control requirement:	The organization:
	a. Keeps an accurate accounting of disclosures of information held in each system of records under its control, including:
	  1. Date, nature, and purpose of each disclosure of a record; and
	  2. Name and address of the person or agency to which the disclosure was made;
	b. Retains the accounting of disclosures for the life of the record or five years after the disclosure is made, whichever is longer; and
	c. Makes the accounting of disclosures available to the person named in the record upon request.

References:	• The Privacy Act of 1974, 5 U.S.C. § 552a (c) (1), (c)(3), (j), (k).
	Data Quality and Integrity (DI)
DI-1	**Data Quality**
Control requirement:	The organization: a. Confirms to the greatest extent practicable upon collection or creation of PII, the accuracy, relevance, timeliness, and completeness of that information;

(Continued)

Table 4.5 Summary of Privacy Control Families [17] *Continued*

Data Quality and Integrity (DI)	
DI-1	**Data Quality**
	b. Collects PII directly from the individual to the greatest extent practicable;
	c. Checks for, and corrects as necessary, any inaccurate or outdated PII used by its programs or systems [*Assignment: organization-defined frequency*]; and
	d. Issues guidelines ensuring and maximizing the quality, utility, objectivity, and integrity of disseminated information.
References:	• The Privacy Act of 1974, 5 U.S.C. § 552a (c) and (e).
	• Treasury and General Government Appropriations Act for Fiscal Year 2001 (P.L. 106–554), app C § 515, 114 Stat. 2763A-153-4.
	• Paperwork Reduction Act, 44 U.S.C. § 3501.
	• OMB Guidelines for Ensuring and Maximizing the Quality, Objectivity, Utility, and Integrity of Information Disseminated by Federal Agencies (October 2001).
	• OMB Memorandum 07–16, *Safeguarding Against and Responding to the Breach of Personally Identifiable Information*.
	• OMB Memorandum 15–01, *Fiscal Year 2014–2015 Guidance on Improving Federal Information Security and Privacy Management Practices*.
DI-1 (1)	**Data Quality	Validate PII**
Control requirement:	The organization requests that the individual or individual's authorized representative validate PII during the collection process.
References:	• The Privacy Act of 1974, 5 U.S.C. § 552a (c) and (e).
	• Treasury and General Government Appropriations Act for Fiscal Year 2001 (P.L. 106–554), app C § 515, 114 Stat.
	• 2763A-153-4.
	• Paperwork Reduction Act, 44 U.S.C. § 3501.
	• OMB Guidelines for Ensuring and Maximizing the Quality, Objectivity, Utility, and Integrity of Information Disseminated by Federal Agencies (October 2001).
	• OMB Memorandum 07–16, *Safeguarding Against and Responding to the Breach of Personally Identifiable Information*.
	• OMB Memorandum 15–01, *Fiscal Year 2014–2015 Guidance on Improving Federal Information Security and Privacy Management Practices*.
DI-1 (2)	**Data Quality	Re-Validate PII**
Control requirement:	The organization requests that the individual or individual's authorized representative revalidate that PII collected is still accurate [*Assignment: organization-defined frequency*].
References:	• The Privacy Act of 1974, 5 U.S.C. § 552a (c) and (e).
	• Treasury and General Government Appropriations Act for Fiscal Year 2001 (P.L. 106–554), app C § 515, 114 Stat. 2763A-153-4.

(Continued)

Table 4.5 Summary of Privacy Control Families [17] *Continued*

DI-1 (2)	**Data Quality | Re-Validate PII**
	• Paperwork Reduction Act, 44 U.S.C. § 3501.
	• OMB Guidelines for Ensuring and Maximizing the Quality, Objectivity, Utility, and Integrity of Information Disseminated by Federal Agencies (October 2001).
	• OMB Memorandum 07–16, *Safeguarding Against and Responding to the Breach of Personally Identifiable Information*.
	• OMB Memorandum 15–01, *Fiscal Year 2014–2015 Guidance on Improving Federal Information Security and Privacy Management Practices*.
DI-2	**Data Integrity and Data Integrity Board**
Control requirement:	The organization:
	a. Documents processes to ensure the integrity of PII through existing security controls; and
	b. Establishes a Data Integrity Board when appropriate to oversee organizational Computer Matching Agreements and to ensure that those agreements comply with the computer matching provisions of the Privacy Act.
References:	• The Privacy Act of 1974, 5 U.S.C. §§ 552a (a)(8)(A), (o), (p), (u).
	• OMB Circular A-130, Appendix I, *Federal Agency Responsibilities for Maintaining Records About Individuals*.
DI-2 (1)	**Data Integrity and Data Integrity Board | Publish Agreements on Website**
Control requirement:	The organization publishes Computer Matching Agreements on its public website.
References:	• The Privacy Act of 1974, 5 U.S.C. §§ 552a (a)(8)(A), (o), (p), (u).
	• OMB Circular A-130, *Managing Information as a Strategic Resource*.
Data Minimization and Retention (DM)	
DM-1	**Minimization of Personally Identifiable Information**
Control requirement:	The organization:
	a. Identifies the minimum PII elements that are relevant and necessary to accomplish the legally authorized purpose of collection.
	b. Limits the collection and retention of PII to the minimum elements identified for the purposes described in the notice and for which the individual has provided consent; and
	c. Conducts an initial evaluation of PII holdings and establishes and follows a schedule for regularly reviewing those holdings [*Assignment: organization-defined frequency, at least annually*] to ensure that only PII identified in the notice is collected and retained, and that the PII continues to be necessary to accomplish the legally authorized purpose.
References:	• The Privacy Act of 1974, 5 U.S.C. § 552a (e).
	• Section 208(b), E-Government Act of 2002 (P.L. 107–347).
	• OMB Memorandum 03–22, *Guidance for Implementing the Privacy Provisions of the E-Government Act of 2002*.

Table 4.5 Summary of Privacy Control Families [17] *Continued*

Data Minimization and Retention (DM)	
DM-1	**Minimization of Personally Identifiable Information**
	• OMB Memorandum 07–16, *Safeguarding Against and Responding to the Breach of Personally Identifiable Information.*
	• OMB Memorandum 15–01, *Fiscal Year 2014–2015 Guidance on Improving Federal Information Security and Privacy Management Practices.*
DM-1 (1)	**Minimization of Personally Identifiable Information | Locate / Remove / Redact / Anonymize PII**
Control requirement:	The organization, where feasible and within the limits of technology, locates and removes/redacts specified PII and/or uses anonymization and de-identification techniques to permit use of the retained information while reducing its sensitivity and reducing the risk resulting from disclosure.
References:	• The Privacy Act of 1974, 5 U.S.C. § 552a (e).
	• Section 208(b), E-Government Act of 2002 (P.L. 107–347).
	• OMB Memorandum 03–22, *Guidance for Implementing the Privacy Provisions of the E-Government Act of 2002.*
	• OMB Memorandum 07–16, *Safeguarding Against and Responding to the Breach of Personally Identifiable Information.*
	• OMB Memorandum 15–01, *Fiscal Year 2014–2015 Guidance on Improving Federal Information Security and Privacy Management Practices.*
DM-2	**Data Retention and Disposal**
Control requirement:	The organization:
	a. Retains each collection of PII for [*Assignment: organization-defined time period*] to fulfill the purpose(s) identified in the notice or as required by law;
	b. Disposes of, destroys, erases, and/or anonymizes the PII, regardless of the method of storage in accordance with a NARA-approved record retention schedule and in a manner that prevents loss, theft, misuse, or unauthorized access; and
	c. Uses [*Assignment: organization-defined techniques or methods*] to ensure secure deletion or destruction of PII (including originals, copies, and archived records).
References:	• The Privacy Act of 1974, 5 U.S.C. § 552a (e)(1), (c)(2).
	• Section 208(e), E-Government Act of 2002 (P.L. 107–347).
	• 44 U.S.C. Chapters 29, 31, 33.
	• OMB Memorandum 07–16, *Safeguarding Against and Responding to the Breach of Personally Identifiable Information.*
	• OMB Memorandum 15–01, *Fiscal Year 2014–2015 Guidance on Improving Federal Information Security and Privacy Management Practices.*
	• OMB Circular A-130, *Managing Information as a Strategic Resource.*
	• NIST Special Publication 800–88, *Guidelines for Media Sanitization.*

(Continued)

Table 4.5 Summary of Privacy Control Families [17] *Continued*

DM-2 (1)	Data Retention and Disposal	System Configuration
Control requirement:	The organization, where feasible, configures its information systems to record the date PII is collected, created, or updated and when PII is to be deleted or archived under an approved record retention schedule.
References:	• The Privacy Act of 1974, 5 U.S.C. § 552a (e)(1), (c)(2). • Section 208(e), E-Government Act of 2002 (P.L. 107–347). • 44 U.S.C. Chapters 29, 31, 33. • OMB Memorandum 07–16, *Safeguarding Against and Responding to the Breach of Personally Identifiable Information.* • OMB Memorandum 15–01, *Fiscal Year 2014–2015 Guidance on Improving Federal Information Security and Privacy Management Practices.* • OMB Circular A-130, *Managing Information as a Strategic Resource.* • NIST Special Publication 800–88, *Guidelines for Media Sanitization.*
DM-3	**Minimization of PII Used in Testing, Training, and Research**
Control requirement:	The organization: a. Develops policies and procedures for the use of PII for testing, training, and research; and b. Implements controls to protect PII used for testing, training, and research.
References:	• NIST Special Publications 800–122, *Guide to Protecting the Confidentiality of Personally Identifiable Information (PII).*
DM-3 (1)	**Minimization of PII Used in Testing, Training, and Research	Risk Minimization Techniques**
Control requirement:	The organization, where feasible, uses techniques to minimize the risk to privacy of using PII for research, testing, or training.
References:	• NIST Special Publications 800–122, *Guide to Protecting the Confidentiality of Personally Identifiable Information (PII).*
	Individual Participation and Redress (IP)
IP-1	**Consent**
Control requirement:	The organization: a. Provides means, where feasible and appropriate, for individuals to authorize the collection, use, maintaining, and sharing of PII prior to its collection; b. Provides appropriate means for individuals to understand the consequences of decisions to approve or decline the authorization of the collection, use, dissemination, and retention of PII;

(Continued)

Table 4.5 Summary of Privacy Control Families [17] *Continued*

Individual Participation and Redress (IP)	
IP-1	**Consent**
	c. Obtains consent, where feasible and appropriate, from individuals prior to any new uses or disclosure of previously collected PII; and
	d. Ensures that individuals are aware of and, where feasible, consent to all uses of PII not initially described in the public notice that was in effect at the time the organization collected the PII.
References:	• The Privacy Act of 1974, 5 U.S.C. § 552a (b), (e)(3).
	• Section 208(c), E-Government Act of 2002 (P.L. 107–347).
	• OMB Memorandum 03–22, *Guidance for Implementing the Privacy Provisions of the E-Government Act of 2002.*
	• OMB Memorandum 10–22, *Guidance for Online Use of Web Measurement and Customization Technologies.*
IP-1 (1)	**Consent | Mechanisms Support Itemized or Tiered Consent**
Control requirement:	The organization implements mechanisms to support itemized or tiered consent for specific uses of data.
References:	• The Privacy Act of 1974, 5 U.S.C. § 552a (b), (e)(3).
	• Section 208(c), E-Government Act of 2002 (P.L. 107–347).
	• OMB Memorandum 03–22, *Guidance for Implementing the Privacy Provisions of the E-Government Act of 2002.*
	• OMB Memorandum 10–22, *Guidance for Online Use of Web Measurement and Customization Technologies.*
IP-2	**Individual Access**
Control requirement:	The organization:
	a. Provides individuals the ability to have access to their PII maintained in its system(s) of records;
	b. Publishes rules and regulations governing how individuals may request access to records maintained in a Privacy Act system of records;
	c. Publishes access procedures in SORNs; and
	d. Adheres to Privacy Act requirements and OMB policies and guidance for the proper processing of Privacy Act requests.
References:	• The Privacy Act of 1974, 5 U.S.C. §§ 552a (c)(3), (d)(5), (e) (4); (j), (k), (t).
	• OMB Circular A-130, *Managing Information as a Strategic Resource.*
IP-3	**Redress**
Control requirement:	The organization:
	a. Provides a process for individuals to have inaccurate PII maintained by the organization corrected or amended, as appropriate; and
	b. Establishes a process for disseminating corrections or amendments of the PII to other authorized users of the

(Continued)

Table 4.5 Summary of Privacy Control Families [17] *Continued*

IP-3	Redress
	PII, such as external information sharing partners and, where feasible and appropriate, notifies affected individuals that their information has been corrected or amended.
References:	• The Privacy Act of 1974, 5 U.S.C. § 552a (d), (c)(4). • OMB Circular A-130, *Managing Information as a Strategic Resource.*
IP-4	**Complaint Management**
Control requirement:	The organization implements a process for receiving and responding to complaints, concerns, or questions from individuals about the organizational privacy practices.
References:	• OMB Circular A-130, *Management of Federal Information Resource.* • OMB Memorandum 07–16, *Safeguarding Against and Responding to the Breach of Personally Identifiable Information.* • OMB Memorandum 08–09, *New FISMA Privacy Reporting Requirements for FY 2008.* • OMB Memorandum 15–01, *Fiscal Year 2014–2015 Guidance on Improving Federal Information Security and Privacy Management Practices.*
	Security (SE)
SE-1	**Inventory of Personally Identifiable Information**
Control requirement:	The organization: a. Establishes, maintains, and updates [*Assignment: organization-defined frequency*] an inventory that contains a listing of all programs and information systems identified as collecting, using, maintaining, or sharing PII; and b. Provides each update of the PII inventory to the CIO or information security official [*Assignment: organization-defined frequency*] to support the establishment of information security requirements for all new or modified information systems containing PII.
References:	• The Privacy Act of 1974, 5 U.S.C. § 552a (e) (10). • Section 208(b)(2), E-Government Act of 2002 (P.L. 107–347). • OMB Memorandum 03–22, *Guidance for Implementing the Privacy Provisions of the E-Government Act of 2002.* • OMB Circular A-130, *Managing Information as a Strategic Resource.* • FIPS Publication 199, *Standards for Security Categorization of Federal Information and Information Systems.*

(Continued)

Table 4.5 Summary of Privacy Control Families [17] *Continued*

Security (SE)	
SE-1	**Inventory of Personally Identifiable Information**
	• NIST Special Publications 800−37, *Guide for Applying the Risk Management Framework to Federal Information Systems: A Security Life Cycle Approach.* • NIST Special Publications 800−122, *Guide to Protecting the Confidentiality of Personally Identifiable Information (PII).*
SE-2	**Privacy Incident Response**
Control requirement:	The organization: a. Develops and implements a Privacy Incident Response Plan; and b. Provides an organized and effective response to privacy incidents in accordance with the organizational Privacy Incident Response Plan.
References:	• The Privacy Act of 1974, 5 U.S.C. § 552a (e), (i)(1), and (m). • Federal Information Security Modernization Act of 2014 (FISMA) Public Law No. 113−293. • OMB Memorandum 06−19, *Reporting Incidents Involving Personally Identifiable Information and Incorporating the Cost for Security in Agency Information Technology Investments.* • OMB Memorandum 07−16, *Safeguarding Against and Responding to the Breach of Personally Identifiable Information.* • NIST Special Publication 800-37, *Guide for Applying the Risk Management Framework to Federal Information Systems: A Security Life Cycle Approach.*
TR-1	**Privacy Notice**
Control requirement:	The organization: a. Provides effective notice to the public and to individuals regarding: (i) its activities that impact privacy, including its collection, use, sharing, safeguarding, maintenance, and disposal of PII; (ii) authority for collecting PII; (iii) the choices, if any, individuals may have regarding how the organization uses PII and the consequences of exercising or not exercising those choices; and (iv) the ability to access and have PII amended or corrected if necessary; b. Describes: (i) the PII the organization collects and the purpose(s) for which it collects that information; (ii) how the organization uses PII internally; (iii) whether the organization shares PII with external entities, the categories of those entities, and the purposes for such sharing; (iv) whether individuals have the ability to consent

(Continued)

Table 4.5 Summary of Privacy Control Families [17] *Continued*

TR-1	Privacy Notice
	to specific uses or sharing of PII and how to exercise any such consent; (v) how individuals may obtain access to PII for the purpose of having it amended or corrected, where appropriate; and (vi) how the PII will be protected; and c. Revises its public notices to reflect changes in practice or policy that affect PII or changes in its activities that impact privacy, before or as soon as practicable after the change.
References:	• The Privacy Act of 1974, 5 U.S.C. § 552a (e)(3), (e)(4); • Section 208(b), E-Government Act of 2002 (P.L. 107–347). • OMB Memorandum 03–22, *Guidance for Implementing the Privacy Provisions of the E-Government Act of 2002*. • OMB Memorandum 07–16, *Safeguarding Against and Responding to the Breach of Personally Identifiable Information*. • OMB Memorandum 10–22, *Guidance for Online Use of Web Measurement and Customization Technologies*. • OMB Memorandum 10–23, *Guidance for Agency Use of Third-Party Websites and Applications*. • OMB Memorandum 15–01, *Fiscal Year 2014–2015 Guidance on Improving Federal Information Security and Privacy Management Practices*. • ISE Privacy Guidelines.[37]
TR-1	**Privacy Notice	Real-Time or Layered Notice**
Control requirement:	The organization provides real-time and/or layered notice when it collects PII.
References:	• The Privacy Act of 1974, 5 U.S.C. § 552a (e)(3), (e)(4); • Section 208(b), E-Government Act of 2002 (P.L. 107–347). • OMB Memorandum 03–22, *Guidance for Implementing the Privacy Provisions of the E-Government Act of 2002*. • OMB Memorandum 07–16, *Safeguarding Against and Responding to the Breach of Personally Identifiable Information*. • OMB Memorandum 10–22, *Guidance for Online Use of Web Measurement and Customization Technologies*. • OMB Memorandum 10–23, *Guidance for Agency Use of Third-Party Websites and Applications*.

(Continued)

[37]Information Sharing Environment. Available from: http://www.ise.gov.

Table 4.5 Summary of Privacy Control Families [17] *Continued*

TR-1	**Privacy Notice | Real-Time or Layered Notice**
	• OMB Memorandum 15–01, *Fiscal Year 2014–2015 Guidance on Improving Federal Information Security and Privacy Management Practices*. • ISE Privacy Guidelines.[38]
TR-2	**System of Records Notices and Privacy Act Statements**
Control requirement:	The organization: a. Publishes SORNs in the Federal Register, subject to required oversight processes, for systems containing PII; b. Keeps SORNs current; and c. Includes Privacy Act Statements on its forms that collect PII, or on separate forms that can be retained by individuals, to provide additional formal notice to individuals from whom the information is being collected.
References:	• The Privacy Act of 1974, 5 U.S.C. § e(3). • OMB Circular A-130, *Managing Information as a Strategic Resource*.
TR-2 (1)	**System of Records Notices and Privacy Act Statements | Public Website Publication**
Control requirement:	The organization publishes SORNs on its public website.
References:	• The Privacy Act of 1974, 5 U.S.C. § e(3). • OMB Circular A-130, *Managing Information as a Strategic Resource*.
TR-3	**Dissemination of Privacy Program Information**
Control requirement:	The organization: a. Ensures that the public has access to information about its privacy activities and is able to communicate with its SAOP/CPO; and b. Ensures that its privacy practices are publicly available through organizational websites or otherwise.
References:	• The Privacy Act of 1974, 5 U.S.C. § 552a. • Section 208, E-Government Act of 2002 (P.L. 107–347). • OMB Memorandum 03–22, *Guidance for Implementing the Privacy Provisions of the E-Government Act of 2002*. • OMB Memorandum 10–23, *Guidance for Agency Use of Third-Party Websites and Applications*.

(Continued)

[38]Information Sharing Environment. Available from: http://www.ise.gov.

Table 4.5 Summary of Privacy Control Families [17] *Continued*

Use Limitation (UL)	
UL-1	**Internal Use**
Control requirement:	The organization uses PII internally only for the authorized purpose(s) identified in the Privacy Act and/or in public notices.
References:	• The Privacy Act of 1974, 5 U.S.C. § 552a (a)(7), (b)(1).
UL-2	**Information Sharing with Third Parties**
Control requirement:	The organization: a. Shares PII externally, only for the authorized purposes identified in the Privacy Act and/or described in its notice(s) or in a manner compatible with those purposes; b. Where appropriate, enters into Memoranda of Understanding, Memoranda of Agreement, Letters of Intent, Computer Matching Agreements, or similar agreements, with third parties that specifically describe the PII covered and specifically enumerate the purposes for which the PII may be used; c. Monitors, audits, and trains its staff on the authorized uses and sharing of PII with third parties and on the consequences of unauthorized use or sharing of PII; and d. Evaluates any proposed new instances of sharing PII with third parties to assess whether they are authorized and whether additional or new public notice is required.
References:	• The Privacy Act of 1974, 5 U.S.C. § 552a (a)(7), (b), (c), (e)(3)(C), (o). • ISE Privacy Guidelines.

DATA BREACHES, IMPACTS, AND CONSEQUENCES

Data breaches[39] involving PII extend beyond the individual[40] involved (e.g., identity theft[41]) and can produce significant impacts for the CSP and/or the federal agency. The organizational impacts can include lost revenue and unbudgeted costs

---

[39]From Wood, D. GAO Report 07–737, Data Breaches Are Frequent, but Evidence of Resulting Identity Theft Is Limited; However, the Full Extent Is Unknown. Washington, DC: US General Accountability Office; 2007. *"An organization's unauthorized or unintentional exposure, disclosure, or loss of sensitive personal information, which can include personally identifiable information such as Social Security numbers (SSN) or financial information such as credit card numbers."*

[40]The Privacy Rights Clearinghouse (PRC) is a nonprofit consumer organization that seeks to raise consumers' awareness of how technology affects personal privacy, and to document privacy complaints. The PRC maintains the Chronology of Data Breaches located at http://www.privacyrights.org/data-breach.

[41]*Federal Identity Theft Laws.* Available from: http://www.ojp.usdoj.gov/ovc/pubs/ID_theft/idtheft-laws.html.

associated with responding to the incident, or even a loss of credibility, confidence, and trust from existing customers or the public.

NOTE

On May 10, 2006, Executive Order 13402, *"Strengthening Federal Efforts to Protect Against Identity Theft,"* was issued to create a Presidential Identity Theft Task Force to review and advise on the execution of the policy[42] set forth by the President of the United States for *"Safeguarding Against and Responding to the Breach of Personally Identifiable Information."* As a result of the Task Force, OMB issued a policy reiterating the privacy and security requirements for federal agencies under the Privacy Act (and other laws, executive orders, regulations, and policies), and required federal agencies to develop and implement breach notification policies.

In addition, it highlighted new technical controls that were to supplement those already required under US laws and policies. For example, OMB established additional security requirements for the protection of all federal information (regardless of whether it was covered under the Privacy Act). These security requirements included:

- encryption using NIST-certified cryptographic modules[43] to mobile computers/devices,
- two-factor authentication for remote access,
- enforcement of a "time-out" capability requiring re-authentication after 30 minutes of inactivity, and
- logging and verification of all data extracts from database containing sensitive information, including the verification of destruction after 90 days (if no longer being used).

Data breaches can also occur for a variety of reasons. Some occur due to intentional actions such as theft of information; others are due to negligence or accidents. Intentional actions involve breaches such as hacking, employee theft, theft of physical equipment, or deception or misrepresentation to obtain unauthorized data. Negligence or accidental losses include loss of laptop computers or other hardware, loss of data tapes, unintentional exposure on the Internet, or improper disposal of data [20].

---

[42]From Federal Register Vol. 71, No. 93, Executive Order 13402 [Internet]. Washington, DC: US Government Printing Office [cited October 2, 2011]. Available from: edocket.access.gpo.gov/2006/pdf/06-4552.pdf. *"It is the policy of the United States to use Federal resources effectively to deter, prevent, detect, investigate, proceed against, and prosecute unlawful use by persons of the identifying information of other persons."*

[43]*Cryptographic Module Validation Program (CMVP).* Available from: http://csrc.nist.gov/groups/STM/cmvp/index.html.

EPIC FAIL

Data Security Breaches

On May 7, 2007, the Congressional Research Services (CRS) reported on personal data security breaches to Congress through a report titled "Data Security Breaches: Context and Incident Summaries." The breaches were not only due to illegal activity such as hacking or unauthorized employee accesses, but also due to poor security and privacy practices such as lost laptops and posting of personal data to public websites. Data security breaches have covered business, education, financial, government, and healthcare industries:

Business

- March 2007—Hacker broke into the website of Johnny's Selected Seeds (Winslow, ME) and stole credit card information in which 20 were used fraudulently [21].
- February 2007—TJ Maxx computer systems were hacked, which resulted in drivers' license numbers, names, and addresses being compromised [21].

Education

- April 2007—Ohio State University's firewall was bypassed by hackers using foreign Internet in which the names, Social Security numbers, employee identification numbers, and birthdates of current and former staff members were stolen [21].
- April 2007—University of California, San Francisco's campus server was compromised over a two-year period in which the names, Social Security numbers, and bank accounts for students, faculty, and staff were allegedly affected [21].

Financial

- December 2006—TD Ameritrade's computers were hacked by criminals using stolen customer accounts requiring them to cover approximately $4 million in fraudulent transactions [21].
- December 2005—Scottrade Inc. was hacked through the Internet in which the customers' names, birth dates, driver's license numbers, phone numbers, bank names, bank routing information, bank account numbers, and Scottrade account numbers were allegedly stolen [21].

Government

- June 2015—OPM discovered that the background investigation records of current, former, and prospective federal employees and contractors had been stolen [22].
- February 2007—Personal information (names and Social Security numbers) were inadvertently posted to Connecticut State Administrative Services Department's website [21].
- November 2006—Bowling Green Ohio Police Department inadvertent published personal data (names, Social Security numbers, and phone numbers) to website [21].

Healthcare

- March 2007—Westerly Hospital in Westerly, RI, allegedly posted patients' confidential information (name, Social Security number, and insurance information) posted on public website [21].
- Ohio Board of Nursing posted the names and Social Security numbers of nurses to their website twice in one month [21].

Table 4.6 Key Security and Privacy Issues and CSP Actions [4]

Issues	CSP Actions
Governance	Align federal agency practices pertaining to the policies, procedures, and standards used for application development and service provisioning in the cloud computing environment.
Compliance	Understand the various types of federal laws and regulations that may impose security and privacy obligations.
Trust	Allow the federal agency visibility into the security and privacy controls and processes employed.
Architecture	Provide the federal agency with technical details into the technologies used to provision the cloud services.
Identity and access management	Review in-place safeguards against the federal agency's requirements to ensure it provides adequate security for authentication and authorization, and other identity and access management functions.
Software isolation	Understand the federal agency's requirements and potential risk associated with using the cloud service virtualization and other logical isolation techniques.
Data protection	Understand the federal agency's data management requirements to include access control and protection at-rest or in-transit, and deposition.
Availability	Understand the federal agency's availability, data backup and recovery, and disaster recovery requirements.
Incident response	Align with the federal agency's incident response procedures.

Consequences and accountability are important aspects to ensure compliance with federal privacy laws and policies that lead to the adequate handling and safeguarding of PII. To address this necessity, OMB requires federal agencies to develop and implement a rules and consequences policy that facilitates the training and enforcement of adherence by employees, contractors, or others involved in handling PII collected and stored by the federal government, other federal government agencies, or service providers on a federal agency's behalf.

SECURITY AND PRIVACY ISSUES

Overcoming security and privacy issues in public cloud computing requires a federal agency to gain a better understanding of their risks and the necessary security and privacy requirements that need to exist. Using situational analysis techniques such as SWOT[44] (Strengths, Weaknesses, Opportunities, and Threats), a federal agency can analyze the different public cloud service offerings from various CSPs. The analysis can be used to determine if privacy and security-related issues, identified in Table 4.6, believed to have long-term significance for cloud

[44]The European Network Information Security Agency (ENISA) *Security & Resilience in Government Clouds* provides an example of using SWOT as a tool as an initial analyzes of different cloud models. Available from: http://www.enisa.europa.eu/act/rm/emerging-and-future-risk/deliverables/security-and-resilience-in-governmental-clouds.

computing [4] exist. In addition, any applicable service agreements (or a separate contract)[45] used can be updated to ensure that the CSP satisfies the federal agency's security and privacy requirements.

SUMMARY

Public cloud computing presents many opportunities for the federal government to reduce costs and improve operational efficiency. But it requires clear understanding of the security and privacy requirements and examining the risks of the types of information that will be placed in the cloud and requiring an appropriate level of assurance through the application of security service and privacy controls. Although cloud computing is evolving, the application of appropriate frameworks such as the FEA-SPP and tools such as PIAs can assist in predicting the implications and consequences of collecting and storing privacy in a public cloud service.

REFERENCES

[1] Kundra V. Federal cloud computing strategy. Washington, DC: Executive Office of the President, Office of Management and Budget; 2011.
[2] Federal Chief Information Officers Council. Privacy Committee, Web 2.0/Cloud Computing Subcommittee. Privacy recommendations for the use of cloud computing by federal departments and agencies. Washington, DC: Executive Office of the President, Office of Management and Budget; 2010.
[3] Federal Chief Information Officers Council. Federal enterprise architecture security and privacy profile (FEA-SPP), version 3.0. Washington, DC: Executive Office of the President, Office of Management and Budget; 2011.
[4] Jansen W, Grance T. NIST Special Publication (SP) 800−144, guidelines on security and privacy in public cloud computing. Maryland: National Institute of Standards and Technology; 2011.
[5] Mell P, Grance T. NIST Special Publication (SP) 800−145, the NIST definition of cloud computing. Maryland: National Institute of Standards and Technology; 2011.
[6] The Smart Grid Interoperability Panel (SGIP), Cyber Security Working Group. Interagency Report (IR) 7628, guidelines for smart grid security. Maryland: National Institute of Standards and Technology; 2010.
[7] Records, computers and the rights of citizens [Internet]. Washington, DC: US Department of Health & Human Services [cited September 28 2011]. <http://www.justice.gov/opcl/docs/rec-com-rights.pdf>.

---

[45]The Federal CIO Council and Chief Acquisition Officers Council in coordination with the Federal Cloud Compliance Committee to developed Creating Effective Cloud Computing Contracts for the Federal Government: Best Practices for Acquiring IT as a Service, which discusses "Privacy" in contracts (pp. 16−23).

[8] OECD Guidelines on the Protection of Privacy and Transborder Flows of Personal Data [Internet]. Paris: Organisation for Economic Co-operation and Development; [cited September 28 2011]. <http://www.oecd.org/internet/interne-teconomy/oecdguidelinesontheprotectionofprivacyandtransborderflowsofpersonal-data.htm>.

[9] Johnson C. Office of Management and Budget (OMB) memorandum 07–16. Safeguarding against and responding to the breach of personally identifiable information. Washington, DC: Executive Office of the President, Office of Management and Budget; 2007.

[10] Overview of the Privacy Act of 1974, 2010 Edition [Internet]. Washington, DC: US Department of Justice [cited September 28 2011]. <http://www.justice.gov/opcl/1974privacyactoverview.htm>.

[11] Privacy Act of 1974 [Internet]. Washington, DC: US Government Printing Office [cited October 10 2011]. <http://www.gpo.gov/fdsys/pkg/USCODE-2011-title5/html/USCODE-2011-title5-partI-chap5-subchapII-sec552a.htm>.

[12] Federal CIO. Council and Chief Acquisition Officers Council. Creating Effective Cloud Computing Contracts for the Federal Government. Washington, DC: Executive Office of the President, Office of Management and Budget; 2012.

[13] Privacy act issuances [Internet]. Washington, DC: US Government Printing Office [cited October 14 2011]. <https://www.gpo.gov/fdsys/browse/collection.action?collectionCode=PAI>.

[14] Federal Chief Information Officers Council, Privacy Committee. Web 2.0/Cloud Computing Subcommittee. Privacy recommendations for the use of cloud computing by federal departments and agencies. Washington, DC: Executive Office of the President, Office of Management and Budget; 2010.

[15] McCallister E, Grance T, Scarfone K. NIST Special Publication (SP) 800–122, Guide to protecting the confidentiality of Personally Identifiable Information (PII). Maryland: National Institute of Standards and Technology; 2010.

[16] Evans D, Bond P, Bement A. Federal Information Processing Standards (FIPS) 199 Standards for security categorization of federal information and information systems. Maryland: National Institute of Standards and Technology; 2004.

[17] Joint Task Force Transformation Initiative Interagency Working Group. NIST Special Publication (SP) 800–53 revision 4 (initial public draft), Security and privacy controls for federal information system and organizations. Maryland: National Institute of Standards and Technology; 2012.

[18] Federal Chief Information Officers Council. Federal enterprise architecture security and privacy profile (FEA-SPP), version 3.0. Washington, DC: Office of Management and Budget; 2011.

[19] Federal Privacy Recommendations for the use of cloud computing by federal departments and agencies. Chief Information Officers Council, Privacy Committee, Web 2.0/Cloud Computing Subcommittee. Washington, DC: Executive Office of the President, Office of Management and Budget; 2010.

[20] Wood D. Personal information: data breaches are frequent, but evidence resulting identity theft is limited; however, the full extent is unknown. Washington, DC: US Government Accountability Office; 2007.

[21] Tehan R. Data security breaches: context and incident summaries. Washington, DC: Congressional Research Service (CRS); 2007.

[22] Cybersecurity Resource Center [Internet]. Washington, DC: US Office of Personnel Management [cited September 2 2016]. <https://www.opm.gov/cybersecurity/cyber-security-incidents/>.

Applying the NIST risk management framework

INFORMATION IN THIS CHAPTER:

- Introduction to FISMA
- Risk Management Framework Overview
- NIST RMF Process

INTRODUCTION TO FISMA

The Federal Information Security Modernization Act (FISMA)[1] was signed into law on December 18, 2014 in Public Law 1136283. FISMA 2014 extended the provisions of FISMA 2002, which permanently reauthorized the framework laid out in the Government Information Security Reform Act (GISRA) of 2000, which expired in November 2002 [1]. FISMA is divided into multiple sections, each of which will be briefly described in this section.

PURPOSE

FISMA 2002 was built upon several existing federal laws designed to ensure the security of federal information and information systems. These federal laws include the Computer Security Act of 1987 (Public Law 100−35),[2] Paperwork

---

[1]The Federal Information Security Modernization Act (FISMA) of 2014 replaced the Federal Information Security Management Act of 2002, signed into law on December 17, 2002 as part of the E-Government Act of 2002 (Public Law 107-347).

[2]From 100th Congress. Public Law 100−235, Computer Security Act of 1987 (40 U.S.C. 759 note). Washington, DC: US Congress; 1987. *"To provide for a computer standards program within the National Bureau of Standards to provide for Government-wide computer security, and to provide for the training in security matters of persons who are involved in the management, operation, and use of Federal computer systems, and for other purposes."*

Reduction Act of 1995 (Public Law 104–13),[3] and Information Technology Management Reform Act of 1996 (i.e., Clinger-Cohen Act, Public Law 104–106, Division E).[4] FISMA 2014 codified the role of the Secretary of the Department of Homeland Security (DHS), and the operational role of DHS through the issuance of Binding Operational Directives (BODs)[5] and the requirement for the use of automated tools.

The purpose of FISMA, as outlined in Section 3551,[6] is covered in six major objectives. In this chapter, the focus will be on 1–4:

1. Establishment of a comprehensive framework for ensuring the effectiveness of security controls over information resources that support federal operations and assets.
2. Provide effective government-wide management and oversight of security-related risks, including coordination of information security efforts throughout the civilian, national security, and law enforcement communities.
3. Development and maintenance of a minimum set of required security controls to protect federal information and information systems.

---

[3]From 104th Congress. Paperwork Reduction Act of 1995. Washington, DC: US Congress; 1995. In part it ensured *"the creation, collection, maintenance, use, dissemination, and disposition of information by or for the Federal Government is consistent with applicable laws, including laws relating to the privacy and confidentiality, including section 552a of title 5, security of information, including the Computer Security Act of 1987 (Public Law 100–235); and access to information, including section 552 of title 5."*

[4]Public Law 104–106, Information Technology Management Reform Act of 1996 (also known as the Clinger–Cohen Act) directed the National Institute of Standards and Technology (NIST) to develop standards, guidelines, and associated methods and techniques for federal computer systems. The standards and guidelines issued by NIST, known as Federal Information Processing Standards (FIPS), are used government-wide and developed when there are compelling federal government requirements and there are no existing voluntary standards to address the federal requirements for the interoperability of different systems, the portability of data and software, and computer security.

[5]From the National Protection and Programs Directorate (NPPD) Office of Cybersecurity and Communications Assistant Secretary, Andy Ozment. Protection to Partnership: Funding the DHS role in Cybersecurity [Internet]. Washington, DC: US Department of Homeland Security [cited March 2, 2016]. Available from: https://www.dhs.gov/news/2015/04/15/written-testimony-nppd-senate-appropriations-subcommittee-homeland-security-hearing. *"Across the Federal Government, each department and agency is responsible for managing its own cybersecurity. However, under the Federal Information Security Modernization Act(FISMA) of 2014, DHS is provided with the authority to administer the implementation of federal cybersecurity policies. In order to carry out this important responsibility, DHS is authorized to issue binding operational directives, monitor agency cybersecurity practices, and provide operational and technical assistance."*

[6]Section 3551 defined the purpose of the Subchapter II—Information Security.

4. Provide a mechanism for improved oversight of federal agency information security programs, including through automated security tools to continuously diagnose[7] and improve security.

5. Utilization of commercially developed information security products for protecting critical information infrastructures.

6. Selection of commercially developed hardware and software information security solutions should be left to individual federal agencies.

ROLES AND RESPONSIBILITIES

The assignment of roles and responsibilities for information security within the federal government was clarified or reiterated within FISMA to cover *policy*, *procurement*, *standards*, and *incident response*. Although FISMA was the last major legislative framework, over the years the foundation has been built upon by a series of executive orders, directives, policies, regulations, standards and guidelines. Within FISMA, several specific roles were identified:

- Director of Office of Management and Budget (OMB).
- Secretary of Department of Homeland Security (DHS)
- National Institute of Standards and Technology (NIST).
- Federal Agencies:
  - Head of Agency or equivalent.
  - Chief Information Officer (CIO).
  - Senior Agency Information Security Officer (SAISO).

In this section, each role will be discussed as it relates to the responsibilities described in FISMA.

Director of OMB

OMB has as one of its key roles[8] the responsibility to implement and enforce government-wide policies. Through FISMA, the Director of OMB was given the

---

[7]From the US Department of Homeland Security. Continuous Diagnostic and Mitigation (CDM) [Internet]. Washington, DC: US Department of Homeland Security [cited March 2, 2016]. Available from: https://www.dhs.gov/cdm. *"The Continuous Diagnostics and Mitigation (CDM) program is a dynamic approach to fortifying the cybersecurity of government networks and systems. CDM provides federal departments and agencies with capabilities and tools that identify cybersecurity risks on an ongoing basis, prioritize these risks based upon potential impacts, and enable cybersecurity personnel to mitigate the most significant problems first. Congress established the CDM program to provide adequate, risk-based, and cost-effective cybersecurity and more efficiently allocate cybersecurity resources. The CDM program enables government entities to expand their continuous diagnostic capabilities by increasing their network sensor capacity, automating sensor collections, and prioritizing risk alerts."*

[8]For additional information on the function of the Office of Management and Budget (OMB), see http://www.whitehouse.gov/omb/organization_mission.

authority for overseeing the federal agency implementation and enforcement of security policies and practices. The authorities included:

- Developing and overseeing the implementation of policies, principles, standards, and guidelines on information security (including ensuring timely adoption and compliance by federal agencies).
- Requiring federal agencies to identify and provide for the information security protection for federal information systems and information, commensurate with the risk and magnitude of the harm resulting from the unauthorized access, use, disclosure, disruption, modification, or destruction.
- Ensuring that the DHS Secretary carries out their authorities and functions.
- Coordinating and developing standards and guidelines.
- Overseeing and enforcing federal agency compliance with FISMA requirements.
- Coordinating information security policies and procedures with related information resources management policies and procedures.
- Reporting annually to Congress on compliance by federal agencies with FISMA requirements (no later than March 1).[9]

These authorities were limited with respect to national security systems (NSSs),[10] except as they relate to budgetary actions and annual reporting to Congress. In this chapter, only those aspects of NSSs related to the NIST Risk Management Framework (RMF) will be discussed.[11]

---

[9]The annual FISMA report includes: summary of findings of annual independent evaluations (e.g., Office of Inspector General Audits), assessment of adoption, and compliance with the NIST standards and guidelines, significant deficiencies in federal agency information security practices, any planned remediation actions to address deficiencies, and summary of a report developed by the NIST.

[10]From E-Government Act of 2002 [Internet]. Washington, DC: US Government Printing Office [cited December 5, 2011]. Available from: http://www.gpo.gov/fdsys/pkg/PLAW-107publ347/html/PLAW-107publ347.htm. "*Any information system whose function, operations, or use involves intelligence activities, involves cryptographic activities related to national security, involves command and control of military forces, involves equipment that is an integral part of a weapon or weapons system, is critical to the fulfillment of military or intelligence missions (excluding any system that is used for administrative and business applications), or is protected at all times by procedures established for information that have been specifically authorized under criteria established by an Executive Order or an Act of Congress to be kept classified in the interest of national defense or foreign policy.*"

[11]From NIST Special Publication (SP) 800-53, Revision 4 Update Announcement [Internet]. Maryland: National Institute of Standards and Technology [cited December 7, 2011]. Available from: http://csrc.nist.gov/groups/SMA/fisma/documents/800-53-Rev4_announcement.pdf. "*As part of the ongoing cyber security partnership among the United States Department of Defense, the Intelligence Community, and the Federal Civil Agencies, five foundational publications are being developed by the partnership's Joint Task Force to create a unified information security framework for the federal government and its contractors.*"

Secretary of DHS

DHS has the responsibility for the operational aspects of federal agency cybersecurity with respect to the federal information systems. Through FISMA, the Director of DHS was given the authority for:

- Assisting the Director of OMB.
- Developing and overseeing the implementation of binding operational directives (BODs) to federal agencies to implement the policies, principles, standards, and guidelines developed by the Director of OMB.
- Monitoring federal agency implement of information security policies and practices.
- Convening meeting with senior agency officials to help ensure effective implementation of information security policies and practices.
- Coordinating Government-wide efforts on information security policies and practices.
- Providing operational and technical assistance to federal agencies in implementing policies, principles, standards, and guidelines on information security.
- Ensuring the operation of a central Federal information security incident response center.

NIST

NIST, under FISMA, was assigned the responsibility to develop standards, guidelines, and associated methods and techniques for federal agencies. These standards and guidelines include the minimum requirements for providing adequate information security for federal information systems (excluding national security systems):

- Standards to be used for categorizing information and information systems based on objectives of providing an adequate level of information security (*Federal Information Processing Standard (FIPS) PUB 199, Standards for Security Categorization of Federal Information and Information Systems*).[12]
- Guidelines recommending the types of information and information systems (*NIST Special Publication (SP) 800-60 Revision 1, Volume I and II: Guide for Mapping Types of Information and Information System to Security Categories*).
- Minimum information security requirements (*Federal Information Processing Standard (FIPS) PUB 200, Minimum Security Requirements for Federal*

---

[12]From Joint Task Force Transformation Initiative, NIST Special Publication (SP) 800-53 Revision 4, Security and Privacy Controls for Federal Information System and Organizations. Maryland: National Institute of Standards and Technology; 2013. *"To comply with the federal standard, organizations first determine the security category of their information system in accordance with FIPS Publication 199, Standards for Security Categorization of Federal Information and Information Systems, derive the information system impact level from the security category in accordance with FIPS 200, and then apply the appropriately tailored set of baseline security controls in NIST Special Publication 800-53, Security and Privacy Controls for Federal Information Systems and Organizations."*

Information and Information Systems[13] *and NIST Special Publication (SP) 800-53 Revision 4, Security and Privacy Controls for Federal Information Systems and Organizations).*

NIST was also given the responsibility for developing guidelines for the detection and handling of information security incidents (*NIST Special Publication (SP) 800-61 Revision 2, Computer Security Incident Handling Guide*), and guidelines for identifying an information system as a national security system (*NIST Special Publication (SP) 800-59, Guideline for Identifying an Information System as a National Security System*).[14]

Federal Agencies

Federal agencies are required to comply with the provisions defined in FISMA. As part of their obligation, they must ensure for the protection of federal information and information systems commensurate with the risk and magnitude of harm resulting from *unauthorized access, use, disclosure, disruption, modification,* or *destruction* [2]. This includes complying with information security standards[15] for non-NSSs and standards and guidelines[16] for NSSs. Federal agencies must also ensure that information security is an integrated part of their strategic planning and operational planning processes so there is alignment of goals and objectives.

Head of Agency or Equivalent

The Head of the Agency (or the highest-level senior official), in an effort to establish commitment and accountability for information security, was given the

---

[13]From Joint Task Force Transformation Initiative, NIST Special Publication (SP) 800-53 Revision 4, Security and Privacy Controls for Federal Information System and Organizations. Maryland: National Institute of Standards and Technology; 2013. "FIPS Publication 200, Minimum Security Requirements for Federal Information and Information Systems, is a mandatory federal standard developed by NIST in response to FISMA."

[14]From Certification and Accreditation Transformation [Internet]. Washington, DC: Department of the Navy [cited December 27, 2011]. Available from: http://www.doncio.navy.mil/chips/ArticleDetails.aspx?ID=3005. *DoDI 8510.01 aligns with the risk management processes included in NIST SP 800-37 ("Guide for Applying the Risk Management Framework to Federal Information Systems: A Security Life Cycle Approach") and describes the DoD risk management process, the DoD Information Assurance Risk Management Framework (DIARMF).*

[15]From Evans, D., Bond, P., Bement, A. Federal Information Processing Standard (FIPS) PUB 199, Standards for Security Categorization of Federal Information and Information Systems. Maryland: National Institute of Standards and Technology; 2004. *"Federal Information Processing Standards Publications (FIPS PUBS) are issued by the National Institute of Standards and Technology (NIST) after approval by the Secretary of Commerce pursuant to Section 5131 of the Information Technology Management Reform Act of 1996 (Public Law 104–106) and the Federal Information Security Management Act of 2002 (Public Law 107–347)."*

[16]From the Committee on National Security Systems (CNSS) [Internet]. Maryland: CNSS [cited December 8, 2011]. Available from: https://www.cnss.gov/CNSS/about/history.cfm. *"The CNSS (formerly named the National Security Telecommunications and Information Systems Security Committee (NSTISSC)) was established by National Security Directive (NSD)-42, National Policy for the Security of National Security Telecommunications and Information Systems."*

responsibility for ensuring senior agency officials (e.g., *authorizing officials*) provide for the protection of federal information and information systems for which they have budgetary oversight, or which support the mission and/or business operations [3]. Protections include:

- Conducting risk assessments;
- Categorizing information and information systems;
- Implementing security policies and procedures; and
- Periodically testing and evaluating security controls and techniques.

The Head of the Agency must ensure that security policies, procedures, and practices are adequate. To support this requirement, the Head of the Agency is required to designate a Federal Agency CIO with the authority for the compliance of FISMA. The Federal Agency CIO, in turn, designates his or her information technology (IT) security responsibilities to a Senior Agency Information Security Officer (SAISO),[17] who is both qualified and trained in information security. These IT security responsibilities include:

- Developing and maintaining an information security program;
- Developing and maintaining information security policies, procedures, and controls;
- Training and overseeing personnel with significant information security responsibilities; and
- Assisting authorizing officials (AO).

Federal Agency Information Security Program

Federal agencies are also required to establish an agency-wide information security program. The program developed by the federal agency must address the following requirements:

- Periodically assessing the risk and magnitude of the harm that could result from the unauthorized access, use, disclosure, disruption, modification, or destruction of information and information systems that support the operations and assets of the agency, which may include using automated tools consistent with NIST standards and guidelines;
- Developing security policies and procedures;
- Developing subordinate plans for providing adequate information security for networks, facilities, and systems or groups of information systems;
- Providing security awareness training to inform personnel, including contractors and other users of information systems that support the operations and assets of the agency;

---

[17]In most federal agencies the title for this role is the Chief Information Security Officer (CISO).

- Developing a process for planning, implementing, evaluating, and documenting remedial action to address any deficiencies in the information security policies, procedures, and practices of the agency;
- Developing procedures for detecting, reporting, and responding to security incidents, including an incident response capability; and
- Developing plans and procedures to ensure continuity of operations for information systems that support the operations and assets of the agency.

Federal Agency Independent Evaluations and Reporting

On an annual basis, federal agencies are required by law to conduct an independent evaluation of their information security program to ensure its effectiveness. The independent evaluations involve the testing of the effectiveness of the organization's policies, procedures, and practices, and an assessment compliance with FISMA, including any supporting federal policies, procedures, standards, and guidelines. The results of the independent evaluations are sent through the Head of the Agency to the Director of OMB. The Director of OMB includes information from all independent evaluations across the federal government and develops a comprehensive summary in a government-wide report that is submitted to Congress.[18]

TIP

To support federal agencies in evaluating their programs, NIST developed the Program Review for Information Security Management Assistance (PRISMA).[19] The PRISMA methodology uses "a standardized approach to review and measure the information security posture of an information security program" [4]. The PRISMA process includes 11 steps that cover both *preparation* and *execution*.

Preparation Steps:

- Review initiation.
- Review scope definition.
- Planning.
- Kickoff meeting.

Execution Steps:

- Review execution.
- Review documentation.
- Interviews.
- Environmental influences and constraints.
- Team negotiations.
- Analysis, report generation, and review.

---

[18]OMB reports to Congress no later than March 1st of each year.
[19]*Program Review for Information Security Management Assistance (PRISMA)*. Available from: http://csrc.nist.gov/groups/SMA/prisma/index.html.

RISK MANAGEMENT FRAMEWORK OVERVIEW

The NIST RMF[20] is a flexible, risk-based approach that is driven by the organization's information security program, and supports the management of risk[21] by facilitating the sharing[22] of information. The NIST RMF objectives [4] include:

- Building information security capabilities into federal information systems;
- Maintaining awareness of the security state of information systems through ongoing continuous monitoring; and
- Providing essential information to key stakeholders to facilitate decisions regarding the acceptance of risk.

Risk management is an essential element of the NIST RMF, which requires linking risks to an organization-wide information security program. This enables the organization to have a broader view of risks, including those across all information systems within the enterprise. Since the NIST RMF is a more technical approach, organizations will need to ensure that risk-based decisions are considered from a strategic viewpoint where the impact to the organization's goals and objectives is more visible.

For the NIST RMF to be effective, the organization needs to identify and communicate program-level security requirements that all information systems within the enterprise should meet. This also limits the duplication of risk management activities where common capabilities can be integrated or even shared by each information system within the overall organization-wide information security program. In this section, we will briefly discuss the role of the risk management when applying the NIST RMF and how closely aligning the system development life cycle (SDLC) processes enables security-related information produced during the SDLC to be reused to support the risk management process.

---

[20]The NIST RMF was developed by the Joint Task Force Transformation Initiative (JTFTI) Working Group, a partnership with stakeholders from the US Department of Defense (DoD), Intelligence Community (IC), and NIST, as a common framework for government-wide risk management.

[21]From Joint Task Force Transformation Initiative Interagency Working Group. NIST Special Publication (SP) 800-37 Revision 1, Guide for Applying the Risk Management Framework to Federal Information Systems: A Security Life Cycle Approach. Maryland: National Institute of Standards and Technology; 2010. *"Risk management can be viewed as a holistic activity that is fully integrated into every aspect of the organization—from senior leaders providing the strategic vision and top-level goals and objectives for the organization, to mid-level leaders planning and managing projects, to individuals on the front lines developing, implementing, and operating the systems supporting the organization's core missions and business processes."*

[22]From Joint Task Force Transformation Initiative Interagency Working Group. NIST Special Publication (SP) 800-37 Revision 1, Guide for Applying the Risk Management Framework to Federal Information Systems: A Security Life Cycle Approach. Maryland: National Institute of Standards and Technology; 2010. *"Reciprocity is the mutual agreement among participating organizations to accept each other's security assessments in order to reuse information system resources and/or to accept each other's assessed security posture in order to share information."*

THE ROLE OF RISK MANAGEMENT

The effective application of the NIST RMF requires the integration of risk management[23] activities at different levels within an organization. As illustrated in Fig. 5.1, the risk management process begins at the organizational level (*Tier 1*) where the governance structure and risk management strategy are developed.

The risk management strategy[24] supports the organization's strategic goals and objectives. To link the risk management strategy with the mission and business processes (*Tier 2*), risk management should be addressed as a part of the enterprise architecture.[25] Finally, at the information system level (*Tier 3*), the appropriate safeguards and countermeasures are applied to the information and information system through the selection, implementation, and assessment of security controls that have traceability to the security requirements[26] established by the organization and allocated within the information security architecture. This alignment between the NIST RMF and the SDLC is critical to ensure there is an early integration of security with the appropriate inputs from stakeholders across the organization.

---

[23]From Joint Task Force Transformation Initiative Interagency Working Group. NIST Special Publication (SP) 800-39, Managing Information Security Risk: Organization, Mission, and Information System View. Maryland: National Institute of Standards and Technology; 2011. *"The program and supporting processes to manage information security risk to organizational operations (including mission, functions, image, reputation), organizational assets, individuals, other organizations, and the Nation, and includes: (i) establishing the context for risk-related activities; (ii) assessing risk; (iii) responding to risk once determined; and (iv) monitoring risk over time."*

[24]The Risk Management Strategy will be discussed in detail in Chapter 6, Risk Management.

[25]From Joint Task Force Transformation Initiative Interagency Working Group. NIST Special Publication (SP) 800-37 Revision 1, Guide for Applying the Risk Management Framework to Federal Information Systems: A Security Life Cycle Approach. Maryland: National Institute of Standards and Technology; 2010. *"Organizations may define certain security capabilities needed to satisfy security requirements and provide appropriate mission and business protection. Security capabilities are typically defined by bringing together a specific set of safeguards/countermeasures (i.e., security controls) derived from the appropriately tailored baselines that together produce the needed capability."*

[26]From Joint Task Force Transformation Initiative, NIST Special Publication (SP) 800-53 Revision 4, Security and Privacy Controls for Federal Information System and Organizations. Maryland: National Institute of Standards and Technology; 2013. *"The term security requirement is used by different communities and groups in different ways and may require additional explanation to establish the particular context for the various use cases. It is important to define the context for each use of the term security requirement so the respective communities (including individuals responsible for policy, architecture, acquisition, engineering, and mission/business protection) can clearly communicate their intent."*

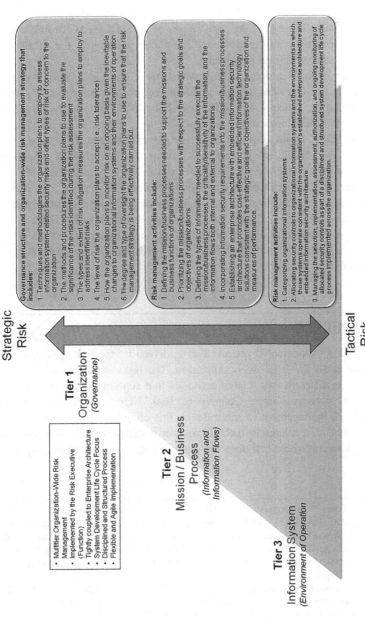

Strategic
Risk

Governance structure and organization-wide risk management strategy that includes:

1. Techniques and methodologies the organization plans to employ to assess information system-related security risks and other types of risk of concern to the organization
2. The methods and procedures the organization plans to use to evaluate the significance of the risks identified during the risk assessment
3. The types and extent of risk mitigation measures the organization plans to employ to address identified risks
4. The level of risk the organization plans to accept (i.e., risk tolerance)
5. How the organization plans to monitor risk on an ongoing basis given the inevitable changes to organizational information systems and their environments of operation
6. The degree and type of oversight the organization plans to use to ensure that the risk management strategy is being effectively carried out.

Risk management activities include:

1. Defining the mission/business processes needed to support the missions and business functions of organizations
2. Prioritizing the mission/business processes with respect to the strategic goals and objectives of organizations
3. Defining the types of information needed to successfully execute the mission/business processes, the criticality/sensitivity of the information, and the information flows both internal and external to organizations
4. Incorporating information security requirements into the mission/business processes
5. Establishing an enterprise architecture with embedded information security architecture that promotes cost-effective and efficient information technology solutions consistent with the strategic goals and objectives of the organization and measures of performance.

Risk management activities include:

1. Categorizing organizational information systems
2. Allocating security controls to organizational information systems and the environments in which those systems operate consistent with the organization's established enterprise architecture and embedded information security architecture
3. Managing the selection, implementation, assessment, authorization, and ongoing monitoring of allocated security controls as part of a disciplined and structured system development life cycle process implemented across the organization.

Tactical
Risk

Tier 1
Organization
(Governance)

Tier 2
Mission / Business
Process
(Information and
Information Flows)

Tier 3
Information System
(Environment of Operation)

- Multitier Organization-Wide Risk Management
- Implemented by the Risk Executive (Function)
- Tightly coupled to Enterprise Architecture
- System Development Life Cycle Focus
- Disciplined and Structured Process
- Flexible and Agile Implementation

FIGURE 5.1

Tier risk management approach.

THE NIST RMF AND THE SYSTEM DEVELOPMENT LIFE CYCLE

As previously discussed, the alignment of activities included in the NIST RMF with a traditional SDLC[27] ensures risk management becomes an integrated part of the information system life cycle. At each phase of the SDLC, as illustrated in Fig. 5.2, specific security considerations are integrated, starting at the initiation phase where requirements definition begins.

Security requirements[28] addressed later within the SDLC instead of including them in the original system design could unnecessarily increase costs and delay the authorization process. By defining NIST RMF activities within the context of the system development process, weaknesses, and deficiencies identified early in the SDLC could improve the effectiveness of security testing performed later in the NIST RMF (e.g., assessing and monitoring security controls). Since information systems typically exist at some phase of the SDLC and will continue to evolve throughout their life cycle, integrating the NIST RMF into the life cycle process enables risks to be mitigated or eliminated through information security and risk management-related activities. For example, the security-related information produced through development security testing may be reused later in SDLC (e.g., implementation/assessment or the operation/maintenance phases).

NIST RMF PROCESS

The NIST RMF is a task-oriented process that is driven by the risk management activities applied at all levels of the organization. The tasks addressed within the NIST RMF include different risk-related activities that support the organization's risk management strategy. Since Chapter 6, Risk Management, will cover enterprise-wide risk management in more detail, this chapter will limit the focus of risk management as it relates to the information system (*Tier 3*), as shown in Fig. 5.1. The risk management activities included in Fig. 5.3 involve applying the

---

[27]From Joint Task Force Transformation Initiative Interagency Working Group. NIST Special Publication (SP) 800-37 Revision 1, Guide for Applying the Risk Management Framework to Federal Information Systems: A Security Life Cycle Approach. Maryland: National Institute of Standards and Technology; 2010. *"There are typically five phases in a generic system development life cycle including: (i) initiation; (ii) development/acquisition; (iii) implementation; (iv) operation/ maintenance; and (v) disposal."*

[28]From Kissel, R., Stine K., Scholl, M., Rossman, H., Fahlsing, J., Gulick. NIST Special Publication (SP) 800-64 Revision 2, Security Considerations in the System Development Lifecycle. Maryland: National Institute of Standards and Technology; 2008. *"Security requirements are a subset of the overall functional and nonfunctional (e.g., quality, assurance) requirements levied on an information system and are incorporated into the system development life cycle simultaneously with the functional and nonfunctional requirements."*

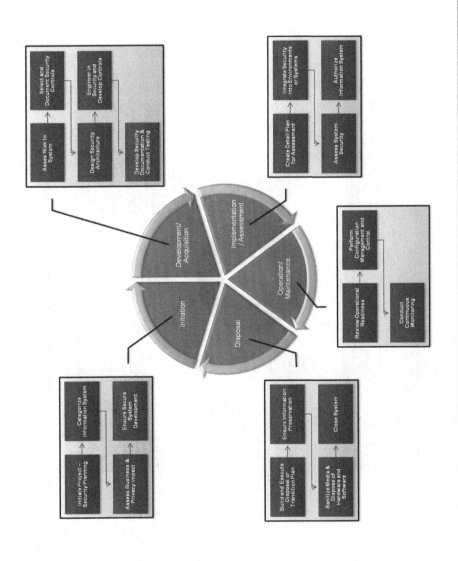

FIGURE 5.2

Security consideration in the system development life cycle (SDLC).

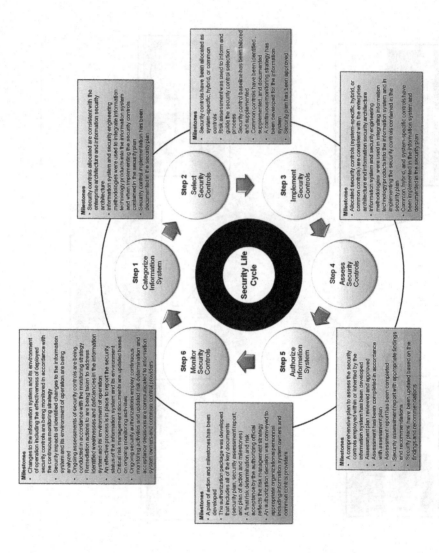

FIGURE 5.3

Risk management framework.

steps included within the NIST RMF as a part of a security life cycle approach. The steps performed within the NIST RMF include:

- categorizing the information and information system;
- selecting the security control baseline;
- implementing the selected security controls;
- assessing the security controls;
- authorizing information system operation; and
- monitoring the security controls.

INFORMATION SYSTEM CATEGORIZATION

The *categorization* of the information system is the first step in the NIST RMF (*Step 1*), and one of the most essential activities[29] required for the selection of a baseline set of security controls (and privacy controls, where applicable). As discussed earlier in the chapter, FISMA tasked NIST with the responsibility to develop standards and guidelines. The standards included procedures for categorizing information and information systems, and the guidelines for categorizing the different types[30] of federal information that will be processed, stored, or transmitted within the information system. The first step in the NIST RMF (*Step 1*), as shown in Table 5.1, includes three major tasks. In this section, the discussion will primarily focus on the first task (1-1).

The security categorization process is driven by the need for federal agencies (or others operating on behalf of federal agencies) to identify the types of information[31] that will be processed, stored, or transmitted in the information system, a critical requirement for understanding the security objectives (confidentiality,[32]

[29]From Evans, D., Bond, P., Bement, A. Federal Information Processing Standard (FIPS) PUB 199, Standards for Security Categorization of Federal Information and Information Systems. Maryland: National Institute of Standards and Technology; 2004. *"Security categories are to be used in conjunction with vulnerability and threat information in assessing the risk to an organization."*

[30]From Evans, D., Bond, P., Bement, A. Federal Information Processing Standard (FIPS) PUB 199, Standards for Security Categorization of Federal Information and Information Systems. Maryland: National Institute of Standards and Technology; 2004. *"Information type is a specific category of information (e.g., privacy, medical, proprietary, financial, investigative, contractor sensitive, security management) defined by an organization or, in some instances, by a specific law, Executive order, or directive, policy, or regulation."*

[31]From Evans, D., Bond, P., Bement, A. Federal Information Processing Standard (FIPS) PUB 199, Standards for Security Categorization of Federal Information and Information Systems. Maryland: National Institute of Standards and Technology; 2004. *"FIPS 199 applies to all information within the federal government other than that information that has been determined pursuant to Executive Order 12958, as amended by Executive Order 13292, or any predecessor order, or by the Atomic Energy Act of 1954, as amended, to require protection against unauthorized disclosure and is marked to indicate its classified status and all federal information systems other than those information systems designated as national security systems."*

[32]From E-Government Act of 2002 [Internet]. Washington, DC: US Government Printing Office [cited December 9, 2011]. Available from: http://www.gpo.gov/fdsys/pkg/PLAW-107publ347/html/PLAW-107publ347.htm. *"Preserving authorized restrictions on information access and disclosure, including means for protecting personal privacy and proprietary information."*

Table 5.1 NIST RMF Step 1 Activities [3]

Task	Name	Activities	References
1-1	Security categorization	• Categorize the information system • Document the results of the security categorization in the security plan	• FIPS 199 • NIST SP 800-30 • NIST SP 800-39 • NIST SP 800-59 • NIST SP 800-60 • CNSS Instruction 1253
1-2	Information system description	• Describe the information system (including the system boundary) • Document the description in the security plan	
1-3	Information system registration	• Register the information system with appropriate organizational program/management offices	

integrity,[33] and availability[34]). In addition, the security categorization process also ensures that the selected security controls implemented provide the adequate security[35] to meet the organization's security objectives. As will be discussed in detail in this chapter, the application of a standardized approach to categorizing information systems enables a common framework to be used across the federal government for the management and oversight of information systems and in reports relating to agency-specific information security to OMB and government-wide information security to Congress.

---

[33]From E-Government Act of 2002 [Internet]. Washington, DC: US Government Printing Office [cited 2011 Dec 9]. Available from: http://www.gpo.gov/fdsys/pkg/PLAW-107publ347/html/PLAW-107publ347.htm. "*Guarding against improper information modification or destruction, and includes ensuring information non-repudiation and authenticity.*"

[34]From E-Government Act of 2002 [Internet]. Washington, DC: US Government Printing Office; [cited December 9, 2011]. Available from: http://www.gpo.gov/fdsys/pkg/PLAW-107publ347/html/PLAW-107publ347.htm. "*Ensuring timely and reliable access to and use of information.*"

[35]From Office of Management and Budget (OMB.) Managing Information as a Strategic Resource [Internet]. Washington, DC: Executive Office of the President, Office of Management and Budget [cited November 6, 2016]. Available from: https://www.whitehouse.gov/sites/default/files/omb/assets/OMB/circulars/a130/a130revised.pdf. "*Adequate security means security protections commensurate with the risk resulting from the unauthorized access, use, disclosure, disruption, modification, or destruction of information. This includes ensuring that information hosted on behalf of an agency and information systems and applications used by the agency operate effectively and provide appropriate confidentiality, integrity, and availability protections through the application of cost-effective security controls.*"

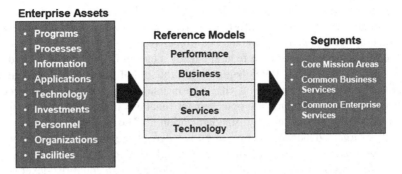

FIGURE 5.4

Enterprise asset mapping [18].

The application of the security categorization process becomes complex when external information system services[36] are used by federal agencies in processing, transmitting, or storing information collected or maintained on behalf of the federal government. In these instances, a federal agency's reliance upon an external service does not limit its overall responsibility for ensuring the security categorization of the external service being used is consistent with the different types of information that will be used within the service to support its mission or business needs. Without an understanding of the security categorization of the information being used in the external service, the federal agency will not be able to determine the necessary requirements that must be used by the service provider to ensure that the service operates at a security level consistent with the federal agency's minimum assurance requirements.

Relationship between the NIST RMF and the Federal Enterprise Architecture

The enterprise architecture is a management practice employed to maximize the effectiveness of mission/business process and information resources [5]. As illustrated in Fig. 5.4, the enterprise assets identified within the enterprise architecture are mapped to the individual federal agency's mission and business processes through the reference models provided in the Federal Enterprise

---

[36]From Joint Task Force Transformation Initiative Interagency Working Group. NIST Special Publication (SP) 800-37 Revision 1, Guide for Applying the Risk Management Framework to Federal Information Systems: A Security Life Cycle Approach. Maryland: National Institute of Standards and Technology; 2010. *"A service for which the organization typically no direct control over the application of required security controls or the assessment of security control effectiveness."*

Architecture (FEA)[37] and the resulting segment architecture.[38] The application of the mapping ensures the information resources are properly aligned with each federal agency's strategic goals and objectives.

The relationship between the federal agency's enterprise architecture[39] and the application of the NIST RMF begins with the initial security categorization. Security categorization provides a vital step in integrating security into the business and information technology management functions and establishes the foundation for information security standardization.[40] The security categorization process is largely dependent upon the knowledge of the information supporting the federal government. By utilizing a framework similar to the one depicted in Fig. 5.5, the security categorization process is adopted as an enterprise-level viewpoint for "each type of information as identified from the FEA Performance Reference Model (PRM)[41] and Business Reference Model (BRM)[42] analysis" [6]. This produces a government-wide approach for evaluating the "level of potential impact values assigned to the respective security objectives" [7] (i.e., confidentiality, integrity, and availability) that are used for establishing the information security and privacy requirements in the security control selection step of the NIST RMF (*Step 3*). The results provide for a strong linkage between the mission, the information, and the information systems with a focus on the cost-effective application of information security [8].

---

[37]From Federal Chief Information Officers Council. Federal Enterprise Architecture Security and Privacy Profile (FEA-SPP), version 3.0. Washington, DC: Office of Management and Budget; 2011. *"The FEA is a business-based framework for government-wide improvement. The goals of the FEA are to locate and reduce or eliminate duplicative investments, discover areas where investments should be made, and identify where departments and agencies can collaborate to improve government operations or services."*

[38]From Federal Chief Information Officers Council. Federal Enterprise Architecture Security and Privacy Profile (FEA-SPP), version 3.0. Washington, DC: Office of Management and Budget; 2011. *"Segment architecture drives decisions for a business case or group of business cases supporting a core mission area or common or shared service."*

[39]From Federal Chief Information Officers Council. Federal Enterprise Architecture Security and Privacy Profile (FEA-SPP), version 3.0. Washington, DC: Office of Management and Budget; 2011. *"A strategic information asset base which defines the mission, the information necessary to perform the mission and the transitional processes for implementing new technologies in response to the changing mission needs."*

[40]From Federal Chief Information Officers Council. Federal Enterprise Architecture Security and Privacy Profile (FEA-SPP), Version 3.0. Washington, DC: Office of Management and Budget; 2011.

[41]From Federal Chief Information Officers Council. Federal Enterprise Architecture Security and Privacy Profile (FEA-SPP), Version 3.0. Washington, DC: Office of Management and Budget; 2011. *Performance Reference Model (PRM) is information that helps agencies monitor the performance of an investment and/or program.*

[42]From Federal Chief Information Officers Council. Federal Enterprise Architecture Security and Privacy Profile (FEA-SPP), version 3.0. Washington, DC: Office of Management and Budget; 2011. *Business Reference Model (BRM) is information that helps agencies understand what primary business functions are provided to citizens through the definition of business areas, lines of business, and subfunctions.*

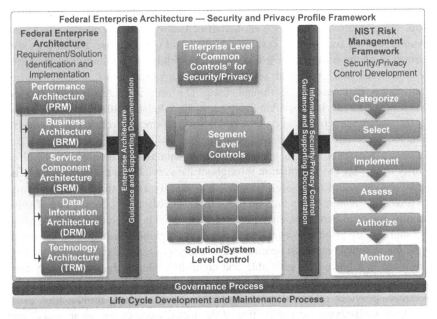

FIGURE 5.5

Federal enterprise architecture—security and privacy profile framework [6].

Shared Responsibility and the Chain of Trust

In general, the application of the NIST RMF requires a shared responsibility[43] and a chain of trust.[44] The relationship between federal agencies and service providers requires operating through terms and conditions defined in a contract, which includes detailed security control requirements or managed through a

---

[43]From Badger, L., Bernstein, D., Bohn, R., de Vaulx, F., Hogan, M., Mao, J., et al. NIST Special Publication (SP) 500-293, US Government Cloud Computing Technology Roadmap, Volume I. Maryland: National Institute of Standards and Technology; 2014. *"The cloud provider and the cloud consumer have differing degrees of control over the computing resources in a cloud system. Compared to traditional IT systems, where one organization has control over the whole stack of computing resources and the entire life cycle of the systems, cloud providers and cloud consumers collaboratively design, build, deploy, and operate cloud-based systems. The split of control means both parties now share the responsibilities in providing adequate protections to the cloud-based systems."*

[44]From Joint Task Force Transformation Initiative Interagency Working Group. NIST Special Publication (SP) 800-37 Revision 1, Guide for Applying the Risk Management Framework to Federal Information Systems: A Security Life Cycle Approach. Maryland: National Institute of Standards and Technology; 2010. *"A chain of trust requires that the organization establish and retain a level of confidence that each participating service provider in the potentially complex consumer-provider relationship provides adequate protection for the services rendered to the organization."*

service level agreement (SLA).[45] Service providers handling federal information or operating information systems on behalf of the federal government must meet the same security requirements as federal agencies [3]. Therefore, the security categorization of the information can provide a common understanding of the security objectives that drive the selection and compensation of security control requirements that need to be implemented. The security categorization process also ensures that service providers have some knowledge of the types of information that will be processed, and the potential overall impact to the federal government, should certain adverse events occur.

Service providers have a responsibility in maintaining an adequate level of security to protect the information throughout the service life cycle. However, the overall responsibility to ensure that sufficient security exists to meet the information protection requirements falls on the authorizing official.[46] For a chain of trust, operating under a shared responsibility model, to exist between the federal government and service providers, confidence needs to be gained through an understanding of the security controls implemented in the service and its environment. This confidence is achieved by verifiable and credible evidence that the security controls are operating effectively. Trust becomes even more important under complex consumer—provider relationships that are introduced such as multivendor situations. By establishing a clear definition of the security objectives, an analysis[47] can be performed to determine which participant, consumer or provider, would be most appropriate to implement the necessary security controls based on the differing degrees of ownership and control over the information system.

Overview of the Security Categorization Process

The goal of the security categorization process is to understand, identify, and categorize both the information and information systems used to process, store, or transmit the information, so that an appropriate level of information security can

---

[45]From Jansen, W., Grance, T. NIST Special Publication (SP) 800-144, Guidelines on Security and Privacy in Public Cloud Computing. Maryland: National Institute of Standards and Technology; 2011. *"An SLA represents the understanding between the cloud subscriber and cloud provider about the expected level of service to be delivered and, in the event that the provider fails to deliver the service at the level specified, the compensation available to the cloud subscriber."*

[46]From Joint Task Force Transformation Initiative Interagency Working Group. NIST Special Publication (SP) 800-37 Revision 1, Guide for Applying the Risk Management Framework to Federal Information Systems: A Security Life Cycle Approach. Maryland: National Institute of Standards and Technology; 2010. *"The authorizing official is a senior official or executive with the authority to formally assume responsibility for operating an information system at an acceptable level of risk to organizational operations and assets, individuals, other organizations, and the Nation."*

[47]From Badger, L., Bernstein, D., Bohn, R., de Vaulx, F., Hogan, M., Mao, J., et al. NIST Special Publication (SP) 500-293, US Government Cloud Computing Technology Roadmap, Volume I. Maryland: National Institute of Standards and Technology; 2014. *"This analysis needs to include considerations from a service model perspective, where different service models imply different degrees of control between cloud providers and cloud consumers."*

be applied. The level of information security is determined, in part, through an assessment of the potential impact[48] to the information in the event that there was a compromise (e.g., breach of security), which caused a loss in confidentiality, integrity, or availability. The results of this process enable federal agencies to understand and communicate their protection requirements as a consequence (e.g., degradation of primary mission functions or capabilities, financial loss, etc.) to an adverse impact to their mission and business processes. In addition, by managing the risk at the enterprise level, the information security needs can be applied more effectively across the federal government by an aggregation of the sensitivity/criticality of information using a standardized and common language. This ensures that information systems supporting multiple federal agency mission areas or supporting federal agencies as a shared business service[49] operate based on the highest level of impact to the federal government.

The security categorization process requires input from across all stakeholders. For this process to be successful the federal agency needs to ensure that coordination and collaboration exist among all parties involved (e.g., information owners, information security practitioners, enterprise architects, capital planning, etc.). Since the output of this process will be an input to the remaining steps in the NIST RMF (*Steps 2–6*), oversight is critical to ensure any errors can be validated to prevent or minimize overprotection or potentially increasing organizational risk by underprotecting the information resources.

Before the categorization process can begin, information to support the categorization process needs to be collected, including the specific organizational-specific policies, procedures, and other relevant documentation relating to risk management that would help the organization understand impacts associated with the loss of confidentiality, integrity, and availability. As depicted in Fig. 5.6, the categorization process is a multistep activity that begins with the identification of information types and concludes with the assignment of security categories and impact levels to information and information systems[50] that will be used as the basis for establishing the initial baseline set of security controls.

---

[48]From Stine, K., Kissel, R., Barker, W., Fahlsing, J., Gulick J. NIST Special Publication (SP) 800-60 Revision 1, Volume I: Guide for Mapping Types of Information and Information Systems to Security Categories. Maryland: National Institute of Standards and Technology; 2008. "*An incorrect information system impact can result in the agency either over protecting the information system thus wasting valuable security resources, or under protecting the information system and placing important operations and assets at risk.*"

[49]From Office of Management and Budget (OMB). Federal Information Technology Shared Services Strategy. Washington, DC: Executive Office of the President, Office of Management and Budget; 2012. "*A function that is provided for consumption by multiple organizations within or between Federal Agencies.*"

[50]From US Code, Title 44, Chapter 35: Coordination of Federal Information Policy [Internet]. Washington, DC: US Government Printing Office [cited December 11, 2011]. Available from: http://www.gpo.gov/fdsys/pkg/PLAW-107publ347/html/PLAW-107publ347.htm. "*An information system is a discrete set of information resources organized for the collection, processing, maintenance, use, sharing, dissemination, or disposition of information.*"

Step 1

Identify Information Types

- Document the agency's business and mission areas
- Identify all of the information types that are input, stored, processed, and/or output from each system
- Document applicable information types for the identified information system along with the basis for the information type selection

Step 2

Select Provisional Impact Levels

- Select the security impact levels for the identified information types
- Determine the security category (SC) for each information type
- Document the provisional impact level of confidentiality, integrity, and availability associated with the system's information type

Step 3

Review Provisional Impact Levels

- Review the appropriateness of the provisional impact levels based on the organization, environment, mission, use, and data sharing
- Adjust the impact levels as necessary
- Document all adjustments to the impact levels and provide the rationale or justification for the adjustments

Step 3

Adjust/Finalize Information Impact Levels

- Adjust the impact levels as necessary
- Document all adjustments to the impact levels and provide the rationale or justification for the adjustments

Step 4

Assign System Security Category

- Review identified security categorizations for the aggregate of information types
- Determine the system security categorization by identifying the security impact level high water mark for each of the security
- Adjust the security impact level high water mark for each system security objective, as necessary
- Assign the overall information system impact level based on the highest impact level for the system security objectives
- Follow the agency's oversight process for reviewing, approving, and documenting all determinations or decisions

FIGURE 5.6

Security categorization process.

Identify Information Types

In July 2001, OMB issued *Citizen-Centered E-Government: Developing the Action Plan*,[51] which established an E-Government Task Force to "identify priority actions that achieve strategic improvements in government and set in motion a transformation of government around citizen needs" [9]. The task force published the E-Government Strategy[52] that focused on achieving improvements across multiple business areas of service within the federal government and reforming the efficiency and effectiveness of the federal government's interaction with individual citizens, businesses, other state and local governments, and even internally within the federal government itself. As part of the assessment[53] performed by the task force, a business architecture, shown in Fig. 5.7, was created as a framework to "describe how the federal government interfaces with citizens, what functions and lines of business the government performs, and the key business processes used" [9].

As the foundation for the FEA BRM,[54] the FEA Program Management Office (FEAPMO) "leveraged previous Federal architecture efforts, in particular the business architecture designed as a part of the 2001 e-government Task Force's effort, as starting points for designing the government-wide model" [10]. Since its initial release, the business architecture has been through multiple revisions. The BRM version 2.0, depicted in Fig. 5.8, reflects four business areas (functions): services for citizens, mode of delivery, support delivery of services, and management of government resources. The BRM is a framework that uses a structured tiered hierarchical representation for describing the common business areas within the federal government.

The federal government's dependence on IT to support various mission and business functions requires federal agencies to understand the appropriate security controls that need to be implemented. The security controls are identified through an assessment of potential impacts should there be a breach of security (i.e., a loss of confidentiality) [7]. Therefore, the first step in the security categorization process requires the identification of information types be processed, transmitted, or stored in the information system. Since the BRM is periodically updated[55] to provide a government-wide view of the various business areas and functions across the

---

[51]*Office of Management and Budget (OMB) Memorandum 01-28.* Available from: http://www.whitehouse.gov/omb/memoranda_m01-28

[52]*E-Government Strategy: Simplified Delivery of Services to Citizens.* Available from: https://www.whitehouse.gov/sites/default/files/omb/inforeg/egovstrategy.pdf.

[53]From E-Government Task Force. E-Government Strategy. Washington, DC: Executive Office of the President, Office of Management and Budget; 2002. *The assessment applied the approach of the Federal Chief Information Officers Council, using the enterprise architecture to establish a "roadmap to achieve an agency's mission through optimal performance of its core business processes within an efficient IT environment."*

[54]The Business Reference Model (BRM) version 1.0 was published in July 2002 and version 2.0 was published in June 2003.

[55]*FEA BRM Version 3.0.* Available from: http://www.whitehouse.gov/sites/default/files/omb/assets/egov_docs/fea_brmv3_wdefinitions_20120622_final.xlsx.

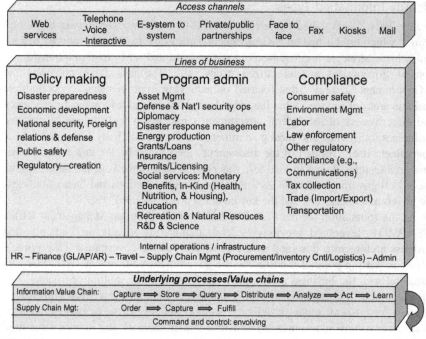

FIGURE 5.7

Business architecture [9].

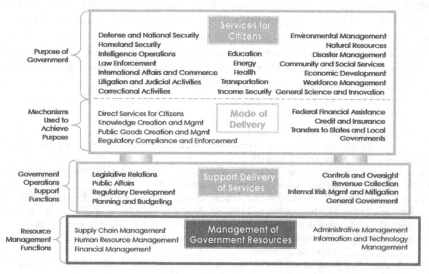

FIGURE 5.8

Business reference model 2.0 [11].

federal government, NIST used the BRM as the basis for the taxonomy of information types[56] for federal agencies to reference[57] when mapping the information types used in the information system. The integration of the enterprise architecture developed by the federal agency can provide a useful starting point to ensure the categorization is consistent with the mission and business objectives.

TIP

The types of activities [8] associated with the identification of information types are:

- Document the agency's business and mission areas.
- Identify all of the information types that are input, stored, processed, and/or output from each system.
- Identify *Mission-based* Information Type categories based on supporting FEA Lines of Business.
- As applicable, identify *Management and Support* Information Type categories based on supporting FEA Lines of Business.
- Specify applicable subfunctions for the identified *Mission-based* and *Management and Support* categories.
- As necessary, identify other required information types.
- Document applicable information types for the identified information system along with the basis for the information-type selection.

Select Provisional Impact Values for Each Information Type

Once the information types have been identified and documented, the provisional impact levels need to be selected and assigned to the security objectives of each information type. The provisional impact levels[58] are based on the potential impacts included in Table 5.2. From the provisional impact levels, an initial security categorization is characterized using the following format:

Security Category $_{\text{information type}}$ = {(**confidentiality**, *impact*), (**integrity**, *impact*), (**availability**, *impact*)}.

---

[56]From Stine, K., Kissel, R., Barker, W., Fahlsing, J., Gulick, J. NIST Special Publication (SP) 800-60 Revision 1, Volume I: Guide for Mapping Types of Information and Information Systems to Security Categories. Maryland: National Institute of Standards and Technology; 2008. *NIST Special Publication (SP) 800-60 (Volume I & II) provides guidelines for agencies to use in categorizing information and information systems by "recommending the types of information and information systems to be included in each such category of potential impact."*

[57]There are instances where information used in an information system may not be captured in the BRM, which will require federal agencies to conduct additional research when characterizing the information so that appropriate impact levels can be assigned to the security categories.

[58]The provisional impact for each information type is documented in Volume II of NIST SP 800-60.

Table 5.2 Potential Impact Levels [7]

Potential Impact	Definition
Low	• The potential impact is *low* if the loss of confidentiality, integrity, or availability could be expected to have a *limited* adverse effect on organizational operations, organizational assets, or individuals.
Moderate	• The potential impact is *moderate* if the loss of confidentiality, integrity, or availability could be expected to have a *serious* adverse effect on organizational operations, organizational assets, or individuals. • A serious adverse effect means that, for example, the loss of confidentiality, integrity, or availability might: (i) cause a significant degradation in mission capability to an extent and duration that the organization is able to perform its primary functions, but the effectiveness of the functions is significantly reduced; (ii) result in significant damage to organizational assets; (iii) result in significant financial loss; or (iv) result in significant harm to individuals that does not involve loss of life or serious life-threatening injuries.
High	• The potential impact is *high* if the loss of confidentiality, integrity, or availability could be expected to have a *severe or catastrophic* adverse effect on organizational operations, organizational assets, or individuals. • A severe or catastrophic adverse effect means that, for example, the loss of confidentiality, integrity, or availability might: (i) cause a severe degradation in or loss of mission capability to an extent and duration that the organization is not able to perform one or more of its primary functions; (ii) result in major damage to organizational assets; (iii) result in major financial loss; or (iv) result in severe or catastrophic harm to individuals involving loss of life or serious life-threatening injuries.

NOTE

The types of activities [8] associated with the selection of provisional impact levels are:

• Select the security impact levels for the identified information types from the recommended provisional impact levels for each identified information type or from FIPS 199 criteria.
• Determine the security category (SC) for each information type: SC information type = {(confidentiality, impact), (integrity, impact), (availability, impact)}.
• Document the provisional impact level of confidentiality, integrity, and availability associated with the system's information type.

TIP

The common factors for selecting impact levels include [8]:

• Confidentiality Factors
  ◦ How can a malicious adversary use the unauthorized disclosure of information to do limited/serious/severe harm to agency operations, agency assets, or individuals?

(Continued)

> **TIP (CONTINUED)**
> - How can a malicious adversary use the unauthorized disclosure of information to gain control of agency assets that might result in unauthorized modification of information, destruction of information, or denial of system services that would result in limited/serious/severe harm to agency operations, agency assets, or individuals?
> - Would unauthorized disclosure/dissemination of elements of the information type violate laws, executive orders, or agency regulations?
> - Integrity Factors
>   - How can a malicious adversary use the unauthorized modification or destruction of information to do limited/serious/severe harm to agency operations, agency assets, or individuals?
>   - Would unauthorized modification/destruction of elements of the information type violate laws, executive orders, or agency regulations?
> - Availability Factors
>   - How can a malicious adversary use the disruption of access to or use of information to do limited/serious/severe harm to agency operations, agency assets, or individuals?
>   - Would disruption of access to or use of elements of the information type violate laws, executive orders, or agency regulations?

Adjust the Information Type's Provisioning Impact Value and Security Category

After the provisional impact levels have been selected, adjustments can be applied (as required) to the information types using information about the information system's environment such as the federal agency's mission, how the information will be used, and interfaces with other systems outside of the authorization boundary[59] (or information system boundary). Other considerations might also include special factors specific to each security category as it applies to the organization or individuals,[60] should a specific breach of security occur. When all of the adjustments to the provisional impact levels have been made for an information type, the highest impact value from each of the selected security objectives becomes the overall security categorization for the information type. As an example, the security categorization for the following information type would be *Moderate* (see Table 5.3).

---

[59]From Joint Task Force Transformation Initiative Interagency Working Group. NIST Special Publication (SP) 800-37 Revision 1, Guide for Applying the Risk Management Framework to Federal Information Systems: A Security Life Cycle Approach. Maryland: National Institute of Standards and Technology; 2010. *"All components of an information system to be authorized for operation by an authorizing official and excludes separately authorized systems, to which the information system is connected."*

[60]From Evans, D., Bond, P., Bement, A. Federal Information Processing Standard (FIPS) PUB 199, Standards for Security Categorization of Federal Information and Information Systems. Maryland: National Institute of Standards and Technology; 2004. *"Adverse effects on individuals may include, but are not limited to, loss of the privacy to which individuals are entitled under law."*

Table 5.3 Potential Impact Levels [7]

Security Objective	Potential Impact		
	Low	Moderate	High
Confidentiality Preserving authorized restrictions on information access and disclosure, including means for protecting personal privacy and proprietary information [44 U.S.C., SEC. 3542]	The unauthorized disclosure of information could be expected to have a *limited* adverse effect on organizational operations, organizational assets, or individuals	The unauthorized disclosure of information could be expected to have a *serious* adverse effect on organizational operations, organizational assets, or individuals	The unauthorized disclosure of information could be expected to have a *severe or catastrophic* adverse effect on organizational operations, organizational assets, or individuals
Integrity Guarding against improper information modification or destruction, and includes ensuring information nonrepudiation and authenticity [44 U.S.C., SEC. 3542]	The unauthorized modification or destruction of information could be expected to have a *limited* adverse effect on organizational operations, organizational assets, or individuals	The unauthorized modification or destruction of information could be expected to have a *serious* adverse effect on organizational operations, organizational assets, or individuals	The unauthorized modification or destruction of information could be expected to have a *severe or catastrophic* adverse effect on organizational operations, organizational assets, or individuals
Availability Ensuring timely and reliable access to and use of information [44 U.S.C., SEC. 3542]	The disruption of access to or use of information or an information system could be expected to have a *limited* adverse effect on organizational operations, organizational assets, or individuals	The disruption of access to or use of information or an information system could be expected to have a *serious* adverse effect on organizational operations, organizational assets, or individuals	The disruption of access to or use of information or an information system could be expected to have a *severe or catastrophic* adverse effect on organizational operations, organizational assets, or individuals

Security Category $_{\text{information type}}$ = {(**confidentiality**, *moderate*), (**integrity**, *moderate*), (**availability**, *low*)}.

TIP

The types of activities [8] associated with the review of the provisional impact levels and the adjustment and finalization of the information impact levels include:

- Reviewing the appropriateness of the provisional impact levels based on the organization, environment, mission, use, and data sharing.

(Continued)

Determine the System Security Impact Level

The final step in the security categorization process is the assignment of an overall security impact level[61] to the information system using the high-water mark.[62] As an example, the security categorization for the following information system would be *Moderate*.

> Security Category $_{\text{information type}}$ = {(**confidentiality**, *moderate*), (**integrity**, *moderate*), (**availability**, *low*)}.

> Security Category $_{\text{information type}}$ = {(**confidentiality**, *not applicable*), (**integrity**, *low*), (**availability**, *low*)}.

> Security Category $_{\text{information system}}$ = {(**confidentiality**, *moderate*), (**integrity**, *moderate*), (**availability**, *low*)}.

> **TIP**
>
> The types of activities [8] associated with the assignment of a system security category based on the aggregate of information types include:
>
> - Reviewing identified security categorizations for the aggregate of information types.
>
> *(Continued)*

---

[61]From Stine, K., Kissel, R., Barker, W., Fahlsing, J., Gulick, J. NIST Special Publication (SP) 800-60 Revision 1, Volume I: Guide for Mapping Types of Information and Information Systems to Security Categories. Maryland: National Institute of Standards and Technology; 2008. *"Impact levels (plural), as used here, refers to low, moderate, high, or not applicable values assigned to each security objective (i.e., confidentiality, integrity, and availability) used in expressing the security category of an information type or information systems. The value of not applicable only applies to information types and not to information systems."*

[62]The highest values from among the security objectives from all information types identified.

> **TIP (CONTINUED)**
>
> - Determining the system security categorization by identifying the security impact level high-water mark for each of the security objectives (confidentiality, integrity, availability): SC System X = {(confidentiality, impact), (integrity, impact), (availability, impact)}.
> - Adjusting the security impact level high-water mark for each system security objective (as necessary).
> - Assigning the overall information system impact level based on the highest impact level for the system security objectives (confidentiality, integrity, availability).
> - Following the agency's oversight process for reviewing, approving, and documenting all determinations or decisions.

However, similar to the focus on adjusting security categories for information types, the system security objectives can also be adjusted, based on the application of several factors such as the aggregation of different types of data (change of the information sensitivity when integrated with other information types) and critical system functionality (interconnection of the system with other information systems and the dependence of the information by other information systems to support a specific mission/business function). In addition, there are other factors that relate to the specific context of the information and the information system (e.g., information that would be subject to privacy laws and policies, supporting infrastructure that stores, processes, or transmits (flows) information within or across the network or system components).

SECURITY CONTROLS SELECTION

The security control selection is the next step in the NIST RMF (*Step 2*) and includes three major tasks, included in Table 5.4. In this section, most of the focus will be spent on the second and third task. The second task includes the security control selection process that begins with the initial security control baseline[63] and concludes with a final set of security controls that will be implemented.[64] The third task involves the development of a strategy to monitor the selected security controls as part of an information security continuous monitoring (ISCM)[65] program.

---

[63]From Joint Task Force Transformation Initiative, NIST Special Publication (SP) 800-53 Revision 4, Security and Privacy Controls for Federal Information System and Organizations. Maryland: National Institute of Standards and Technology; 2013. *"Baseline controls are the starting point for the security control selection process."*

[64]From Joint Task Force Transformation Initiative, NIST Special Publication (SP) 800-53 Revision 4, Security and Privacy Controls for Federal Information System and Organizations. Maryland: National Institute of Standards and Technology; 2013. *"For legacy systems, some or all of the security controls selected may already be implemented."*

[65]From Dempsey, K., Chawla, N., Johnson, A., Johnston, R., Jones, A., Orebaugh, A., et al. NIST Special Publication (SP) 800-137, Information Security Continuous Monitoring (ISCM) for Federal Information System and Organizations. Maryland: National Institute of Standards and Technology; 2011. *ISCM is "maintaining ongoing awareness of information security, vulnerabilities, and threats to support organizational risk management decisions."*

Table 5.4 NIST RMF Step 2 Activities [3]

Task	Name	Activities	References
2-1	Common control identification	• Identify the security controls that are provided by the organization as common controls for organizational information systems • Document the controls in a security plan (or equivalent document)	• FIPS 199 • FIPS 200 • NIST SP 800-18 • NIST SP 800-30 • NIST SP 800-53 • CNSS Instruction 1253
2-2	Security control selection	• Select the security controls for the information system • Document the controls in the security plan	• FIPS 199 • FIPS 200 • NIST SP 800-18 • NIST SP 800-30 • NIST SP 800-53 • CNSS Instruction 1253
2-3	Monitoring strategy	• Develop a strategy for the continuous monitoring of security control effectiveness and any proposed/actual changes to the information system and its environment of operations	• NIST SP 800-30 • NIST SP 800-39 • NIST SP 800-53 • NIST SP 800-53A • NIST SP 800-117 • NIST SP 800-126 • NIST SP 800-128 • NIST SP 800-137 • CNSS Instruction 1253
2-4	Security plan approval	• Review and approve the security plan	• NIST SP 800-18 • NIST SP 800-30 • NIST SP 800-53 • CNSS Instruction 1253

TIP

For legacy information systems (including service providers), a gap analysis [12] can be performed as follows:

1. Reconfirm (or update) the security categorization;
2. Review the existing security plan (considering any updates to the security categorization); and
3. Implement security controls in the updated security plan with specific attention given to any new security controls or enhancements.

The initial security control baseline consists of a minimum set of security requirements derived from among the 17[66] security-related areas included in Table 5.5.

---

[66]The PM family of security controls relates to an organizational information security program, and therefore they may not be specific to only one information system.

Table 5.5 Security Control Families [6]

Class[a]	Acronym	Name	Activities
Management	PM	Program management	Organization-wide information security program management controls that are independent of any particular information system and are essential for managing information security programs (e.g., Information Security Program Plan)
Management	RA	Risk assessment	Assessing the risk to organizational operations, assets, and individuals resulting from the operation of information systems, and the processing, storage, or transmission of information
Management	PL	Planning	Developing, documenting, updating, and implementing security plans for systems
Management	SA	System and services acquisition	Allocating resources to protect systems, employing SDLC processes, employing software usage and installation restrictions, and ensuring that third-party providers employ adequate security measures to protect outsourced information, applications, or services
Management	CA	Certification and accreditation and security assessments	Assessing security controls for effectiveness, implementing plans to correct deficiencies and to reduce vulnerabilities, authorizing the operation of information systems and system connections, and monitoring system security controls
Operational	PS	Personnel security	Ensuring that individuals in positions of authority are trustworthy and meet security criteria, ensuring that information and information systems are protected during personnel actions, and employing formal sanctions for personnel failing to comply with security policies and procedures
Operational	PE	Physical and environmental protection	Ensuring that individuals in positions of authority are trustworthy and meet security criteria, ensuring that information and information systems are protected during personnel actions, and employing formal sanctions for personnel failing to comply with security policies and procedures
Operational	CP	Contingency planning	Establishing and implementing plans for emergency response, backup operations, and postdisaster recovery of information systems
Operational	CM	Configuration management	Establishing baseline configurations and inventories of systems, enforcing security configuration settings for products, monitoring and controlling changes to baseline configurations, and to components of systems throughout their SDLC
Operational	MA	Maintenance	Performing periodic and timely maintenance of systems, and providing effective controls on the tools, techniques, mechanisms, and personnel that perform system maintenance

Operational	SI	System and information integrity	Identifying, reporting, and correcting information and system flaws in a timely manner, providing protection from malicious code, and monitoring system security alerts and advisories
Operational	MP	Media protection	Protecting information in printed form or on digital media, limiting access to information to authorized users, and sanitizing or destroying digital media before disposal or reuse
Operational	IR	Incident response	Establishing operational incident handling capabilities for information systems, and tracking, documenting, and reporting incidents to appropriate officials
Operational	AT	Awareness and training	Ensuring that managers and users of information systems are made aware of the security risks associated with their activities and of applicable laws, policies, and procedures related to security, and ensuring that personnel are trained to carry out their assigned information security-related duties
Technical	IA	Identification and authentication	Identifying and authenticating the identities of users, processes, or devices that require access to information systems
Technical	AC	Access control	Limiting information system access to authorized users, processes acting on behalf of authorized users, or devices (including other information systems), and to types of transactions and functions that authorized users are permitted to exercise
Technical	AU	Audit and accountability	Creating, protecting, and retaining information system audit records that are needed for the monitoring, analysis, investigation, and reporting of unlawful, unauthorized, or inappropriate information system activity, and ensuring that the actions of individual users can be traced so that the individual users can be held accountable for their actions
Technical	SC	System and communications protection	Monitoring, controlling, and protecting communications at external and internal boundaries of information systems, and employing architectural designs, software development techniques, and systems engineering principles to promote effective security

aNIST SP 800-53 Revision 4 removes the labels that provide a class distinction between security controls as many security controls have management, operational, and technical aspects.

"The 17 areas represent a broad-based, balanced information security program that addresses the management, operational, and technical aspects of protecting federal information and information systems" [13]. The determination of which requirements from within each area will be included in the initial security control baseline is based on the impact level for the information system following the security categorization process in the NIST RMF (*Step 1*).

The security control selection process includes multiple steps beginning with the selection of the initial security control baseline. Once the baseline has been determined, the next step involves tailoring the initial security control baseline. As illustrated in Fig. 5.9, to ensure the resulting security controls required for the information system achieve cost-effective, risk-based security, and any rationale and tailoring is an integral part of the organization's risk management process.[67] In addition, any changes to the baseline needs to be supported by documentation[68] that addresses decisions[69] made for adjusting the initial security control baseline such as through an assessment of risk within the information system and operating environment.

Tailoring the Initial Baseline

The tailoring process involves the customization of the initial security control baseline.[70] This process uses three[71] primary mechanisms to adjust the baseline to more closely align the security control requirements to the actual information system and/or operating environment:

- *Scoping considerations*—specific considerations on the applicability and implementation of specific security controls;
- *Compensating security controls*—management, operational, and technical controls implemented in lieu of an identified security controls in the initial security control baseline;
- *Organization-defined parameters*—parameters applied to portions of a security control to support specific organization requirements or objectives.

---

[67]The NIST Risk Management Process will be discussed in detail in Chapter 6, Risk Management.

[68]From Joint Task Force Transformation Initiative. NIST Special Publication (SP) 800-53 Revision 4, Security and Privacy Controls for Federal Information System and Organizations. Maryland: National Institute of Standards and Technology; 2013. *"The level of detail required in documenting tailoring decisions in the security control selection process is at the discretion of organizations and reflects the FIPS 199 impact levels of the respective information systems implementing or inheriting the controls."*

[69]Tailoring decisions should be documented in the security plan (or a related document).

[70]From Joint Task Force Transformation Initiative. NIST Special Publication (SP) 800-53 Revision 4, Security and Privacy Controls for Federal Information System and Organizations. Maryland: National Institute of Standards and Technology; 2013. *"Organizations have flexibility in applying the baseline security controls in accordance with the guidance provided in Special Publication 800-53. This allows organizations to tailor the relevant security control baseline so that it more closely aligns with their mission and business requirements and environments of operation."*

[71]The tailing process includes other optional mechanisms to modify appropriately and align the controls more closely with the specific conditions within the organization such as supplementing the baseline with additional security controls and enhancements, and providing additional specification information for control implementation.

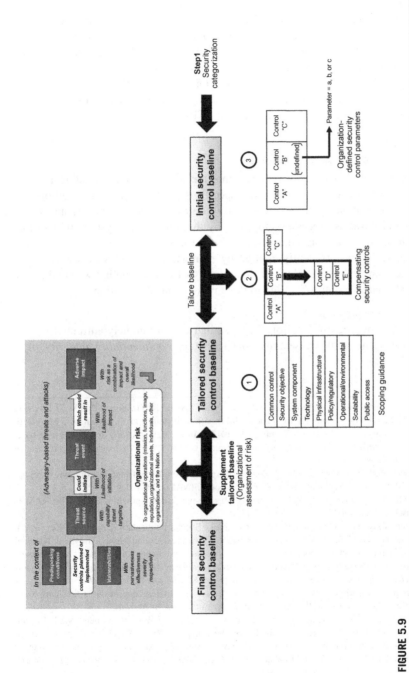

FIGURE 5.9

Security controls selection process.

In addition, the concept of overlays[72] provides a process for tailoring based on an organizational-specific set of security controls that have been identified to supplement the baseline for a community-wide use or to address specialized requirements, technologies, or unique missions/environments of operation [12]. For example, the Federal Risk and Authorization Management Program (FedRAMP) utilizes the security controls for low- and moderate-impact[73] (and high-impact[74]) information systems and contains controls and enhancements above the NIST baseline that addresses the unique elements deemed necessary for the government-wide use of cloud computing [19].

Applying Scoping Considerations

Scoping ensures that security requirements are identified for providing an adequate level of protection by providing specific security terms and conditions for addressing the implementation of security controls based on the organization's mission and business processes supported by the information system. In addition, the application of scoping considerations[75] can ensure that security controls are cost-effectively and efficiently applied by eliminating unnecessary security controls. There are several scoping considerations that can be applied when adjusting the initial security control baseline to the environment of operation:

- Use of common controls;[76]
- Downgrading security controls for those that do not uniquely attribute to high-water mark for the security objectives (i.e., *confidentiality, integrity,* or *availability*);

---

[72]From Joint Task Force Transformation Initiative. NIST Special Publication (SP) 800-53 Revision 4, Security and Privacy Controls for Federal Information System and Organizations. Maryland: National Institute of Standards and Technology; 2013. *"An overlay is a fully specified set of security controls, control enhancements, and supplemental guidance derived from the application of tailoring guidance."*

[73]Low- and Moderate-Impact Security Control Baselines. Available from: https://www.fedramp. gov/files/2015/03/FedRAMP-Rev-4-Baseline-Workbook-FINAL062014.xlsx.

[74]FedRAMP High Baseline. Available from: https://www.fedramp.gov/files/2015/12/FedRAMP_ HHH_Baseline_Final-for-Public-Release-121715.xlsx.

[75]From Joint Task Force Transformation Initiative. NIST Special Publication (SP) 800-53 Revision 4, Security and Privacy Controls for Federal Information System and Organizations. Maryland: National Institute of Standards and Technology; 2013. *"The application of scoping considerations can eliminate unnecessary security controls from the initial security control baselines and help to ensure that organizations select only those controls that are needed to provide the appropriate level of protection for organizational information systems— protection based on the missions and business functions being supported by those systems and the environments in which the systems operate."*

[76]From Joint Task Force Transformation Initiative Interagency Working Group. NIST Special Publication (SP) 800-37 Revision 1, Guide for Applying the Risk Management Framework to Federal Information Systems: A Security Life Cycle Approach. Maryland: National Institute of Standards and Technology; 2010. *"Common controls are security controls that are inherited by one or more organizational information systems."*

- Allocation and placement of security controls applicable to specific information system components;
- Removal of security controls that are technology-dependent;
- Application of security control for those areas that support the physical infrastructure used to provide direct protection;
- Employment of security controls based on the laws, directives, policies, and so on that govern the information types and the information system;
- Employment of security controls that are consistent with the assumption about the operational environment;
- Implementation of security controls based on the scalability associated with the specific impact level; and
- Application of security controls where public access is granted.

Selecting Compensating Security Controls

Compensation is the function of implementing one or more security controls as an alternative to a security control in the initial security control baseline. Although there are many circumstances that could occur where compensation would be required, the most important aspect of using compensation is to have a clear understanding of the risks associated with not implementing the recommended security control. The compensating security control(s) should provide, at minimum, a comparable level of protection and mitigate any risk introduced through the removal of the control from the initial security control baseline.

NOTE

Compensating controls should only be employed if [12]:

- The organization selects the compensating control from NIST Special Publication 800–53, or if an appropriate compensating control is not available, the organization adopts a suitable compensating control from another source;
- The organization provides supporting rationale for how the compensating control delivers an equivalent security capability for the information system and why the related baseline security control could not be employed; and
- The organization assesses and formally accepts the risk associated with employing the compensating control in the information system.

Assigning Security Control Parameter Values

Organization-defined parameters are included in portions of security controls to offer flexibility in the implementation. The parameters enable the security control requirements to be completed with specific values that could come from within the organization or as prescribed by federal laws, executive orders, directives, and policies that govern the type of information or information system, or other sources such as industry "best practices." In situations where the prescribed parameters are more restrictive, they should be applied to the maximum extent possible. In addition, if there are variations to recommended parameters, the differences should be documented to ensure that the organization has some understanding of the risk and can apply the necessary compensating controls to mitigate risks that are determined to be unacceptable.

Supplementing the Tailored Baseline

Once the initial baseline has been tailored (if necessary), the tailored baseline (or initial baseline if no tailoring was performed) should be reviewed to ensure that it provides the adequate protection and any identified organization risk[77] that exists is mitigated. Enhancing security control baselines by selecting additional security controls or supplementing the baseline security controls with enhancements can occur due to specific situations such as advanced persistent threat, cross-domain services, mobility, classified and sensitive information. There may also be situations where security controls cannot be sufficiently applied, requiring alternative strategies by placing restrictions[78] on the use of the information systems and specific information technologies.

Identifying additional security controls can be accomplished through the definition of requirements or conducting a gap analysis. Requirements definition involves an evaluation of the risk assessment to establish requirements through an analysis of threat information or attack potential. Whereas, a gap analysis focuses on characterizing the security requirements through an assessment of the existing security capabilities and determining the types of threats[79] that can likely be prevented. As an example, Fig. 5.10 provides an illustration of the framework in which "effectively withstand cyber attacks from adversaries with the stated capabilities or attack potential, organizations strive to achieve a certain level of defensive capability or cyber preparedness"[80] [12]. However, in either approach,

---

[77]Joint Task Force Transformation Initiative, NIST Special Publication (SP) 800-53 Revision 3, Recommended Security Controls for Federal Information System and Organizations. Maryland: National Institute of Standards and Technology; 2010. *"The risk assessment provides important inputs to determine the sufficiency of the security controls."*

[78]From Joint Task Force Transformation Initiative. NIST Special Publication (SP) 800-53 Revision 4, Security and Privacy Controls for Federal Information System and Organizations. Maryland: National Institute of Standards and Technology; 2013. *"Restrictions include: limiting the information that information systems can process, store, or transmit or the manner in which organizational missions/ business functions are automate; prohibiting external access to organizational information by removing selected information system components from networks (i.e., air gapping); and prohibiting moderate- or high-impact information on organizational information system components to which the public has access, unless an explicit risk determination is made authorizing such access."*

[79]From Joint Task Force Transformation Initiative. NIST Special Publication (SP) 800-53 Revision 4, Security and Privacy Controls for Federal Information System and Organizations. Maryland: National Institute of Standards and Technology; 2013. *"Credible threat information (or make reasonable assumptions) about the activities of adversaries with certain capabilities or attack potential (e.g., skill levels, expertise, available resources)."*

[80]Cyber preparedness, in general, is the process of characterizing the threat source's intent and motivations to ensure a commensurate level of security capabilities exists to defend against an attack. NIST Special Publication (SP) 800-30 Revision 1, Appendix D ("Threat Sources") provides an example of a threat taxonomy that can be used as a starting point for building a tailored list of threat sources.

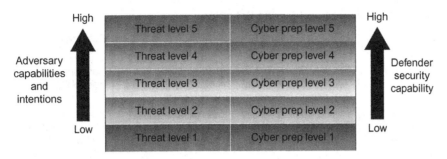

FIGURE 5.10

Cyber preparedness [14].

the goal is to use the information from the analysis to identify security controls and/or enhancements, which will be required to attain the appropriate level of preparedness.

Documenting the Tailoring and Supplementation Process

The rationale for the decisions made throughout the tailoring and supplementation process resulting in an adjustment to the initial security control baseline should be documented. Table 5.6 provides an example of the type of information that should be used when tailoring the security control baseline and for determining if any impacts would occur to a federal agency's mission or business based on the changes in the security control baseline. In addition, the information documented could be used by the authorizing official to make a credible, risk-based decision as part of the authorization step of the NIST RMF (*Step 5*). This information is also important for understanding any risk-based decisions that were made so they can be evaluated if any changes occur during the monitoring step of the NIST RMF (*Step 6*).

Continuous Monitoring Strategy

Continuous monitoring planning[81] starts with the development of a continuous monitoring strategy[82] during the security control selection process. During this

---

[81]From Joint Task Force Transformation Initiative Interagency Working Group. NIST Special Publication (SP) 800-37 Revision 1, Guide for Applying the Risk Management Framework to Federal Information Systems: A Security Life Cycle Approach. Maryland: National Institute of Standards and Technology; 2010. *"The implementation of a robust continuous monitoring program allows an organization to understand the security state of the information system over time and maintain the initial security authorization in a highly dynamic environment of operation with changing threats, vulnerabilities, technologies, and mission/business functions."*

[82]From Joint Task Force Transformation Initiative Interagency Working Group. NIST Special Publication (SP) 800-37 Revision 1, Guide for Applying the Risk Management Framework to Federal Information Systems: A Security Life Cycle Approach. Maryland: National Institute of Standards and Technology; 2010. *"The strategy defines how changes to the information system will be monitored, how security impact analyses will be conducted, and the security status reporting requirements including recipients of the status reports."*

Table 5.6 Documenting Tailoring Rationale

Control	Tailoring Guidance	Rationale
[Control Number and Name]	**Select tailoring guidance** {*Common Control*}, {*Security Objective*}, {*System Component*}, {*Technology*}, {*Physical Infrastructure*}, {*Policy/Regulatory*}, {*Operational/Environmental*}, {*Scalability*}, or {*Public Access*}	[Scoping Consideration]: *rationale*
[Control Number and Name]	**Compensating control**	[Compensating control(s)]: *rationale*
[Control Number and Name]	**Supplemental control**	[Risk]: *rationale*

step, the strategy focuses on defining "how changes to the information system will be monitored and how the security impact analyses will be conducted" [3]. In addition, the strategy includes the identification of any volatile security controls and the frequency at which those security controls should be monitored over time. This also requires establishing the approach for conducting assessments (e.g., automated techniques and tools such as Secure Content Automation Protocol (SCAP),[83] architectures to support dynamic monitoring and reporting such as the Continuous Asset Evaluation, Situational, Awareness, and Risk Scoring (CAESARS)[84] Framework Extension (FE),[85] and manual assessments).

Allocating Security Controls

Defining the information system boundary[86] during the security categorization process requires understanding the scope of protection for the system components

---

[83]Security Content Automation Protocol (SCAP). Available from: http://scap.nist.gov.

[84]From US Department of Homeland Security (DHS), National Cyber Security Division (NCSD), Federal Network Security (FNS) [Internet]. Washington, DC: US Department of Homeland Security [cited December 13, 2011]. Available from: http://www.dhs.gov/files/publications/gc_1285952885143.shtm. "*CAESARS represents a solution for making assessments on a continuous or nearly continuous basis; this is a prerequisite for moving IT security management from isolated assessments, supporting infrequent authorization decisions, to continuous risk management.*"

[85]NIST Interagency Report (IR) 7756 (Draft), *CAESARS Framework Extension: An Enterprise Continuous Monitoring Technical Reference Architecture*. Available from: http://csrc.nist.gov/publications/drafts/nistir-7756/Draft-NISTIR-7756_second-public-draft.pdf.

[86]From Joint Task Force Transformation Initiative Interagency Working Group. NIST Special Publication (SP) 800-37 Revision 1, Guide for Applying the Risk Management Framework to Federal Information Systems: A Security Life Cycle Approach. Maryland: National Institute of Standards and Technology; 2010. "*Well-defined boundaries establish the scope of protection for organizational information systems (i.e., what the organization agrees to protect under its direct management control or within the scope of its responsibilities) and include the people, processes, and information technologies that are part of the systems supporting the organization's missions and business processes.*"

allocated to the information system and interfaces between interconnected systems. This boundary definition activity is critical for fully understanding and clarifying any shared roles and responsibilities for implementing, monitoring, and assessing security controls allocated[87] as part of the security control selection process. However, clarifying roles and responsibilities is not only important as it relates to establishing the ownership of the security controls, but can also help with determining the security-related information that needs to be shared when communicating[88] between security control owners. Although only a conceptual model, Fig. 5.11 does provide a high-level illustration of the potential flow of information when allocating security controls, and when assigning ownership for common capabilities that support more than one information system (i.e., common controls or portions of controls in a hybrid controls situation). In addition, establishing a definition of the authorization boundary and the level of control of the resources can provide a clear delineation of the specific security controls being inherited such as system components that may be used by an organization, but may be outside the direct control of the authorizing official. For security control allocation to be successful, in most cases it requires building trusted relationships based on the sharing of evidence that specific security controls are implemented correctly and operating effectively, including any assessment results (or a summary) and information collected as part of an ongoing continuous monitoring program. The sharing of information ensures changes that could impact the information system inheriting the common controls (or hybrid portions) are understood and any identified risks through the risk management process can be accepted or mitigated through the application of compensating controls.

Decomposition

Decomposition enables complex information systems and security controls to be allocated among more manageable subsystems,[89] thereby enabling subsystems to

---

[87]From Joint Task Force Transformation Initiative Interagency Working Group. NIST Special Publication (SP) 800-37 Revision 1, Guide for Applying the Risk Management Framework to Federal Information Systems: A Security Life Cycle Approach. Maryland: National Institute of Standards and Technology; 2010. *"Allocation is a term used to describe the process an organization employs: (i) to determine whether security controls are defined as system-specific, hybrid, or common; and (ii) to assign security controls to specific information system components responsible for providing a particular security capability (e.g., router, server, remote sensor)."*

[88]From Joint Task Force Transformation Initiative Interagency Working Group. NIST Special Publication (SP) 800-37 Revision 1, Guide for Applying the Risk Management Framework to Federal Information Systems: A Security Life Cycle Approach. Maryland: National Institute of Standards and Technology; 2010. *"Communication regarding the security status of common (inherited) controls is essential irrespective of whether the common control provider is internal or external to the organization."*

[89]From Joint Task Force Transformation Initiative Interagency Working Group. NIST Special Publication (SP) 800-37 Revision 1, Guide for Applying the Risk Management Framework to Federal Information Systems: A Security Life Cycle Approach. Maryland: National Institute of Standards and Technology; 2010. *"A subsystem is a major subdivision of an information system consisting of information, information technology, and personnel that perform one or more specific functions."*

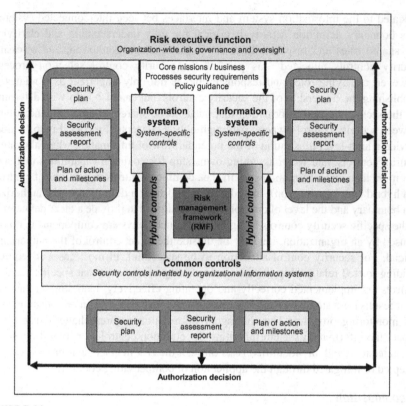

FIGURE 5.11

Security control allocation [3].

be viewed independently[90] and security controls can be allocated, based on security objectives or common capabilities or functions in the information system architecture. This type of approach could also more effectively focus security controls to achieve a more cost-effective application of the risk management processes such as conducting assessments[91] and ongoing continuous monitoring. Subsystems may be

---

[90]From Joint Task Force Transformation Initiative Interagency Working Group. NIST Special Publication (SP) 800-37 Revision 1, Guide for Applying the Risk Management Framework to Federal Information Systems: A Security Life Cycle Approach. Maryland: National Institute of Standards and Technology; 2010. *"Separately categorizing each subsystem does not change the overall categorization of the information system."*

[91]From Joint Task Force Transformation Initiative Interagency Working Group. NIST Special Publication (SP) 800-37 Revision 1, Guide for Applying the Risk Management Framework to Federal Information Systems: A Security Life Cycle Approach. Maryland: National Institute of Standards and Technology; 2010. *"The organization can: (i) issue a single authorization for the entire complex information system (to include bundling assessment results from individual subsystem assessments and any additional assessment results at the system level); or (ii) implement a strategy for managing the risk associated with connecting separately authorized information systems when viewed as a system of systems."*

dynamic, where they may be provisioned or de-provisioned rapidly as required, or may not reside within the information system but only at a specific point in the information system life cycle. In other cases, the subsystems may be controlled and managed by a service provider outside of the authorization boundary or outside of the control of the organization. In these situations, establishing subsystems enables parts of the information system that are more volatile or not within the control of the federal agency or service provider to be monitored differently based on the federal agency's assurance requirements to ensure that required security controls continue to operate at an acceptable level of risk over time.

SECURITY CONTROLS IMPLEMENTATION

In this step of the NIST RMF (*Step 3*), both the tasks included in Table 5.7 will be covered together due to their close relationship (i.e., implementation of the security controls and documentation of their implementation may occur concurrently). To enable the efficient and cost-effective implementation of security controls, some knowledge of the existing and target information security architecture[92] may be required. The information security architecture serves to influence security controls allocated to system components within the information

Table 5.7 NIST RMF Step 3 Activities [3]

Task	Name	Activities	References
3-1	Security control implementation	• Implement the security controls specified in the security plan	• FIPS 200 • NIST SP 800-30 • NIST SP 800-53 • NIST SP 800-53A • CNSS Instruction 1253
3-2	Security control documentation	• Document the security control implementation, as appropriate, in the security plan, providing a functional description of the control implementation (including planned inputs, expected behavior, and expected outputs)	• NIST SP 800-18 • NIST SP 800-53 • CNSS Instruction 1253

---

[92]From Joint Task Force Transformation Initiative, NIST Special Publication (SP) 800-53 Revision 4, Security and Privacy Controls for Federal Information System and Organizations. Maryland: National Institute of Standards and Technology; 2013. *"The information security architecture includes an architectural description, the placement/allocation of security functionality (including security controls), security-related information for external interfaces, information being exchanged across the interfaces, and the protection mechanisms associated with each interface."*

system during the security control selection process. In addition, the allocation of security controls should be based on "best practices" focused on identifying specific system components for providing a security capability. Documenting the security control implementation in the security plan provides a functional description of the security controls (i.e., planned inputs, expected behavior, and expected outputs) both from an organizational perspective (management and operational security controls) and a system perspective (operational and technical security controls). In addition, the security plan documents a description of any inheritance (common security controls), shared ownership (hybrid security controls), and the system-specific security controls allocated to system components within the information system boundary. The level of detail for documenting security controls implementation should commensurate with the impact level assigned to the information system, but should at least provide traceability of decisions prior to and after deployment of the information system and be sufficient to support control assessment [3].

Implementing and Documenting Security Controls

As discussed earlier in the chapter, the integration of security early in the SDLC enables architects and engineers to integrate security controls into the information security architecture[93] by applying overlapping, defense-in-depth protective layers,[94] through the use of security engineering principles,[95] and secure coding methodologies.[96] Additionally, the implementation of risk management activities (e.g., development testing and evaluation[97]) ensures that information security planning is performed in parallel with the information system development to identify any weaknesses and deficiencies that will need to be mitigated, thereby maximizing the reuse of the assessment results in later phases of the SDLC and achieving a more cost-effective balance between the implementation of security controls and the management of risk. In addition, security control allocation, both

---

[93]In a legacy information system, a "*gap analysis*" can be used to understand any limitation in the existing information security architecture where security controls are not functioning properly so that corrective actions can be planned and compensating controls can be identified to provide adequate protection for any unacceptable risks.

[94]For information on defense-in-depth protective layers, see the National Security Agency (NSA), Defense in Depth White Paper. Available from: www.nsa.gov/ia/_files/support/defenseindepth.pdf.

[95]For information on the security engineering principle, see NIST SP 800-27 Rev A. Available from: http://csrc.nist.gov/publications/nistpubs/800-27A/SP800-27-RevA.pdf.

[96]From US Department of Homeland Security, National Cyber Security Division (NCSD), Strategic Initiatives Branch [Internet]. Washington, DC: US Department of Homeland Security [cited December 15, 2011]. Available from: https://buildsecurityin.us-cert.gov/bsi/home.html. "*Build Security In is a collaborative effort that provides practices, tools, guidelines, rules, principles, and other resources that software developers, architects, and security practitioners can use to build security into software in every phase of its development.*"

[97]From Joint Task Force Transformation Initiative Interagency Working Group. NIST Special Publication (SP) 800-37 Revision 1, Guide for Applying the Risk Management Framework to Federal Information Systems: A Security Life Cycle Approach. Maryland: National Institute of Standards and Technology; 2010. "*Developmental testing and evaluation activities include, for example, design and code reviews, application scanning, and regression testing.*"

between the security control owners (e.g., common control providers) and information system components, requires identifying any dependencies from the security control selection process. This activity is essential to ensure that any changes to the planned security controls resulting from the infeasibility or impracticability of their implementation, can be updated in the security plan documentation to capture any risk-based decision-making and accurately describe compensating security controls that will be implemented to minimize the impact associated with unacceptable risks.

> **NOTE**
>
> What is the purpose of the system security plan?
>
> "The purpose of the system security plan is to provide an overview of the security requirements of the system and describe the controls in place or planned for meeting those requirements. The system security plan also delineates responsibilities and expected behavior of all individuals who access the system. The system security plan should be viewed as documentation of the structured process of planning adequate, cost-effective security protection for a system" [3].

SECURITY CONTROLS ASSESSMENT

The security controls implemented and documented in the previous steps are essential components for conducting an effective assessment.[98] The security controls assessment step in the NIST RMF (*Step 4*) involves the preparation, execution, and reporting of the security controls effectiveness in the information system. This section will summarize the assessment-related tasks in Table 5.8. The assessment tasks are dependent on the close collaboration and cooperation of the security assessor[99] and the organization to ensure that there is an appropriate level of depth[100] and coverage[101] applied when evaluating

---

[98]From Joint Task Force Transformation Initiative, NIST Special Publication (SP) 800-53A Revision 1, Guide for Assessing the Security Controls for Federal Information System and Organizations. Maryland: National Institute of Standards and Technology; 2010. *"Partial assessments of security controls can be conducted in the initial phases of system development life cycle to promote early detection of weakness and deficiencies and a more cost-effective approach to risk mitigation."*

[99]From Joint Task Force Transformation Initiative, NIST Special Publication (SP) 800-53 Revision 4, Security and Privacy Controls for Federal Information System and Organizations. Maryland: National Institute of Standards and Technology; 2013. *"The individual, group, or organization responsible for conducting a security control assessment."*

[100]From Joint Task Force Transformation Initiative, NIST Special Publication (SP) 800-53 Revision 4, Security and Privacy Controls for Federal Information System and Organizations. Maryland: National Institute of Standards and Technology; 2013. *"An attribute associated with an assessment method that addresses the rigor and level of detail associated with the application of the method."*

[101]From Joint Task Force Transformation Initiative, NIST Special Publication (SP) 800-53 Revision 4, Security and Privacy Controls for Federal Information System and Organizations. Maryland: National Institute of Standards and Technology; 2013. *"An attribute associated with an assessment method that addresses the scope or breadth of the assessment objects included in the assessment (e.g., types of objects to be assessed and the number of objects to be assessed by type)."*

Table 5.8 NIST RMF Step 4 Activities [3]

Task	Name	Activities	References
4-1	Assessment preparation	• Develop, review, and approve a plan to assess the security controls	• NIST SP 800-53A
4-2	Security control assessment	• Assess the security controls in accordance with the assessment procedures defined in the security assessment plan	• NIST SP 800-53A • NIST SP 800-115
4-3	Security assessment report	• Prepare the security assessment report documenting the issues, findings, and recommendations from the security control assessment	• NIST SP 800-53A
4-4	Remediation actions	• Conduct the initial remediation actions on security controls based on the findings and recommendations of the security assessment report • Reassess remediated control(s), as appropriate	• NIST SP 800-30 • NIST SP 800-53A

the security controls effective against the organization's identified assurance requirements.[102]

Assessment Preparation

Prior to beginning the assessment activities, expectations should be appropriately set through the development of a security assessment plan (SAP). Preparatory activities should be planned together, by the organization undergoing the assessment and the provider conducting the assessment, to limit any unexpected issues and to gain a clear understanding of the level of effort required. Fig. 5.12 provides an example list of preparatory activities that guide the completion of the assessment plan. In addition, the organization should also provide the security assessor with the following types of information:

- Organizational chart (or description of organizational personnel responsible for security policies and procedures);
- Policies and procedures that relate to the information system;
- Organizational chart (or description of organizational personnel responsible for security control implementation); and
- Artifacts, where available, that provide an understanding of security controls such as the security plan, risk assessment, continuous monitoring plan, plan of action and milestones (POA&Ms), accreditation decision letter (if already

---

[102]From Joint Task Force Transformation Initiative Interagency Working Group. NIST Special Publication (SP) 800-37 Revision 1, Guide for Applying the Risk Management Framework to Federal Information Systems: A Security Life Cycle Approach. Maryland: National Institute of Standards and Technology; 2010. *"Assurance requirements address the quality of the design, development, and implementation of the security functions in the information system."*

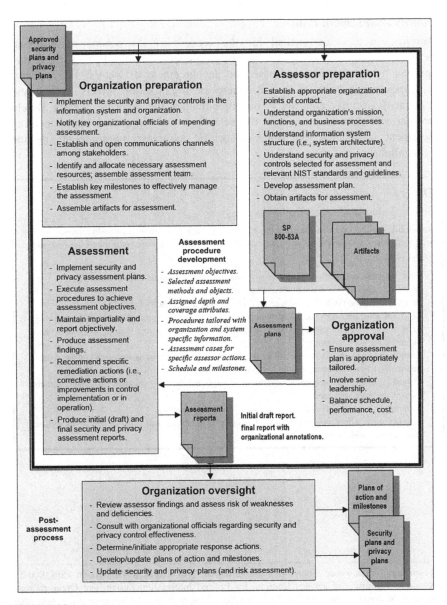

FIGURE 5.12

Security controls assessment process [16].

under an existing accreditation), privacy impact assessment (PIA), contingency plan, configuration management plan, security configuration checklists, and/or interconnection system agreements (ISAs, MOU (*Memorandum of Understanding*), contracts, etc.).

Security Assessment Plan

Planning activities are critical for the success of the security assessment. The SAP,[103] developed by the security assessor, should be reviewed and approved by the organization based on an agreement of what is in scope for the assessment. Similar to *Step 2*, where the organization selects, tailors, and supplements security controls to be implemented, the security assessor should also perform similar activities by selecting, tailoring, and supplementing assessment procedures that address specific assurance requirements by the organization.

TIP

Select, Tailor, Customize, Optimize

As a guide, and to improve the effectiveness in executing assessments, an assessor should seek to find ways to save time and money when conducting assessments through the following steps [16]:

- Select assessment methods[104] and objects that match the assurance requirements.
- Select the appropriate depth and coverage attributes.[105]
- Identify common controls to reduce redundancy and duplication of effort.
- Customize security-specific assessment procedures to closely match the operating environment (and utilizing supplemental guidance in the NIST Security Controls Catalog to establish an intent of the security control).
- Identify assessment results that are applicable for reuse (previous assessments) or through more efficiency in sequencing the current assessment.
- Adjust assessment procedures to accommodate external service providers based on contracts or service-level agreements.
- Develop assessment procedures[106] for custom security controls.
- Identify areas where assessment procedures can be combined and consolidated to maximize cost savings without compromising quality.

---

[103]From Joint Task Force Transformation Initiative, NIST Special Publication (SP) 800-53 Revision 4, Security and Privacy Controls for Federal Information System and Organizations. Maryland: National Institute of Standards and Technology; 2013. *"The security assessment plan and privacy assessment plan provide the objectives for the security and privacy control assessments, respectively, and a detailed roadmap of how to conduct such assessments."*
[104]Examine, interview, and test.
[105]Basic, focused, and comprehensive.
[106]In situations where security controls not included in Security Control Catalog (NIST Special Publication (SP) 800-53, Appendix F) were included in the security control baseline, the assessor may have to develop custom security assessment procedures. In these situations, NIST Special Publication (SP) 800-53A can be used as a guide.

Assessing Security Controls

Conducting security assessments,[107] which will be discussed in more detail in later chapters, is described briefly in this section. The security assessment execution is primarily organized and executed by the security assessor, with the organization's support. Therefore, the key focus will be on making the assurance case.[108]

When conducting the security assessment, the security assessor needs to obtain evidence[109] to facilitate the security assessor in making an objective determination of security control effectiveness, based on the criteria (i.e., expect input, behavior, and outcome) identified in the assessment procedures. Since the key focus will be on making the assurance case, the evidence should come directly from the information system or operating environment, or from a third-party evaluation of the product or technology such as a common criteria evaluation.[110] In addition, automated tools and techniques could be used to improve the quality of the security assessment through an increase in the sampling size and coverage.

Reporting Assessment Results

Reporting on the security control assessment results, including any issues, weaknesses and deficiencies, and recommendations, is performed through the security assessment report (SAR).[111] The SAR works together with the security plan (including risk assessment) and POA&Ms to provide an overall picture of the security state and risk posture for the information system. The specific reporting format for security assessment results is organizationally dependent, but should provide enough detail to enable the authorizing official to establish a credible, risk-based decision. In addition to findings, the SAR also includes key recommendations for addressing the findings.[112] Evidence produced during

---

[107]From Joint Task Force Transformation Initiative Interagency Working Group. NIST Special Publication (SP) 800-37 Revision 1, Guide for Applying the Risk Management Framework to Federal Information Systems: A Security Life Cycle Approach. Maryland: National Institute of Standards and Technology; 2010. *"Security control assessments determine the extent to which the controls are implemented correctly, operating as intended, and producing the desired outcome with respect to meeting the security requirements for the information system."*

[108]From US Department of Homeland Security, National Cyber Security Division (NCSD), Strategic Initiatives Branch [Internet]. Washington, DC: US Department of Homeland Security [cited December 17, 2011]. Available from: https://buildsecurityin.us-cert.gov/articles/knowledge/assurance-cases/arguing-security-creating-security-assurance-cases. *"An assurance case is a body of evidence organized into an argument demonstrating that some claim about a system holds, i.e. is assured."*

[109]Supporting information about the claims of security controls implemented within information system.

[110]For more information on the Common Criteria Evaluation and Validation Scheme (CCEVS), see http://www.niap-ccevs.org/.

[111]The security assessment report is one component of the security authorization package that is used by the authorizing official to make an authorization decision.

[112]Depending on when the security assessment was performed in the SDLC (e.g., development/test), initial reports of findings of a *"delta"* could be resolved during the information system development.

the security assessment should be retained by the organization for reuse in future security assessment-related activities either through manual or automated consumption.[113]

INFORMATION SYSTEM AUTHORIZATION

The next step in the NIST RMF (*Step 5*) concludes with an authorization decision[114] for the information system to operate (or continue to operate, for legacy systems). This section will present the tasks outlined in Table 5.9, with primary emphasis being placed on planning corrective actions and the authorization process.

Table 5.9 NIST RMF Step 5 Activities [3]

Task	Name	Activities	References
5-1	Plan of action and milestones	• Prepare the plan of action and milestones based on the findings and recommendations of the security assessment report excluding any remediation action taken	• OMB M-02-01 • NIST SP 800-30 • NIST SP 800-53A
5-2	Security authorization package	• Assemble the security authorization package • Submit the package to the authorizing official for adjudication	
5-3	Risk determination	• Determine the risk to organizational operations (including mission, functions, image, or reputation), organizational assets, individuals, other organizations, or the Nation	• NIST SP 800-30 • NIST SP 800-39
5-4	Risk acceptance	• Determine if the risk to organizational operation, organizational assets, individuals, other organizations, or the Nation is acceptable	• NIST SP 800-53A

[113]From Cloud Security Alliance (CSA), CloudAudit Working Group [Internet]. Washington, DC: Cloud Security Alliance [cited December 19, 2011]. Available from: https://cloudsecurityalliance. org/wp-content/uploads/2011/12/GRC-Stack-CSA-Congress-2011-part-1.pptx. *Automated emerging specifications such as CloudAudit can be used to provide "a structure for organizing assertions and supporting documentation for specific controls across different compliance frameworks in a way that simplifies discovery by humans and tools."*

[114]From Joint Task Force Transformation Initiative Interagency Working Group. NIST Special Publication (SP) 800-37 Revision 1, Guide for Applying the Risk Management Framework to Federal Information Systems: A Security Life Cycle Approach. Maryland: National Institute of Standards and Technology; 2010. *"The security authorization decision indicates to the information system owner whether the system is: (i) authorized to operate; or (ii) not authorized to operate."*

Corrective Action Planning

The POA&Ms[115] receive input from the SAR[116], and is one of three key documents presented in the authorization package to the authorizing official. The POA&Ms include a set of tasks focused on correcting weaknesses or deficiencies discovered during the security controls assessment,[117] or security testing (e.g., periodic vulnerability scanning, penetration testing, etc.). In addition, POA&Ms document corrective actions for security weaknesses and deficiencies found during other types of reviews done by, for, or on behalf of the federal agency, including Government Accountability Office (GAO) audits, financial system audits, and critical infrastructure vulnerability assessments [17].

Developing a Risk Mitigation Strategy

A strategy for risk mitigation[118] planning is important when prioritizing corrective actions as part of an organization-wide risk management function. The prioritization[119] should take input from other activities within the NIST RMF, such as security categorization. In addition, other inputs can also influence the risk mitigation strategy, such as the security controls (i.e., where the security weaknesses or deficiencies exist), impacts of the weaknesses and deficiencies on the overall security state of the information system, and the risk mitigation approach used by the organization to address weaknesses and deficiencies [3].

---

[115]From Daniels, M. Office of Management and Budget (OMB) Memorandum 02-01, Guidance for Preparing and Submitting Security Plans of Action and Milestones. Washington, DC: Executive Office of the President, Office of Management and Budget; 2001. *"A plan of action and milestones (POA&M) is a tool that identifies tasks that need to be accomplished. It details resources required to accomplish the elements of the plan, any milestones in meeting the task, and scheduled completion dates for the milestones."*

[116]From Joint Task Force Transformation Initiative Interagency Working Group. NIST Special Publication (SP) 800-37 Revision 1, Guide for applying the risk management framework to federal information systems: A security life cycle approach. Maryland: National Institute of Standards and Technology; 2010. *"The security assessment report provides visibility into specific weaknesses and deficiencies in the security controls employed within or inherited by the information system that could not reasonably be resolved during system development."*

[117]From Joint Task Force Transformation Initiative Interagency Working Group. NIST Special Publication (SP) 800-37 Revision 1, Guide for Applying the Risk Management Framework to Federal Information Systems: A Security Life Cycle Approach. Maryland: National Institute of Standards and Technology; 2010. *"All security weaknesses and deficiencies identified during the security control assessment are documented in the security assessment report to maintain an effective audit trail."*

[118]From Joint Task Force Transformation Initiative Interagency Working Group. NIST Special Publication (SP) 800-39, Managing Information Security Risk: Organization, Mission, and Information System View. Maryland: National Institute of Standards and Technology; 2011. *"Prioritizing, evaluating, and implementing the appropriate risk-reducing controls/countermeasures recommended from the risk management process."*

[119]From Joint Task Force Transformation Initiative Interagency Working Group. NIST Special Publication (SP) 800-37 Revision 1, Guide for Applying the Risk Management Framework to Federal Information Systems: A Security Life Cycle Approach. Maryland: National Institute of Standards and Technology; 2010. *"A risk assessment guides the prioritization process for items included in the plan of action and milestones."*

Documenting POA&Ms

The authorizing official uses POA&Ms as an oversight management tool for tracking corrective actions for a specific information system. In addition, the organization can also use consolidated POA&Ms from across all of the information system to identify common weaknesses and deficiencies to effectively allocate resources for organization-wide security improvements. Therefore, POA&Ms should provide enough details[120] to enable the organization to identify, assess, prioritize, and monitor the correction of weaknesses and deficiencies both in federal and contractor systems.[121] POA&M details[122] should include:

- Brief description of the weakness.[123]
- Identity of the organization held responsible for resolving the weakness.
- Estimated funding resources required to resolve the weakness.
- Scheduled completion date for resolving the weakness.
- Key milestones[124] with completion dates.
- Milestone changes.
- The source of the weakness.
- Status.[125]

---

[120]From Daniels, M. Office of Management and Budget (OMB) Memorandum 02-01, Guidance for Preparing and Submitting Security Plans of Action and Milestones. Washington, DC: Executive Office of the President, Office of Management and Budget; 2001. *OMB has developed POA&M guidance that provides specific instructions and examples for the POA&Ms.*

[121]From Bolten, J. Office of Management and Budget (OMB) Memorandum 04-25, FY 2004 Reporting Instructions for the Federal Information Security Management Act. Washington, DC: Executive Office of the President, Office of Management and Budget; 2004. *The agency is responsible for ensuring that the contractor corrects weaknesses discovered through self-assessments and independent assessments. Any weaknesses are to be reflected in the agency's POA&M.*

[122]From Bolten, J. Office of Management and Budget (OMB) Memorandum 04-25, FY 2004 Reporting Instructions for the Federal Information Security Management Act. Washington, DC: Executive Office of the President, Office of Management and Budget; 2004. *The exact format prescribed in the POA&M examples in M-04-25 are no longer required, but, all of the associated data elements must be included in the POA&Ms.*

[123]From Daniels, M. Office of Management and Budget (OMB) Memorandum 02-01, Guidance for Preparing and Submitting Security Plans of Action and Milestones. Washington, DC: Executive Office of the President, Office of Management and Budget; 2001. *"Description of the weaknesses. Sensitive descriptions of specific weaknesses are not necessary, but sufficient data must be provided to permit oversight and tracking. Where it is necessary to provide more sensitive data, the POA&M should note the fact of its special sensitivity."*

[124]From Daniels, M. Office of Management and Budget (OMB) Memorandum 02-01, Guidance for Preparing and Submitting Security Plans of Action and Milestones. Washington, DC: Executive Office of the President, Office of Management and Budget; 2001. *A milestone will identify specific requirements to correct an identified weakness.*

[125]From Daniels, M. Office of Management and Budget (OMB) Memorandum 02-01, Guidance for Preparing and Submitting Security Plans of Action and Milestones. Washington, DC: Executive Office of the President, Office of Management and Budget; 2001. *Ongoing or completed. "Completed" should be used only when a weakness has been fully resolved and the corrective action has been tested. Include the date of completion.*

Security Authorization Approaches

The security authorization process is based on three different approaches.[126] The first, and most commonly used, is the traditional approach, which involves only *one* authorizing official. In this approach, a single authorizing official has both the responsibility and accountability for accepting security risks. Next is the joint authorization[127] approach, which includes a shared interest, usually between multiple authorizing officials because the information system ties directly into the strategic mission or business processes. In this approach, the authorizing officials are collectively responsible and accountable for accepting the security risks.

The final approach is used when the mission or business processes are supported by more than one federal agency. This approach is known as the leveraged authorization approach and can be used to authorize an information system, commonly a shared service,[128] that can be used by more than one agency based on the original authorization package without requiring reauthorization by the leveraging organization.

Owing to the complexity in implementing the leveraged authorization approach, it is the one used least often of the three, but offers the most cost savings.[129] The leveraging organization, usually through an assigned authorizing official, leverages the original authorization[130] by accepting the risks, and

---

[126]From Joint Task Force Transformation Initiative Interagency Working Group. NIST Special Publication (SP) 800-37 Revision 1, Guide for Applying the Risk Management Framework to Federal Information Systems: A Security Life Cycle Approach. Maryland: National Institute of Standards and Technology; 2010. *"Organizations can choose from three different approaches when planning for and conducting security authorizations to include: (i) an authorization with a single authorizing official; (ii) an authorization with multiple authorizing officials; or (iii) leveraging an existing authorization."*

[127]From Joint Task Force Transformation Initiative Interagency Working Group. NIST Special Publication (SP) 800-37 Revision 1, Guide for Applying the Risk Management Framework to Federal Information Systems: A Security Life Cycle Approach. Maryland: National Institute of Standards and Technology; 2010. *"Collaborating on the security categorization, selection of security controls, plan for assessing the controls to determine effectiveness, plan of action and milestones, and continuous monitoring strategy, is necessary for a successful joint authorization."*

[128]From Office of Management and Budget (OMB). Federal Information Technology Shared Services Strategy. Washington, DC: Executive Office of the President, Office of Management and Budget; 2012. *"A function that is provided for consumption by multiple organizations within or between Federal Agencies."*

[129]From Joint Task Force Transformation Initiative Interagency Working Group. NIST Special Publication (SP) 800-37 Revision 1, Guide for Applying the Risk Management Framework to Federal Information Systems: A Security Life Cycle Approach. Maryland: National Institute of Standards and Technology; 2010. *"The leveraged authorization approach provides opportunities for significant cost savings and avoids a potentially costly and time-consuming authorization process by the leveraging organization."*

[130]From Joint Task Force Transformation Initiative Interagency Working Group. NIST Special Publication (SP) 800-37 Revision 1, Guide for Applying the Risk Management Framework to Federal Information Systems: A Security Life Cycle Approach. Maryland: National Institute of Standards and Technology; 2010. *"When reviewing the authorization package, the leveraging organization considers risk factors such as the time elapsed since the authorization results were produced, the environment of operation (if different from the environment of operation reflected in the authorization package), the criticality/sensitivity of the information to be processed, stored, or transmitted, as well as the overall risk tolerance of the leveraging organization."*

assesses only those additional requirements beyond the original security control baseline established by the original.[131] For example, if the leveraging organization determines that there is insufficient information in the authorization package or inadequate security measures in place for establishing an acceptable level of risk, the leveraging organization may negotiate for additional security measures[132] and/or security-related information [3].

Another option that may be used by an organization when multiple instances of the same information system (or subsystem) are deployed in a number of different operational environments is the application of a type authorization [3]. In a type authorization a single authorizing package is used to reflect a common view for all of the instances deployed across all locations where the information system is hosted (also known as site-specific controls[133]).

Security Authorization Process

The security authorization process is the most involved step in the NIST RMF (*Step 5*) because it requires the direct or indirect input from each of the previous steps in the NIST RMF (*categorization, security control selection, security control implementation*, and *security control assessment*) to make the authorization decision. This process begins with the assembly of the authorization package, where the key and supporting documents needed to make the authorization decision are prepared. After the security authorization package has been assembled, the determination of risk involves an analysis of information gathered from across the organization to provide the authorizing official with enough credible information to support a risk-based decision.

The authorization package includes both key and supporting documents.[134] Fig. 5.13 illustrates the three key minimum documents that are required by the

---

[131]From Joint Task Force Transformation Initiative Interagency Working Group. NIST Special Publication (SP) 800-37 Revision 1, Guide for Applying the Risk Management Framework to Federal Information Systems: A Security Life Cycle Approach. Maryland: National Institute of Standards and Technology; 2010. *"The term owning organization refers to the federal agency or subordinate organization that owns the authorization package."*

[132]From Joint Task Force Transformation Initiative Interagency Working Group. NIST Special Publication (SP) 800-37 Revision 1, Guide for Applying the Risk Management Framework to Federal Information Systems: A Security Life Cycle Approach. Maryland: National Institute of Standards and Technology; 2010. *"Additional security measures may include, for example, increasing the number of security controls, conducting additional assessments, implementing compensating controls, or establishing constraints on the use of the information system or services provided by the system."*

[133]From Joint Task Force Transformation Initiative Interagency Working Group. NIST Special Publication (SP) 800-37 Revision 1, Guide for Applying the Risk Management Framework to Federal Information Systems: A Security Life Cycle Approach. Maryland: National Institute of Standards and Technology; 2010. *"Site-specific controls are typically implemented by an organization as common controls."*

[134]From Joint Task Force Transformation Initiative Interagency Working Group. NIST Special Publication (SP) 800-37 Revision 1, Guide for Applying the Risk Management Framework to Federal Information Systems: A Security Life Cycle Approach. Maryland: National Institute of Standards and Technology; 2010. *"The authorizing official determines what additional supporting documentation or references may be required to be included in the authorization package."*

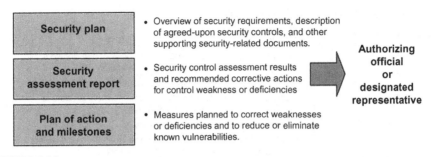

FIGURE 5.13

Security authorization package [3].

authorizing official: *security plan*, *SAR*, and *POA&Ms*. These three documents are considered the most accurate representation of the security state of the information system and are based on the information derived from activities performed throughout the execution of the NIST RMF.

For security controls inherited in whole or in part by another organization (common control provider) or an external service provider, security risk-related information[135] may be shared with the authorizing official to supplement the authorization package and assist in making an authorization decision. For all of the key documents included in the authorization package, the owner of the information system or provider of common controls generally has the responsibility of the packaging and submitting the security authorization package.

Risk determination is a critical activity in the authorization process that involves reviewing the documents in the security authorization package. During this activity, the authorizing official will likely place significant importance on the security assessment report [3], but will also use information gathered through other risk management activities to understand the organization's overall risk exposure[136] from operating the information system. In addition, the authorizing official will likely rely upon additional input from the other parts of the

---

[135]From Joint Task Force Transformation Initiative Interagency Working Group. NIST Special Publication (SP) 800-37 Revision 1, Guide for Applying the Risk Management Framework to Federal Information Systems: A Security Life Cycle Approach. Maryland: National Institute of Standards and Technology; 2010. *"Risk-related information includes the criticality of organizational missions and/or business functions supported by the information system and the risk management strategy for the organization."*

[136]From Joint Task Force Transformation Initiative Interagency Working Group. NIST Special Publication (SP) 800-37 Revision 1, Guide for Applying the Risk Management Framework to Federal Information Systems: A Security Life Cycle Approach. Maryland: National Institute of Standards and Technology; 2010. *"Risk exposure is the degree to which an organization is threatened by the potential adverse effects on organizational operations and assets, individuals, other organizations, or the Nation."*

Table 5.10 Authorization Decisions [3]

Decision	Specification
Authorization to operate	• Acceptance[a] of risk to organizational operations and assets, individuals, other organizations, and the Nation
	• Issued for an information system or common controls inherited
	• Authorized for a specified period of time (termination date is established as a condition of authorization)
	• Includes terms and conditions (*optional*)
Denial of authorization to operate	• Nonacceptance of risk to organizational operations and assets, individuals, other organizations, and the Nation
	• Immediate steps cannot be taken to reduce the risk to an acceptable level (*major weaknesses or deficiencies in security controls*)
	• Issued for an information system or common controls inherited
	• All activities halted for operational information systems
	• Inheritance not approved for common control providers within the organization
	• Revise the plan of action and milestones to ensure that appropriate measures are taken to correct the identified weaknesses or deficiencies
Authorization rescission	• Special case of a denial of authorization to operate
	• Specific violation of:
	• Federal/organizational security policies, directives, regulations, standards, guidance, or practices
	• The terms and conditions of the original authorization

[a]From Joint Task Force Transformation Initiative Interagency Working Group. NIST Special Publication (SP) 800-37 Revision 1, Guide for Applying the Risk Management Framework to Federal Information Systems: A Security Life Cycle Approach. Maryland: National Institute of Standards and Technology; 2010. "*The explicit acceptance of risk is the responsibility of the authorizing official and cannot be delegated to other officials within the organization.*"

organization such as the organization's risk executive[137] and other organizational assessments of risk to assist in making the final determination, in addition to the documents in the security authorization package. "The information system-related security risk information derived from the execution of the NIST RMF is available to the risk executive (function) for use in formulating and updating the organization-wide risk management strategy" [3].

The risk determination concludes in a final determination of an authorization decision as defined in Table 5.10. The authorization decision is achieved through a balance of the security considerations identified through the execution of the

---

[137]From Joint Task Force Transformation Initiative Interagency Working Group. NIST Special Publication (SP) 800-39, Managing Information Security Risk: Organization, Mission, and Information System View. Maryland: National Institute of Standards and Technology; 2011. "*An individual or group within an organization that helps to ensure that: (i) security risk-related considerations for individual information systems, to include the authorization decisions for those systems, are viewed from an organization-wide perspective with regard to the overall strategic goals and objectives of the organization in carrying out its missions and business functions and (ii) managing risk from individual information systems is consistent across the organization, reflects organizational risk tolerance, and is considered along with other organizational risks affecting mission/business success.*"

NIST RMF, with mission and operational needs for the information system [3]. The security considerations are based on the contents of the authorization package, input from the risk executive, and any other supporting information as determined by the authorizing official.

After the final authorization decision has been made, the decision is communicated to the system owner or common controls provider. The authorization decision document includes not only the authorization decision, but may also include any applicable terms and conditions[138] and a termination date. As an alternative, instead of establishing a termination date (time-drive reauthorizations[139]), the organization could also require the implementation of a continuous monitoring program (event-driven reauthorization[140]) that provides the capability to continuously make risk determinations and acceptance. For example, "if the maximum authorization period for an information system is three years, then an organization establishes a continuous monitoring strategy for assessing a subset of the security controls employed within and inherited by the system during the authorization period. This strategy allows all security controls designated in the respective security plans to be assessed at least one time by the end of the three-year period" [3].

NOTE

As discussed in OMB Memorandum 11–33, *FY 2011 Reporting Instructions for the Federal Information Security Management Act and Agency Privacy Management*, OMB waived the requirements for a reauthorization every three years.

20. Is a security reauthorization still required every three years or when an information system has undergone significant change as stated in OMB Circular A 130?[141]

(Continued)

---

[138]From Joint Task Force Transformation Initiative Interagency Working Group. NIST Special Publication (SP) 800-37 Revision 1, Guide for Applying the Risk Management Framework to Federal Information Systems: A Security Life Cycle Approach. Maryland: National Institute of Standards and Technology; 2010. *"The terms and conditions for the authorization provide a description of any limitations or restrictions placed on the operation of the information system or the implementation of common controls that must be followed by the system owner or common control provider."*

[139]From Joint Task Force Transformation Initiative Interagency Working Group. NIST Special Publication (SP) 800-37 Revision 1, Guide for Applying the Risk Management Framework to Federal Information Systems: A Security Life Cycle Approach. Maryland: National Institute of Standards and Technology; 2010. *"Time-driven reauthorizations occur when the authorization termination date is reached."*

[140]From Joint Task Force Transformation Initiative Interagency Working Group. NIST Special Publication (SP) 800-37 Revision 1, Guide for Applying the Risk Management Framework to Federal Information Systems: A Security Life Cycle Approach. Maryland: National Institute of Standards and Technology; 2010. *"Event-driven reauthorizations can occur when there is a significant change to an information system or its environment of operation."*

[141]See Office of Management and Budget (OMB) Circular A-130, https://www.whitehouse.gov/sites/default/files/omb/assets/OMB/circulars/a130/a130revised.pdf. In accordance with FISMA, Office of Management and Budget (OMB) Circular A-130 was updated on July 28, 2016 to modernize the policy to provide more timely and relevant guidance to agencies and ensure that the federal IT ecosystem operates more securely and more efficiently.

> **NOTE (CONTINUED)**
>
> *No. Rather than enforcing a static, three-year reauthorization process, agencies are expected to conduct ongoing authorizations of information systems through the implementation of continuous monitoring programs. Continuous monitoring programs thus fulfill the three-year security reauthorization requirement, so a separate reauthorization process is not necessary. In an effort to implement a more dynamic, risk-based security authorization process, agencies should follow the guidance in NIST Special Publication 800-37, Revision 1. Agencies should develop and implement continuous monitoring strategies for all information systems. Agency officials should monitor the security state of their information systems on an ongoing basis with a frequency sufficient to make ongoing risk-based decisions on whether to continue to operate the systems within their organizations. Continuous monitoring programs and strategies should address: (i) the effectiveness of deployed security controls; (ii) changes to information systems and the environments in which those systems operate; and (iii) compliance to federal legislation, directives, policies, standards, and guidance with regard to information security and risk management. Agencies will be required to report the security state of their information systems and results of their ongoing authorizations through CyberScope in accordance with the data feeds defined by DHS.*
>
> Organizational information systems may move from a static, point-in-time authorization process to a dynamic, near real-time ongoing authorization process when the following conditions are satisfied [20]:
>
> - *Condition 1*—In accordance with the RMF, the information system has been granted an initial authorization to operate by the AO as a result of a complete, zero-base review of the system and has entered the operations/maintenance phase of the system development life cycle.
> - *Condition 2*—An organizational ISCM program is in place that monitors all implemented security controls with the appropriate degree of rigor and at the appropriate frequencies specified by the organization in accordance with the ISCM strategy and NIST guidance.

For an ongoing authorization[142] to be successful,[143] the continuous monitoring program needs to integrate information security and risk management into the organization's SDLC. The continuous monitoring NIST RMF (*Step 6*) is aligned with the NIST SDLC operations and maintenance (O&M) phase. The application of configuration management and control policies and procedures identifies changes to the information system, and any automated tools and techniques employed ensures that security controls are continuously assessed for

---

[142]In June 2014, NIST published guidance on ongoing authorization to supplement NIST SP 800-37 Revision 1 support the transition of information security program to near real-time risk management in "*Supplemental Guidance on Ongoing Authorization: Transitioning to Near Real-Time Risk Management.*" Available from: http://csrc.nist.gov/publications/nistpubs/800-37-rev1/nist_oa_guidance.pdf.

[143]From Joint Task Force Transformation Initiative Interagency Working Group. NIST Special Publication (SP) 800-37 Revision 1, Guide for Applying the Risk Management Framework to Federal Information Systems: A Security Life Cycle Approach. Maryland: National Institute of Standards and Technology; 2010. "*The authorizing official maintains sufficient knowledge of the current security state of the information system (including the effectiveness of the security controls employed within and inherited by the system) to determine whether continued operation is acceptable based on ongoing risk determinations, and if not, which step or steps in the Risk Management Framework needs to be re-executed in order to adequately mitigate the additional risk.*"

effectiveness. In addition, the use of automation also supports the concept of "near real-time" ongoing authorizations.[144]

If a management-driven continuous monitoring strategy is applied during the continuous monitoring step, the authorization decision can be streamlined. For example, if reauthorization actions result in either a time-driven (*termination date*) or event-driven (*significant change*[145]) trigger, and information produced as a result of the ongoing assessment activities continued to demonstrate the effectiveness of the security controls, the only action required for reauthorization might include making updates to the original authorization package and resubmission to the authorizing official for risk acceptance.

SECURITY CONTROLS MONITORING

The final step in NIST RMF (*Step 6*) focuses on those activities that support the ongoing authorization of the information system. Through the integration of risk management in an organization-wide ISCM program, the security state can be monitored on an ongoing basis. The discussion on development and maintenance of an ISCM program and on specific types of tools, techniques, and technologies will be presented in more detail in later chapters. Therefore, this section limits the discussion to cover only those activities included in Table 5.11 as they relate to the continuous assessment of security controls and updates to risk management documents to support the ongoing risk determination, mitigation, and acceptance.

Managing information risk on an ongoing basis requires a rigorous organizational continuous monitoring[146] strategy and program designed to maintain a security authorization over an extended period of time. Continuous monitoring is a concept in which the security impacts to changes in the information system and the

---

[144]From Joint Task Force Transformation Initiative Interagency Working Group. NIST Special Publication (SP) 800-37 Revision 1, Guide for Applying the Risk Management Framework to Federal Information Systems: A Security Life Cycle Approach. Maryland: National Institute of Standards and Technology; 2010. *"Formal reauthorization actions are avoided in situations where the continuous monitoring process provides authorizing officials the necessary information to manage the potential risk arising from changes to the information system or its environment of operation."*

[145]From Joint Task Force Transformation Initiative Interagency Working Group. NIST Special Publication (SP) 800-37 Revision 1, Guide for Applying the Risk Management Framework to Federal Information Systems: A Security Life Cycle Approach. Maryland: National Institute of Standards and Technology; 2010. *"A significant change is defined as a change that is likely to affect the security state of an information system."*

[146]From Joint Task Force Transformation Initiative Interagency Working Group. NIST Special Publication (SP) 800-37 Revision 1, Guide for Applying the Risk Management Framework to Federal Information Systems: A Security Life Cycle Approach. Maryland: National Institute of Standards and Technology; 2010. *"The monitoring program allows an organization to: (i) track the security state of an information system on a continuous basis and (ii) maintain the security authorization for the system over time in highly dynamic environments of operation with changing threats, vulnerabilities, technologies, and missions/business processes."*

Table 5.11 NIST RMF Step 6 Activities [3]

Task	Name	Activities	References
6-1	Information system and environment changes	• Determine the security impact of proposed or actual changes to the information system and its environment of operation	• NIST SP 800-30 • NIST SP 800-53A • NIST SP 800-128
6-2	Ongoing security control assessments	• Assess a selected subset of the technical, management, and operational security controls employed within and inherited by the information system in accordance with the organization-defined monitoring strategy	• NIST SP 800-53A • NIST SP 800-137
6-3	Ongoing remediation actions	• Conduct remediation actions based on the results of ongoing monitoring activities, assessment of risk, and outstanding items in the plan of action and milestones	• NIST SP 800-30 • NIST SP 800-53 • NIST SP 800-53A • CNSS Instruction 1253
6-4	Key updates	• Update the security plan, security assessment report, and plan of action and milestones based on the results of the continuous monitoring process	• NIST SP 800-118 • NIST SP 800-53 • NIST SP 800-53A • NIST SP 800-137
6-5	Security status reporting	• Report the security status of the information system (including the effectiveness of security controls employed within and inherited by the system) to the authorizing official and other appropriate organizational officials on an ongoing basis in accordance with the monitoring strategy	• NIST SP 800-53A • NIST SP 800-137
6-6	Ongoing risk determination and acceptance	• Review the reported security status of the information system (including the effectiveness of security controls employed within and inherited by the system) on an ongoing basis in accordance with the monitoring strategy to determine whether the risk to organizational operation, organizational assets, individuals, other organizations, or the Nation remains acceptable	• NIST SP 800-30 • NIST SP 800-39
6-7	Information system removal and decommissioning	• Implement an information system decommissioning strategy, when needed, which executes required actions when a system is removed from service	• NIST SP 800-30 • NIST SP 800-53A • NIST 800-64

operating environment are managed and controlled. In addition to conducting security impact analyses, the organization can also use automated tools to provide security status-related information to organizational officials in "near real-time" in order to assist the authorizing official in making cost-effective, risk-based decisions regarding the use and operation of the information system. Through a disciplined approach to continuous monitoring, the organization can more efficiently determine the affects on changes to the security state of the information system and the necessary corrective actions and/or risk mitigations that need to be put in place.

TIP

An effective organization-wide continuous monitoring program [3] includes:

- Configuration management and control processes.
- Security impact analyses on proposed or actual changes.
- Assessment of selected security controls.
- Security status reporting.
- Active involvement by authorizing officials.

Determining Security Impact

Over time, information systems can be susceptible to changes. The application of configuration management and control processes[147] requires documenting[148] and assessing the impact[149] on changes (*proposed* or *actual*). The assessment of the impact to the security state of the information throughout the SDLC is an important part of maintaining an ongoing security authorization. However, not all

---

[147]From Joint Task Force Transformation Initiative Interagency Working Group. NIST Special Publication (SP) 800-37 Revision 1, Guide for Applying the Risk Management Framework to Federal Information Systems: A Security Life Cycle Approach. Maryland: National Institute of Standards and Technology; 2010. *"A disciplined and structured approach to managing, controlling, and documenting changes to an information system or its environment of operation is an essential element of an effective security control monitoring program."*

[148]From Joint Task Force Transformation Initiative Interagency Working Group. NIST Special Publication (SP) 800-37 Revision 1, Guide for Applying the Risk Management Framework to Federal Information Systems: A Security Life Cycle Approach. Maryland: National Institute of Standards and Technology; 2010. *"It is important to record any relevant information about specific changes to hardware, software, or firmware such as version or release numbers, descriptions of new or modified features/capabilities, and security implementation guidance, or any changes to the environment of operation for the information system (e.g., modifications to hosting networks and facilities, mission/business use of the system, threats), or changes to the organizational risk management strategy."*

[149]Johnson, A., Dempsey, K., Ross, R., Gupta, S., Bailey, D. NIST Special Publication (SP) 800-128, Guide for Security-Focused Configuration Management of Information System. Maryland: National Institute of Standards and Technology; 2011. *"Security impact analysis is the analysis conducted by qualified staff within an organization to determine the extent to which changes to the information system affect the security posture of the system."*

changes (e.g., routine changes or scheduled maintenance) will impact the security state of the information system or the environment. Through a consistent application of configuration management and controls processes similar to Fig. 5.14, all changes going through the continuous monitoring process will be required to undergo an assessment of risk to support an ongoing authorization based on an understanding of the impacts to those changes.

Ongoing Security Controls Assessments

The monitoring strategy is developed during the security control selection step of the NIST RMF (*Step 2*). The strategy is focused on establishing criteria[150] for selecting which security controls employed within or inherited by the information system should be monitored as part of the continuous monitoring program. The determination of which security controls to assess and the frequency of monitoring requires obtaining input from a variety of sources [3] to include:

- Risk assessments (including current threat and vulnerability information),
- History of cyber attacks,
- Results of previous security assessments, and
- Operational requirements.

In addition, factors such as security control volatility[151] and POA&Ms[152] can also be useful. For example, "security controls that are subject to the direct effects or side effects of frequent changes in hardware, software, and/or firmware components of an information system would, therefore, likely be controls with higher volatility" [3].

The continuous assessments of security controls identified for ongoing monitoring could produce weaknesses or deficiencies in addition to those discovered during the initial security authorization process. These corrective actions (and

---

[150]From Joint Task Force Transformation Initiative Interagency Working Group. NIST Special Publication (SP) 800-37 Revision 1, Guide for Applying the Risk Management Framework to Federal Information Systems: A Security Life Cycle Approach. Maryland: National Institute of Standards and Technology; 2010. *"The selection criteria reflect the priorities and importance of the information system to organizational operations and assets, individuals, other organizations, and the Nation."*

[151]From Joint Task Force Transformation Initiative Interagency Working Group. NIST Special Publication (SP) 800-37 Revision 1, Guide for Applying the Risk Management Framework to Federal Information Systems: A Security Life Cycle Approach. Maryland: National Institute of Standards and Technology; 2010. *"Security control volatility is a measure of how frequently a control is likely to change over time subsequent to its implementation."*

[152]From Joint Task Force Transformation Initiative Interagency Working Group. NIST Special Publication (SP) 800-37 Revision 1, Guide for Applying the Risk Management Framework to Federal Information Systems: A Security Life Cycle Approach. Maryland: National Institute of Standards and Technology; 2010. *"Security controls identified in the plan of action and milestones are also a priority in the continuous monitoring process, due to the fact that these controls have been deemed to be ineffective to some degree."*

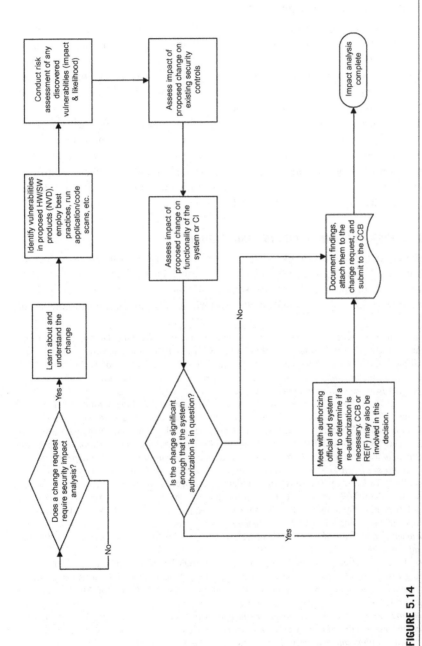

FIGURE 5.14

Configuration management and control flow—security impact analyses [15].

recommendations) will follow a similar strategy for risk mitigation[153] planning discussed in the NIST RMF (*Step 5*), including updates in the POA&Ms.[154]

Key Updates and Status Reporting

During continuous monitoring, results of security control assessments modifications to security control implementations, or changes to the information system may require updates to key documents in the authorization package.[155] Fig. 5.12 provides recommendations on when potential updates may be required for each document to support the ongoing authorization of the information system or to facilitate near real-time risk management.

On an ongoing basis, results of the continuous monitoring activities are reported to the authorizing official by the system owner (or common controls provider). The frequency of updates through security status reports may be based on the monitoring strategy, and could occur more frequently when significant changes occur to the information system or significant deficiencies[156] (or material weaknesses) are identified (see Table 5.12).

Ongoing Risk Determination and Acceptance

The status update reports by the system owner (or common controls provider) are reviewed by the authorizing official on an ongoing basis. The status reports are coordinated with the organization's senior information security officer and the risk executive that provide input to the authorizing official in determining if the

---

[153]From Joint Task Force Transformation Initiative Interagency Working Group. NIST Special Publication (SP) 800-39, Managing Information Security Risk: Organization, Mission, and Information System View. Maryland: National Institute of Standards and Technology; 2011. "*Prioritizing, evaluating, and implementing the appropriate risk-reducing controls/countermeasures recommended from the risk management process.*"

[154]From Joint Task Force Transformation Initiative Interagency Working Group. NIST Special Publication (SP) 800-37 Revision 1, Guide for Applying the Risk Management Framework to Federal Information Systems: A Security Life Cycle Approach. Maryland: National Institute of Standards and Technology; 2010. "*Security controls that are modified, enhanced, or added during the continuous monitoring process are reassessed by the assessor to ensure that appropriate corrective actions are taken to eliminate weaknesses or deficiencies or to mitigate the identified risk.*"

[155]From Joint Task Force Transformation Initiative Interagency Working Group. NIST Special Publication (SP) 800-37 Revision 1, Guide for Applying the Risk Management Framework to Federal Information Systems: A Security Life Cycle Approach. Maryland: National Institute of Standards and Technology; 2010. "*The documents in the authorization package are considered 'living documents' and updated accordingly based on actual events that may affect the security state of the information system.*"

[156]From Lew, J. Office of Management and Budget (OMB) Memorandum 11-33, FY 2011 Reporting Instructions for the Federal Information Security Management Act and Agency Privacy Management. Washington, DC: Executive Office of the President, Office of Management and Budget; 2011. "*A significant deficiency is a weakness in an agency's overall information systems security program or management control structure, or within one or more information systems, that significantly restricts the capability of the agency to carry out its mission or compromises the security of its information, information systems, personnel, or other resources, operations, or assets.*"

Table 5.12 Key Document Updates

Key Document	Definition [3]	Owner	When to Update?
Security Plan	• An overview of the security requirements; describes the security controls in place or planned for meeting those requirements • Information to understand the intended or actual implementation of each security control employed within or inherited by the information system • Supporting appendices or, as references to appropriate sources, other risk- and security-related documents such as a • risk assessment; • privacy impact assessment (PIA); • system interconnection agreements; • contingency plan; • security configurations; • configuration management plan; • incident response plan; and • continuous monitoring strategy	Information system owner or common control provider	Whenever events[a] dictate changes (or modifications) to security controls
Security Assessment Report (SAR)	• A list of recommended corrective actions for any weaknesses or deficiencies identified in the security controls	Security control assessor	Whenever changes[b] are made to security controls (and additional assessment activities are performed)
Plan of Action and Milestones (POA&Ms)	• Describes the specific measures planned: (i) to correct weaknesses or deficiencies noted in the security controls during the assessment; and (ii) to address known vulnerabilities in the information system • Content and structure of plans of action and milestones are informed by the organizational risk management strategy developed as part of the risk executive (function) and is consistent with the plans of action and milestones process established by the organization and any specific requirements defined in federal policies, directives, memoranda, or regulations	Information system owner or common control provider	At least quarterly,[c] whenever changes occur to the POA&M status such as progress made, and to address vulnerabilities discovered during security impact analyses or continuous monitoring

[a]From Joint Task Force Transformation Initiative Interagency Working Group. NIST Special Publication (SP) 800-37 Revision 1, Guide for Applying the Risk Management Framework to Federal Information Systems: A Security Life Cycle Approach. Maryland: National Institute of Standards and Technology; 2010. *"Updates to the security plan may be triggered by a variety of events, including for example: (i) a vulnerability scan of the information system or vulnerability assessment of the environment of operation; (ii) new threat information; (iii) weaknesses or deficiencies discovered in currently deployed security controls after an information system breach; (iv) a redefinition of mission priorities or business objectives invalidating the results of the previous security categorization process; and (v) a change in the information system (e.g., adding new hardware, software, or firmware; establishing new connections) or its environment of operation (e.g., moving to a new facility)."*

[b]From Joint Task Force Transformation Initiative Interagency Working Group. NIST Special Publication (SP) 800-37 Revision 1, Guide for Applying the Risk Management Framework to Federal Information Systems: A Security Life Cycle Approach. Maryland: National Institute of Standards and Technology; 2010. *"Updates to the security assessment report help to ensure that the information system owner, common control provider, and authorizing officials maintain the appropriate awareness with regard to security control effectiveness."*

[c]From Bolten, J. Office of Management and Budget (OMB) Memorandum 0425, FY 2004 Reporting Instructions for the Federal Information Security Management Act. Washington, DC: Executive Office of the President, Office of Management and Budget; 2004. *"Program officials shall regularly (at least quarterly and at the direction of the CIO) update the agency CIO on their progress to enable the CIO to monitor agency-wide remediation efforts and provide the agency's quarterly update to OMB [per FY2011 FAQ on FISMA Reporting (M-11-33)—No FISMA submissions will be accepted outside of CyberScope]".*

risk to the information system continues to be acceptable. The use of automated tools can assist in capturing, maintaining, and presenting (i.e., quantifying and visually displaying) security status information to support "near real-time" risk management, by communicating the overall risk posture. If automation is not available, a summary of the key changes to the documents included in the authorization package should be used by the authorizing official to understand and determine if changes would affect the original authorization decision (i.e., affects on the mission or business) for using and operating the information system.

SUMMARY

In this chapter, FISMA was introduced as a basis for understanding the key requirements for federal information security programs, including the roles and responsibilities for managing information security risks. The implementation of FISMA requires the application of organization-wide risk management activity. The management of risk is a complex and multifaceted activity requiring risks to be addressed at the strategic and tactical levels, and through different viewpoints. Integrating risk management into the organization's SDLC will result in the consistent application of risk management processes and procedures. Although this chapter limited the discussion of risk management process and decision making at the organizational level (which will be covered in the next chapter), the NIST RMF and related risk management and security tasks were covered in detail for managing risks from an information system perspective.

REFERENCES

[1] Bolten J. Office of Management and Budget (OMB). FY 2003 report to Congress on federal government information security management. Washington, DC: Office of Management and Budget; 2004.

[2] E-Government Act of 2002 [Internet]. Washington, DC: US Government Printing Office [cited December 5, 2011]. <http://www.gpo.gov/fdsys/pkg/PLAW-107publ347/html/PLAW-107publ347.htm>.

[3] Joint Task Force Transformation Initiative Interagency Working Group. NIST Special Publication (SP) 800-37 revision 1, guide for applying the risk management framework to federal information systems: a security life cycle approach. Maryland: National Institute of Standards and Technology; 2010.

[4] Brown P, Kissel R. NIST Interagency Report (IR) 7358, program review for information security management assistance. Maryland: National Institute of Standards and Technology; 2007.

[5] Joint Task Force Transformation Initiative Interagency Working Group. NIST Special Publication (SP) 800-39, managing information security risk: organization, mission, and information system view. Maryland: National Institute of Standards and Technology; 2011.

[6] Federal Chief Information Officers Council. Federal enterprise architecture security and privacy profile (FEA-SPP), version 3.0. Washington, DC: Office of Management and Budget; 2011.

[7] Evans D, Bond P, Bement A. Federal Information Processing Standard (FIPS) PUB 199, Standards for Security Categorization of Federal Information and Information Systems. Maryland: National Institute of Standards and Technology; 2004.

[8] Stine K, Kissel R, Barker W, Fahlsing J, Gulick J. NIST Special Publication (SP) 800-60 Revision 1, Volume I: Guide for Mapping Types of Information and Information Systems to Security Categories. Maryland: National Institute of Standards and Technology; 2008.

[9] E-Government Task Force. E-Government Strategy. Washington, DC: Executive Office of the President, Office of Management and Budget; 2002.

[10] Federal Enterprise Architecture Program Management Office (FEAPMO). Business reference model (BRM) version 1.0. Washington, DC: Executive Office of the President, Office of Management and Budget; 2002.

[11] Federal Enterprise Architecture Program Management Office (FEAPMO). Consolidated reference model version 2.3. Washington, DC: Executive Office of the President, Office of Management and Budget; 2007.

[12] Joint Task Force Transformation Initiative. NIST Special Publication (SP) 800-53 Revision 4, Security and Privacy Controls for Federal Information Systems and Organizations. Maryland: National Institute of Standards and Technology; 2013.

[13] Gutierrez C, Jeffrey W. FIPS 200, minimum security requirements for federal information and information systems. Maryland: National Institute of Standards and Technology; 2006.

[14] Ross R. FISMA Implementation project [Internet]. Maryland: National Institute of Standards and Technology [cited December 21, 2011]. <www.nasa.gov/ppt/482348main_2010_Monday_2_ross.ppt>.

[15] Johnson A, Dempsey K, Ross R, Gupta S, Bailey D. NIST Special Publication (SP) 800-128, Guide for security-focused configuration management of information system. Maryland: National Institute of Standards and Technology; 2011.

[16] Joint Task Force Transformation Initiative. NIST Special Publication (SP) 800-53A Revision 4, Assessing Security and Privacy Controls in Federal Information Systems and Organizations: Building Effective Assessment Plan. Maryland: National Institute of Standards and Technology; 2014.

[17] Daniels M. Office of Management and Budget (OMB). Memorandum 02-01, Guidance for preparing and submitting security plans of action and milestones. Washington, DC: Executive Office of the President, Office of Management and Budget; 2001.

[18] Federal Enterprise Architecture Program Management Office (FEAPMO). FEA practice guidance. Washington, DC: Executive Office of the President, Office of Management and Budget; 2006.

[19] FedRAMP Program Management Office (PMO). FedRAMP FAQ [Internet]. Washington, DC: US General Services Administration [cited December 20, 2011]. <http://www.gsa.gov/portal/category/102439#12>.

[20] Dempsey K, Ross R, Stine K. Supplemental guidance on ongoing authorization: transitioning to near real-time risk management. Maryland: National Institute of Standards and Technology; 2014.

Risk management

6

INFORMATION IN THIS CHAPTER:

- Introduction to Risk Management
- Federal Information Security Risk Management Practices
- Overview of Enterprise-Wide Risk Management
- NIST Risk Management Process
- Comparing the NIST and ISO/IEC Risk Management Processes

INTRODUCTION TO RISK MANAGEMENT

The role of risk management within the federal government has evolved from focusing primarily on the assessment of risk[1] associated within a single information system[2] to an integration of risk-related activities that involves all levels[3] of

---

[1]From Joint Task Force Transformation Initiative Interagency Working Group. NIST Special Publication (SP) 800-30 Revision 1, Guide for Conducting Risk Assessments. Maryland: National Institute of Standards and Technology; 2011. *"Risk is a measure of the extent to which an entity is threatened by a potential circumstance or event, and is typically a function of: (i) the adverse impacts that would arise if the circumstance or event occurs and (ii) the likelihood of occurrence."*

[2]From Sterne, D., Balenson, D., Branstad, M., Jaworski, L., Lee, M.P., Pfleeger, C., et at. NIST SP 800-12, An Introduction to Computer Security: The NIST Handbook. Maryland: National Institute of Standards and Technology; 1995. *"Risk management is made up of two primary and one underlying activities; risk assessment and risk mitigation are the primary activities and uncertainty analysis is the underlying one."*

[3]From Joint Task Force Transformation Initiative Interagency Working Group. NIST SP 800-39, Managing Information Security Risk: Organization, Mission, and Information System View. Maryland: National Institute of Standards and Technology; 2011. *The integration of risk management as an organizational function focuses on a three-tiered approach: organization level (tier 1); mission/business process level (tier 2); and information system level (tier 3).*

Federal Cloud Computing. DOI: http://dx.doi.org/10.1016/B978-0-12-809710-6.00006-8

the organization.[4] By recognizing that organizations[5] are operating in highly complex, interconnected environments using state-of-the-art and legacy information systems [1], the application of the risk management process becomes more important to ensure the responsibility for information security risk management exists as an organization-wide activity. This organization-wide activity extends from those responsible for the strategic planning to those that operate the information systems in support of the mission and business operations. In Chapter 5, Applying the National Institute of Standards and Technology (NIST) Risk Management Framework (RMF), risk management was discussed from the perspective of the information system through the NIST RMF[6] to integrate risk management activities into the NIST system development life cycle (SDLC).[7] Risk management in this chapter will examine risk management from a broader perspective. By discussing risk management as a holistic process that can include multiple perspectives (i.e., organization, mission and business process, and information system), we can obtain an understanding of how it would be applied across the entire organization or across multiple organizations.

Enterprise Risk Management (ERM) is facilitated through the organization's risk management processes[8] to ensure that the management of risk is applied

---

[4]From Joint Task Force Transformation Initiative Interagency Working Group. NIST SP 800-39, Managing Information Security Risk: Organization, Mission, and Information System View. Maryland: National Institute of Standards and Technology; 2011. *Risk management is "the program and supporting processes to manage information security risk to organizational operations (including mission, functions, image, reputation), organizational assets, individuals, other organizations, and the Nation, and includes: (i) establishing the context for risk-related activities; (ii) assessing risk; (iii) responding to risk once determined; and (iv) monitoring risk over time."*

[5]From Joint Task Force Transformation Initiative Interagency Working Group. NIST Special Publication (SP) 800-39, Managing Information Security Risk: Organization, Mission, and Information System View. Maryland: National Institute of Standards and Technology; 2011. *"The term organization describes an entity of any size, complexity, or positioning within an organizational structure (e.g., a federal agency or, as appropriate, any of its operational elements) that is charged with carrying out assigned mission/business processes and that uses information systems in support of those processes."*

[6]From Joint Task Force Transformation Initiative Interagency Working Group. NIST Special Publication (SP) 800-39, Managing Information Security Risk: Organization, Mission, and Information System View. Maryland: National Institute of Standards and Technology; 2011. *The Risk Management Framework (RMF) provides a structured process that integrates risk management activities into the system development life cycle. The RMF operates primarily at tier 3 but also interacts with tier 1 and tier 2 (e.g., providing feedback from authorization decisions to the risk executive (function), disseminating updated risk information to authorizing officials, common control providers, and information system owners).*

[7]The NIST SDLC process includes five phases: initiation, development/acquisition, implementation, operation/maintenance, and disposal.

[8]From Joint Task Force Transformation Initiative Interagency Working Group. NIST Special Publication (SP) 800-39, Managing Information Security Risk: Organization, Mission, and Information System View. Maryland: National Institute of Standards and Technology; 2011. *"The NIST risk management process is complementary to and should be used as part of a more comprehensive Enterprise Risk Management (ERM) program."*

consistently across the enterprise. An ERM program is integrated across the organization through a comprehensive set of processes and practices that focus on managing organizational risk.[9] For risk management to be effective in managing security risks, it is essential that those with the responsibility for executing the mission and business operations have a clear understanding of their associated roles and responsibilities within the information security program.

An effective risk management program is driven from a "top-down" approach where the commitment and support for the program is enabled through the prioritization and allocation of resources needed for the program. In addition to resourcing risk management, the risk management strategy needs to be developed and communicated by the organization's senior management to ensure that the risk management processes and practices are supported by the governance structure that links information system security risks to organizational impacts.[10] The organization's senior management/executives play a critical role to ensure that information security risks are considered from an organizational perspective. Their role includes [1]:

- Assigning risk management responsibilities;
- Recognizing and understanding that management of information security risks is an ongoing activity;
- Establishing and communicating the risk tolerance[11] throughout the organization; and
- Ensuring accountability for risk management decisions and effective, organization-wide risk management programs.

---

[9]From Joint Task Force Transformation Initiative Interagency Working Group. NIST Special Publication (SP) 800-39, Managing Information Security Risk: Organization, Mission, and Information System View. Maryland: National Institute of Standards and Technology; 2011. *"Organizational risk can include many types of risk (e.g., program management risk, investment risk, budgetary risk, legal liability risk, safety risk, inventory risk, supply chain risk, and security risk)."*

[10]From Joint Task Force Transformation Initiative Interagency Working Group. NIST Special Publication (SP) 800-39, Managing Information Security Risk: Organization, Mission, and Information System View. Maryland: National Institute of Standards and Technology; 2011. *"Information systems are subject to serious threats that can have adverse effects on organizational operations (i.e., missions, functions, image, or reputation), organizational assets, individuals, other organizations, and the Nation by exploiting both known and unknown vulnerabilities to compromise the confidentiality, integrity, or availability of the information being processed, stored, or transmitted by those systems."*

[11]From Joint Task Force Transformation Initiative Interagency Working Group. NIST Special Publication (SP) 800-39, Managing Information Security Risk: Organization, Mission, and Information System View. Maryland: National Institute of Standards and Technology; 2011. *"Risk tolerance is the level of risk or degree of uncertainty that is acceptable to organizations and is a key element of the organizational risk frame."*

FEDERAL INFORMATION SECURITY RISK MANAGEMENT PRACTICES

Risk management is not a new concept within the federal government. As early as 1974, guidelines have been developed to support federal agencies in integrating risk management practices into federal security programs. For example, the National Bureau of Standards (NBS)[12] published the *Guidelines for Automatic Data Processing Physical Security and Risk Management* for the purpose of assisting automatic data processing (ADP) facility managers in developing physical security programs. These guidelines provided procedures for risk management—related activities such as conducting a risk analysis (risk assessment) and the selection and implementation of security measures (risk mitigation). This early risk management philosophy became the foundations by which federal information security programs were built.[13] As chronicled in Table 6.1, over the

Table 6.1 Chronology of Federal Information Security Risk Management References

Date	Title and Description	Author
June 1974	*Guidelines for Automatic Data Processing Physical Security and Risk Management* provided "a handbook for use by Federal organizations in structuring physical security and risk management programs for their ADP facilities" [2].	NBS
May 1975	*Computer Security Guidelines for Implementing the Privacy Act of 1974* provided "a handbook for use by Federal organizations in implementing any computer safeguards which they must adopt in order to implement the Act" [3]. It included conducting Security Risk Assessments.	NBS
August 1979	*Guidelines for Automatic Data Processing Risk Analysis* provided the first formal set of guidelines for federal agencies when performing a risk analysis.	NBS
October 1989	*Guide for Selecting Automated Risk Analysis Tools* "assisted managers in selecting the most appropriate risk analysis tool" [4]. Although excluding specific focus on conducting risks analyses, it did cover the elements[a] of risk analysis for the purpose of selecting a tool.	National Institute of Standards and Technology (NIST)

(Continued)

---

[12]NBS became the National Institute of Standards and Technology (NIST) in 1988.
[13]From Stoneburner, G., Goguen, A., Feringa, A. NIST Special Publication (SP) 800-30, Risk Management Guide for Information Technology Systems. Maryland: National Institute of Standards and Technology; 2002. *"Risk management encompasses three processes: risk assessment, risk mitigation, and evaluation and assessment."*

Table 6.1 Chronology of Federal Information Security Risk Management References *Continued*

Date	Title and Description	Author
January 1991	*Computers at Risk*[b] recommended the development of Generally Accepted System Security Principles (GASSP).	National Research Council (NRC) of the National Academies of Science (NAS)
October 1992	*A Framework for Computer Security Risk Management* provided a computer security risk management framework (RMF) developed in collaboration among NIST/National Security Agency (NSA), other countries, and the private sector.	Dr. Stuart Karzke (NIST)
October 1995	*An Introduction to Computer Security: The NIST Handbook* provided "assistance in securing computer-based resources by explaining important concepts, cost consideration and interrelationships of security controls" [5]. In addition, it included a chapter focused specifically on risk management.	NIST
September 1996	*Generally Accepted Principles and Practices for Securing Information Technology Systems* that provided security principles (used by individuals responsible for security at the system and organizational level) and practices[c] to be applied in the use, protection, and design of government information and data systems [6]. *The NIST Handbook* is a companion reference that was used as the basis for identifying common practices that support building an IT security program.	US GAO
May 1998	*Information Security Management, Learning From Leading Organizations* highlighted five management principles that were implemented by leading private sector organizations: assessing risk, establishing a central management focal point, implementing appropriate policies and procedures, promoting awareness, and monitoring and evaluating policy and control effectiveness. These principles aligned with the embodied framework established by the Federal Information Security Management Act (FISMA).	US GAO
November 1999	*Information Security Risk Assessment, Practices of Leading Organizations* was published to "identify and describe (1) information security risk assessment methods and (2) related critical success factors that could be considered by federal agencies to improve their own processes" [7].	US GAO
November 2000	*Federal Information Technology Security Assessment Framework* provided a method for agency officials when assessing status of their security programs and identify improvements.	NIST
July 2002	*Risk Management Guide for Information Technology Systems* provided a foundation for developing a risk management program.	NIST

(Continued)

Table 6.1 Chronology of Federal Information Security Risk Management References *Continued*

Date	Title and Description	Author
March 2011	*Managing Information Security Risk: Organization, Mission, and Information System View* provided guidance for managing information security risk with specific details of assessing, responding to, and monitoring risk on an ongoing basis [8].	NIST
September 2011	*Guide for Conducting Risk Assessments* refocused from the previous publication to address risk assessments as part of the RMF [9].	NIST

[a]*Asset identification, threat assessment, vulnerability assessment, and safeguard effectiveness.*
[b]*"Computers at Risk: Safe Computing in the Information Age," National Academy Press (1991), was a report of the System Security Study Committee (formed in 1990 by the Computer Science and Telecommunications Board). Available from: http://www.nap.edu/catalog.php?record_id = 1581.*
[c]*NIST used the Organization for Economic Co-Operation and Development's (OECD) "Guidelines for the Security of Information Systems" when developing the principles for federal information systems. The OECD document was updated in 2002 and renamed from the original publication in 1992 to "OECD Guidelines for the Security of Information System and Networks."*

years, the federal government's viewpoint on risk management has changed, requiring the practices to evolve from a tactical to a strategic focus.

Risk management practices are a critical part of federal information security that requires addressing continuous changes in the sophistication and complexity of the threat environment. In the past, federal agencies have been required to rely upon only risk assessments as a tool for integrating risk management activities within their certification and accreditation (C&A)[14] processes [10] (also referred to security assessment and authorization) and as the foundation[15] for managing risks within their information security programs. However, federal risk management processes are maturing. By adopting a government-wide approach, federal risk management programs are becoming more comprehensive through the use of continuous monitoring tools and techniques to gather security-related information to manage risks. Therefore, throughout the remainder of this chapter, the focus will shift to discussing a holistic, enterprise perspective to managing risk and the role of risk management in supporting a government-wide approach to security assessment, authorization, and continuous monitoring.

[14]From Joint Task Force Transformation Initiative Interagency Working Group. NIST Special Publication (SP) 800-37 Revision 1, Guide for Applying the Risk Management Framework to Federal Information Systems: A Security Life Cycle Approach. Maryland: National Institute of Standards and Technology; 2010. *"The Joint Task Force Transformation Initiative Working Group transformed the traditional Certification and Accreditation (C&A) process into the six-step Risk Management Framework (RMF)."*
[15]From Crumpacker, J. Information Security Risk Assessment, Practices of Leading Organizations. Washington, DC: US Government Accountability Office; 1999. *"Risk assessments provide the foundation for other elements of the risk management cycle through which appropriate policies are developed and cost-effective techniques to implement these policies are selected."*

OVERVIEW OF ENTERPRISE-WIDE RISK MANAGEMENT

Enterprise-wide risk management consists of a structured approach for consistently and continuously applying risk management practices for managing risk[16] beyond the information system boundary. By examining the components that make up the federal government's viewpoint of an organization-wide risk management program, a model can be established that will be useful for integrating these components into existing federal government and private sector risk management programs. As previously discussed, risk management within the federal government has primarily focused on managing risk at the information system level. This system level approach is not adequate when risks need to be communicated across the different levels of the organization or between multiple organizations. For risk management to be effective as a strategic and tactical tool used by the organization(s) in making risk decisions, they need to be able to manage risk across the complex environments in which information systems operate. In this section, an overview will be provided of the integrated, enterprise-wide risk management[17] methodology, and how it is applied in the context of the organization(s)[18] supported by the information system. In addition, to provide a broader context, the next section will include a brief comparison of both the practices and processes used in the federal government and in the private sector using international risk management standards.

COMPONENTS OF THE NIST RISK MANAGEMENT PROCESS

The risk management process (or cycle)[19] consists of four components that provide a structured, process-oriented approach for managing risks. Each of the four

---

[16]From Joint Task Force Transformation Initiative Interagency Working Group. NIST Special Publication (SP) 800-39, Managing Information Security Risk: Organization, Mission, and Information System View. Maryland: National Institute of Standards and Technology; 2011. *"Risk refers to information security risk from the operation and use of organizational information systems including the processes, procedures, and structures within organizations that influence or affect the design, development, implementation, and ongoing operation of those systems."*

[17]From Joint Task Force Transformation Initiative Interagency Working Group. NIST Special Publication (SP) 800-39, Managing Information Security Risk: Organization, Mission, and Information System View. Maryland: National Institute of Standards and Technology; 2011. *"Integrated, enterprise-wide risk management includes, for example, consideration of: (i) the strategic goals/objectives of organizations; (ii) organizational missions/business functions prioritized as needed; (iii) mission/business processes; (iv) enterprise and information security architectures; and (v) system development life cycle processes."*

[18]From Joint Task Force Transformation Initiative Interagency Working Group. NIST Special Publication (SP) 800-39, Managing Information Security Risk: Organization, Mission, and Information System View. Maryland: National Institute of Standards and Technology; 2011. *"Any entity of any size, complexity, or positioning with an organizational structure that is charged with carrying out assigned mission/business processes and that uses information system in support of those processes."*

[19]From Office of Electricity Delivery and Energy Reliability. Electricity Sector Cybersecurity Risk Management Process Guideline. Washington, DC: US Department of Energy. *"The risk management cycle is a comprehensive process that requires organizations to (1) frame risk (i.e., establish the context for risk-based decisions), (2) assess risk, (3) respond to risk once determined, and (4) monitor risk on an ongoing basis, using effective organizational communications and an iterative feedback loop for continuous improvement in the risk-related activities of organizations."*

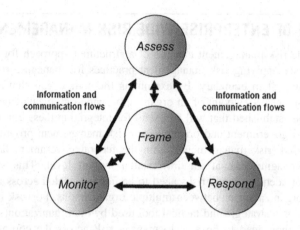

FIGURE 6.1

Components of the risk management process.

components of the risk management process ensures that risk is managed in an integrated process that requires the involvement of the entire organization. Historically, the federal government included only two of the four components of risk management—risk assessment and risk response. In this approach to risk management, as illustrated in Fig. 6.1, two additional components have been added: risk framing and risk monitoring.

Risk Framing

Establishing a risk context (or framing) is a critical first step in risk management that requires describing the risk environment. The environment includes risk assumptions,[20] risk constraints,[21] risk tolerance,[22] priorities/trade-offs,[23] and the

---

[20]From Joint Task Force Transformation Initiative Interagency Working Group. NIST Special Publication (SP) 800-39, Managing Information Security Risk: Organization, Mission, and Information System View. Maryland: National Institute of Standards and Technology; 2011. *"Assumptions about the threats, vulnerabilities, consequences/impact, and likelihood of occurrence that affect how risk is assessed, responded to, and monitored over time."*

[21]From Joint Task Force Transformation Initiative Interagency Working Group. NIST Special Publication (SP) 800-39, Managing Information Security Risk: Organization, Mission, and Information System View. Maryland: National Institute of Standards and Technology; 2011. *"Constraints on the risk assessment, response, and monitoring alternatives under consideration."*

[22]From Joint Task Force Transformation Initiative Interagency Working Group. NIST Special Publication (SP) 800-39, Managing Information Security Risk: Organization, Mission, and Information System View. Maryland: National Institute of Standards and Technology; 2011. *"Levels of risk, types of risk, and degree of risk uncertainty that are acceptable."*

[23]From Joint Task Force Transformation Initiative Interagency Working Group. NIST Special Publication (SP) 800-39, Managing Information Security Risk: Organization, Mission, and Information System View. Maryland: National Institute of Standards and Technology; 2011. *"The relative importance of missions/business functions, trade-offs among different types of risk that organizations face, time frames in which organizations must address risk, and any factors of uncertainty that organizations consider in risk responses."*

trust model.[24] Framing the risk can also include information about any tools or techniques that are used by the organization to support the risk management activities. The output of risk framing is a risk management strategy[25] that provides the organization with a common perspective for managing risks (i.e., assessment, response, or monitoring).

Risk Assessment

The assessment of risk is based on the organization's risk context, and includes activities focused on supporting the identification and determination of risk, and monitoring risk factors.[26] Risks are identified based on a characterization of threats[27] (threat sources and events), vulnerabilities,[28] and predisposing conditions.[29] The risk determination is based on the impact that would result from an event and the likelihood the event would occur. Monitoring risk factors is the maintenance aspect, and includes an ongoing situational awareness of the changes to information used by the organization when making a risk-based decision.

A risk assessment is a tool that can be used organization-wide. Depending on the organizational structure, risk-related information captured at the strategic level (tier 1), as illustrated in Fig. 6.2, can be used at the tactical level (tier 3). By conducting risk

---

[24]Trust models can be formed through evidence-based assurance (validated trust), historical relationships (direct historical trust), third-party assurance (mediated trust), authoritative organizations (mandate trust), or any combination (hybrid trust) of the previous trust models for one organization to obtain the necessary level of trust of the security/risk activities of another organization.

[25]From Joint Task Force Transformation Initiative Interagency Working Group. NIST Special Publication (SP) 800-39, Managing Information Security Risk: Organization, Mission, and Information System View. Maryland: National Institute of Standards and Technology; 2011. *A risk management strategy "addresses how organizations intend to assess risk, respond to risk, and monitor risk—making explicit and transparent the risk perceptions that organizations routinely use in making both investment and operational decisions."*

[26]From Joint Task Force Transformation Initiative Interagency Working Group. NIST Special Publication (SP) 800-30 Revision 1, Guide for Conducting Risk Assessments. Maryland: National Institute of Standards and Technology; 2011. *"Risk factors are characteristics used in risk models as inputs to determining levels of risk in risk assessments and can include threat information, vulnerabilities, and preconditions."*

[27]From Joint Task Force Transformation Initiative Interagency Working Group. NIST Special Publication (SP) 800-30 Revision 1, Guide for Conducting Risk Assessments. Maryland: National Institute of Standards and Technology; 2011. *"An event or situation that has the potential for causing undesirable consequences or impact."*

[28]From Joint Task Force Transformation Initiative Interagency Working Group. NIST Special Publication (SP) 800-30 Revision 1, Guide for Conducting Risk Assessments. Maryland: National Institute of Standards and Technology; 2011. *"Weakness in an information system, system security procedures, internal controls, or implementation that could be exploited by a threat source."*

[29]From Joint Task Force Transformation Initiative Interagency Working Group. NIST Special Publication (SP) 800-30 Revision 1, Guide for Conducting Risk Assessments. Maryland: National Institute of Standards and Technology; 2011. *"A condition that exists within an organization, a mission or business process, enterprise architecture, information system, or environment of operation, which affects (i.e., increases or decreases) the likelihood that threat events, once initiated, result in adverse impacts to organizational operations and assets, individuals, other organizations, or the Nation."*

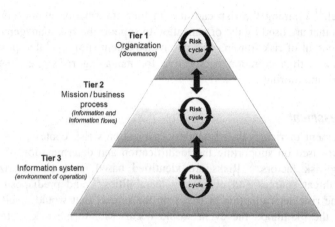

FIGURE 6.2

Multitiered integration of the risk management process.

assessments as a continual risk management activity, threats, vulnerability, likelihood, and impact information can be refined and updated with information at each of the three levels within the organization (governance, mission/business process, and information system). However, to effectively integrate risk assessments at the different levels within the organization, the involvement in the risk assessment activities must extend beyond those responsible for information security. By using an organizational approach to conduct risk assessments, information security risks become an integral part of the organization's overall decision-making process.

Risk Response

After risks have been identified and analyzed, the organization focuses on developing responses[30] to risk. When responding to risks, the organization needs to ensure that the response is consistent with the risk context defined in the risk framing component of risk management. Depending on the level of the organization, the risk response may be different due to the types of risk-related information being evaluated for impact and the specific interpretation of the risk management strategy. For example:

- The focus of risk response at the strategic, organizational level might focus on the actions (e.g., accept risk, avoid risk, and transfer risk) that would be available to the organization based on the risk framing.

---

[30]From Joint Task Force Transformation Initiative Interagency Working Group. NIST Special Publication (SP) 800-39, Managing Information Security Risk: Organization, Mission, and Information System View. Maryland: National Institute of Standards and Technology; 2011. *"The purpose of the risk response component is to provide a consistent, organization-wide, response to risk in accordance with the organizational risk frame by: (i) developing alternative courses of action for responding to risk; (ii) evaluating the alternative courses of action; (iii) determining appropriate courses of action consistent with organizational risk tolerance; and (iv) implementing risk responses based on selected courses of action."*

- Risk responses from the perspective of the mission/business process owners might consider impacts on the ability of the specific organization to accomplish a specific business function that could result in changes to the information security architecture or processes that support the information security program.
- Risk response at the tactical, information system level might focus on specific tasks (plans of action and milestones) that would be undertaken to correct any weaknesses or deficiencies found in security controls to ensure that the system-level risk can be mitigated to an acceptable level.

A key part of risk response that cannot be overlooked is how the responses to risk are communicated outside of the organization such as with external service providers (or even between organizations) who may share some or all of the risks. This may require those service providers (or organizations) to be part of the risk response decision-making process, specifically if it relates to contractual or service-level obligations that have already been established and formalized prior to the risk response decisions.

Risk Monitoring

The purpose of risk monitoring is to address how risk will be monitored. This includes verifying compliance with the risk response decisions by ensuring that the organization implements the risk response measures (and any information security requirements), determines the ongoing effectiveness of risk response measures, and identifies any changes that would impact the risk posture [1]. Risk monitoring activities at the various levels of the organization (or with other organizational entities) should be coordinated and communicated. This can include sharing risk assessment results that would have an organization-wide impact to risk responses being planned or implemented. The organization should also consider the tools and technologies that will be needed to facilitate monitoring and the frequency necessary for effectively monitoring risks, including the changes that would impact responses to risks.

MULTITIERED RISK MANAGEMENT

Most organizations, regardless of the size or type, have a similar structure that includes executive leadership (addressing risk as it relates to the organization's mission and business functions), mission and business management (addressing risk as it relates to the organization's operations), and system management (addressing risk as it relates to the security controls). As illustrated in Fig. 6.2, the integration of the risk management process focuses on the risk management activities[31] at each tier.

---

[31]Activities related to framing risk, assessing risk, responding to risk, and monitoring risk executed at each tier within the context of the organization's governance structure and risk management program.

The information flow between the organizational tiers should be bi-directional. By offering a feedback loop, results of monitoring activities can be shared between organizational tiers at each level within the governance structure (or model[32]). For example, *tier 3* outputs can be used by tier 2 to improve policies, procedures, and practices, and *tier 2* outputs can be used to by tier 1 to improve organizational policies that govern the risk management program and are articulated through the risk management strategy. Not only is the information flow important for the facilitation of internal risk-related information, it can also serve to communicate information from external sources (e.g., peer organizations, service providers) that may improve the strategy to ensure that it is comprehensive.

Tier 1 Risk Management Activities

The organization's governance[33] structure and practices are generally developed from a "top-down" approach. This ensures that the organizational governance (i.e., responsibilities and practices) addresses risk from an organizational viewpoint that is consistent with the strategic goals and objectives. In addition, risk management process should be directed from the senior management (head of a federal agency, corporate executive, etc.) to align the risk decision with the organization's strategic direction. Senior management may also have the overall responsibility for overseeing the achievement of the business objectives and thus they may have the ability to ensure that resources are available and used effectively to manage risk.

> **NOTE**
>
> Five potential outcomes of the governance-related risk management activities [1] include:
>
> - Strategic alignment of risk management decisions consistent with the organization's goals and objectives.
> - Execution of risk management processes (i.e., frame, assess, respond to, and monitor).
> - Effective and efficient allocation of risk management resources.
> - Performance-based outcomes (e.g., risk management metrics) that ensure organizational goals and objectives are being achieved.
> - Optimizing risk management investments to support organizational objectives.

In tier 1, the risk executive (or function) also plays an important role in supporting risk management by determining how decisions made regarding risk are carried through the organization governance.[34]

---

[32]There are three basic types of security governance models: centralized, decentralized, and hybrid.

[33]Applying a consistent and unified governance approach facilitates cost-savings when applying risk management activities and translating risks between business functions.

[34]From Joint Task Force Transformation Initiative Interagency Working Group. NIST Special Publication (SP) 800-39, Managing Information Security Risk: Organization, Mission, and Information System View. Maryland: National Institute of Standards and Technology; 2011. *Risk management decisions include: (i) the types of that are reserved for specific senior management; (ii) the types that are deemed to be organization-wide and the types that can be delegated to subordinate organizations or to other roles in the organization; and (iii) how risk management decisions will be communicated.*

Tier 2 Risk Management Activities

At tier 2, the business/mission processes[35] manage risk based on the components defined in the risk management strategy. Since these processes support the mission/business functions, they must have an awareness of impact. As an example, if a sophisticated cyber attack occurred, the mission/business processes need to be designed to achieve an anticipated level of resiliency. Therefore, a key consideration when defining the mission/business processes is the selection of a risk response strategy that is within the constraints defined in the risk management strategy[36] [1].

Tier 3 Risk Management Activities

The NIST SDLC integrates risk management activities through the application of the NIST RMF. The specific risk management activities at tier 3 are guided by the output of the risk management activities conducted at tier 1 and tier 2, (i.e., where the risk management strategy and the risk response strategy are supported by an information security architecture).[37] In addition, the output of the risk management activities from the other tiers also ensures the information system operates consistently with the information system resiliency[38] requirements.

[35]From Joint Task Force Transformation Initiative Interagency Working Group. NIST Special Publication (SP) 800-39, Managing Information Security Risk: Organization, Mission, and Information System View. Maryland: National Institute of Standards and Technology; 2011. *A risk-aware mission/business process is one that explicitly takes into account the likely risk such a process would cause if implemented by and explicitly accounting for risk when evaluating the mission/business activities.*

[36]From Joint Task Force Transformation Initiative Interagency Working Group. NIST Special Publication (SP) 800-39, Managing Information Security Risk: Organization, Mission, and Information System View. Maryland: National Institute of Standards and Technology; 2011. *Risk response strategies specify the responsible parties, dependencies on other risk response strategies and other factors, implementation timeline, monitoring plans and triggers, and any temporary measures that can be implemented until the response strategy has been fully implemented.*

[37]From Joint Task Force Transformation Initiative Interagency Working Group. NIST Special Publication (SP) 800-39, Managing Information Security Risk: Organization, Mission, and Information System View. Maryland: National Institute of Standards and Technology; 2011. *The information security architecture represents that portion of the enterprise architecture specifically addressing information system resilience and providing architectural information for the implementation of security capabilities.*

[38]From Joint Task Force Transformation Initiative Interagency Working Group. NIST Special Publication (SP) 800-39, Managing Information Security Risk: Organization, Mission, and Information System View. Maryland: National Institute of Standards and Technology; 2011. *Information system resiliency is the ability of an information system to continue to operate under adverse conditions and recover within a time frame consistent with the operational need.*

NIST RISK MANAGEMENT PROCESS

The risk management process can be applied as a tiered model as represented in Fig. 6.3, in which each of the four risk management components, previously

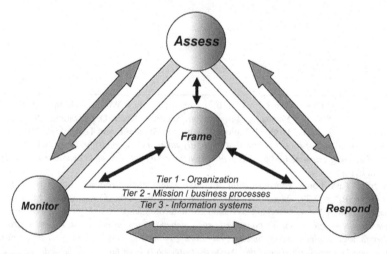

FIGURE 6.3

Tiered application of the risk management process.

[39]From Joint Task Force Transformation Initiative Interagency Working Group. NIST Special Publication (SP) 800-39, Managing Information Security Risk: Organization, Mission, and Information System View. Maryland: National Institute of Standards and Technology; 2011. *The attribute of a person or enterprise that provides confidence to others of the qualification, capabilities, and reliability of that entity to perform specific tasks and fulfill assigned responsibilities.*

discussed, is applied at each tier. Each tier plays a role in the execution of the risk management process where information flows across the tiers bi-directionally. In this section, each risk management process will be described and the specific interactions between the tiers will be highlighted. Although there is no specific order for applying the risk management processes within an organization, this section does address each process within each tier based on the presumption that a "top-down" approach will be used. The approach starts with tier 1 where the risk framing step begins in the risk management cycle and concludes with monitoring risk before moving to the next tier (i.e., tier 2 and tier 3).

FRAMING RISK

In the risk management process, risk framing establishes the risk management strategy that provides a common organization-wide strategy for executing the other steps (assessment, response, and monitoring) of the process that are supported by the commitment of the organizations, senior management. As illustrated in Fig. 6.4, input to risk framing can include laws, policies, directives, regulations, contractual relationships, financial limitations, or information that explicitly (Memorandums of Understanding/Agreement (MOUs/MOAs), governance processes) supports key activities in the risk framing step.

Risk framing activities produce guidance that enables the development of a common perspective on how the organization manages risk. This perspective is established through the assumptions and constraints, level of risk tolerance, and

FIGURE 6.4

Risk framing—inputs, activities, and outputs.

priorities and trade-offs that drive the organizations' decision-making process, and the type/size of the organization. Since risk framing may initially be high level or undefined, a feedback loop should exist to ensure that information from the other steps of the risk management process are used to adjust the original risk factors that contribute to the organization's risk management policies, procedures, standards, and guidance.

The risk framing step also produces the risk framework and risk methodologies[40] that will be used by the organization in tier 2 and tier 3 of the risk management hierarchy and in the execution of the other risk management steps. For example, if the organizational governance structure is centralized,[41] only one framework and methodology may be required, whereas if the organization is decentralized,[42] multiple frameworks and methodologies may be required. By having a common framework and methodology for organization-wide tailoring, it ensures that at least there is a consistent evaluation standard used by the entire organization for assessing risk and prioritizing risks as they are aggregated (or consolidated) from across the organization. This standard can then be applied in the risk assessment step when assessing risks and in the risk response step when courses of action are prioritized and implemented to achieve the most cost-effective strategy for risk mitigation.[43]

ASSESSING RISK

The risk assessment step of the risk management process, as shown in Fig. 6.5, involves two major activities: identifying threats and vulnerabilities and risk determination. This step receives input from the other risk management processes to help the decision-makers at each level of the risk management hierarchy identify, prioritize, and estimate risks. The inputs to the risk assessment step include, for example, the risk assessment methodology (risk framing), different courses of actions (risk response), and new threats and vulnerabilities identified (risk monitoring).

---

[40]From Joint Task Force Transformation Initiative Interagency Working Group. NIST Special Publication (SP) 800-30 Revision 1, Guide for Conducting Risk Assessments. Maryland: National Institute of Standards and Technology; 2011. *A risk assessment methodology is a risk assessment process, together with a risk model, assessment approach, and analysis approach.*

[41]From Joint Task Force Transformation Initiative Interagency Working Group. NIST Special Publication (SP) 800-39, Managing Information Security Risk: Organization, Mission, and Information System View. Maryland: National Institute of Standards and Technology; 2011. *The authority, responsibility, and decision-making powers are vested solely within central bodies that establish the appropriate policies, procedures, and processes.*

[42]From Joint Task Force Transformation Initiative Interagency Working Group. NIST Special Publication (SP) 800-39, Managing Information Security Risk: Organization, Mission, and Information System View. Maryland: National Institute of Standards and Technology; 2011. *The authority, responsibility, and decision-making powers are vested in and delegated to individual subordinate organizations that establish their own policies, procedures, and processes.*

[43]From Joint Task Force Transformation Initiative Interagency Working Group. NIST Special Publication (SP) 800-39, Managing Information Security Risk: Organization, Mission, and Information System View. Maryland: National Institute of Standards and Technology; 2011. *"Prioritizing, evaluating, and implementing the appropriate risk-reducing controls/countermeasures recommended from the risk management process."*

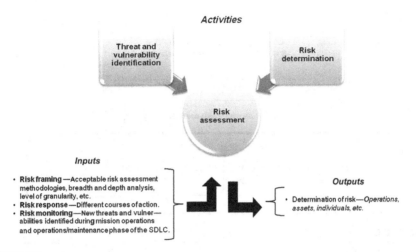

FIGURE 6.5

Risk assessment—inputs, activities, and outputs.

Risk assessments can be a useful source of input for risk-related information when conducted at each of the organizational tiers. Tier 1 and tier 2 apply risk assessments based on information security—related risks associated with organizational governance and management activities, mission/business processes (or enterprise architecture), and funding of information security programs [11]. Tier 3 risk assessment activities focus primarily on support information system—related activities conducted during the implementation of the NIST RMF as discussed in Chapter 5, Applying the NIST Risk Management Framework (i.e., security categorization, security control selection, security control implementation, security control assessments, security authorization, and security control monitoring). Previously, risk assessments were only conducted at tier 3 (information system level). Although, some risk information cannot be assessed effectively at tier 3, such as tier 1 risks associated with the organization-wide security program or tier 2 risks associated with common controls shared across the organization or between entities that have a trusted relationship.

WARNING

According to NIST:

"*... risk assessments are often not precise instruments of measurement and reflect:*

 i. the limitations of specific assessment methodologies, tools, and techniques employed;
 ii. the subjectivity, quality, and trustworthiness of the data used;
 iii. the interpretation of assessment results; and
 iv. the skills and expertise of those individuals or groups conducting the assessments.

Since cost, timeliness, and ease of use are a few of the many important factors in the application of risk assessments, organizations should attempt to reduce the complexity of risk assessments and maximize the reuse of assessment results by sharing risk-related information across their enterprises, whenever possible."

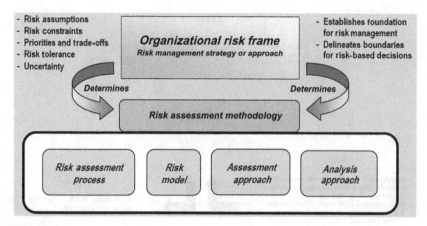

FIGURE 6.6

Components of a risk assessment [13].

As previously noted, inputs to the risk assessment can come from a variety of sources. As illustrated in Fig. 6.6, one of the most important sources is the organizational risk frame that establishes the context for the risk management strategy. The risk management strategy includes "information regarding policies and requirements for conducting risk assessments, specific assessment methodologies to be employed, procedures for selecting risk factors to be considered, scope of the assessments, rigor of analyses, degree of formality, and requirements that facilitate consistent and repeatable risk determinations across the organization" [13]. The risk assessment methodology, a component of the risk management strategy, includes the definition of the risk assessment process, risk model (risk factors and relationships among risk factors), assessment approach (quantitatively,[44] qualitatively,[45] or semi-quantitatively[46]), and an analysis approach (threat-oriented, asset/impact-oriented, or vulnerability-oriented).

RESPONDING TO RISK

The risk response step in Fig. 6.7 includes multiple activities for responding to risk such as identifying courses of actions, evaluating alternative courses of action, and selecting and implementing courses of action. As with risk

---

[44]From Risk Steering Committee. DHS Risk Lexicon. Washington, DC: US Department of Homeland Security; 2010. *"Set of methods, principles, or rules for assessing risk based on non-numerical categories or levels."*

[45]From Risk Steering Committee. DHS Risk Lexicon. Washington, DC: US Department of Homeland Security; 2010. *"Set of methods, principles, or rules for assessing risk based on non-numerical categories or levels."*

[46]From Risk Steering Committee. DHS Risk Lexicon. Washington, DC: US Department of Homeland Security; 2010. *"Set of methods, principles, or rules to assess risk that uses bins, scales, or representative numbers whose values and meanings are not maintained in other contexts."*

Activities

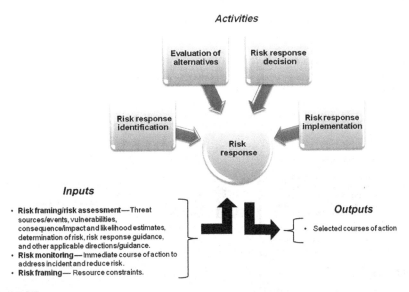

FIGURE 6.7

Risk response—inputs, activities, and outputs.

assessment, the risk response is performed at each level of the risk management hierarchy, with activities performed at specific tiers. For example, risk response identification could require considering organization-wide impacts and therefore might be performed at tier 1, whereas evaluation of alternative courses of action could require an evaluation of impacts to mission/business processes and therefore might be performed at tier 2. Regardless at which tier the activity is performed, the risk decisions receive input from the other risk management processes that are shared and communicated.

MONITORING RISK

The last step in the risk management process involves monitoring risk. Fig. 6.8 illustrates the two activities performed during the risk monitoring step: risk monitoring strategy and risk monitoring. Risk monitoring strategy includes defining the purpose of the risk monitoring program, type of monitoring to be performed (e.g., automated vs. manual) and frequency of monitoring activities. Risk monitoring provides organizations with the means to verify compliance,[47] determine the

---

[47]From Joint Task Force Transformation Initiative Interagency Working Group. NIST Special Publication (SP) 800-39, Managing Information Security Risk: Organization, Mission, and Information System View. Maryland: National Institute of Standards and Technology; 2011. "*Compliance verification ensures that organizations have implemented required risk response measures and that information security requirements derived from and traceable to organizational mission/business functions, federal legislation, directives, regulations, policies, and standards/guidelines are satisfied.*"

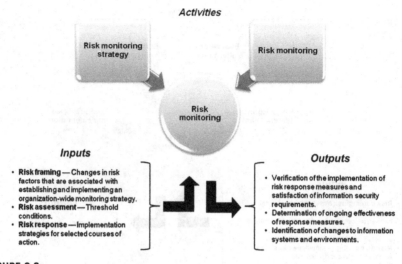

FIGURE 6.8

Risk monitoring—inputs, activities, and outputs.

ongoing effectiveness of risk response measures[48] and identify risk-impacting changes to organizational information systems and environments of operation [1], which is driven by the monitoring strategy.

COMPARING THE NIST AND ISO/IEC RISK MANAGEMENT PROCESSES

Risk management methodologies[49] have been published by many organizations. In this section, a brief examination will be provided on the methodologies

---

[48]From Joint Task Force Transformation Initiative Interagency Working Group. NIST Special Publication (SP) 800-39, Managing Information Security Risk: Organization, Mission, and Information System View. Maryland: National Institute of Standards and Technology; 2011. *"Effectiveness monitoring is employed by organizations to determine if implemented risk response measures have actually been effective in reducing identified risk to the desired level."*

[49]Examples include the Software Engineering Institute (SEI)'s *"Security Quality Requirements Engineering (SQUARE),"* available from: http://www.sei.cmu.edu/library/abstracts/reports/05tr009.cfm; the Software Engineering Institute (SEI)'s *"Operationally Critical Threat, Asset, and Vulnerability Evaluation (OCTAVE),"* available from: http://www.cert.org/octave; the Committee of Sponsoring Organizations of the Treadway Commission (COSO)'s *"Enterprise Risk Management—Integrated Framework,"* available from: http://www.coso.org/erm-integrated-framework.htm; and the Information Systems Audit and Control Association (ISACA)'s *"Risk IT,"* available from: http://www.isaca.org/Knowledge-Center/Risk-IT-IT-Risk-Management/Pages/Risk-IT1.aspx.

Table 6.2 NIST and ISO/IEC Risk Management Standards and Guidelines

ISO/IEC 27001:2005 Information technology—Security techniques—Information security management system—Requirements

ISO/IEC 27002:2005 Information technology—Security techniques—Code of practices for information security management

ISO/IEC 27005:2011[a] Information technology—Security techniques—Information security risk management

ISO/IEC 31000:2009 Risk management—Principles and guidelines

ISO/IEC 31010:2009 Risk management—Risk assessment techniques

NIST SP 800-30 Revision 1[b] Guide for Conducting Risk Assessments

NIST SP 800-37 Revision 1 Guide for Applying the RMF to Federal Information Systems: A Security Life Cycle Approach

NIST SP 800-53 Security and Privacy Controls for Federal Information Systems and Organizations

NIST SP 800-53A Guide for Assessing the Security Controls in Federal Information Systems and Organizations

NIST SP 800-39 Managing Information Security Risk: Organization, Mission, and Information System View

[a]*Replaced ISO/IEC 27005:2008 with the same name.*
[b]*Replaced NIST SP 800-30 with a different title ("Risk Management Guide for Information Technology Systems").*

published by NIST and the International Organization for Standards /International Electrotechnical Commission (ISO/IEC). As a reference, Table 6.2 provides a list of risk management—related standards and guidelines published by NIST and the ISO/IEC, and can be useful as a basis for understanding how each approaches risk management.

Risk management practices are the foundation by which the risk management strategy is communicated through the governance structure. By understanding the general similarities and differences between each approach, it will enable federal agencies following the NIST methodology and private sector organizations following the ISO/IEC methodology to more consistently apply risk management practices across the organizational boundaries. As an example, Fig. 6.9 provides a "high-level" comparison of the key processes included in the NIST and ISO/IEC risk management methodologies.

TIP

NIST plays a critical role in aligning standards where possible with those developed internationally or nationally. Risk management is no exception. The goal of harmonization efforts performed by NIST is to limit "the burden on organizations that must conform to both ISO/IEC standards and NIST standards and guidance" [1].

NIST steps   ISO/IEC steps

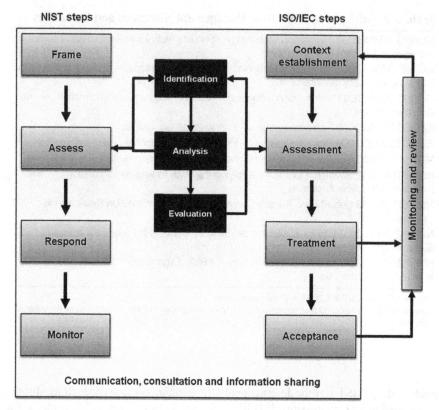

FIGURE 6.9

Comparison of major NIST and ISO/IEC risk management processes.

In *Step 1*, outlined in Table 6.3, both NIST and the ISO/IEC address framing the risk (or establishing the risk context).[50] In the NIST process, risk framing requires the organization to develop a risk management strategy that meets its unique governance structure, mission, and business operations. Although the NIST process presents a more flexible approach, it is limited in providing specific guidance for performing the risk framing activity, whereas the ISO/IEC process provides a more specific set of criteria to use when documenting the risk context.

In the next step, the NIST and the ISO/IEC processes include similar activities for supporting risk identification and risk determination activities. As shown in

[50]From Joint Task Force Transformation Initiative Interagency Working Group. NIST Special Publication (SP) 800-39, Managing Information Security Risk: Organization, Mission, and Information System View. Maryland: National Institute of Standards and Technology; 2011. *Risk framing (or establishing context) includes defining the criteria used by organizations to determine "when risk assessment results do not warrant risk responses, then assessment results could be fed directly to the risk monitoring step as a source of input."*

Table 6.3 Key Process Activities—Step 1

NIST	ISO/IEC
• Development of the risk management strategy • Development of organizational policies, procedures, standards, guidance, and resources	• Setting basic criteria (approach, evaluation, impact, and acceptance) • Defining the scope and boundaries • Establishing an organization

Table 6.4 Key Process Activities—Step 2

NIST	ISO/IEC
• Identify threats and vulnerabilities • Determine risk	• Identify threat • Identify existing controls • Identify vulnerabilities • Identify consequences • Assess consequences • Assess incident likelihood • Determine risk level • Evaluate risks

Table 6.5 Key Process Activities—Step 3

NIST	ISO/IEC
• Identify risk responses • Evaluate response alternatives • Risk response decision • Risk response implementation	• Define a risk treatment plan • Modify risks based on changes in the controls selected

Table 6.4, both focus on the determination of risk through the identification of threats and vulnerabilities and the analysis of the risk-related information to support a risk determination. One specific difference is an additional activity in the ISO/IEC risk assessment process for evaluating risks to determine if any actions should be taken based on the output of risk analysis and risk prioritization. Additionally, both processes apply the context established in Step 1 as an input into the assessment of risk within the risk management process.

In Table 6.5, the risk response (or risk treatment) options are selected for determining which courses of action (e.g., acceptance, avoidance, mitigation, etc.) to apply as a response to a particular risk. During the risk decision process in Step 3, both the NIST and the ISO/IEC recognize that regardless of the decision, there still remains a degree of residual risk that must be addressed and compared against the organization's risk tolerance [1]. However, as shown in Table 6.6, the ISO/IEC process (Step 4), includes an additional activity for the explicit and formal acceptance of residual risk. The NIST process also includes risk acceptance,

Table 6.6 Key Process Activities—Step 4

NIST	ISO/IEC
	• Accept information security risks

Table 6.7 Key Process Activities—Step 5

NIST	ISO/IEC
	• Communicate, share, and exchange risk information

Table 6.8 Key Process Activities—Step 6

NIST	ISO/IEC
• Develop a risk monitoring strategy • Monitor organizational information systems and environments of operation on an ongoing basis	• Monitor and review risk factors

but as a separate course of action (i.e., acceptance of risk in the NIST RMF Step 5 and Step 6) when responding to risk that has been determined to be within the organizational risk tolerance.

Both NIST and the ISO/IEC processes address the ongoing communications and sharing of risk-related information with decision-makers and stakeholders impacted by the risk response decisions. This activity uses the bi-directional pathway to communicate risk information to ensure those with responsibility for implementing the risk decisions understand the actions that must be taken. Unlike the ISO/IEC process shown in Table 6.7, the NIST process does not specifically identify the communication, sharing, and exchanging of risk information as a separate step, rather it is linked to other risk management activities such as risk monitoring where risk-based decisions are made as an integral part of every tier within the organization's risk management hierarchy, that is governance level, mission/business process level, and information system level.

In the final step outlined in Table 6.8, monitoring (Step 6), both the NIST and the ISO/IEC processes focus on monitoring risks (and risk factors) for any changes. The NIST process includes an additional requirement for the development of a formal risk monitoring strategy that serves as a separate function within the monitoring strategy for facilitating monitoring activities through a risk monitoring program. The risk monitoring program includes features such as monitoring for compliance, effectiveness, changes, and type (automated vs. manual) and frequency of monitoring. In the ISO/IEC risk management process, an emphasis is placed on not only monitoring risks and their factors, but also monitoring the risk management process itself to ensure that it is consistently applied and improvements in the process or relevance of risk criteria are integrated into the risk management approach.

SUMMARY

This chapter introduced the topic of organization-wide risk management. Risk management plays a critical role within the federal government, and the cultural adoption of information technology. The adoption of cloud services will need to be addressed by a government-wide approach in which risk management is integrated into the federal information security programs to achieve a "do once, use many times" approach.

In this chapter we also introduced to the federal risk management practices, and how over time, the maturity of these practices evolved. Since both federal agencies and service providers may adopt different risk management processes, understanding where the differences might exist is important to cost-effectively implement risk management programs. Therefore, we concluded with a brief comparison of the harmonization between the federal risk management practices and the international risk management standards.

REFERENCES

[1] Joint Task Force Transformation Initiative Interagency Working Group. NIST Special Publication (SP) 800-39, Managing information security risk: organization, mission, and information system view. Maryland: National Institute of Standards and Technology; 2011.

[2] Davis R. Federal Information Processing Standard (FIPS) Publication 31, Guidelines for automatic data processing physical security and risk management. Maryland: National Bureau of Standards; 1974.

[3] Davis R. Federal Information Processing Standard (FIPS) Publication 41, Computer security guidelines for implementing the privacy act of 1974. Maryland: National Bureau of Standards; 1974.

[4] Gilbert E. NIST Special Publication (SP) 500-174, Guide for selecting automated risk analysis tools. Maryland: National Institute of Standards and Technology; 1989.

[5] Guttman B, Roback E. NIST SP 800-11, An Introduction to Computer Security: The NIST Handbook. Maryland: National Institute of Standards and Technology; 1996.

[6] Swanson M, Guttman B. NIST Special Publication (SP) 800-14, Generally accepted principles and practices for securing information technology systems. Maryland: National Institute of Standards and Technology; 1996.

[7] Brock J. Information security risk assessment, practices of leading organizations. Washington, DC: US Government Accountability Office; 1999.

[8] Joint Task Force Transformation Initiative Interagency Working Group. NIST Special Publication (SP) 800-39, Managing information security risk: organization, mission, and information system view. Maryland: National Institute of Standards and Technology; 2011.

[9] Wilshusen G. Progress made on harmonizing policies and guidance for national security and non-national security systems. Washington, DC: US Government Accountability Office; 2010.

[10] Metheny M. [Internet]. Washington, DC: International information systems security certification consortium [cited January 25, 2012]. http://blog.isc2.org/isc2_blog/2010/12/cloud-adoption-risk-management.html.

[11] Van Roekel S. Security authorization of information system in cloud computing environments. Washington, DC: Executive Office of the President, Office of Management and Budget; 2011.

[12] Jansen W, Grance T. NIST Special Publication (SP) 800-144, Guidelines on Security and Privacy in Public Cloud Computing. Maryland: National Institute of Standards and Technology; 2011.

[13] Joint Task Force Transformation Initiative Interagency Working Group. NIST Special Publication (SP) 800-30 Revision 1, Guide for conducting risk assessments. Maryland: National Institute of Standards and Technology; 2011.

Comparison of federal and international security certification standards

7

INFORMATION IN THIS CHAPTER:

- Introduction
- Overview of Certification and Accreditation
- NIST and ISO/IEC Information Security Standards

INTRODUCTION

Managing information security and compliance requirements on an audit-by-audit basis can be a challenging and difficult task, specifically where security control assessment results and evidence are gathered, analyzed, and reported simultaneously. This duplication of effort can result in significant inefficiencies and an unproductive use of resources. However, the ability to leverage reuse and satisfy multiple compliance and contractual obligations requires a comprehensive information security and compliance framework. Additionally, the framework needs to be able to harmonize compliance requirements across both the federal government and industry.

Federal agencies, contractors, and service providers are required to adhere to a variety of mandates that cut across multiple federal laws, directives, regulations, standards, and policies. In addition to the federal requirements, some service providers are required to support other compliance obligations from a number of different industry security laws, regulations, and standards. The overlap in the security requirements and compliance obligations has resulted in service providers establishing multiple, and sometimes concurrent, information security and risk management programs. Some of these programs even operate independently due to the inferred incapability, resulting in unnecessary redundancies.

The federal government has, itself, struggled with similar problems. Federal information security programs are often complex and continuously changing. In addition, the increasing reliance on external service providers for information technology (IT) services, and the duplication of certification and accreditation (C&A) processes have required the federal government to transform existing processes to one that is more unified, agile, and streamlined. One of the goals of the

Federal Cloud Computing. DOI: http://dx.doi.org/10.1016/B978-0-12-809710-6.00007-X

new process is to unify the different information security frameworks across the federal government and establish a foundational set of common information security standards and guidelines. This new process also requires the involvement of a government-wide effort to continue to identify gaps and standardize federal security requirements, in addition to harmonizing with existing international security standards, thereby creating consistency in security standards and practices to support reciprocity by enabling the federal government to leverage existing authorizations, a necessary requirement for the Federal Risk and Authorization Management Program (FedRAMP).[1]

OVERVIEW OF CERTIFICATION AND ACCREDITATION

The concept of C&A[2] is a well-defined security methodology used both within the US government and internationally.[3] For illustrative purposes, Table 7.1 provides definitions for both *certification* and *accreditation* included in various security standards (and guidelines) used over the years from across the different federal communities (i.e., Civilian Agencies, the Department of Defense (DoD), and the Intelligence Community (IC)).[4] In reviewing the definitions, one can identify a common definitional purpose for the C&A process, even though the policies, procedures, and practices may be uniquely developed to describe how the different C&A processes are implemented for use within each of the federal communities. Therefore, a common definition of the C&A process can be summarized as follows:

> *A process for evaluating (or assessing) the technical and nontechnical security safeguards (or controls) implemented to protect the information technology systems or applications against threats and vulnerabilities to achieve an acceptable level of risk.*

In the next section, we will examine each of the federal C&A processes to gain a better understanding of how the federal government's security practices have evolved over time. In addition, the examination will serve to provide an insight into the significant challenges that exists for establishing and maintaining

---

[1]FedRAMP will be discussed in detail in Chapters 8—9.

[2]Sometimes referred to in the federal government as Security Assessment and Authorization.

[3]As an example is ISO/IEC 27001:2005, originally developed by the British Standards Institute (or the BSI Group's British Standards) BS7799-2:1998 in February 1998, an internationally recognized certification process for an organization's Information Security Management System (ISMS).

[4]From Wilshusen, G. Progress Made on Harmonizing Policies and Guidance or National Security and Non-National Security Systems. Washington, DC: US Government Accountability Office; 2010. *"The intelligence community is a federation of executive branch agencies and organizations that work separately and together to conduct intelligence activities necessary for the conduct of foreign relations and the protection of the national security of the United States."*

Table 7.1 Definitions of Certification and Accreditation

Date	Certification[a]	Accreditation[b]
1983[c]	A technical evaluation that establishes the extent to which a computer system or network design implementation meets a prespecified set of security requirements [1].	The authorization and approval granted to a system or network to process sensitive data in an operational environment [1].
1994	"A comprehensive analysis of the technical and nontechnical security features and other safeguards of a system to establish the extent to which a particular system meets a set of specified security requirements" [2].	"A formal declaration by a designated approving authority (DAA) that an AIS is approved to operate in a particular security mode using a prescribed set of safeguards" [2].
2000	"Comprehensive evaluation of the technical and nontechnical security features of an IS and other safeguards, made in support of the accreditation process, to establish the extent to which a particular design and implementation meets a set of specified security requirements" [3].	"Formal declaration by a Designated Approving Authority (DAA) that an IS is approved to operate in a particular security mode using a prescribed set of safeguards to an acceptable level of risk" [3].
2000	"Comprehensive evaluation of the technical and nontechnical security features of an IS and other safeguards made in support of the accreditation process, to establish the extent to which a particular design and implementation meets a set of specified security requirements" [4].	"Formal declaration by a Designated Approving Authority (DAA) that an IS is approved to operate in a particular security mode using a prescribed set of safeguards at an acceptable level of risk" [4].
2004	"A comprehensive assessment of the management, operational and technical security controls in an information system, made in support of security accreditation, to determine the extent to which the controls are implemented correctly, operating as intended, and producing the desired outcome with respect to meeting the security requirements for the system" [5].	"The official management decision given by a senior agency official to authorize operation of an information system and to explicitly accept the risk to agency operations (including mission, functions, image, or reputation), agency assets, or individuals, based on the implementation of an agreed-upon set of security controls" [5].
2007	"A comprehensive evaluation and validation of a DoD IS to establish the degree to which it complies with assigned IA controls based on standardized procedures" [6].	"A formal statement by a designated accrediting authority (DAA) regarding acceptance of the risk associated with operating a DoD information system (IS) and expressed as an authorization to operate (ATO), interim ATO (IATO), interim authorization to test (IATT), or denial of ATO (DATO)" [6].

(Continued)

Table 7.1 Definitions of Certification and Accreditation *Continued*

Date	Certification[a]	Accreditation[b]
2008	"A comprehensive assessment of the management, operational, and technical security controls in an information technology system, or for a particular item of information technology, made in support of accreditation" [7].	"Official management decisions that explicitly accept a defined level of risk associated with the operation of an information technology system at a particular level of security in a specific environment on behalf of an IC element" [7].
2010	A determination of the "extent to which the controls are implemented correctly, operating as intended, and producing the desired outcome with respect to meeting the security requirements for the information system" [8].	"The official management decision given by a senior organizational official to authorize operation of an information system and to explicitly accept the risk to organizational operations and assets, individuals, other organizations, and the Nation based on the implementation of an agreed-upon set of security controls" [8]
2010	"Comprehensive evaluation of the technical and nontechnical security safeguards of an information system to support the accreditation process that establishes the extent to which a particular design and implementation meets a set of specified security requirements" [9].	"Formal declaration by a Designated Accrediting Authority (DAA) or Principal Accrediting Authority (PAA) that an information system is approved to operate at an acceptable level of risk, based on the implementation of an approved set of technical, managerial, and procedural safeguards" [9].

[a]*Synonymous with security control assessment in some NIST, DoD, and CNSS references.*
[b]*FIPS 39, Glossary for computer systems security.*
[c]*Synonymous with security authorization in some NIST, DoD, and CNSS references.*

a standardized process that will be necessary to achieve reciprocity required for the cost-effective use of FedRAMP provisionally authorized cloud services.[5]

EVOLUTION OF THE FEDERAL C&A PROCESSES

Federal agencies are continuing to improve the ways to which they interconnect information systems. In recent years, federal agencies have begun to use more

---

[5]From Joint Task Force Transformation Initiative Interagency Working Group. NIST Special Publication (SP) 800-37 Revision 1, Guide for Applying the Risk Management Framework to Federal Information Systems: A Security Life Cycle Approach. Maryland: National Institute of Standards and Technology; 2010. "*Reciprocity is the mutual agreement among participating organizations to accept each other's security assessments in order to reuse information system resources and/or to accept each other's assessed security posture in order to share information. Reciprocity is best achieved by promoting the concept of transparency (i.e., making sufficient evidence regarding the security state of an information system).*"

agile development methodologies to maintain pace with quickly evolving technology architectures. Using agile methodologies also enables the federal government to be more adaptable and better equipped to support changes in their mission and business requirements. Similar to the technology changes discussed in Chapter 1, Introduction to the Federal Cloud Computing Strategy, as early as the 1970s, C&A processes used by the federal government have also evolved. The evolution of C&A processes and practices has been established through the development of a number of different standards (and guidelines). However, these processes and practices have also been applied differently, both between federal communities and federal agencies within the same community.[6]

In the remainder of this section, we will focus our discussion through a brief overview of the different C&A processes that have been used across the federal government with the intent of gaining an understanding into how they evolved and were changed. However, this section is not meant to be a comprehensive tutorial of the federal C&A processes, but instead it will serve to provide a summary of how information security and risk management practices have evolved and were implemented independently across the different federal communities.

Civilian agencies

In 1983, the National Bureau of Standards (NBS), now known as National Institute of Standards and Technology (NIST), published the Federal Information Processing Standard (FIPS) PUB 102, "*Guideline for Computer Certification and Accreditation.*" This publication provided federal agencies with a guide for establishing and carrying out a program and a technical process for computer security C&A[7] [1]. The key purpose of the publication was to achieve two main objectives:

- Establishing a program for certification and accreditation (e.g., policies and procedures, and roles and responsibilities); and
- Performing a certification and accreditation (e.g., planning, data collection, evaluation, and reporting findings).

---

[6]From Wilshusen, G. Progress Made on Harmonizing Policies and Guidance or National Security and Non-National Security Systems. Washington, DC: US Government Accountability Office; 2010. "*Prior to efforts to harmonize information security guidance, federal organizations had developed separate, and sometimes disparate, guidance for information security. For example, the National Security Agency used the National Information Systems Certification and Accreditation Process, the intelligence community used DCID 6/3, and DOD used the Department of Defense Information Technology Security Certification and Accreditation Process, which later became the DIACAP.*"

[7]From Burrows, J. Federal Information Processing Standard (FIPS) PUB 102, Guidelines for Computer Security Certification and Accreditation. Maryland: National Institute of Standards and Technology; 1983. "*The quality exhibited by a computer system that embodies its protection against internal failures, human errors, attacks, and natural catastrophes that might cause improper disclosure, modification, destruction, or denial of service.*"

The FIPS PUB 102 C&A process became the standard of practice for use by civilian federal agencies until 2004, when NIST published the first version of the Special Publication (SP) 800-37, *"Guide for the Security Certification and Accreditation of Federal Information Systems."*

During the period between the publication of FIPS PUB 102 and NIST SP 800-37, the Federal Information Security Management Act (FISMA)[8] became law (2002). As a result of the gap in guidance, Office of Management and Budget (OMB) released a memo through the Federal Chief Information Officers (CIO) Council to provide interim guidance for federal agencies until NIST published SP 800-37. This memo gave federal agencies the freedom to use another comparable security certification methodology provided it addressed the requirements covered in NIST SP 800-26 [10].[9]

When the first version of NIST SP 800-37 was published, it became the standard guidance used by civilian federal agencies for non-National Security Systems (NSSs) until the C&A process was revised in February 2010 through an updated version of NIST SP 800-37 (Revision 1). Although this new publication, led by NIST, was created through the Joint Task Force Transformation Initiative (JTFTI) Interagency Working Group. As will be revisited in a later section, the goal of the JTFTI was the development of a common set of core standards and guidelines that would be part of a government-wide C&A transformation effort. This new effort aimed at modernizing the traditional C&A process through the elimination of separate processes and the implementation of a risk-based security authorization approach. This new approach focused on creating a common information security framework that could be used across the federal government.[10] In addition, the focus was to make the process more dynamic by enabling near, real-time risk management and continuous monitoring through a single Risk Management Framework (RMF).[11]

---

[8]FISMA was discussed in detail in Chapter 5, Applying the NIST Risk Management Framework.

[9]NIST Special Publication (SP) 800-26, Security Self-Assessment Guide for Information Technology Systems, published in 2001, built upon the Federal IT Security Assessment Framework published by the Federal CIO Council in 2000 as a tool for use by federal agencies when evaluating their IT security programs. NIST Special Publication (SP) 800-26 was superseded by FIPS 200/ NIST Special Publication (SP) 800-53 (specification of security controls) and NIST Special Publication (SP) 800-53A (assessment of security control effectiveness).

[10]From Joint Task Force Transformation Initiative Interagency Working Group. NIST Special Publication (SP) 800-37 Revision 1, Guide for Applying the Risk Management Framework to Federal Information Systems: A Security Life Cycle Approach. Maryland: National Institute of Standards and Technology; 2010. *"NIST in partnership with the Department of Defense (DoD), the Office of the Director of National Intelligence (ODNI), and the Committee on National Security Systems (CNSS), has developed a common information security framework for the federal government and its contractors."*

[11]The RMF was discussed in detail in Chapter 5, Applying the NIST Risk Management Framework.

Department of Defense (DoD)

In 1994, the National Computer Security Center (NCSC),[12] originally known as the DoD Computer Security Center (CSC), a part of the National Security Agency (NSA), published the *"Introduction to Certification and Accreditation"* (or the "Blue Book"). This book was one of many standards and guidelines included within the *"Rainbow Series"*[13] and provided a high-level introduction for both the DoD and non-DoD communities on the basic concepts and policies associated with C&A, including roles and responsibilities and the risk management process. Following the publication of the "Blue Book," the *"Certification and Accreditation Process Handbook for Certifiers"* was published to provide more focused guidance on creating a "structured process by which to perform a C&A of a system" [10].

However, it was not until 1997 through the Defense-wide Information Security Program (DISSP)[14] that a DoD-wide C&A process was created. This new process, which became known as the Department of Defense Information Technology Security Certification and Accreditation Process (DITSCAP), was expected to be the standard C&A process for use across the DoD. DITSCAP not only established a standard process to certify and accredit information systems, but was also to be used to maintain the security posture of the Defense Information Infrastructure (DII) through an infrastructure approach to C&A [11].

After FISMA became law, the DoD C&A process changed again. In 2006, through an interim instruction, DITSCAP began the transition to a new dynamic process known as the Defense Information Assurance Certification and Accreditation Process (DIACAP). DIACAP, through a final official issuance in 2007, was designed as the DoD-wide C&A process to be used to support the transition of DoD information systems to Global Information Grid (GIG)[15] standards and a net-centric environment. In addition, this new process had the objective of enabling improved information sharing across the DoD through a standard C&A approach that focused on providing specific DoD-wide guidance on managing and disseminating enterprise standards and guidelines for Information Assurance (IA) design, implementation, configuration, validation, operation sustainment, and reporting [12].

---

[12]From Gallagher, P. NCSC-TG-031 Version 1, Certification and Accreditation Process Handbook for Certifiers. Maryland: National Computer Security Center; 1996. *The Introduction to Certification and Accreditation and the Certification and Accreditation Process Handbook for Certifiers were not developed specifically for the DoD, but instead provided guidance that could be used by DoD and Non-DoD agencies and organizations.*

[13]*Rainbow Series.* Available from: http://fas.org/irp/nsa/rainbow.htm.

[14]The Defense-wide Information Security Program (DISSP), currently known as the Defense-wide Information Assurance Program (DIAP), is a part of the Defense Information Systems Agency (DISA), Center for Information Systems Security (CISS).

[15]From England, G. DoDI 8000.01, Management of the Department of Defense Information Enterprise. Washington, DC: Department of Defense; 2009. *"The globally interconnected, end-to-end set of information capabilities for collecting, processing, storing, disseminating, and managing information on demand to warfighters, policy makers, and support personnel."*

Intelligence Community (IC)

The Director of Central Intelligence Directives (DCID), issued by the Director of Central Intelligence (DCI), were formerly used to provide intelligence community-wide policies and guidance, including governing information systems that stored, processed, or transmitted intelligence information. In 1983, DCID 1/16 was published (and later updated in 1988) by the DCI to establish a security policy for the processing, storage, and transmission of US foreign intelligence and counterintelligence in automated information systems (AIS) and networks. Additionally, the criteria in the DoD Trusted Computer System Evaluation Criteria (TCSEC), published by the NCSC in 1985, was identified by DCID 1/16 as the protective measures (administrative, environmental, and technical security requirements) that were required to be met by the AIS to protect sensitive information. However, DCID 1/16 later became superseded by DCID 6/3[16] in 1999, with an implementation manual being published in 2000[17] (and an update in 2002). DCID 6/3 became the first C&A process documented for use by the IC.

DCI policy was used within the IC until the establishment of the Office of the Director of National Intelligence (ODNI) in 2005. In 2008, the ODNI published the Intelligence Community Directive (ICD) 503, which was to supersede DCID 6/3.[18] The ICD 503 was established to implement the strategic goals[19] agreed upon by the IC CIO, the DoD CIO, OMB, and NIST. ICD 503 and other transition guidance in the form of directives and standards directed the use of Committee on National Security Systems (CNSS) policy and guidance, which in turn pointed to the harmonized NIST guidance [13].

Committee on National Security Systems (CNSS)

The CNSS[20] published the National Information Assurance Certification and Accreditation Process (NIACAP) in 2000. The NIACAP process, with similarities

---

[16]DCID 6/3 was developed to be a harmonization with DITSCAP.

[17]DCID 6/3, Manual, Protecting Sensitive Compartmented Information within Information Systems, April 2002.

[18]Although ICD 503 directed the use of polices and guidance created by the CNSS and NIST, respectively, DCID 6/3 is still widely used within the IC.

[19]From Public Affairs Office. ODNI News Release No. 10-07, DNI & DoD Chief Information Officers Announce Certification and Accreditation Transformation Goals. Washington, DC: Office of the Director of National Intelligence; 2007. *One of the goals was the institute of a common C&A that "will ensure system certifications and accreditations accomplished by one agency are valid for all agencies."*

[20]From Office of the Director of National Intelligence [Internet]. Maryland: Committee for National Security Systems, [cited February 15, 2012]. Available from: https://www.cnss.gov/CNSS/about/history. cfm. *"The Committee on National Security Systems (CNSS) originated in 1953 through its predecessor body, the U.S. Communications Security Board (USCSB). In 1990, it was established as the National Security Telecommunications and Information Systems Security Committee (NSTISSC) by National Security Directive (NSD) 42, 'National Policy for the Security of National Security Telecommunications and Information Systems.' This was reaffirmed by Executive Order (E.O.) 13284, 'Amendment of Executive Orders, and Other Actions, in Connection With the Establishment of the Department of Homeland Security' and E.O. 13231, 'Critical Infrastructure Protection in the Information Age' dated October 16, 2001. In 2001, under E.O. 13231, the President redesignated the NSTISSC as CNS."*

to the DITSCAP, was used by Civilian Agencies for NSS[21] for both national tele-communication and information systems. In 2005, the CNSS issued the *"National Policy on Certification and Accreditation of National Security Systems"* to give civilian federal agencies the flexibility to use NIACAP or an alternative C&A process. Since the CNSS is also a part of the JTFTI Interagency Working Group, it is "working with representatives from the Civil, Defense, and Intelligence Community to produce a unified information security framework" [14]. As a first step, CNSS Policy No. 22[22] was issued, establishing a requirement for the use of an organization-wide IA risk management program for all NSSs, which is consistent with the NIST standards and guidelines.

> **NOTE**
>
> Outside of the application of C&A processes on traditional information systems, there also exist C&A processes for interfaces used to control access or transfer information between differing security domains. The Secret and Below Interoperability (SABI) and the Top Secret/Sensitive Compartmented Information (SCI) and Below Interoperability (TSABI) processes have been developed by the DoD and IC for addressing risk associated with operating cross-domain solutions (CDS)[23] that control the connection between networks of different classification levels.
>
> - SABI C&A process follows the DIACAP C&A principles.
> - TSABI C&A process follows the DCID 6/3 C&A principles.
>
> In an effort to unify the two processes, the Unified Cross Domain Management Office (UCDMO), was created "to more effectively share information between security domains—that is, to move information between networks at different clearance (classification) levels throughout the federal government" [15]. The UCDMO, in an effort to unify the security requirements, published the CDS Overlay in December 2011,[24] which provides a single comprehensive set of security control guidance for CDS. The CDS Overlay is based on the NIST SP 800-53 Revision 3 and the CNSS-1253.
>
> In addition, the NIST SP 800-53 Revision 4 described CDSs as potential situations where additional conditions and controls might be required:
>
> *Security control baselines do not assume that information systems have to operate across multiple security policy domains. The baselines assume a flat view of information flows*
>
> *(Continued)*

[21]NSSs were briefly discussed in Chapter 5. However, NIST Special Publication (SP) 800-59, *"Guide for Identifying an Information System as a National Security System,"* provides additional guidance for the identification of NSSs.

[22]From Takai, T. CNSSP No. 22, Policy on Information Assurance Management for National Security Systems. Maryland: Committee on National Security Systems; 2012. *Upon this revision of CNSSP No. 22, CNSS Policy No. 6, "National Policy on Certification and Accreditation of National Security Systems," dated October 2005, and National Security Telecommunications and Information Systems Security Instruction (NSTISSI) 1000, "National Information Assurance Certification and Accreditation Process (NIACAP)" were canceled.*

[23]From Defense Information Systems Agency [Internet]. Maryland: Department of Defense; [cited April 05, 2016]. Available from: http://www.disa.mil/network-services/enterprise-connections/connection-process-guide/disn-service-appendices/cross-domain-solutions. *"A Cross Domain Solution (CDS) is a form of controlled interface that provides the ability to manually and/or automatically access and/or transfer information between different security domains."*

[24]DoD CIO and Assistant Director of National Intelligence and Intelligence Community CIO Memorandum, "Use of Unified Cross Domain Management Office (UCDMO) Baseline Cross Domain Solutions (CDSs)," December 1, 2011.

> **NOTE (CONTINUED)**
>
> *(i.e., the same security policies in different domains when information moves across authorization boundaries). To address cross-domain services and transactions, some subset of the AC-4 security control enhancements can be considered to ensure adequate protection of information when transferred between information systems with different security policies [16].*

TOWARDS A UNIFIED APPROACH TO C&A

As previously mentioned, the JTFTI, led by NIST, with participating members from the Civilian, Defense, and Intelligence Communities, is a joint partnership focused on transforming the federal government's C&A processes. One of the primary goals is to establish a "unified information security framework that harmonizes security standards and guidelines for NSSs and non-NSSs" [13]. This harmonization effort not only eliminates the duplication among the various federal C&A processes, but also aims at reducing the cost associated with managing and operating multiple overlapping C&A processes.

In addition, the unified process enables the government to more effectively share information when responding to the growing number of advanced cyber threats.

> **NOTE**
>
> The DoD Cloud Computing Strategy, published by the DoD CIO,[25] directed leveraging efforts such as FedRAMP, which prescribes the use of the NIST standards and guidelines as a standardized and streamlined C&A process for commercial and federal cloud providers [17].

These cyber threats have led to challenges within the federal government's ability to seamlessly share information and authorizations through reciprocity, effectively limiting the reuse of evidence when verifying the implementation of security controls between interconnected systems. As depicted in Fig. 7.1, the unification of C&A processes establishes a bridge across the various federal communities by harmonizing policies and guidance. This harmonization process focuses on using the NIST standards and guidelines currently applied to non-NSSs, leaving the DoD and IC to shift their focus to addressing the unique security requirements through community-specific[26] policies and guidance.

---

[25]The DoD CIO is also a permanent member of the FedRAMP Joint Authorization Board (JAB), along with the CIO of the US Department of Homeland Security (DHS) and the US General Services Administration (GSA). Available from: https://www.fedramp.gov/files/2015/01/JAB-Charter-2.0.pdf.

[26]From Wilshusen, G. Progress Made on Harmonizing Policies and Guidance or National Security and Non-National Security Systems. Washington, DC: US Government Accountability Office; 2010. *"FISMA provides a further exception to compliance with NIST standards. It permits an agency to use more stringent information security standards if it certifies that its standards are at least as stringent as the NIST standards and are otherwise consistent with policies and guidelines issued under FISMA."*

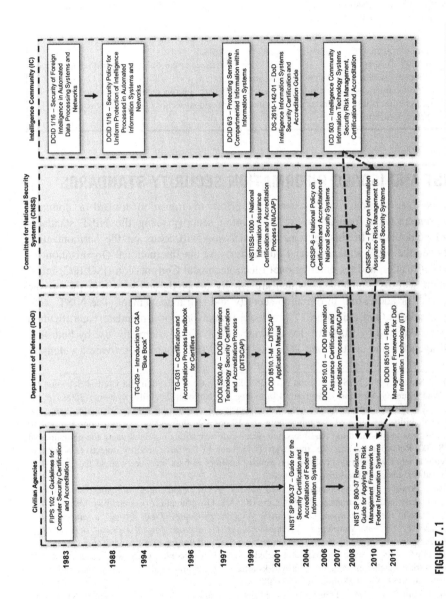

FIGURE 7.1

Civilian agency, DoD, and IC C&A processes.

> **NOTE**
>
> There are several key differences between the information and system categorization steps and the control selection processes described between the CNSS policies and the NIST standards and guidelines. These differences [13] include:
>
> - *System Categorization*—different methodologies[27] are used to categorize the impact associated with information that is stored, processed, or transmitted.
> - *Security Control Selection*—selection of control baselines or control profiles will be conducted differently within each of these communities.
> - *Program Management Controls*—program management controls required for nonnational information security programs will be optional for national security system information security programs.

NIST AND ISO/IEC INFORMATION SECURITY STANDARDS

In the last section, we discussed an effort to transition toward a common government-wide foundation for information security using the NIST standards (and guidelines). In this section, the discussion will focus on the harmonization between the NIST standards (and guidelines) and the International Organization for Standardization and the International Electrotechnical Commission (ISO/IEC) information security standards,[28] which are widely adopted for use within the private sector[29] for addressing information security and risk management. The NIST security standards (and guidelines)[30] provide a framework for a mandatory certification process directed by FISMA[31] to authorize information systems for use by both federal agencies and contractors. Whereas, the ISO/IEC standards provide a voluntary

---

[27]From Shaeffer, R. CNSS Instruction No. 1253, Security Categorization and Control Selection for National Security Systems. Maryland: Committee on National Security Systems; 2009. In the National Security Community, the potential impact levels determined for confidentiality, integrity, and availability are retained, meaning there are 27 possible three-value combinations for NSI or NSS, as opposed to the three possible single-value categorizations obtained using the guidelines in FIPS 200. Retaining the discrete impact levels for each of the three security objectives is done to provide a better granularity in allocating security controls to baselines, and should thereby reduce the need for subsequent tailoring of controls.

[28]From Powner, D. Cyberspace: United States Faces Challenges in Addressing Global Cybersecurity and Governance. Washington, DC: US Government Accountability Office; 2010. *"The IEC and the International Organization for Standardization (ISO), through a joint technical committee (JTC), have developed information security standards for all types of organizations, including commercial enterprises, government agencies, and not-for-profit organizations."*

[29]The ISMS is a systematic approach that includes the policies, peoples, processes practices, and technologies for managing information security risks affecting the confidentiality, integrity, and availability.

[30]FIPS and NIST Special Publication (SP) 800 series.

[31]From Joint Task Force Transformation Initiative Interagency Working Group. NIST Special Publication (SP) 800-53 Revision 4 (Initial Public Draft), Security and Privacy Controls for Federal Information Systems and Organizations. Maryland: National Institute of Standards and Technology; 2012. *"Although the NIST security standards (and guidelines) were developed in response to FISMA they are consistent with ISO/IEC 27001, but provide additional implementation detail for use by the federal government and its contractors."*

Table 7.2 Mapping of Information Security and Risk Management Programs to NIST and ISO/IEC Standards (and Guidelines)

Component	NIST	ISO/IEC
Risk Management (*including Risk Assessment Methodology*)	• NIST SP 800-39—Managing Information Security Risk: Organization, Mission, and Information System View • NIST SP 800-30 Revision 1—Guide for Conducting Risk Assessments	• ISO/IEC 30000—Risk management—Principles and guidelines • ISO/IEC 30010—Risk assessment techniques • ISO/IEC 27005—Information technology—Security techniques—Information security risk management
Information Security Framework	• NIST SP 800-37—Guide for Applying the Risk Management Framework to Federal Information Systems	• ISO/IEC 27001—Information technology—Security techniques—Information security management systems—Requirements
Information Security Controls	• NIST SP 800-53—Security and Privacy Controls for Federal Information Systems and Organizations	• ISO/IEC 27002—Information technology—Security techniques—Code of practices for information security management
Information Security Assessment/Auditing	• NIST SP 800-53A—Guide for Assessing the Security Controls in Federal Information Systems and Organizations, Building Effective Security Assessment Plans	• ISO/IEC 27007—Information technology—Security techniques—Guidelines for information security management systems auditing • ISO/IEC 27008—Information technology—Information technology—Security techniques—Guidelines for auditors on information security management systems controls

certification process for use by non-government organizations to confirm their management system incorporating generally accepted information security best practices. For comparison, Table 7.2 provides a list of major references that have been published by NIST and the ISO/IEC for implementing the different components of a comprehensive information security and risk management program.

In previous chapters we examined both the NIST RMF[32] and the NIST Risk Management[33] process. In this section, the discussion will shift to provide a basic understanding of the relationship between the different information security and risk management standards, focusing on highlighting their compatibility, but limiting the discussion of recommending any specific methods and methodologies for aligning or integrating the different processes. To support the discussion, Fig. 7.2 provides a

---

[32]See Chapter 5, Applying the Risk Management Framework.
[33]See Chapter 6, Risk Management.

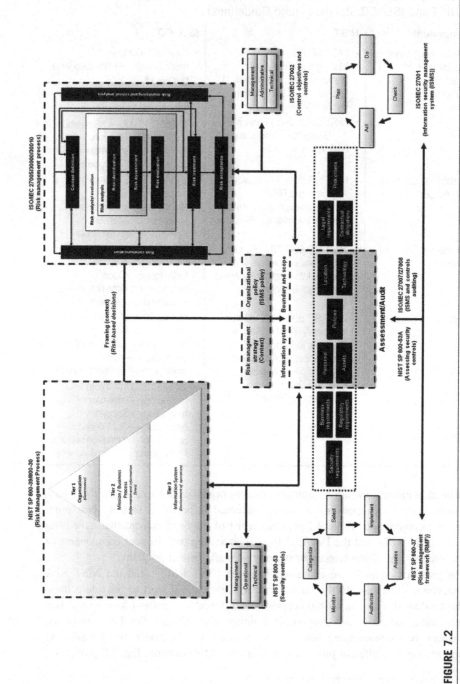

FIGURE 7.2

Relationship between NIST and ISO/IEC information security standards.

point of reference for use by service providers that have already invested in becoming certified or are currently operating under the ISO/IEC standards. By defining the relationship between the different information security and risk management standards, service providers will be better positioned to align their information security programs, and enabling them to reuse their exiting investment.

> **NOTE**
>
> The NIST FISMA Implementation Project includes several initiatives under the second phase (Phase II: Implementation and Assessment Aids) of the project. The ISO Harmonization Initiative focuses on identifying common relationships and mappings of FISMA standards, guidelines, and requirements with: (i) ISO/IEC 27000 series information security management standards; and (ii) ISO/IEC 9000 and 17000 series quality management, and laboratory testing, inspection, and accreditation standards. This harmonization is important for minimizing duplication of effort for organizations that must demonstrate compliance to both FISMA and ISO requirements [18].

BOUNDARY AND SCOPE DEFINITION

The NIST RMF and the ISO/IEC "Plan-Do-Check-Act" (PDCA) focuses on applying a structured, risk-based approach for the integration of information security. Both NIST (800-37 Revision 1—RMF Step 1) and the ISO/IEC (27001—Clause 4.2.1.a) require the identification of a boundary[34] around the information system.[35] However, within the ISO/IEC process, the scope (or boundary) typically includes the organization and the information system that maintains and has control over the information system. To effectively characterize the boundary and scope of protection,[36] processes require the

---

[34]From Joint Task Force Transformation Initiative Interagency Working Group. NIST Special Publication (SP) 800-37 Revision 1, Guide for Applying the Risk Management Framework to Federal Information Systems: A Security Life Cycle Approach. Maryland: National Institute of Standards and Technology; 2010. *Authorization boundary is "all components of an information system to be authorized for operation by an authorizing official and excludes separately authorized systems, to which the information system is connected."*

[35]From Joint Task Force Transformation Initiative Interagency Working Group. NIST Special Publication (SP) 800-37 Revision 1, Guide for Applying the Risk Management Framework to Federal Information Systems: A Security Life Cycle Approach. Maryland: National Institute of Standards and Technology; 2010. *"A discrete set of information resources (e.g., personnel and information technology) organized for the collection, processing, maintenance, use, sharing, dissemination, or disposition of information."*

[36]From Joint Task Force Transformation Initiative Interagency Working Group. NIST Special Publication (SP) 800-37 Revision 1, Guide for Applying the Risk Management Framework to Federal Information Systems: A Security Life Cycle Approach. Maryland: National Institute of Standards and Technology; 2010. *"Well-defined boundaries establish the scope of protection for organizational information systems (i.e., what the organization agrees to protect under its direct management control or within the scope of its responsibilities) and include the people, processes, and information technologies that are part of the systems supporting the organization's missions and business processes."*

organization to define the associated policies,[37] assets, technologies, locations, and personnel.

SECURITY POLICY

After the boundary and scope have been defined, the organization creates an information security policy (addressed through the NIST SP 800-53 XX-1 controls and the *information security management system* (ISMS) policy[38] in ISO/IEC 27001), which establishes the management's direction and principles for governing the information system. In addition, the security policy[39] should, at a minimum, include a purpose and scope (SP 800-53 XX-1 controls), identify the roles and responsibilities (SP 800-53 XX-1 controls and 27001—A.6.1.3), address a statement of compliance that is supported through a management commitment (SP 800-53 XX-1 controls and 27001—A.6.1.1), and coordinate among organizational entities (SP 800-53 XX-1 controls and 27001—A.6.1.2).

> **NOTE**
>
> In NIST SP 800-53, "*Security and Privacy Controls for Federal Information Systems and Organizations*," the first control in each control family[40] (e.g., Access Controls, Identification and Authentication, Incident Response, etc.) requires identifying the policies and procedures that are implemented by the remaining security controls (and control enhancements) included in the family of controls.
>
> The policies may be inherited completely (common control[41]) from the organizational policies or may be derived partially (hybrid control[42]) from an organizational policy that is further defined in an information system-specific policy.

RISK MANAGEMENT STRATEGY (CONTEXT)

Both NIST and ISO/IEC require an organizational policy (or ISMS policy) that aligns with the risk management strategy[43] (or context). The risk management strategy is developed as an output of the risk framing (or context definition). The framing[44] (context) definition is established as a part of the risk management process[45] discussed in Chapter 6, Risk management.

RISK MANAGEMENT PROCESS

Before the allocation[46] of the security controls, the organization needs to understand the risks by conducting a risk assessment. Both NIST (800-37 Revision 1—RMF Step 2) and the ISO/IEC (27001—Clause 4.2.1.d−g) address the selection of security controls before and after the risk assessment. In addition, NIST and the ISO/IEC have a separate function within the risk management process (discussed in see chapter: Risk management) where the risks are evaluated based on criteria established during the framing (or context definition) step. This criterion assists in determining which of the risk response (or risk treatment) options in Table 7.3 would be appropriate as a treatment for the risk.

One notable difference between the NIST and ISO/IEC processes is the explicit requirements for the acceptance of risk defined in the risk treatment plan and the residual risk acceptance. For example, NIST does specify the acceptance of risk; it is performed as a result of the approval of the system security plan (800-37 Revision 1—RMF Step 3) and authorization to operate (800-37 Revision 1—RMF Step 5). However, both the NIST and ISO/IEC risk management processes include the ongoing monitoring where risk management becomes a continual process.[47]

---

[43]From Joint Task Force Transformation Initiative Interagency Working Group. NIST Special Publication (SP) 800-39, Managing Information Security Risk: Organization, Mission, and Information System View. Maryland: National Institute of Standards and Technology; 2011. *"How the organization intends to assess risk, respond to risk, and monitor risks."*

[44]From Joint Task Force Transformation Initiative Interagency Working Group. NIST Special Publication (SP) 800-39, Managing Information Security Risk: Organization, Mission, and Information System View. Maryland: National Institute of Standards and Technology; 2011. *"Describes the environment in which risk-based decisions are made."*

[45]See Chapter 6 for a comparison of the NIST and ISO/IEC Risk Management processes.

[46]Allocation of security controls can occur by assigning responsibility for security controls at each of the three tiers (governance, mission/business process, or information system levels) in the risk management hierarchy.

[47]From Joint Task Force Transformation Initiative Interagency Working Group. NIST Special Publication (SP) 800-39, Managing Information Security Risk: Organization, Mission, and Information System View. Maryland: National Institute of Standards and Technology; 2011. *"Monitor organizational information systems and environments of operation on an ongoing basis to verify compliance, determine effectiveness of risk response measures, and identify changes."*

Table 7.3 Comparison of Options for Risk Response or Treatment

NIST	ISO/IEC
• Risk acceptance	• Risk reduction
• Risk avoidance	• Risk retention
• Risk sharing	• Risk avoidance
• Risk transfer	• Risk transfer

SECURITY OBJECTIVES AND CONTROLS

The selection (and implementation) of control objectives and controls is a similar activity under both the NIST and ISO/IEC processes. The selection process focuses on identifying those control objectives and controls that meet the requirements of the organizational assessment of risk identified during the execution of the risk assessment, in addition to requirements derived from other sources such as business requirements, regulatory requirements, legal requirements, and contractual obligations. One significant difference that exists is in the scope and organization of the security controls included in NIST security control families (800-53—Appendix F) and the ISO/IEC security control clauses (27001—Annex A). In Table 7.4, a mapping is provided that illustrates, the security control clauses in ISO/IEC 27001 and the equivalent security controls in NIST SP 800-53. Although the security control mappings provide a high-level comparison of the gaps between the organization of control objectives and controls included in ISO/IEC 27001 and NIST SP 800-53, "there is still some degree of subjectivity in the mapping analysis because the mappings are not always one-to-one and may not be completely equivalent" [19].

NOTE

The NIST SP 800-53 AC control family is defined as follows:

Organizations must limit information system access to authorized users, processes acting on behalf of authorized users or devices (including other information systems) and to the types of transactions and functions that authorized users are permitted to exercise [19].

The AC-1 security control requirement states:

AC-1 ACCESS CONTROL POLICY AND PROCEDURES

Control: The organization:

a. Develops, documents, and disseminates to [Assignment: organization-defined personnel or roles]:
  1. An access control policy that addresses purpose, scope, roles, responsibilities, management commitment, coordination among organizational entities, and compliance; and
  2. Procedures to facilitate the implementation of the access control policy and associated access controls; and
b. Reviews and updates the current:
  1. Access control policy [Assignment: organization-defined frequency]; and
  2. Access control procedures [Assignment: organization-defined frequency].

(Continued)

> **NOTE (CONTINUED)**
>
> Supplemental guidance: This control addresses the establishment of policy and procedures for the effective implementation of selected security controls and control enhancements in the AC family. Policy and procedures reflect applicable federal laws, Executive Orders, directives, regulations, policies, standards, and guidance. Security program policies and procedures at the organization level may make the need for system-specific policies and procedures unnecessary. The policy can be included as part of the general information security policy for organizations or conversely, can be represented by multiple policies reflecting the complex nature of certain organizations. The procedures can be established for the security program in general and for particular information systems, if needed. The organizational risk management strategy is a key factor in establishing policy and procedures.

Table 7.4 Mapping of ISO/IEC Control Objectives and Controls NIST Controls [16]

ISO/IEC 27001 Controls	NIST SP 800-53 Controls[a]
A.5 Information security policies	
A.5.1 Management direction for information security	
A.5.1.1 Policies for information security	All XX-1 controls
A.5.1.2 Review of the policies for information security	All XX-1 controls
A.6 Organization of information security	
A.6.1 Internal organization	
A.6.1.1 Information security roles and responsibilities	All XX-1 controls, CM-9, CP-2, PS-7, SA-3, SA-9, PM-2, PM-10
A.6.1.2 Segregation of duties	AC-5
A.6.1.3 Contact with authorities	IR-6
A.6.1.4 Contact with special interest groups	SI-5, PM-15
A.6.1.5 Information security in project management	SA-3, SA-9, SA-15
A.6.2 Mobile devices and teleworking	
A.6.2.1 Mobile device policy	AC-17, AC-18, AC-19
A.6.2.2 Teleworking	AC-3, AC-17, PE-17
A.7 Human resources security	
A.7.1 Prior to employment	
A.7.1.1 Screening	PS-3, SA-21
A.7.1.2 Terms and conditions of employment	PL-4, PS-6
A.7.2 During employment	
A.7.2.1 Management responsibilities	PL-4, PS-6, PS-7, SA-9
A.7.2.2 Information security awareness, education, and training	AT-2, AT-3, CP-3, IR-2, PM-13

(Continued)

Table 7.4 Mapping of ISO/IEC Control Objectives and Controls NIST Controls [16] *Continued*

ISO/IEC 27001 Controls	NIST SP 800-53 Controls[a]
A.7.2.3 Disciplinary process	PS-8
A.7.3 Termination and change of employment	
A.7.3.1 Termination or change of employment responsibilities	PS-4, PS-5
A.8 Asset management	
A.8.1 Responsibility for assets	
A.8.1.1 Inventory of assets	CM-8
A.8.1.2 Ownership of assets	CM-8
A.8.1.3 Acceptable use of assets	PL-4
A.8.1.4 Return of assets	PS-4, PS-5
A.8.2 Information classification	
A.8.2.1 Classification of information	RA-2
A.8.2.2 Labeling of information	MP-3
A.8.2.3 Handling of assets	MP-2, MP-4, MP-5, MP-6, MP-7, PE-16, PE-18, PE- 20, SC-8, SC-28
A.8.3 Media handling	
A.8.3.1 Management of removable media	MP-2, MP-4, MP-5, MP-6, MP-7
A.8.3.2 Disposal of media	MP-6
A.8.3.3 Physical media transfer	MP-5
A.9 Access control	
A.9.1 Business requirement of access control	
A.9.1.1 Access control policy	AC-1
A.9.1.2 Access to networks and network services	AC-3, AC-6
A.9.2 User access management	
A.9.2.1 User registration and de-registration	AC-2, IA-2, IA-4, IA-5, IA-8
A.9.2.2 User access provisioning	AC-2
A.9.2.3 Management of privileged access rights	AC-2, AC-3, AC-6, CM-5
A.9.2.4 Management of secret authentication information of users	IA-5
A.9.2.5 Review of user access rights	AC-2
A.9.2.6 Removal or adjustment of access rights	AC-2
A.9.3 User responsibilities	
A.9.3.1 Use of secret authentication information	IA-5
A.9.4 System and application access control	
A.9.4.1 Information access restriction	AC-3, AC-24
A.9.4.2 Secure logon procedures	AC-7, AC-8, AC-9, IA-6
A.9.4.3 Password management system	IA-5
A.9.4.4 Use of privileged utility programs	AC-3, AC-6
A.9.4.5 Access control to program source code	AC-3, AC-6, CM-5

(Continued)

Table 7.4 Mapping of ISO/IEC Control Objectives and Controls NIST Controls [16] *Continued*

ISO/IEC 27001 Controls	NIST SP 800-53 Controls[a]
A.10 Cryptography	
A.10.1 Cryptographic controls	
A.10.1.1 Policy on the use of cryptographic controls	SC-13
A.10.1.2 Key management	SC-12, SC-17
A.11 Physical and environmental security	
A.11.1 Secure areas	
A.11.1.1 Physical security perimeter	PE-3*
A.11.1.2 Physical entry controls	PE-2, PE-3, PE-4, PE-5
A.11.1.3 Securing offices, rooms and facilities	PE-3, PE-5
A.11.1.4 Protecting against external and environmental threats	CP-6, CP-7, PE-9, PE-13, PE-14, PE-15, PE-18, PE- 19
A.11.1.5 Working in secure areas	SC-42(3)*
A.11.1.6 Delivery and loading areas	PE-16
A.11.2 Equipment	
A.11.2.1 Equipment siting and protection	PE-9, PE-13, PE-14, PE-15, PE-18, PE-19
A.11.2.2 Supporting utilities	CP-8, PE-9, PE-10, PE-11, PE-12, PE-14, PE-15
A.11.2.3 Cabling security	PE-4, PE-9
A.11.2.4 Equipment maintenance	MA-2, MA-6
A.11.2.5 Removal of assets	MA-2, MP-5, PE-16
A.11.2.6 Security of equipment and assets off-premises	AC-19, AC-20, MP-5, PE-17
A.11.2.7 Secure disposal or reuse of equipment	MP-6
A.11.2.8 Unattended user equipment	AC-11
A.11.2.9 Clear desk and clear screen policy	AC-11, MP-2, MP-4
A.12 Operations security	
A.12.1 Operational procedures and responsibilities	
A.12.1.1 Documented operating procedures	All XX-1 controls, SA-5
A.12.1.2 Change management	CM-3, CM-5, SA-10
A.12.1.3 Capacity management	AU-4, CP-2(2), SC-5(2)
A.12.1.4 Separation of development, testing, and operational environments	CM-4(1)*, CM-5*
A.12.2 Protection from malware	
A.12.2.1 Controls against malware	AT-2, SI-3
A.12.3 Backup	
A.12.3.1 Information backup	CP-9

(Continued)

Table 7.4 Mapping of ISO/IEC Control Objectives and Controls NIST Controls [16] *Continued*

ISO/IEC 27001 Controls	NIST SP 800-53 Controls[a]
A.12.4 Logging and monitoring	
A.12.4.1 Event logging	AU-3, AU-6, AU-11, AU-12, AU-14
A.12.4.2 Protection of log information	AU-9
A.12.4.3 Administrator and operator logs	AU-9, AU-12
A.12.4.4 Clock synchronization	AU-8
A.12.5 Control of operational software	
A.12.5.1 Installation of software on operational systems	CM-5, CM-7(4), CM-7(5), CM-11
A.12.6 Technical vulnerability management	
A.12.6.1 Management of technical vulnerabilities	RA-3, RA-5, SI-2, SI-5
A.12.6.2 Restrictions on software installation	CM-11
A.12.7 Information systems audit considerations	
A.12.7.1 Information systems audit controls	AU-5*
A.13 Communications security	
A.13.1 Network security management	
A.13.1.1 Network controls	AC-3, AC-17, AC-18, AC-20, SC-7, SC-8, SC-10
A.13.1.2 Security of network services	CA-3, SA-9
A.13.1.3 Segregation in networks	AC-4, SC-7
A.13.2 Information transfer	
A.13.2.1 Information transfer policies and procedures	AC-4, AC-17, AC-18, AC-19, AC-20, CA-3, PE-17, SC-7, SC-8, SC-15
A.13.2.2 Agreements on information transfer	CA-3, PS-6, SA-9
A.13.2.3 Electronic messaging	SC-8
A.13.2.4 Confidentiality or nondisclosure agreements	PS-6
A.14 System acquisition, development and maintenance	
A.14.1 Security requirements of information systems	
A.14.1.1 Information security requirements analysis and specification	PL-2, PL-7, PL-8, SA-3, SA-4
A.14.1.2 Securing application services on public networks	AC-3, AC-4, AC-17, SC-8, SC-13
A.14.1.3 Protecting application services transactions	AC-3, AC-4, SC-7, SC-8, SC-13
A.14.2 Security in development and support processes	
A.14.2.1 Secure development policy	SA-3, SA-15, SA-17
A.14.2.2 System change control procedures	CM-3, SA-10, SI-2

(Continued)

Table 7.4 Mapping of ISO/IEC Control Objectives and Controls NIST Controls [16] *Continued*

ISO/IEC 27001 Controls	NIST SP 800-53 Controls[a]
A.14.2.3 Technical review of applications after operating platform changes	CM-3, CM-4, SI-2
A.14.2.4 Restrictions on changes to software packages	CM-3, SA-10
A.14.2.5 Secure system engineering principles	SA-8
A.14.2.6 Secure development environment	SA-3*
A.14.2.7 Outsourced development	SA-4, SA-10, SA-11, SA-12, SA-15
A.14.2.8 System security testing	CA-2, SA-11
A.14.2.9 System acceptance testing	SA-4, SA-12(7)
A.14.3 Test data	
A.14.3.1 Protection of test data	SA-15(9)*
A.15 Supplier relationships	
A.15.1 Information security in supplier relationships	
A.15.1.1 Information security policy for supplier relationships	SA-12
A.15.1.2 Address security within supplier agreements	SA-4, SA-12
A.15.1.3 Information and communication technology supply chain	SA-12
A.15.2 Supplier service delivery management	
A.15.2.1 Monitoring and review of supplier services	SA-9
A.15.2.2 Managing changes to supplier services	SA-9
A.16 Information security incident management	
A.16.1 Managing of information security incidents and improvements	
A.16.1.1 Responsibilities and procedures	IR-8
A.16.1.2 Reporting information security events	AU-6, IR-6
A.16.1.3 Reporting information security weaknesses	SI-2
A.16.1.4 Assessment of and decision on information security events	AU-6, IR-4
A.16.1.5 Response to information security incidents	IR-4
A.16.1.6 Learning from information security incidents	IR-4
A.16.1.7 Collection of evidence	AU-4*, AU-9*, AU-10(3)*, AU-11*
A.17 Information security aspects of business continuity management	

(Continued)

Table 7.4 Mapping of ISO/IEC Control Objectives and Controls NIST Controls [16] *Continued*

ISO/IEC 27001 Controls	NIST SP 800-53 Controls[a]
A.17.1 Information security continuity	
A.17.1.1 Planning information security continuity	CP-2
A.17.1.2 Implementing information security continuity	CP-6, CP-7, CP-8, CP-9, CP-10, CP-11, CP-13
A.17.1.3 Verify, review, and evaluate information security continuity	CP-4
A.17.2 Redundancies	
A.17.2.1 Availability of information processing facilities	CP-2, CP-6, CP-7
A.18 Compliance	
A.18.1 Compliance with legal and contractual requirements	
A.18.1.1 Identification of applicable legislation and contractual requirements	All XX-1 controls
A.18.1.2 Intellectual property rights	CM-10
A.18.1.3 Protection of records	AC-3, AC-23, AU-9, AU-10, CP-9, SC-8, SC-8(1), SC-13, SC-28, SC-28(1)
A.18.1.4 Privacy and protection of personal information	Appendix J Privacy controls
A.18.1.5 Regulation of cryptographic controls	IA-7, SC-12, SC-13, SC-17
A.18.2 Information security reviews	
A.18.2.1 Independent review of information security	CA-2(1), SA-11(3)
A.18.2.2 Compliance with security policies and standards	All XX-1 controls, CA-2
A.18.2.3 Technical compliance review	CA-2

[a]*indicates that the ISO/IEC control does not fully satisfy the intent of the NIST control.*

Examining the mapping in Table 7.4, the AC family of controls are distributed among the various security control clauses (27001—Annex A). For example, AC-1 is covered in multiple ISO/IEC control objectives and controls. Table 7.5 provides a mapping of AC-1 to the ISO/IEC standards covered in the multiple control objectives and controls.

Once the control objectives and controls have been selected, they need to be documented through a System Security Plan (*800-37 Revision 1—RMF Step 2*) and the Statement of Applicability (*27001—Clause 4.2.1.j*). Although the specification of the formats may differ, the specific scope as outlined in Table 7.6 provides a general comparison of the requirements.

Table 7.5 Example Comparison of NIST (AC-1) and ISO/IEC (27001) Requirements

NIST	ISO/IEC
Control: The organization develops, disseminates, and reviews/updates [Assignment: organization-defined frequency]: a. A formal, documented access control policy that addresses purpose, scope, roles, responsibilities, management commitment, coordination among organizational entities, and compliance; and	• A.5.1.1 Information security policy • A.5.1.2 Review of the information security policy • A.6.1.1 Information security roles and responsibilities • A.9.1.1 Access control policy • A.12.1.1 Documented operating procedures • A.18.1.1 Identification of applicable legislation and contractual requirements
b. Formal, documented procedures to facilitate the implementation of the access control policy and associated access controls. Supplemental Guidance: This control is intended to produce the policy and procedures that are required for the effective implementation of selected security controls and control enhancements in the access control family. The policy and procedures are consistent with applicable federal laws, Executive Orders, directives, policies, regulations, standards, and guidance. Existing organizational policies and procedures may make the need for additional specific policies and procedures unnecessary. The access control policy can be included as part of the general information security policy for the organization. Access control procedures can be developed for the security program in general and for a particular information system, when required. The organizational risk management strategy is a key factor in the development of the access control policy.	• A.18.2.2 Compliance with security policies and standards

Table 7.6 Comparison of SSP and SOA Requirements

NIST	ISO/IEC
• Security control title • Security controls implemented or planned to be implemented • Scoping guidance applied and what type of consideration • Indication of common control and the responsible party for its implementation	• Selected control objective and controls • Reason for selection • Identification of those currently implemented • Exclusions and justification of exclusion

SUMMARY

This chapter introduced the federal C&A processes. These processes, which have evolved over time, have been used by federal agencies to certify and accredit their information systems. More recently, these processes have followed a multiyear process of convergences into a single unified process, led by NIST and supplemented by community-driven requirements to accommodate specific security requirements and information sensitivity.

In addition to the federal certification standards, the ISO/IEC has developed a comparable set of standards that have been used by the private sector and internationally, and includes a similar process for certifying the organizations' information systems. The ISO/IEC process requires the implementation, operation, monitoring, review, and maintenance of an ISMS that is adequately protected based on information security requirements determined by a risk assessment and other applicable requirements (e.g., business, regulatory, contractual, and legal).

As the security and compliance requirements consistently grow and change, organizations will have to adjust their approaches, tools, and techniques to ensure that not only their security programs can respond to the changes in the threat environment, but can also leverage the efficiency and effectiveness of unified information security frameworks to assist them in addressing multiple security laws, regulation, and standards.

REFERENCES

[1] Burrows J. Federal Information Processing Standard (FIPS) PUB 102, Guidelines for computer security certification and accreditation. Maryland: National Institute of Standards and Technology; 1983.

[2] Gallagher P. NCSC-TG-029, Introduction to certification and accreditation. Maryland: National Computer Security Center; 1994.

[3] Gallagher P NSTISSI No. 1000, National Information Assurance Certification and Accreditation Process (NIACAP). Maryland: National Security Telecommunications and Information Systems Security Committee; 2000.

[4] Money A. DoD 8510.1-M, Department of Defense Information Technology Security Certification and Accreditation Process (DIACAP): application manual. Washington, DC: Department of Defense; 2000.

[5] Ross R, Swanson M, Stoneburnder G, Katzke S, Johnson A. NIST Special Publication (SP) 800-37, Guide for the security certification and accreditation of federal information systems. Maryland: National Institute of Standards and Technology; 2004.

[6] Grimes J. DoDI 8510.01, DoD Information Assurance Certification and Accreditation Process (DIACAP). Washington, DC: Department of Defense; 2007.

[7] McConnell JM. ICD Number 503, Intelligence community information technology system security risk management, certification, and accreditation. Washington, DC: Office of the Director of National Intelligence; 2008.

[8] Joint Task Force Transformation Initiative Interagency Working Group. NIST Special Publication (SP) 800-37 Revision 1, Guide for applying the risk management framework to federal information systems: a security life cycle approach. Maryland: National Institute of Standards and Technology; 2010.

[9] Shaeffer R. CNSS Instruction No. 4009, National Information Assurance (IA) glossary.. Maryland: Committee on National Security Systems; 2010.

[10] Forman M. Guidance to Assist Agencies with Certification and Accreditation. Washington, DC: Executive Office of the President, Office of Management and Budget; 2003.

[11] Valletta A. DoDI 5200.40, DoD Information Assurance Certification and Accreditation Process (DIACAP). Virginia: Department of Defense; 1997.

[12] Grimes J. DoDI 8510.01, DoD Information Assurance Certification and Accreditation Process (DIACAP). Virginia: Department of Defense; 2007.

[13] Wilshusen G. Progress made on harmonizing policies and guidance or national security and non-national security systems. Washington, DC: US Government Accountability Office; 2010.

[14] Takai T. CNSSP No. 22, Policy on information assurance management for national security systems. Maryland: Committee on National Security Systems; 2012.

[15] Public Affairs Office. ODNI News Release No. 08-07, DoD CIO and DNI CIO establish new office to enhance information sharing between DoD and the intelligence community. Washington, DC: Office of the Director of National Intelligence; 2007.

[16] Joint Task Force Transformation Initiative Interagency Working Group. NIST Special Publication (SP) 800-53 Revision 4, Security and privacy controls for federal information systems and organizations. Maryland: National Institute of Standards and Technology; 2013.

[17] Takai T. Cloud Computing Strategy. Washington, DC: US Department of Defense; 2012.

[18] NIST FISMA Implementation Project [Internet]. Maryland: National Institute of Standards and Technology [cited August 24, 2012] <http://csrc.nist.gov/groups/SMA/fisma/overview.html#phases>.

[19] Gutierrez C, Jeffrey W. Federal Information Processing Standard (FIPS) PUB 200, Minimum security requirements for federal information and information systems. Maryland: National Institute of Standards and Technology; 2006.

FedRAMP primer

8

INFORMATION IN THIS CHAPTER:

- Introduction to FedRAMP
- FedRAMP Overview
- FedRAMP Policy Memo
- FedRAMP Governance and Stakeholders
- FedRAMP Security Assessment Framework
- Third Party Assessment Organization Program

INTRODUCTION TO FEDRAMP

In mid-2009, an interagency effort,[1] created under the Federal Cloud Computing Initiative, was established to focus on solving a single problem statement—*How do we best perform security authorization and continuous monitoring for outsourced and multiagency systems?* [1]. This problem included addressing barriers to the adoption of cloud computing solutions and the cost-effective consolidation of data centers and applications. Traditionally, federal agencies have independently conducted risk management activities through the certification and accreditation (C&A) of their information systems (either residing within the federal agency accreditation boundary or operated by a contractor on their behalf). Applying this same model to shared services could greatly reduce the overall cost benefit.

There are other issues and challenges associated with applying a singular authorization model such as the incompatibility between different federal agency security policies, differences in acquisition and compliance processes, and an

---

[1]The interagency effort was conducted within the Cloud Computing Security Working Group that included members from across the government to include: the National Institute of Standards and Technology (NIST), US Department of Defense (DoD), US Department of Education (ED), US Department of Energy (DOE), US Department of Health and Human Services (HHS), US Department of Homeland Security (DHS), US Department of Housing and Urban Development (HUD), US Department of Justice (DOJ), US Department of Labor (DOL), US General Services Administration (GSA), Office of Management and Budget (OMB), Social Security Administration (SSA), and the United States Postal Service (USPS).

Federal Cloud Computing. DOI: http://dx.doi.org/10.1016/B978-0-12-809710-6.00008-1

inconsistent and variable application of federal information security and privacy requirements. These issues and challenges are not necessarily new to the federal government, and they existed in the lifecycle of traditional federal information technology (IT) environments. However, the issues and challenges become more amplified when applied at a larger scale to shared and outsourced information systems, such as a shared services approach that focuses on improving government-wide operational efficiency and effectiveness. Without adopting a more centralized methodology the benefits become less achievable and could potentially inhibit adoption of cloud computing solutions.

The solution—an initiative that would provide joint authorization and continuous security monitoring services using a unified, government-wide risk management approach that federal agencies across the government could leverage [1]. This initiative, known as the Federal Risk and Authorization Management Program (FedRAMP),[2] was designed to focus on three main areas: *authorization*, *continuous monitoring*, and *federal security requirements*. The initial goal of FedRAMP was to establish a unified risk management process that:

- Increased security of cloud solutions through a common assessment approach;
- Eliminated duplication of effort and achieved cost-savings through efficiency;
- Enabled rapid acquisition through leveraged authorizations;
- Improved reuse of authorization packages based on a common set of security requirements;
- Facilitated use of shared services across multiple federal agencies; and
- Integrated a government-wide security approach.

In addition to the benefits of unifying under a common implementation of the NIST Risk Management Framework (RMF), commercial service providers also benefited because they only had to perform a single assessment to obtain a Provisional Authorization To Operate (P-ATO).[3] Since the FedRAMP program also included a single government-wide governance body, federal agencies could leverage the P-ATOs, greatly reducing their effort because they do not have to individually initiate independent risk management activities.[4]

In November 2010, the FedRAMP Program Management Office (PMO) released the *Proposed Security Assessment & Authorization for US Government Cloud Computing*. This initial framework was based on 18 months of collaboration with stakeholders across the public and private sector. However, the proposed solution was also developed for the purpose of encouraging a discussion around the "best" approach by gathering "input, knowledge, and experience" [2] necessary for framing the security control requirements and processes for cloud

---

[2]*FedRAMP Program Management Office (PMO)*. Available from: http://www.fedramp.gov.
[3]There are two paths in the FedRAMP Program: *Joint Authorization Board (JAB) Provisional Authorization to Operate (P-ATO)* and *Agency ATO*.
[4]Chapter 5, Applying the NIST Risk Management Framework discussed the risk management activities involved in the application of the Risk Management Framework (RMF).

computing environments. The FedRAMP program continued to evolve for the next 13 months until December 8, 2011[5] when the Federal Chief Information Officer (CIO)[6] published a memorandum titled *Security Authorization of Information Systems in Cloud Computing Environments*, which established the federal policy for the protection of federal information in cloud services. The memorandum also described the components of the FedRAMP effort, and established milestones for the program and the policy governing the adoption by federal agencies [3].

FEDRAMP OVERVIEW

As previously discussed, the FedRAMP program was established through an Office of Management and Budget (OMB) memorandum in December 2011. The FedRAMP program is the first government-wide security authorization program, developed to standardize how Federal Information Security Modernization Act (FISMA)[7] would be applied[8] to cloud computing services—government or commercial. FedRAMP requirements are mandatory for federal agencies and Cloud Service Provider (CSP), and provide a common framework to security assessment, authorization, and continuous monitoring of cloud services, but uses the same framework federal agencies currently use to perform security authorizations of their IT systems and services. Additionally, federal agencies are still required to issue an authorization to operate for use of the cloud service.

The purpose of FedRAMP is to:

- Ensure that cloud systems used by Government entities have adequate safeguards;
- Eliminate duplication of effort and reduce risk management costs; and
- Enable rapid and cost-effective Government procurement of information systems/services [6].

The results of the FedRAMP program are cloud service authorizations that can be leveraged across multiple federal agencies.

---

[5]*OMB Releases FedRAMP Policy Memo.* Available from: https://www.fedramp.gov/files/2015/03/fedrampmemo.pdf.
[6]Vivek Kundra, the first US Federal CIO appointed in March 2009, resigned in June 2011, and was replaced by Steven VanRoekel.
[7]FedRAMP does not replace FISMA, but is based upon the same standards and guidelines produced through the implementation of FISMA.
[8]From FedRAMP Online Training—Introduction to FedRAMP [Internet]. Washington, DC: US General Services Administration [cited 2016 May 8]. Available from: https://www.fedramp.gov/resources/training/. *"FedRAMP focus is to ensure the rigorous security standards of FISMA are appliance while introducing efficiencies to the process for cloud system (key of which is reuse)."*

FEDRAMP POLICY MEMO

The FedRAMP "Policy Memo"[9] established the governing federal policy for the secure adoption and government-wide use of cloud services. The memorandum describes the framework for implementing the FedRAMP components that includes:

- A standard set of security requirements for provisional[10] authorization and ongoing monitoring;
- A conformity assessment program for third-party assessment[11];
- An assembly of security experts from across government to review authorization documents[12] to support the risk-based decisions by the Joint Authorization Board (JAB)[13];
- Standardized contract language that integrates FedRAMP requirements into the federal government acquisition process; and
- An authoritative central repository for storing authorization documents.

As illustrated in Fig. 8.1, the FedRAMP "Policy Memo" is represented at the top of the FedRAMP document hierarchy, providing the highest level of governance. The governance processes defined in the FedRAMP Security Assessment Framework (SAF), previously the FedRAMP Concept of Operations (CONOPS), are supported by the foundational elements, which include: (i) security assessment templates and guidelines; (ii) the Third Party Assessment Organization (3PAO) program description and application; and (iii) the three parallel ongoing monitoring mechanisms (*automated/manual data feeds*, *annual attestation*, and *event/incident handling*). The foundational elements provide the FedRAMP PMO with the key functions needed to meet the operating capability for the program.

---

[9]FedRAMP is a supplementary policy to OMB A-130 for security authorizations.

[10]From Shive, D., McCormack, L., Halvorsen, T. Federal Risk and Authorization Management Program (FedRAMP) Joint Authorization Board (JAB) Charter Version 2.0. Washington, DC: FedRAMP Program Management Office, US General Services Administration; 2016. *"The JAB will provide the technical knowledge and skills to provide a government-wide baseline approach to address the security needs associated with placing Federal data in cloud computing solutions. Additionally, the JAB will provide joint provisional security authorizations of cloud solutions using this baseline approach. This provisional authorization will create an authorization package that can be leveraged by individual agencies across the Federal Government to grant an Authority to Operate at their respective organizations."*

[11]From FedRAMP PMO. Assessors [Internet]. Washington, DC: US General Services Administration [cited March 17, 2012]. Available from: https://www.fedramp.gov/participate/assessors/. *"The American Association for Laboratory Accreditation (A2LA) accredits FedRAMP assessors with the FedRAMP PMO providing final approval."*

[12]Documents included in the authorizing package include: Security Plan, Security Assessment Report, Plan of Action and Milestones, and Continuous Monitoring Plan.

[13]As discussed in Chapter 5, Applying the NIST Risk Management Framework, the authorization package includes three key documents, the Security Plan, Security Assessment Report, and the Plan of Action and Milestones. The authorizing official defines that additional supporting documents are required.

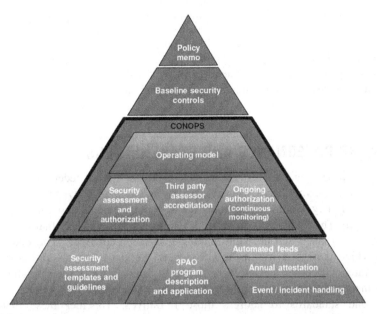

FIGURE 8.1

Document hierarchy [4].

The scope of coverage for the FedRAMP "Policy Memo" is inclusive of almost all cloud services, regardless of the service and deployment models[14] or whether the cloud service is commercial[15] or noncommercial.[16] In addition, the memorandum is applied government-wide,[17] with the exception of

[14]As defined in NIST Special Publication (SP) 800-145, *The NIST Definition of Cloud Computing.*

[15]From US General Services Administration Federal Acquisition Regulation (FAR) Subpart 2.1 [Internet]. Washington, DC: US General Services Administration [cited March 13, 2012]. Available from: https://www.acquisition.gov/far/html/Subpart%202_1.html#wp1145508. *"Commercial item" has multiple requirements as defined in FAR 2.101 such as any item, other than real property, that is of a type customarily used by the general public or by non-governmental entities for purposes other than governmental purposes sold, leased, or licensed to the general public or has been offered for sale, lease or license to the general public.*

[16]Noncommercial includes those products or services that do not fall under the definition of a "commercial item" and are primarily governed by FAR Part 13 ($100,000 and less) and FAR 15 (over $100,000).

[17]From VanRoekel, S. Office of Management and Budget (OMB) Memorandum, Security Authorization of Information System in Cloud Computing Environments. Washington, DC: Executive Office of the President, Office of Management and Budget; 2011. "This includes Executive departments and agencies not subject to the Federal Acquisition Regulation."

the following conditions in which the requirements under the FISMA[18] still apply:

- A private cloud[19] deployment model;
- On-premises (i.e., within a Federal facility[20]); and
- Cloud services are not provided to any external entity.[21]

FEDRAMP GOVERNANCE AND STAKEHOLDERS

OMB, which has government-wide management oversight of federal information/ IT (including privacy and security), is the governing body that issued the FedRAMP Policy Memo that defines the key requirements and capabilities of the program. The FedRAMP program is also governed by a JAB that acts as the primary governance and decision making body for FedRAMP. The FedRAMP PMO, which is housed within the US General Services Administration (GSA), collaborates with other stakeholders to identify high priority security and identity management initiatives and develop recommendations for policies, procedures, and standards to address those initiatives. Together these different stakeholders within the Executive Branch work to develop, manage, and operate the program.

- Other governing bodies of FedRAMP include:
  - National Institute of Standards and Technology (NIST), which provides technical assistance to the 3PAO process, maintains FISMA standards (refer to Chapter 5, *Applying the NIST Risk Management Framework*) and establishes related technical standards.
  - Federal CIO Council disseminates FedRAMP information to Federal Agency CIOs and other representatives through cross-agency communication and events.

---

[18]FISMA was discussed in detail in Chapter 5, Applying the NIST Risk Management Framework.
[19]From Mell, P., Grance, T. NIST Special Publication (SP) 800-145, The NIST Definition of Cloud Computing. Maryland: National Institute of Standards and Technology; 2011. *"The cloud infrastructure is provisioned for exclusive use by a single organization"*.
[20]From US General Services Administration FAR Subpart 2.1 [Internet]. Washington, DC: US General Services Administration [cited March 13, 2012]. Available from: https://www.acquisition. gov/far/current/html/Subpart%202_1.html. *Pursuant to 48 C.F.R. 2.101, federally controlled facilities are buildings or leased space under the jurisdiction, custody or control of a department or agency, including those spaces included in commercial buildings shared with nongovernment tenants and/or contractor-operated under a management and operating contract.*
[21]From VanRoekel, S. Office of Management and Budget (OMB) Memorandum, Security Authorization of Information System in Cloud Computing Environments. Washington, DC: Executive Office of the President, Office of Management and Budget; 2011. *External entities, depending on where in the federal government hierarchy the cloud service is deployed, includes external users and could include bureaus, components, or subordinate organizations within a federal agency.*

- US Department of Homeland Security (DHS) manages the FedRAMP continuous monitoring strategy, including data feed criteria, reporting structure, threat notification coordination, and incident response. DHS monitors and reports on security incidents and provides monitoring. Additionally, DHS updates requirements for FISMA reporting.

PRIMARY STAKEHOLDERS

The four key primary federal government stakeholders for FedRAMP include the DHS, the JAB, the FedRAMP PMO, and the federal agencies.[22] Each of the primary stakeholders shares some responsibility for implementing the FedRAMP "Policy Memo". Fig. 8.2 presents a high-level overview of the stakeholders and a workflow that highlights the interactions and relationships existing between each participating CSP and 3PAO.

DHS

The DHS National Protection and Programs Directorate (NPPD)[23] includes several divisions, but one specifically, the Office of Cybersecurity and Communications (CS&C), focuses on the "security, resiliency, and reliability of the nation's cyber and communications infrastructure."[24] The CS&C includes the National Cyber Security Division (NCSD),[25] which has the primary objective of protecting and securing cyberspace and cyber assets, and includes a function specifically focusing on the security of federal networks.

In July 2010, through the Director of OMB, the Special Assistant to the President and Cybersecurity Coordinator, published OMB Memorandum 10−28[26,27] to clarify the cybersecurity responsibilities and activities. This memo set out the lines of responsibility and authority to reduce overlap and ensure the cost-effective application of resources needed for the government-wide coordination of cybersecurity efforts. In addition, the memo aligned cybersecurity-related

---

[22]Federal agencies use the FedRAMP process when conducting risk assessments, security authorizations, and granting an ATO to a cloud service.

[23]*National Protection and Programs Directorate (NPPD)*. Available from: http://www.dhs.gov/about-national-protection-and-programs-directorate.

[24]*Office of Cybersecurity and Communications (CS&C)*. Available from: http://www.dhs.gov/office-cybersecurity-and-communications.

[25]Functions within the NCSD include the national cyberspace response system, which seeks to protect the national cyber infrastructure, the federal network security branch, and cyber risk management programs.

[26]*Clarifying Cybersecurity Responsibilities and Activities of the Executive Office of the President and Department of Homeland Security*. Available from: https://www.whitehouse.gov/sites/default/files/omb/assets/memoranda_2010/m10-28.pdf.

[27]OMB Circular A-130, *Managing Information as a Strategic Resource*, was revised on July 28, 2016, rescinding, OMB Memorandum 10-28, but incorporated the principle of this memorandum and requirements of the Federal Information Security Modernization Act (FISMA) of 2014.

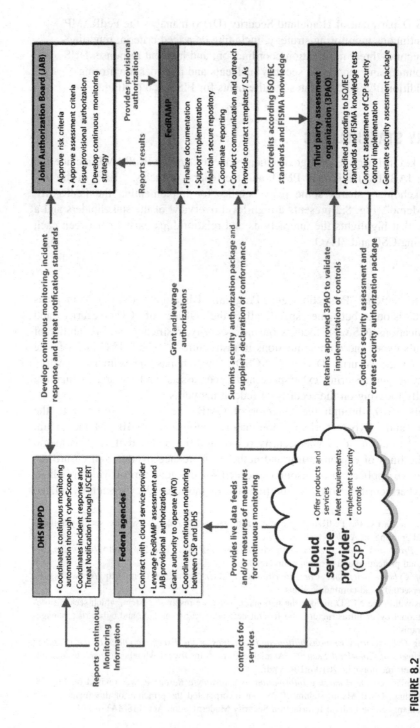

FIGURE 8.2

FedRAMP stakeholder roles and interactions [4].

roles and responsibilities (see (a)), including limitations (see (b) and (c)) for the implementation of FISMA[28]:

- Section 3543(a)—The Director of OMB "shall oversee agency information security policies and practices, including developing and overseeing the implementation of policies, principles, standards, and guidelines on information security" [5].
- Section 3543(b) and (c)—Limitations associated with National Security Systems (NSSs) and Department of Defense (DoD), and Intelligence Community (IC) information systems.

The responsibilities assigned under this memorandum were inherited by the FedRAMP "Policy Memo" and gave the DHS the responsibility under FedRAMP for four key areas:

- Government-wide and agency-specific cybersecurity assistance;
- Cybersecurity operations and incident response coordination;
- Continuous monitoring standards development[29];
- Trusted Internet Connection (TIC) program implementation.[30]

JAB

The JAB was chartered under a joint agreement[31] between the CIOs of GSA, DHS, and DoD with the objective of:

- Defining and regularly reviewing the security authorization requirements;
- Approving accreditation criteria for the 3PAOs;
- Establishing the criteria for the queue that will prioritize authorization package review;
- Reviewing authorization packages;
- Granting provisional authorizations;
- Ensuring reviews and updates of provisional authorization;
- Establishing mechanisms for the maintenance of the security authorization requirements.

The JAB is comprised of Authorizing Officials (AOs) and AO-designated technical representatives from GSA, DHS, and DoD, and is supported through the

---

[28]FISMA was discussed in detail in Chapter 5, Applying the NIST Risk Management Framework.

[29]In September 2010, the DHS Federal Network Security branch published the Continuous Asset Evaluation, Situational Awareness and Risk Scoring (CAESARS) architectural reference framework, which has been adopted by NIST through Interagency Reports as an Enterprise Continuous Monitoring Reference Model (also known as the CAESARS Framework Extension).

[30]The TIC program was original published as an OMB Initiative in Office of Management and Budget (OMB) Memorandum 08-05 with the focus of optimizing federal network services into a common solution for the federal government.

[31]*FedRAMP JAB Charter.* Available from: https://www.fedramp.gov/files/2015/01/JAB-Charter-2.0.pdf.

FedRAMP PMO that operates within the GSA, Office of Citizens Services and Innovative Technologies (OCSIT).

FedRAMP PMO

The FedRAMP PMO is a critical operational function that provides most of the administrative and technical support for FedRAMP processes and frameworks,[32] to include facilitating the implementation of the security assessment and authorization (SA&A) processes in the NIST RMF,[33] excluding the actual authorization. In addition, the FedRAMP PMO operates most of the programmatic functions of the FedRAMP processes and activities that support the key components included in Fig. 8.1 of the FedRAMP operating model such as:

- 3PAO conformity assessment program.
- Authorization package queue.
- Education and outreach.
- Authorization repository.
- Security assessment templates and guidelines, to include Memorandums of Understanding (MOUs)/Memorandums of Agreement (MOAs) and standard contract language and Service Level Agreements (SLAs).

Federal Agencies

The role of the federal agency in FedRAMP is as a federal customer, which uses the processes (e.g., SAF, NIST RMF, etc.), and documentation (e.g., FedRAMP templates, NIST standards and guidelines, FedRAMP authorization packages, etc.) to procure and use cloud services to meet the objectives of the "Cloud First" policy, originally discussed in the *25 Point Implementation Plan to Reform Federal Information Technology Management*[34] and further defined in the *Federal Cloud Computing Strategy.*[35] The federal agency, as a party within a contract[36] for cloud services, is to use FedRAMP as a cost-effective mechanism

---

[32](a) Security and privacy requirements harmonization, (b) federal agency guidance, (c) security authorization initiation requests, (d) authorization package leveraging, and (e) continuous monitoring.
[33]NIST RMF was discussed in detail in Chapter 5, Applying the NIST Risk Management Framework.
[34]*25 Point Implementation Plan to Reform Federal Information Technology Management.* Available from: https://cio.gov/wp-content/uploads/downloads/2012/09/25-Point-Implementation-Plan-to-Reform-Federal-IT.pdf.
[35]*Federal Cloud Computing Strategy.* Available from: https://www.whitehouse.gov/sites/default/files/omb/assets/egov_docs/federal-cloud-computing-strategy.pdf.
[36]Cloud services can be a "public cloud" or a federal "community cloud" that provides shared services. For example, the Bureau of the Public Debt, Administrative Resource Center (BPD-ARC), a part of the US Treasury, provides Government-to-Government Shared Services that provides services leveraged by other federal agencies. For more information on the BPD-ARC, visit: https://arc.publicdebt.treas.gov/.

for the secure adoption of cloud services that are within the scope of the FedRAMP "Policy Memo."

FEDRAMP ACCELERATED PROCESS

The FedRAMP Accelerated process was announced on March 28, 2016, with the focus of improving the timeline for completing the FedRAMP JAB P-ATO.[37] In the process, a FedRAMP 3PAO conducts a readiness (capabilities) assessment or "pre-audit" before completing the security assessment and JAB review. As illustrated in Fig. 8.3, the FedRAMP PMO will conduct Readiness Assessment Review of the Readiness Assessment Report (RAR).[38]

The RAR "identifies the minimum FedRAMP requirements necessary for all CSPs to meet to attain a FedRAMP ATO. CSPs who have a RAR approved by the FedRAMP PMO will be deemed "FedRAMP Ready" in the FedRAMP Marketplace" [16].

The FedRAMP Readiness Assessment and RAR provide information on the organizational processes and the security capabilities of the CSP system. This information assists the FedRAMP PMO in determining the readiness of the CSP system in achieving a P-ATO. The 3PAO submits the RAR to the FedRAMP PMO with an attestation.[39] To achieve a "FedRAMP Ready," the CSP would go through an assessment that focuses on key capabilities based on federal mandates[40] (see Table 8.1) and FedRAMP requirements[41] (see Table 8.2 through 8.8) that must be met by the CSP.

---

[37]The FedRAMP Readiness Assessment is only applicable to FedRAMP JAB P-ATO and is only encouraged for use in the Agency ATO path.

[38]*The FedRAMP Readiness Assessment Report Template.* Available from: https://www.fedramp. gov/files/2016/08/FedRAMP-Readiness-Assessment-Report-Template_080916.docx.

[39]From FedRAMP Program Management Office (PMO). Readiness Assessment Report Template. Washington, DC: US General Services Administration; 2016. *"To be considered FedRAMP-Ready, the CSP must meet all of the requirements in Section 4.1, Federal Mandates. In addition, the 3PAO must assess the CSP's ability to meet the requirements in Section 4.2, FedRAMP Requirements. The 3PAO must use its expert judgment to subjectively evaluate the CSP's overall readiness and factor this evaluation into its attestation."*

[40]From FedRAMP Program Management Office (PMO). Readiness Assessment Report Template. Washington, DC: US General Services Administration; 2016. *"Federal Manages, identifies a small set of the Federal mandates a CSP must satisfy. FedRAMP will not waive any of these requirements."*

[41]From FedRAMP Program Management Office (PMO). Readiness Assessment Report Template. Washington, DC: US General Services Administration; 2016. *"Federal Requirements, identifies an excerpt of the most compelling requirements from the National Institute of Science and Technology (NIST) Special Publication (SP) 800 series documents and FedRAMP guidance. A CSP is unlikely to achieve a FedRAMP Authorization if any of these requirements are not met."*

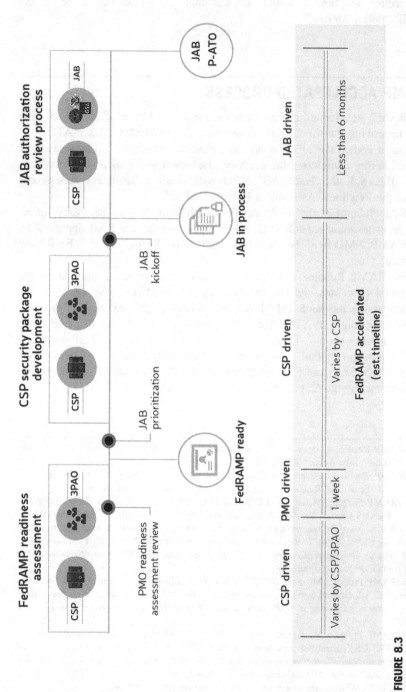

FIGURE 8.3

FedRAMP accelerated [15].

Table 8.1 Federal Mandates [16]

Are FIPS 140-2 Validated or National Security Agency (NSA)-Approved cryptographic modules consistently used?

Can the system fully support user authentication via Agency Common Access Card (CAC) or Personal Identity Verification (PIV) credentials?

Is the system operating at the minimum eAuth level for its FIPS-199 designated level of operation (Level 3 for Moderate, Level 4 for High)?

Does the CSP have the ability to consistently remediate High vulnerabilities in 30 days and Moderate vulnerabilities in 90 days?

Does the CSP and system meet Federal Records Management Requirements, including the ability to support record holds, National Archives and Records Administration (NARA) requirements, and Freedom of Information Act (FOIA) requirements?

Table 8.2 FedRAMP Requirements—Approved Cryptographic Modules [SC-13] [16]

Are Data at Rest [SC-28] cryptographic modules FIPS 140-2 Validated or NSA-Approved?

Are Transmission [SC-8 (1), SC-12, SC-12(2, 3)] cryptographic modules FIPS 140-2 Validated or NSA-Approved?

Are Remote Access [AC-17 (2)] cryptographic modules FIPS 140-2 Validated or NSA-Approved?

Are Authentication [IA-5 (1), IA-7] cryptographic modules FIPS 140-2 Validated or NSA-Approved?

Are Digital Signatures/Hash [CM-5 (3)] cryptographic modules FIPS 140-2 Validated or NSA-Approved

Table 8.3 FedRAMP Requirements—Transport Layer Security [NIST SP 800-52, Revision 1] [16]

Do cryptographic modules use Secure Sockets Layer (SSL)?

Do cryptographic modules use Transport Layer Security (TLS) 1.0?

Do cryptographic modules use TLS 1.1?

Do cryptographic modules use TLS 1.2?

Table 8.4 FedRAMP Requirements—Identification and Authentication, Authorization, and Access Control [16]

Does the system identify and authorize users in a manner that cannot be repudiated and which sufficiently reduces the risk of impersonation? [IA-2]

Does the system require multifactor authentication (MFA) for administrative accounts and functions? [IA-2, IA-2(1), IA-2(3)]

Does the system uniquely identify each individual user? [IA-4, IA-4(4)]

Does the system fully comply with eAuth Level 3 or higher? [NIST SP 800-63]

Does the system restrict non-authorized personnel's access to resources? [AC-6(2)]

Does the system restrict non-privileged users from performing privileged function? [AC-6(10)]

Does the system ensure secure separation of customer data? [SC-4]

Does the system ensure secure separation of customer processing environments? [SC-2, SC-3]

Table 8.5 FedRAMP Requirements—Audit, Alerting, Malware, and Incident Response [16]

Does the system have the capability to detect, contain, and eradicate malicious software? [SI-3, SI-3 (1), SI-3 (2), SI-3 (7), MA-3 (2)]

Does the system store audit data in a tamper-resistant manner, which meets chain of custody and any e-discovery requirements? [AU-7, AU-9]

Does the CSP have the capability to detect unauthorized or malicious use of the system, including insider threat and external intrusions? [SI-4, SI-4 (4), SI-7, SI-7 (7)]

Does the CSP have an Incident Response Plan, and is it tested at least annually? [IR-3, IR-8]

Does the CSP have the capability to perform code analysis scans for code written in-house (non-COTS products)? [SA-11 (1), SA-11 (8)]

Does the CSP implement automated mechanisms for incident handling and reporting? [IR-4 (1), IR-6 (1)]

Does the CSP retain online audit records for at least 90 days to provide support for after-the-fact investigations of security incidents and offline for at least one year to meet regulatory and organizational information retention requirements? [AU-7, AU-7 (1), AU-11]

Does the CSP have the capability to notify customers and regulators of confirmed incidents in a timeframe consistent with all legal, regulatory, or contractual obligations? [*FedRAMP Incident Communications Procedures*]

Table 8.6 FedRAMP Requirements—Contingency Planning and Disaster Recovery [16]

Does the CSP have the capability to recover the system to a known and functional state following an outage, breach, DoS attack, or disaster? [CP-2, CP-2 (2), CP-2 (3), CP-9, CP-10]

Does the CSP have a Contingency Plan, and is a functional test completed at least annually (for moderate systems) in accordance with NIST Special Publication 800-34? [CP-2, CP-8]

Does the system have alternate storage and processing facilities? [CP-6, CP-7]

Does the system have or use alternate telecommunications providers? [CP-8, CP-8 (2)]

Does the system have backup power generation or other redundancy? [PE-11]

Does the CSP have SLAs in place with all telecommunications providers? [CP-8 (1)]

Table 8.7 FedRAMP Requirements—Configuration and Risk Management [16]

Does the CSP maintain a current, complete, and accurate baseline configuration of the information system? [CM-2]

Does the CSP maintain a current, complete, and accurate inventory of the information system software, hardware, and network components? [CM-8]

Does the CSP have a Configuration Management Plan? [CM-9, CM-11]

Does the CSP follow a formal change control process that includes a security impact assessment? [CM-3, CM-4]

Does the CSP employ automated mechanisms to detect inventory and configuration changes? [CM-2(2), CM-6(1), CM-8(3)]

Does the CSP prevent unauthorized changes to the system? [CM-5, CM-5(1), CM-5(5)]

(Continued)

Table 8.7 FedRAMP Requirements—Configuration and Risk Management [16]
Continued

Does the CSP establish configuration settings for products employed that reflect the most restrictive mode consistent with operational requirements? [CM-6]
Does the CSP ensure that checklists for configuration settings are Security Content Automation Protocol (SCAP)-validated or SCAP-compatible (if validated checklists are not available)? [CM-6]
Does the CSP perform authenticated operating system/ infrastructure, web, and database vulnerability scans at least monthly, as applicable? [RA-5]
Does the CSP adhere to a risk management program that is incorporated system-wide and can support the timely remediation of vulnerabilities? [RA-5, *FedRAMP Continuous Monitoring Guide*]

Table 8.8 FedRAMP Requirements—Data Center Security [16]

Does the CSP restrict physical system access to only authorized personnel? [PE-2 through PE-6, PE-8]
Does the CSP monitor and log physical access to the information system, and maintain access records? [PE-6, PE-8]
Does the CSP monitor and respond to physical intrusion alarms and surveillance equipment [PE-6 (1)]

FEDRAMP SECURITY ASSESSMENT FRAMEWORK

The initial version of the FedRAMP CONOPS was published on February 7, 2012. The CONOPS leveraged the initial draft of the FedRAMP SA&A processes[42] and similarly included: *security assessment, security authorization*, and *continuous monitoring*. However, through the maturity of the program, the initial processes were expanded to address those core process elements that will be governed by FedRAMP to support several important outputs:

- Adequacy of information security for cloud services.
- Implementation of a common risk management approach.
- Improved procurement of cloud services.

After the FedRAMP program achieved full operating capability in 2014, the FedRAMP CONOPS was rewritten as the FedRAMP SAF. The FedRAMP SAF was built upon the NIST RMF[43] described in NIST SP 800-37 Revision 1, *Guide for Applying the Risk Management Framework to Federal Information Systems*, and follows the same SA&A processes used by federal agencies when conducting

---

[42]Proposed Security Assessment & Authorization for US Government Cloud Computing.
[43]NIST RMF was discussed in detail in Chapter 5, Applying the NIST Risk Management Framework.

their own security assessment and authorizations. However, the FedRAMP program simplified the NIST RMF by creating four phases that encompass the six steps as described in the NIST RMF.

NOTE

Federal agencies are required to assess and authorize information system in accordance with FISMA. The FedRAMP SAF provides a structured approach for use by CSPs and the federal government. The FedRAMP SAF also offers a catalyst for developing similar processes and practices that will be used by the private sector when adopting cloud services. By offering a similar model for conducting due diligence when evaluating the information security, risk management, and compliance of cloud services, the Cloud Security Alliance (CSA) developed the Open Certification Framework (OCF)[44], a program for flexible, incremental, and multilayered cloud provider certification according to the CSA's industry-leading security guidance and control objectives. The FedRAMP operates under a "do once, use many times" concept, where the CSA OCF operates under a "certify-once, use-often" concept. However, both models can also be used as options by CSPs, saving both time and cost associated with consumer due diligence activities. In addition, by leveraging cloud services that have been reviewed under the FedRAMP and OCF model, cloud consumers can reduce the need to perform their own due diligence, potentially accelerating the development and deployment of new products and services (Tables 8.9 and 8.10).

Table 8.9 FedRAMP Requirements—Policies and Procedures [16]

Does the CSP have an Access Control Policy and Procedures [AC-1]?

Does the CSP have an Awareness and Training Policy and Procedures [AT-1]?

Does the CSP have an Audit and Accountability Policy and Procedures [AU-1]?

Does the CSP have a Security Assessment and Authorization Policy and Procedures [CA-1]?

Does the CSP have a Configuration Management Policy and Procedures [CM-1]?

Does the CSP have a Contingency Planning Policy and Procedures [CP-1]?

Does the CSP have an Identification and Authentication Policy and Procedures [IA-1]?

Does the CSP have an Incident Response Policy and Procedures [IR-1]?

Does the CSP have a Maintenance Policy and Procedures [MA-1]?

Does the CSP have a Media Protection Policy and Procedures [MP-1]?

Does the CSP have a Physical and Environmental Policy and Procedures [PE-1]?

Does the CSP have a Planning Policy and Procedures [PL-1]?

Does the CSP have a Personnel Security Policy and Procedures [PS-1]?

Does the CSP have a Risk Assessment Policy and Procedures [RA-1]?

Does the CSP have a System and Services Acquisition Policy and Procedures [SA-1]?

Does the CSP have a System and Communications Protection Policy and Procedures [SC-1]?

Does the CSP have a System and Information Integrity Policy and Procedures [SI-1]?

(Continued)

---

[44]Cloud Security Alliance [Internet]. [cited May 3, 2016]. <https://cloudsecurityalliance.org/group/open-certification/#_overview>. *"The Cloud Security Alliance (CSA) Security, Trust and Assurance Registry (STAR) program is the industry's leading trust mark for cloud security. The CSA Open Certification Framework (OCF) is a program for flexible, incremental and multilayered CSP certifications according to the CSA's industry leading security guidance. The OCF/STAR program comprises a global cloud computing assurance framework with a scope of capabilities, flexibility of execution, and completeness of vision that far exceeds the risk and compliance objectives of other security audit and certification programs."*

> **NOTE (CONTINUED)**
>
> **Table 8.10** FedRAMP Requirements—Security Awareness Training [16]
>
> Does the CSP train personnel on security awareness and role-based security responsibilities? [AT-2, AT-2(2), AT-3]?

As previously illustrated in Fig. 8.2, FedRAMP requires the interaction of multiple participants. The FedRAMP SAF further elaborated on the role of each participant in Table 8.11.

The FedRAMP SAF provides the high-level overview and operating model that encompasses four key phases that govern the life cycle of a cloud computing service within FedRAMP. As shown in Fig. 8.4, the FedRAMP SAF focuses on phases that include: *document, assess, authorize, and monitor.*

Table 8.11 Major FedRAMP Participants

Participant	Role and Responsibility
Federal Agency Customer (or Contractor operating on behalf of a Federal Agency)	The Cloud Consumer for a cloud service that will be used to store, process, or transmit federal information is required to follow the FedRAMP process as part of the acquisition process.
Cloud Service Provider (CSP)	The Cloud Provider that will be providing the cloud service to a federal agency (or contractor operating on behalf of a federal agency) is required to meet the FedRAMP security requirements and agency-specific requirements (where applicable).
Third Party Assessment Organization (3PAO)	The Cloud Auditor that will be providing the independent assessment of cloud service is required to validate and attest to the quality and compliance of the CSP based on its security authorization package.
Joint Authorization Board (JAB)	The JAB is the authorizing body that reviews the security authorization package and grants provisional authority to operate (ATO).
FedRAMP Program Management Office (PMO)	The FedRAMP PMO is a program management function that manages the security assessment, authorization, and continuous monitoring processes.

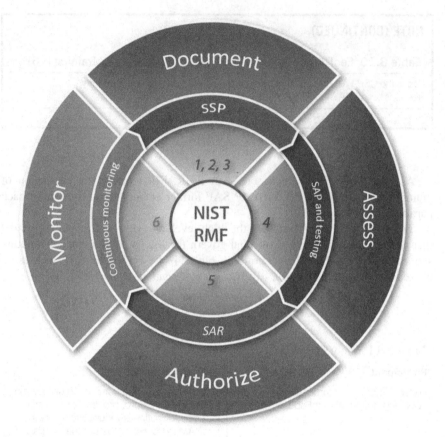

FIGURE 8.4

FedRAMP SAF [6].

FEDRAMP SECURITY ASSESSMENT FRAMEWORK PHASES

FISMA requires federal agencies to ensure the protection of federal information and information systems. The accountability for this requirement cannot be transferred to the FedRAMP PMO, but instead, as illustrated in Fig. 8.2, it is shared between the FedRAMP PMO and the federal agency based on the scope of the evaluation (i.e., FedRAMP security requirements baseline vs the agency-specific security and privacy requirements). The FedRAMP SAF used in conducting the SA&A of cloud services are designed to be compatible with the existing risk management practices already defined by NIST and used in traditional IT environments or FedRAMP-exempt cloud solutions. Therefore, only the differences within the FedRAMP SAF and the NIST RMF[45] will be discussed in this section.

---

[45]NIST RMF was discussed in detail in Chapter 5, Applying the NIST Risk Management Framework.

Document Phase

The FedRAMP JAB, in collaboration with the Federal CIO Council and Federal Chief Information Security Officer (CISO) community, defined three additional sets of security control baselines that extend the existing NIST security control baselines[46] for low-,[47] moderate-,[48] and high-impact[49] cloud-based information systems. As will be discussed in more detail in Chapter 9, The FedRAMP Cloud Computing Security Requirements, these minimum security controls have been tailored and supplemented to establish a standardized set of security requirements considered to provide adequate protection for federal information within cloud computing environments. In addition to the initial tailoring of the NIST security control baselines by the JAB (i.e., applying the *scoping guidance* and specifying government-wide *organization-defined parameters*), CSPs also have the responsibility for completing additional tailoring for the application of security controls that may differ from the FedRAMP security control requirements (i.e., specifying *compensating security controls*). For example, in Table 8.12, the security controls selection process (NIST RMF Step 2) maps to one additional FedRAMP deliverable: *Control Implementation Summary (CIS)*.

The CIS is used by the CSPs to document "control implementation responsibility and implementation status of the FedRAMP security controls. The scope of the CIS template includes a description of all management, operational, and technical FedRAMP security controls that are documented in the SSP at the determined impact level (Moderate or Low) by the CSP" [14].

NOTE

Initiating a Request

Initiating a request,[50] is the initial steps for CSPs and involves completing a brief request form that provides a summary of information on the CSP and the cloud service to include:

- CSP Name.
- CSP Website.
- CSP Points of Contact.

(Continued)

---

[46]From Joint Task Force Transformation Initiative, NIST Special Publication (SP) 800-53 Revision 4, Security and Privacy Controls for Federal Information System and Organizations. Maryland: National Institute of Standards and Technology; 2013. *"Organizations have flexibility in applying the baseline security controls in accordance with the guidance provided in Special Publication 800-53. This allows organizations to tailor the relevant security control baseline so that it more closely aligns with their mission and business requirements and environments of operation."*
[47]*FedRAMP Low Security Controls.* Available from: https://www.fedramp.gov/files/2016/07/FedRAMP-Low-HHH-Baseline-Controls-2016-05-18.xlsx.
[48]*FedRAMP Moderate Security Controls.* Available from: https://www.fedramp.gov/files/2016/07/FedRAMP-Moderate-HHH-Baseline-Controls-2016-05-18.xlsx.
[49]*FedRAMP High Security Controls.* Available from: https://www.fedramp.gov/files/2016/07/FedRAMP-High-HHH-Baseline-Controls-2016-05-18.xlsx.
[50]The FedRAMP initiation can be performed by both the sponsoring federal agency and the CSP. Available from: http://survey.clicktools.com/app/survey/response.jsp.

Table 8.12 NIST RMF and FedRAMP Document Phase/Deliverables

FedRAMP Phase	FedRAMP Deliverables	NIST RMF Step
Document	• FIPS 199 Categorization[a]	RMF Step 1—Categorize Information System • *Task 1.1*—Security Categorization • *Task 1.2*—Information System Description • *Task 1.2*—Information System Registration
	• Control Implementation Summary (CIS)[b]	RMF Step 2—Select Security Controls • *Task 2.1*—Common Control Identification • *Task 2.2*—Security Control Selection • *Task 2.3*—Monitoring Strategy • *Task 2.4*—Security Plan Approval
	• System Security Plan (SSP)[c] • Rules of Behavior (RoB)[d] • Information System Security Policies • IT Contingency Plan (CP)[e] • Configuration Management (CM) Plan • Incident Response Plan (IRP) • E-Authentication Workbook[f] • Privacy Threshold Analysis (PTA) and Privacy Impact Assessment (PIA)[g]	RMF Step 3—Implement Security Controls • *Task 3.1*—Security Control Implementation • *Task 3.2*—Security Control Documentation

[a]FedRAMP Program Management Office (PMO). Templates [Internet]. Washington, DC: US General Services Administration [cited April 29, 2016]. <https://www.fedramp.gov/resources/templates-3/>. "*The Federal Information Processing Standard 199 (FIPS-199) Categorization (Security Categorization) report is a key document in the security authorization package developed for submission to the Federal Risk and Authorization Management Program (FedRAMP) authorizing officials. The FIPS-199 Categorization report includes the determination of the security impact level for the cloud environment that may host any or all of the service models (Information as a Service (IaaS), Platform as a Service (PaaS), and Software as a Service (SaaS)). The ultimate goal of the security categorization is for the cloud service provider (CSP) to be able to select and implement the FedRAMP security controls applicable to its environment.*"

[b]FedRAMP Program Management Office (PMO). Templates [Internet]. Washington, DC: US General Services Administration [cited April 29, 2016]. <https://www.fedramp.gov/resources/templates-3/>. "*This document provides a sample format for preparing the Control Implementation Summary (CIS) Report for the CSP information system. The CSP may modify the format as necessary to comply with its internal policies and Federal Risk and Authorization Management Program (FedRAMP) requirements.*"

(Continued)

Table 8.12 NIST RMF and FedRAMP Document Phase/Deliverables
Continued

^cFedRAMP Program Management Office (PMO). Templates [Internet]. Washington, DC: US General Services Administration [cited April 29, 2016]. <https://www.fedramp.gov/resources/templates-3/>. *"This document details a cloud systems security controls. The plan (template) is written in accordance with National Institute of Standards and Technology (NIST) Special Publication (SP) 800-18, Revision 1, Guide for Developing Security Plans for Information Technology Systems."*

^dFedRAMP Program Management Office (PMO). Templates [Internet]. Washington, DC: US General Services Administration [cited April 29, 2016]. <https://www.fedramp.gov/resources/templates-3/>. *"Rules of Behavior describe security controls associated with user responsibilities and certain expectations of behavior for following security policies, standards, and procedures. Security control PL-4 requires Cloud Service Providers to implement Rules of Behavior."*

^eFedRAMP Program Management Office (PMO). Templates [Internet]. Washington, DC: US General Services Administration [cited April 29, 2016]. <https://www.fedramp.gov/resources/templates-3/>. *"This document supports Information Technology (IT) Contingency Plan requirements for the Federal Risk and Authorization Management Program (FedRAMP)" and "This document details a cloud systems security controls. The plan (template) is written in accordance with National Institute of Standards and Technology (NIST) Special Publication (SP) 800-18, Revision 1, Guide for Developing Security Plans for Information Technology Systems."*

^fFedRAMP Program Management Office (PMO). Templates [Internet]. Washington, DC: General Services Administration [cited April 29, 2016]. <https://www.fedramp.gov/resources/templates-3/.> *"This document details a cloud systems security controls. The Electronic Authentication template will provide an overview of the authentication level for the CSP system in accordance with OMB Memo M-04-04."*

^gFedRAMP Program Management Office (PMO). Templates [Internet]. Washington, DC: US General Services Administration [cited April 29, 2016]. <https://www.fedramp.gov/resources/templates-3/>. *"This document is intended to be used by Cloud Service Providers (CSPs) for assessing privacy concerns. Personally Identifiable Information (PII) as defined in OMB Memo M-07-16 refers to information that can be used to distinguish or trace an individual's identity, either alone or when combined with other personal or identifying information that is linked or linkable to a specific individual. A CSP performs a Privacy Threshold Analysis annually to determine if PII is collected by any of the system components. A CSP conducts a Privacy Impact Assessment (PIA) to analyze each system component to determine if any components collect PII, the type of PII collected, and the functions that collect it."*

NOTE (CONTINUED)
- CSP System Information (Name, Brief Description of the Service Provided by the System, FedRAMP Readiness, Cloud Service Model, Cloud Deployment Model, and FIPS-199 Categorization).
- Indication of Previous System Authorizations and if a Third Party Assessor is used.

Documenting security controls, described in Table 8.2 maps to the corresponding NIST RMF Step 3 (*Implement Security Controls*). In this phase, the CSP implements the required security controls and documents the implementation in the System Security Plan (SSP). The SSP provides the JAB with the necessary visibility through the functional descriptions of how the security controls have been integrated into the cloud service and the operating environment. "The functional description of the security control implementation includes *planned inputs, expected behavior, and expected outputs* where appropriate, typically for those technical controls that are employed in the hardware, software, or firmware components of the information system" [7]. The SSP describes the controls implemented, and also provides a method for communicating to the JAB those security controls that have been planned or compensated by the CSP.

Before the security control implementations can be described, the CSP needs to identify the information system components included within the operating environment. Since cloud environments can be configured differently and encompass different layers (e.g., a single provider operates the IaaS layer, a single or different provider operates the IaaS and PaaS layers, or a single provider operates all layers or only the SaaS layer), it is important for the CSP to accurately reflect the security control boundary layer to ensure gaps do not exist between each layer.

TIP

The FedRAMP PMO identified the following list of questions [13] to assist CSPs in describing the scope of the boundary for their cloud service. Below is a subset of those questions:

- Does the cloud service leverage an existing provisional authorization?
- Do tenants share the same virtual LANs (VLAN(s))?
- Are virtual machine zones isolated on unique network segments?
- Are separate physical network adapters used to isolate virtual machine zones?
- Is layer-2 isolation performed?
- Are firewalls used to provide isolation between tenants?
- Are router access control lists (ACLs) used to provide isolation between tenants?
- Are network zones used, and if so, how are those zones defined?
- Do you have the capability to identify the geographic location where the customer data is stored?
- Do you have the capability for a federal agency customer to identify the geographic location where its data are stored?
- Is live migration used, and if so, is it performed manually or automatically?
- If live migration is automated, what rules are used to govern the migration?

Identified below are the outputs from the steps included within the SAF document phase when documenting security controls.

Major Milestone Outputs

Documentation of the security controls implemented in the cloud service as included within the approved baseline security controls allocated and described in the SSP and supporting documentation.

Assess Phase

In this step of the SAF phase, as outlined in Table 8.13, the CSP works directly with a contracted accredited[51] 3PAO. The 3PAO is responsible for performing an independent and qualified assessment of the security controls using the artifacts

---

[51]List of accredited 3PAOs can be found at FedRAMP.gov. Available from: http://www.fedramp.gov/marketplace/accredited-3paos/.

Table 8.13 NIST RMF and FedRAMP Assess Phase/Deliverables

FedRAMP Phase	FedRAMP Deliverable	NIST RMF Step
Assess • *Step 1*—Develop Testing Plan • *Step 2*—Audit Control Implementations • *Step 3*—Perform Vulnerability/ Penetration Testing	• 3PAO Designation Form • Security Assessment Plan (SAP) • Security Assessment Test Cases • Security Assessment Report (SAR)	RMF Step 4—Assess Security Controls • *Task 4.1*—Assessment Preparation • *Task 4.2*—Security Control Assessment • *Task 4.3*—Security Assessment Report • *Task 4.4*—Remediation Actions

Identified below are the outputs from the steps included within the SAF assess phase when performing the security assessment.

included in the security assessment package. The assessment-related activities performed in this step are consistent with those included within the NIST RMF Step 4 and involve a collaborative relationship between the CSP and the 3PAO to ensure assessor independence is maintained. The output of this task involves making a determination of the extent to which the controls are implemented correctly, operate as intended, and produce the desired outcome with respect to meeting the FedRAMP security requirements [7].

Major Milestone Outputs

- Approved security assessment plan used to assess the security control employed within or inherited by the cloud service.
- SAR that identifies the findings and recommendations based on an assessment of the security controls implemented within the cloud service.
- Plan of action and milestones (POA&Ms) that include remediation action for correcting weaknesses and deficiencies in the cloud service.

Authorize Phase

The next phase in the SAF, as outlined in Table 8.14, is the assembly of the documentation by the CSP into a security authorization package that includes the Supplier's Declaration of Conformation.[52] In addition to the authorization activities included in NIST RMF Step 4, the CSP also has responsibility in

---

[52]From Global Standards Information, Supplier's Declaration of Conformity [Internet]. Maryland: National Institute of Standards and Technology [cited March 22, 2012]. Available from: http://gsi.nist. gov/global/index.cfm/L1-5/L2-45/A-208. *"A Supplier's Declaration of Conformity (SDOC) is a first party assessment in which a supplier or manufacturer provides written assurance of conformity."*

Table 8.14 NIST RMF and FedRAMP Assess Phase/Deliverables

FedRAMP Phase	FedRAMP Deliverable	NIST RMF Step
Authorize • *Step 1*—Develop Plan of Action and Milestones (POA&Ms) • *Step 2*—Compile All Updated and Final Documentation • *Step 3*—Answer Questions from Final Risk Assessment • *Step 4*—Accept the Documented Findings and Make Any Updated to POA&Ms • *Step 5*—Accept Provisional Authorization	• Plan of Action and Milestones (POA&Ms) • Finalized Security Assessment Package[a] • Supplier's Declaration of Conformity (SDOC)[b]	RMF Step 5—Authorize Information System • *Task 5.1*—Plan of Action and Milestones • *Task 5.2*—Security Authorization Package • *Task 5.3*—Risk Determination • *Task 5.4*—Risk Acceptance

Identified below are the outputs from the steps included within the SAF authorize when finalizing the security assessment package and receiving an authorization decision.
[a]*Complete package of all security assessment deliverables and related evidence.*
[b]*From Global Standards Information, Supplier's Declaration of Conformity [Internet]. Maryland: National Institute of Standards and Technology [cited March 22. 2012]. Available from: < http://gsi. nist.gov/global/index.cfm/L1-5/L2-45/A-208>. "CSPs verify and attest to the trust of the implemented security controls as detailed in their assessment package."*

documenting a remediation plan (or POA&Ms),[53] which is performed in NIST RMF Step 5. After reviewing the security assessment report (SAR) generated by the 3PAO, the CSP is required to prepare POA&Ms[54] that require establishing the tasks, resources required to complete the task, and the schedule for remediating any findings of weaknesses and deficiencies. The 3PAO SAR and the POA&Ms are two of the three key documents in the security authorization package submitted and reviewed by the JAB when making a risk-based decision for granting a provisional authorization.

The JAB reviews the security authorization package and makes the final risk-based decision when granting a provisional authorization. This risk determination is based on an accumulation of risk-related information that is used by the JAB when assessing the risk to the federal government when using the cloud service.

---

[53]From FedRAMP Program Management Office (PMO), FedRAMP Plan of Action and Milestones Template. Washington, DC: US General Services Administration; 2012. *"The plan of action and milestones (POA&M) is one of three key documents in the security authorization package and describes the specific tasks that are planned: (i) to correct any weaknesses or deficiencies in the security controls noted during the assessment; and (ii) to address the residual vulnerabilities in the information system."*
[54]From FedRAMP Program Management Office (PMO), FedRAMP Plan of Action and Milestones Template Completion Guide v1.1. Washington, DC: US General Services Administration; 2015. *"High and critical risk findings identified following Provisional Authorization through continuous monitoring activities must be mitigated within 30 days after identification. Moderate findings shall have a mitigation date within 90 days of Provisional Authorization date or within 90 days of identification as part of continuous monitoring activities."*

Major Milestone Output
- Security assessment package that includes the key documents used in making an authorization decision—the SSP, SAR, and POA&Ms.
- Provisional ATO letter[55] that includes the risk determination and acceptance decision by the JAB for cloud service.

Leveraging the ATO

Leveraging is an authorization approach,[56] previously discussed in Chapter 5, Applying the NIST Risk Management Framework, which is used when one federal agency accepts the authorization package of another federal agency. The leveraging federal agency's AO reviews and accepts the risk based on a determination of the risk for using the cloud service to support their specific mission and business processes and use the cloud service to store, process, or transmit their information. In this FedRAMP phase, the final acceptance of risk (or ATO) is granted by the leveraging federal agency[57] accepting the provisional ATO for cloud service. This includes the agreement of the control responsibility as allocated by the CSPs in the CIS, as discussed earlier in this chapter.

Monitor Phase

In the final phase, ongoing assessment and authorization (also known as continuous monitoring), the JAB determines if the security controls implemented are still effective and the provisional authorization should be maintained.[58] This determination is based on three keys areas: *operational visibility, change control process*, and *incident response*. The operational visibility focuses on periodic assessment of a select subset of security controls to ensure security controls implemented by CSPs continue to be effective. The change control process relates to the CSPs' ability to understand security impacts associated with changes to the cloud service. Incident response focuses on identifying new threats and vulnerabilities and the response and mitigate activities for

---

[55]From FedRAMP Program Management Office (PMO). FedRAMP Security Assessment Framework Version 2.1. Washington, DC: US General Services Administration; 2015. *"CSPs with an authorization are required to implement continuous monitoring, continue to meet the FedRAMP requirements, and maintain an appropriate risk level associated with a Low and Moderate security impact level in order to maintain an authorization. If the CSP fails to maintain its risk posture and comply with FedRAMP continuous monitoring, the JAB AO or the Agency AO can choose to revoke the CSPs authorization."*

[56]Three authorization approaches are available by AOs when conducting authorizations: (1) traditional single AO ATO, (2) multiple AO ATO, and (3) leveraged ATO.

[57]There are four types of security assessment package categories that will be maintained in the FedRAMP repository.

[58]From FedRAMP Program Management Office (PMO), Continuous Monitoring Strategy & Guide, Version 2.0. Washington, DC: US General Services Administration; 2014. *"To maintain an authorization that meets the FedRAMP requirements, CSPs must monitor their security controls, assess them on a regular basis, and demonstrate that the security posture of their service offering is continuously acceptable."*

incidences. Continuous monitoring will be discussed in detail in later chapters. However, in this section, a high-level overview will be provided as it relates to the FedRAMP SAF.

Operational Visibility

Operational visibility focuses on three sources of information for determining the security and risk posture of cloud services to demonstrate continued compliance through the automation to enable oversight and monitoring. Originally included in the reporting instructions[59] to federal agencies in April 2010, a three-tiered approach[60] was introduced as a method for federal agencies to effectively and "continuously monitor security-related information across the enterprise in a manageable and actionable way" [8]. To enable near-real-time monitoring, CyberScope was introduced as the platform for submitting data feeds (automated and manual) and to enable OMB and DHS[61] to conduct government-wide benchmarking through a set of questions/ metrics[62] that describe each on the federal agencies' security posture.

As part of the continuous monitoring requirements, CSPs are required to submit similar types of data elements to federal agencies to use in meeting their reporting requirements and to give the FedRAMP PMO operational visibility into the security posture of cloud services. In addition, CSPs are required to conduct an annual re-assessment of a subset of the security controls identified in the FedRAMP baseline and submit an annual self-attestation report.

Change Control

Changes to an operational environment are inevitable as a system undergoes routine maintenance. However, some changes may cause significant impacts to the security posture of the cloud service.[63] Therefore, the CSP is required

---

[59]Office of Management and Budget (OMB) Memorandum 10-15, *FY 2010 Reporting Instructions for the Federal Information Security Management Act and Agency Privacy Management*. Available from: www.whitehouse.gov/sites/default/files/omb/assets/memoranda_2010/m10-15.pdf.

[60]From Zients, J., Kundra, V., Schmidt, H. Office of Management and Budget (OMB) Memorandum 10-15, FY 2010 Reporting Instructions for the Federal Information System Management Act and Agency Privacy Management. Washington, DC: Executive Office of the President, Office of Management and Budget; 2010. "*The three-tiered approached is a result of the task force established in September 2009 to develop new, outcome-focused metrics for information security performance for Federal agencies.*"

[61]In July 2010, through the responsibilities outlined in OMB Memorandum 10-28, Clarifying Cybersecurity Responsibilities and Activities of the Executive Office of the President and the Department of Homeland Security, DHS was given the primary responsibility for operational aspects of cybersecurity with respect to the federal information system covered under FISMA 2002 as defined in Section 3545.

[62]In February 2012, DHS published the FY 2012 Chief Information Officer Federal Information Security Management Act Reporting Metrics, which requires federal agencies to report on cloud services. Available from: http://www.dhs.gov/xlibrary/assets/nppd/ciofismametricsfinal.pdf.

[63]Depending on the cloud service and deployment model, changes to the cloud service could affect other services or applications within the cloud stack.

to report "changes in the CSP's point of contact with FedRAMP, changes in the CSP's risk posture, changes to any applications residing on the cloud system, and/or changes to the cloud system infrastructure" [6], and submit any residual artifacts associated with significant changes such as the SSP, security impacts analysis, and a re-assessment by a 3PAO to the FedRAMP PMO.

Incident Response

Incident response plans ensure there is bilateral communication on incidents between the CSP and the federal government. Depending on the type of incident and the scope of the impact, a single incident could impact multiple federal agencies leveraging the cloud service [9]. The notification of incidents and coordination with the United States Computer Emergency Readiness Team (US-CERT)[64] and federal agency Security Operations Centers (SOCs) ensures that there is a managed response and escalation of incidences.

THIRD PARTY ASSESSMENT ORGANIZATION PROGRAM

Conformity assessments[65] are not new to the federal government. As discussed in Chapter 2, Cloud computing standards, the federal government has a role in supporting standards development.[66] For example, NIST,[67] which chairs the Interagency Committee on Standards Policy (ISCP),[68] has the responsibility[69] of coordinating public and private sector standards and conformity assessment activities. In the 3PAO Program, the FedRAMP PMO in coordination with NIST designed "a conformity assessment process for use with FedRAMP to ensure the independence of and the management and the technical quality of 3PAOs uses a standard and consistent

---

[64]*US-CERT*. Available from: http://www.us-cert.gov.

[65]From Global Standards Information, Federal Register, Vol. 65, No. 155, Guidance on Federal Conformity Assessment Activities. Maryland: National Institute of Standards and Technology; 2000. "*Conformity assessment means any activity concerned with determining directly or indirectly that requirements are fulfilled.*"

[66]Office of Management and Budget (OMB) Circular No A-119, *Federal Participation in the Development and Use of Voluntary Consensus Standards and in Conformity Assessment Activities.* Available from: http://www.whitehouse.gov/omb/circulars_a119.

[67]NIST, a US government's standards agency, collaborates with other standards development organizations (SDOs) such as the American National Standards Institute (ANSI), which is the representative for the United States in the International Organization for Standards (ISO).

[68]*Interagency Committee on Standards Policy (ICSP)*. http://standards.gov/icsp/query/index.cfm.

[69]Reference Section 12 of the *National Technology Transfer and Advancement Act (NTAA) of 1995.* Available from: https://www.gpo.gov/fdsys/pkg/PLAW-104publ113/pdf/PLAW-104publ113.pdf.

security assessment process" [10]. The conformity assessment process[70] gives the federal government the confidence of the security in using cloud services through:

- the conformance with an established set of security standards and requirements;
- a consistently applied security assessment process; and
- the use of a structured approach when granting provisional ATOs.

In the FedRAMP process, the 3PAO[71] plays a critical role in providing the FedRAMP JAB with an independent evaluation (or inspection[72]) to ensure that the cloud service meets FedRAMP security requirements through a conformity assessment[73] process. To ensure that assessments of cloud services are conducted in a unified and standard approach, enabling a "do once, use many times" approach, organizations conducting the security assessments will need to be accredited to ensure that they meet the minimum requirements of independence and competence.[74]

> **TIP**
>
> Independent assessors or assessment teams must be capable of conducting an impartial assessment. What qualifies an assessor or assessment team as being capable of presenting results in a manner that would enable the JAB in making a "credible, risk-based decision" is determined through the 3PAO program. In addition to the 3PAO program, "CSPs should establish minimum
>
> *(Continued)*

---

[70]ISO/IEC 17020:1998, General Criteria for the operation of various types of bodies performing inspection. ISO/IEC 17020:1998 has been withdrawn and replaced by the revised version ISO/ IEC 17020:2012, Conformity assessment—Requirements for the operation of various types of bodies performing inspection—http://www.iso.org/iso/iso_catalogue/catalogue_tc/catalogue_detail.htm? csnumber=52994.

[71]From FedRAMP Program Management Office (PMO). Independent Assessors [Internet]. Washington, DC: US General Services Administration [cited April 24, 2016]. Available from: https://www.fedramp.gov/participate/3paos/. *"Independent assessors perform initial and periodic assessments of cloud systems to ensure they meet FedRAMP requirements."*

[72]From Global Standards Information, Federal Register, Vol. 65, No. 155, Guidance on Federal Conformity Assessment Activities. Maryland: National Institute of Standards and Technology; 2000. *"Inspection is defined as the evaluation by observation and judgment accompanied as appropriate by measurement, testing or gauging of the conformity of a product, process or service to specified requirements."*

[73]From Global Standards Information, Conformity Assessment [Internet]. Maryland: National Institute of Standards and Technology [cited March 17, 2012]. Available from: http://gsi.nist.gov/global/index. cfm/L1-5/L2-45. *"Conformity assessment procedures provide a means of ensuring that the products, services, systems, persons, or bodies have certain required characteristics, and that these characteristics are consistent from product to product, service to service, system to system, etc."*

[74]Breitenberg, M. NISTIR 6014, The ABC's of the US Conformity Assessment System. Maryland: National Institute of Standards and Technology; 1997. *"A prescribed set of rules, conditions, or requirements concerning definitions of terms; classification of components; specification of materials, performance, or operations; delineation of procedures; or measurement of quantity and quality in describing materials, products, systems, services, or practices."*

> **TIP (CONTINUED)**
>
> personnel requirements such as the CCSK with other credentials like the CISSP, CAP, CSSLP, etc. The CSP could have some level of assurance that the assessor conducting the assessment has evidence of cloud security knowledge" [11].
>
> *The criteria of an independent assessor(s) or assessment team within the Cloud should include a mix of skills and proficiencies …*
>
> *… a key criteria that should be included as part of the selection criterion when identifying qualified and "capable" independent assessors or members of an assessment team is certifications that establish a baseline of cloud security knowledge [12].*

SUMMARY

In this chapter, FedRAMP was introduced through a detailed discussion of the program goals and objectives, and its role in supporting the secure adoption of cloud computing services. The program's governing documents (i.e., Policy Memo, RAR, SAF) provide insight into how the program operates. In addition, the primary stakeholders were also briefly discussed as it relates to their roles and responsibilities for the governance and execution of FedRAMP phases. The FedRAMP Accelerated process was presented, which includes a readiness (capabilities) assessment or "pre-audit" to determine if a CSP is "FedRAMP Ready." Through a review of the FedRAMP phases defined within the FedRAMP SAF, a mapping to NIST RMF provides context into the similarities and differences between the FedRAMP implementation of those processes defined in NIST standards and guidance references. Finally, the FedRAMP 3PAO program was introduced highlighting the role of the 3PAO in ensuring CSPs are in conformance with the FedRAMP security and privacy requirements.

REFERENCES

[1] Mel P. ISACA national capital area chapter, Session #4: federal risk and authorization management program (FedRAMP). Gaithersburg, MD: National Institute of Standards and Technology; 2010.

[2] Kundra V. Proposed security assessment & authorization for US government cloud computing, draft version 0.96.. Washington, DC: CIO Council; 2010.

[3] VanRoekel S. Office of Management and Budget (OMB) memorandum, security authorization of information system in cloud computing environments. Washington, DC: Executive Office of the President, Office of Management and Budget; 2011.

[4] FedRAMP Program Management Office (PMO). Federal risk and authorization management program (FedRAMP), agency day. Washington, DC: US General Services Administration; 2012.

[5] E-Government Act of 2002 [Internet]. Washington, DC: US Government Printing Office; [cited Dec 5, 2011]. <http://www.gpo.gov/fdsys/pkg/PLAW-107publ347/html/PLAW-107publ347.htm>.

[6] FedRAMP Program Management Office (PMO). FedRAMP Security Assessment Framework Version 2.1. Washington, DC: US General Services Administration; 2015.

[7] Joint Task Force Transformation Initiative Interagency Working Group. NIST SP 800-37 Revision 1, Guide for Applying the Risk Management Framework to Federal Information Systems: A Security Life Cycle Approach. Gaithersburg, MD: National Institute of Standards and Technology; 2010.

[8] Zients J, Kundra V, Schmidt H. Office of Management and Budget (OMB) memorandum 10−15, FY 2010 reporting instructions for the federal information system management act and agency privacy management. Washington, DC: Executive Office of the President, Office of Management and Budget; 2010.

[9] FedRAMP Program Management Office (PMO). Continuous Monitoring Strategy & Guide, Version 2.0. Washington, DC: US General Services Administration; 2014.

[10] FedRAMP Program Management Office (PMO). General FedRAMP FAQ [Internet]. Washington, DC: US General Services Administration [cited Mar 15, 2011]. <http://www.gsa.gov/portal/content/118887>.

[11] Metheny M. Selecting a 3PAO with assessors that have the certificate of cloud security knowledge (CCSK) [Internet]. Palm Harbor, FL: International Information Systems Security Certification Consortium (ISC)2 Blog [cited April 1, 2012]. <http://blog.isc2.org/isc2_blog/2012/04/selecting-a-3pao-with-assessors-that-have-the-certificate-of-cloud-security-knowledge-ccsk.html>.

[12] Metheny, M. Selecting an Independent Third Party Assessor [Internet]. Washington, DC: FedRAMP.net [cited April 1, 2012]. <http://www.fedramp.net/selecting-an-independent-third-party-assessor.pdf>.

[13] FedRAMP Program Management Office (PMO). Guide to Understanding FedRAMP Version 1.0. Washington, DC: US General Services Administration; 2012.

[14] FedRAMP Program Management Office (PMO). Control Implementation Summary (CIS)Template Version 2.1. Washington, DC: US General Services Administration; 2012.

[15] FedRAMP Program Management Office (PMO), FedRAMP Accelerated Process Overview. [Internet]. Washington, DC: US General Services Administration [cited September 9, 2016]. <https://www.fedramp.gov/participate/fedramp-accelerated-process/>.

[16] FedRAMP Program Management Office (PMO). Readiness Assessment Report Template. Washington, DC: US General Services Administration; 2016.

The FedRAMP cloud computing security requirements

9

INFORMATION IN THIS CHAPTER:

- Security Control Selection Process
- FedRAMP Cloud Computing Security Requirements
- Federal Laws, Executive Orders, Policies, Directives, Regulations, Standards, and Guideline

SECURITY CONTROL SELECTION PROCESS

The Federal Risk and Authorization Management Program (FedRAMP) Joint Authorization Board (JAB) selected security controls from the National Institute of Standards and Technology (NIST) Special Publication (SP) 800-53 low, moderate, and high security control baselines and supplemented with additional security controls and enhancements to address the unique risks to cloud computing environments. These risks included multitenancy, visibility, control/responsibility, shared resource pooling, and trust [1]. The FedRAMP security control baselines were developed through a multistep process focused on defining a standardized set of security requirements for the cost-effective, authorization of cloud services for use by the federal government. As discussed in Chapter 5, Applying the NIST Risk Management Framework, the security control selection process involves the application of three steps:

- Selecting the initial security control baseline.
- Tailoring the security control baseline.
- Supplementing the security control baseline.

Since the FedRAMP program is meant to be a consistent, government-wide approach to security assessment and authorization, the final security control baselines creates a government-wide overlay[1] that identifies specific security requirements for "cloud-based information systems that are uniformly applied to all federal agencies procuring or implementing cloud services" [2].

---

[1]From Joint Task Force Transformation Initiative, NIST Special Publication (SP) 800-53 Revision 4, Security and Privacy Controls for Federal Information System and Organizations. Maryland: National Institute of Standards and Technology; 2013. "*An overlay is a fully specified set of security controls, control enhancements, and supplemental guidance derived from the application of tailoring guidance*".

Federal Cloud Computing. DOI: http://dx.doi.org/10.1016/B978-0-12-809710-6.00009-3

SELECTING THE SECURITY CONTROL BASELINE

The FedRAMP security control baselines operates at the low-, moderate-, or high-impact level, where low, moderate, and high categorization is equally applied across all of the security objectives (*confidentiality*, *integrity*, and *availability*) for the cloud service.

For cloud services applying the FedRAMP low baseline, the security control baseline was developed based on the following security categorization:

> SECURITY CATEGORY _{cloud service} = {(**confidentiality**, *low*), (**integrity**, *low*), (**availability**, *low*)}

where the value for potential impact to the loss of confidentiality, integrity, and availability is low.

For cloud services applying the FedRAMP moderate baseline, the security control baseline was developed based on following security categorization:

> SECURITY CATEGORY _{cloud service} = {(**confidentiality**, *moderate*), (**integrity**, *moderate*), (**availability**, *moderate*)}

where the value for potential impact to the loss of confidentiality, integrity, and availability is moderate.

For cloud services applying the FedRAMP high baseline, the security control baseline was developed based on following security categorization:

> SECURITY CATEGORY _{cloud service} = {(**confidentiality**, *high*), (**integrity**, *high*), (**availability**, *high*)}

where the value for potential impact to the loss of confidentiality, integrity, and availability is high.

TAILORING AND SUPPLEMENTING SECURITY CONTROL BASELINE

The FedRAMP security control baselines[2] were developed through the application of the NIST Risk Management Framework (RMF)[3] tailoring process. As discussed previously, the tailoring process is the second step of the security control selection process and includes the assignment of specific values to the organization-defined security control parameters.[4] Some security controls

---

[2]From Joint Task Force Transformation Initiative, NIST Special Publication (SP) 800-53 Revision 4, Security and Privacy Controls for Federal Information System and Organizations. Maryland: National Institute of Standards and Technology; 2013. *"Baseline controls are the starting point for the security control selection process."*

[3]Chapter 5 discussed the risk management activities involved in the application of the Risk Management Framework (RMF).

[4]From Joint Task Force Transformation Initiative, NIST Special Publication (SP) 800-53 Revision 4, Security and Privacy Controls for Federal Information System and Organizations. Maryland: National Institute of Standards and Technology; 2013. *"Organizations may choose to define specific values for security control parameters in policies, procedures, or guidance (which may be applicable to more than one information system) referencing the source documents in the security plan in lieu of explicitly completing the assignment/selection statements within the control as part of the plan."*

included within NIST SP 800-53, Appendix F—Security Control Catalog, have embedded parameters[5] that are designed to provide flexibility when defining the specification for the security control and enhancement(s) necessary to support the definition of government-wide security requirements for the secure use of cloud computing services.

After the initial security control baseline was tailored, the FedRAMP JAB supplemented the baseline with additional security controls and enhancements identified as necessary to sufficiently protect federal information within a cloud computing environment. In addition to the requirements defined in the FedRAMP security controls, the FedRAMP JAB defined additional requirements through security control addendum [2].

FEDRAMP CLOUD COMPUTING OVERLAY

The FedRAMP cloud computing overlay[6] is a government-wide set of security controls that are based on a focused look at the security capabilities and requirements needed to protect federal information within low-, moderate-, and high-impact cloud services. The application of an overlay does not limit Cloud Service Providers (CSPs) or federal agencies from tailoring or supplementing the FedRAMP security control baselines, rather it creates a "community-wide or specialized set of security controls for information system and organizations" [2] based on a consensus[7] of those within the community that the requirements should be broadly applied to multiple information systems (and cloud services) that meet a specific target characteristic (i.e., the FedRAMP control baselines can be further refined based on a specific service or deployment model).

---

[5]From Joint Task Force Transformation Initiative. NIST Special Publication (SP) 800-53 Revision 4, Security and Privacy Controls for Federal Information System and Organizations. Maryland: National Institute of Standards and Technology; 2013. *"Assignment and selection statements provide organizations with the capability to specialize security controls and control enhancements based on organizational security requirements or requirements originating in federal laws, Executive Orders, directives, policies, regulations, standards, or guidelines. Organization-defined parameters used in assignment and selection statements in the basic security controls apply also to all control enhancements associated with those controls."*
[6]From Joint Task Force Transformation Initiative, NIST Special Publication (SP) 800-53 Revision 4, Security and Privacy Controls for Federal Information System and Organizations. Maryland: National Institute of Standards and Technology; 2013. *"An overlay is a fully specified set of security controls, control enhancements, and supplemental guidance derived from the application of tailoring guidance."*
[7]From Joint Task Force Transformation Initiative, NIST Special Publication (SP) 800-53 Revision 4, Security and Privacy Controls for Federal Information System and Organizations. Maryland: National Institute of Standards and Technology; 2013. *"The overlay concept is most effective when communities of interest work together to create consensus-based overlays that are not duplicative."*

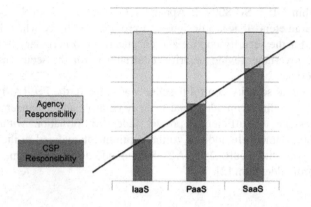

FIGURE 9.1

Security control responsibilities [3].

FEDRAMP CLOUD COMPUTING SECURITY REQUIREMENTS

The FedRAMP "Policy Memo," as discussed in Chapter 8, FedRAMP Primer, is the overarching policy that covers all commercial and noncommercial cloud services, including all cloud deployment and service models with the exception[8] of a private cloud operating on-premise, and which provides services to only the owning organization (i.e., no external users, including other organizational entities within the same federal agency). Since CSPs can operate as either a public (i.e., federal or state government) or private sector organization, or both, potentially complex cloud relationships can be created where security control assignment and ownership can be difficult to determine. Therefore, all stakeholders should participate in planning and coordinating the development of cloud-specific contracts (or other end user agreements).[9]

The scope of the contracts (or agreements) should provide a clear definition of the governance over the cloud service environment (i.e., the policies, procedures, standards, guidelines, and roles and responsibilities that would be applied). In addition, the contracts (or agreements) should provide a clear delineation of the security control responsibility,[10] similar to Fig. 9.1, including any applicable

---

[8]From FedRAMP Program Management Office (PMO). Is FedRAMP mandatory? [Internet]. Washington, DC: US General Services Administration [cited May 6, 2016]. Available from: https://www.fedramp.gov/resources/faqs/is-fedramp-mandatory/. "*Private cloud deployments intended for single organizations and implemented fully within Federal facilities are the only exception.*"

[9]From Federal CIO Council, Chief Acquisition Officer Council. Creating Effective Cloud Computing Contracts for the Federal Government: Best Practices for Acquiring IT as a Service. Washington, DC: Federal CIO Council; 2012. "*Any contract provisions regarding controlling law, jurisdiction, and indemnification arising out of a Federal agency's use of a CSP environment must align with Federal statutes, policies, and regulations; and compliance should be defined before a contract award. This may be done through a separate document or be included in the actual contract.*"

[10]From FedRAMP Program Management Office (PMO). FedRAMP Concept of Operations (CONOPS) Version 1.1. Washington, DC: US General Services Administration; 2012. "*The FedRAMP Control Implementation Summary (CIS) summarizes the control ownership and indicates which controls are owned and managed by the CSP and which controls are owned and managed by the leveraging agency.*"

policies and procedures that would satisfy the requirements for the security controls. As an example, the FedRAMP Security Assessment Framework (SAF), requires CSPs to submit information security policies governing their cloud service, as described in the System Security Plan (SSP),[11] to the FedRAMP PMO as part of the FedRAMP security authorization process.

The delineation should include any applicable policies and procedures that would apply to the implementation of the FedRAMP security controls. Since CSPs are required to submit information security policies and procedures governing their cloud service as described in the FedRAMP SSP[12] template to the FedRAMP PMO as part of the FedRAMP security authorization process, CSPs should at minimum have established security policies that govern all of FedRAMP security requirements that are applicable to their cloud service layer.

The assignment of responsibility for security controls is an essential activity that requires identifying situations where there is potential shared responsibilities (or hybrid controls). For example, a CSP may implement the Incident Response Policy and Procedures security control (IR-1) as a hybrid control with the policy portion of the control deemed to be common and applied as a corporate responsibility, and the procedures portion of the control deemed to be system-specific [2]. The FedRAMP PMO established the Control Implementation Summary (CIS) document to be completed by the CSP to aid in communicating the ownership and responsibility of the security controls between the CSP and the federal agency customer.

POLICY AND PROCEDURES

The Federal Information Security Modernization Act (FISMA)[13] requires the highest-level senior executive within an organization (e.g., head of the federal agency, chief executive officer) with the overall responsibility to provide for the information security protections and to ensure the development, implementation,

---

[11]From FedRAMP Program Management Office (PMO). FedRAMP Concept of Operations (CONOPS) Version 1.1. Washington, DC: US General Services Administration; 2012. *"The SSP details the security authorization boundary, how the implementations address each required control and enhancement in the selected control baseline, descriptions of roles and responsibilities, and expected behavior of individuals with system access."*

[12]From FedRAMP Program Management Office (PMO). FedRAMP Concept of Operations (CONOPS) Version 1.1. Washington, DC: US General Services Administration; 2012. *"The SSP details the security authorization boundary, how the implementations address each required control and enhancement in the selected control baseline, descriptions of roles and responsibilities, and expected behavior of individuals with system access."*

[13]FISMA was discussed in detail in Chapter 5, Applying the Risk Management Framework.

and maintenance of information security policies, procedures, and control techniques. The policies, procedures, and control techniques must address all applicable requirements, including those issued by the Office of Management and Budget (OMB) and the NIST, except where authority is delegated to other organizations (e.g., the Secretary of Defense for US Department of Defense (DoD) information systems).

In each of the security control families (e.g., security assessment and authorization, configuration management, access control), the first control, identified as the "XX-1" security controls, requires the development of security policies[14] that address the requirements that must be implemented within information system or by the organization.[15] The CSP's security policies should include at minimum the purpose[16] of the policy, the scope,[17] the roles and responsibilities,[18] and compliance.[19] The FedRAMP "Policy Memo"[20] issued by the OMB defines

[14]From Joint Task Force Transformation Initiative, NIST Special Publication (SP) 800-53 Revision 4, Security and Privacy Controls for Federal Information System and Organizations. Maryland: National Institute of Standards and Technology; 2013. *"The policies and procedures are consistent with applicable federal laws, Executive Orders, directives, policies, regulations, standards, and guidance."*

[15]From Joint Task Force Transformation Initiative. NIST Special Publication (SP) 800-37 Revision 1, Guide for Applying the Risk Management Framework to Federal Information Systems: A Security Life Cycle Approach. Maryland: National Institute of Standards and Technology; 2010. *"The federal agency or subordinate organization that owns the authorization package. The information system may not be owned by the same organization that owns the authorization package, for example, in situations where the system/services are provided by an external provider."*

[16]From Burrows, J., McNulty, F., Katzke, S., Gilbert, I., Steinauer, D. NIST Special Publication (SP) 800-12, An Introduction to Computer Security: The NIST Handbook. Maryland: National Institute of Standards and Technology; 1995. *"Program policy normally includes a statement describing why the program is being established. This may include defining the goals of the program."*

[17]From Burrows, J., McNulty, F., Katzke, S., Gilbert, I., Steinauer, D. NIST Special Publication (SP) 800-12, An Introduction to Computer Security: The NIST Handbook. Maryland: National Institute of Standards and Technology; 1995. *"Program policy should be clear as to which resources-including facilities, hardware, and software, information, and personnel—the computer security program covers."*

[18]From Burrows, J., McNulty, F., Katzke, S., Gilbert, I., Steinauer, D. NIST Special Publication (SP) 800-12, An Introduction to Computer Security: The NIST Handbook. Maryland: National Institute of Standards and Technology; 1995. *"Once the computer security program is established, its management is normally assigned to either a newly-created or existing office."*

[19]From Burrows, J., McNulty, F., Katzke, S., Gilbert, I., Steinauer, D. NIST Special Publication (SP) 800-12, An Introduction to Computer Security: The NIST Handbook. Maryland: National Institute of Standards and Technology; 1995. *"Addresses two issues, general compliance, to ensure meeting the requirements to establish a program and the responsibilities assigned therein to various organizational components and the use of specified penalties and disciplinary actions."*

[20]The FedRAMP "Policy Memo" includes all of the key components of a policy such as purpose, scope, roles and responsibility, and compliance.

the government-wide security program,[21] and the security and authorization policy for addressing the security and authorization of cloud computing environments. Through the implementation of an information security program plan,[22] the organization can effectively centralize those security controls deemed independent of a particular cloud service and instead manage them as part of the overarching information security program.

TIP

Standards, Guidelines, and Procedures

To assist CSPs and federal agencies in implementing policies, standards, guidelines, and procedures should be used. Standards and guidelines, such as those developed by NIST under a statutory responsibility, establish minimum requirements promulgated from legislative mandates "to support the implementation of and compliance with FISMA" [4]. Whereas other standards and guidelines such as the NIST SPs, Defense Information System Agency (DISA) Security Technical Implementation Guides (STIGs),[23] or National Security Agency (NSA) Information Assurance (IA) Mitigation Guidelines[24] focus on providing specific methods or techniques for ensuring the security of a solution. Standards and guidelines can focus on a general concept such as server security,[25] secure communication[26] or secure operations,[27] while others may target a specific technology (i.e., virtualization[28] or IPv6[29]) or security feature (i.e., encryption[30] or security automation[31]). Procedures are more scoped to the operating environment (i.e., operational personnel, facility, and system operations) and provide the detailed steps that address how the policies, standards, and guidelines are applied within an operational context such as credential management or performing audit log management.

---

[21]From Joint Task Force Transformation Initiative, NIST Special Publication (SP) 800-53 Revision 4, Security and Privacy Controls for Federal Information System and Organizations. Maryland: National Institute of Standards and Technology; 2013. *"Security program policies and procedures at the organization level may make the need for system-specific policies and procedures."*

[22]From Joint Task Force Transformation Initiative, NIST Special Publication (SP) 800-53 Revision 4, Security and Privacy Controls for Federal Information System and Organizations. Maryland: National Institute of Standards and Technology; 2013. *"The security plans for individual information systems and the organization-wide information security program plan together, provide complete coverage for all security controls employed within the* organization."

[23]*Security Technical Implementation Guides (STIGs) Security Checklists*. Available from: http://iase.disa.mil/stigs/.

[24]*IA Mitigation Guidance*. Available from: http://www.nsa.gov/ia/mitigation_guidance/index.shtml.

[25]NIST Special Publication (SP) 800-123, *Guide to General Server Security*. Available from: http://nvlpubs.nist.gov/nistpubs/Legacy/SP/nistspecialpublication800-123.pdf.

[26]NIST Special Publication (SP) 800-113, *Guide to SSL VPNs*. Available from: http://nvlpubs.nist.gov/nistpubs/Legacy/SP/nistspecialpublication800-113.pdf.

[27]NIST Special Publication (SP) 800-128, *Guide for Security-Focused Configuration Management of Information Systems*. Available from: http://nvlpubs.nist.gov/nistpubs/Legacy/SP/nistspecialpublication800-128.pdf.

[28]NIST Special Publication (SP) 800-125, *Guide to Security for Full Virtualization Technologies*. Available from: http://nvlpubs.nist.gov/nistpubs/Legacy/SP/nistspecialpublication800-125.pdf.

[29]NIST Special Publication (SP) 800-119, *Guidelines for the Secure Deployment of IPv6*. Available from: http://nvlpubs.nist.gov/nistpubs/Legacy/SP/nistspecialpublication800-119.pdf.

[30]NIST Special Publication (SP) 800-130, *A Framework for Designing Cryptographic Key Management Systems*. Available from: http://nvlpubs.nist.gov/nistpubs/SpecialPublications/NIST.SP.800-130.pdf.

[31]NIST Special Publication (SP) 800-126, *The Technical Specific for the Security Content Automation Protocol (SCAP)*. Available from: http://nvlpubs.nist.gov/nistpubs/Legacy/SP/nistspecialpublication800-126r2.pdf.

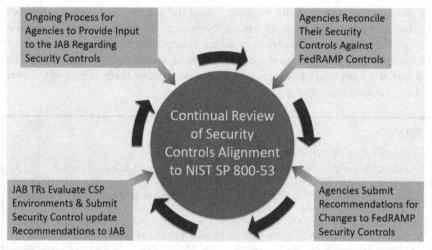

FIGURE 9.2

Maintenance of security controls [5].

HARMONIZING FEDRAMP REQUIREMENTS

The FedRAMP "Policy Memo" established a standard set of security requirements that would be used for the authorization and ongoing continuous monitoring of cloud services.[32] In addition, the FedRAMP security requirements could be supplemented with additional federal agency-specific security and privacy requirements, or even incur changes through updates to NIST SP 800-53 and by the JAB[33] review process. Therefore, a harmonization governance process,[34] similar to Fig. 9.2, may be used by the FedRAMP PMO to maintain and elicit changes to the FedRAMP security controls, to include changes in security control requirements.

---

[32]At the time of the FedRAMP memo publication, only NIST-defined low- and moderate-impact information systems were considered within scope of FedRAMP.

[33]From VanRoekel, S. Office of Management and Budget (OMB) Memorandum, Security Authorization of Information System in Cloud Computing Environments. Washington, DC: Executive Office of the President, Office of Management and Budget; 2011. *The JAB shall "define and regularly review the FedRAMP security authorization requirements in accordance with the Federal Information Security Management Act of 2002 (FISMA) and DHS guidance."*

[34]From VanRoekel, S. Office of Management and Budget (OMB) Memorandum, Security Authorization of Information System in Cloud Computing Environments. Washington, DC: Executive Office of the President, Office of Management and Budget; 2011. *The FedRAMP PMI will create "a methodology for harmonizing agency-specific security and privacy controls with the FedRAMP security authorization requirements."*

Through a continual review process[35] input from multiple sources can be used by the JAB to harmonize the FedRAMP security controls as part of a review and adjudication. Example input could include feedback from federal agencies on the adequacy of the FedRAMP security control requirements, an evaluation by JAB Technical Representatives (TRs) of CSP environments, or the reconciliation with federal agency-specific security and privacy requirements. In addition, all federal agencies (and contractors)[36] are required to be in compliance with NIST publications[37] one year[38] date of publication. Therefore, changes to the NIST SP 800-53 could also require changes and updates to the FedRAMP security controls.

ASSURANCE OF EXTERNAL SERVICE PROVIDERS COMPLIANCE

FISMA requires agencies to provide security protections "...commensurate with the risk and magnitude of harm resulting from unauthorized access, use, disclosure, disruption, modification, or destruction of information collected or maintained by or on behalf of the agency; and information systems used or operated by an agency or other organization on behalf of an agency" [6]. In addition, OMB requires federal agencies to ensure appropriate information security oversight capabilities exist for contractors and other users with privileged access to federal data and systems.

CSPs, regardless of the deployment and service model, are required to meet the same requirements when processing, storing, or transmitting federal information or are operating on behalf of the federal government. The integration of FedRAMP security requirements into the terms and conditions of contracts and service-level agreements (SLAs),[39] provides a mechanism when defining roles and responsibilities. The FedRAMP PMO provides standard contract clauses,[40] control-specific

---

[35]From Coleman, C., Spires, R, Takai, T. Federal Risk and Authorization Management Program Joint Authorization Board Charter Version 1.0. Washington, DC: FedRAMP Program Management Office, US General Services Administration; 2012. *"The JAB will work with the FedRAMP PMO to establish methods for regular input by Executive departments and agencies to ensure the FedRAMP security authorization requirements are meeting the needs of the Federal government."*

[36]From FedRAMP Program Management Office (PMO). FedRAMP Standard Contract Language, Washington, DC: US General Services Administration; 2012. *"Contractor shall refer to cloud service providers, or contract holders who are providing cloud computing services to the Federal Government through this contract."*

[37]From Lew, J. Office of Management and Budget (OMB) Memorandum 11-33, FY 2011 Reporting Instructions for the Federal Information Security Management Act and Agency Privacy Management. Washington, DC: Executive Office of the President, Office of Management and Budget; 2011. *"For information systems under development or for legacy systems undergoing significant changes, agencies are expected to be in compliance with the NIST publications immediately upon deployment of the information system."*

[38]From Lew, J. Office of Management and Budget (OMB) Memorandum 11-33, FY 2011 Reporting Instructions for the Federal Information Security Management Act and Agency Privacy Management. Washington, DC: Executive Office of the President, Office of Management and Budget; 2011. *"The one year compliance date for revisions to NIST publications applies to new and/or updated material in the publications."*

[39]Example sources for defining service levels can include the Open Data Center Alliance (ODCA) Usage Models available from: https://opendatacenteralliance.org/accelerating-adoption/usage-models/.

[40]FedRAMP Standard Contract Clauses. Available from: https://www.fedramp.gov/files/2015/03/FedRAMP_Standard_Contractual_Clauses_062712_0.pdf.

contract clauses,[41] and accompanying SLA guidance[42] covering all FedRAMP requirements [3]. Although CSPs are responsible for ensuring compliance with the FedRAMP security requirements, the overall responsibility for mitigating risks in using cloud services is retained with the federal agency customer.

NOTE

The Federal Acquisition Regulation (FAR) covers the acquisition of IT supplies and services used by federal agencies. The requirements within the FAR include applicable provisions with references to address information security and privacy as part of the acquisition process. These requirements include the following:

- FAR 7.103(u)—"Ensuring that agency planners on information technology acquisitions comply with the information technology security requirements in the Federal Information Security Management Act (44 US C. 3544), OMB's implementing policies including Appendix III of OMB Circular A-130, and guidance and standards from the Department of Commerce's National Institute of Standards and Technology" [7].
- FAR 11.102—"Agencies shall select existing requirements documents or develop new requirements documents that meet the needs of the agency in accordance with the guidance contained in the Federal Standardization Manual, FSPM-0001; for DoD components, DoD 4120.24-M, Defense Standardization Program Policies and Procedures; and for IT standards and guidance, the Federal Information Processing Standards Publications (FIPS PUBS)" [8].
- FAR 39.101(d)—"In acquiring information technology, agencies shall include the appropriate information technology security policies and requirements, including use of common security configurations available from the National Institute of Standards and Technology's website at http://checklists.nist.gov. Agency contracting officers should consult with the requiring official to ensure the appropriate standards are incorporated" [9].
- FAR 52.239-1(a)—"Contractor shall not publish or disclose in any manner, without the Contracting Officer's written consent, the details of any safeguards either designed or developed by the Contractor under this contract or otherwise provided by the Government."[43]
- FAR 52.239-1(b)—"To the extent required to carry out a program of inspection to safeguard against threats and hazards to the security, integrity, and confidentiality of Government data, the Contractor shall afford the Government access to the Contractor's facilities, installations, technical capabilities, operations, documentation, records, and databases."[44]
- FAR 52.239-1(c)—"If new or unanticipated threats or hazards are discovered by either the Government or the Contractor, or if existing safeguards have ceased to function, the discoverer shall immediately bring the situation to the attention of the other party."[45]

---

[41]FedRAMP Control-Specific Contract Clauses. Available from: https://www.fedramp.gov/files/2015/03/FedRAMP_Standard_Contractual_Clauses_062712_0.pdf.

[42]In February 2012, the Federal CIO Council and the Chief Acquisition Officers Council published a best practices guide for "*Creating Effective Cloud Computing Contracts for the Federal Government*" to provide federal agencies with best practices for acquiring IT as a service.

[43]US General Services Administration. FAR Subpart 7.1 [Internet]. Washington, DC: US General Services Administration [cited March 13, 2012]. Available from: https://www.acquisition.gov/far/html/52_233_240.html.

[44]US General Services Administration. FAR Subpart 7.1 [Internet]. Washington, DC: US General Services Administration [cited March 13, 2012]. Available from: https://www.acquisition.gov/far/html/52_233_240.html.

[45]US General Services Administration. FAR Subpart 7.1 [Internet]. Washington, DC: US General Services Administration [cited March 13, 2012]. Available from: https://www.acquisition.gov/far/html/52_233_240.html.

APPROACHES TO IMPLEMENTING FEDRAMP SECURITY CONTROLS

Decisions made as part of the security control selection process are driven by the organization's determination of the adequate protection for a given information system within a target operating environment. The decisions made during the risk management activities aid in establishing the risk-based information such as assumptions, constraints, and rationale needed for addressing security within the information system. This information supports the implementation of security controls based on a risk-based approach that requires an understanding of the potential impacts to the organization's mission or business processes and those organizations that rely upon the information system. The potential impact is based on the compromise of one or more security objectives[46] (i.e., loss of confidentiality, integrity, or availability).

Some information systems are in the development process (i.e., *new development*), while others may already be in production (i.e., *legacy*). Depending on the state of the information system, security controls may be part of the initial requirements definition or applied as part of the change management function. If the information system is in the development process, the integration of security controls can be applied as part of the normal system development life cycle (SDLC).[47] However, if the information system is already in production, a gap analysis approach can be used to assist the organization in fully understanding what is in-place and what additional security controls will need to be applied to address the differences in the requirements gap. In some circumstances, compensating security controls may even need to be identified and applied where existing security controls that are already in-place have been determined to be insufficient to effectively mitigate potential risks.

CSPs can apply similar techniques when implementing the FedRAMP security controls. Since cloud environments may present different risks than traditional IT environments, the CSP should conduct an additional analysis to identify where the gap exists (i.e., within the different cloud service models and technology implementations) and who has the overall responsibility (CSP or federal agency) for addressing the weaknesses or deficiencies. As an example, Fig. 9.3 illustrates a high-level gap analysis exercise CSPs could use to identify the gaps in their security capabilities and features based on what is built-in.

---

[46]From Joint Task Force Transformation Initiative, NIST Special Publication (SP) 800-53 Revision 4 (Initial Public Draft), Security and Privacy Controls for Federal Information System and Organizations. Maryland: National Institute of Standards and Technology; 2012. *"Security controls are typically deployed as a unified set to achieve a desired security capability. The loss of one security objective (e.g. integrity) can adversely affect the other objectives (e.g. confidentiality and availability). When selecting security controls for nondisclosure purposes, organizations consider the security categorization of user data and system-level data—where system data may require stronger protection in the form of additional security controls."*

[47]NIST Special Publication (SP) 800-64 Revision 2, *Security Considerations in the System Development Life Cycle*. Available from: http://nvlpubs.nist.gov/nistpubs/Legacy/SP/nistspecialpublication800-64r2.pdf.

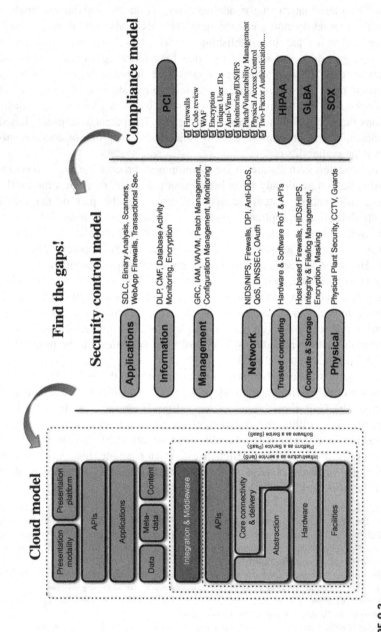

FIGURE 9.3

Cloud security reference model [10].

The gap analysis exercise includes the following three steps [10]:

1. Classifying the service against cloud model (e.g., IaaS, PaaS, or SaaS).
2. Map the existing security architecture against the cloud model.
3. Map the FedRAMP security requirements (identified as the compliance model) against the security architecture and the cloud model.

Using the steps in the gap analysis exercise, CSPs can use the preliminary information to complete the first three steps of the NIST RMF,[48] including determining the potential gaps in achieving the target FedRAMP security control baselines (low-, moderate-, or high-impact) based on their own application of the information security categorization process when completing the Federal Information Processing Standards (FIPS) 199 worksheet. In addition, this information can help them begin the process of documenting the CIS, as discussed in Chapter 8, FedRAMP Primer.

> **TIP**
>
> Some CSPs have already aligned with other regulatory or industry control frameworks such as ISO/IEC 27001/27002, ISACA COBIT, PCI DSS, and NIST 800-53. Therefore the Cloud Security Alliance (CSA) Cloud Control Matrix (CCM)[49] provides an industry consensus framework that has been developed as a tool,[50] for use by CSPs to integrate FedRAMP into their existing integrated security framework and to assist CSPs in conducting a crosswalk to determine the differences in their existing security and compliance program with the FedRAMP security requirements.

FEDRAMP SECURITY CONTROL REQUIREMENTS

The FedRAMP security control requirements provide the minimum security control baseline requirements for cloud computing environments. These security controls were based on the minimum assurance requirements included in the NIST SP 800-53 [2] and the FedRAMP Security Controls [11]. Table 9.1 provides summary of the security controls assigned to each of the security control baselines (*low, moderate, and high*) based on impact.

---

[48]Chapter 5 discussed the risk management activities involved in the application of the Risk Management Framework (RMF).
[49]Cloud Security Alliance (CSA) Cloud Control Matrix (CCM). Available from: https://cloudsecurityalliance.org/group/cloud-controls-matrix//.
[50]NIST Special Publication (SP) 800-53 Revision 4 (Initial Public Draft), Appendix H provides a security control mapping between NIST Special Publication (SP) 800-53 controls and ISO/IEC 27001 (Annex A) controls.

Table 9.1 Summary of Required Security Controls [12]

Control ID	Control Description	Impact Level		
		Low	Moderate	High
AC	**Access Control**			
AC-1	Access Control Policy and Procedures	AC-1	AC-1	AC-1
AC-2	Account Management	AC-2	AC-2 (1) (2) (3) (4) (5) (7) (9) (10) (12)	AC-2 (1) (2) (3) (4) (5) (7) (9) (10) (11) (12) (13)
AC-3	Access Enforcement	AC-3	AC-3	AC-3
AC-4	Information Flow Enforcement	Not Selected	AC-4 (21)	AC-4 (8) (21)
AC-5	Separation of Duties	Not Selected	AC-5	AC-5
AC-6	Least Privilege	Not Selected	AC-6 (1) (2) (5) (9) (10)	AC-6 (1) (2) (3) (5) (7) (8) (9) (10)
AC-7	Unsuccessful Logon Attempts	AC-7	AC-7	AC-7 (2)
AC-8	System Use Notification	AC-8	AC-8	AC-8
AC-10	Concurrent Session Control	Not Selected	AC-10	AC-10
AC-11	Session Lock	Not Selected	AC-11 (1)	AC-11 (1)
AC-12	Session Termination	Not Selected	AC-12	AC-12 (1)
AC-14	Permitted Actions without Identification or Authentication	AC-14	AC-14	AC-14
AC-17	Remote Access	AC-17	AC-17 (1) (2) (3) (4) (9)	AC-17 (1) (2) (3) (4) (9)
AC-18	Wireless Access	AC-18	AC-18 (1)	AC-18 (1) (3) (4) (5)
AC-19	Access Control for Mobile Devices	AC-19	AC-19 (5)	AC-19 (5)
AC-20	Use of External Information Systems	AC-20	AC-20 (1) (2)	AC-20 (1) (2)
AC-21	Information Sharing	Not Selected	AC-21	AC-21
AC-22	Publicly Accessible Content	AC-22	AC-22	AC-22
AT	**Awareness and Training**			
AT-1	Security Awareness and Training Policy and Procedures	AT-1	AT-1	AT-1
AT-2	Security Awareness Training	AT-2	AT-2 (2)	AT-2 (2)
AT-3	Role-Based Security Training	AT-3	AT-3	AT-3 (3) (4)
AT-4	Security Training Records	AT-4	AT-4	AT-4

(Continued)

Table 9.1 Summary of Required Security Controls [12] *Continued*

AU	Audit and Accountability			
AU-1	Audit and Accountability Policy and Procedures	AU-1	AU-1	AU-1
AU-2	Audit Events	AU-2	AU-2 (3)	AU-2 (3)
AU-3	Content of Audit Records	AU-3	AU-3 (1)	AU-3 (1) (2)
AU-4	Audit Storage Capacity	AU-4	AU-4	AU-4
AU-5	Response to Audit Processing Failures	AU-5	AU-5	AU-5 (1) (2)
AU-6	Audit Review, Analysis and Reporting	AU-6	AU-6 (1) (3)	AU-6 (1) (3) (4) (5) (6) (7) (10)
AU-7	Audit Reduction and Report Generation	Not Selected	AU-7 (1)	AU-7 (1)
AU-8	Time Stamps	AU-8	AU-8 (1)	AU-8 (1)
AU-9	Protection of Audit Information	AU-9	AU-9 (2) (4)	AU-9 (2) (3) (4)
AU-10	Nonrepudiation	Not Selected	Not Selected	AU-10
AU-11	Audit Record Retention	AU-11	AU-11	AU-11
AU-12	Audit Generation	AU-12	AU-12	AU-12 (1) (3)
CA	**Security Assessment and Authorization**			
CA-1	Security Assessment and Authorization Policies and Procedures	CA-1	CA-1	CA-1
CA-2	Security Assessments	CA-2 (1)	CA-2 (1) (2) (3)	CA-2 (1) (2) (3)
CA-3	System Interconnections	CA-3	CA-3 (3) (5)	CA-3 (3) (5)
CA-5	Plan of Action and Milestones	CA-5	CA-5	CA-5
CA-6	Security Authorization	CA-6	CA-6	CA-6
CA-7	Continuous Monitoring	CA-7	CA-7 (1)	CA-7 (1) (3)
CA-8	Penetration Testing	Not Selected	CA-8 (1)	CA-8 (1)
CA-9	Internal System Connections	CA-9	CA-9	CA-9
CM	**Configuration Management**			
CM-1	Configuration Management Policy and Procedures	CM-1	CM-1	CM-1
CM-2	Baseline Configuration	CM-2	CM-2 (1) (2) (3) (7)	CM-2 (1) (2) (3) (7)

(Continued)

Table 9.1 Summary of Required Security Controls [12] *Continued*

CM	Configuration Management			
CM-3	Configuration Change Control	Not Selected	CM-3	CM-3 (1) (2) (4) (6)
CM-4	Security Impact Analysis	CM-4	CM-4	CM-4 (1)
CM-5	Access Restrictions for Change	Not Selected	CM-5 (1) (3) (5)	CM-5 (1) (2) (3) (5)
CM-6	Configuration Settings	CM-6	CM-6 (1)	CM-6 (1) (2)
CM-7	Least Functionality	CM-7	CM-7 (1) (2) (5)	CM-7 (1) (2) (5)
CM-8	Information System Component Inventory	CM-8	CM-8 (1) (3) (5)	CM-8 (1) (2) (3) (4) (5)
CM-9	Configuration Management Plan	Not Selected	CM-9	CM-9
CM-10	Software Usage Restrictions	CM-10	CM-10 (1)	CM-10 (1)
CM-11	User-Installed Software	CM-11	CM-11	CM-11 (1)
CP	**Contingency Planning**			
CP-1	Contingency Planning Policy and Procedures	CP-1	CP-1	CP-1
CP-2	Contingency Plan	CP-2	CP-2 (1) (2) (3) (8)	CP-2 (1) (2) (3) (4) (5) (8)
CP-3	Contingency Training	CP-3	CP-3	CP-3 (1)
CP-4	Contingency Plan Testing	CP-4	CP-4 (1)	CP-4 (1) (2)
CP-6	Alternate Storage Site	Not Selected	CP-6 (1) (3)	CP-6 (1) (2) (3)
CP-7	Alternate Processing Site	Not Selected	CP-7 (1) (2) (3)	CP-7 (1) (2) (3) (4)
CP-8	Telecommunications Services	Not Selected	CP-8 (1) (2)	CP-8 (1) (2) (3) (4)
CP-9	Information System Backup	CP-9	CP-9 (1) (3)	CP-9 (1) (2) (3) (5)
CP-10	Information System Recovery and Reconstitution	CP-10	CP-10 (2)	CP-10 (2) (4)
IA	**Identification and Authentication**			
IA-1	Identification and Authentication Policy and Procedures	IA-1	IA-1	IA-1
IA-2	Identification and Authentication (Organizational Users)	IA-2 (1) (12)	IA-2 (1) (2) (3) (5) (8) (11) (12)	IA-2 (1) (2) (3) (4) (5) (8) (9) (11) (12)
IA-3	Device Identification and Authentication	Not Selected	IA-3	IA-3
IA-4	Identifier Management	IA-4	IA-4 (4)	IA-4 (4)

Table 9.1 Summary of Required Security Controls [12] *Continued*

IA	Identification and Authentication			
IA-5	Authenticator Management	IA-5 (1) (11)	IA-5 (1) (2) (3) (4) (6) (7) (11)	IA-5 (1) (2) (3) (4) (6) (7) (8) (11) (13)
IA-6	Authenticator Feedback	IA-6	IA-6	IA-6
IA-7	Cryptographic Module Authentication	IA-7	IA-7	IA-7
IA-8	Identification and Authentication (Non-Organizational Users)	IA-8 (1) (2) (3) (4)	IA-8 (1) (2) (3) (4)	IA-8 (1) (2) (3) (4)
IR	**Incident Response**			
IR-1	Incident Response Policy and Procedures	IR-1	IR-1	IR-1
IR-2	Incident Response Training	IR-2	IR-2	IR-2 (1) (2)
IR-3	Incident Response Testing	Not Selected	IR-3 (2)	IR-3 (2)
IR-4	Incident Handling	IR-4	IR-4 (1)	IR-4 (1) (2) (3) (4) (6) (8)
IR-5	Incident Monitoring	IR-5	IR-5	IR-5 (1)
IR-6	Incident Reporting	IR-6	IR-6 (1)	IR-6 (1)
IR-7	Incident Response Assistance	IR-7	IR-7 (1) (2)	IR-7 (1) (2)
IR-8	Incident Response Plan	IR-8	IR-8	IR-8
IR-9	Information Spillage Response	Not Selected	IR-9 (1) (2) (3) (4)	IR-9 (1) (2) (3) (4)
MA	**Maintenance**			
MA-1	System Maintenance Policy and Procedures	MA-1	MA-1	MA-1
MA-2	Controlled Maintenance	MA-2	MA-2	MA-2 (2)
MA-3	Maintenance Tools	Not Selected	MA-3 (1) (2) (3)	MA-3 (1) (2) (3)
MA-4	Nonlocal Maintenance	MA-4	MA-4 (2)	MA-4 (2) (3) (6)
MA-5	Maintenance Personnel	MA-5	MA-5 (1)	MA-5 (1)
MA-6	Timely Maintenance	Not Selected	MA-6	MA-6
MP	**Media Protection**			
MP-1	Media Protection Policy and Procedures	MP-1	MP-1	MP-1
MP-2	Media Access	MP-2	MP-2	MP-2
MP-3	Media Marking	Not Selected	MP-3	MP-3
MP-4	Media Storage	Not Selected	MP-4	MP-4

(Continued)

Table 9.1 Summary of Required Security Controls [12] *Continued*

MP	**Media Protection**			
MP-5	Media Transport	Not Selected	MP-5 (4)	MP-5 (4)
MP-6	Media Sanitization	MP-6	MP-6 (2)	MP-6 (1) (2) (3)
MP-7	Media Use	MP-7	MP-7 (1)	MP-7 (1)
PE	**Physical and Environmental Protection**			
PE-1	Physical and Environmental Protection Policy and Procedures	PE-1	PE-1	PE-1
PE-2	Physical Access Authorizations	PE-2	PE-2	PE-2
PE-3	Physical Access Control	PE-3	PE-3	PE-3 (1)
PE-4	Access Control for Transmission Medium	Not Selected	PE-4	PE-4
PE-5	Access Control for Output Devices	Not Selected	PE-5	PE-5
PE-6	Monitoring Physical Access	PE-6	PE-6 (1)	PE-6 (1) (4)
PE-8	Visitor Access Records	PE-8	PE-8	PE-8 (1)
PE-9	Power Equipment and Cabling	Not Selected	PE-9	PE-9
PE-10	Emergency Shutoff	Not Selected	PE-10	PE-10
PE-11	Emergency Power	Not Selected	PE-11	PE-11 (1)
PE-12	Emergency Lighting	PE-12	PE-12	PE-12
PE-13	Fire Protection	PE-13	PE-13 (2) (3)	PE-13 (1) (2) (3)
PE-14	Temperature and Humidity Controls	PE-14	PE-14 (2)	PE-14 (2)
PE-15	Water Damage Protection	PE-15	PE-15	PE-15 (1)
PE-16	Delivery and Removal	PE-16	PE-16	PE-16
PE-17	Alternate Work Site	Not Selected	PE-17	PE-17
PE-18	Location of Information System Components	Not Selected	Not Selected	PE-18
PL	**Planning**			
PL-1	Security Planning Policy and Procedures	PL-1	PL-1	PL-1
PL-2	System Security Plan	PL-2	PL-2 (3)	PL-2 (3)
PL-4	Rules of Behavior	PL-4	PL-4 (1)	PL-4 (1)
PL-8	Information Security Architecture	Not Selected	PL-8	PL-8

(Continued)

Table 9.1 Summary of Required Security Controls [12] *Continued*

PS	**Personnel Security**			
PS-1	Personnel Security Policy and Procedures	PS-1	PS-1	PS-1
PS-2	Position Risk Designation	PS-2	PS-2	PS-2
PS-3	Personnel Screening	PS-3	PS-3 (3)	PS-3 (3)
PS-4	Personnel Termination	PS-4	PS-4	PS-4 (2)
PS-5	Personnel Transfer	PS-5	PS-5	PS-5
PS-6	Access Agreements	PS-6	PS-6	PS-6
PS-7	Third-Party Personnel Security	PS-7	PS-7	PS-7
PS-8	Personnel Sanctions	PS-8	PS-8	PS-8
RA	**Risk Assessment**			
RA-1	Risk Assessment Policy and Procedures	RA-1	RA-1	RA-1
RA-2	Security Categorization	RA-2	RA-2	RA-2
RA-3	Risk Assessment	RA-3	RA-3	RA-3
RA-5	Vulnerability Scanning	RA-5	RA-5 (1) (2) (3) (5) (6) (8)	RA-5 (1) (2) (3) (4) (5) (6) (8) (10)
SA	**System and Services Acquisition**			
SA-1	System and Services Acquisition Policy and Procedures	SA-1	SA-1	SA-1
SA-2	Allocation of Resources	SA-2	SA-2	SA-2
SA-3	System Development Life Cycle	SA-3	SA-3	SA-3
SA-4	Acquisition Process	SA-4	SA-4 (1) (2) (8) (9) (10)	SA-4 (1) (2) (8) (9) (10)
SA-5	Information System Documentation	SA-5	SA-5	SA-5
SA-8	Security Engineering Principles	Not Selected	SA-8	SA-8
SA-9	External Information System Services	SA-9	SA-9 (1) (2) (4) (5)	SA-9 (1) (2) (4) (5)
SA-10	Developer Configuration Management	Not Selected	SA-10 (1)	SA-10 (1)
SA-11	Developer Security Testing and Evaluation	Not Selected	SA-11 (1) (2) (8)	SA-11 (1) (2) (8)
SA-12	Supply Chain Protection	Not Selected	Not Selected	SA-12
SA-15	Development Process, Standards and Tools	Not Selected	Not Selected	SA-15
SA-16	Developer-Provided Training	Not Selected	Not Selected	SA-16
SA-17	Developer Security Architecture and Design	Not Selected	Not Selected	SA-17

(Continued)

Table 9.1 Summary of Required Security Controls [12] *Continued*

SC	System and Communications Protection			
SC-1	System and Communications Protection Policy and Procedures	SC-1	SC-1	SC-1
SC-2	Application Partitioning	Not Selected	SC-2	SC-2
SC-3	Security Function Isolation	Not Selected	Not Selected	SC-3
SC-4	Information in Shared Resources	Not Selected	SC-4	SC-4
SC-5	Denial of Service Protection	SC-5	SC-5	SC-5
SC-6	Resource Availability	Not Selected	SC-6	SC-6
SC-7	Boundary Protection	SC-7	SC-7 (3) (4) (5) (7) (8) (12) (13) (18)	SC-7 (3) (4) (5) (7) (8) (10) (12) (13) (18) (20) (21)
SC-8	Transmission Confidentiality and Integrity	Not Selected	SC-8 (1)	SC-8 (1)
SC-10	Network Disconnect	Not Selected	SC-10	SC-10
SC-12	Cryptographic Key Establishment and Management	SC-12	SC-12 (2) (3)	SC-12 (1) (2) (3)
SC-13	Cryptographic Protection	SC-13	SC-13	SC-13
SC-15	Collaborative Computing Devices	SC-15	SC-15	SC-15
SC-17	Public Key Infrastructure Certificates	Not Selected	SC-17	SC-17
SC-18	Mobile Code	Not Selected	SC-18	SC-18
SC-19	Voice Over Internet Protocol	Not Selected	SC-19	SC-19
SC-20	Secure Name/Address Resolution Service (Authoritative Source)	SC-20	SC-20	SC-20
SC-21	Secure Name/Address Resolution Service (Recursive or Caching Resolver)	SC-21	SC-21	SC-21
SC-22	Architecture and Provisioning for Name/Address Resolution Service	SC-22	SC-22	SC-22
SC-23	Session Authenticity	Not Selected	SC-23	SC-23 (1)
SC-24	Fail in Known State	Not Selected	Not Selected	SC-24
SC-28	Protection of Information at Rest	Not Selected	SC-28 (1)	SC-28 (1)
SC-39	Process Isolation	SC-39	SC-39	SC-39

(Continued)

Table 9.1 Summary of Required Security Controls [12] *Continued*

SI	System and Information Integrity			
SI-1	System and Information Integrity Policy and Procedures	SI-1	SI-1	SI-1
SI-2	Flaw Remediation	SI-2	SI-2 (2) (3)	SI-2 (1) (2) (3)
SI-3	Malicious Code Protection	SI-3	SI-3 (1) (2) (7)	SI-3 (1) (2) (7)
SI-4	Information System Monitoring	SI-4	SI-4 (1) (2) (4) (5) (14) (16) (23)	SI-4 (1) (2) (4) (5) (11) (14) (16) (18) (19) (20) (22) (23) (24)
SI-5	Security Alerts, Advisories, and Directives	SI-5	SI-5	SI-5 (1)
SI-6	Security Function Verification	Not Selected	SI-6	SI-6
SI-7	Software, Firmware, and Information Integrity	Not Selected	SI-7 (1) (7)	SI-7 (1) (2) (5) (7) (14)
SI-8	Spam Protection	Not Selected	SI-8 (1) (2)	SI-8 (1) (2)
SI-10	Information Input Validation	Not Selected	SI-10	SI-10
SI-11	Error Handling	Not Selected	SI-11	SI-11
SI-12	Information Handling and Retention	SI-12	SI-12	SI-12
SI-16	Memory Protection	SI-16	SI-16	SI-16

In the following sections, the security requirements for each security control family are provided.

Access Controls (AC)	
AC-1	**Access Control Policy and Procedures**

Control Requirement:	The Cloud Service Provider (CSP):
	 a. Develops, documents, and disseminates to *CSP-defined personnel or roles*:
	    1. An access control policy that addresses purpose, scope, roles, responsibilities, management commitment, coordination among organizational entities, and compliance; and
	    2. Procedures to facilitate the implementation of the access control policy and associated access controls; and
	 b. Reviews and updates the current:
	    1. Access control policy *at least every three (3) years;*[51] and
	    2. Access control procedures *at least annually.*[52]

(Continued)

---

[51]High-Impact Security Requirement: *at least annually.*

[52]High-Impact Security Requirement: *at least annually, or whenever a significant change occurs.*

Continued

AC-2	Account Management
Control Requirement:	The Cloud Service Provider (CSP):

The Cloud Service Provider (CSP):

a. Identifies and selects the *CSP-defined information system account types* to support organizational missions/business functions.

b. Assigns account managers for information system accounts.

c. Establishes conditions for group and role membership.

d. Specifies authorized users of the information system, group and role membership, and access authorizations (i.e., privileges) and other attributes (as required) for each account.

e. Requires approvals by *CSP-defined personnel or roles* for requests to create information system accounts.

f. Creates, enables, modifies, disables, and removes information system accounts in accordance with *CSP-defined procedures or conditions*.

g. Monitors the use of information system accounts.

h. Notifies account managers:

    1. When accounts are no longer required;

    2. When users are terminated or transferred; and

    3. When individual information system usage or need-to-know changes.

i. Authorizes access to the information system based on:

    1. A valid access authorization;

    2. Intended system usage; and

    3. Other attributes as required by the organization or associated missions/business functions.

j. Reviews accounts for compliance with account management requirements *at least annually*.[53]

k. Establishes a process for reissuing shared/group account credentials (if deployed) when individuals are removed from the group.

Control Enhancements:

1. The Cloud Service Provider (CSP) employs automated mechanisms to support the management of information system accounts.

2. The information system automatically disables temporary and emergency accounts after *no more than thirty (30) days for temporary and emergency account types*.[54]

3. The information system automatically disables inactive user accounts after *ninety (90) days*.[55]

    Additional FedRAMP Requirements—Low/Moderate

    The Cloud Service Provider (CSP) defines the time period for nonuser accounts (e.g., accounts associated with devices). The time periods are approved and accepted by the Joint Authorization Board/ Authorizing Official (JAB)/AO.

(Continued)

---

[53]High-Impact Security Requirement: *monthly for privileged access, every six (6) months for non-privileged access.*

[54]High-Impact Security Baseline: *24 hours from last use.*

[55]High-Impact Security Baseline: *thirty-five (35) days for user accounts.*

Continued

Additional FedRAMP Requirements—High

　The Cloud Service Provider (CSP) defines the time period for nonuser accounts (e.g., accounts associated with devices). The time periods are approved and accepted by the JAB/AO. Where user management is a function of the service, reports of activity of consumer users shall be made available.

4. The information system automatically audits account creation, modification, disabling, and removal actions and notifies *Cloud Service Provider (CSP)-defined personnel or roles.*[56]

5. [57]The Cloud Service Provider (CSP) requires that users log out when *CSP-defined time-period of expected inactivity or description of when to log out.*[58]

7. The Cloud Service Provider (CSP):

　a. Establishes and administers privileged user accounts in accordance with a role-based access scheme that organizes allowed information system access and privileges into roles.

　b. Monitors privileged role assignments.

　c. Takes *CSP-defined actions*[59] when privileged role assignments are no longer appropriate.

9. If shared/group accounts are deployed, only permits the use of shared/group accounts that meet *Cloud Service Provider (CSP)-defined conditions for establishing shared/group accounts.*[60]

10. [61]If shared/group accounts are deployed, the information system terminates shared/group account credentials when members leave the group.

11. The information system enforces *Cloud Service Provider (CSP)-defined circumstances and/or usage conditions for CSP-defined information system accounts.*

(Continued)

---

[56]High-Impact Security Requirement: *CSP and/or CSP system owner.*

[57]FedRAMP Program Management Office (PMO). FedRAMP High System Security Plan (SSP) Template. Washington, DC: US General Services Administration; 2016. "*Should use a shorter timeframe than AC-12.*"

[58]High-Impact Security Requirement: *inactivity is anticipated to exceed fifteen (15) minutes.*

[59]High-Impact Security Requirement: *disables/revokes access within a CSP specified timeframe.*

[60]High-Impact Security Requirement: *CSP defined need with justification statement that explains why such accounts are necessary.*

[61]FedRAMP Program Management Office (PMO). FedRAMP High System Security Plan (SSP) Template. Washington, DC: US General Services Administration; 2016. "*Required if shared/group accounts are deployed.*"

Continued

	12. [62] For privileged accounts, the Cloud Service Provider (CSP):
	  a. Monitors information system accounts for *CSP-defined atypical usage*; and
	  b. Reports atypical usage of information system accounts to *a minimum, the Information System Security Officer (ISSO) and/or similar role within the CSP*.
	13. The *Cloud Service Provider (CSP)* disables accounts of users posing a significant risk within *one (1) hour* of discovery of the risk.

AC-3	**Access Enforcement**
Control Requirement:	The information system enforces approved authorizations for logical access to information and system resources in accordance with applicable access control policies.
AC-4	**Information Flow Enforcement**
Control Requirement:	The information system enforces approved authorizations for controlling the flow of information within the system and between interconnected systems based on *Cloud Service Provider (CSP)-defined information flow control policies.*
Control Enhancements:	8. The information system enforces information flow control using *Cloud Service Provider (CSP)-defined security policy filters* as a basis for flow control decisions for *CSP-defined information flows.* 21. The information system separates information flows logically or physically using *Cloud Service Provider (CSP)-defined mechanisms and/or techniques* to accomplish *CSP-defined required separations by types of information.*
AC-5[63]	**Separation of Duties**

Control Requirement:	The *Cloud Service Provider (CSP)*:
	  a. Separates *CSP-defined duties of individuals*;
	  b. Documents separation of duties of individuals; and
	  c. Defines information system access authorizations to support separation of duties.

(Continued)

---

[62]FedRAMP Program Management Office (PMO). FedRAMP High System Security Plan (SSP) Template. Washington, DC: US General Services Administration; 2016. *"Required for privileged accounts."*

[63]FedRAMP Program Management Office (PMO). FedRAMP High System Security Plan (SSP) Template. Washington, DC: US General Services Administration; 2016. *"CSPs have the option to provide a separation of duties matrix as an attachment to the SSP. Directions for attaching the Separation of Duties Matrix document may be found in Section 15.11 Attachment 11 — Separation of Duties Matrix."*

Continued

AC-6	**Least Privilege**
Control Requirement:	The Cloud Service Provider (CSP) employs the concept of least privilege, allowing only authorized accesses for users (and processes acting on behalf of users), which are necessary to accomplish assigned tasks in accordance with organizational missions and business functions.
Control Enhancements:	1. The Cloud Service Provider (CSP) explicitly authorizes access to *CSP-defined security functions (deployed in hardware, software, and firmware) and security-relevant information.*[64]
	2. [65]The Cloud Service Provider (CSP) requires that users of information system accounts, or roles, with access to *all security functions*, use nonprivileged accounts or roles, when accessing nonsecurity functions.
	3. The *Cloud Service Provider (CSP)* authorizes network access to *all privileged commands* only for *CSP-defined compelling operational needs* and documents the rationale for such access in the security plan for the information system.
	5. The *Cloud Service Provider (CSP)* restricts privileged accounts on the information system to *CSP-defined personnel or roles*.
	7. The *Cloud Service Provider (CSP)*:
	a. Reviews *at a minimum, annually* the privileges assigned to *all users with privileges* to validate the need for such privileges; and
	b. Reassigns or removes privileges, if necessary, to correctly reflect organizational mission/business needs.
	8. The information system prevents *any software except software explicitly documented* from executing at higher privilege levels than users executing the software.
	9. The information system audits the execution of privileged functions.
	10. The information system prevents non-privileged users from executing privileged functions to include disabling, circumventing, or altering implemented security safeguards/countermeasures.
AC-7	**Unsuccessful Logon Attempts**
Control Requirement:	The information system:
	a. Enforces a limit of *no more than three* consecutive invalid logon attempts by a user during a *fifteen (15)-minute time period*; and
	b. Automatically *locks the account/node for thirty (30) minutes*;[66] *locks the account/node until released by an administrator; or delays next logon prompt according to Cloud Service Provider (CSP)-defined delay algorithm* when the maximum number of unsuccessful attempts is exceeded.

(Continued)

---

[64]High-Impact Security Requirement: *all functions not publicly accessible and all security-relevant information not publicly available.*

[65]FedRAMP Program Management Office (PMO). FedRAMP High System Security Plan (SSP) Template. Washington, DC: US General Services Administration; 2016. *"Examples of security functions include but are not limited to: establishing system accounts, configuring access authorizations (i.e., permissions, privileges), setting events to be audited, and setting intrusion detection parameters, system programming, system and security administration, other privileged functions."*

[66]High-Impact Security Requirement: *not more than three (3) or until unlocked by an administrator.*

Continued

AC-7	Unsuccessful Logon Attempts
Control Enhancements:	2. The information system purges/wipes information from *mobile devices as defined by Cloud Service Provider (CSP) policy* based on *CSP-defined purging/wiping requirements/techniques* after *three (3)* consecutive, unsuccessful device logon attempts.
AC-8[67]	System Use Notification
Control Requirement:	The information system: a. Displays to users *Cloud Service Provider (CSP)-defined system use notification message or banner* before granting access to the system that provides privacy and security notices consistent with applicable federal laws, Executive Orders, directives, policies, regulations, standards, and guidance and states that: 1. Users are accessing a US Government information system; 2. Information system usage may be monitored, recorded, and subject to audit; 3. Unauthorized use of the information system is prohibited and subject to criminal and civil penalties; and 4. Use of the information system indicates consent to monitoring and recording; b. Retains the notification message or banner on the screen until users acknowledge the usage conditions and take explicit actions to log on to or further access the information system; and c. [68]For publicly accessible systems: 1. Displays system use information *Cloud Service Provider (CSP)-defined conditions*, before granting further access; 2. Displays references, if any, to monitoring, recording, or auditing that are consistent with privacy accommodations for such systems that generally prohibit those activities; and 3. Includes a description of the authorized uses of the system. **Additional FedRAMP Requirements** • The Cloud Service Provider (CSP) shall determine elements of the cloud environment that require the System Use Notification control. The elements of the cloud environment that require System Use Notification are approved and accepted by the JAB/AO. • The CSP shall determine how System Use Notification is going to be verified and provide appropriate periodicity of the check. The System Use Notification verification and periodicity are approved and accepted by the JAB/AO.

(Continued)

---

[67]FedRAMP Program Management Office (PMO). FedRAMP High System Security Plan (SSP) Template. Washington, DC: US General Services Administration; 2016. *"If performed as part of a Configuration Baseline check, then the % of items requiring setting that are checked and that pass (or fail) check can be provided."*

[68]FedRAMP Program Management Office (PMO). FedRAMP High System Security Plan (SSP) Template. Washington, DC: US General Services Administration; 2016. *"If performed as part of a Configuration Baseline check, then the % of items requiring setting that are checked and that pass (or fail) check can be provided."*

Continued

AC-8[67]	**System Use Notification**
	• If not performed as part of a Configuration Baseline check, then there must be documented agreement on how to provide results of verification and the necessary periodicity of the verification by the CSP. The documented agreement on how to provide verification of the results are approved and accepted by the JAB/AO.
AC-10	**Concurrent Session Control**
Control Requirement:	The information system limits the number of concurrent sessions for each *Cloud Service Provider (CSP) account and/or account type* to *three (3) sessions for privileged access and two (2) sessions for non-privileged access.*
AC-11	**Session Lock**
Control Requirement:	The information system: a. Prevents further access to the system by initiating a session lock after *fifteen (15) minutes* of inactivity or upon receiving a request from a user; and b. Retains the session lock until the user reestablishes access using established identification and authentication procedures.
Control Enhancements:	1. The information system conceals, via the session lock, information previously visible on the display with a publicly viewable image.
AC-12	**Session Termination**
Control Requirement:	The information system automatically terminates a user session after *Cloud Service Provider (CSP)-defined conditions or trigger events requiring session disconnect.*
Control Enhancements:	1.[69] The information system: a. Provides a logout capability for user-initiated communications sessions whenever authentication is used to gain access to *Cloud Service Provider (CSP)-defined information resources*; and b. Displays an explicit logout message to users indicating the reliable termination of authenticated communications sessions.

(Continued)

---

[69]FedRAMP Program Management Office (PMO). FedRAMP High System Security Plan (SSP) Template. Washington, DC: US General Services Administration; 2016. *"Testing for logout functionality (OTG-SESS-006).* https://www.owasp.org/index.php/Testing_for_logout_functionality_%28OTG-SESS-006%29."

Continued

AC-14	Permitted Actions without Identification and Authentication
Control Requirement:	The Cloud Service Provider (CSP): a. Identifies *CSP user actions* that can be performed on the information system without identification or authentication consistent with organizational missions/business functions; and b. Documents and provides supporting rationale in the security plan for the information system, user actions not requiring identification or authentication.
AC-17	**Remote Access**
Control Requirement:	The Cloud Service Provider (CSP): a. Establishes and documents usage restrictions, configuration/connection requirements, and implementation guidance for each type of remote access allowed; and b. Authorizes remote access to the information system prior to allowing such connections.

Control Enhancements:	1. The information system monitors and controls remote access methods.
	2. The information system implements cryptographic mechanisms to protect the confidentiality and integrity of remote access sessions.
	3. The information system routes all remote accesses through *Cloud Service Provider (CSP)-defined number* managed network access control points.
	4. The Cloud Service Provider (CSP):
	    a. Authorizes the execution of privileged commands and access to security-relevant information via remote access only for *CSP-defined needs*; and
	    b. Documents the rationale for such access in the security plan for the information system.
	9. The Cloud Service Provider (CSP) provides the capability to expeditiously disconnect or disable remote access to the information system within a *Cloud Service Provider (CSP)-defined time period no greater than fifteen (15) minutes*.[70]

AC-18	**Wireless Access**
Control Requirement:	The Cloud Service Provider (CSP): a. Establishes usage restrictions, configuration/connection requirements, and implementation guidance for wireless access; and b. Authorizes wireless access to the information system prior to allowing such connections.
Control Enhancements:	1. The information system protects wireless access to the system using authentication of *users and/or devices* and encryption.

(Continued)

---

[70]High-Impact Security Requirement: *fifteen (15) minutes.*

Continued

AC-18	**Wireless Access**
	3. The Cloud Service Provider (CSP) disables, when not intended for use, wireless networking capabilities internally embedded within information system components prior to issuance and deployment. 4. The Cloud Service Provider (CSP) identifies and explicitly authorizes users allowed to independently configure wireless networking capabilities. 5. The Cloud Service Provider (CSP) selects radio antennas and calibrates transmission power levels to reduce the probability that usable signals can be received outside of organization-controlled boundaries.
AC-19	**Access Control for Mobile Devices**
Control Requirement:	The Cloud Service Provider (CSP): a. Establishes usage restrictions, configuration requirements, connection requirements, and implementation guidance for organization-controlled mobile devices; and b. Authorizes the connection of mobile devices to organizational information systems.
Control Enhancements:	5. The Cloud Service Provider (CSP) employs *full-device encryption and/or container encryption* to protect the confidentiality and integrity of information on CSP-*defined mobile devices*.
AC-20	**Use of External Information Systems**
Control Requirement:	The Cloud Service Provider (CSP) establishes terms and conditions, consistent with any trust relationships established with other organizations owning, operating, and/or maintaining external information systems, allowing authorized individuals to: a. Access the information system from the external information systems; and b. Process, store, and/or transmit organization-controlled information using the external information systems.

Control Enhancements:	1. The Cloud Service Provider (CSP) permits authorized individuals to use an external information system to access the information system or to process, store, or transmit organization-controlled information only when the organization:
	
	    a. Verifies the implementation of required security controls on the external system as specified in the organization's information security policy and security plan; or
	
	    b. Retains approved information system connection or processing agreements with the organizational entity hosting the external information system.
	
	2. The Cloud Service Provider (CSP) *restricts or prohibits* the use of organization-controlled portable storage devices by authorized individuals on external information systems.

(Continued)

Continued

AC-21	Information Sharing
Control Requirement:	The Cloud Service Provider (CSP): a. Facilitates information sharing by enabling authorized users to determine whether access authorizations assigned to the sharing partner match the access restrictions on the information for *CSP-defined information sharing circumstances where user discretion is required*; and b. Employs *CSP automated mechanisms or manual processes* to assist users in making information sharing/collaboration decisions.
AC-22	Publicly Accessible Content
Control Requirement:	The Cloud Service Provider (CSP): a. Designates individuals authorized to post information onto a publicly accessible information system; b. Trains authorized individuals to ensure that publicly accessible information does not contain nonpublic information; c. Reviews the proposed content of information prior to posting onto the publicly accessible information system to ensure that nonpublic information is not included; and d. Reviews the content on the publicly accessible information system for nonpublic information *at least quarterly* and removes such information, if discovered.
Awareness and Training (AT)	
AT-1	Security Awareness and Training Policy and Procedures

Control Requirement:	The Cloud Service Provider (CSP):
	a. Develops, documents, and disseminates to *CSP-defined personnel or roles*:
	  1. A security awareness and training policy that addresses purpose, scope, roles, responsibilities, management commitment, coordination among organizational entities, and compliance; and
	  2. Procedures to facilitate the implementation of the security awareness and training policy and associated security awareness and training controls; and
	b. Reviews and updates the current:
	  1. Security awareness and training policy *at least every three (3) years*;[71] and
	  2. Security awareness and training procedures *at least annually*.[72]

AT-2	Security Awareness Training
Control Requirement:	The Cloud Service Provider (CSP) provides basic security awareness training to information system users (including managers, senior executives, and contractors): a. As part of initial training for new users; b. When required by information system changes; and c. *At least annually* thereafter.

(Continued)

---

[71]High-Impact Security Requirement: *at least annually.*
[72]High-Impact Security Requirement: *at least annually, or whenever a significant change occurs.*

Continued

AT-2	Security Awareness Training
Control Enhancements:	2. The Cloud Service Provider (CSP) includes security awareness training on recognizing and reporting potential indicators of insider threat.
AT-3	**Role-Based Security Training**
Control Requirement:	The Cloud Service Provider (CSP) provides role-based security training to personnel with assigned security roles and responsibilities: a. Before authorizing access to the information system or performing assigned duties; b. When required by information system changes; and c. *At least annually* thereafter.
Control Enhancements:	3. The Cloud Service Provider (CSP) includes practical exercises in security training that reinforce training objectives. 4. The Cloud Service Provider (CSP) provides training to its personnel on *malicious code indicators as defined by organization incident policy/capability* to recognize suspicious communications and anomalous behavior in organizational information systems.
AT-4	**Security Training Records**
Control Requirement:	The Cloud Service Provider (CSP): a. Documents and monitors individual information system security training activities including basic security awareness training and specific information system security training; and b. Retains individual training records for *at least one (1) year*.[73]
	Audit and Accountability (AU)
AU-1	**Audit and Accountability Policy and Procedures**
Control Requirement:	The Cloud Service Provider (CSP): a. Develops, documents, and disseminates to *CSP-defined personnel or roles*: 1. An audit and accountability policy that addresses purpose, scope, roles, responsibilities, management commitment, coordination among organizational entities, and compliance; and 2. Procedures to facilitate the implementation of the audit and accountability policy and associated audit and accountability controls; and b. Reviews and updates the current: 1. Audit and accountability policy *at least every three (3) years*;[74] and 2. Audit and accountability procedures *at least annually*.[75]

(Continued)

[73]High-Impact Security Requirement: *at least five (5) years or 5 years after completion of a specific training program.*
[74]High-Impact Security Requirement: *at least annually.*
[75]High-Impact Security Requirement: *at least annually, or whenever a significant change occurs.*

Continued

AU-2	Auditable Events
Control Requirement:	The Cloud Service Provider (CSP): a. Determines that the information system is capable of auditing the following events: *Successful and unsuccessful account logon events, account management events, object access, policy change, privilege functions, process tracking, and system events. For web applications: all administrator activity, authentication checks, authorization checks, data deletions, data access, data changes, and permission changes*; b. Coordinates the security audit function with other organizational entities requiring audit-related information to enhance mutual support and to help guide the selection of auditable events; c. Provides a rationale for why the auditable events are deemed to be adequate to support after-the-fact investigations of security incidents; and d. Determines that the following events are to be audited within the information system: *CSP-defined subset of the auditable events defined in AU-2 a. to be audited continually for each identified event.* **Additional FedRAMP Requirements** • Coordination between service provider and consumer shall be documented and accepted by the JAB/AO.
Control Enhancements:	3.[76]The Cloud Service Provider (CSP) reviews and updates the auditable events *annually or whenever there is a change in the threat environment.*
AU-3	Content of Audit Records
Control Requirement:	The information system generates audit records containing information that establishes what type of event occurred, when the event occurred, where the event occurred, the source of the event, the outcome of the event, and the identity of any individuals or subjects associated with the event.
Control Enhancements:	1. The information system generates audit records containing the following additional information: *Cloud Service Provider (CSP)-defined additional, more detailed information.*[77] **Additional FedRAMP Requirements** • The Cloud Service Provider (CSP) defines audit record types include: *session, connection, transaction, or activity duration; for client−server transactions, the number of bytes received and bytes sent; additional informational messages to diagnose or identify the event; characteristics that describe or identify the object or resource being acted upon; individual identities of group account users; full-text of privileged commands.* • The audit record types are approved and accepted by the JAB/AO. 2. The information system provides centralized management and configuration of the content to be captured in audit records generated by *all network, data storage, and computing devices.*

(Continued)

---

[76]FedRAMP Program Management Office (PMO). FedRAMP High System Security Plan (SSP) Template. Washington, DC: US General Services Administration; 2016. *"Annually or whenever changes in the threat environment are communicated to the service provider by the JAB/AO."*

[77]FedRAMP Program Management Office (PMO). FedRAMP High System Security Plan (SSP) Template. Washington, DC: US General Services Administration; 2016. *"For client-server transactions, the number of bytes sent and received gives bidirectional transfer information that can be helpful during an investigation or inquiry."*

Continued

AU-4	**Audit Storage Capacity**
Control Requirement:	The Cloud Service Provider (CSP) allocates audit record storage capacity in accordance with *CSP-defined audit record storage requirements*.
AU-5	**Response to Audit Processing Failures**
Control Requirement:	The information system: a. Alerts *Cloud Service Provider (CSP)-defined personnel or roles* in the event of an audit processing failure; and b. Takes the following additional actions: *CSP-defined actions to be taken; (overwrite oldest record)*.
Control Enhancements:	1. The information system provides a warning to *Cloud Service Provider (CSP)-defined personnel, roles, and/or locations* within *CSP-defined time period* when allocated audit record storage volume reaches *CSP-defined percentage* of repository maximum audit record storage capacity. 2. The information system provides an alert in *Cloud Service Provider (CSP)-defined real-time* to *CSP personnel with authority to address failed audit events* when the following audit failure events occur: *audit failure events requiring real-time alerts, as defined by organization audit policy*.
AU-6	**Audit Review, Analysis, and Reporting**
Control Requirement:	The Cloud Service Provider (CSP): a. Reviews and analyzes information system audit records *at least weekly* for indications of *CSP-defined inappropriate or unusual activity*; and b. Reports findings to *CSP-defined personnel or roles*. **Additional FedRAMP Requirements** • The Cloud Service Provider (CSP) defines audit record types include: defines audit record types coordination between service provider and consumer shall be documented and accepted by the JAB/AO. In multitenant environments, capability and means for providing review, analysis, and reporting to consumer for data pertaining to consumer shall be documented.
Control Enhancements:	1. The Cloud Service Provider (CSP) employs automated mechanisms to integrate audit review, analysis, and reporting processes to support organizational processes for investigation and response to suspicious activities. 3. The Cloud Service Provider (CSP) analyzes and correlates audit records across different repositories to gain organization-wide situational awareness. 4. The information system provides the capability to centrally review and analyze audit records from multiple components within the system.

(Continued)

Continued

AU-6	Audit Review, Analysis, and Reporting
	5. The Cloud Service Provider (CSP) integrates analysis of audit records with analysis of *vulnerability scanning information; performance data; information system monitoring information; penetration test data; and/or data/information collected from other sources* to further enhance the ability to identify inappropriate or unusual activity.
	6. The Cloud Service Provider (CSP) correlates information from audit records with information obtained from monitoring physical access to further enhance the ability to identify suspicious, inappropriate, unusual, or malevolent activity.
	Additional FedRAMP Requirements • Coordination between service provider and consumer shall be documented and accepted by the JAB/AO.
	7. The Cloud Service Provider (CSP) specifies the permitted actions for each *information system process; role; and/or user* associated with the review, analysis, and reporting of audit information.
	10. The Cloud Service Provider (CSP) adjusts the level of audit review, analysis, and reporting within the information system when there is a change in risk-based on law enforcement information, intelligence information, or other credible sources of information.
AU-7	**Audit Reduction and Report Generation**
Control Requirement:	The information system provides an audit reduction and report generation capability that: a. Supports on-demand audit review, analysis, and reporting requirements and after-the-fact investigations of security incidents; and b. Does not alter the original content or time ordering of audit records.
Control Enhancements:	1. The information system provides the capability to process audit records for events of interest based on *Cloud Service Provider (CSP)-defined audit fields within audit records.*
AU-8	**Time Stamps**
Control Requirement:	The information system: a. Uses internal system clocks to generate time stamps for audit records; and b. Records time stamps for audit records that can be mapped to Coordinated Universal Time (UTC) or Greenwich Mean Time (GMT) and meets *one (1) second granularity of time measurement.*

(Continued)

Continued

AU-8	Time Stamps
Control Enhancements:	1.[78]The information system: a. Compares the internal information system clocks *at least hourly* with *authoritative time source:* http://tf.nist.gov/tf-cgi/servers.cgi; and b. Synchronizes the internal system clocks to the authoritative time source when the time difference is greater than *Cloud Service Provider (CSP)-defined time period*. **Additional FedRAMP Requirements** • The Cloud Service Provider (CSP) selects primary and secondary time servers used by the NIST Internet time service. The secondary server is selected from a different geographic region than the primary server. • The Cloud Service Provider (CSP) synchronizes the system clocks of network computers that run operating systems other than Windows to the Windows Server Domain Controller emulator or to the same time source for that server.
AU-9	**Protection of Audit Information**
Control Requirement: Control Enhancements:	The information system protects audit information and audit tools from unauthorized access, modification, and deletion. 2. The information system backs up audit records *at least weekly* onto a different system or media than the system being audited. 3. The information system implements cryptographic mechanisms to protect the integrity of audit information and audit tools. 4. The Cloud Service Provider (CSP) authorizes access to management of audit functionality to only *CSP-defined subset of privileged users*.
AU-10	**Non-repudiation**
Control Requirement:	The information system protects against an individual (or process acting on behalf of an individual) falsely denying having performed *minimum actions including the addition, modification, deletion, approval, sending, or receiving of data*.
AU-11	**Audit Record Retention**
Control Requirement:	The Cloud Service Provider (CSP) retains audit records for *at least ninety (90) days*[79] to provide support for after-the-fact investigations of security incidents and to meet regulatory and organizational information retention requirements.

(Continued)

---

[78]FedRAMP Program Management Office (PMO). FedRAMP High System Security Plan (SSP) Template. Washington, DC: US General Services Administration; 2016. *"The service provider selects primary and secondary time servers used by the NIST Internet time service, or by a Stratum-1 time server. The secondary server is selected from a different geographic region than the primary server. If using Windows Active Directory, all servers should synchronize time with the time source for the Windows Domain Controller. If using some other directory services (e.g., LDAP), all servers should synchronize time with the time source for the directory server."*

[79]High-Impact Security Requirement: *at least one (1) year.*

AU-11	Audit Record Retention
	Additional FedRAMP Requirements
	• The Cloud Service Provider (CSP) retains audit records online for at least ninety (90) days and further preserves audit records off-line for a period that is in accordance with National Archives and Records Administration (NARA) requirements.

AU-12	Audit Generation
Control Requirement:	The information system:
	a. Provides audit record generation capability for the auditable events defined in AU-2 a. at *all information system components where audit capability is deployed/available*;
	b. Allows Cloud *Service Provider (CSP)-defined personnel or roles* to select which auditable events are to be audited by specific components of the information system; and
	c. Generates audit records for the events defined in AU-2 d. with the content defined in AU-3.
Control Enhancements:	1. The information system compiles audit records from *all network, data storage, and computing devices* into a system-wide (logical or physical) audit trail that is time-correlated to within *Cloud Service Provider (CSP)-defined level of tolerance for relationship between time stamps of individual records in the audit trail*.3. The information system provides the capability for *Cloud Service Provider (CSP)-defined individuals or roles with audit configuration responsibilities* to change the auditing to be performed on *all network, data storage, and computing devices* based on *CSP-defined threat situations* within *CSP-defined time thresholds*.

Security Assessment and Authorization (CA)	
CA-1	Security Assessment and Authorization Policy and Procedures
Control Requirement:	The Cloud Service Provider (CSP):
	a. Develops, documents, and disseminates to *CSP-defined personnel or roles*:
	1. A security assessment and authorization policy that addresses purpose, scope, roles, responsibilities, management commitment, coordination among organizational entities, and compliance; and
	2. Procedures to facilitate the implementation of the security assessment and authorization policy and associated security assessment and authorization controls; and
	b. Reviews and updates the current:
	1. Security assessment and authorization policy *at least every three (3) years*;[80] and
	2. Security assessment and authorization procedures *at least annually*.[81]

(Continued)

---

[80]High-Impact Security Requirement: *at least annually.*

[81]High-Impact Security Requirement: *at least annually, or whenever a significant change occurs.*

Continued

CA-2	Security Assessments

Control Requirement:	The Cloud Service Provider (CSP):
	a. Develops a security assessment plan that describes the scope of the assessment including:
	  1. Security controls and control enhancements under assessment;
	  2. Assessment procedures to be used to determine security control effectiveness; and
	  3. Assessment environment, assessment team, and assessment roles and responsibilities;
	b. Assesses the security controls in the information system and its environment of operation *at least annually* to determine the extent to which the controls are implemented correctly, operating as intended, and producing the desired outcome with respect to meeting established security requirements;
	c. Produces a security assessment report that documents the results of the assessment; and
	d. Provides the results of the security control assessment to *CSP-defined individuals or roles to include the FedRAMP PMO.*

Control Enhancements:	1. The Cloud Service Provider (CSP) employs assessors or assessment teams with *CSP-defined level of independence* to conduct security control assessments. **Additional FedRAMP Requirements** • Must use an accredited 3PAO for JAB authorization. 2. The Cloud Service Provider (CSP) includes as part of security control assessments, *at least annually, announced or unannounced, in-depth monitoring; vulnerability scanning; malicious user testing; insider threat assessment; performance/load testing; or CSP-defined other forms of security assessment.* **Additional FedRAMP Requirements** • To include "announced," "vulnerability scanning to occur at least annually." 3. The Cloud Service Provider (CSP) accepts the results of an assessment of *CSP-defined information system* performed by *any FedRAMP Accredited 3PAO* when the assessment meets the conditions the JAB/AO in the FedRAMP Secure Repository.
CA-3	System Interconnections
Control Requirement:	The Cloud Service Provider (CSP): a. Authorizes connections from the information system to other information systems through the use of Interconnection Security Agreements; b. Documents, for each interconnection, the interface characteristics, security requirements, and the nature of the information communicated; and c. Reviews and updates Interconnection Security Agreements *at least annually*[82] and on input from FedRAMP.

(Continued)

---

[82]High-Impact Security Requirement: *at east annually and on input from FedRAMP.*

Continued

CA-3	System Interconnections
Control Enhancements:	3. The Cloud Service Provider (CSP) prohibits the direct connection of an *CSP unclassified, nonnational security system* to an external network without the use of *Boundary Protections which meet Trusted Internet Connection (TIC) requirements*[83]. 5.[84] The Cloud Service Provider (CSP) employs *allow-all, deny-by-exception or deny-all, permit-by-exception*[85] policy for allowing *CSP-defined information systems*[86] to connect to external information systems.
CA-5	**Plan of Action and Milestones**
Control Requirement:	The Cloud Service Provider (CSP): a. Develops a plan of action and milestones (POA&Ms) for the information system to document the CSP's planned remedial actions to correct weaknesses or deficiencies noted during the assessment of the security controls and to reduce or eliminate known vulnerabilities in the system; and b. Updates existing POA&Ms *at least monthly* based on the findings from security controls assessments, security impact analyses, and continuous monitoring activities. **Additional FedRAMP Requirements** • POA&Ms must be provided at least monthly.
CA-6	**Security Authorization**
Control Requirement:	The Cloud Service Provider (CSP): a. Assigns a senior-level executive or manager as the authorizing official for the information system; b. Ensures that the authorizing official authorizes the information system for processing before commencing operations; and c. Updates the security authorization[87] *at least every three (3) years or when a significant change occurs.*

(Continued)

---

[83]FedRAMP Program Management Office (PMO). FedRAMP High System Security Plan (SSP) Template. Washington, DC: US General Services Administration; 2016. *"Refer to Appendix H – Cloud Considerations of the TIC 2.0 Reference Architecture document* [https://www.fedramp.gov/files/2015/04/TIC_Ref_Arch_v2-0_2013.pdf]."

[84]FedRAMP Program Management Office (PMO). FedRAMP High System Security Plan (SSP) Template. Washington, DC: US General Services Administration; 2016. *"For JAB Authorization, CSPs shall include details of this control in their Architecture Briefing."*

[85]High-Impact Security Requirement: *deny-all, permit by exception.*

[86]High-Impact Security Requirement: *any systems.*

[87]FedRAMP Program Management Office (PMO). FedRAMP High System Security Plan (SSP) Template. Washington, DC: US General Services Administration; 2016. *"Significant change is defined in NIST Special Publication 800-37 Revision 1, Appendix F (SP 800-37). The service provider describes the types of changes to the information system or the environment of operations that would impact the risk posture. The types of changes are approved and accepted by the JAB/AO."*

Continued

CA-7[88]	Internal System Connections
Control Requirement:	The Cloud Service Provider (CSP) develops a continuous monitoring strategy and implements a continuous monitoring program that includes: a. Establishment of *CSP-defined metrics* to be monitored; b. Establishment of *CSP-defined frequencies* for monitoring and *CSP-defined frequencies* for assessments supporting such monitoring; c. Ongoing security control assessments in accordance with the organizational continuous monitoring strategy; d. Ongoing security status monitoring of organization-defined metrics in accordance with the organizational continuous monitoring strategy; e. Correlation and analysis of security-related information generated by assessments and monitoring; f. Response actions to address results of the analysis of security-related information; and g. Reporting the security status of organization and the information system to *meet Federal and FedRAMP requirements CSP-defined frequency* at a *CSP-defined frequency*. **Additional FedRAMP Requirements** • Operating *System* Scans: at least monthly. • Database and Web Application Scans: at least monthly. • All scans performed by Independent Assessor: at least annually.
Control Enhancements:	1. The Cloud Service Provider (CSP) employs assessors or assessment teams with *CSP-defined level of independence* to monitor the security controls in the information system on an ongoing basis. 3. The Cloud Service Provider (CSP) employs trend analyses to determine if security control implementations, the frequency of continuous monitoring activities, and/or the types of activities used in the continuous monitoring process need to be modified based on empirical data.
CA-8	Penetration Testing
Control Requirement:	The Cloud Service Provider (CSP) conducts penetration testing *at least annually* on *CSP-defined information systems or system components*.
Control Enhancements:	1. The Cloud Service Provider (CSP) employs an independent penetration agent or penetration team to perform penetration testing on the information system or system components.

(Continued)

---

[88]FedRAMP Program Management Office (PMO). FedRAMP High System Security Plan (SSP) Template. Washington, DC: US General Services Administration; 2016. *"CSPs must provide evidence of closure and remediation of a high vulnerability within the timeframe for standard POA&M updates."*

Continued

CA-9	Internal System Connections
Control Requirement:	The Cloud Service Provider (CSP): a. Authorizes internal connections of *CSP-defined information system components or classes of components* to the information system; and b. Documents, for each internal connection, the interface characteristics, security requirements, and the nature of the information communicated.
	Configuration Management (CM)
CM-1	Configuration Management Policy and Procedures

Control Requirement:	The Cloud Service Provider (CSP):
	a. Develops, documents, and disseminates to *CSP-defined personnel or roles*:
	  1. A configuration management policy that addresses purpose, scope, roles, responsibilities, management commitment, coordination among organizational entities, and compliance; and
	  2. Procedures to facilitate the implementation of the configuration management policy and associated configuration management controls; and
	b. Reviews and updates the current:
	  1. Configuration management policy *at least every three (3) years*;[89] and
	  2. Configuration management procedures *at least annually*.[90]

CM-2	Baseline Configuration
Control Requirement:	The Cloud Service Provider (CSP) develops, documents, and maintains under configuration control, a current baseline configuration of the information system.

Control Enhancements:	1. The Cloud Service Provider (CSP) reviews and updates the baseline configuration of the information system:
	  a. *At least annually or when a significant change occurs*;[91]
	  b. When required due *to include when directed by the JAB*; and
	  c. As an integral part of information system component installations and upgrades.

(Continued)

---

[89]High-Impact Security Requirement: *at least annually.*
[90]High-Impact Security Requirement: *at least annually, or whenever a significant change occurs.*
[91]FedRAMP Program Management Office (PMO). FedRAMP High System Security Plan (SSP) Template. Washington, DC: US General Services Administration; 2016. *"Significant change is defined in NIST Special Publication 800-37 Revision 1, Appendix F, Page F-7."*

Continued

CM-2	**Baseline Configuration**
	2. The Cloud Service Provider (CSP) employs automated mechanisms to maintain an up-to-date, complete, accurate, and readily available baseline configuration of the information system.
	3. The Cloud Service Provider (CSP) retains *CSP-defined previous versions of baseline configurations of the information system*[92] to support rollback.
	7. The Cloud Service Provider (CSP):
	a. Issues *CSP-defined information systems, system components, or devices* with *CSP-defined configurations* to individuals traveling to locations that the organization deems to be of significant risk; and
	b. Applies *CSP-defined security safeguards* to the devices when the individuals return.
CM-3	**Configuration Change Control**
Control Requirement:	The Cloud Service Provider (CSP):
	a. Determines the types of changes to the information system that are configuration-controlled;
	b. Reviews proposed configuration-controlled changes to the information system and approves or disapproves such changes with explicit consideration for security impact analyses;
	c. Documents configuration change decisions associated with the information system;
	d. Implements approved configuration-controlled changes to the information system;
	e. Retains records of configuration-controlled changes to the information system for *CSP-defined time period*;[93]
	f. Audits and reviews activities associated with configuration-controlled changes to the information system; and
	g. Coordinates and provides oversight for configuration change control activities through *Additional FedRAMP Requirements* that convenes *CSP-defined frequency* and/or *CSP-defined configuration change conditions*.
	Additional FedRAMP Requirements
	• The Cloud Service Provider (CSP) establishes a central means of communicating major changes to or developments in the information system or environment of operations that may affect its services to the federal government and associated service consumers (e.g., electronic bulletin board, web status page). The means of communication are approved and accepted by the JAB/AO.

(Continued)

---

[92]High-Impact Security Requirement: *CSP defined previous versions of baseline configurations of the previously approved baseline configuration of IS components.*

[93]FedRAMP Program Management Office (PMO). FedRAMP High System Security Plan (SSP) Template. Washington, DC: US General Services Administration; 2016. *"In accordance with record retention policies and procedures."*

Continued

CM-3	Configuration Change Control

Control Enhancements:	1. The Cloud Service Provider (CSP) employs automated mechanisms to:
	  a. Document proposed changes to the information system;
	  b. Notify *CSP-defined configuration management approval authorities* of proposed changes to the information system and request change approval;
	  c. Highlight proposed changes to the information system that have not been approved or disapproved by *CSP agreed-upon time period*;
	  d. Prohibit changes to the information system until designated approvals are received;
	  e. Document all changes to the information system; and
	  f. Notify *CSP-defined configuration management approval authorities* when approved changes to the information system are completed.
	2. The Cloud Service Provider (CSP) tests, validates, and documents changes to the information system before implementing the changes on the operational system.
	4. The Cloud Service Provider (CSP) requires an information security representative to be a member of the *configuration control board (CCB) or similar (as defined in CM-3)*.
	6. The Cloud Service Provider (CSP) ensures that cryptographic mechanisms used to provide *all security safeguards that rely on cryptography* are under configuration management.

CM-4	Security Impact Analysis
Control Requirement:	The Cloud Service Provider (CSP) analyzes changes to the information system to determine potential security impacts prior to change implementation.
Control Enhancements:	1. The Cloud Service Provider (CSP) analyzes changes to the information system in a separate test environment before implementation in an operational environment, looking for security impacts due to flaws, weaknesses, incompatibility, or intentional malice.
CM-5	Access Restrictions for Change
Control Requirement:	The Cloud Service Provider (CSP) defines, documents, approves, and enforces physical and logical access restrictions associated with changes to the information system.
Control Enhancements:	1. The information system enforces access restrictions and supports auditing of the enforcement actions. 2. The Cloud Service Provider (CSP) reviews information system changes *at least every thirty (30) days* and *CSP-defined circumstances* to determine whether unauthorized changes have occurred.

(Continued)

Continued

CM-5	Access Restrictions for Change
	3. The information system prevents the installation of *CSP-defined software and firmware components* without verification that the component has been digitally signed using a certificate[94] that is recognized and approved by the organization.
	5. The Cloud Service Provider (CSP):
	a. Limits privileges to change information system components and system-related information within a production or operational environment; and
	b. Reviews and reevaluates privileges *at least quarterly.*

CM-6[95]	Configuration Settings
Control Requirement:	The Cloud Service Provider (CSP):
	a. Establishes and documents configuration settings for information technology products employed within the information system using standards defined in Additional FedRAMP Requirements that reflect the most restrictive mode consistent with operational requirements.
	Additional FedRAMP Requirements
	• The Cloud Service Provider (CSP) shall use the Center for Internet Security guidelines (Level 1) to establish configuration settings or establishes its own configuration settings if United States Government Configuration Baseline (USGCB) is not available. If no recognized USGCB is available for the technology in use, the CSP should create their own baseline and include a justification statement as to how they came up with the baseline configuration settings.
	• The Cloud Service Provider (CSP) shall ensure that checklists for configuration settings are Security Content Automation Protocol (SCAP) validated or SCAP compatible (if validated checklists are not available).
	b. Implements the configuration settings;
	c. Identifies, documents, and approves any deviations from established configuration settings for CSP-defined information system components based on CSP-defined operational requirements; and
	d. Monitors and controls changes to the configuration settings in accordance with organizational policies and procedures.
Control Enhancements:	1. The Cloud Service Provider (CSP) employs automated mechanisms to centrally manage, apply, and verify configuration settings for *CSP-defined information system components*.
	2. The Cloud Service Provider (CSP) employs *CSP-defined security safeguards* to respond to unauthorized changes to *CSP-defined configuration settings*.

(Continued)

---

[94]FedRAMP Program Management Office (PMO). FedRAMP High System Security Plan (SSP) Template. Washington, DC: US General Services Administration; 2016. *"If digital signatures/certificates are unavailable, alternative cryptographic integrity checks (hashes, self-signed certs, etc.) can be used."*

[95]FedRAMP Program Management Office (PMO). FedRAMP High System Security Plan (SSP) Template. Washington, DC: US General Services Administration; 2016. *"Information on the USGCB checklists can be found at:* http://usgcb.nist.gov/usgcb_faq.html#usgcbfaq_usgcbfdcc.*"*

Continued

CM-7[96],[97]	Least Functionality
Control Requirement:	The Cloud Service Provider (CSP): a. Configures the information system to provide only essential capabilities; and b. Prohibits or restricts the use of the following functions, ports, protocols, and/or services in accordance with the *USGCB*. **Additional FedRAMP Requirements** • The Cloud Service Provider (CSP) shall use the Center for Internet Security guidelines (Level 1) to establish list of prohibited or restricted functions, ports, protocols, and/or services or establishes its own list of prohibited or restricted functions, ports, protocols, and/or services if USGCB is not available. If no recognized USGCB is available for the technology in use, the CSP should create their own baseline and include a justification statement as to how they came up with the baseline configuration settings.
Control Enhancements:	1. The Cloud Service Provider (CSP): a. Reviews the information system *at least monthly* to identify unnecessary and/or nonsecure functions, ports, protocols, and services; and b. Disables *CSP-defined functions, ports, protocols, and services within the information system deemed to be unnecessary and/or nonsecure.* 2.[98]The information system prevents program execution in accordance with *CSP-defined policies regarding software program usage and restriction and/or rules authorizing the terms and conditions of software program usage.* 5. The Cloud Service Provider (CSP): a. Identifies *CSP-defined software programs authorized to execute on the information system;* b. Employs a deny-all, permit-by-exception policy to allow the execution of authorized software programs on the information; and c. Reviews and updates the list of authorized software programs *at least annually or when there is a change.*[99]
CM-8	Information System Component Inventory
Control Requirement:	The Cloud Service Provider (CSP): a. Develops and documents an inventory of information system components that: 1. Accurately reflects the current information system;

(Continued)

---

[96]FedRAMP Program Management Office (PMO). FedRAMP High System Security Plan (SSP) Template. Washington, DC: US General Services Administration; 2016. *"Information on the USGCB checklists can be found at:* http://usgcb.nist.gov/usgcb_faq.html#usgcbfaq_usgcbfdcc.*"*

[97]FedRAMP Program Management Office (PMO). FedRAMP High System Security Plan (SSP) Template. Washington, DC: US General Services Administration; 2016. *"Partially derived from AC-17 (8).*"

[98]FedRAMP Program Management Office (PMO). FedRAMP High System Security Plan (SSP) Template. Washington, DC: US General Services Administration; 2016. *"This control shall be implemented in a technical manner on the information system to only allow programs to run that adhere to the policy (i.e., white listing). This control is not to be based off of strictly written policy on what is allowed or not allowed to run.*"

[99]High-Impact Security Requirement: *at least quarterly or when there is a change.*

CM-8	Information System Component Inventory
	2. Includes all components within the authorization boundary of the information system;
	3. Is at the level of granularity deemed necessary for tracking and reporting; and
	4. Includes *CSP-defined information deemed necessary to achieve effective information system component accountability*; and
	b. Reviews and updates the information system component inventory *at least monthly*.
	Additional FedRAMP Requirements
	• Must be provided at least monthly or when there is a change.
Control Enhancements:	1. The Cloud Service Provider (CSP) updates the inventory of information system components as an integral part of component installations, removals, and information system updates.
	2. The Cloud Service Provider (CSP) employs automated mechanisms to help maintain an up-to-date, complete, accurate, and readily available inventory of information system components.
	3. The Cloud Service Provider (CSP):
	a. Employs automated mechanisms continuously, using automated mechanisms with a maximum five-minute delay in detection to detect the presence of unauthorized hardware, software, and firmware components within the information system; and
	b. Takes the following actions when unauthorized components are detected: disables network access by such components, isolates the components, and/or notifies CSP-defined personnel or roles.
	4. The Cloud Service Provider (CSP) includes in the information system component inventory information, a means for identifying by *name and/or position and role* individuals responsible/accountable for administering those components.
	5. The Cloud Service Provider (CSP) verifies that all components within the authorization boundary of the information system are not duplicated in other information system inventories.
CM-9	**Configuration Management Plan**
Control Requirement:	The Cloud Service Provider (CSP) develops, documents, and implements a configuration management plan for the information system that:
	a. Addresses roles, responsibilities, and configuration management processes and procedures;
	b. Establishes a process for identifying configuration items throughout the system development life cycle (SDLC) and for managing the configuration of the configuration items;
	c. Defines the configuration items for the information system and places the configuration items under configuration management; and
	d. Protects the configuration management plan for unauthorized disclosure and modification.

(Continued)

Continued

CM-10	Software Usage Restrictions
Control Requirement:	The Cloud Service Provider (CSP): a. Uses software and associated documentation in accordance with contract agreements and copyright laws; b. Tracks the use of software and associated documentation protected by quantity licenses to control copying and distribution; and c. Controls and documents the use of peer-to-peer file sharing technology to ensure that this capability is not used for the unauthorized distribution, display, performance, or reproduction of copyrighted work.
Control Enhancements:	1. The Cloud Service Provider (CSP) establishes *CSP-defined restrictions* on the use of open source software.
CM-11	User-Installed Software
Control Requirement:	The Cloud Service Provider (CSP): a. Establishes *CSP-defined policies* governing the installation of software by users; b. Enforces software installation policies through *CSP-defined methods*; and c. Monitors policy compliance *continuously (via CM-7 (5))*.
Control Enhancements	1. The information system alerts *Cloud Service Provider (CSP)-* defined personnel or roles when the unauthorized installation of software is detected.
Contingency Planning (CP)	
CP-1	Contingency Planning Policy and Procedures

Control Requirement:	The Cloud Service Provider (CSP):
	a. Develops, documents, and disseminates to *CSP-defined personnel or roles*:
	  1. A contingency planning policy that addresses purpose, scope, roles, responsibilities, management commitment, coordination among organizational entities, and compliance; and
	  2. Procedures to facilitate the implementation of the contingency planning policy and associated contingency planning controls; and
	b. Reviews and updates the current:
	  1. Contingency planning policy *at least every three (3) years*;[100] and
	  2. Contingency planning policy *at least annually*.[101]

(Continued)

[100]High-Impact Security Requirement: *at least annually.*
[101]High-Impact Security Requirement: *at least annually, or whenever a significant change occurs.*

Continued

CP-2	Contingency Plan
Control Requirement:	The Cloud Service Provider (CSP): a. Develops a contingency plan for the information system that: 1. Identifies essential missions and business functions and associated contingency requirements; 2. Provides recovery objectives, restoration priorities, and metrics; 3. Addresses contingency roles, responsibilities, assigned individuals with contact information; 4. Addresses maintaining essential missions and business functions despite an information system disruption, compromise, or failure; 5. Addresses eventual, full information system restoration without deterioration of the security safeguards originally planned and implemented; and 6. Is reviewed and approved by *CSP-defined personnel or roles*; b. Distributes copies of the contingency plan to *CSP-defined key contingency personnel (identified by name and/or by role) and organizational elements*; c. Coordinates contingency planning activities with incident handling activities; d. Reviews the contingency plan for the information system *at least annually*; e. Updates the contingency plan to address changes to the organization, information system, or environment of operation and problems encountered during contingency plan implementation, execution, or testing; f. Communicates contingency plan changes to *CSP-defined key contingency personnel (identified by name and/or by role) and organizational elements*; and g. Protects the contingency plan from unauthorized disclosure and modification. **Additional FedRAMP Requirements** • For JAB authorizations the contingency lists include designated FedRAMP personnel.
Control Enhancements:	1. The Cloud Service Provider (CSP) coordinates contingency plan development with organizational elements responsible for related plans. 2. The Cloud Service Provider (CSP) conducts capacity planning so that necessary capacity for information processing, telecommunications, and environmental support exists during contingency operations. 3. The Cloud Service Provider (CSP) plans for the resumption of essential missions and business functions within the *CSP-defined time period* of contingency plan activation.

(Continued)

Continued

	4. The Cloud Service Provider (CSP) for the resumption of all missions and business functions within the *time period defined in CSP and organization SLA* of contingency plan activation.
	5. The Cloud Service Provider (CSP) plans for the continuance of essential missions and business functions with little or no loss of operational continuity and sustains that continuity until full information system restoration at primary processing and/or storage sites.
	8. The Cloud Service Provider (CSP) identifies critical information system assets supporting essential missions and business functions.
CP-3	**Contingency Training**
Control Requirement:	The Cloud Service Provider (CSP) provides contingency training to information system users consistent with assigned roles and responsibilities:
	a. Within *ten (10) days* of assuming a contingency role or responsibility;
	b. When required by information system changes; and
	c. *At least annually* thereafter.
Control Enhancements:	1. The Cloud Service Provider (CSP) incorporates simulated events into contingency training to facilitate effective response by personnel in crisis situations.
CP-4	**Contingency Plan Testing**
Control Requirement:	The Cloud Service Provider (CSP):
	a. Tests the contingency plan for the information system *at least annually for moderate- and high-impact systems or at least every three (3) years for low-impact systems* using *functional exercises for moderate- and high-impact systems or classroom exercises/table-top written tests for low-impact systems* to determine the effectiveness of the plan and the organizational readiness to execute the plan;
	Additional FedRAMP Requirements
	• The Cloud Service Provider (CSP) develops test plans in accordance with NIST Special Publication 800-34 (as amended) and provides plans to FedRAMP prior to initiating testing. Test plans are approved and accepted by the JAB/AO prior to initiating testing.
	b. Reviews the contingency plan test results; and
	c. Initiates corrective actions, if needed.
Control Enhancements:	1. The Cloud Service Provider (CSP) coordinates contingency plan testing and/or exercises with organizational elements responsible for related plan.
	2. The Cloud Service Provider (CSP) tests the contingency plan at the alternate processing site:
	a. To familiarize contingency personnel with the facility and available resources; and
	b. To evaluate the capabilities of the alternate processing site to support contingency operations.

Continued

CP-6	Alternate Storage Site
Control Requirement:	The Cloud Service Provider (CSP): a. Establishes an alternate storage site including necessary agreements to permit the storage and retrieval of information system backup information; and b. Ensures that the alternate storage site provides information security safeguards equivalent to that of the primary site.
Control Enhancements:	1. The Cloud Service Provider (CSP) identifies an alternate storage site that is separated from the primary storage site to reduce susceptibility to the same threats. 2. The Cloud Service Provider (CSP) configures the alternate storage site to facilitate recovery operations in accordance with recovery time and recovery point objectives. 3. The Cloud Service Provider (CSP) identifies potential accessibility problems to the alternate storage site in the event of an area-wide disruption or disaster and outlines explicit mitigation actions.
CP-7	Alternate Processing Site
Control Requirement:	The Cloud Service Provider (CSP): a. Establishes an alternate processing site including necessary agreements to permit the transfer and resumption of CSP-defined *information system operations* for essential missions/business functions within a time period consistent with the *Additional FedRAMP Requirements and* when the primary processing capabilities are unavailable; **Additional FedRAMP Requirements** • The Cloud Service Provider (CSP) defines a time period consistent with the recovery time objectives and business impact analysis. b. Ensures that equipment and supplies required to transfer and resume operations are available at the alternate processing site or contracts are in-place to support delivery to the site within the organization-defined time period for transfer/resumption; and c. Ensures that the alternate processing site provides information security safeguards equivalent to that of the primary site.
Control Enhancements:	1. [102]The Cloud Service Provider (CSP) identifies an alternate processing site that is separated from the primary processing site to reduce susceptibility to the same threats.

(Continued)

[102]FedRAMP Program Management Office (PMO). FedRAMP High System Security Plan (SSP) Template. Washington, DC: US General Services Administration; 2016. *"The Cloud Service Provider (CSP) may determine what is considered a sufficient degree of separation between the primary and alternate processing sites, based on the types of threats that are of concern. For one particular type of threat (i.e., hostile cyber attack), the degree of separation between sites will be less relevant."*

Continued

CP-7	Alternate Processing Site
	2. The Cloud Service Provider (CSP) identifies potential accessibility problems to the alternate processing site in the event of an area-wide disruption or disaster and outlines explicit mitigation actions.
	3. The Cloud Service Provider (CSP) develops alternate processing site agreements that contain priority-of-service provisions in accordance with organizational availability requirements (including recovery time objectives).
	4. The Cloud Service Provider (CSP) prepares the alternate processing site so that the site is ready to be used as the operational site supporting essential missions and business functions.
CP-8	**Telecommunications Services**
Control Requirement:	The Cloud Service Provider (CSP) establishes alternate telecommunications services including necessary agreements to permit the resumption of *CSP-defined information system operations* for essential missions and business functions within *CP-8 Additional FedRAMP Requirements* when the primary telecommunications capabilities are unavailable at either the primary or alternate processing or storage sites.
	Additional FedRAMP Requirements
	• The Cloud Service Provider (CSP) defines a time period consistent with the business impact analysis.
Control Enhancements:	1. The Cloud Service Provider (CSP):
	a. Develops primary and alternate telecommunications service agreements that contain priority-of-service provisions in accordance with organizational availability requirements (including recovery time objectives); and
	b. Requests telecommunications service priority for all telecommunications services used for national security emergency preparedness in the event that the primary and/or alternate telecommunications services are provided by a common carrier.
	2. The Cloud Service Provider (CSP) obtains alternate telecommunications services to reduce the likelihood of sharing a single point of failure with primary telecommunications services.
	3. The Cloud Service Provider (CSP) obtains alternate telecommunications services from providers that are separated from primary service providers to reduce susceptibility to the same threats.
	4. The Cloud Service Provider (CSP):
	a. Requires primary and alternate telecommunications service providers to have contingency plans;
	b. Reviews provider contingency plans to ensure that the plans meet organizational contingency requirements; and
	c. Obtains evidence of contingency testing/training by providers *annually*.

(Continued)

Continued

CP-9	Information System Backup
Control Requirement:	The Cloud Service Provider (CSP): a. Conducts backups of user-level information contained in the information system *daily incremental* and *weekly full*. **Additional FedRAMP Requirements** • The Cloud Service Provider (CSP) maintains at least three backup copies of user-level information (at least one of which is available online). b. Conducts backups of system-level information contained in the information system *daily incremental* and *weekly full*; **Additional FedRAMP Requirements** • The Cloud Service Provider (CSP) maintains at least three backup copies of system-level information (at least one of which is available online). c. Conducts backups of information system documentation including security-related documentation *daily incremental* and *weekly full*; and **Additional FedRAMP Requirements** • The Cloud Service Provider (CSP) maintains at least three backup copies of information system documentation including security information (at least one of which is available online). d. Protects the confidentiality, integrity, and availability of backup information at storage locations. **Additional FedRAMP Requirements** • The Cloud Service Provider (CSP) shall determine what elements of the cloud environment require the Information System Backup control. • The Cloud Service Provider (CSP) shall determine how Information System Backup is going to be verified and appropriate periodicity of the check.
Control Enhancements:	1. The Cloud Service Provider (CSP) tests backup information *at least annually* to verify media reliability and information integrity. 2. The Cloud Service Provider (CSP) uses a sample of backup information in the restoration of selected information system functions as part of contingency plan testing. 3. The Cloud Service Provider (CSP) stores backup copies of *CSP-defined critical information system software and other security-related information* in a separate facility or in a fire-rated container that is not collocated with the operational system. 5. The Cloud Service Provider (CSP) transfers information system backup information to the alternate storage site *time period and transfer rate consistent with the recovery time and recovery point objectives defined in the service provider and organization SLA*.

(Continued)

Continued

CP-10	Information System Recovery and Reconstitution
Control Requirement:	The Cloud Service Provider (CSP) provides for the recovery and reconstitution of the information system to a known state after a disruption, compromise, or failure.
Control Enhancements:	2. The information system implements transaction recovery for systems that are transaction-based.
	4. The Cloud Service Provider (CSP) provides the capability to restore information system components within the *time period consistent with the restoration time periods defined in the service provider and organization SLA* from configuration-controlled and integrity-protected information representing a known, operational state for the components.
	Identification and Authentication (IA)
IA-1	Identification and Authentication Policy and Procedures
Control Requirement:	The Cloud Service Provider (CSP):
	a. Develops, documents, and disseminates to *CSP-defined personnel or roles*:
	1. An identification and authentication policy that addresses purpose, scope, roles, responsibilities, management commitment, coordination among organizational entities, and compliance; and
	2. Procedures to facilitate the implementation of the identification and authentication policy and associated identification and authentication controls; and
	b. Reviews and updates the current:
	1. Identification and authentication policy *at least every three (3) years*;[103] and
	2. Identification and authentication procedures *at least annually*.[104]
IA-2	Identification and Authentication (Organizational Users)
Control Requirement:	The information system uniquely identifies and authenticates organizational users (or processes acting on behalf of organizational users).
Control Enhancements:	1. The information system implements multifactor authentication for network access to privileged accounts.
	2. The information system implements multifactor authentication for network access to non-privileged accounts.
	3. The information system implements multifactor authentication for local access to privileged accounts.

(Continued)

[103]High-Impact Security Requirement: *at least annually.*
[104]High-Impact Security Requirement: *at least annually, or whenever a significant change occurs.*

Continued

IA-2	Identification and Authentication (Organizational Users)
	4. The information system implements multifactor authentication for local access to non-privileged account.
	5. The Cloud Service Provider (CSP) requires individuals to be authenticated with an individual authenticator when a group authenticator is employed.
	8. The information system implements replay-resistant authentication mechanisms for network access to privileged accounts.
	9. The information system implements replay-resistant authentication mechanisms for network access to nonprivileged accounts.
	11. [105]The information system implements multifactor authentication for remote access to privileged and non-privileged accounts such that one of the factors is provided by a device separate from the system gaining access and the device meets *CSP-defined strength of mechanism requirements*.
	12. [106]The information system accepts and electronically verifies Personal Identity Verification (PIV) credentials.
IA-3	**Device Identification and Authentication**
Control Requirement:	The information system uniquely identifies and authenticates *CSP-defined specific and/or types of devices* before establishing a *local, remote, or network* connection.
IA-4	**Identifier Management**
Control Requirement:	The Cloud Service Provider (CSP) manages information system identifiers by:
	a. Receiving authorization from *CSP-defined personnel or roles* to assign an individual, group, role, or device identifier;
	b. Selecting an identifier that identifies an individual, group, role, or device;
	c. Assigning the identifier to the intended individual, group, role, or device;
	d. Preventing reuse of identifiers for *at least two (2) years*; and
	e. Disabling the identifier after *ninety (90) days*[107] *for user identifiers and in accordance with the Additional FedRAMP requirements*.

(Continued)

---

[105]FedRAMP Program Management Office (PMO). FedRAMP High System Security Plan (SSP) Template. Washington, DC: US General Services Administration; 2016. *"PIV = separate device. Please refer to NIST SP 800-157 Guidelines for Derived Personal Identity Verification (PIV) Credentials. FIPS 140-2 means validated by the Cryptographic Module Validation Program (CMVP)."*
[106]FedRAMP Program Management Office (PMO). FedRAMP High System Security Plan (SSP) Template. Washington, DC: US General Services Administration; 2016. *"Include Common Access Card (CAC), i.e., the DoD technical implementation of PIV/FIPS 201/HSPD-12."*
[107]High-Impact Security Requirement: *thirty-five (35) days.*

Continued

IA-4	Identifier Management
Control Enhancements:	**Additional FedRAMP Requirements** • The Cloud Service Provider (CSP) defines time period of inactivity for device identifiers. 4. The Cloud Service Provider (CSP) manages individual identifiers by uniquely identifying each individual as *contractors or foreign nationals*.
IA-5	**Authenticator Management**
Control Requirement:	The Cloud Service Provider (CSP) manages information system authenticators by: a. Verifying, as part of the initial authenticator distribution, the identity of the individual, group, role, or device receiving the authenticator; b. Establishing initial authenticator content for authenticators defined by the organization; c. Ensuring that authenticators have sufficient strength of mechanism for their intended use; d. Establishing and implementing administrative procedures for initial authenticator distribution, for lost/compromised or damaged authenticators, and for revoking authenticators; e. Changing default content of authenticators prior to information system installation; f. Establishing minimum and maximum lifetime restrictions and reuse conditions for authenticators; g. Changing/refreshing authenticators *to include sixty (60) days for passwords*. h. Protecting authenticator content from unauthorized disclosure and modification; i. Requiring individuals to take, and having devices implement, specific security safeguards to protect authenticators; and j. Changing authenticators for group/role accounts when membership to those accounts changes. **Additional FedRAMP Requirements** • Authenticators must be compliant with NIST SP 800-63-2 Electronic Authentication Guideline assurance Level 4. Link to publication: http://nvlpubs.nist.gov/nistpubs/SpecialPublications/NIST.SP.800-63-2.pdf.
Control Enhancements:	1. The information system, for password-based authentication: a. Enforces minimum password complexity of *case sensitive, minimum of twelve (12) characters, and at least one each of upper-case letters, lower-case letters, numbers, and special characters*; b. Enforces at least the following number of changed characters when new passwords are created: *at least one (1)*;[108]

(Continued)

---

[108]High-Impact Security Requirement: *at least fifty percent (50%)*.

Continued

IA-5	Authenticator Management
	c. Stores and transmits only cryptographically protected passwords;
	d. Enforces password minimum and maximum lifetime restrictions of *one (1) day minimum, sixty (60) day maximum*;
	e. Prohibits password reuse for *twenty-four* (24) generations; and
	f. Allows the use of a temporary password for system logons with an immediate change to a permanent password.
	2. The information system, for public key infrastructure (PKI)-based authentication:
	a. Validates certifications by constructing and verifying a certification path to an accepted trust anchor including checking certificate status information;
	b. Enforces authorized access to the corresponding private key;
	c. Maps the authenticated identity to the account of the individual or group; and
	d. Implements a local cache of revocation data to support path discovery and validation in case of inability to access revocation information via the network.
	3. The Cloud Service Provider (CSP) requires that the registration process to receive all *hardware/biometric (multifactor authenticators)* be conducted *in person* before *CSP-defined registration authority* with authorization by *CSP-defined personnel or roles*.
	4. [109]The Cloud Service Provider (CSP) employs automated tools to determine if password authenticators are sufficiently strong to satisfy *CSP-defined requirements*.
	6. The Cloud Service Provider (CSP) protects authenticators commensurate with the security category of the information to which use of the authenticator permits access.
	7. The Cloud Service Provider (CSP) ensures that unencrypted static authenticators are not embedded in applications or access scripts or stored on function keys.
	8. The Cloud Service Provider (CSP) implements *different authenticators on different systems* to manage the risk of compromise due to individuals having accounts on multiple information systems.
	11. The information system, for hardware token-based authentication, employs mechanisms that satisfy *Cloud Service Provider (CSP)-defined token quality requirements*.
	13. The information system prohibits the use of cached authenticators after *Cloud Service Provider (CSP)-defined time period*.

(Continued)

[109]FedRAMP Program Management Office (PMO). FedRAMP High System Security Plan (SSP) Template. Washington, DC: US General Services Administration; 2016. *"If automated mechanisms which enforce password authenticator strength at creation are not used, automated mechanisms must be used to audit strength of created password authenticators."*

Continued

IA-6	Authenticator Feedback
Control Requirement:	The information system obscures feedback of authentication information during the authentication process to protect the information from possible exploitation/use by unauthorized individuals.

IA-7	Cryptographic Module Authentication
Control Requirement:	The information system implements mechanisms for authentication to a cryptographic module that meet the requirements of applicable federal laws, Executive Orders, directives, policies, regulations, standards, and guidance for such authentication.

IA-8	Identification and Authentication (Non-Organizational Users)
Control Requirement:	The information system uniquely identifies and authenticates non-organizational users (or processes acting on behalf of non-organizational users).
Control Enhancements:	1. The information system accepts and electronically verifies Personal Identity Verification (PIV) credentials from other federal agencies.
	2. The information system accepts only Federal Identity, Credential, and Access Management (FICAM)-approved third-party credentials.
	3. The Cloud Service Provider (CSP) employs only FICAM-approved information system components in *CSP-defined information systems* to accept third-party credentials.
	4. The information system conforms to FICAM-issued profiles.

Incident Response (IR)	

IR-1	Incident Response Policy and Procedures
Control Requirement:	The Cloud Service Provider (CSP):
	a. Develops, documents, and disseminates to *CSP-defined personnel or roles*:
	1. An incident response policy that addresses purpose, scope, roles, responsibilities, management commitment, coordination among organizational entities, and compliance; and
	2. Procedures to facilitate the implementation of the incident response policy and associated incident response controls; and
	b. Reviews and updates the current:
	1. Incident response policy *at least every three (3) years*;[110] and
	2. Incident response procedures *at least annually*.[111]

IR-2	Incident Response Training
Control Requirement:	The Cloud Service Provider (CSP) provides incident response training to information system users consistent with assigned roles and responsibilities:
	a. Within to *CSP-defined time period*[112] of assuming an incident response role or responsibility;

(Continued)

---

[110]High-Impact Security Requirement: *at least annually.*

[111]High-Impact Security Requirement: *at least annually, or whenever a significant change occurs.*

[112]High-Impact Security Requirement: *ten (10) days.*

Continued

IR-2	Incident Response Training
Control Enhancements:	b. When required by information system changes; and c. *At least annually* thereafter. 1. The Cloud Service Provider (CSP) incorporates simulated events into incident response training to facilitate effective response by personnel in crisis situations. 2. The Cloud Service Provider (CSP) employs automated mechanisms to provide a more thorough and realistic incident response training environment.
IR-3	**Incident Response Testing**
Control Requirement:	The Cloud Service Provider (CSP) tests the incident response capability for the information system *at least annually*[113] using tests in accordance with the *Additional FedRAMP Requirements* to determine the incident response effectiveness and documents the results. **Additional FedRAMP Requirements** • The Cloud Service Provider (CSP) defines tests and/or exercises in accordance with NIST Special Publication 800-61 (as amended). For JAB authorization, the service provider provides test plans to the JAB/AO annually. Test plans are approved and accepted by the JAB/AO prior to the test commencing.
Control Enhancements:	2. The Cloud Service Provider (CSP) coordinates incident response testing with organizational elements responsible for related plans.
IR-4	**Incident Handling**
Control Requirement:	The Cloud Service Provider (CSP): a. Implements an incident handling capability for security incidents that includes preparation, detection and analysis, containment, eradication, and recovery; b. Coordinates incident handling activities with contingency planning activities; and c. Incorporates lessons learned from ongoing incident handling activities into incident response procedures, training, and testing/exercises, and implements the resulting changes accordingly. **Additional FedRAMP Requirements** • The Cloud Service Provider (CSP) ensures that individuals conducting incident handling meet personnel security requirements commensurate with the criticality/sensitivity of the information being processed, stored, and transmitted by the information system.
Control Enhancements:	1. The Cloud Service Provider (CSP) employs automated mechanisms to support the incident handling process.

(Continued)

---

[113]High-Impact Security Requirement: *at least every six (6) months.*

Continued

IR-4	Incident Handling
	2. The Cloud Service Provider (CSP) includes dynamic reconfiguration of *all network, data storage, and computing devices* as part of the incident response capability.
	3. The Cloud Service Provider (CSP) identifies *CSP-defined classes of incidents* and *CSP-defined actions to take in response to classes of incident* to ensure continuation of organizational missions and business functions.
	4. The Cloud Service Provider (CSP) correlates incident information and individual incident responses to achieve an organization-wide perspective on incident awareness and response.
	6. The Cloud Service Provider (CSP) implements incident handling capability for insider threats.
	8. The Cloud Service Provider (CSP) coordinates with *external organizations including consumer incident responders and network defenders and the appropriate Computer Incident Response Team (CIRT)/Computer Emergency Response Team (CERT) (such as US-CERT, DoD CERT, IC CERT)* to correlate and share *CSP incident information* to achieve a cross-organization perspective on incident awareness and more effective incident responses.
IR-5	**Incident Monitoring**
Control Requirement:	The Cloud Service Provider (CSP) tracks and documents information system security incidents.
Control Enhancements:	1. The Cloud Service Provider (CSP) employs automated mechanisms to assist in the tracking of security incidents and in the collection and analysis of incident information.
IR-6	**Incident Reporting**
Control Requirement:	The Cloud Service Provider (CSP):
	a. Requires personnel to report suspected security incidents to the organizational incident response capability within *US-CERT incident reporting timelines as specified in NIST SP800-61 (as amended)*; and
	b. Reports security incident information to *CSP-defined authorities*.
	Additional FedRAMP Requirements
	• Report security incident information according to FedRAMP Incident Communications Procedure.
Control Enhancements:	1. The Cloud Service Provider (CSP) employs automated mechanisms to assist in the reporting of security incidents.
IR-7	**Incident Response Assistance**
Control Requirement:	The Cloud Service Provider (CSP) provides an incident response support resource, integral to the organizational incident response capability that offers advice and assistance to users of the information system for the handling and reporting of security incidents.

(Continued)

Continued

IR-7	Incident Response Assistance

Control Enhancements:	1. The Cloud Service Provider (CSP) employs automated mechanisms to increase the availability of incident response–related information and support.
	
	2. The Cloud Service Provider (CSP):
	   a. Establishes a direct, cooperative relationship between its incident response capability and external providers of information system protection capability; and
	   b. Identifies organizational incident response team members to the external providers.

IR-8	**Incident Response Plan**

Control Requirement:	The Cloud Service Provider (CSP):
	a. Develops an incident response plan that:
	   1. Provides the organization with a roadmap for implementing its incident response capability;
	   2. Describes the structure and organization of the incident response capability;
	   3. Provides a high-level approach for how the incident response capability fits into the overall organization;
	   4. Meets the unique requirements of the organization, which relate to mission, size, structure, and functions;
	   5. Defines reportable incidents;
	   6. Provides metrics for measuring the incident response capability within the organization;
	   7. Defines the resources and management support needed to effectively maintain and mature an incident response capability; and
	   8. Is reviewed and approved by *CSP-defined personnel or roles*;
	b. Distributes copies of the incident response plan in accordance with *Additional FedRAMP Requirements*.
	
	Additional FedRAMP Requirements
	• The Cloud Service Provider (CSP) defines a list of incident response personnel (identified by name and/or by role) and organizational elements. The incident response list includes designated FedRAMP personnel.
	c. Reviews the incident response plan *at least annually*.
	d. Updates the incident response plan to address system/organizational changes or problems encountered during plan implementation, execution, or testing.
	e. Communicates incident response plan changes to personnel in accordance with *Additional FedRAMP Requirements*.

(Continued)

Continued

IR-8	Incident Response Plan
	Additional FedRAMP Requirements • The Cloud Service Provider (CSP) defines a list of incident response personnel (identified by name and/or by role) and organizational elements. The incident response list includes designated FedRAMP personnel. f. Protects the incident response plan from unauthorized disclosure and modification.
IR-9	**Information Spillage Response**
Control Requirement:	The Cloud Service Provider (CSP) responds to information spills by: a. Identifying the specific information involved in the information system contamination; b. Alerting *CSP-defined personnel or roles* of the information spill using a method of communication not associated with the spill; c. Isolating the contaminated information system or system component; d. Eradicating the information from the contaminated information system or component; e. Identifying other information systems or system components that may have been subsequently contaminated; and f. Performing other *CSP-defined actions*.
Control Enhancements:	1. The Cloud Service Provider (CSP) assigns *CSP-defined personnel or roles* with responsibility for responding to information spills. 2. The Cloud Service Provider (CSP) provides information spillage response training *CSP-defined frequency*.[114] 3. The Cloud Service Provider (CSP) implements *CSP-defined procedures* to ensure that organizational personnel impacted by information spills can continue to carry out assigned tasks while contaminated systems are undergoing corrective actions. 4. The Cloud Service Provider (CSP) employs *CSP-defined security safeguards* for personnel exposed to information not within assigned access authorizations.
	Maintenance (MA)
MA-1	**System Maintenance Policy and Procedures**

Control Requirement:	The Cloud Service Provider (CSP):
	a. Develops, documents, and disseminates to *CSP-defined personnel or roles*:
	  1. A system maintenance policy that addresses purpose, scope, roles, responsibilities, management commitment, coordination among organizational entities, and compliance; and
	  2. Procedures to facilitate the implementation of the system maintenance policy and associated system maintenance controls; and

(Continued)

---

[114]High-Impact Security Requirement: *at least annually.*

Continued

Maintenance (MA)	
MA-1	**System Maintenance Policy and Procedures**
	b. Reviews and updates the current: 　　1. System maintenance policy *at least every three (3) years*;[115] and 　　2. System maintenance procedures *at least annually*.[116]
MA-2	**Controlled Maintenance**
Control Requirement:	The Cloud Service Provider (CSP): a. Schedules, performs, documents, and reviews records of maintenance and repairs on information system components in accordance with manufacturer or vendor specifications and/or organizational requirements; b. Approves and monitors all maintenance activities, whether performed on-site or remotely and whether the equipment is serviced on-site or removed to another location; c. Requires that *CSP-defined personnel or roles* explicitly approve the removal of the information system or system components from organizational facilities for off-site maintenance or repairs; d. Sanitizes equipment to remove all information from associated media prior to removal from organizational facilities for off-site maintenance or repairs; e. Checks all potentially impacted security controls to verify that the controls are still functioning properly following maintenance or repair actions; and f. Includes *CSP-defined maintenance-related information* in organizational maintenance records.
Control Enhancements:	2. The Cloud Service Provider (CSP): a. Employs automated mechanisms to schedule, conduct, and document maintenance and repairs; and b. Produces up-to-date, accurate, and complete records of all maintenance and repair actions requested, scheduled, in process, and completed.
MA-3	**Maintenance Tools**
Control Requirement: Control Enhancements:	The Cloud Service Provider (CSP) approves, controls, and monitors information system maintenance tools. 1. The Cloud Service Provider (CSP) inspects the maintenance tools carried into a facility by maintenance personnel for improper or unauthorized modifications. 2. The Cloud Service Provider (CSP) checks media-containing diagnostic and test programs for malicious code before the media are used in the information system.

(Continued)

---

[115]High-Impact Security Requirement: *at least annually.*
[116]High-Impact Security Requirement: *at least annually, or whenever a significant change occurs.*

Continued

MA-3	Maintenance Tools

	3. The Cloud Service Provider (CSP) prevents the unauthorized removal of maintenance equipment containing organizational information by:
	  a. Verifying that there is no organizational information contained on the equipment;
	  b. Sanitizing or destroying the equipment;
	  c. Retaining the equipment within the facility; or
	  d. Obtaining an exemption from *the information owner* explicitly authorizing removal of the equipment from the facility.

MA-4	**Nonlocal Maintenance**

Control Requirement:	The Cloud Service Provider (CSP):
	  a. Approves and monitors nonlocal maintenance and diagnostic activities;
	  b. Allows the use of nonlocal maintenance and diagnostic tools only as consistent with organizational policy and documented in the security plan for the information system;
	  c. Employs strong authenticators in the establishment of nonlocal maintenance and diagnostic sessions;
	  d. Maintains records for nonlocal maintenance and diagnostic activities; and
	  e. Terminates session and network connections when nonlocal maintenance is completed.

Control Enhancements:	2. The Cloud Service Provider (CSP) documents in the security plan for the information system, the policies and procedures for the establishment and use of nonlocal maintenance and diagnostic connections.
	3. The Cloud Service Provider (CSP):
	  a. Requires that nonlocal maintenance and diagnostic services be performed from an information system that implements a security capability comparable to the capability implemented on the system being serviced; or
	  b. Removes the component to be serviced from the information system prior to nonlocal maintenance or diagnostic services, sanitizes the component (with regard to organizational information) before removal from organizational facilities, and after the service is performed, inspects and sanitizes the component (with regard to potentially malicious software) before reconnecting the component to the information system.
	6. The information system implements cryptographic mechanisms to protect the integrity and confidentiality of nonlocal maintenance and diagnostic communications.

MA-5	**Maintenance Personnel**
Control Requirement:	The Cloud Service Provider (CSP): a. Establishes a process for maintenance of personnel authorization and maintains a list of authorized maintenance organizations or personnel;

Continued

MA-5	**Maintenance Personnel**
	b. Ensures that non-escorted personnel performing maintenance on the information system have required access authorizations; and
	c. Designates organizational personnel with required access authorizations and technical competence to supervise the maintenance activities of personnel who do not possess the required access authorizations.
Control Enhancements:	1. The Cloud Service Provider (CSP):
	a. Implements procedures for the use of maintenance personnel who lack appropriate security clearances or are not US citizens, which include the following requirements:
	1. Maintenance personnel who do not have needed access authorizations, clearances, or formal access approvals are escorted and supervised during the performance of maintenance and diagnostic activities on the information system by approved organizational personnel who are fully cleared, have appropriate access authorizations, and are technically qualified.
	2. Prior to initiating maintenance or diagnostic activities by personnel who do not have needed access authorizations, clearances, or formal access approvals, all volatile information storage components within the information system are sanitized and all nonvolatile storage media are removed or physically disconnected from the system and secured; and
	b. Develops and implements alternate security safeguards in the event an information system component cannot be sanitized, removed, or disconnected from the system.
	Additional FedRAMP Requirements
	• Only MA-5 (1)(a)(1) is required by FedRAMP moderate and high baselines.
MA-6	**Timely Maintenance**
Control Requirement:	The Cloud Service Provider (CSP) obtains maintenance support and/or spare parts for *CSP-defined information system components* within *CSP-defined time period* of failure.
	Media Protection (MP)
MP-1	**Media Protection Policy and Procedures**
Control Requirement:	The Cloud Service Provider (CSP):
	a. Develops, documents, and disseminates to *CSP-defined personnel or roles*:
	1. A media protection policy that addresses purpose, scope, roles, responsibilities, management commitment, coordination among organizational entities, and compliance; and
	2. Procedures to facilitate the implementation of the media protection policy and associated media protection controls; and

(Continued)

Continued

Media Protection (MP)	
MP-1	**Media Protection Policy and Procedures**

	b. Reviews and updates the current:
	   1. Media protection policy *at least every three (3) years;*[117] and
	   2. Media protection procedures *at least annually.*[118]

MP-2	**Media Access**
Control Requirement:	The Cloud Service Provider (CSP) restricts access to *CSP-defined types of digital and/or nondigital media* to *CSP-defined personnel or roles.*
MP-3	**Media Markings**
Control Requirement:	The Cloud Service Provider (CSP): a. Marks information system media indicating the distribution limitations, handling caveats, and applicable security markings (if any) of the information; and b. [119] Exempts *no removable media types* from marking as long as the media remain within *CSP-defined controlled areas.*
MP-4	**Media Storage**

Control Requirement:	The Cloud Service Provider (CSP):
	a. Physically controls and securely stores *all types of digital and nondigital media with sensitive information* within controlled areas in accordance with *Additional FedRAMP Requirements.*
	   Additional FedRAMP Requirements
	   • The Cloud Service Provider (CSP) defines controlled areas within facilities where the information and information system reside.
	b. Protects information system media until the media are destroyed or sanitized using approved equipment, techniques, and procedures.

MP-5	**Media Transport**

Control Requirement:	The Cloud Service Provider (CSP):
	a. Protects and controls *all media with sensitive information* during transport outside of controlled areas using *digital media, encryption using a FIPS 140-2-validated encryption module; for nondigital media, secured in locked container;*
	   Additional FedRAMP Requirements
	   • The Cloud Service Provider (CSP) defines security measures to protect digital and nondigital media in transport. The security measures are approved and accepted by the JAB/AO.

(Continued)

---

[117]High-Impact Security Requirement: *at least annually.*

[118]High-Impact Security Requirement: *at least annually, or whenever a significant change occurs.*

[119]High-Impact Security Requirement: *Second parameter in MP-3(b)-2 is not applicable.*

Continued

MP-5	Media Transport
	b. Maintains accountability for information system media during transport outside of controlled areas;
	c. Documents activities associated with the transport of information system media; and
	d. Restricts the activities associated with the transport of information system media to authorized personnel.
Control Enhancements:	4. The information system employs cryptographic mechanisms to protect the confidentiality and integrity of information stored on digital media during transport outside of controlled areas.
MP-6	**Media Sanitization**
Control Requirement:	The Cloud Service Provider (CSP):
	a. Sanitizes *CSP-defined information system media* prior to disposal, release out of organizational control, or release for reuse using *CSP-defined sanitization techniques and procedures*[120] in accordance with applicable federal and organizational standards and policies; and
	b. Employs sanitization mechanisms with strength and integrity commensurate with the classification or classification of the information.
Control Enhancements:	1. The Cloud Service Provider (CSP) approves, tracks, documents, and verifies media sanitization and disposal actions.
	2. [121] The Cloud Service Provider (CSP) tests sanitization equipment and procedures *at least annually*[122] to verify that the intended sanitization is being achieved.
	3. The Cloud Service Provider (CSP) applies nondestructive sanitization techniques to portable storage devices prior to connecting such devices to the information system under the following circumstances: *CSP-defined circumstances requiring sanitization of portable storage devices.*
MP-7	**Media Use**
Control Requirement:	The Cloud Service Provider (CSP) *restricts or prohibits* the use of *CSP-defined types of information system media* on *CSP-defined information systems or system components* using *CSP-defined security safeguards.*
Control Enhancements:	1. The Cloud Service Provider (CSP) prohibits the use of portable storage devices in organizational information systems when such devices have no identifiable owner.

(Continued)

---

[120]High-Impact Security Requirement: *techniques and procedures IAW NIST SP 800-88 and Section 5.9: Reuse and Disposal of Storage Media and Hardware.*

[121]FedRAMP Program Management Office (PMO). FedRAMP High System Security Plan (SSP) Template. Washington, DC: US General Services Administration; 2016. *"Equipment and procedures may be tested or evaluated for effectiveness."*

[122]High-Impact Security Requirement: *at least annually.*

Continued

Physical and Environmental Protection (PE)	
PE-1	**Physical and Environmental Protection Policy and Procedures**

Control Requirement:	The Cloud Service Provider (CSP):
	a. Develops, documents, and disseminates to *CSP-defined personnel or roles*:
	   1. A physical and environmental protection policy that addresses purpose, scope, roles, responsibilities, management commitment, coordination among organizational entities, and compliance; and
	   2. Procedures to facilitate the implementation of the physical and environmental protection policy and associated physical and environmental protection controls; and
	b. Reviews and updates the current:
	   1. Physical and environmental protection policy *at least every three (3) years*;[123] and
	   2. Physical and environmental protection procedures *at least annually*.[124]

PE-2	**Physical Access Authorizations**
Control Requirement:	The Cloud Service Provider (CSP): a. Develops, approves, and maintains a list of individuals with authorized access to the facility where the information system resides; b. Issues authorization credentials for facility access; c. Reviews the access list detailing authorized facility access by individuals *at least annually*;[125] and d. Removes individuals from the facility access list when access is no longer required.
PE-3	**Physical Access Control**

Control Requirement:	The Cloud Service Provider (CSP):
	a. Enforces physical access authorizations at *CSP-defined entry/ exit points to the facility where the information system resides* by;
	   1. Verifying individual access authorizations before granting access to the facility; and
	   2. Controlling ingress/egress to the facility using *CSP-defined physical access control systems/devices and guards*;
	b. Maintains physical access audit logs for *CSP-defined entry/exit points*;
	c. Provides *CSP-defined security safeguards* to control access to areas within the facility officially designated as publicly accessible;

(Continued)

---

[123]High-Impact Security Requirement: *at least annually.*
[124]High-Impact Security Requirement: *at least annually, or whenever a significant change occurs.*
[125]High-Impact Security Requirement: *at least every ninety (90) days.*

Continued

PE-3	**Physical Access Control**
	d. Escorts visitors and monitors visitor activity *in all circumstances within restricted access area where the information system resides*; e. Secures keys, combinations, and other physical access devices; f. Inventories *CSP-defined physical access devices at least annually*; and g. Changes combinations and keys *at least annually* and/or when keys are lost, combinations are compromised, or individuals are transferred or terminated.
Control Enhancements:	1. The Cloud Service Provider (CSP) enforces physical access authorizations to the information system in addition to the physical access controls for the facility at *CSP-defined physical spaces containing components of the information system*.
PE-4	**Access Control for Transmission Medium**
Control Requirement:	The Cloud Service Provider (CSP) controls physical access to *CSP-defined information system distribution and transmission lines* within organizational facilities using *CSP-defined security safeguards*.
PE-5	**Access Control for Output Devices**
Control Requirement:	The Cloud Service Provider (CSP) controls physical access to information system output devices to prevent unauthorized individuals from obtaining the output.
PE-6	**Monitoring Physical Access**
Control Requirement:	The Cloud Service Provider (CSP): a. Monitors physical access to the facility where the information system resides to detect and respond to physical security incidents; b. Reviews physical access logs *at least monthly* and upon occurrence of *CSP-defined events or potential indications of events*; and c. Coordinates results of reviews and investigations with the organization's incident response capability.
Control Enhancements:	1. The Cloud Service Provider (CSP) monitors physical intrusion alarms and surveillance equipment. 4. The Cloud Service Provider (CSP) monitors physical access to the information system in addition to the physical access monitoring of the facility as *CSP-defined physical spaces containing one or more components of the information system*.
PE-8	**Visitor Access Records**
Control Requirement:	The Cloud Service Provider (CSP): a. Maintains visitor access records to the facility where the information system resides *for a minimum of one (1) year*; and b. Reviews visitor access records *at least monthly*.

(Continued)

Continued

PE-8	Visitor Access Records
Control Enhancements:	1. The Cloud Service Provider (CSP) employs automated mechanisms to facilitate the maintenance and review of visitor access records.
PE-9	**Power Equipment and Cabling**
Control Requirement:	The Cloud Service Provider (CSP) protects power equipment and power cabling for the information system from damage and destruction.
PE-10	**Emergency Shutoff**
Control Requirement:	The Cloud Service Provider (CSP): a. Provides the capability of shutting off power to the information system or individual system components in emergency situations; b. Places emergency shutoff switches or devices in *CSP-defined location by information system or system component* to facilitate safe and easy access for personnel; and c. Protects emergency power shutoff capability from unauthorized activation.
PE-11	**Emergency Power**
Control Requirement:	The Cloud Service Provider (CSP) provides a short-term uninterruptible power supply to facilitate *an orderly shutdown of the information system and/or transition of the information system to long-term alternate power* in the event of a primary power source loss.
Control Enhancements:	1. The Cloud Service Provider (CSP) provides a long-term alternate power supply for the information system that is capable of maintaining minimally required operational capability in the event of an extended loss of the primary power source.
PE-12	**Emergency Lighting**
Control Requirement:	The Cloud Service Provider (CSP) employs and maintains automatic emergency lighting for the information system that activates in the event of a power outage or disruption and that covers emergency exits and evacuation routes within the facility.
PE-13	**Fire Protection**
Control Requirement:	The Cloud Service Provider (CSP) employs and maintains fire suppression and detection devices/systems for the information system that are supported by an independent energy source.
Control Enhancements:	1. The Cloud Service Provider (CSP) employs fire detection devices/systems for the information system that activate automatically and notify CSP *building maintenance/physical security personnel* and CSP emergency responders with incident response responsibilities in the event of a fire.

(Continued)

Continued

PE-13	Fire Protection
	2. The Cloud Service Provider (CSP) employs fire suppression devices/systems for the information system that provide automatic notification of any activation *CSP-defined personnel or roles* and *CSP-defined emergency responders*.
	3. The Cloud Service Provider (CSP) employs an automatic fire suppression capability for the information system when the facility is not staffed on a continuous basis.
PE-14	**Temperature and Humidity Controls**
Control Requirement:	The Cloud Service Provider (CSP):
	a. Maintains temperature and humidity levels within the facility where the information system resides *consistent with American Society of Heating, Refrigerating, and Air-conditioning Engineers (ASHRAE) document titled "Thermal Guidelines for Data Processing Environments"*; and
	Additional FedRAMP Requirements:
	• The Cloud Service Provider (CSP) measures temperature at server inlets and humidity levels by dew point.
	b. Monitors temperature and humidity levels *continuously*.
Control Enhancements:	2. The Cloud Service Provider (CSP) employs temperature and humidity monitoring that provides an alarm or notification of changes potentially harmful to personnel or equipment.
PE-15	**Water Damage Protection**
Control Requirement:	The Cloud Service Provider (CSP) protects the information system from damage resulting from water leakage by providing master shutoff or isolation valves that are accessible, working properly, and known to key personnel.
Control Enhancements:	1. The Cloud Service Provider (CSP) employs automated mechanisms to detect the presence of water in the vicinity of the information system and alerts *CSP building maintenance/physical security personnel*.
PE-16	**Delivery and Removal**
Control Requirement:	The Cloud Service Provider (CSP) authorizes, monitors, and controls *all information system components* entering and exiting the facility and maintains records of those items.
PE-17	**Alternate Work Site**
Control Requirement:	The Cloud Service Provider (CSP):
	a. Employs *CSP-defined security controls* at alternate work sites;
	b. Assesses as feasible, the effectiveness of security controls at alternate work sites; and

(Continued)

Continued

PE-17	Alternate Work Site
	c. Provides a means for employees to communicate with information security personnel in case of security incidents or problems.
PE-18	**Location of Information System Components**
Control Requirement:	The Cloud Service Provider (CSP) positions information system components within the facility to minimize potential damage from *physical and environmental hazards identified during threat assessment* and to minimize the opportunity for unauthorized access.
	Planning (PL)
PL-1	**Security Planning Policy and Procedures**

Control Requirement:	The Cloud Service Provider (CSP):
	 a. Develops, documents, and disseminates to *CSP-defined personnel or roles*:
	   1. A security planning policy that addresses purpose, scope, roles, responsibilities, management commitment, coordination among organizational entities, and compliance; and
	   2. Procedures to facilitate the implementation of the security planning policy and associated security planning controls; and
	 b. Reviews and updates the current:
	   1. Security planning policy *at least every three (3) years*;[126] and
	   2. Security planning procedures *at least annually*.[127]

PL-2	**System Security Plan**

Control Requirement:	The Cloud Service Provider (CSP):
	 a. Develops a security plan for the information system that:
	   1. Is consistent with the organization's enterprise architecture;
	   2. Explicitly defines the authorization boundary for the system;
	   3. Describes the operational context of the information system in terms of missions and business processes;
	   4. Provides the security categorization of the information system including supporting rationale;
	   5. Describes the operational environment for the information system and relationships with or connections to other information;
	   6. Provides an overview of the security requirements for the system;
	   7. Identifies any relevant overlays, if applicable;

(Continued)

[126]High-Impact Security Requirement: *at least annually.*
[127]High-Impact Security Requirement: *at least annually, or whenever a significant change occurs.*

Continued

PL-2	**System Security Plan**
	8. Describes the security controls in-place or planned for meeting those requirements including a rationale for the tailoring decisions; and
	9. Is reviewed and approved by the authorizing official or designated representative prior to plan implementation;
	b. Distributes copies of the security plan and communicates subsequent changes to the plan to *CSP-defined personnel or roles*;
	c. Reviews the security plan for the information system *at least annually*;
	d. Updates the plan to address changes to the information system/ environment of operation or problems identified during plan implementation or security control assessments; and
	e. Protects the security plan from unauthorized disclosure and modification.
Control Enhancements:	3. The Cloud Service Provider (CSP) plans and coordinates security-related activities affecting the information system with *CSP-defined individuals or groups* before conducting such activities in order to reduce the impact on other organizational entities.
PL-4	**Rules of Behavior**
Control Requirement:	The Cloud Service Provider (CSP):
	a. Establishes and makes readily available to individuals requiring access to the information system, the rules that describe their responsibilities and expected behavior with regard to information and information system usage;
	b. Receives a signed acknowledgment from such individuals, indicating that they have read, understood, and agreed to abide by the rules of behavior, before authorizing access to information and the information system;
	c. Reviews and updates the rules of behavior *at least every three (3) years*;[128] and
	d. Requires individuals who have signed a previous version of the rules of behavior to read and resign when the rules of behavior are revised/updated.
Control Enhancements:	1. The Cloud Service Provider (CSP) includes in the rules of behavior, explicit restrictions on the use of social media/networking sites and posting organizational information on public websites.
PL-8	**Information Security Architecture**
Control Requirement:	The Cloud Service Provider (CSP):
	a. Develops an information security architecture for the information system that:
	1. Describes the overall philosophy, requirements, and approach to be taken with regard to protecting the confidentiality, integrity, and availability of organizational information;

(Continued)

---

[128]High-Impact Security Requirement: *annually.*

Continued

PL-8	**Information Security Architecture**
	2. Describes how the information security architecture is integrated into and supports the enterprise architecture; and
	3. Describes any information security assumptions about, and dependencies on, external services;
	b. [129] Reviews and updates the information security architecture[130] *at least annually* to reflect updates in the enterprise architecture; and
	c. Ensures that planned information security architecture changes are reflected in the security plan, the security Concept of Operations (CONOPS), and organizational procurements/ acquisitions.
	Personnel Security (PS)
PS-1	**Personnel Security Policy and Procedures**
Control Requirement:	The Cloud Service Provider (CSP): a. Develops, documents, and disseminates to *CSP-defined personnel or roles*: 1. A personnel security policy that addresses purpose, scope, roles, responsibilities, management commitment, coordination among organizational entities, and compliance; and 2. Procedures to facilitate the implementation of the personnel security policy and associated personnel security controls; and b. Reviews and updates the current: 1. Personnel security policy *at least every three (3) years*;[131] and 2. Personnel security procedures *at least annually*.[132]
PS-2	**Position Risk Designation**
Control Requirement:	The Cloud Service Provider (CSP): a. Assigns a risk designation to all positions; b. Establishes screening criteria for individuals filling those positions; and c. Reviews and revises position risk designations *at least every three (3) years*.[133]

(Continued)

---

[129]FedRAMP Program Management Office (PMO). FedRAMP High System Security Plan (SSP) Template. Washington, DC: US General Services Administration; 2016. *"Significant change is defined in NIST Special Publication 800-37 Revision 1, Appendix F, on Page F-7."*
[130]High-Impact Security Requirement: *at least annually or when a significant change occurs*
[131]High-Impact Security Requirement: *at least annually.*
[132]High-Impact Security Requirement: *at least annually, or whenever a significant change occurs.*
[133]High-Impact Security Requirement: *at least annually.*

Continued

PS-3	Personnel Screening
Control Requirement:	The Cloud Service Provider (CSP): a. Screens individuals prior to authorizing access to the information system; and b. Rescreens individuals *for national security clearances; a reinvestigation is required during the 5th year for top secret security clearance, the 10th year for secret security clearance, and 15th year for confidential security clearance. For moderate risk law enforcement and high-impact public trust level, a reinvestigation is required during the 5th year. There is no reinvestigation for other moderate risk positions or any low risk positions.*
Control Enhancements:	3. The Cloud Service Provider (CSP) ensures that individuals accessing an information system processing, storing, or transmitting information requiring special protection: a. Have valid access authorizations that are demonstrated by assigned official government duties; and b. Satisfy *personnel screening criteria—as required by specific information.*
PS-4	**Personnel Termination**
Control Requirement:	The Cloud Service Provider (CSP), upon termination of individual employment: a. Disables information system access the *same day*;[134] b. Terminates/revokes any authenticators/credentials associated with the individual; c. Conducts exit interviews that include a discussion of *CSP-defined information security topics*; d. Retrieves all security-related organizational information system-related property; e. Retains access to organizational information and information systems formerly controlled by terminated individual; and f. Notifies *CSP-defined personnel or roles* within *CSP-defined time period.*
Control Enhancements:	2. The Cloud Service Provider (CSP) employs automated mechanisms to notify *access control personnel responsible for disabling access to the system* upon termination of an individual.
PS-5	**Personnel Transfer**
Control Requirement:	The Cloud Service Provider (CSP): a. Reviews and confirms ongoing operational need for current logical and physical access authorizations to information systems/facilities when individuals are reassigned or transferred to other positions within the organization; b. Initiates *CSP-defined transfer or reassignment actions* within *CSP-defined time period following the formal transfer action*;[135] c. Modifies access authorization as needed to correspond with any changes in operational need due to reassignment or transfer; and d. Notifies *CSP-defined personnel or roles* within *five days of the formal transfer action (DoD 24 hours).*

(Continued)

---

[134]High-Impact Security Requirement: within *eight (8) hours.*
[135]High-Impact Security Requirement: *twenty-four (24) hours.*

Continued

PS-6	Access Agreements

Control Requirement:	The Cloud Service Provider (CSP):
	a. Develops and documents access agreements for organizational information systems;
	b. Reviews and updates the access agreements *at least annually*; and
	c. Ensures that individuals requiring access to organizational information and information systems:
	  1. Sign appropriate access agreements prior to being granted access; and
	  2. Re-sign access agreements to maintain access to organizational information systems when access agreements have been updated or *at least annually*.[136]

PS-7	Third-Party Personnel Security
Control Requirement:	The Cloud Service Provider (CSP): a. Establishes personnel security requirements including security roles and responsibilities for third-party providers; b. Requires third-party providers to comply with personnel security policies and procedures established by the organization; c. Documents personnel security requirements; d. Requires third-party providers to notify *CSP-defined personnel or roles* of any personnel transfers or terminations of third-party personnel who possess organizational credentials and/or badges, or who have information system privileges the *same day*;[137] and e. Monitors provider compliance.
PS-8	Personnel Sanctions
Control Requirement:	The Cloud Service Provider (CSP): a. Employs a formal sanctions process for personnel failing to comply with established information security policies and procedures; and b. Notifies *CSP-defined personnel or roles*[138] within *CSP-defined time period* when a formal employee sanctions process is initiated, identifying the individual sanctioned and the reason for the sanction.

(Continued)

[136]High-Impact Security Requirement: *at least annually and any time there is a change to the user's level of access.*
[137]High-Impact Security Requirement: *terminations: immediately; transfers: within twenty-four (24) hours.*
[138]High-Impact Security Requirement: *at a minimum, the ISSO and/or similar role within the organization.*

Continued

Risk Assessment (RA)	
RA-1	**Risk Assessment Policy and Procedures**

Control Requirement:	The Cloud Service Provider (CSP):
	a. Develops, documents, and disseminates to *CSP-defined personnel or roles*:
	   1. A risk assessment policy that addresses purpose, scope, roles, responsibilities, management commitment, coordination among organizational entities, and compliance; and
	   2. Procedures to facilitate the implementation of the risk assessment policy and associated risk assessment controls; and
	b. Reviews and updates the current:
	   1. Risk assessment policy *at least every three (3) years*;[139] and
	   2. Risk assessment procedures *at least annually*.[140]

RA-2	**Security Categorization**
Control Requirement:	The Cloud Service Provider (CSP): a. Categorizes information and the information system in accordance with applicable Federal Laws, Executive Orders, directives, policies, regulations, standards, and guidance; b. Documents the security categorization results (including supporting rationale) in the security plan for the information system; and c. Ensures that the security categorization decision is reviewed and approved by the authorizing official or authorizing official designated representative.
RA-3[141]	**Risk Assessment**
Control Requirement:	The Cloud Service Provider (CSP): a. Conducts an assessment of risk, including the likelihood and magnitude of harm, from the unauthorized access, use, disclosure, disruption, modification, or destruction of the information system and the information it processes, stores, or transmits; b. Documents risk assessment results in *security plan; risk assessment report;* or *security assessment report;* c. Reviews risk assessment results *at least every three (3) years or when a significant change occurs;* d. Disseminates risk assessment results to *CSP-defined personnel or roles*; and

(Continued)

---

[139]High-Impact Security Requirement: *at least annually.*

[140]High-Impact Security Requirement: *at least annually, or whenever a significant change occurs.*

[141]FedRAMP Program Management Office (PMO). FedRAMP High System Security Plan (SSP) Template. Washington, DC: US General Services Administration; 2016. *"Significant change is defined in NIST Special Publication 800-37 Revision 1, Appendix F."*

Continued

RA-3[141]	**Risk Assessment**
	Additional FedRAMP Requirements • Include all Authoring Officials and FedRAMP ISSOs. e. Updates the risk assessment *at least every three (3) years or when a significant change occurs* or whenever there are significant changes to the information system or environment of operation (including the identification of new threats and vulnerabilities), or other conditions that may impact the security state of the system.
RA-5	**Vulnerability Scanning**

Control Requirement:	The Cloud Service Provider (CSP):
	a. Scans for vulnerabilities in the information system and hosted applications *monthly operating system/infrastructure and monthly web applications and databases* and when new vulnerabilities potentially affecting the system/applications are identified and reported;
	Additional FedRAMP Requirements
	• An accredited independent assessor scans operating systems/ infrastructure, web applications, and databases once annually.
	
	b. Employs vulnerability scanning tools and techniques that promote interoperability among tools and automate parts of the vulnerability management process by using standards for:
	    1. Enumerating platforms, software flaws, and improper configurations;
	    2. Formatting and making transparent, checklists and test procedures; and
	    3. Measuring vulnerability impact;
	c. Analyzes vulnerability scan reports and results from security control assessments;
	d. Remediates legitimate vulnerabilities; *high-risk vulnerabilities mitigated within thirty (30) days from date of discovery; moderate risk vulnerabilities mitigated within ninety (90) days from date of discovery*, in accordance with an organizational assessment of risk; and
	e. Shares information obtained from the vulnerability scanning process and security control assessments with *CSP-defined personnel or roles* to help eliminate similar vulnerabilities in other information systems (i.e., systemic weaknesses or deficiencies).
	
	Additional FedRAMP Requirements
	• To include the Risk Executive; for JAB authorizations to include FedRAMP ISSOs.

Control Enhancements:	1. The Cloud Service Provider (CSP) employs vulnerability scanning tools that include the capability to readily update the list of information system vulnerabilities to be scanned. 2. The Cloud Service Provider (CSP) updates the information system vulnerabilities scanned *prior to a new scan*.

(Continued)

Continued

RA-5	Vulnerability Scanning
	3. The Cloud Service Provider (CSP) employs vulnerability scanning procedures that can demonstrate the breadth and depth of coverage (i.e., information system components scanned and vulnerabilities checked).
	4. The Cloud Service Provider (CSP) determines what information about the information system is discoverable by adversaries and subsequently *notify appropriate CSP personnel and follow procedures for organization and CSP-defined corrective actions*.
	5. The Cloud Service Provider (CSP) includes privileged access authorization to *operating systems, databases, web applications* for selected *all scans*.
	6. [142]The Cloud Service Provider (CSP) employs automated mechanisms to compare the results of vulnerability scans over time to determine trends in information system vulnerabilities.
	8. [143]The Cloud Service Provider (CSP) reviews historic audit logs to determine if a vulnerability identified in the information system has been previously exploited.
	Additional FedRAMP Requirements
	• This enhancement is required for all high vulnerability scan findings.
	10. [144]The Cloud Service Provider (CSP) correlates the output from vulnerability scanning tools to determine the presence of multivulnerability/multihop attack vectors.
	System and Services Acquisition (SA)
SA-1	**System and Services Acquisition Policy and Procedures**

Control Requirement:	The Cloud Service Provider (CSP):
	 a. Develops, documents, and disseminates to *CSP-defined personnel or roles*:
	   1. A system and services acquisition policy that addresses purpose, scope, roles, responsibilities, management commitment, coordination among organizational entities, and compliance; and
	   2. Procedures to facilitate the implementation of the system and services acquisition policy and associated system and services acquisition controls; and

(Continued)

---

[142]FedRAMP Program Management Office (PMO). FedRAMP High System Security Plan (SSP) Template. Washington, DC: US General Services Administration; 2016. *"Include in Continuous Monitoring ISSO digest/report to JAB."*

[143]FedRAMP Program Management Office (PMO). FedRAMP High System Security Plan (SSP) Template. Washington, DC: US General Services Administration; 2016. *"While scanning tools may label findings as high or critical, the intent of the control is based around NIST's definition of high vulnerability."*

[144]FedRAMP Program Management Office (PMO). FedRAMP High System Security Plan (SSP) Template. Washington, DC: US General Services Administration; 2016. *"If multiple tools are not used, this control is not applicable."*

Continued

System and Services Acquisition (SA)	
SA-1	**System and Services Acquisition Policy and Procedures**
	b. Reviews and updates the current:
	1. System and services acquisition policy *at least every three (3) years;*[145] and
	2. System and services acquisition procedures *at least annually.*[146]
SA-2	**Allocation of Resources**
Control Requirement:	The Cloud Service Provider (CSP):
	a. Determines information security requirements for the information system or information system service in mission/business process planning;
	b. Determines, documents, and allocates the resources required to protect the information system or information system service as part of its capital planning and investment control process; and
	c. Establishes a discrete line item for information security in organizational programming and budgeting documentation.
SA-3	**System Development Life Cycle**
Control Requirement:	The Cloud Service Provider (CSP):
	a. Manages the information system using *CSP-defined SDLC* that incorporates information security considerations;
	b. Defines and documents information security roles and responsibilities throughout the SDLC;
	c. Identifies individuals having information security roles and responsibilities; and
	d. Integrates the organizational information security risk management process into SDLC activities.
SA-4	**Acquisition Process**
Control Requirement:	The Cloud Service Provider (CSP) includes the following requirements, descriptions, and criteria,[147] explicitly or by reference, in the acquisition contract for the information system, system component, or information system service in accordance with applicable federal laws, Executive Orders, directives, policies, regulations, standards, guidelines, and organizational mission/business needs:
	a. Security functional requirements;
	b. Security strength requirements;
	c. Security assurance requirements;

(Continued)

[145]High-Impact Security Requirement: *at least annually.*
[146]High-Impact Security Requirement: *at least annually, or whenever a significant change occurs.*
[147]FedRAMP Program Management Office (PMO). FedRAMP High System Security Plan (SSP) Template. Washington, DC: US General Services Administration; 2016. "*The use of Common Criteria (ISO/IEC 15408) evaluated products is strongly preferred. See* http://www.niap-ccevs.org/vpl or http://www.commoncriteriaportal.org/products.html."

Continued

SA-4	Acquisition Process
	d. Security-related documentation requirements;
	e. Requirements for protecting security-related documentation;
	f. Description of the information system development environment and environment in which the system is intended to operate; and
	g. Acceptance criteria.
Control Enhancements:	1. The Cloud Service Provider (CSP) requires the developer of the information system, system component, or information system service to provide a description of the functional properties of the security controls to be employed.
	2. The Cloud Service Provider (CSP) requires the developer of the information system, system component, or information system service to provide design and implementation information for the security controls to be employed that includes: *security-relevant external system interfaces and high-level design; CSP-defined design/implementation information*[148] *at CSP-defined level of detail.*
	8. The Cloud Service Provider (CSP) requires the developer of the information system, system component, or information system service[149] to produce a plan for the continuous monitoring of security control effectiveness that contains *at least the minimum requirement as defined in control CA-7.*
	9. The Cloud Service Provider (CSP) requires the developer of the information system, system component, or information system service to identify early in the SDLC, the functions, ports, protocols, and services intended for organizational use.
	10. The Cloud Service Provider (CSP) employs only information technology products on the FIPS 201-approved products list for Personal Identity Verification (PIV) capability implemented within organizational information systems.
SA-5	Information System Documentation
Control Requirement:	The Cloud Service Provider (CSP): a. Obtains administrator documentation for the information system, system component, or information system service that describes: 1. Secure configuration, installation, and operation of the system, component, or service;

(Continued)

---

[148]High-Impact Security Requirement: *at a minimum to include security-relevant external system interfaces; high-level design; low-level design; source code or network and data flow diagram; and/or CSP defined design/implementation information.*

[149]FedRAMP Program Management Office (PMO). FedRAMP High System Security Plan (SSP) Template. Washington, DC: US General Services Administration; 2016. *"CSP must use the same security standards regardless of where the system component or information system service is acquired."*

Continued

SA-5	Information System Documentation
	2. Effective use and maintenance of security functions/mechanisms; and
	3. Known vulnerabilities regarding configuration and use of administrative (i.e., privileged) functions;
	b. Obtains user documentation for the information system, system component, or information system service that describes:
	1. User-accessible security functions/mechanisms and how to effectively use those security functions/mechanisms;
	2. Methods for user interaction, which enables individuals to use the system, component, or service in a more secure manner; and
	3. User responsibilities in maintaining the security of the system, component, or service;
	c. Documents attempts to obtain information system, system component, or information system service documentation when such documentation is either unavailable or nonexistent and *CSP-defined actions* in response;
	d. Protects documentation as required, in accordance with the risk management strategy; and
	e. Distributes documentation to *CSP-defined personnel or* roles.[150]
SA-8	**Security Engineering Principles**
Control Requirement:	The Cloud Service Provider (CSP) applies information system security engineering principles in the specification, design, development, implementation, and modification of the information system.
SA-9[151]	**External Information System Services**
Control Requirement:	The Cloud Service Provider (CSP):
	a. Requires that providers of external information system services comply with organizational information security requirements and employ *FedRAMP Security Controls Baseline(s) if Federal information is processed or stored within the external system* in accordance with applicable federal laws, Executive Orders, directives, policies, regulations, standards, and guidance;
	b. Defines and documents government oversight and user roles and responsibilities with regard to external information system services; and

(Continued)

---

[150]High-Impact Security Requirement: *at a minimum, the ISSO (or similar role within the organization).*

[151]FedRAMP Program Management Office (PMO). FedRAMP High System Security Plan (SSP) Template. Washington, DC: US General Services Administration; 2016. *"See the FedRAMP Documents page under Key Cloud Service Provider (CSP) Documents > Continuous Monitoring Strategy Guide* https://www.FedRAMP.gov/resources/documents."

Continued

SA-9[151]	**External Information System Services**
	c. Employs *Federal/FedRAMP Continuous Monitoring requirements must be met for external systems where federal information is processed or stored* to monitor security control compliance by external service providers on an ongoing basis.
Control Enhancements:	1. The Cloud Service Provider (CSP):
	a. Conducts an organizational assessment of risk prior to the acquisition or outsourcing of dedicated information security services; and
	b. Ensures that the acquisition or outsourcing of dedicated information security services is approved by Cloud Service Provider (CSP)-*defined personnel or roles.*
	2. The Cloud Service Provider (CSP) requires providers of *all external systems where federal information is processed or stored* to identify the functions, ports, protocols, and other services required for the use of such services.
	4. The Cloud Service Provider (CSP) employs *CSP-defined security safeguards* to ensure that the interests of *all external systems where federal information is processed or stored* are consistent with and reflect organizational interests.
	5. [152]The Cloud Service Provider (CSP) restricts the location of information processing, *information data, and information services* to *CSP-defined locations* based on *CSP-defined requirements or conditions.*
SA-10	**Developer Configuration Management**
Control Requirement:	The Cloud Service Provider (CSP) requires the developer of the information system, system component, or information system service to:
	a. Perform configuration management during system, component, or service *development, implementation, and operation*;
	b. Document, manage, and control the integrity of changes to *CSP-defined configuration items under configuration management*;
	c. Implement only organization-approved changes to the system, component, or service;
	d. Document approved changes to the system, component, or service and the potential security impacts of such changes; and
	e. Track security flaws and flaw resolution within the system, component, or service and report findings to CSP-defined *personnel*.

(Continued)

---

[152]FedRAMP Program Management Office (PMO). FedRAMP High System Security Plan (SSP) Template. Washington, DC: US General Services Administration; 2016. "*System services refer to FTP, Telnet, and TFTP etc.*"

Continued

SA-10	Developer Configuration Management
	Additional FedRAMP Requirements: For JAB authorizations, track security flaws and flaw resolution within the system, component, or service and report findings to organization-defined personnel, to include FedRAMP ISSOs.
Control Enhancements:	1. The Cloud Service Provider (CSP) requires the developer of the information system, system component, or information system service to enable integrity verification of software and firmware components.
SA-11	Developer Security Testing and Evaluation
Control Requirement:	The Cloud Service Provider (CSP) requires the developer of the information system, system component, or information system service to: a. Create and implement a security assessment plan; b. Perform *unit; integration; system;* and/or *regression* testing/evaluation at *CSP-defined depth and coverage*; c. Produce evidence of the execution of the security assessment plan and the results of the security testing/evaluation; d. Implement a verifiable flaw remediation process; and e. Correct flaws identified during security testing/evaluation.
Control Enhancements:	1. The Cloud Service Provider (CSP) requires the developer of the information system, system component, or information system service to employ static code analysis tools to identify common flaws and document the results of the analysis. **Additional FedRAMP Requirements:** • (Requirement for SA-11 (1) or SA-11 (8) or both)**:** The Cloud Service Provider (CSP) documents in the Continuous Monitoring Plan, how newly developed code for the information system is reviewed. 2. The Cloud Service Provider (CSP) requires the developer of the information system, system component, or information system service to perform threat and vulnerability analyses and subsequent testing/evaluation of the as-built system, component, or service. 8. The Cloud Service Provider (CSP) requires the developer of the information system, system component, or information system service to employ dynamic code analysis tools to identify common flaws and document the results of the analysis.
SA-12	Supply Chain Protection
Control Requirement:	The Cloud Service Provider (CSP) protects against supply chain threats to the information system, system component, or information system service by employing *CSP-defined personnel security requirements, approved hardware/software vendor list/process, and secure SDLC procedures* as part of a comprehensive, defense-in-breadth information security strategy.

Continued

SA-15	Development Process, Standards, and Tools

Control Requirement:	The Cloud Service Provider (CSP):
	a. Requires the developer of the information system, system component, or information system service to follow a documented development process that:
	    1. Explicitly addresses security requirements;
	    2. Identifies the standards and tools used in the development process;
	    3. Documents the specific tool options and tool configurations used in the development process; and
	    4. Documents, manages, and ensures the integrity of changes to the process and/or tools used in development; and
	b. Reviews the development process, standards, tools, and tool options/configurations *as needed and as dictated by the current threat posture* to determine if the process, standards, tools, and tool options/configurations selected and employed can satisfy CSP-*defined security requirements.*

SA-16	Developer-Provided Training
Control Requirement:	The Cloud Service Provider (CSP) requires the developer of the information system, system component, or information system service to provide *CSP-defined training* on the correct use and operation of the implemented security functions, controls, and/or mechanisms.
SA-17	Developer Security Architecture and Design
Control Requirement:	The Cloud Service Provider (CSP) requires the developer of the information system, system component, or information system service to produce a design specification and security architecture that: a. Is consistent with and supportive of the organization's security architecture that is established within and is an integrated part of the organization's enterprise architecture; b. Accurately and completely describes the required security functionality, and the allocation of security controls among physical and logical components; and c. Expresses how individual security functions, mechanisms, and services work together to provide required security capabilities and a unified approach to protection.
	System and Communications Protection (SC)
SC-1	System and Communications Protection Policy and Procedures
Control Requirement:	The Cloud Service Provider (CSP): a. Develops, documents, and disseminates to *CSP-defined personnel or roles*: 1. A system and communications protection policy that addresses purpose, scope, roles, responsibilities, management commitment, coordination among organizational entities, and compliance; and

Continued

	2. Procedures to facilitate the implementation of the system and communications protection policy and associated system and communications protection controls; and
	b. Reviews and updates the current:
	   1. System and communications protection policy *at least every three (3) years;*[153] and
	   2. System and communications protection procedures *at least annually*[154]

SC-2	**Application Partitioning**
Control Requirement:	The information system separates user functionality (including user interface services) from information system management functionality.
SC-3	**Security Function Isolation**
Control Requirement:	The information system isolates security functions from nonsecurity functions.
SC-4	**Information in Shared Resources**
Control Requirement:	The information system prevents unauthorized and unintended information transfer via shared system resources.
SC-5	**Denial of Service Protection**
Control Requirement:	The information system protects against or limits the effects of the following types of denial of service attacks: *CSP-defined types of denial of service attacks or reference to source for such information* by employing *CSP-defined security safeguards.*
SC-6	**Resource Availability**
Control Requirement:	The information system protects the availability of resources by allocating *CSP-defined resources* by *priority; quota;* and/or *CSP-defined security safeguards.*
SC-7	**Boundary Protection**
Control Requirement:	The information system: a. Monitors and controls communications at the external boundary of the system and at key internal boundaries within the system; and b. Implements subnetworks for publicly accessible system components that are *physically or logically* separated from internal organizational networks; and c. Connects to external networks or information systems only through managed interfaces consisting of boundary protection devices arranged in accordance with organizational security architecture.

(Continued)

---

[153]High-Impact Security Requirement: *at least annually.*
[154]High-Impact Security Requirement: *at least annually, or whenever a significant change occurs.*

Continued

SC-7	Boundary Protection

Control Enhancements:	3. The Cloud Service Provider (CSP) limits the number external network connections to the information system.
	
	4. The Cloud Service Provider (CSP):
	
	  a. Implements a managed interface for each external telecommunication service;
	
	  b. Establishes a traffic flow policy for each managed interface;
	
	  c. Protects the confidentiality and integrity of the information being transmitted across each interface;
	
	  d. Documents each exception to the traffic flow policy with a supporting mission/business need and duration of that need; and
	
	  e. Reviews exceptions to the traffic flow policy *at least annually*[155] and removes exceptions that are no longer supported by an explicit mission/business need.
	
	5. The information system at managed interfaces denies network traffic by default and allows network communications traffic by exception (i.e., deny-all, permit by exception).
	
	7. The information system, in conjunction with a remote device, prevents the device from simultaneously establishing nonremote connections with the system and communicating via some other connection to resources in external networks.
	
	8. The information system routes *CSP-defined internal communications traffic* to *CSP-defined external networks* through authenticated proxy servers at managed interfaces.
	
	10. The Cloud Service Provider (CSP) prevents the unauthorized exfiltration of information across managed interfaces.
	
	12. The Cloud Service Provider (CSP) implements *CSP-defined host-based boundary protection mechanisms*[156] at *CSP-defined information system components*.
	
	13. [157]The Cloud Service Provider (CSP) isolates *SC-7 (13) in accordance with Additional FedRAMP Requirements* from other

(Continued)

---

[155]High-Impact Security Requirement: *at least every ninety (90) days or whenever there is a change in the threat environment that warrants a review of the exceptions.*

[156]High-Impact Security Requirement: *Host Intrusion Prevention System (HIPS), Host Intrusion Detection System (HIDS), or minimally a host-based firewall.*

[157]FedRAMP Program Management Office (PMO). FedRAMP High System Security Plan (SSP) Template. Washington, DC: US General Services Administration; 2016. *"Examples include: information security tools, mechanisms, and support components such as, but not limited to PKI, patching infrastructure, cyber defense tools, special purpose gateway, vulnerability tracking systems, internet access points (IAPs); network element and data center administrative/management traffic; Demilitarized Zones (DMZs), Server farms/computing centers, centralized audit log servers etc."*

Continued

SC-7	**Boundary Protection**
	internal information system components, by implementing physically separate subnetworks with managed interfaces to other components of the system.
	Additional FedRAMP Requirements:
	• The Cloud Service Provider (CSP) defines key information security tools, mechanisms, and support components associated with system and security administration and isolates those tools, mechanisms, and support components from other internal information system components via physically or logically separate subnets.
	18. The information system fails securely in the event of an operational failure of a boundary protection device.
	20. The information system provides the capability to dynamically isolate/segregate *Cloud Service Provider (CSP)- defined information system components* from other components of the system.
	21. The *Cloud Service Provider (CSP)* employs boundary protection mechanisms to separate *CSP-defined information system components* supporting *CSP-defined mission and/or business functions.*
SC-8	**Transmission Confidentiality and Integrity**
Control Requirement:	The information system protects the *confidentiality and integrity* of transmitted information.
Control Enhancements:	1. The information system implements cryptographic mechanisms to *prevent unauthorized disclosure of information and detect changes to information* during transmission unless otherwise protected by *a hardened or alarmed carrier Protective Distribution System (PDS).*
SC-10	**Network Disconnect**
Control Requirement:	The information system terminates the network connection associated with a communications session at the end of the session or after *no longer than 30 minutes for RAS-based sessions or no longer than 60 minutes for noninteractive user sessions*[158] of inactivity.

(Continued)

[158]High-Impact Security Requirement: *no longer than ten (10) minutes for privileged sessions and no longer than fifteen (15) minutes for user sessions.*

SC-12[159]	**Cryptographic Key Establishment and Management**
Control Requirement:	The Cloud Service Provider (CSP) establishes and manages cryptographic keys for required cryptography employed within the information system in accordance with *CSP-defined requirements for key generation, distribution, storage, access, and destruction*.
Control Enhancements:	1. The Cloud Service Provider (CSP) maintains availability of information in the event of the loss of cryptographic keys by users. 2. The Cloud Service Provider (CSP) produces, controls, and distributes symmetric cryptographic keys using *NIST FIPS-compliant* key management technology and processes. 3. The Cloud Service Provider (CSP) produces, controls, and distributes asymmetric cryptographic keys using *NSA-approved key management technology and processes; approved PKI Class 3 certificates or prepositioned keying material; or approved PKI Class 3 or Class 4 certificates and hardware security tokens that protect the user's private key.*
SC-13	**Cryptographic Protection**
Control Requirement:	The information system implements *FIPS-validated or NSA-approved cryptograph* in accordance with applicable federal laws, Executive Orders, directives, policies, regulations, and standards.
SC-15	**Collaborative Computing Devices**
Control Requirement:	The information system: a. Prohibits remote activation of collaborative computing devices with the following exceptions: *no exceptions* and b. Provides an explicit indication of use to users physically present at the devices. **Additional FedRAMP Requirements:** • The information system provides *disablement* (instead of physical disconnect) of collaborative computing devices in a manner that supports ease of use.
SC-17	**Public Key Infrastructure Certificates**
Control Requirement:	The Cloud Service Provider (CSP) issues public key certificates under a *CSP-defined certificate policy* or obtains public key certificates from an approved service provider.
SC-18	**Mobile Code**
Control Requirement:	The Cloud Service Provider (CSP): a. Defines acceptable and unacceptable mobile code and mobile code technologies; b. Establishes usage restrictions and implementation guidance for acceptable mobile code and mobile code technologies; and c. Authorizes, monitors, and controls the use of mobile code within the information system.
SC-19	**Voice Over Internet Protocol**
Control Requirement:	The Cloud Service Provider (CSP): a. Establishes usage restrictions and implementation guidance for Voice over Internet Protocol (VoIP) technologies based on the

(Continued)

---

[159]FedRAMP Program Management Office (PMO). FedRAMP High System Security Plan (SSP) Template. Washington, DC: US General Services Administration; 2016. "*Federally approved and validated cryptography.*"

Continued

SC-19	Voice Over Internet Protocol
	potential to cause damage to the information system if used maliciously; and
	b. Authorizes, monitors, and controls the use of VoIP within the information system.
SC-20	**Secure Name/Address Resolution Service (Authoritative Source)**
Control Requirement:	The information system:
	a. Provides additional data origin authentication and integrity verification artifacts along with the authoritative name resolution data the system returns in response to external name/address resolution queries; and
	b. Provides the means to indicate the security status of child zones and (if the child supports secure resolution services) to enable verification of a chain of trust among parent and child domains, when operating as part of a distributed, hierarchical namespace.
SC-21	**Secure Name/Address Resolution Service (Recursive or Caching Resolver)**
Control Requirement:	The information system requests and performs data origin authentication and data integrity verification on the name/address resolution responses the system receives from authoritative sources.
SC-22	**Architecture and Provisioning for Name/Address Resolution Service**
Control Requirement:	The information systems that collectively provide name/address resolution service for an organization are fault-tolerant and implement internal/external role separation.
SC-23	**Session Authenticity**
Control Requirement:	The information system protects the authenticity of communications sessions.
Control Enhancements:	1. The information system invalidates session identifiers upon user logout or other session termination.
SC-24	**Fail in Known State**
Control Requirement:	The information system fails to a Cloud Service Provider (CSP)-*defined known state* for *CSP types of failures* preserving *CSP-defined system state information* in failure.
SC-28[160]	**Protection of Information at Rest**
Control Requirement:	The information system protects the *confidentiality and integrity* of *CSP-defined information at rest*.
Control Enhancements:	1. The information system implements cryptographic mechanisms to prevent unauthorized disclosure and modification of *CSP-defined information* on *all information system components storing customer data deemed sensitive*.

(Continued)

---

[160]FedRAMP Program Management Office (PMO). FedRAMP High System Security Plan (SSP) Template. Washington, DC: US General Services Administration; 2016. *"The organization supports the capability to use cryptographic mechanisms to protect information at rest."*

Continued

SC-39	Process Isolation
Control Requirement:	The information system maintains a separate execution domain for each executing process.
System and Information Integrity (SI)	
SI-1	**System and Information Integrity Policy and Procedures**

Control Requirement:	The Cloud Service Provider (CSP):
	a. Develops, documents, and disseminates to *CSP-defined personnel or roles*:
	  1. A system and information integrity policy that addresses purpose, scope, roles, responsibilities, management commitment, coordination among organizational entities, and compliance; and
	  2. Procedures to facilitate the implementation of the system and information integrity policy and associated system and information integrity controls; and
	b. Reviews and updates the current:
	  1. System and information integrity policy *at least every three (3) years*;[161] and
	  2. System and information integrity procedures *at least annually*.[162]

SI-2	**Flaw Remediation**
Control Requirement:	The Cloud Service Provider (CSP): a. Identifies, reports, and corrects information system flaws; b. Tests software and firmware updates related to flaw remediation for effectiveness and potential side effects before installation; c. Installs security-relevant software and firmware updates within *thirty (30) days of release of updates* of the release of the updates; and d. Incorporates flaw remediation into the organizational configuration management process.

Control Enhancements:	1. The Cloud Service Provider (CSP) centrally manages the flaw remediation process.
	2. The Cloud Service Provider (CSP) employs automated mechanisms *at least monthly* to determine the state of information system components with regard to flaw remediation.
	3. The Cloud Service Provider (CSP):
	  a. Measures the time between flaw identification and flaw remediation; and
	  b. Establishes *CSP-defined benchmarks* for taking corrective actions.

(Continued)

---

[161]High-Impact Security Requirement: *at least annually.*
[162]High-Impact Security Requirement: *at least annually, or whenever a significant change occurs.*

Continued

SI-3	Malicious Code Protection

Control Requirement:	The Cloud Service Provider (CSP):
	
	a. Employs malicious code protection mechanisms at information system entry and exit points to detect and eradicate malicious code;
	
	b. Updates malicious code protection mechanisms whenever new releases are available in accordance with organizational configuration management policy and procedures;
	
	c. Configures malicious code protection mechanisms to:
	  1. Perform periodic scans of the information system *at least weekly* and real-time scans of files from external sources *to include endpoints* as the files are downloaded, opened, or executed in accordance with organizational security policy; and
	  2. Send *alert to administrator or CSP-defined personnel*[163] in response to malicious code detection; and
	
	d. Addresses the receipt of false positives during malicious code detection and eradication and the resulting potential impact on the availability of the information system.

Control Enhancements:	1. The Cloud Service Provider (CSP) centrally manages malicious code protection mechanisms. 2. The information system automatically updates malicious code protection mechanisms. 7. The information system implements nonsignature-based malicious code detection mechanisms.
SI-4[164]	Information System Monitoring

Control Requirement:	The Cloud Service Provider (CSP):
	a. Monitors the information system to detect:
	  1. Attacks and indicators of potential attacks in accordance with *CSP-defined monitoring objectives*; and
	  2. Unauthorized local, network, and remote connections;
	
	b. Identifies unauthorized use of the information system through *CSP-defined techniques and methods*;
	
	c. Deploys monitoring devices:
	  1. Strategically within the information system to collect organization-determined essential information; and
	  2. At ad hoc locations within the system to track specific types of transactions of interest to the organization;
	
	d. Protects information obtained from intrusion-monitoring tools from unauthorized access, modification, and deletion;

(Continued)

[163]High-Impact Security Requirement: *to include blocking and quarantining malicious code and alerting administrator or defined security personnel near-real-time.*
[164]FedRAMP Program Management Office (PMO). FedRAMP High System Security Plan (SSP) Template. Washington, DC: US General Services Administration; 2016. *"See US-CERT Incident Response Reporting Guidelines."*

Continued

SI-4[164]	Information System Monitoring
	e. Heightens the level of information system monitoring activity whenever there is an indication of increased risk to organizational operations and assets, individuals, other organizations, or the Nation based on law enforcement information, intelligence information, or other credible sources of information; and
	f. Obtains legal opinion with regard to information system monitoring activities in accordance with applicable federal laws, Executive Orders, directives, policies, or regulations; and
	g. Provides *CSP-defined information system monitoring information to CSP-defined personnel or roles as needed and/or CSP-defined frequency.*
Control Enhancements:	1. The Cloud Service Provider (CSP) connects and configures individual intrusion detection tools into an information system-wide intrusion detection system.
	2. The Cloud Service Provider (CSP) employs automated tools to support near real-time analysis of events.
	4. The information system monitors inbound and outbound communications traffic *continually* for unusual or unauthorized activities or conditions.
	5. [165]The information system alerts *CSP-defined personnel or roles* when the following indications of compromise or potential compromise occur: *CSP-defined compromise indicators.*
	11. The Cloud Service Provider (CSP) analyzes outbound communications traffic at the external boundary of the information system and selected CSP-defined interior points within the system (e.g., subnetworks, subsystems) to discover anomalies.
	14. The Cloud Service Provider (CSP) employs a wireless intrusion detection system to identify rogue wireless devices and to detect attack attempts and potential compromises/breaches to the information system.
	16. The Cloud Service Provider (CSP) correlates information from monitoring tools employed throughout the information system.
	18. The Cloud Service Provider (CSP) analyzes outbound communications traffic at the external boundary of the information system (i.e., system perimeter) and at *CSP-defined interior points within the system (e.g., subnetworks, subsystems)* to detect covert exfiltration of information.

(Continued)

---

[165]FedRAMP Program Management Office (PMO). FedRAMP High System Security Plan (SSP) Template. Washington, DC: US General Services Administration; 2016. "*In accordance with the incident response plan.*"

Continued

SI-4[164]	**Information System Monitoring**
	19. The Cloud Service Provider (CSP) implements *CSP-defined additional monitoring* of individuals who have been identified by *CSP-defined sources* as posing an increased level of risk.
	20. The Cloud Service Provider (CSP) implements *CSP-defined additional monitoring* of privileged users.
	22. The information system detects network services that have not been authorized or approved by *Cloud Service Provider (CSP)-defined authorization or approval processes* and *audits and/or alerts CSP-defined personnel or roles*.
	23. The Cloud Service Provider (CSP) implements *CSP-defined host-based monitoring mechanisms* at *CSP-defined information system components*.
	24. The information system discovers, collects, distributes, and uses indicators of compromise.
SI-5	**Security Alerts, Advisories, and Directives**
Control Requirement:	The Cloud Service Provider (CSP):
	a. Receives information system security alerts, advisories, and directives from *to include US-CERT* on an ongoing basis;
	b. Generates internal security alerts, advisories, and directives as deemed necessary;
	c. Disseminates security alerts, advisories, and directives to *include system security personnel and administrators with configuration/ patch-management responsibilities*; and
	d. Implements security directives in accordance with established time frames, or notifies the issuing organization of the degree of noncompliance.
Control Enhancements:	1. The Cloud Service Provider (CSP) employs automated mechanisms to make security alert and advisory information available throughout the organization.
SI-6	**Security Functionality Verification**
Control Requirement:	The information system:
	a. Verifies the correct operation of Cloud Service Provider (CSP)-defined security functions;
	b. Performs this verification to include upon system startup and/or restart at least monthly;
	c. Notifies to include system administrators and security personnel of failed security verification tests; and
	d. Shuts the information system down; restarts the information system; and/or to include notification of system administrators and security personnel when anomalies are discovered.

(Continued)

Continued

SI-7	Software, Firmware, and Informatio Integrity
Control Requirement:	The Cloud Service Provider (CSP) employs integrity verification tools to detect unauthorized changes to *CSP-defined software, firmware, and information*.
Control Enhancements:	1. The information system performs an integrity check of *CSP-defined software, firmware, and information: at startup; at security-relevant events; and/or at least monthly*.
	2. The Cloud Service Provider (CSP) employs automated tools that provide notification to *CSP-defined personnel or roles* upon discovering discrepancies during integrity verification.
	5. The information system automatically *shuts the information system down; restarts the information system; and/or implements Cloud Service Provider (CSP)-defined security safeguard* when integrity violations are discovered.
	7. The Cloud Service Provider (CSP) incorporates the detection of unauthorized *CSP-defined security-relevant changes to the information system* into the organizational incident response capability.
	14. The Cloud Service Provider (CSP):
	a. Prohibits the use of binary or machine-executable code from sources with limited or no warranty and without the provision of source code; and
	b. Provides exceptions to the source code requirement only for compelling mission/operational requirements and with the approval of the authorizing official.
SI-8	**Spam Protection**
Control Requirement:	The Cloud Service Provider (CSP):
	a. Employs spam protection mechanisms at information system entry and exit points to detect and take action on unsolicited messages; and
	b. Updates spam protection mechanisms when new releases are available in accordance with organizational configuration management policy and procedures.
Control Enhancements:	1. The Cloud Service Provider (CSP) centrally manages spam protection mechanisms.
	2. The Cloud Service Provider (CSP) automatically updates spam protection mechanisms.
SI-10	**Information Input Validation**
Control Requirement:	The information system checks the validity of CSP-defined *information inputs*.

(Continued)

Continued

SI-11	Error Handling
Control Requirement:	The information system: a. Generates error messages that provide information necessary for corrective actions without revealing information that could be exploited by adversaries; and b. Reveals error messages only to *Cloud Service Provider (CSP)-defined personnel or roles*.
SI-12	**Information Handling and Retention**
Control Requirement:	The Cloud Service Provider (CSP) handles and retains information within the information system and information output from the system in accordance with applicable federal laws, Executive Orders, directives, policies, regulations, standards, and operational requirements.
SI-16	**Memory Protection**
Control Requirement:	The information system implements *Cloud Service Provider (CSP)-defined security safeguards* to protect its memory from unauthorized code execution.

FEDERAL LAWS, EXECUTIVE ORDERS, POLICIES, DIRECTIVES, REGULATIONS, STANDARDS AND GUIDELINES

The security controls in NIST Special Publication 800-53 are designed to facilitate compliance with applicable federal laws, Executive Orders, directives, policies, regulations, standards, and guidance. Compliance is not about adhering to static checklists or generating unnecessary FISMA reporting paperwork. Rather, compliance necessitates organizations executing due diligence with regard to information security and risk management. Information security due diligence includes using all appropriate information as part of an organization-wide risk management program to effectively use the tailoring guidance and inherent flexibility in NIST publications so that the selected security controls documented in organizational security plans meet the mission and business requirements of organizations. Using the risk management tools and techniques that are available to organizations is essential in developing, implementing, and maintaining the safeguards and countermeasures with the necessary and sufficient strength of mechanism to address the current threats to organizational operations and assets, individuals, other organizations, and the Nation. Employing effective risk-based processes, procedures, and technologies will help ensure that all federal information systems and organizations have the necessary resilience to support ongoing federal responsibilities, critical infrastructure applications, and continuity of government. [2]

FEDERAL LAWS AND EXECUTIVE ORDERS

- 18 U.S.C. § 1080, Computer Fraud and Abuse Act (PL 99-474)
- 44 U.S.C. § 101, E-Government Act (P.L. 107-347), December 2002
- 44 U.S.C. § 101, Federal Information Security Modernization Act (P.L. 113-283), December 2014
- 44 U.S.C. § 3501, Paperwork Reduction Act (P.L. 104-13), May 1995
- 5 U.S.C. § 552a, Privacy Act of 1974 (P.L. 93-579), December 1974
- 5 U.S.C. § 552, Freedom of Information Act As Amended in 2002 (PL 104-232)
- U.S.C. § 552, As Amended By Public Law No. 104-231, 110 Stat. 3048, Electronic Freedom of Information Act Amendments of 1996
- 15 U.S.C. § 1601, Health Insurance Portability and Accountability Act (P.L. 104-191), August 1996
- 44 U.S.C. § 31, Records Management by Federal Agencies
- 50 U.S.C. § 1805, USA Freedom Act (P.L. 114-13), October 2015
- Executive Order 13556, Controlled Unclassified Information, November 2010

FEDERAL POLICIES, DIRECTIVES, AND REGULATIONS

- Code of Federal Regulations, Title 5, Administrative Personnel, Section 731.106, *Designation of Public Trust Positions and Investigative Requirements* (5 C.F.R. 731.106)
- Code of Federal Regulations, Part 5 Administrative Personnel, Subpart C—*Employees Responsible for the Management or Use of Federal Computer Systems*, Section 930.301 through 930.305 (5 C.F.R. 930.301-305)
- Department of Homeland Security, National Infrastructure Protection Plan (NIPP), 2009
- Federal Continuity Directive 1 (FCD 1), *Federal Executive Branch National Continuity Program and Requirements*, February 2008
- Executive Office of the President of the United States and Federal CIO Council, *Federal Identity, Credential, and Access Management (FICAM) Roadmap and Implementation Guidance*, December 2011
- Homeland Security Presidential Directive 7, *Critical Infrastructure Identification, Prioritization, and Protection*, December 2003
- Homeland Security Presidential Directive 12, *Policy for a Common Identification Standard for Federal Employees and Contractors*, August 2004
- Homeland Security Presidential Directive 20 (National Security Presidential Directive 51), *National Continuity Policy*, May 2007
- National Communications System (NCS) Directive 3-10, *Minimum Requirements for Continuity Communications Capabilities*, July 2007
- Office of Management and Budget Circular A-108, *Responsibilities for the Maintenance of Records About Individuals by Federal Agencies*

- Office of Management and Budget Circular A-123, *Management's Responsibility for Internal Controls*
- Office of Management and Budget Circular A-130, Appendix III, Transmittal Memorandum #4, *Management of Federal Information Resources*, November 2000
- Office of Management and Budget, Federal Enterprise Architecture Program Management Office, *FEA Consolidated Reference Model Document*, Version 2.3, October 2007
- Office of Management and Budget, *Federal Segment Architecture Methodology (FSAM)*, January 2009
- Office of Management and Budget Memorandum 01-05, *Guidance on Inter-Agency Sharing of Personal Data—Protecting Personal Privacy*, December 2000
- Office of Management and Budget Memorandum 02-01, *Guidance for Preparing and Submitting Security Plans of Action and Milestones*, October 2001
- Office of Management and Budget Memorandum 03-19, *Reporting Instructions for the Federal Information Security Management Act and Updated Guidance on Quarterly IT Security Reporting*, August 2003
- Office of Management and Budget Memorandum 03-22, *OMB Guidance for Implementing the Privacy Provisions of the E-Government Act of 2002*, September 2003
- Office of Management and Budget Memorandum 04-04, *E-Authentication Guidance for Federal Agencies*, December 2003
- Office of Management and Budget Memorandum 04-26, *Personal Use Policies and File Sharing Technology*, September 2004
- Office of Management and Budget Memorandum 05-08, *Designation of Senior Agency Officials for Privacy*, February 2005
- Office of Management and Budget Memorandum 05-24, *Implementation of Homeland Security Presidential Directive (HSPD) 12—Policy for a Common Identification Standard for Federal Employees and Contractors*, August 2005
- Office of Management and Budget Memorandum 06-15, *Safeguarding Personally Identifiable Information*, May 2006
- Office of Management and Budget Memorandum 06-16, *Protection of Sensitive Information*, June 2006
- Office of Management and Budget Memorandum 06-19, *Reporting Incidents Involving Personally Identifiable Information and Incorporating the Cost for Security in Agency Information Technology Investments*, July 2006
- Office of Management and Budget Memorandum, *Recommendations for Identity Theft Related Data Breach Notification Guidance*, September 2006
- Office of Management and Budget Memorandum 07-11, *Implementation of Commonly Accepted Security Configurations for Windows Operating Systems*, March 2007
- Office of Management and Budget Memorandum 07-16, *Safeguarding Against and Responding to the Breach of Personally Identifiable Information*, May 2007

- Office of Management and Budget Memorandum 07-18, *Ensuring New Acquisitions Include Common Security Configurations*, June 2007
- Office of Management and Budget Memorandum 08-22, *Guidance on the Federal Desktop Core Configuration (FDCC)*, August 2008
- Office of Management and Budget Memorandum 08-23, *Securing the Federal Government's Domain Name System Infrastructure*, August 2008
- The White House, Office of the Press Secretary, *Designation and Sharing of Controlled Unclassified Information (CUI)*, May 2008
- The White House, Office of the Press Secretary, *Classified Information and Controlled Unclassified Information*, May 2009
- Office of Management and Budget Memorandum 11-11, *Continued Implementation of Homeland Security Presidential Directive (HSPD) 12— Policy for a Common Identification Standard for Federal Employees and Contractors*, February 2011
- Office of Management and Budget Memorandum, *Requirements for Accepting Externally Issued Identity Credentials*, October 2011
- Office of Management and Budget Memorandum 11-33, *FY 2011 Reporting Instructions for the Federal Information Security Management Act and Agency Privacy Management*, September 2011
- Office of Management and Budget Memorandum 12-18, *Managing Government Records Directive*, August 2012
- Office of Management and Budget Memorandum 12-20, *FY 2012 Reporting Instructions for the Federal Information Security Management Act and Agency Privacy Management*, September 2012
- Office of Management and Budget Memorandum 14-03, *Enhancing the Security of Federal Information and Information Systems*, November 2013
- Office of Management and Budget Memorandum 14-04, *Fiscal Year 2013 Reporting Instructions for the Federal Information Security Management Act and Agency Privacy Management*, November 2013
- Office of Management and Budget Memorandum 15-01, *Fiscal Year 2014—2015 Guidance on Improving Federal Information Security and Privacy Management Practices*, October 2014
- Office of Management and Budget Memorandum 16-04, *Fiscal Year 2015—2016 Guidance on Federal Information Security and Privacy Management Requirements*, October 2015
- Office of Management and Budget Memorandum 16-04, *Cyber Security and Implementation Plan (CSIP) for the Federal Civilian Government*, October 2015
- Office of Management and Budget Circular A-123, *Management's Responsibility for Enterprise Risk Management and Internal Control*, July 2016
- Office of Management and Budget Circular A-130, *Managing Federal Information as a Strategic Resource*, July 2016

FEDERAL STANDARDS

- International Organization for Standardization/International Electrotechnical Commission 27001:2005, Security techniques—*Information security management systems—Requirements*
- International Organization for Standardization/International Electrotechnical Commission 15408-1:2009, *Information technology—Security techniques—Evaluation criteria for IT security—Part 1: Introduction and general model.*
- International Organization for Standardization/International Electrotechnical Commission 15408-2:2008, *Information technology—Security techniques—Evaluation criteria for IT security—Part 2: Security functional requirements*
- International Organization for Standardization/International Electrotechnical Commission 15408-3:2008, *Information technology—Security techniques—Evaluation criteria for IT security—Part 3: Security assurance requirements*
- National Institute of Standards and Technology Federal Information Processing Standards Publication 140-2, *Security Requirements for Cryptographic Modules*, May 2001
- National Institute of Standards and Technology Federal Information Processing Standards Publication 140-3, *Security Requirements for Cryptographic Modules (DRAFT)*, December 2009
- National Institute of Standards and Technology Federal Information Processing Standards Publication 180-4, *Secure Hash Standard (SHS)*, March 2012
- National Institute of Standards and Technology Federal Information Processing Standards Publication 186-4, *Digital Signature Standard (DSS)*, July 2013
- National Institute of Standards and Technology Federal Information Processing Standards Publication 188, *Standard Security Label for Information Transfer*, September 1994
- National Institute of Standards and Technology Federal Information Processing Standards Publication 197, *Advanced Encryption Standard (AES)*, November 2001
- National Institute of Standards and Technology Federal Information Processing Standards Publication 198-1, *The Keyed-Hash Message Authentication Code (HMAC)*, July 2008
- National Institute of Standards and Technology Federal Information Processing Standards Publication 199, *Standards for Security Categorization of Federal Information and Information Systems*, February 2004
- National Institute of Standards and Technology Federal Information Processing Standards Publication 200, *Minimum Security Requirements for Federal Information and Information Systems*, March 2006
- National Institute of Standards and Technology Federal Information Processing Standards Publication 201-12 *Personal Identity Verification (PIV) of Federal Employees and Contractors*, August 2013
- National Institute of Standards and Technology Federal Information Processing Standards Publication 202, *SHA-3 Standard: Permutation-Based Hash and Extendable-Output Functions*, August 2015

FEDERAL GUIDELINES AND INTERAGENCY REPORTS

- National Institute of Standards and Technology Special Publication 800-12, *An Introduction to Computer Security: The NIST Handbook*, October 1995
- National Institute of Standards and Technology Special Publication 800-13, *Telecommunications Security Guidelines for Telecommunications Management Network*, October 1995
- National Institute of Standards and Technology Special Publication 800-14, *Generally Accepted Principles and Practices for Securing Information Technology Systems*, September 1996
- National Institute of Standards and Technology Special Publication 800-15, *Minimum Interoperability Specification for PKI Components (MISPC)*, Version 1, January 1998
- National Institute of Standards and Technology Special Publication 800-16, Revision 1, *Information Security Training Requirements: A Role- and Performance-Based Model (DRAFT)*, March 2014
- National Institute of Standards and Technology Special Publication 800-17, *Modes of Operation Validation System (MOVS): Requirements and Procedures*, February 1998
- National Institute of Standards and Technology Special Publication 800-18, Revision 1, *Guide for Developing Security Plans for Federal Information Systems*, February 2006
- National Institute of Standards and Technology Special Publication 800-19, *Mobile Agent Security*, October 1999
- National Institute of Standards and Technology Special Publication 800-20, *Modes of Operation Validation System for the Triple Data Encryption Algorithm (TMOVS): Requirements and Procedures*, October 1999
- National Institute of Standards and Technology Special Publication 800-22, Revision 1a, *A Statistical Test Suite for Random and Pseudorandom Number Generators for Cryptographic Applications*, April 2010
- National Institute of Standards and Technology Special Publication 800-23, *Guidelines to Federal Organizations on Security Assurance and Acquisition/Use of Tested/Evaluated Products*, August 2000
- National Institute of Standards and Technology Special Publication 800-25, *Federal Agency Use of Public Key Technology for Digital Signatures and Authentication*, October 2000
- National Institute of Standards and Technology Special Publication 800-27, Revision A, *Engineering Principles for Information Technology Security (A Baseline for Achieving Security)*, June 2004
- National Institute of Standards and Technology Special Publication 800-28, Version 2, *Guidelines on Active Content and Mobile Code*, March 2008
- National Institute of Standards and Technology Special Publication 800-29, *A Comparison of the Security Requirements for Cryptographic Modules in FIPS 140-1 and FIPS 140-2*, June 2001

- National Institute of Standards and Technology Special Publication 800-30, Revision 1, *Guide for Conducting Risk Assessments*, September 2012
- National Institute of Standards and Technology Special Publication 800-32, *Introduction to Public Key Technology and the Federal PKI Infrastructure*, February 2001
- National Institute of Standards and Technology Special Publication 800-33, *Underlying Technical Models for Information Technology Security*, December 2001
- National Institute of Standards and Technology Special Publication 800-34, Revision 1, *Contingency Planning Guide for Federal Information Systems*, May 2010
- National Institute of Standards and Technology Special Publication 800-35, *Guide to Information Technology Security Services*, October 2003
- National Institute of Standards and Technology Special Publication 800-36, *Guide to Selecting Information Security Products*, October 2003
- National Institute of Standards and Technology Special Publication 800-37, Revision 1, *Guide for Applying the Risk Management Framework to Federal Information Systems: A Security Life Cycle Approach*, February 2010
- National Institute of Standards and Technology Special Publication 800-38G, *Recommendation for Block Cipher Modes of Operation: Methods for Format-Preserving Encryption*, March 2016
- National Institute of Standards and Technology Special Publication 800-38F, *Recommendation for Block Cipher Modes of Operation: Methods for Key Wrapping*, December 2012
- National Institute of Standards and Technology Special Publication 800-38E, *Recommendation for Block Cipher Modes of Operation: The XTS-AES Mode for Confidentiality on Storage Devices*, January 2010
- National Institute of Standards and Technology Special Publication 800-38D, *Recommendation for Block Cipher Modes of Operation: Galois/Counter Mode (GCM) and GMAC*, November 2007
- National Institute of Standards and Technology Special Publication 800-38C, *Recommendation for Block Cipher Modes of Operation: the CCM Mode for Authentication and Confidentiality*, May 2004
- National Institute of Standards and Technology Special Publication 800-38B, *Recommendation for Block Cipher Modes of Operation: The CMAC Mode for Authentication*, May 2005
- National Institute of Standards and Technology Special Publication 800-38A— Addendum, *Recommendation for Block Cipher Modes of Operation: Three Variants of Ciphertext Stealing for CBC Mode*, October 2010
- National Institute of Standards and Technology Special Publication 800-39, *Managing Information Security Risk: Organization, Mission, and Information System View*, March 2011
- National Institute of Standards and Technology Special Publication 800-40, Revision 3, *Guide on Firewalls and Firewall Policy*, July 2013

- National Institute of Standards and Technology Special Publication 800-41, Revision 1, *Guidelines on Firewalls and Firewall Policy*, September 2009
- National Institute of Standards and Technology Special Publication 800-44, Version 2, *Guidelines on Securing Public Web Servers*, September 2007
- National Institute of Standards and Technology Special Publication 800-45, Version 2, *Guidelines on Electronic Mail Security*, February 2007
- National Institute of Standards and Technology Special Publication 800-46, Revision 2, *Guide to Enterprise Telework, Remote Access, and Bring Your Own Device (BYOD) Security*, July 2016
- National Institute of Standards and Technology Special Publication 800-47, *Security Guide for Interconnecting Information Technology Systems*, August 2002
- National Institute of Standards and Technology Special Publication 800-48, Revision 1, *Guide to Securing Legacy IEEE 802.11 Wireless Networks*, July 2008
- National Institute of Standards and Technology Special Publication 800-49, *Federal S/MIME V3 Client Profile*, November 2002
- National Institute of Standards and Technology Special Publication 800-50, *Building an Information Technology Security Awareness and Training Program*, October 2003
- National Institute of Standards and Technology Special Publication 800-51, Revision 1, *Guide to Using Vulnerability Naming Schemes*, February 2011
- National Institute of Standards and Technology Special Publication 800-52, Revision 1, *Guidelines for the Selection, Configuration, and Use of Transport Layer Security (TLS) Implementations*, April 2014
- National Institute of Standards and Technology Special Publication 800-53, Revision 4, *Security and Privacy Controls for Federal Information Systems and Organizations*, April 2013
- National Institute of Standards and Technology Special Publication 800-53A, Revision 4, *Guide for Assessing the Security Controls in Federal Information Systems and Organizations: Building Effective Security Assessment Plans*, December 2014
- National Institute of Standards and Technology Special Publication 800-54, *Border Gateway Protocol Security*, July 2007
- National Institute of Standards and Technology Special Publication 800-55, Revision 1, *Performance Measurement Guide for Information Security*, July 2008
- National Institute of Standards and Technology Special Publication 800-56C, *Recommendation for Key Derivation through Extraction-then-Expansion*, November 2011
- National Institute of Standards and Technology Special Publication 800-56B, Revision 1, *Recommendation for Pair-Wise Key Establishment Schemes Using Integer Factorization Cryptography*, September 2014

- National Institute of Standards and Technology Special Publication 800-56A, Revision 2, *Recommendation for Pair-Wise Key Establishment Schemes Using Discrete Logarithm Cryptography*, May 2013
- National Institute of Standards and Technology Special Publication 800-57 Part 3, *Recommendation for Key Management Part 3*, January 2015
- National Institute of Standards and Technology Special Publication 800-57 Part 2, *Recommendation for Key Management Part 2*, August 2005
- National Institute of Standards and Technology Special Publication 800-57, Revision 4 Part 1, *Recommendation for Key Management Part 1*, January 2016
- National Institute of Standards and Technology Special Publication 800-58, *Security Considerations for Voice Over IP Systems*, January 2005
- National Institute of Standards and Technology Special Publication 800-59, *Guideline for Identifying an Information System as a National Security System*, August 2003
- National Institute of Standards and Technology Special Publication 800-60, Revision 1, *Guide for Mapping Types of Information and Information Systems to Security Categories*, August 2008
- National Institute of Standards and Technology Special Publication 800-61, Revision 2, *Computer Security Incident Handling Guide*, August 2012
- National Institute of Standards and Technology Special Publication 800-63-2, *Electronic Authentication Guideline*, August 2013
- National Institute of Standards and Technology Special Publication 800-63-3, *Digital Authentication Guideline (DRAFT)*, May 2016
- National Institute of Standards and Technology Special Publication 800-64, Revision 2, *Security Considerations in the System Development Life Cycle*, October 2008
- National Institute of Standards and Technology Special Publication 800-65, *Integrating IT Security into the Capital Planning and Investment Control Process*, January 2005
- National Institute of Standards and Technology Special Publication 800-66, Revision 1, *An Introductory Resource Guide for Implementing the Health Insurance Portability and Accountability Act (HIPAA) Security Rule*, October 2008
- National Institute of Standards and Technology Special Publication 800-67, Revision 1, *Recommendation for the Triple Data Encryption Algorithm (TDEA) Block Cipher*, January 2012
- National Institute of Standards and Technology Special Publication 800-70, Revision 3, *National Checklist Program for IT Products—Guidelines for Checklist Users and Developers*, December 2015
- National Institute of Standards and Technology Special Publication 800-73-4, *Interfaces for Personal Identity Verification*, May 2015
- National Institute of Standards and Technology Special Publication 800-76-2, *Biometric Specification for Personal Identity Verification*, July 2013

- National Institute of Standards and Technology Special Publication 800-77, *Guide to IPsec VPNs*, December 2005
- National Institute of Standards and Technology Special Publication 800-78-4, *Cryptographic Algorithms and Key Sizes for Personal Identity Verification (PIV)*, May 2015
- National Institute of Standards and Technology Special Publication 800-79-2, *Guidelines for the Accreditation of Personal Identity Verification Card Issuers (PCI) and Derived PIV Credential Issuers (DPCI)*, July 2015
- National Institute of Standards and Technology Special Publication 800-81-2, *Secure Domain Name System (DNS) Deployment Guide*, September 2013
- National Institute of Standards and Technology Special Publication 800-82, Revision 2, *Guide to Industrial Control Systems (ICS) Security*, May 2015
- National Institute of Standards and Technology Special Publication 800-83, Revision 1, *Guide to Malware Incident Prevention and Handling for Desktops and Laptops*, July 2013
- National Institute of Standards and Technology Special Publication 800-84, *Guide to Test, Training, and Exercise Programs for IT Plans and Capabilities*, September 2006
- National Institute of Standards and Technology Special Publication 800-86, *Guide to Integrating Forensic Techniques into Incident Response*, August 2006
- National Institute of Standards and Technology Special Publication 800-88, Revision 1, *Guidelines for Media Sanitization*, December 2014
- National Institute of Standards and Technology Special Publication 800-89, *Recommendation for Obtaining Assurances for Digital Signature Applications*, November 2006
- National Institute of Standards and Technology Special Publication 800-90C, *Recommendation for Random Bit Generator (RBG) Constructions (DRAFT)*, January 2016
- National Institute of Standards and Technology Special Publication 800-90B, *Recommendation for the Entropy Sources Used for Random Bit Generation (DRAFT)*, January 2016
- National Institute of Standards and Technology Special Publication 800-90A, Revision 1, *Recommendation for Random Number Generation Using Deterministic Random Bit Generators*, June 2015
- National Institute of Standards and Technology Special Publication 800-92, *Guide to Computer Security Log Management*, September 2006
- National Institute of Standards and Technology Special Publication 800-94, *Guide to Intrusion Detection and Prevention Systems (IDPS)*, February 2007
- National Institute of Standards and Technology Special Publication 800-94 Revision 1, *Guide to Intrusion Detection and Prevention Systems (IDPS) (DRAFT)*, July 2012
- National Institute of Standards and Technology Special Publication 800-95, *Guide to Secure Web Services*, August 2007

- National Institute of Standards and Technology Special Publication 800-97, *Establishing Robust Security Networks: A Guide to IEEE 802.11i*, February 2007
- National Institute of Standards and Technology Special Publication 800-98, *Guidelines for Securing Radio Frequency Identification (RFID) Systems*, April 2007
- National Institute of Standards and Technology Special Publication 800-100, *Information Security Handbook: A Guide for Managers*, October 2006
- National Institute of Standards and Technology Special Publication 800-101, Revision 1, *Guidelines Mobile Device Forensics*, May 2014
- National Institute of Standards and Technology Special Publication 800-106, *Randomized Hashing Digital Signatures*, February 2009
- National Institute of Standards and Technology Special Publication 800-107, Revision 1, *Recommendation for Applications Using Approved Hash Algorithms*, August 2012
- National Institute of Standards and Technology Special Publication 800-108, *Recommendation for Key Derivation Using Pseudorandom Functions*, October 2009
- National Institute of Standards and Technology Special Publication 800-111, *Guide to Storage Encryption Technologies for End User Devices*, November 2007
- National Institute of Standards and Technology Special Publication 800-113, *Guide to SSL VPNs*, July 2008
- National Institute of Standards and Technology Special Publication 800-114, Revision 1, *User's Guide to Teleworking and Bring Your Own Device (BYOD) Security*, March 2016
- National Institute of Standards and Technology Special Publication 800-115, *Technical Guide to Information Security Testing and Assessment*, September 2008
- National Institute of Standards and Technology Special Publication 800-116, *A Recommendation for the Use of PIV Credentials in Physical Access Control Systems (PACS)*, November 2008
- National Institute of Standards and Technology Special Publication 800-116, Revision 1, *A Recommendation for the Use of PIV Credentials in Physical Access Control Systems (PACS) (DRAFT)*, December 2015
- National Institute of Standards and Technology Special Publication 800-117, Version 1.0, *Guide to Adopting and Using the Security Content Automation Protocol (SCAP)*, July 2010
- National Institute of Standards and Technology Special Publication 800-119, *Guidelines for the Secure Deployment of IPv6*, December 2010
- National Institute of Standards and Technology Special Publication 800-120, *Recommendation for EAP Methods Used in Wireless Network Access Authentication*, September 2009

- National Institute of Standards and Technology Special Publication 800-121, Revision 1, *Guide to Bluetooth Security*, June 2012
- National Institute of Standards and Technology Special Publication 800-122, *Guide to Protecting the Confidentiality of Personally Identifiable Information (PII)*, April 2010
- National Institute of Standards and Technology Special Publication 800-123, *Guide to General Server Security*, July 2008
- National Institute of Standards and Technology Special Publication 800-124, Revision 1, *Guidelines for Managing the Security of Mobile Devices in the Enterprise*, June 2013
- National Institute of Standards and Technology Special Publication 800-125, *Guide to Security for Full Virtualization Technologies*, January 2011
- National Institute of Standards and Technology Special Publication 800-125A, *Guide to Security for Full Virtualization Technologies (DRAFT)*, October 2014
- National Institute of Standards and Technology Special Publication 800-125B, *Secure Virtual Network Configuration for Virtual Machine (VM) Protection*, March 2016
- National Institute of Standards and Technology Special Publication 800-126, Revision 2, *The Technical Specification for the Security Content Automation Protocol (SCAP): SCAP Version 1.2*, September 2011
- National Institute of Standards and Technology Special Publication 800-126, Revision 3, *The Technical Specification for the Security Content Automation Protocol (SCAP): SCAP Version 1.3 (DRAFT)*, July 2016
- National Institute of Standards and Technology Special Publication 800-126A, Revision 3, *SCAP 1.3 Component Specification Version Updates (DRAFT)*, July 2016
- National Institute of Standards and Technology Special Publication 800-128, *Guide for Security-Focused Configuration Management of Information Systems*, August 2011
- National Institute of Standards and Technology Special Publication 800-132, *Recommendation for Password-Based Key Derivation Part: Storage Applications*, December 2010
- National Institute of Standards and Technology Special Publication 800-133, *Recommendation for Cryptographic Key Generation*, December 2012
- National Institute of Standards and Technology Special Publication 800-137, *Information Security Continuous Monitoring for Federal Information Systems and Organizations*, September 2011
- National Institute of Standards and Technology Special Publication 800-142, *Practical Combinatorial Testing*, October 2010
- National Institute of Standards and Technology Special Publication 800-144, *Guidelines for Security and Privacy in Public Cloud Computing*, December 2011

- National Institute of Standards and Technology Special Publication 800-145, *The NIST Definition of Cloud Computing*, September 2011
- 111. National Institute of Standards and Technology Special Publication 800-146, *Cloud Computing Synopsis and Recommendations*, May 2012
- National Institute of Standards and Technology Special Publication 800-147, *Basic Input/Output System (BIOS) Protection Guidelines*, April 2011
- National Institute of Standards and Technology Special Publication 800-147B, *BIOS Protection Guidelines for Servers*, April 2014
- National Institute of Standards and Technology Special Publication 800-150, *Guide to Cyber Threat Information Sharing (DRAFT)*, April 2016
- National Institute of Standards and Technology Special Publication 800-153, *Guidelines for Securing Wireless Local Area Networks (WLANs)*, September 2011
- National Institute of Standards and Technology Special Publication 800-154, *Guide to Data-Centric System Threat Modeling (DRAFT)*, March 2016
- National Institute of Standards and Technology Special Publication 800-160, *Systems Security Engineering: An Integrated Approach to Building Trustworthy Resilient Systems (DRAFT)*, May 2016
- National Institute of Standards and Technology Special Publication 800-161, *Supply Chain Risk Management Practices for Federal Information Systems and Organizations*, April 2015
- National Institute of Standards and Technology Special Publication 800-162, *Guide to Attribute Based Access Control (ABAC) Definition and Considerations*, January 2014
- National Institute of Standards and Technology Special Publication 800-163, *Vetting the Security of Mobile Applications*, January 2015
- National Institute of Standards and Technology Special Publication 800-167, *Guide to Application Whitelisting*, June 2015
- National Institute of Standards and Technology Special Publication 800-171, *Protecting Controlled Unclassified Information in Nonfederal Information Systems and Organizations*, June 2015
- National Institute of Standards and Technology Special Publication 800-171, Revision 1, *Protecting Controlled Unclassified Information in Nonfederal Information Systems and Organizations (DRAFT)*, August 2016
- National Institute of Standards and Technology Special Publication 800-175B, *Guideline for Using Cryptographic Standards in the Federal Government: Cryptographic Mechanisms (DRAFT)*, March 2016
- National Institute of Standards and Technology Special Publication 800-175A, *Guideline for Using Cryptographic Standards in the Federal Government: Directives, Mandates and Policies (DRAFT)*, April 2016
- National Institute of Standards and Technology Special Publication 800-177, *Trustworthy Email (DRAFT)*, March 2016
- National Institute of Standards and Technology Special Publication 800-179, *Guide to Securing Apple OS X 10.10 Systems for IT Professionals: A NIST Security Configuration Checklist (DRAFT)*, June 2016

- National Institute of Standards and Technology Special Publication 800-180, *NIST Definition of Microservices, Application Containers and System Virtual Machines (DRAFT)*, February 2016
- National Institute of Standards and Technology Special Publication 800-184, *Guide for Cybersecurity Event Recovery (DRAFT)*, June 2016
- National Institute of Standards and Technology Special Publication 800-185, *SHA-3 Derived Functions: cSHAKE, KMAC, TuppleHash, and ParallelHash (DRAFT)*, August 2016
- National Institute of Standards and Technology Special Publication 800-188, *De-Identifying Government Datasets (DRAFT)*, August 2016
- National Institute of Standards and Technology Interagency Report 7622, *Notional Supply Chain Risk Management Practices for Federal Information Systems*, October 2012
- National Institute of Standards and Technology Interagency Report 7692, *Specification for the Open Checklist Interactive Language (OCIL) Version 2.0*, April 2011
- National Institute of Standards and Technology Interagency Report 7693, *Specification for Asset Identification 1.1*, June 2011
- National Institute of Standards and Technology Interagency Report 7694, *Specification for the Asset Reporting Format 1.1*, June 2011
- National Institute of Standards and Technology Interagency Report 7696, *Common Platform Enumeration: Naming Specification Version 2.3*, August 2011
- National Institute of Standards and Technology Interagency Report 7696, *Common Platform Enumeration: Name Matching Specification Version 2.3*, August 2011
- National Institute of Standards and Technology Interagency Report 7697, *Common Platform Enumeration: Dictionary Specification Version 2.3*, August 2011
- National Institute of Standards and Technology Interagency Report 7698, *Common Platform Enumeration: Applicability Language Specification Version 2.3*, August 2011
- National Institute of Standards and Technology Interagency Report 7756, *CAESARS Framework Extension: An Enterprise Continuous Monitoring Technical Reference Architecture (DRAFT)*, January 2012
- National Institute of Standards and Technology Interagency Report 7799, *Continuous Monitoring Reference Model Workflow, Subsystem, and Interface Specifications (DRAFT)*, January 2012
- National Institute of Standards and Technology Interagency Report 7848, *Specification for the Asset Summary Reporting Format 1.0 (DRAFT)*, May 2012
- National Institute of Standards and Technology Interagency Report 7946, *CVSS Implementation Guidance*, September 2013
- National Institute of Standards and Technology Interagency Report 7956, *Cryptographic Key Management Issues and Challenges in Cloud Services*, September 2013

- National Institute of Standards and Technology Interagency Report 7966, *Security of Automated Access Management Using Secure Shell (SSH)*, October 2015
- National Institute of Standards and Technology Interagency Report 8006, *NIST Cloud Computing Forensic Science Challenges (DRAFT)*, June 2014
- National Institute of Standards and Technology Interagency Report 8011, *Automation Support for Security Control Assessments (DRAFT)*, February 2016
- National Institute of Standards and Technology Interagency Report 8058, *Security Content Automation Protocol (SCAP) Version 1.2 Content Style Guide: Best Practices for Creating and Maintaining SCAP 1.2 Content (DRAFT)*, May 2015
- National Institute of Standards and Technology Interagency Report 8112, *Attribute Metadata (DRAFT)*, August 2016
- National Institute of Standards and Technology Interagency Report 8114, *Report on Lightweight Cryptography (DRAFT)*, August 2016

SUMMARY

This chapter provided a detailed discussion of the FedRAMP security controls, including the security selection process used by the JAB. In addition, specific issues regarding roles and responsibilities were highlighted as it relates to the delineation of responsibility for security controls and situations where shared responsibilities would require defining the scope that would need to be addressed in governing policies and procedures. The governance and maintenance of the FedRAMP security requirements were briefly discussed, focusing on the application of a harmonizing process to incorporate industry feedback and agency-specific security and privacy. Finally, the FedRAMP security control requirements were described, to include potential approaches for implementing the security controls, both in existing or new cloud services with an emphasis on applying a gap analysis or integrating them through a traditional SDLC.

REFERENCES

[1] FedRAMP Program Management Office (PMO). FedRAMP security controls preface [Internet]. Washington, DC: US General Services Administration [cited May 10, 2016]. <https://www.fedramp.gov/files/2015/03/FedRAMP-Security-Controls-Preface-FINAL-1.pdf>.
[2] Joint Task Force Transformation Initiative, NIST Special Publication (SP) 800-53 Revision 4, Security and Privacy Controls for Federal Information System and Organizations. Maryland: National Institute of Standards and Technology; 2013.

[3] FedRAMP Program Management Office (PMO). FedRAMP concept of operations (CONOPS) Version 1.1. Washington, DC: US General Services Administration; 2012.

[4] NIST Computer Security Division, Computer Security Resource Center [Internet]. Washington, DC: US General Services Administration [cited March 4, 2012]. <http://csrc.nist.gov/groups/SMA/fisma/index.html>.

[5] FedRAMP Program Management Office (PMO). Federal risk and authorization management program (FedRAMO), security controls briefing. Washington, DC: US General Services Administration; 2012.

[6] E-Government Act of 2002 [Internet]. Washington, DC: US Government Printing Office; [cited March 10, 2012]. <http://www.gpo.gov/fdsys/pkg/PLAW-107publ347/html/PLAW-107publ347.html>.

[7] US General Services Administration. FAR Subpart 7.1 [Internet]. Washington, DC: US General Services Administration; [cited March 13, 2012]. <https://www.acquisition.gov/far/current/html/Subpart%207_1.html>.

[8] US General Services Administration. FAR Subpart 7.1 [Internet]. Washington, DC: US General Services Administration; [cited March 13, 2012]. <https://www.acquisition.gov/far/html/Subpart%2011_1.html>.

[9] US General Services Administration. FAR Subpart 7.1 [Internet]. Washington, DC: US General Services Administration; [cited March 13, 2012]. <https://www.acquisition.gov/far/html/Subpart%2039_1.html>.

[10] Cloud Security Alliance Working Group. Security guidance for critical areas of focus in cloud computing V3.0. Washington, DC: Cloud Security Alliance; 2011.

[11] FedRAMP Program Management Office (PMO). FedRAMP security controls [Internet]. Washington, DC: US General Services Administration [cited March 3, 2011]. <https://www.fedramp.gov/files/2015/03/FedRAMP-Rev-4-Baseline-Workbook-FINAL062014.xlsx>.

[12] FedRAMP Program Management Office (PMO). FedRAMP High System Security Plan (SSP) Template [Internet]. Washington, DC: US General Services Administration [cited September 8, 2016]. <https://www.fedramp.gov/files/2016/07/FedRAMP-SSP-Template-High-2016-06-20-v01-00.docx>.

Security testing: vulnerability assessments and penetration testing

10

INFORMATION IN THIS CHAPTER:

- Introduction to Security Testing
- Vulnerability Assessment
- Penetration Testing
- FedRAMP Vulnerability Scan and Penetration Testing Requirements

INTRODUCTION TO SECURITY TESTING

Security testing is one type of assessment method[1] used for determining if the information system being assessed meets the security objectives.[2] Security testing as defined by the National Institute of Standards and Technology (NIST) is the "process of exercising one or more assessment objects under specified conditions to compare actual with expected behavior, the results of which are used to support the determination of security control existence, functionality, correctness, completeness, and potential for improvement over time" [1]. Security testing can be used to determine if technical mechanisms or organizational activities meet a set of predefined specifications or can be used to evaluate security controls to determine if they can be circumvented.[3]

Security testing can be conducted using manual or automated techniques. Both testing techniques have advantages and disadvantages. Manual security testing is not only time-consuming; it can also be more expensive than automated testing. Automated testing uses tools to execute tests and automate tasks, thereby improving the efficiency of security testing. Automated tools can also improve the time to

---

[1]Testing, examination, and interviewing.

[2]Confidentiality, integrity, and availability.

[3]From Joint Task Force Transformation Initiative Interagency Working Group. NIST Special Publication (SP) 800-53A Revision 4, Assessing Security and Privacy Controls in Federal Information Systems and organizations. Maryland: National Institute of Standards and Technology; 2014. *"Penetration testing is a specific type of assessment in which assessors simulate the actions of a given class of attacker by using a defined set of documentation (that is, the documentation representative of what that class of attacker is likely to possess) and working under other specific constraints to attempt to circumvent the security features of an information system."*

Federal Cloud Computing. DOI: http://dx.doi.org/10.1016/B978-0-12-809710-6.00010-X

complete security testing, and can be more frequently updated based on new types of vulnerabilities and exploits. However, automated security testing reduces the types of testing techniques (e.g., social engineering[4]) that can be performed based on the limitation of automated tools to mimic human behavior. Therefore, both manually and automated testing should be considered against the depth and coverage required for the security testing.

TIP

Security testing can be differentiated by the depth[5] and coverage[6] of the testing conducted. Depth and coverage are factors in the level of effort and the rigor and scope of the security testing.

Depth
The three values for the depth attribute are [1]:

- **Basic testing:** Test methodology (also known as black box testing) that assumes no knowledge of the internal structure and implementation detail of the assessment object. This type of testing is conducted using a functional specification for mechanisms and a high-level process description for activities. Basic testing provides a level of understanding of the security controls necessary for determining whether the controls are implemented and free of obvious errors.
- **Focused testing:** Test methodology (also known as gray box testing) that assumes some knowledge of the internal structure and implementation detail of the assessment object. This type of testing is conducted using a functional specification and limited system architectural information (e.g., high-level design) for mechanisms and a high-level process description and high-level description of integration into the operational environment for activities. Focused testing provides a level of understanding of the security controls necessary for determining whether the controls are implemented and free of obvious errors and whether there are increased grounds for confidence that the controls are implemented correctly and operating as intended.
- **Comprehensive testing:** Test methodology (also known as white box testing) that assumes explicit and substantial knowledge of the internal structure and implementation detail of the assessment object. This type of testing is conducted using a functional specification, extensive

(Continued)

---

[4]From Scarfone, K., Souppaya, M., Cody, A., Orebaugh, A. NIST Special Publication (SP) 800-115, Technical Guide to Information Security Testing and Assessment. Maryland: National Institute of Standards and Technology; 2008. *"Social engineering is an attempt to trick someone into revealing information (e.g., a password) that can be used to attack systems or networks. It is used to test the human element and user awareness of security, and can reveal weaknesses in user behavior—such as failing to follow standard procedures."*

[5]From Joint Task Force Transformation Initiative Interagency Working Group. NIST Special Publication (SP) 800-53A Revision 4, Assessing Security and Privacy Controls in Federal Information Systems and organizations. Maryland: National Institute of Standards and Technology; 2014. *"An attribute associated with an assessment method that addresses the rigor and level of detail associated with the application of the method."*

[6]From Joint Task Force Transformation Initiative Interagency Working Group. NIST Special Publication (SP) 800-53A Revision 4, Assessing Security and Privacy Controls in Federal Information Systems and organizations. Maryland: National Institute of Standards and Technology; 2014. *"An attribute associated with an assessment method that addresses the scope or breadth of the assessment objects included in the assessment (e.g., types of objects to be assessed and the number of objects to be assessed by type)."*

TIP (CONTINUED)

system architectural information (e.g., high-level design, low-level design) and implementation representation (e.g., source code, schematics) for mechanisms, and a high-level process description and detailed description of integration into the operational environment for activities. Comprehensive testing provides a level of understanding of the security controls necessary for determining whether the controls are implemented and free of obvious errors and whether there are further increased grounds for confidence that the controls are implemented correctly and operating as intended on an ongoing and consistent basis, and that there is support for continuous improvement in the effectiveness of the controls.

Coverage

The three values for the coverage attribute are [1]:

- **Basic testing:** Testing that uses a representative sample of assessment objects (by type and number within type) to provide a level of coverage necessary for determining whether the security controls are implemented and free of obvious errors.
- **Focused testing:** Testing that uses a representative sample of assessment objects (by type and number within type) and other specific assessment objects deemed particularly important to achieving the assessment objective to provide a level of coverage necessary for determining whether the security controls are implemented and free of obvious errors and whether there are increased grounds for confidence that the controls are implemented correctly and operating as intended.
- **Comprehensive testing:** Testing that uses a sufficiently large sample of assessment objects (by type and number within type) and other specific assessment objects deemed particularly important to achieving the assessment objective to provide a level of coverage necessary for determining whether the security controls are implemented and free of obvious errors and whether there are further increased grounds for confidence that the controls are implemented correctly and operating as intended on an ongoing and consistent basis, and that there is support for continuous improvement in the effectiveness of the controls.

VULNERABILITY ASSESSMENT

The purpose of a vulnerability assessment (scanning) is to examine an information system or product, with the intent of identifying inadequate security measures and vulnerabilities.[7] In addition to vulnerabilities, vulnerability assessments can also include network discovery, network port, and service identification.[8] These types

---

[7]From Joint Task Force Transformation Initiative Interagency Working Group. NIST Special Publication (SP) 800-53A Revision 4, Assessing Security and Privacy Controls in Federal Information Systems and organizations. Maryland: National Institute of Standards and Technology; 2014. *"Weakness in an information system, system security procedures, internal controls, or implementation that could be exploited or triggered by a threat source."*

[8]From Scarfone, K., Souppaya, M., Cody, A., Orebaugh, A. NIST Special Publication (SP) 800-115, Technical Guide to Information Security Testing and Assessment. Maryland: National Institute of Standards and Technology; 2008. *"Network port and service identification involves using a port scanner to identify network ports and services operating on active hosts—such as FTP and HTTP—and the application that is running each identified service, such as Microsoft Internet Information Server (IIS) or Apache for the HTTP service."*

of assessments differ from penetration testing, discussed in the next section, which attempts to simulate a specific attack to exploit vulnerabilities in the target environment. Although, vulnerability assessments can help to inform a penetration test, they are often performed on a more regular basis to provide an initial prioritized list of vulnerabilities or used as part of the deployment of new information systems or products. The results of a vulnerability assessment include not only the vulnerabilities identified, but also the information on how to remediate discovered vulnerabilities.

Vulnerability scanning[9] can be performed on operating systems, network devices, databases, and web applications and custom software,[10] depending on the types of tools used and the scope of the assessment. During the vulnerability scanning, target hosts are identified and information about the hosts are collected[11] for analysis (e.g., operating system type, installed applications, and open ports). The analysis[12] of the information collected from vulnerability scanning can be evaluated manually through human interpretation or automatically through the vulnerability scanner[13] to assist in identifying outdated software, missing patches, misconfigurations, and policy compliance rules.

[9]From Joint Task Force Transformation Initiative Interagency Working Group. NIST Special Publication (SP) 800-53 Revision 4, Security and privacy controls for federal information systems and organizations. Maryland: National Institute of Standards and Technology; 2013. *"Vulnerability scanning includes, for example: (i) scanning for patch levels; (ii) scanning for functions, ports, protocols, and services that should not be accessible to users or devices; and (iii) scanning for improperly configured or incorrectly operating information flow control mechanisms."*

[10]From Scarfone, K., Souppaya, M., Cody, A., Orebaugh, A. NIST Special Publication (SP) 800-115, Technical Guide to Information Security Testing and Assessment. Maryland: National Institute of Standards and Technology; 2008. *"Application security can be assessed in a number of ways, ranging from source code review to penetration testing of the implemented application."*

[11]Credentialed (or authenticated) vulnerability assessments can extract vulnerability information from the host using those credentials; whereas noncredentialed vulnerability assessments only look at network services exposed by the host (i.e., do not provide all known operating system and application vulnerabilities).

[12]From Scarfone, K., Souppaya, M., Cody, A., Orebaugh, A. NIST Special Publication (SP) 800-115, Technical Guide to Information Security Testing and Assessment. Maryland: National Institute of Standards and Technology; 2008. *"A useful resource to reference throughout the analysis phase is the NIST National Vulnerability Database (NVD). NVD is a database that contains information on Common Vulnerabilities and Exposures (CVE), a list of standardized names for known vulnerabilities. The NVD scores vulnerabilities with the Common Vulnerability Scoring System (CVSS) and provides additional information regarding the vulnerability and additional resources to reference for mitigation recommendations (e.g., vendor Web sites)."*

[13]From Joint Task Force Transformation Initiative Interagency Working Group. NIST Special Publication (SP) 800-53 Revision 4, Security and privacy controls for federal information systems and organizations. Maryland: National Institute of Standards and Technology; 2013. *"Organizations consider using tools that express vulnerabilities in the Common Vulnerabilities and Exposures (CVE) naming convention and that use the Open Vulnerability Assessment Language (OVAL) to determine/test for the presence of vulnerabilities."*

Vulnerability assessments reports produced from vulnerability scanners may utilize different methods to score[14] vulnerabilities, resulting in different risk levels for the same vulnerability. Additionally, vulnerability scanners only identify and report vulnerabilities on a host-by-host basis and do not take into account the environment in which the vulnerability resides. Reliance on vulnerability scanners to evaluate and report results to assign risk would need to be weighed against the potential for vulnerabilities identified on individual hosts to be assigned a lower or higher risk level than would actually exist. Therefore, some human interpretation would be required in appropriately evaluating and assigning risk levels for vulnerabilities identified, rather than relying solely on the risk levels assigned by the vulnerability scanner.

The security categorization[15] of the information system guides the frequency and comprehensiveness,[16] and the type of information system components to be included in a vulnerability assessment. Additionally, the location, exposure, and criticality of the information system components also helps inform the vulnerability assessment. For example, a vulnerability scan of a public facing web application may require a different approach than an internal web application, which is not publically accessible. Further, vulnerability scanning of custom software application[17] may require a different approach than a commercial-off-the-shelf (COTS) software application.

> **NOTE**
>
> NIST Special Publication 800-53 has established a requirement for a low, moderate, and high-impact information systems to include regularly and/or random vulnerability scanning as part of the security practices. In this section, the specific vulnerability scanning requirements are presented for information system categorized as low, moderate, or high in accordance with Federal Information Processing Standard (FIPS) 199.
>
> *(Continued)*

---

[14]The Common Vulnerability Scoring System (CVSS) was developed to provide a way to characterize vulnerabilities and score them using a standardized method through a common algorithm to produce a severity rating. CVSS uses three metrics groups to characterize a vulnerability (base, temporal, and environmental); however, only the base metric groups examines the exploitability and impact of vulnerabilities. For more information on CVSS, visit https://www.first.org/cvss.

[15]Chapter 5, Applying the NIST risk management framework, discussed the FIPS 199 security categorization process in the application of the Risk Management Framework (RMF).

[16]From Scarfone, K., Souppaya, M., Cody, A., Orebaugh, A. NIST Special Publication (SP) 800-115, Technical Guide to Information Security Testing and Assessment. Maryland: National Institute of Standards and Technology; 2008. *"Most vulnerability scanners allow the assessor to perform different levels of scanning that vary in terms of thoroughness. While more comprehensive scanning may detect a greater number of vulnerabilities, it can slow the overall scanning process. Less comprehensive scanning can take less time, but identifies only well-known vulnerabilities."*

[17]From Joint Task Force Transformation Initiative Interagency Working Group. NIST Special Publication (SP) 800-53 Revision 4, Security and privacy controls for federal information systems and organizations. Maryland: National Institute of Standards and Technology; 2013. *"Vulnerability analyses for custom software applications may require additional approaches such as static analysis, dynamic analysis, binary analysis, or a hybrid of the three approaches."*

> **NOTE (CONTINUED)**
> ### Low, Moderate, or High Security Category
> RA-5 vulnerability scanning:
>   The organization:
>
> a. Scans for vulnerabilities in the information system and hosted applications [Assignment: organization-defined frequency and/or randomly in accordance with organization-defined process] and when new vulnerabilities potentially affecting the system/applications are identified and reported.
> b. Employs vulnerability scanning tools and techniques that facilitate interoperability among tools and automate parts of the vulnerability management process by using standards for:
>   1. Enumerating platforms, software flaws, and improper configurations;
>   2. Formatting checklists and test procedures; and
>   3. Measuring vulnerability impact.
> c. Analyzes vulnerability scan reports and results from security control assessments.
> d. Remediates legitimate vulnerabilities [Assignment: organization-defined response times] in accordance with an organizational assessment of risk.
> e. Shares information obtained from the vulnerability scanning process and security control assessments with [Assignment: organization-defined personnel or roles] to help eliminate similar vulnerabilities in other information systems (i.e., systemic weaknesses or deficiencies).
>
> ### Moderate, or High Security Category
> RA-5 (1) Vulnerability Scanning | Update Tool Capability
>   The organization employs vulnerability scanning tools that include the capability to readily update the information system vulnerabilities to be scanned.
> RA-5 (2) Vulnerability Scanning | Update by Frequency/Prior to New Scan/When Identified
>   The organization updates the information system vulnerabilities scanned organization-defined frequency prior to a new scan, or when new vulnerabilities are identified and reported.
> RA-5 (5) Vulnerability Scanning | Privileged Access
>   The information system implements privileged access authorization to organization-identified information system components for selected organization-defined vulnerability scanning activities.
>
> ### High Security Category
> RA-5 (4) Vulnerability Scanning | Discoverable Information
>   The organization determines what information about the information system is discoverable by adversaries and subsequently takes organization-defined corrective actions.

The overall outcome of the vulnerability assessment should be identifying sources of potential vulnerabilities. The vulnerabilities should be analyzed to inform the vulnerability management program of which vulnerabilities need to be patched or mitigated. The vulnerability management program should focus on characterizing and prioritizing the vulnerabilities to prevent attackers from not only compromising a host or device, but also use of the compromised host or device to in turn compromise other hosts or devices (also known as "lateral movement"[18]). As presented in Table 10.1,

---

[18]FedRAMP PMO. FedRAMP Penetration Test Guidance Version 1.0.1. Washington, DC: US General Services Administration; 2015. *"Perform further discovery and enumeration to identify hosts on the network that may only respond to the compromised system. Leverage compromised systems and credentials to pivot to additional hosts with the intent of gaining unauthorized access to management systems."*

Table 10.1 Description of the Attacks Steps [2]

Attack Step	Attacker Action	Defender Action
1. Gain internal entry	The attacker is outside the target boundaries and seeks entry. **Examples include:** Spear phishing email sent; DDoS attack against gov. initiated.	• Limit attacks or negative events from even initiating in, or having the ability to impact, the local environment. **Examples include:** Multifactor authentication; SPAM filters; access control lists for routers/firewalls; link encryption and virtual private networks (VPNs); authoritative Domain Name System (DNS) to prevent poisoning; gateway level antimalware applications.
2. Initiate attack internally	The attacker is inside the boundary and initiates attack on some object internally. **Examples include:** User opens spear phishing email or clicks on attachment; laptop lost or stolen; user installs unauthorized software or hardware.	• Limit initiating condition from occurring in local environment. **Examples include:** Educating users not to click on attachments; maintaining positive control of assets; restricting privileges for software installation or removable media. • Limit precipitating event from resulting in attack. **Examples include:** Preventing automatic execution of code on removable media; educating users not to share passwords; educating users not to send unencrypted *personally identifiable information (PII)* outside of the enterprise; host-level antimalware applications that blocks before execution.
3. Gain foothold	The attacker has gained entry to the object and achieves enough actual compromise to gain a foothold, but without persistence. **Examples include:** Unauthorized user successfully logs in with authorized credentials; browser exploit code successfully executed in memory and call back initiated; person gains unauthorized access to server room.	• Limit vulnerable conditions that attack/threat exploits. **Examples include:** Patching; implementation of common secure configurations. • Limit successful completion of exploitation attempt. **Examples include:** DEP (data execution prevention); recompiling techniques; removing default passwords and accounts; multifactor authentication; disabling accounts; redundant communication paths. • Limit successful foothold on object. **Examples include:** Detect attempts; blocking access attempts to known bad DNS domains; reviewing audit and event logs.

(Continued)

Table 10.1 Description of the Attacks Steps [2] *Continued*

Attack Step	Attacker Action	Defender Action

4. Gain persistence	The attack has gained a foothold on the object and now achieves persistence.
	
	Examples include: Malware installed on host that survives reboot or log off; Basic Input/Output System (BIOS) or kernel modified; new/privileged account created for unauthorized user; unauthorized person issued credentials/allowed access.
		• Limit persistent compromise of asset.
		  Examples include: Application whitelisting; malware/intrusion prevention tools; virtualization and sandboxing; one-time password systems; requiring hardware tokens for authentication.
		• Detect persistence; respond and recover.
		  Examples include: File reputation services; file integrity checking; blocking known malicious command and control channels; reviewing audit and event logs; advanced behavioral analysis techniques.

5. Example control—escalate or propagate	The attacker has persistence on the object and seeks to expand control by escalation of privileges on the object or propagation to another object.
	
	Examples include: Administrator privileges hijacked or stolen; administrator's password used by unauthorized party; secure configuration is changed and/or audit function is disabled; authorized users access resources they do not need to perform job; process or program that runs as root is compromised or hijacked.
		• Limit escalation of privileges or access propagation to other assets.
		  Examples include: Restricting privileges for accounts, programs, and processes; implementing and following configuration change control processes; using hardware tokens or two-factor authentication for privileged actions.
		• Detect escalation or propagation activity; respond and recover.
		  Examples include: Use of intrusion detection system (IDS) tools; reviewing audit and event logs.

6. Achieve attack objective	The attacker achieves an objective. Loss of confidentiality, integrity, or availability of data or system capability.
	
	Examples include: Exfiltration of files; modification of database entries; deletion of file or application; denial of service; disclosure of PII.
		• Minimize impact from successful attack.
		  Examples include: Use of data loss prevention tools; laptop and media encryption; outbound boundary filtering; educating users to protect critical information; restricting access to critical information and resources; file and transaction (e.g., email) encryption; link encryption/VPNs.
		• Detect impact from successful attack; respond and recover.
		  Example methods include: Use of auditing and insider threat tools; network event and analysis tools.

the steps of a compromise can be articulated from the viewpoint of the malicious attacker to assist in determining what defender actions should be taken to counter the attack actions.

PENETRATION TESTING

Beyond vulnerability assessments, there may be a requirement to attempt to exploit vulnerabilities to mimic real-world attacks. Penetration testing[19] is another type of security testing that requires the penetration tester to "simulate the actions of a given class of attacker by using a defined set of documentation (i.e., the documentation representative of what that class of attacker is likely to possess) and working under other specific constraints to attempt to circumvent the security features of an information system" [1]. In addition, penetration testing can assist in prioritizing[20] vulnerabilities in hosts or devices based on the potential for being compromised. Further, the penetration testing can also be used to test the controls in-place to resist or detect potential attacks.

TIP

During the attack phase of penetration testing, vulnerabilities identified in the discovery phase tested to determine if they can be exploited. Although not a complete list, vulnerabilities can generally fall into one of the following types of categories [3]:

- **Misconfigurations.** Misconfigured security settings, particularly insecure default settings, are usually easily exploitable.
- **Kernel flaws.** Kernel code is the core of an open source (OS), and enforces the overall security model for the system—so any security flaw in the kernel puts the entire system in danger.
- **Buffer overflows.** A buffer overflow occurs when programs do not adequately check input for appropriate length. When this occurs, arbitrary code can be introduced into the system and executed with the privileges—often at the administrative level—of the running program.
- **Insufficient input validation.** Many applications fail to fully validate the input they receive from users.
- **Symbolic links.** A symbolic link (symlink) is a file that points to another file. Operating systems include programs that can change the permissions granted to a file.

(Continued)

---

[19]From Joint Task Force Transformation Initiative Interagency Working Group. NIST Special Publication (SP) 800-53 Revision 4, Security and privacy controls for federal information systems and organizations. Maryland: National Institute of Standards and Technology; 2013. *"Penetration testing is a test methodology in which assessors, typically working under specific constraints, attempt to circumvent or defeat the security features of an information system."*
[20]From Scarfone, K., Souppaya, M., Cody, A., Orebaugh, A. NIST Special Publication (SP) 800-115, Technical Guide to Information Security Testing and Assessment. Maryland: National Institute of Standards and Technology; 2008. *"The prioritization helps to determine effective strategies for eliminating the identified vulnerabilities and mitigating associated risks."*

TIP (CONTINUED)

- **File descriptor attacks.** File descriptors are numbers used by the system to keep track of files in lieu of filenames. Specific types of file descriptors have implied uses. When a privileged program assigns an inappropriate file descriptor, it exposes that file to compromise.
- **Race conditions.** Race conditions can occur during the time a program or process has entered into a privileged mode. A user can time an attack to take advantage of elevated privileges while the program or process is still in the privileged mode.
- **Incorrect file and directory permissions.** File and directory permissions control the access assigned to users and processes. Poor permissions could allow many types of attacks, including the reading or writing of password files or additions to the list of trusted remote hosts.

NOTE

NIST Special Publication 800-53 has established a requirement for high security categorized information systems to include penetration testing as part of the security practices. In this section, the vulnerability scanning requirements are presented for information systems categorized as high in accordance with FIPS 199.

High Security Category

CA-8 Penetration Testing:

The organization conducts penetration testing [Assignment: organization-defined frequency[21]] on [Assignment: organization-defined information systems or system components].

Penetration testing is best described in a phase-oriented approach. As depicted in Figs. 10.1 and 10.2, NIST outlines four basic phases of penetration

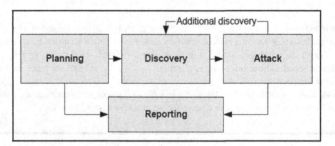

FIGURE 10.1

Four phases of penetration testing [3].

[21]From Joint Task Force Transformation Initiative Interagency Working Group. NIST Special Publication (SP) 800-53 Revision 4, Security and privacy controls for federal information systems and organizations. Maryland: National Institute of Standards and Technology; 2013. *"Penetration testing exercises can be scheduled and/or random in accordance with organizational policy and organizational assessments of risk."*

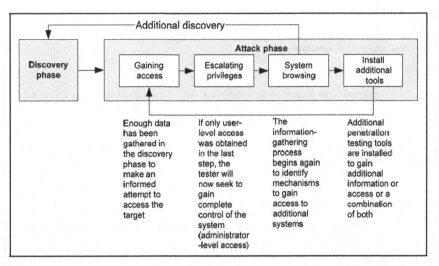

FIGURE 10.2

Attack phase steps with loopback to discovery phase [3].

testing: *planning*; *discovery*; *attack*; *reporting*. During the planning phase, the rules of engagement (ROE[22]) is developed, which includes the goals and rules of the penetration testing. The discovery phase includes information gathering (e.g., port/service identification, hostname/IP address information, employee name/contact information, and application information) and scanning (e.g., vulnerability assessment[23]). After the discovery phase, the attack phase, similar to the attack steps in Table 10.1, focus on exploiting[24] vulnerabilities. Although not all exploits will allow the tester to gain escalated privileges, the attack phase could include expanding the knowledge of the network and other vulnerabilities that could potentially allow the tester to gain additional accesses, change system state to achieve escalated privileges, or install additional tools.

---

[22]From Scarfone, K., Souppaya, M., Cody, A., Orebaugh, A. NIST Special Publication (SP) 800-115, Technical Guide to Information Security Testing and Assessment. Maryland: National Institute of Standards and Technology; 2008. *"Detailed guidelines and constraints regarding the execution of information security testing. The ROE is established before the start of a security test, and gives the test team authority to conduct defined activities without the need for additional permissions."*
[23]From Scarfone, K., Souppaya, M., Cody, A., Orebaugh, A. NIST Special Publication (SP) 800-115, Technical Guide to Information Security Testing and Assessment. Maryland: National Institute of Standards and Technology; 2008. *"Vulnerability scanners check only for the possible existence of a vulnerability."*
[24]From Scarfone, K., Souppaya, M., Cody, A., Orebaugh, A. NIST Special Publication (SP) 800-115, Technical Guide to Information Security Testing and Assessment. Maryland: National Institute of Standards and Technology; 2008. *"Exploit programs or scripts are specialized tools for exploiting specific vulnerabilities."*

TIP

Rules of engagement template [3]:

1. **Introduction**
    1.1. **Purpose**
        Identifies the purpose of the document as well as the organization being tested, the group conducting the testing (or, if an external entity, the organization engaged to conduct the testing), and the purpose of the security test.
    1.2. **Scope**
        Identifies test boundaries in terms of actions and expected outcomes.
    1.3. **Assumptions and limitations**
        Identifies any assumptions made by the organization and the test team. These may relate to any aspect of the test to include the test team, installation of appropriate safeguards for test systems, and so on.
    1.4. **Risks**
        Inherent risks exist when conducting information security tests—particularly in the case of intrusive tests. This section should identify these risks, as well as mitigation techniques and actions to be employed by the test team to reduce them.
    1.5. **Document structure**
        Outlines the ROE's structure, and describes the content of each section.
2. **Logistics**
    2.1. **Personnel**
        Identifies by name all personnel assigned to the security testing task, as well as key personnel from the organization being tested. This section should include a table with all points of contact (POC) for the test team, appropriate management personnel, and the incident response team. If applicable, security clearances or comparable background check details should also be provided.
    2.2. **Test schedule**
        Details the schedule of testing, and includes information such as critical tests and milestones. This section should also address hours during which the testing will take place—for example, it may be prudent to conduct technical testing of an operational site during evening hours rather than during peak business periods.
    2.3. **Test site**
        Identifies the location or locations from which testing is authorized. If testing will occur on the organization's site, building and equipment access should be discussed. Physical access should cover requirements such as badges, escorts, and security personnel that the testers may encounter. Equipment access should address areas such as level of access (user or administrator) to the systems and/or network, and physical access to computer rooms or specific racks that these rooms contain. Areas to which the test team will not be given access should be identified here as well. If testing will be conducted from a remote location such as a rented server farm or test lab, details of the test site architecture should be included in this section.
    2.4. **Test equipment**
        Identifies equipment that the test team will use to conduct the information security tests. This section should also identify the method of differentiating between the organization's systems and the systems conducting the testing—for example, if the test team's systems are identified by MAC, keeping track of test systems could be handled through use of network discovery software. In addition to hardware, tools authorized for use on the network should be identified. It would also be appropriate to include a write-up of each tool in an appendix.

(Continued)

TIP (CONTINUED)

3. **Communication strategy**

   3.1. **General communication**

   Discusses frequency and methods of communication. For example, identify meeting schedule, locations, and conference call information if appropriate.

   3.2. **Incident handling and response**

   This section is critical in the event that an incident occurs on the network while testing is in progress. Criteria for halting the information security testing should be provided, as should details on the test team's course of action in the event that a test procedure negatively impacts the network or an adversary attacks the organization while testing is underway. The organization's incident response call tree/chain of command should be provided in a quick-reference format. A process for reinstating the test team and resuming testing should also be provided.

4. **Target system/network**

   Identifies the systems and/or networks to be tested throughout the information security testing process. Information should include authorized and unauthorized IP addresses or other distinguishing identifiers, if appropriate, for the systems (servers, workstations, firewalls, routers, etc.), operating systems, and any applications to be tested. It is also crucial to identify any system not authorized for testing—this is referred to as the "exclude list."

5. **Testing execution**

   This section is specific to test type and scope, but should detail allowable and unallowable activities and include a description of the information security testing methodology. If necessary, an assessment plan should be developed that complements the ROE—this could be either an appendix or a separate document.

   5.1. **Nontechnical test components**

   Identifies nontechnical test activities that will take place, and includes information to help identify the types of policies, procedures, and other documents that should be reviewed. If interviews or site surveys are to be conducted, guidelines should be established for advance approval of the interview list and questions. If physical security of information systems is in the scope of the testing, procedures should be determined and a form—with appropriate signatures and contact information—generated for the test team to show to law enforcement or onsite security personnel in the event that they are questioned.

   5.2. **Technical test components**

   Includes the type of technical testing to be conducted (e.g., network scanning, discovery, penetration testing); discusses whether files are authorized to be installed, created, modified, and/or executed to facilitate testing; and explains the required actions for those files once testing is completed. Any additional information regarding the technical testing of the organization's systems and networks should also be included in this section. Significant detail should be included on what activities will occur on the target network to ensure that all parties are aware of what is authorized and to be expected as a result of the testing.

   5.3. **Data handling**

   Identifies guidelines for gathering, storing, transmitting, and destroying test data, and establishes detailed, unambiguous requirements for data handling. Keep in mind that data results from any type of information security test will identify vulnerabilities that an adversary can exploit, and should be considered sensitive.

   (Continued)

TIP (CONTINUED)

6. **Reporting**

Details reporting requirements and the report deliverables expected to be provided throughout the testing process and at its conclusion. Minimum information to be provided in each report (e.g., vulnerabilities and recommended mitigation techniques) and the frequency with which the reports will be delivered (e.g., daily status reports) should be included. A template may be provided as an appendix to the ROE to demonstrate report format and content.

7. **Signature page**

Designed to identify accountable parties and ensure that they know and understand their responsibilities throughout the testing process. At a minimum, the test team leader and the organization's senior management (Chief Security Officer (CSO), Chief Information Security Officer (CISO), Chief Information Officer (CIO), etc.) should sign the ROE stating that they understand the test's scope and boundaries.

FEDRAMP VULNERABILITY SCAN AND PENETRATION TESTING REQUIREMENTS

The Federal Risk and Authorization Program (FedRAMP) requirements were discussed in detail in Chapter 8, FedRAMP Primer and Chapter 9, The FedRAMP Cloud Computing Security Requirements. In this section, the focus will be on the specific FedRAMP requirements for vulnerability scanning[25] and penetration testing.[26] As part of the security testing, FedRAMP requires monthly automated scanning of the operating systems/infrastructure, web applications, and databases. In addition, annual automated scanning of the operating systems/infrastructure, web applications, and databases and penetration testing must be performed by an accredited independent assessor.[27]

TIP

Cloud Services Provider (CSPs) should ensure that Third-Party Assessment Organizations (3PAOs) use the same type of vulnerabilities scanning tools to conduct the vulnerability assessment to ensure that the CSP can obtain the same results during mitigation and continuous monitoring. This becomes especially critical when closing out findings.

FedRAMP requires the Cloud Services Provider (CSP), for a Joint Authorization Board Provisional Authorization To Operate (JAB P-ATO), the initial vulnerability

---

[25]*FedRAMP JAB P-ATO Vulnerability Scan Requirements Guide. Version 1.0.* Available from: https://www.fedramp.gov/files/2015/01/FedRAMP-JAB-P-ATO-Vulnerability-Scan-Requirements-Guide-v1-0.pdf

[26]*FedRAMP Penetration Test Guidance, Version 1.0.1.* Available from: https://www.fedramp.gov/files/2015/01/FedRAMP-PenTest-Guidance-v-1-0.pdf

[27]Third-Party Assessment Organization (3PAO).

scans be performed by a 3PAO. After the initial vulnerability scanning, the CSP is required to continue monthly using the same tools used by the 3PAO until all vulnerabilities have been eliminated or mitigated. The requirements for vulnerability scanning include [4]:

- **Authentication/Credential scan**—Vulnerability scans must be performed using system credentials that allow full access to the systems.
- **Enable all nondestructive plug-ins**—To ensure that all vulnerabilities are discovered, the scanner must be configured to scan for all nondestructive findings.
- **Full system boundary scanning**—Each scan must include all components within the system boundary.
- **Scanner signatures up-to-date**—The vulnerability scanner used must be up-to-date and includes the latest revisions of the vulnerability signatures.
- **Provide summary of scanning**—Each scan submission must be accompanied by a summary[28] of the scanning performed.
- **POA&M all findings**—Findings within the scans must all be addressed in the Plan of Action and Milestones (POA&Ms) or other risk acceptance request and maintained until the vulnerabilities have been remediated and validated.

TIP

Vulnerability scanning submission requirements [4]:

- Vulnerability scan data
  - Raw scan files (Format: XML, CSV, or other structure data format)
  - Exported summary reports (Format: PDF, Microsoft Word, or other standard readable documents)
    - Summary reports should include: *Executive Summary*, *Detailed Summary*, and *Inventory Report*.
  - Current inventory (Format: Excel, CSV, or XML)
    - Identifies all components within the authorization boundary and
    - Vulnerability scans and inventory should patch (e.g., IP address, hostnames, or other unique identifier).

Similar to vulnerability scanning, FedRAMP also requires annual penetration testing[29] by an independent penetration agent or team (i.e., 3PAO) as part of the

---

[28]From FedRAMP PMO. FedRAMP Penetration Test Guidance Version 1.0.1. Washington, DC: US General Services Administration; 2015. *"The summary must include a listing of all the scan files submitted, which scanning tools were used, and a short summary of the purpose of the scan (e.g., monthly scans, re-scans, verification scans, etc.). In addition, the summary should discuss the configuration settings of the scanner, including if the signatures were limited for targeted, verifications scans or if the scope of the scan excluded certain components or IP addresses."*

[29]From FedRAMP PMO. FedRAMP Penetration Test Guidance Version 1.0.1. Washington, DC: US General Services Administration; 2015. *"A penetration test is a proactive and authorized exercise to break through the security of an IT system. The main objective of a penetration test is to identify exploitable security weaknesses in an information system. These vulnerabilities may include service and application flaws, improper configurations, and risk end-user behavior. A penetration test also may evaluation an organization's security policy compliance, its employees' security awareness, and the organization's ability to identify and response to security incidents."*

initial and annual security assessment. FedRAMP also requires the CSP classify the cloud service as Software as a Service (SaaS), Platform as a Service (PaaS), and/or Infrastructure as a Service (IaaS), and the scope include all components, and associated services and access path—both internal[30] and external[31]. The identification of the methods and techniques that will be used to test the exploitation of devices and/or services will need to be documented in the ROE. In addition, all of the attack vectors[32] (discussed later in this section) must be included as part of the penetration test, and documented in the Penetration Test Plan.

The ROE[33] is developed by the 3PAO in accordance with NIST SP 800-115, Appendix B[34] and approved by the CSP Authorizing Official prior to testing. The ROE includes the following information [5]:

- Local computer incident response team or capability and their requirements for exercising the penetration test;
- Physical penetration constraints;
- Acceptable pre-text for social engineering; and
- Summary and reference to any third-party agreements, including POC for third parties that may be affected by the penetration test.

The penetration test plan is developed by the 3PAO, and includes the following information [5]:

- A description of the approach, constraints and methodology for each planned attach;
- A detailed test schedule that specifies the start and end date; and
- Technical POC with a backup for each subsystem and/or application that may be included in the penetration test.

[30]From Scarfone, K., Souppaya, M., Cody, A., Orebaugh, A. NIST Special Publication (SP) 800-115, Technical Guide to Information Security Testing and Assessment. Maryland: National Institute of Standards and Technology; 2008. *"Insider scenarios simulate the actions of a malicious insider."*

[31]From Scarfone, K., Souppaya, M., Cody, A., Orebaugh, A. NIST Special Publication (SP) 800-115, Technical Guide to Information Security Testing and Assessment. Maryland: National Institute of Standards and Technology; 2008. *"Outsider scenarios simulate the outsider-attacker who has little or no specific knowledge of the target and who works entirely from assumptions."*

[32]From FedRAMP PMO. FedRAMP Penetration Test Guidance Version 1.0.1. Washington, DC: US General Services Administration; 2015. *3PAOs may include additional attack vectors believed to be appropriate.*

[33]From FedRAMP Program Management Office (PMO). FedRAMP Security Assessment Plan Template. Washington, DC: US General Services Administration; 2016. *"A Rules of Engagement (RoE) document is designed to describe proper notifications and disclosures between the owner of a tested systems and an independent assessor. In particular, a RoE includes information about targets of automated scans and IP address origination information of automated scans (and other testing tools)."*

[34]Available from: http://csrc.nist.gov/publications/nistpubs/800-115/SP800-115.pdf

> **NOTE**
>
> **FedRAMP ROE/Test Plan (TP) requirements** [5]
>
> The 3PAO is required to develop the ROE and TP based on the parameters and system information provided by the CSP, and includes the following information:
>
> - System scope
>   Provide a description of the boundaries and scope of the cloud service system, along with any identified supporting services or systems. System scope should account for all IP addresses, Uniform Resource Locators (URLs), devices, components, software, and hardware.
> - Assumptions and limitations
>   Provide a description of the assumptions, dependencies, and limitations that may have an impact on penetration activities or results. Include references to local and federal legal constraints that may be relevant to testing or results. Assumptions also include any assumed agreement, or access to third-party software, systems, or facilities.
> - Testing schedule
>   Provide a schedule that describes testing phases, initiation/completion dates, and allows for tracking of penetration testing deliverables.
> - Testing methodology
>   The methodology section will address relevant penetration testing activities.
> - Relevant personnel
>   Provide a list of key personnel involved in the management and execution of the penetration test. This list should include, at a minimum:
>   - System Owner (CSP)
>   - Trusted Agent (CSP)
>   - Penetration Test Team Lead (3PAO)
>   - Penetration Test Team Member(s) (3PAO)
>   - Escalation Points of Contact (CSP or 3PAO)
> - Incident response procedures
>   Provide a description of the chain of communication and procedures to be followed, should an event requiring incident response intervention be initiated during penetration testing.
> - Evidence handling procedures
>   Provide a description of procedures for transmission and storage of penetration test evidence collected during the course of the assessment.

FedRAMP requires not only logical penetration testing to exploit vulnerabilities in the cloud service, but also physical testing to verify locked doors, alarm systems, and guards providing the physical protection of the information technology (IT) environment. In addition, the security policies and procedures are tested to ensure that CSP personnel are notified in the event of a physical security incident. Security incidents, both physical and logical, should be tested for different types of attackers [5]:

- Internal—employees or users who are employed by the CSP, including both privileged and nonprivileged users;
- External—users and nonusers of the cloud service who are not employed by the CSP;

- Trusted—users[35] with approved access right to the cloud service; and
- Untrusted—nonusers[36] of the cloud service.

The attack avenues (or vectors) seek to identify paths at which the cloud service can be compromised by the different types of attackers, leading to the unauthorized disclosure of information (loss of confidentiality); unauthorized modification or destruction of information (loss of integrity); and disruption of access to or use of information or an information system (loss of availability). Table 10.2 outlines the different attack vectors identified and developed by FedRAMP for use by 3PAOs.

Table 10.2 Attack Vector [5]

Title	Description
External to Corporate—External Untrusted to Internal Untrusted	An Internet-based attack attempting to gain useful information about or access to the cloud service through an external corporate network owned and operated by the CSP.
External to Cloud Service—External Untrusted to External Trusted	An Internet-based attack as an un-credentialed third party attempting to gain unauthorized access to the cloud service.
Cloud Service to CSP Management System—External Trusted to Internal Trusted	An external attack as a credentialed cloud service user attempting to access the CSP management system or infrastructure.
Tenant to Tenant—External Trusted to External Trusted	An external attack as a credential cloud service user, originating from a tenant environment instance attempting to access or compromise a secondary tenant instance within the cloud service.
Corporate to CSP Management System—Internal Untrusted to Internal Trusted	An internal attack attempting to access the target management system from a system with an identified and simulated security weakness on the CSP corporate network that mimics a malicious device.
Mobile Application—External Untrusted to External Trusted	An attack that emulates a mobile application user attempting to access the CSP cloud service or the CSP's cloud service's mobile application.

---

[35]From FedRAMP PMO. FedRAMP Penetration Test Guidance Version 1.0.1. Washington, DC: US General Services Administration; 2015. *Trusted users include both internal CSP employees with management access to the cloud service, as well as external users with credentialed access to the tenant environment.*

[36]From FedRAMP PMO. FedRAMP Penetration Test Guidance Version 1.0.1. Washington, DC: US General Services Administration; 2015. *"Non-users include both internal CSP employees who lack credentialed access to the cloud service, as well as any individual attempting to access the cloud service."*

There are many methodologies and frameworks that exist to support the 3PAO in conducting penetration testing activities, whether the target IT environment is an operating system, web application, or underlying network infrastructure:

GENERAL

- Open Source Security Testing Methodology Manual (OSSTMM)[37]
- Penetration Testing Execution Standard (PTES)[38]
- NIST Technical Guide to Information Security Testing and Assessment (NIST SP 800-115)
- PCI Data Security Standard (PCI DSS)—Penetration Testing Guidance[39]

WEB APPLICATION

- Open Web Application Security Project (OWASP)[40]

SOCIAL ENGINEERING

- Social Engineering Framework[41]

The *FedRAMP penetration testing methodology* as depicted in Figure 10.3, aligns with the many guidelines in industry best practices and frameworks. Although, it is up to the 3PAO to determine which methodology and test practices are best suited for the penetration testing based on the types of technologies included within scope, and the cloud service type (SaaS, PaaS, and/or IaaS).

TIP

The FedRAMP penetration testing methodology elements include [5]:

- **Scoping**
- **Information gathering and discovery**
    - Web application/API testing information gathering/discovery
        - Perform Internet searches to identify any publicly available information on the target web application
        - Identify the target application architecture
        - Identify account roles and authorization boundary
        - Map all content and functionality

(Continued)

---

[37]Available from: http://www.isecom.org
[38]Available from: http://www.pentest-standard.org
[39]Available from: https://www.pcisecuritystandards.org/documents/Penetration_Testing_Guidance_March_2015.pdf
[40]Available from: https://www.owasp.org
[41]Available from: http://www.social-engineer.org/framework/se-tools/computer-based/social-engineer-toolkit-set/

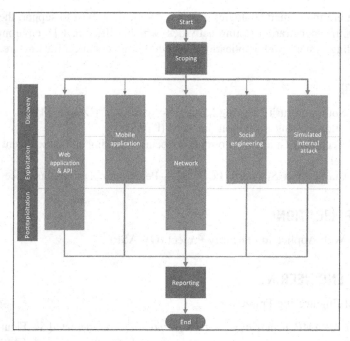

FIGURE 10.3

Elements of the FedRAMP penetration testing methodology [5].

TIP (CONTINUED)

- Identify all user-controlled input entry points
- Perform web application server configuration checks.
- Mobile application information gathering/discovery
  - Perform Internet search to identify any publically available information on the target web application
  - Map all content and functionality
  - Identify all permission sets requested by the application.
- Network information gathering/discovery
  - Perform Open Source Intelligence (OSINT) gathering activities
  - Enumerate and inventory live network endpoints
  - Enumerate and inventory network service availability
  - Fingerprint operating systems and network services
  - Perform vulnerability identification
- Social engineering information gathering/discovery
  - Perform Internet searches to identify CSP personnel of interest responsible for target system management.
- Simulated internal attack information gathering/discovery
  - Perform a scoping exercise with the CSP to determine potential attack vectors
  - Perform vulnerability identification.
- **Exploitation**
  - Web application/API exploitation

(Continued)

TIP (CONTINUED)

- Authentication and session management
- Authorization
- Application logic
- Input validation.
  - Mobile application exploitation
    - Authorization
    - Data storage
    - Information disclosure.
  - Network exploitation
    - Attach scenarios
    - Exploitation
    - Record results.
  - Social engineering exploitation
    - Spear phishing exercise.
  - Simulated internal attack exploitation
    - Escalate administrative privileges
    - Recording results.
- **Postexploitation**[42]
  - Web application/API postexploitation
    - Unauthorized management access
    - Unauthorized data access.
  - Mobile application post-exploitation
  - Network postexploitation
    - Gain situational awareness
    - Privileged escalation
    - Lateral movement
    - Identification and exfiltration of sensitive systems or data.
  - Social engineering postexploitation
  - Simulated internal attack postexploitation
- **Reporting**[43]

TIP

The Penetration Testing Report must include the following information sections [5]:

- **Scope of target System**
  Outlines the target system that was tested and if any deviations were made from the ROE/TP.
- **Attack vectors addressed during the penetration test**
  Describes the attack vector(s) tested and the threat model(s) following for executing the penetration test.

(Continued)

---

[42]From FedRAMP PMO. FedRAMP Penetration Test Guidance Version 1.0.1. Washington, DC: US General Services Administration; 2015. *Escalation of privileges; Lateral movement; and Identification and exfiltration of sensitive systems or data.*

[43]From FedRAMP PMO. FedRAMP Penetration Test Guidance Version 1.0.1. Washington, DC: US General Services Administration; 2015. Penetration test assessment activates and results must be organized and compiled into comprehensive Penetration Testing Report to be included in the Security Assessment Report (SAR).

TIP (CONTINUED)

- **Timeline for penetration test activity**

    Documents when the penetration testing activity was performed.
- **Actual tests performed and results**

    Documents the actual tests performed to address the penetration test requirements outlined in the Penetration Test Report, and documents the results of each test.
- **Findings and evidence**

    Findings include a description of the issues, the impact on the target system, a recommend on the CSP, a risk rating, and relevant evidence to provide context for each findings.
- **Access paths**

    Describes the access paths[44] and the impact if multiple vulnerabilities could be coupled to form a sophisticated attack against the CSP.

SUMMARY

In this chapter, security testing assessment methods were introduced, and the differentiation between automated and manual techniques. In addition, a review of two types of security testing, vulnerability scanning and penetration testing were provided, including the ROE for documenting the purpose of the security test, and detailed guidelines and constraints regarding the execution of security testing. Finally, the FedRAMP security testing requirements were discussed with the focus on vulnerability and penetration testing activities.

REFERENCES

[1] Joint Task Force Transformation Initiative Interagency Working Group. NIST Special Publication (SP) 800-53A Revision 4, Assessing Security and Privacy Controls in Federal Information Systems and organizations. Maryland: National Institute of Standards and Technology; 2014.

[2] Dempsey K, Eavy P, Moore G. NIST Interagency Report (IR), Automation Support for Security Control Assessments., Volume 1: Overview. Maryland: National Institute of Standards and Technology; 2016.

[3] Scarfone K, Souppaya M, Cody A, Orebaugh A. NIST Special Publication (SP) 800-115, Technical Guide to Information Security Testing and Assessment. Maryland: National Institute of Standards and Technology; 2008.

[4] FedRAMP PMO. FedRAMP JAB P-ATO Vulnerability Scan Requirements Guide Version 1.0. Washington, DC: US General Services Administration; 2015.

[5] FedRAMP PMO. FedRAMP Penetration Test Guidance Version 1.0.1. Washington, DC: US General Services Administration; 2015.

---

[44]From FedRAMP PMO. FedRAMP Penetration Test Guidance Version 1.0.1. Washington, DC: US General Services Administration; 2015. *"Attack paths are chains of attack vectors, exploitations, and post-exploitations."*

Security assessment and authorization: Governance, preparation, and execution

11

INFORMATION IN THIS CHAPTER:

- Introduction to the Security Assessment Process
- Governing the Security Assessment
- Preparing for the Security Assessment
- Executing the Security Assessment Plan

INTRODUCTION TO THE SECURITY ASSESSMENT PROCESS

The security assessment process is a key component of the National Institute of Standards and Technology Risk Management Framework (NIST RMF)[1] and the Federal Risk and Authorization Management Program (FedRAMP).[2] FedRAMP[3] enables the adoption and use of cloud services through a cost-effective, risk-based approach that ensures security assessments are an integral part of the system development life cycle (SDLC).[4] FedRAMP also enables federal agencies to benefit from the application of a security risk model that allows them to leverage the authorization through a unified, consistent security assessment framework.

---

[1]Chapter 5 discussed the risk management activities involved in the application of the Risk Management Framework (RMF).

[2]FedRAMP Program Management Office (PMO). FedRAMP Security Assessment Framework Version 2.1. Washington, DC: US General Services Administration; 2015. *"FedRAMP is a Government-wide program that provides a standardized approach to security assessment, authorization, and continuous monitoring for cloud products and services."*

[3]Chapter 8 discussed the FedRAMP process areas.

[4]From Kissel, R., Stine, K., Scholl, M., Rossman, H., Fahlsing, J., Gulick, J. NIST Special Publication (SP) 800-64 Revision 2, Security Considerations in the System Development Life Cycle. Maryland: National Institute of Standards and Technology; 2008. *"Security planning in the initiation phase should include preparations for the entire system life cycle, including the identification of key security milestones and deliverables, and tools and technologies. Special consideration should be given to items that may need to be procured (e.g. test/assessment tools)."*

The goal of a security assessment is to establish confidence that the security controls employed within the information system (or those inherited) have been effectively implemented and are operating as intended. Security assessments conducted at different stages throughout the SDLC[5] can benefit organizations by reducing costs through the reuse of evidence produced through the design, implementation, and testing of the required security controls. By identifying the gaps in security requirements early in the SDLC process,[6] some security controls can be more cost-effectively designed and implemented within the information security architecture,[7] and tested[8] prior to being fully integrated into the production operating environment.

The authorization step relies on the quality of the evidence and the results of the security assessment documented in the security assessment report (SAR).[9] The SAR is one of the three key documents presented to the

[5]From Joint Task Force Transformation Initiative, NIST Special Publication (SP) 800-53A Revision 4, Assessing Security and Privacy Controls in Federal Information Systems and Organizations. Maryland: National Institute of Standards and Technology; 2014. *"Conducting security control assessments in parallel with the development/acquisition and implementation phases of the life cycle permits the identification of weaknesses and deficiencies early and provides the most cost-effective method for initiating corrective actions. The results of security control assessments carried out during system development and implementation can also be used (consistent with reuse criteria) during the security authorization process to avoid system fielding delays or costly repetition of assessments."*

[6]From Joint Task Force Transformation Initiative, NIST Special Publication (SP) 800-53A Revision 4, Assessing Security and Privacy Controls in Federal Information Systems and Organizations. Maryland: National Institute of Standards and Technology; 2014. *"There are typically five phases in a generic system development life cycle: (i) initiation; (ii) development/ acquisition; (iii) implementation; (iv) operations and maintenance; and (v) disposition (disposal)."*

[7]From Kissel, R., Stine, K., Scholl, M., Rossman, H., Fahlsing, J., Gulick, J. NIST Special Publication (SP) 800-64 Revision 2, Security Considerations in the System Development Life Cycle. Maryland: National Institute of Standards and Technology; 2008. *"Schematic of security integration providing details on where, within the system, security is implemented and shared."*

[8]From Kissel, R., Stine, K., Scholl, M., Rossman, H., Fahlsing, J., Gulick, J. NIST Special Publication (SP) 800-64 Revision 2, Security Considerations in the System Development Life Cycle. Maryland: National Institute of Standards and Technology; 2008. For example, *"testing of basic security controls during functional testing may reduce or eliminate issues earlier in the development cycle (e.g. mandatory access controls, secure code development, and firewalls)."*

[9]From Joint Task Force Transformation Initiative Interagency Working Group. NIST Special Publication (SP) 800-30 Revision 1, Guide for Conducting Risk Assessments. Maryland: National Institute of Standards and Technology; 2011. *"Organizations can use the results from security control assessments to inform risk assessments. Organizations use the results from risk assessments to help determine the severity of such vulnerabilities which in turn, can guide and inform organizational risk responses (e.g., prioritizing risk response activities, establishing milestones for corrective actions). Organizations can use risk assessment results to provide risk-related information to authorizing officials."*

authorizing official (AO)[10] when making a credible, risk-based decision.[11] The AO uses the information from the security assessment results[12] as a factor for assuming responsibility[13] for the information systems operation and the information that will be processed, stored, or transmitted within the information system. Through an analysis of the risk associated with the weaknesses and deficiencies identified during the security assessment, the AO can use the judgment of the assessor to make a determination if they are deemed to be acceptable. This reliance on the quality and reliability of the results of the security assessment places a significant importance on the selection of the independent security assessment provider (or security assessor).[14] The security assessment provider must be qualified and competent in conducting security assessments and capable of assessing the security controls, including compiling the evidence needed to demonstrate the effectiveness of the security controls employed within the information system. In addition, the security assessor must be able to effectively present the evidence in a manner that enables a risk-based decision to be made.

In this chapter, the NIST RMF Step 4 (*Assessment*) and Step 5 (*Authorization*) steps will be discussed, with the focus on assisting organizations in developing

---

[10]The FedRAMP Joint Authorization Board (JAB) only grants a provisional authorization for cloud services that have undergone a FedRAMP assessment with an *accredited* Third Party Assessment Organization (3PAO) that enables federal agencies to accept the risk-based decision for granting their own authorization, or federal agencies can conduct their own assessment utilizing the FedRAMP assessment process and a 3PAO for making a risk-based decision.

[11]From Joint Task Force Transformation Initiative Interagency Working Group. NIST Special Publication (SP) 800-37 Revision 1, Guide for Applying the Risk Management Framework to Federal Information Systems: A Security Life Cycle Approach. Maryland: National Institute of Standards and Technology; 2010. *"Risk assessments (either formal or informal) are employed at the discretion of the organization to provide needed information on threats, vulnerabilities, and potential impacts as well as the analyses for the risk mitigation recommendations."*

[12]From Joint Task Force Transformation Initiative, NIST Special Publication (SP) 800-53A Revision 4, Assessing Security and Privacy Controls in Federal Information Systems and Organizations. *Maryland*: National Institute of Standards and Technology; 2014. *"The results of security control assessments carried out during system development and implementation can also be used (consistent with reuse criteria) during the security authorization process."*

[13]From Joint *Task* Force Transformation Initiative Interagency Working Group. NIST Special Publication (SP) 800-37 Revision 1, Guide for Applying the Risk Management Framework to Federal Information Systems: A Security Life Cycle Approach. Maryland: National Institute of Standards and Technology; 2010. *"The explicit acceptance of risk is the responsibility of the authorizing official and cannot be delegated to other officials within the organization."*

[14]From Joint Task Force Transformation Initiative, NIST Special Publication (SP) 800-53A Revision 4, Assessing Security and Privacy Controls in Federal Information Systems and Organizations. Maryland: National Institute of Standards and Technology; 2014. *"An independent assessor is any individual or group capable of conducting an impartial assessment of security controls and privacy controls employed within or inherited by an information system."*

their organization-wide strategy[15] by presenting a framework for managing security assessments. The framework includes three key areas:

- Governance.
- Preparation.
- Execution.

> **NOTE**
>
> The FedRAMP provides a structured, policy-driven process for building a trusted relationship between Cloud Service Providers (CSPs) and federal agency customers. In addition, it supports the acceleration, and secure adoption and use of commercial and noncommercial cloud services through a cost-effective, risk-based approach to security authorization by integrating security assessment as a part of the SDLC. FedRAMP also enables federal agencies to benefit from the application of a security risk model that allows them to leverage the authorization through a unified, consistent security assessment framework.

GOVERNANCE IN THE SECURITY ASSESSMENT

The security assessment policy establishes the governance for the security assessment process. The policy, at a minimum, should cover the requirements for the security assessment preparation and execution, the methodology by which the security assessment is directed and guided, and the roles and responsibilities. The security assessment methodology establishes a repeatable framework for conducting security assessments through the consistent and structured application of assessment procedures, processes, methods, and practices [1]. The methodology[16] also addresses the approach the organization will use for determining the reuse of security assessment results and how the security assessment will be conducted.

---

[15]From Joint Task Force Transformation Initiative, NIST Special Publication (SP) 800-53A Revision 4, Assessing Security and Privacy Controls in Federal Information Systems and Organizations. Maryland: National Institute of Standards and Technology; 2014. *"Organizations are encouraged to develop a broad-based, organization-wide strategy for conducting security and privacy assessments, facilitating more cost-effective and consistent assessments across the inventory of information systems."*

[16]*NIST* Special Publication (SP) 800-115, *Technical Guide to Information Security Testing and Assessment*, Appendix E includes some example methodologies. Available from: http://nvlpubs. nist.gov/nistpubs/Legacy/SP/nistspecialpublication800-115.pdf.

There are generally two primary roles in security assessments, the *security assessment customer* and the *security assessment provider*.[17] Security assessment customers and providers can be from the same organization or the provider can be contracted from a public or private entity outside of the customer organization. However, to ensure the effectiveness and efficiency of security assessments, a degree of independence is critical, specifically for reusing previous assessment results.[18] For example, security assessment-related documentation and evidence could be produced from testing conducted as an integrated part of the SDLC[19] or from third-party testing [20] "if an information system component product is identified as providing support for the implementation of a particular security control" [2].

Security assessments can also include assessment results from other security assessments performed from outside of the organization. In these situations, factors relating to the security assessment results for security controls outside of the boundary for the information system being assessed must consider the credibility of the results being inherited,[21] *partially* or *completely*, at the organization level

---

[17]From Joint Task Force Transformation Initiative Interagency Working Group. NIST Special Publication (SP) 800-37 Revision 1, Guide for Applying the Risk Management Framework to Federal Information Systems: A Security Life Cycle Approach. Maryland: National Institute of *Standards* and Technology; 2010. *"The security assessment provider can be an individual, group, or organization responsible for conducting a comprehensive assessment of the management, operational, and technical security controls employed within or inherited by an information system to determine the overall effectiveness of the controls (i.e. the extent to which the controls are implemented correctly, operating as intended, and producing the desired outcome with respect to meeting the security requirements for the system)."*

[18]From Joint Task Force Transformation Initiative, NIST Special Publication (SP) 800-53A Revision 4, Assessing Security and Privacy Controls in Federal Information Systems and Organizations. Maryland: National Institute of Standards and Technology; 2014. *"Organizations can take advantage of previous assessment results whenever possible, to reduce the overall cost of assessments and to make the assessment process more efficient."*

[19]From Joint Task Force Transformation Initiative, NIST Special Publication (SP) 800-53A Revision 4, Assessing Security and Privacy Controls in *Federal* Information Systems and Organizations. Maryland: National Institute of Standards and Technology; 2014. *"Assessment results can be obtained from many activities that occur routinely during the system development life cycle to reduce the overall cost of assessments and to make the assessment process more efficient."*

[20]From The Common Criteria Evaluation and Validation Scheme [Internet]. Maryland: National Security Agency [cited April 08, 2012]. Available from: http://www.niap-ccevs.org. Examples include National Information Assurance Partnership (NIAP)/Common Criteria Evaluation and *Validation* Scheme (CCEVS) is *"a national program for the evaluation of information technology products for conformance to the International Common Criteria for Information Technology Security Evaluation."*

[21]From Joint Task Force Transformation Initiative, NIST Special Publication (SP) 800-53A Revision 4, Assessing Security and Privacy Controls in *Federal* Information Systems and Organizations. Maryland: National Institute of Standards and Technology; 2014. *"Security control assessments and privacy control assessments include common controls that are the responsibility of organizational entities other than the information system owner inheriting the controls or hybrid controls where there is shared responsibility among the system owner and designated organizational entities."*

(i.e., information security program) rather than the information at system level to preserve impartiality. From an organizational perspective, security assessments, where there is a shared responsibility[22] conducted by different parts of the same organization, require an appropriate level of independence to ensure the segregation of responsibilities and accountability for maintaining security assessment results.

NOTE

In the FedRAMP Policy Memo, the Office of Management and Budget (OMB) defined four key stakeholders:

- Joint Authorization Board (JAB)—US Department of Defense (DoD), US General Services Administration (GSA), and US Department of Homeland Security (DHS).
- FedRAMP Program Management Office (PMO).
- DHS.
- Federal Agencies.

The FedRAMP PMO described the role of these four stakeholders in the frequently asked question (FAQ) [3]. *"Who are the key FedRAMP organizations?"* In addition, several other roles described in the FAQ were identified as having a direct and indirect responsibility within FedRAMP. The other roles include:

- NIST.
- Federal Chief Information Officer (CIO) Council.
- Third Party Assessor Organizations (3PAO).
- CSPs.

The JAB approves the accreditation criteria for 3PAOs to provide independent assessments of CSPs' implementation of the FedRAMP security authorization requirements [4]. NIST, which has been given responsibilities under Federal Information Security Modernization Act (FISMA),[23] is tasked with developing the standards and guidelines used within FedRAMP. NIST also plays a supplementary support function indirectly supporting FedRAMP through the establishment of training frameworks[24] and education programs.[25] The FedRAMP PMO coordinates and collaborates with the NIST to develop and implement a formal conformity assessment program[26] to accredit 3PAOs to provide independent assessments of how CSPs implement the FedRAMP requirements [5].

---

[22]From Joint Task Force Transformation Initiative, NIST Special Publication (SP) 800-53A Revision 4, Assessing Security and Privacy Controls in *Federal* Information Systems and Organizations. Maryland: National Institute of Standards and Technology; 2014. *"Assessments of common controls that are managed by the organization and support multiple information systems."*
[23]*FISMA* was discussed in detail in Chapter 5, Applying the Risk Management Framework.
[24]NIST in leading the National Initiative for Cybersecurity Education (NICE) developed a unified framework for the cybersecurity workforce. Available from: http://csrc.nist.gov/nice/framework/.
[25]From Applying the Risk Management Framework to Federal Information Systems Training [Internet]. Maryland: National Institute of Standards and Technology [cited April 10, 2012]. Available from: http://csrc.nist.gov/groups/SMA/fisma/rmf-training.html. *NIST developed a training program designed to "provide people new to risk management with an overview of a methodology for managing organizational risk—the Risk Management Framework (RMF)."*
[26]From VanRoekel, S. Office of Management and Budget (OMB) Memorandum, Security Authorization of Information System in Cloud Computing Environments. Washington, DC: Executive Office of the President, Office of Management and Budget; 2011. *"A conformity assessment program provides the capability of producing consistent independent, third-party assessments of security controls implemented by CSPs."*

NOTE

Why is FedRAMP accrediting 3PAOs? [6]

Although there currently is no standard or guidance for choosing a 3PAO, the FedRAMP PMO and NIST have designed a conformity assessment process to ensure the independence of and the management and technical quality of 3PAOs using a standard and consistent security assessment process.

How does a company become a 3PAO? [3]

The American Association for Laboratory Accreditation (A2LA) accredits FedRAMP 3PAOs with the FedRAMP PMO providing final approval. Please contact A2LA for more information on becoming an accredited FedRAMP 3PAO.

When is a 3PAO required? [6]

CSPs that go through FedRAMP must use a 3PAO to provide an independent verification and validation of the security implementations required by FedRAMP. FedRAMP provisional authorizations must include an assessment by a FedRAMP-accredited 3PAO to ensure a consistent assessment process.

Is the use of FedRAMP approved 3PAO require for assessment? [3]

A FedRAMP approved 3PAO is required for FedRAMP JAB P-ATO (Provisional *Authorization to* Operate) and CSP supplied packages, but is optional for FedRAMP Agency Authorization packages.

PREPARING FOR THE SECURITY ASSESSMENT

Security assessments can be a challenging, time-consuming, and costly activity if the security assessment customer does not appropriately plan and prepare for the security assessment activities. Even before selecting the security assessment provider, the security assessment customer needs to understand its objectives and the information needed to support decisions regarding the impact associated with using an information system. In addition, security assessments can become even more complex, specifically in multilevel or multiservice provider relationships, where security assessment activities may be distributed between more than one service provider. Therefore, more focus is required to be placed on the coordination activities, to ensure sufficient information is made available to the security assessor. This situation may also require either working through requests from the other service providers to participate in a security assessment of all of the security controls or to obtain the security assessment results[27] to be included within the current security assessment to inform the security assessment customer.

---

[27]*Depending* on the length of time between the last assessment and the current assessment, inheritance of assessment results could require additional time to ensure that the assessment results are still valid by validating the completeness, accuracy, and reliability.

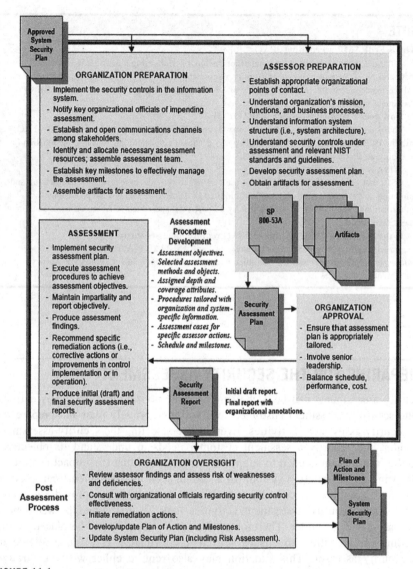

FIGURE 11.1

Security controls assessment overview [2].

From the initiation of the security assessment,[28] both parties' involvement is essential to ensure the preparatory (*pre-assessment*) activities conclude with an executable plan for the assessment. As illustrated in Fig. 11.1, the security assessment process requires the participation from both the assessment customer

---

[28]Process for determining how effectively an object of the assessment meets identified security objectives.

and the security assessment provider. During the security assessment,[29] the security assessment team will rely heavily on the participation and knowledge of the security assessment customer to ensure that there is an impartial and objective report of the security control effectiveness, and also a quality assessment, which provides key information needed for decision-makers. This information includes details about the deficiencies and weaknesses that, if compromised (i.e., security controls designed to assure the level of confidentiality, integrity, and availability), could impact mission and business functions supported through the use of the information system. After the security assessment (*post-assessment*), the SAR is generated to build an assurance case.[30] The SAR provides a summary of the security-related information needed for establishing a credible, risk-based decision.

SECURITY ASSESSMENT CUSTOMER RESPONSIBILITIES

The customer of the security assessment plays an essential role in the proper planning of the security assessment activities. The security assessment customer is responsible for implementing the security controls, but also has the responsibility of appropriately selecting a qualified security assessment provider, and in determining the objective and scope of the security assessment. In parallel with the preparation activities, the security assessment customer should, at minimum, conduct its own security readiness review.[31] The security readiness review ensures that the appropriate security-related information has been organized in a manner that can be easily evaluated by the security assessor. The security assessor uses the security-related information to gain an understanding of the organization's mission and business functions, how those functions are supported by the information system, and how the security controls have been implemented to meet the minimum assurance requirements. The information provided by the security assessment customer should also include a description of any security

[29]From Joint Task Force Transformation Initiative, NIST Special Publication (SP) 800-53A Revision 4, Assessing Security and Privacy Controls in Federal Information Systems and Organizations. Maryland: National Institute of Standards and Technology; 2014. *"Security control assessments and privacy control assessments are not about checklists, simple pass-fail results, or generating paperwork to pass inspections or audits-rather, security controls assessments are the principle vehicle used to verify that the implementers and operators of the information system are meeting their state security goals and objectives."*

[30]From Joint Task Force Transformation Initiative, NIST Special Publication (SP) 800-53A Revision 4, Assessing Security and Privacy Controls in Federal Information Systems and Organizations. Maryland: National Institute of Standards and Technology; 2014. *"An assurance case is a body of evidence organized into an argument demonstrating that some claim about an information system holds (i.e. is assured)."*

[31]Appendix F of NIST Interagency Report (IR) 7328, *Security Assessment Provider Requirements and Customer Responsibilities*, provides a sample "Customer Readiness Review Checklist."

controls that have not been fully implemented or are planned to ensure the necessary scope is clearly understood for developing an effective security assessment plan (SAP).[32]

TIP

FedRAMP Readiness Process [7]

- The FedRAMP readiness process is used to determine a CSP's eligibility for the JAB Process Provisional Authorization process.
- To be eligible the CSP must:
  - Have an understanding of the FISMA and FedRAMP requirements and process.
  - Be able to commit the resources needed to complete a FedRAMP assessment.
  - Have the ability to implement the FedRAMP control baseline.
  - Meet FedRAMP requirements for the level of detail in documenting the control implementation.

Readiness Process Roles [7]

- CSP
  - Provide information about the cloud system, documentation, and make updates in response to comments from FedRAMP.
  - Learn about the FedRAMP process.
- FedRAMP Readiness and Development Team
  - Review incoming applications and initiates contact with CSPs.
  - Coordinate the readiness process.
  - Perform a completeness check and reviews the CSP's initial documentation.
  - Provide comments and feedback on documentation to the CSP.
  - Recommend to director or project manager of whether to kick-off the full FedRAMP assessment.
  - FedRAMP director/FedRAMP manager.
  - Make a final decision of whether the CSP starts the full FedRAMP assessment.

SELECTING A SECURITY ASSESSMENT PROVIDER

The security assessment customer must use its "best judgment" when selecting a security assessment provider to ensure that there is an adequate level of independence or there is no conflict of interest, and the security

---

[32]From Joint Task Force Transformation Initiative, NIST Special Publication (SP) 800-53A Revision 4, Assessing Security and Privacy Controls in Federal Information Systems and Organizations. Maryland: National Institute of Standards and Technology; 2014. *"The security assessment plan and privacy assessment plan provides the objectives for the security control assessment."*

assessment provider has the necessary technical expertise (i.e., knowledge,[33] skills,[34] and abilities[35]). The independence[36] is critical when multiple organizations are responsible for the security control implementations. Therefore, the security assessment customer should determine the most appropriate approach to ensure that there is a necessary separation[37] between the security assessment provider and those involved in the development, operations, and management of the information system. This is specifically important when the security assessment customer used a different security assessment provider to develop evidence that will be reused in the current security assessment, or uses the same provider for other security-related services such as implementing remediations/mitigations. In these situations, having the security assessment results reviewed by an independent expert could assist in verifying that they are accurate and complete to ensure they are still valid as an objective determination of the state of the security control implementation and effectiveness.

TIP

The FedRAMP 3PAO[38] program was established to accredit organizations based on establishing their ability to meet the requirements of ISO/IEC 17020:1998[39] and to demonstrate the technical

(Continued)

---

[33]From Dodaro, G. Federal Information Systems Control Audit Manual: Volume I—Financial Statement Audits. Washington, DC: US Government Accountability Office; 1999. *"Organized body of information, facts, principles, or procedures."*

[34]From Dodaro, G. Federal Information Systems Control Audit Manual: Volume I—Financial Statement Audits. Washington, DC: US Government Accountability Office; 1999. *"Demonstrable and implies a degree of proficiency."*

[35]From Metheny, M. FedRAMP 3PAO Program—Have We Heard of This Idea Before? [Internet]. Florida: International Information Systems Security Certification Consortium (ISC)2 Blog [cited April 22, 2012]. Available from: http://blog.isc2.org/isc2_blog/2012/04/fedramp-3pao-program-have-we-heard-of-this-idea-before.html. *"An ability is the power to perform a job function while applying or using the essential knowledge."*

[36]FISMA requires audits to be performed annually through an independent evaluation.

[37]From Government Auditing Standards [Internet]. Washington, DC: US Government Accountability Office [cited April 12, 2012]. Available from: http://www.gao.gov/govaud/govaudhtml/index.html. *"Audit organizations that provide nonaudit services must evaluate whether providing the services creates an independence impairment either in fact or appearance with respect to entities they audit."*

[38]From Federal Risk and Authorization Management Program (FedRAMP) [Internet]. Washington, DC: US General Services Administration [cited April 16, 2012]. Available from: https://www.fedramp.gov/marketplace/accredited-3paos. *"Accredited independent assessors—Third Party Assessment Organizations (3PAOs) have demonstrated independence and technical competency required to test security implementations and collect representative evidence."*

[39]General criteria for the operation of various types of bodies performing inspections—superseded by ISO/IEC 17020:2012.

412 **CHAPTER 11** Security assessment and authorization

> ## TIP (CONTINUED)
>
> competence[40] necessary for conducting security assessment of cloud services. The goal of the conformity assessment[41] process is to ensure the qualified 3PAO:
>
> - Uses a methodology that is aligned with the NIST standards and processes for ensuring that cloud services meet the federal government's minimum security requirements.
> - Applies a consistent and standardized process for conducting security assessments.

Security Assessment Planning

The security assessment customer also plays a central role in ensuring that the security assessment is conducted effectively and efficiently. In its role, the security assessment customer must ensure that it is not only ready for the security assessment by performing its own readiness review, but it also needs to provide the necessary information (e.g., evidence of prior assessments and artifacts describing security control implementation) and make the resources (e.g., information system access and knowledgeable personnel) available to support the security assessment. The security-relevant information helps security assessors understand the scope of the information system and the security controls being assessed. The more complete and accurate the information, the more tailored the security assessor can make the SAP and supporting assessment procedures. Therefore, prior to the security assessment, the security assessment customer should identify the scope of the assessment and the system components that will be the target of the security assessment. For example, scoping the security assessment could include identifying the number and types of components (i.e., a homogeneous environment that has been consistently configured generally may require less depth or coverage) and determining resource requirements (i.e., accessibility/complexity of the operating environment and use of automated tools versus manual evaluation or inspections techniques).

After the scoping has been completed, the security assessment customer should focus on gathering the security-relevant information for the security assessment provider to evaluate so that a realistic schedule can be developed for conducting the security assessment. Security-relevant information gathered and

---

[40]From Metheny, M. FedRAMP 3PAO Program—Have We Heard of This Idea Before? [Internet]. Florida: International Information Systems Security Certification Consortium (ISC)2 Blog [cited April 22, 2012]. Available from: http://blog.isc2.org/isc2_blog/2012/04/fedramp-3pao-program-have-we-heard-of-this-idea-before.html. *"An assessor requires more than pure security knowledge, but also a supplemental knowledge of cloud computing."*

[41]From FedRAMP Program Management Office (PMO). FedRAMP Concept of Operations (CONOPS) Version 1.1. Washington, DC: US General Services Administration; 2012. *"A methodology to demonstrate capability in meeting requirements relating to a product, process, system, person or body as defined by ISO/IEC 17020."*

provided during the security assessment planning can include the following types of information:

- Organizational and system-specific security policies and procedures.
- Descriptions of security control implementation and roles and responsibilities for security controls (e.g., system security plan, standard operating procedures, system diagrams, design documents service level agreements, interconnection agreements, contracts, accreditation packages for common controls, etc.).
- Documents that were developed in support of security control implementation (e.g., contingency plan, risk assessments, incident response plans, plan of action, milestones, etc.).
- Any extracts from the information system (e.g., audit logs, configuration settings, firewall and intrusion detection/prevention rulesets,[42] evidence generated from previous security assessments, etc.).
- Inventories and hardware/software specifications.

> **TIP**
>
> The Cloud Security Alliance (CSA) CloudAudit[43] is an example of the type of framework that could be used by security assessment customers and leveraged to automate the collection of information (i.e., assertions and artifacts) needed to support a security assessment. "The goal of CloudAudit was to provide a common interface and namespace that allows enterprises who are interested in streamlining their audit processes (cloud or otherwise) as well as cloud computing providers to automate the Audit, Assertion, Assessment, and Assurance of their infrastructure (IaaS), platform (PaaS), and application (SaaS) environments and allow authorized consumers of their services to do likewise via an open, extensible and secure interface and methodology." [8]

During the security assessment, the security assessor may require assistance from security assessment customer personnel who may have knowledge about how security controls are managed or were integrated into the information system and the operational environment. The security assessment customer should make available key personnel who would need to be interviewed or participate (i.e., conducting security testing) in the security assessment. Depending on the scope of the assessment, coordination and collaboration may be required to limit impacts on the security assessment customer's ongoing operations or existing customers that rely on the services provided by the target information system. Therefore, participation by the security assessment customer is essential to ensure

---

[42]From Scarfone, K., Souppaya, M., Cody, A., Orebaugh, A. NIST Special Publication (SP) 800-115, Technical Guide to Information Security Testing and Assessment. Maryland: National Institute of Standards and Technology; 2008. *"A ruleset is a collection of rules or signatures that network traffic or system activity is compared against to determine what action to take."*

[43]From CoudAudit [Internet]. Washington, DC: Cloud Security Alliance [cited August 26, 2012]. Available from: https://cloudsecurityalliance.org/group/cloudaudit/. *"The goal of CloudAudit is to provide a common interface and namespace that allows enterprises who are interested in streamlining their audit processes (cloud or otherwise)."*

that security assessment activities being performed in support of the security assessment are aligned with the agreed-to schedule and milestones.

SECURITY ASSESSMENT PROVIDER RESPONSIBILITIES

The security assessment provider should have a management structure that can deliver a quality security assessment and the technical capabilities to effectively execute the given security assessment. The results of the security assessment execution should provide key decision-makers within the security assessment customer organization (or organizational official(s) that are responsible for making the authorization decision[44]) with the needed security-related information (and supporting evidence) to make a credible, risk-based decision. These security assessment results are compiled by the security assessment provider through the execution of a variety of methods[45] and techniques and supported by the management structure[46] and operational/management systems to ensure the consistency and reliability of the security assessment process, and the quality, accuracy, and completeness of the security-related information.

> **NOTE**
>
> 3PAO accreditation[47] by FedRAMP includes an assessment by the A2LA.[48] A2LA performs an initial assessment of each 3PAO required for accreditation by FedRAMP, a yearly surveillance, and a full re-assessment every two years for continued accreditation.
>
> *(Continued)*

[44]From Joint Task Force Transformation Initiative Interagency Working Group. NIST Special Publication (SP) 800-37 Revision 1, Guide for Applying the Risk Management Framework to Federal Information Systems: A Security Life Cycle Approach. Maryland: National Institute of Standards and Technology; 2010. *"The authorization decision document conveys the final security authorization decision from the authorizing official to the information system owner or common control provider, and other organizational officials, as appropriate. The authorization decision document contains the following information: (i) authorization decision; (ii) terms and conditions for the authorization; and (iii) authorization termination date. The security authorization decision indicates to the information system owner whether the system is: (i) authorized to operate; or (ii) not authorized to operate. The terms and conditions for the authorization provide a description of any specific limitations or restrictions placed on the operation of the information system or inherited controls that must be followed by the system owner or common control provider. The authorization termination date, established by the authorizing official, indicates when the security authorization expires."*

[45]Assessment methods include testing (exercising an assessment object to compare results—expected vs actual), examining (process used to facilitate understanding how a security control is implemented by examining an assessment object), and interviewing (process used to facilitate understanding how a security control is implemented by conducting interview with organizational personnel).

[46]A framework for managing, planning, and assuring the quality of the assessment.

[47]A list of accredited 3PAOs can be found at: https://www.fedramp.gov/marketplace/accredited-3paos/

[48]Available from: http://www.a2la.org/appsweb/fedramp.cfm

NOTE (CONTINUED)

The A2LA assessment ensures that 3PAOs meet the FedRAMP requirements of ISO 17020 (as revised) and FedRAMP specific knowledge requirements related to the FedRAMP Security Assessment Framework. The A2LA provides an assessment report to FedRAMP that documents the 3PAO:

- Is competent to perform inspections of CSP documents
- Has a documented and fully operational quality system
- Quality system meets the standards of ISO/IEC 17020-2012
- Is operating in accordance with its quality system A2LA also assesses 3PAOs with specific FedRAMP and FISMA knowledge.

A 3PAO must demonstrate technical competence through reviews of System Security Plans, creation of an SAP, and documenting the results in Security Assessment Test Cases as well as a Security Assessment Report. [9]

FedRAMP 3PAOs must maintain a management system and technical competence and capability to ensure assessment of cloud services are performed consistently and in compliance with the FedRAMP requirements. The FedRAMP management and technical requirements are summarized as follows:

Management Requirements [10]:

- Conducting inspections and maintain a quality management system in accordance with ISO/IEC 17020.
- Ensuring that the security assessment team members are competent in performing security assessments.
- Ensuring the protection of proprietary information received as part of the assessment.

Technical Requirements [10]:

- Maintaining knowledge, understanding, and competency in the application of the FedRAMP program security assessment standards, guidelines, and requirements and cloud-based information system-related technologies and practices.
- Maintaining knowledge and understanding in the use of NIST publications and programs.
- Selecting personnel that collectively have the relevant knowledge, skills, and abilities for conducting a security assessment on a given cloud-based information system.
- Preparing an SAP consistent with the FedRAMP requirement, including reviewing the SAP with the cloud service provider.
- Conducting a security assessment with the SAP and preparing a SAR consistent with the FedRAMP requirements.

The requirements established by the FedRAMP PMO ensure that the resulting security assessment results and supporting evidence can be leveraged by multiple federal agencies through a single FedRAMP security authorization package.

Selection of Security Assessment Team Members

Similar to the security assessment customer role of selecting a security assessment provider, the security assessment provider has an obligation of conducting due diligence when selecting team members who have the knowledge and expertise in conducting an assessment of the target information system, including experience with the technologies, and also familiarity with the applicable governing federal information security laws, directives, policies, standards, and guidelines.[49]

Developing the Security Assessment Plan

The SAP provides the roadmap for executing the security assessment. In the SAP, the rules[50] by which the security assessment provider conducts the security assessment are documented to ensure the security assessment customer understands and agrees to the scope of the assessment and also the types of activities that will be performed. The SAP could also include any applicable assumptions and legal considerations (i.e., limitations of liability or nondisclosures to protect both the security assessment customer should any significant issues that occur during or after the assessment). Although the primary responsibility for the development of the SAP is usually the security assessment provider, it should be developed in collaboration with the security assessment customer to ensure the following key points are covered:

- *Scope*—number of components and locations, the types of assessment (or objective), and the depth/coverage.
- *Authorizations*—networks and systems identified by IP address or range and hostname.
- *Logistics*—resource requirements, availability of the location and environment, and testing tools.
- *Data handling*—storage and physical/logical safeguards for data stored at-rest and during transmission, and destruction/sanitization of data after the assessment.
- *Incident response*—definition of the incident and actions that should be taken or guidelines that should be followed by all parties.

The development of the SAP also requires completing several steps to address the key points are covered either within the SAP directly or referenced externally in other contractual documents (e.g., authorization memorandum, engagement or arrangement letter, service agreement, rules of engagement (ROE), service contracts, etc.).

Identify In-Scope Security Controls

The security assessor in the development of the SAP must first consider the type of assessment, complete or partial, and the security controls described in the system security plan (SSP), in-place or planned, for meeting the security

---

[49]As an example, the (ISC)^2 Certified Authorization Professional (CAP) certification can assist in selected qualified security assessors by measuring their knowledge, skills, abilities, and experience with the NIST Risk Management Framework (RMF).

[50]From Scarfone, K., Souppaya, M., Cody, A., Orebaugh, A. NIST Special Publication (SP) 800-115, Technical Guide to Information Security Testing and Assessment. Maryland: National Institute of Standards and Technology; 2008. *"Detailed guidelines and constraints regarding the execution of information security testing."*

assessment customer's security requirements. A *complete assessment* is usually performed during the initial authorization or where significant changes have occurred and the scope of the changes cannot be isolated to a specific set of controls and therefore all security controls will be in-scope for the security assessment. A *partial assessment* only focuses on a subset of security controls. The subset of security controls can be those selected as part of the continuous (or ongoing) monitoring activities, security testing performed as part of the normal SDLC, which includes assessing a specific set of security controls implemented within the change control process (assuming the scope of the change can be bounded), or where previous assessments occurred and were leveraged, but additional security controls were included to supplement the security control baseline to address unique organizational security requirements. After the purpose of the security assessment has been determined, the SSP and the continuous monitoring strategy[51] are reviewed to select the security controls that would be considered in-scope for the assessment and be used for the remainder of the steps in the SAP development.

Select Assessment Procedures

The security controls identified in the previous step are used by the security assessment provider in selecting the initial set of security assessment procedures.[52] Assessment procedures provide a framework for building assurance cases by demonstrating the effectiveness of security controls implemented within the current operating environment. For each security control selected in the SSP, a complementary assessment procedure is selected. For example, Table 11.1 provides the assessment procedure for CA-2 (*Security Assessment*).

Assessment procedures include one or more objectives for the assessment. The assessment objectives consist of a series of determination statements,[53] which map to the functionality of the security control and assist the security assessor in demonstrating the extent to which a security control is implemented correctly, operates as intended, and produces the desired outcome. In addition, within each assessment objective, methods and objects are used by the security assessment

---

[51]Continuous Monitoring is discussed in detailed in Chapter 12, Strategies for Continuous Monitoring.

[52]NIST Special Publication (SP) 800-53A Revision 4, Appendix F contains a catalog of assessment procedures that are used as a starting point for further tailoring and supplementation.

[53]From Joint Task Force Transformation Initiative, NIST Special Publication (SP) 800-53A Revision 4, Assessing Security and Privacy Controls in Federal Information Systems and Organizations. Maryland: National Institute of Standards and Technology; 2014. *"The determination statements are linked to the content of the security control (i.e. the security control functionality) to ensure traceability of assessment results back to the fundamental control requirements."*

Table 11.1 Example Assessment Procedure

CA-2	Security Assessment		
Assessment Objective: Determine if the organization:			
CA-2(a)	develops a security assessment plan that describes the scope of the assessment including:		
	CA-2(a)(1)	security controls and control enhancements under assessment;	
	CA-2(a)(2)	assessment procedures to be used to determine security control effectiveness;	
	CA-2(a)(3)	CA-2(a)(3)[1]	assessment environment;
		CA-2(a)(3)[2]	assessment team;
		CA-2(a)(3)[3]	assessment roles and responsibilities;
CA-2(b)	CA-2(b)[1]	defines the frequency to assess the security controls in the information system and its environment of operation;	
	CA-2(b)[2]	assesses the security controls in the information system with the organization-defined frequency to determine the extent to which the controls are implemented correctly, operating as intended, and producing the desired outcome with respect to meeting established security requirements;	
CA-2(c)	produces a security assessment report that documents the results of the assessment;		
CA-2(d)	CA-2(d)[1]	defines individuals or roles to whom the results of the security control assessment are to be provided; and	
	CA-2(d)[2]	provides the results of the security control assessment to organization-defined individuals or roles.	

Potential Assessment Methods and Objects:

Examine: [Select from: Security assessment and authorization policy; procedures addressing security assessment planning; procedures addressing security assessments; security assessment plan; other relevant documents or records].

Interview: [Select from: Organizational personnel with security assessment responsibilities; organizational personnel with information security responsibilities].

Test: [Select from: Automated mechanisms supporting security assessment, security assessment plan development, and/or security assessment reporting].

provider during the security assessment. The assessment methods[54] and objects[55] together define the specific actions taken and items selected by the security assessor to produce a finding (or determination of effectiveness) for the security assessment. In Table 11.1, the assessment method for the CA-2 assessment objective contains three different types of assessment methods, *examine, interview,* and *test.* The security assessor can use one or all methods to make a determination if the assessment objective is achieved. For the examination assessment method, the security assessor can choose from the identified assessment objects (or other objects not included on the list) to produce the necessary information for the assessor to make a determination of the assessment objective.

TIP

Assessment procedures can form the basis for developing assessment cases.[56] Assessment cases provide a tool for security assessment customers (e.g., federal agency, CSP, communities of interest, etc.) by providing a specific set of assessor actions. The assessment cases represent the specific viewpoint of the community that developed them and present the necessary actions that should be taken to cost-effectively conduct the security assessment. Similar to the security control selection process,[57] tailoring and supplementation is applied to the baseline assessment cases.

Tailor Assessment Procedures

Assessment tailoring involves customizing the assessment procedure to more closely reflect the characteristics of the information system and the operating environment. Customization may be conducted at the organizational level, information system level, or both. The goal of tailoring assessment procedures is to produce the most accurate representation of the security assessment actions necessary to make a determination in the most cost-effective manner. Some assessment procedures may require more tailoring than others or, depending on the phase of the SDLC in which the security assessment is being performed, the assessment procedures may be tailored to focus on a specific aspect of the

---

[54]From Joint Task Force Transformation Initiative, NIST Special Publication (SP) 800-53A Revision 4, Assessing Security and Privacy Controls in Federal *Information* Systems and Organizations. Maryland: National Institute of Standards and Technology; 2014. *"Similar to the security control selection process, tailoring and supplementation is applied to the baseline assessment cases."*

[55]From Joint Task Force Transformation Initiative, NIST Special Publication (SP) 800-53A Revision 4, Assessing Security and Privacy Controls in Federal *Information* Systems and Organizations. Maryland: National Institute of Standards and Technology; 2014. *"The item (i.e. specifications, mechanisms, activities, individuals) upon which an assessment method is applied during an assessment."*

[56]NIST *Special* Publication (SP) 800-53A Revision 4, Appendix H contains more information on Assessment Cases.

[57]NIST RMF Step 2 (*Security* Control *Selection*) was discussed in detail in Chapter 5, Applying the Risk Management Framework.

information system. For example, security assessments conducted during the development/acquisition phase can be tailored to focus on testing very specific functionality to identify deficiencies or weaknesses that may be more costly to remediate in later phases of the SDLC process.

Tailoring involves applying considerations[58] to help guide the selection of potential activities focused on during the assessment. The security assessment customer may provide guidance to assist the security assessor in determining the level of the assessment tailoring that is appropriate for the given assessment.

The level of tailoring could also depend on factors such as the available timing and scope for the security assessment. In this chapter, we will only focus on two of the tailoring considerations:

- Selecting assessment methods and objects.
- Selecting depth and coverage attributes.

Selecting Assessment Methods and Objects

Security assessors have various options available when selecting assessment methods and objects. Each assessment procedure provides potential options. However, assessors are not necessarily limited to those included in the baseline assessment procedures to obtain the evidence needed to support the determination of security control effectiveness. The actions performed by the security assessors and the types of objects selected for the assessment can be obtained by reviewing the information provided by the security assessment customer as part of the preparatory activities. For example, the SSP and supporting artifacts provided to the security assessors could provide valuable insight into how a particular security control was implemented and what types of methods (e.g., examine, interview, and test) and objects (e.g., specifications, mechanisms, activities, and individuals) would be required for producing evidence and a determination of security control effectiveness.

Selecting Depth and Coverage Attributes

Security assessors also have options for defining the depth and coverage of assessment procedures. The depth and coverage attributes[59] represent the rigor and scope of the assessment and impact the level of effort required for conducting the security assessment. The more detailed the assessment activities, the more resource-intensive and time-consuming. However, the more detailed the security assessment, the greater the level of assurance that a particular security control implemented within the information system meets the required

---

[58]NIST Special Publication (SP) 800-53A Revision 4, Section 3.2.3 contains a list of consideration for tailoring assessment procedures that could include: (1) selecting assessment method and object, (2) selecting depth and coverage attribute values, (3) identifying common controls, (4) developing information system/platform-specific and organization-specific assessments, (5) incorporating assessment results from previous *assessments*, and (6) obtaining evidence from external providers.
[59]Basic, focused, and comprehensive.

security objectives. Although not specifically identifiable[60] in assessment procedures like the methods and objects, the depth and coverage become important factors when building the assurance case during the security assessment execution.

Supplementing Assessment Procedures

The security assessment provider may need to supplement the assessment procedures where security controls unique to an organization or information system do not exist in the baseline security controls (or the assessment procedures do not exist). This could occur where the organization has supplemented the baseline security controls to adequately mitigate organizational-specific risks. In this situation, the additional security controls documented in the SSP would require the security assessor in collaboration with the security assessment customer to develop new assessment procedures.

Optimize Assessment Procedures

Optimizing security assessments involves the consolidation or sequencing of assessment procedures to reduce the cost of an associated security assessment. In this activity, the security assessor organizes the assessment procedures in the most efficient way that would enable executing assessment methods and selecting the assessment objects in a manner most likely to produce the desired evidence. For example, some assessment procedures may focus on different aspects of the same control, or different security controls may be integrated into the same components or be related. Therefore, sequencing assessment procedures may facilitate efficiency and reuse of security assessment results.

Finalize and Approve Assessment Plan

Once the SAP has been completed and the assessment procedures have been selected, tailored, and optimized, the security assessment provider must obtain approval from the security assessment customer. This approval acknowledges acceptance and gives the security assessor permission to begin executing the SAP in accordance with the schedule and milestones.

EXECUTING THE SECURITY ASSESSMENT PLAN

The formal approval of the SAP gives the security assessment provider the authorization to begin conducting the security assessment. The SAP utilizes a

---

[60]NIST Special Publication (SP) 800-53A Revision 4, Appendix D contains detailed information on the depth and coverage. In addition, examples of how *depth* and coverage are applied are shown in the "Potential Assessors Evidence Gathering Actions" in NIST Special Publication (SP) 800-53A Revision 4, Appendix H.

variety of methods, techniques, and tools during the course of executing the assessment procedures. The assessment procedures provide the necessary information for determining the depth and scope, and will enable the security assessor to select the appropriate testing methodology for the particular type of security assessment. For example, where the security assessment requires conducting penetration testing,[61] the security assessor usually focuses on a scoped and controlled set of components that attempt to identify an attacker (or class of attackers). Since the attackers must operate under constraints, the characterization of the attacker and the tools and techniques[62] will be very specialized to the assessment procedure being executed.

TIP

The FedRAMP Security Controls Baseline for Moderate-Impact cloud services requires the CSP in CA-7 (*Continuous Monitoring*) to plan, schedule, and conduct assessments annually that include unannounced penetration testing and in-depth monitoring to ensure compliance with all vulnerability mitigation plans [11]. In addition, in RA-5 (*Vulnerability Scanning*), the CSP is required to employ an independent penetration agent or penetration team to conduct a vulnerability analysis, perform penetration testing based on the analysis of the vulnerabilities to determine their exploitability[63] [11].

The assessment procedures for CA and RA will likely evaluate compliance of the CSP by examining the risk assessment and security assessment policies and procedure, the continuous monitoring plan, vulnerability scan results, and records of vulnerability mitigations and penetration to determine if the CSP, given the existing vulnerabilities within the cloud service, conducted penetration testing (where applicable). The security assessor could conduct formal interviews with CSP personnel that would have the role and responsibility for coordinating and supporting penetration testing, and ensuring the testing was conducted in accordance with the vulnerability mitigation procedures.

During the security assessment, results are produced and documented through actions associated with each assessment objective where selected methods and objects were applied. The security assessment results establish a conclusion about the determination of whether the objectives for the security control have been achieved. The evidence to support the determination is

---

[61]From Joint Task Force Transformation Initiative, NIST Special Publication (SP) 800-53A Revision 4, Assessing Security and Privacy Controls in Federal Information Systems and Organizations. Maryland: National Institute of Standards and Technology; 2014. "*A test methodology in which assessors, using all available documentation (e.g. system design, source code, manuals) and working under specific constraints, attempt to circumvent the security features of an information system.*"
[62]The Penetration Testing Execution Standard (PTES) Technical Guidelines is an example resource that assists in developing procedures when conducting penetration testing. Available from: http://www.pentest-standard.org/index.php/PTES_Technical_Guidelines.
[63]Chapter 10 discussed the FedRAMP requirements for Vulnerability Scanning and Penetration Testing.

collected and a summary is documented by the security assessor that provides the basis for the finding. Since the findings are meant to be unbiased and objective, the security assessor must present in detail the rationale for why a particular assessment objective was documented as either satisfied (S) or other than satisfied (O).[64] The rationale for establishing an "O" finding may be due to issues other than the security control ineffectiveness. The other issues could include the inability of the security assessor to make a determination where information was insufficient or the unavailability of a particular information system component under examination that was needed for making the determination.

For the security assessment results produced, the security assessment customer should review the findings with specific emphasis on those determinations that result in an "O" finding to determine the significance and to assist in prioritizing findings when developing corrective actions based on the recommendations provided by the security assessor. In addition, the review of the findings may also give an indication that there was a lack of understanding by the security assessor of how the security controls were implemented in the SSP and the security assessment customer may need to provide further clarification to ensure that the most accurate reflection of the effectiveness of the security controls is documented in the SAR.

SUMMARY

This chapter provided an introduction to the application of the NIST RMF security assessment process. A three-step framework was presented that covered governing the assessment, preparing for the assessment, and executing the assessment. Additionally, the roles and responsibilities for the security assessment provider and security assessment customer were discussed as they relate to the assessment framework. Finally, the assessment process was covered to address specific factors at each stage of the assessment, to include planning the assessment, executing the assessment, and reporting the security assessment results.

---

[64]From Joint Task Force Transformation Initiative, NIST Special Publication (SP) 800-53A Revision 4, Assessing Security and Privacy Controls in Federal Information Systems and Organizations. Maryland: National Institute of Standards and Technology; 2014. *"For each finding of other than satisfied, assessors indicate which parts of the security control are affected by the finding (i.e. aspects of the control that were deemed not satisfied or were not able to be assessed) and describe how the control differs from the planned or expected state."*

REFERENCES

[1] Scarfone K, Souppaya M, Cody A, Orebaugh A. NIST Special Publication (SP) 800-115, Technical Guide to Information Security Testing and Assessment. Maryland: National Institute of Standards and Technology; 2008.

[2] Joint Task Force Transformation Initiative. NIST Special Publication (SP) 800-53A Revision 1, Guide for assessing the security controls in federal information systems and organizations. Maryland: National Institute of Standards and Technology; 2010.

[3] FedRAMP Frequently Asked Questions (FAQs) [Internet]. Washington, DC: US General Services Administration [cited May 2, 2016]. Available from: https://www.fedramp.gov/resources/faqs/.

[4] VanRoekel S. Office of Management and Budget (OMB) Memorandum, Security Authorization of Information System in Cloud Computing Environments. Washington, DC: Executive Office of the President, Office of Management and Budget; 2011.

[5] VanRoekel S. Office of Management and Budget (OMB) Memorandum, Security Authorization of Information System in Cloud Computing Environments. Washington, DC: Executive Office of the President, Office of Management and Budget; 2011.

[6] FedRAMP Frequently Asked Questions (FAQs) [Internet]. Washington. DC: US General Services Administration [cited August 28, 2012]. Available from: http://www.gsa.gov/portal/category/102439.

[7] FedRAMP Process for Determining Readiness of a CSP [Internet]. Washington, DC: US General Services Administration [cited September 8, 2016]. Available from: https://www.fedramp.gov/files/2015/03/Quick-Guide-to-The-FedRAMP-Readiness-Process-08152014.pptx.

[8] CloudAudit Working Group [Internet]. Washington, DC: Cloud Security Alliance [cited June 25, 2016]. <https://cloudsecurityalliance.org/group/cloudaudit/>.

[9] FedRAMP Program Management Office (PMO). FedRAMP 3PAO Obligation and Performance Guide Version 1.0. Washington, DC: US General Services Administration; 2015.

[10] FedRAMP 3PAO Application [Internet]. Washington, DC: US General Services Administration [cited April 11, 2012]. <http://www.gsa.gov/graphics/staffoffices/FedRAMP_3PAO_Application_Materials_010412_Final.zip>.

[11] FedRAMP Security Controls [Internet]. Washington, DC: US General Services Administration [cited April 14, 2012]. <https://www.fedramp.gov/resources/documents-2016/>.

Strategies for continuous monitoring

12

INFORMATION IN THIS CHAPTER:

- Introduction to Continuous Monitoring
- The Continuous Monitoring Process
- Continuous Monitoring within FedRAMP

INTRODUCTION TO CONTINUOUS MONITORING

Continuous[1] monitoring (CM)[2] is an organizational-wide activity that supports risk management by enabling an organization to understand and maintain its information security and risk posture through the collection, analysis, monitoring, and reporting of security-related information. To be effective, CM needs to be driven by the organization's management to ensure that it is managed as a part of the enterprise-wide risk management activity. This ensures that monitoring is considered outside the context of a single information system, but rather as an integrated part of the organization's risk management function. CM begins by defining the CM strategy. The CM strategy links to the organizational strategies, goals, and objectives, and ensures that there is a common understanding of organizational-wide risk tolerance. The risk tolerance is used when determining how to develop and execute a CM program that includes tasks[3] such as *collecting*

---

[1]From Dempsey, K., Nirali, C., Johnson, A., Johnston, R., Jones, A., Orebaugh, A., et al. NIST Special Publication (SP) 800-137, Information Security Continuous Monitoring (ISCM) for Federal Information Systems and Organizations. Maryland: National Institute of Standards and Technology; 2011. *"Security controls and organizational risks are assessed and analyzed at a frequency sufficient to support risk-based security decisions to adequately protect organization information."*

[2]From Dempsey, K., Nirali, C., Johnson, A., Johnston, R., Jones, A., Orebaugh, A., et al. NIST Special Publication (SP) 800-137, Information Security Continuous Monitoring (ISCM) for Federal Information Systems and Organizations. Maryland: National Institute of Standards and Technology; 2011. *"Information security monitoring (ISCM) is defined as maintaining ongoing awareness of information security, vulnerability, and threats to support organization risk management decisions."*

[3]Note, this is not a complete list of activities that can be included within an organization's continuous monitoring program needed to maintain a situational awareness of the information system and operating environment.

Federal Cloud Computing. DOI: http://dx.doi.org/10.1016/B978-0-12-809710-6.00012-3

and reporting on metrics, conducting and reporting security control assessments, planning, controlling, and maintaining change management and configuration control, conducting risk assessments and prioritizing risk responses.

> **NOTE**
>
> CM is not necessarily a new requirement for the federal government. Historically, as far back as 1995, the National Institute of Standards and Technology (NIST) introduced the concept, as one of two activities[4] used to support operational assurance.[5] At that time, monitoring was simply defined as an "ongoing activity that checks on the system, its users, or the environment" [1]. In 1996, Office of Management and Budget (OMB) Circular A-130, Appendix III,[6] a government-wide policy was established for federal agencies to review security controls on an ongoing basis through the use of technical tools and techniques.[7] The Federal Information Security Management Act (FISMA) codified CM, by requiring federal agencies to monitor, test, and evaluate information security controls. However, it was not until the publication of the first revision of NIST SP 800-37 that the federal agencies had a systematic model for applying CM within the context of the System Development Life Cycle (SDLC). The NIST security certification and accreditation (C&A) process introduced CM in the fourth phase.[8]
>
> NIST further published CM guidance in NIST SP 800-137[9] to address assessment and analysis of security control effectiveness and of organizational security status in accordance with organizational risk tolerance. [2] This guidance was established in government-wide policy[10] in the most recent revised version of OMB Circular A-130.[11]

[4]The difference between system audits and monitoring focused on the notion of "real time."

[5]From Guttman, B., Rockback, E. NIST Special Publication (SP) 800-12, An Introduction to Computer Security: The NIST Handbook. Maryland: National Institute of Standards and Technology; 1995. *"Operational assurance is the process of reviewing an operational system to see that the security controls, both automated and manual, are functioning correctly and effectively."*

[6]*Office of Management and Budget (OMB) Circular A-130*, Appendix III. Available from: https://www.whitehouse.gov/sites/default/files/omb/assets/omb/circulars/a130/a130trans4.pdf.

[7]From Office of Management and Budget (OMB). OMB Memorandum Circular A-130, Appendix III, Security of Federal Automated Information Resources. Washington: Executive Office of the President, Office of Management and Budget; 2000. *"Example included virus scanners, vulnerability assessment products, and penetration testing."*

[8]The CM program addressed three tasks: *configuration management and control, security control monitoring, and status reporting and documentation.*

[9]Information Security Continuous Monitoring (ISCM) for Federal Information Systems and Organizations. Available from: http://nvlpubs.nist.gov/nistpubs/Legacy/SP/nistspecialpublication800-137.pdf.

[10]Office of Management and Budget (OMB). OMB A-130, Managing Federal Information as a Strategic Resource. Washington, DC: Executive Office of the President, Office of Management and Budget; 2016. *"Agencies must develop ISCM strategy and implement ISCM activities in accordance with applicable statutes, directives, policies, instructions, regulations, standards, and guidelines. The ISCM strategies must document all available security and privacy controls selected and implemented by agencies, including the frequency of and degree of rigor associated with the monitoring process."*

[11]*Managing Federal Information as a Strategic Resource.* Available from: https://www.whitehouse.gov/sites/default/files/omb/assets/OMB/circulars/a130/a130revised.pdf.

The broader CM activity within an organization is implemented through the execution of three major foundational elements:

- Organizational governance.
- CM strategy.
- CM program.

These elements operate together to ensure that CM is conducted as an organizational-wide activity that includes the participation from both those responsible for defining the strategy for the organization and those responsible for the day-to-day management and monitoring of information systems. A common CM approach across the organization enables each level of the organization to more effectively communicate and share information that would support a cost-efficient, resilient, and timely[12] risk management strategy. The increasing reliance on information technology (IT) for supporting the organization's mission and as a critical part of its business operations requires accurate and up-to-date information for making continuous risk-based decisions. Using a standardized CM approach enables the security- and risk-related information to be produced both cost-effectively and efficiently through a managed set of resources and processes.

ORGANIZATIONAL GOVERNANCE

The management of risk requires a "top-down" approach, led by management, with the establishment of the CM strategy. The CM strategy, as illustrated in Fig. 12.1, is implemented through a comprehensive CM program.

The role of governance[13] is to ensure that the CM strategy is consistently applied through a CM program across the organization. The process for implementing CM, briefly introduced in this section and discussed in detail later in this chapter, requires an effective integration into the organization's governance structure. Governance manages the CM strategy and program through the CM processes, which include:

- Defining a strategy for continuous monitoring;
- Developing and implementing a CM program;
- Analyzing data and reporting findings;

---

[12]From Dempsey, K., Nirali, C., Johnson, A., Johnston, R., Jones, A., Orebaugh, A., et al. NIST Special Publication (SP) 800-137, Information Security Continuous Monitoring (ISCM) for Federal Information Systems and Organizations. Maryland: National Institute of Standards and Technology; 2011. "*Risk management decisions, assessment and responses need to be able to scale with emerging security issues, and any decision-making needs to be based on the most relevant and accurate information.*"

[13]Governance models are discussed in detail in Chapter 6, Risk Management.

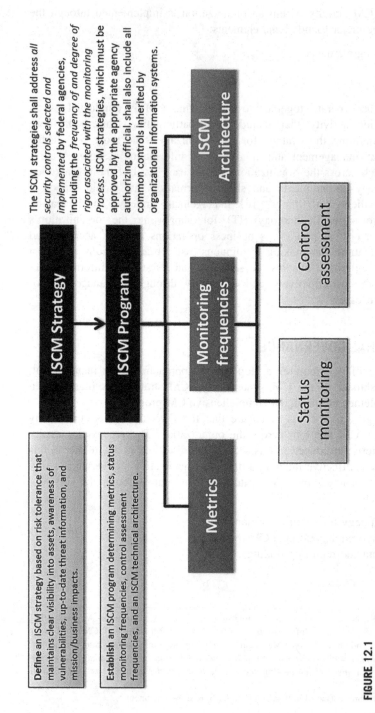

The ISCM strategies shall address *all security controls selected and implemented* by federal agencies, including the *frequency of and degree of rigor associated with the monitoring Process.* ISCM strategies, which must be approved by the appropriate agency authorizing official, shall also include all common controls inherited by organizational information systems.

ISCM Strategy

ISCM Program

ISCM Architecture

Monitoring frequencies

Control assessment

Status monitoring

Metrics

Define an ISCM strategy based on risk tolerance that maintains clear visibility into assets, awareness of vulnerabilities, up-to-date threat information, and mission/business impacts.

Establish an ISCM program determining metrics, status monitoring frequencies, control assessment frequencies, and an ISCM technical architecture.

FIGURE 12.1

ISCM program components.

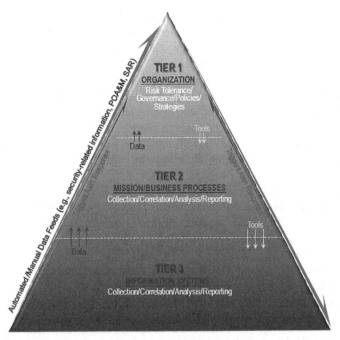

FIGURE 12.2

Organization-wide view of CM [2].

- Responding to findings; and
- Reviewing and updating[14] the Information Security Continuous Monitoring (ISCM) strategy and program [2].

In Fig. 12.2, the organization-wide view focuses on illustrating how CM supports the risk-based decisions made at the various levels within an organization. In the three-tiered model, tier 1 focuses on strategic CM activities that support governance[15] decisions based on security-related information from the implementation of CM activities at tiers 2 and 3. The model also represents the alignment that must exist between the CM process and the risk management process, as discussed in Chapter 6, so that the monitoring strategy produces information that

---

[14]The CM strategy and program are viewed for relevance and are revised as needed to increase visibility into assets and awareness of vulnerabilities.

[15]From Joint Task Force Transformation Initiative. NIST Special Publication (SP) 800-39, Managing Information Security Risk: Organization, Mission, and Information System View. Maryland: National Institute of Standards and Technology; 2011. "*Governance is the set of responsibilities and practices exercised by those responsible for an organization (e.g. the board of directors and executive management in a corporation, the head of a federal agency) with the express goal of: (i) providing strategic direction; (ii) ensuring that organizational mission and business objectives are achieved; (iii) ascertaining that risks are managed appropriately; and (iv) verifying that the organization's resources are used responsibly.*"

is relevant and useful when making risk-related decisions at each organizational tier. Tier 1 addresses risk management from a strategic perspective by developing a governance policy that drives the CM strategy and communicates the organization's risk management strategy. In tier 2, CM security-related information is dependent on the specific importance of the mission/business processes to the overall organizational goals and objectives. Therefore, it is critical to have an understanding of the security impacts to ensure appropriate implementation of CM activities for information systems that support mission/business processes. In tier 3, CM activities focus on the information system-level security controls to ensure they implement the organization security requirements and continue to be effective over time.

Metrics[16] developed at each tier guide the collection of security-related information used in making risk-based decisions. Therefore, it is important for organizations to select the most appropriate tools and techniques[17] that present information in a format that will be useful for a specific organizational tier. The format also enables the data that will be collected,[18] correlated, analyzed, and reported to be effectively communicated to provide stakeholders with the most accurate indication of the security posture.[19] Since metrics are a key part[20] of CM, the organization may need to refine and update[21] the metrics so they

---

[16]From Dempsey, K., Nirali, C., Johnson, A., Johnston, R., Jones, A., Orebaugh, A., et al. NIST Special Publication (SP) 800-137, Information Security Continuous Monitoring (ISCM) for Federal Information Systems and Organizations. Maryland: National Institute of Standards and Technology; 2011. *"Metrics are designed to present information in a context that is meaningful for each tier."*

[17]From Dempsey, K., Nirali, C., Johnson, A., Johnston, R., Jones, A., Orebaugh, A., et al. NIST Special Publication (SP) 800-137, Information Security Continuous Monitoring (ISCM) for Federal Information Systems and Organizations. Maryland: National Institute of Standards and Technology; 2011. *"Organization-wide monitoring cannot be efficiently achieved through manual processes alone or through automated processes alone."*

[18]From Dempsey, K., Nirali, C., Johnson, A., Johnston, R., Jones, A., Orebaugh, A., et al. NIST Special Publication (SP) 800-137, Information Security Continuous Monitoring (ISCM) for Federal Information Systems and Organizations. Maryland: National Institute of Standards and Technology; 2011. *"Data collection primarily occurs at the information systems tier."*

[19]From Federal Network Security Branch. Continuous Monitoring and Risk Scoring (CM/RS) Concept of Operations (CONOPS) for Supporting Agency Cyber Security Operations. Washington: US Department of Homeland Security; 2011. *"Security posture is the state of effectiveness to agency implemented security controls."*

[20]From Dempsey, K., Nirali, C., Johnson, A., Johnston, R., Jones, A., Orebaugh, A., et al. NIST Special Publication (SP) 800-137, Information Security Continuous Monitoring (ISCM) for Federal Information Systems and Organizations. Maryland: National Institute of Standards and Technology; 2011. *"Care must be taken in determining how best to use security-related information from individual information systems in calculating organizational metrics for security and risk."*

[21]From Dempsey, K., Nirali, C., Johnson, A., Johnston, R., Jones, A., Orebaugh, A., et al. NIST Special Publication (SP) 800-137, Information Security Continuous Monitoring (ISCM) for Federal Information Systems and Organizations. Maryland: National Institute of Standards and Technology; 2011. *"Organizations, security architectures, operational security capabilities, and monitoring processes will improve and mature over time to better respond to the dynamic threat and vulnerability landscape."*

"continue to be relevant, meaningful, actionable, and supportive of risk management decisions made by organizational officials at all tiers" [2].

In addition, federal agencies have legislative and regulatory drivers for capturing metrics that enable them to measure[22] the performance of security related to their program goals and objectives. The Government Performance Results Act (GPRA) Modernization Act[23] requires a quarterly performance assessment of all government programs to assess performance and improvement. The long-term strategic planning[24] described in the GPRA Modernization Act requires federal agencies to define performance goals[25] and objectives, and the performance objectives that are reported on quarterly. Each performance plan includes "a balanced set of performance indicators to be used in measuring or assessing progress toward each performance goal" [3]. FISMA[26] requires federal agencies to report[27] on the status of their information security programs. The annual FISMA report summarizes the performance of the federal agency's program to secure all of your agency's information and information systems [4].

CM STRATEGY

The CM strategy aligns the CM activities with the organization-wide risk management strategy.[28] Through an understanding of the organization's strategic goals and objectives, the CM requirements can be developed to address the monitoring and assessment frequency of security controls, and customize status reporting to ensure consistency across the organization. This further supports each of the organizational tier's information needs required for

---

[22]NIST uses "measures" to refer to the results of data collection, analysis, and reporting. Available from: http://csrc.nist.gov/publications/nistpubs/800-55-Rev1/SP800-55-rev1.pdf.

[23]The Government Performance Results Act (GPRA) of 1993 was modernized in 2010. Available from: http://www.whitehouse.gov/omb/mgmt-gpra/gplaw2m.

[24]From Chew, E., Swanson, M., Stine, K., Bartol, N., Brown, A., Robinson, W. NIST Special Publication (SP) 800-55 Revision 1, Performance Management. Maryland: National Institute of Standards and Technology; 2011. *"Information security must be explicitly tied to at least one goal or objective in the strategic planning process to demonstrate importance in accomplishing the agency's mission."*

[25]From GPRA Modernization Act of 2010 [Internet]. Washington: US Government Printing Office [cited April 28, 2012]. Available from: http://www.gpo.gov/fdsys/pkg/PLAW-111publ352/pdf/PLAW-111publ352.pdf. *"Strategic plans include outcome-oriented goals and objectives, and a description of how the goals and objectives are achieved through operational processes, skills and technology, and human capital, etc."*

[26]FISMA is discussed in detail in Chapter 5, Applying the Risk Management Framework.

[27]Status reporting is performed annually and requires federal agencies to summarize the performance of their security programs used to secure all information and information systems.

[28]From Dempsey, K., Nirali, C., Johnson, A., Johnston, R., Jones, A., Orebaugh, A., et al. NIST Special Publication (SP) 800-137, Information Security Continuous Monitoring (ISCM) for Federal Information Systems and Organizations. Maryland: National Institute of Standards and Technology; 2011. *"The ISCM strategy is developed and implemented to support risk management in accordance with organizational risk tolerance."*

making risk-based decisions. For the strategy to be effective and support the organization's risk management function, it needs to be comprehensive, broadly encompassing the technology, processes, procedures, operating environment, and people [2].

The organization's information requirements can be different at each of the organizational tiers, requiring strategies tailored specifically to a tier. Therefore, to meet the goal of maintaining consistency across the organization, the implementation of the organization-wide CM strategy needs to be driven by the leadership to ensure that the CM strategy evolves as requirements for information change at each tier. In addition to enabling information reuse across the organization, a consistent understanding of the CM strategy ensures a cost-effective implementation of the processes, procedures, tools, and techniques to all organizational information systems, achieving a broad organization-wide situational awareness. The CM strategy can also help the organization use an integrated approach to more efficiently react, such as by changes in a single information system or in the organization's threat environment.

TIP

The CM strategy [2] should:

- Reflect the organization's risk tolerance (including helping set priorities and consistent management of risk);
- Include metrics that provide meaningful indications of security status at all organizational tiers;
- Ensure continued effectiveness of all security controls;
- Address verifying compliance with information security requirements derived from organizational missions/business functions, federal legislation, directives, regulations, policies, and standards/guidelines;
- Be informed by all organizational IT assets and aids to maintain visibility into the security of the assets;
- Ensure knowledge and control of changes to organizational systems and environments of operation; and
- Maintain awareness of threats and vulnerabilities.

An organization-wide CM strategy provides a comprehensive view of the CM requirements of all organizational tiers. These requirements may be derived from multiple sources including the key metrics and the frequency of security controls monitoring and assessments deemed necessary to provide an indication of the information security and risk posture. CM strategies can also be developed at a specific tier[29] to address local requirements. However, to enable an organization-

---

[29]From Dempsey, K., Nirali, C., Johnson, A., Johnston, R., Jones, A., Orebaugh, A., et al. NIST Special Publication (SP) 800-137, Information Security Continuous Monitoring (ISCM) for Federal Information Systems and Organizations. Maryland: National Institute of Standards and Technology; 2011. "*A continuous monitoring strategy for an individual system may also include metrics related to its potential impact on other systems.*"

wide approach to CM, tier-specific strategies will need to be driven from a consistent application of the methodologies and practices used at the higher organizational tiers (i.e., tier 3 strategies should encompass tier 2 policies, procedures, and processes). This ensures that any condition that would require the tier-specific strategy to be updated also triggers additional updates to strategies in the higher tiers so that security-related information captured at the lower tiers maintains relevance in supporting organization-wide risk-based decisions across the organization.

NOTE

In July 2010, OMB released a policy[30] that clarified the roles and responsibilities for cybersecurity. In this policy, the Department of Homeland Security (DHS)[31] was identified as having the responsibility for implementing the operational aspects of the cybersecurity of civilian federal information systems.[32] The scope of responsibility as it relates to CM included the government-wide and agency-specific monitoring and assessment of areas such as cybersecurity operations and incident response [5]. In addition, DHS's role was further clarified in a Federal Information Security Memorandum[33] published in August 2011 in which federal agencies were required to report[34] to DHS on metrics through automated[35] or manual data feeds. For example, starting in 2012, DHS started publishing Annual FISMA Reporting Metrics.[36] Within the annual FISMA reporting metrics, CM was identified as a "key element to managing an information security program is having accurate information about security postures, activities and threats" [6]. Finally, the Federal Information Security Modernization Act

(Continued)

---

[30]Office of Management and Budget (OMB) Memorandum 10−28, *Clarifying Cybersecurity Responsibilities and Activities of the Executive Office of the President and the Department of Homeland Security (DHS)*. Available from: www.whitehouse.gov/omb/assets/memoranda_2010/m10-28.pdf.

[31]From Zients, J., Kundra, V., Schmidt, H. Office of Management and Budget (OMB) Memorandum 10−15, FY 2010 Reporting Instructions for the Federal Information System Management Act and Agency Privacy Management. Washington: Executive Office of the President, Office of Management and Budget; 2010. *"DHS will provide additional operational support to federal agencies in securing federal systems."*

[32]FISMA was discussed in detail in Chapter 5, Applying the Risk Management Framework.

[33]From Lew, J. Office of Management and Budget (OMB) Memorandum 11−33, FY 2011 Reporting Instructions for the Federal Information System Management Act and Agency Privacy Management. Washington: Executive Office of the President, Office of Management and Budget; 2011. *"The Department of Homeland Security issues Federal Information Security Memoranda to inform federal departments and agencies of their responsibilities, required actions, and effective dates to achieve federal information security policies."*

[34]From Lew, J. Office of Management and Budget (OMB) Memorandum 11−33, FY 2011 Reporting Instructions for the Federal Information System Management Act and Agency Privacy Management. Washington: Executive Office of the President, Office of Management and Budget; 2011. *"The reporting requirements will mature over time as the efforts of the Chief Information Officer (CIO) Council's Continuous Monitoring Working Group (CMWG), in collaboration with the agencies, evolve and additional metrics and capabilities are developed."*

[35]Security automation is discussed in Chapter 6, Cost-Effective Compliance Using Security Automation.

[36]Annual FISMA Reporting Metrics. Available from: https://www.dhs.gov/fisma.

> **NOTE (CONTINUED)**
>
> of 2014 codified DHS's role[37] in administering the implementation of information security policies for federal agencies, overseeing agencies' compliance with those policies, and assisting OMB in developing those policies. [7]

CM PROGRAM

Although more tactically focused, the organization's CM program facilitates the implementation of the CM strategy. The scope of the program should be designed to address the sufficiency in security-related information to support risk-based decisions. This can be accomplished by defining metrics and frequencies[38] of monitoring and assessment that produce the needed information. The development of a Continuous Monitoring Plan[39] facilitates the implementation of the CM program. The Continuous Monitoring Plan also addresses the integration of CM activities and metrics to support the CM strategy through the identification of security controls necessary for monitoring to ensure their effectiveness[40] over time.

As previously mentioned, metrics provide a guide for collecting security-related information. The types of metrics defined for the organization reflect the security objectives for the organization, mission/business processes, and/or information systems. In addition, metrics can also be defined at any organizational tier. Therefore, the organization will need to ensure that the frequency of monitoring, if not consistent across the organizational tiers, has a linkage between the security-related information requirements.

---

[37]Federal Information Security Modernization Act (FISMA) [Internet]. Washington, DC: US Department of Homeland Security; [cited July 17, 2016]. <https://www.dhs.gov/fisma>. *"Department authority to develop and oversee the implementation of binding operational directives to other agencies, in coordination and consistent with OMB policies and practices."*

[38]The frequency of monitoring and assessment should be sufficient to meet the organization's security assurance requirements. NIST Special Publication (SP) 800-53, Appendix E, discusses security assurance.

[39]From VanRoekel, S. Security Authorization of Information Systems in Cloud Computing Environments. Washington: Executive Office of the President, Office of Management and Budget; 2011. *"Authorization packages contain the body of evidence needed by authorizing officials to make risk-based decisions regarding the information systems providing cloud services. This includes, as a minimum, the Security Plan, Security Assessment Report, Plan of Action and Milestones and a Continuous Monitoring Plan."*

[40]From Dempsey, K., Nirali, C., Johnson, A., Johnston, R., Jones, A., Orebaugh, A., et al. NIST Special Publication (SP) 800-137, Information Security Continuous Monitoring (ISCM) for Federal Information Systems and Organizations. Maryland: National Institute of Standards and Technology; 2011. *"The measure of correctness of implementation (i.e. how consistently the control implementation complies with the security plan) and how well the security plan meets organizational needs in accordance with current risk tolerance."*

THE CONTINUOUS MONITORING PROCESS

For CM to be an effective tool and operate as a source of information for supporting the management of risk, the organization needs to ensure that the requirements and activities at each level of the organization are addressed in the CM strategy. This enables risk management activities to more closely reflect the type of security-related information collected as part of the CM program and used for making risk-based decisions. As an example, Fig. 12.3 provides a high-level illustration of the alignment that should exist between the CM strategy and the organizational tiers. In addition, it also depicts the inputs that can be potential sources for deriving requirements that need to be addressed by the strategy for implementing an organization-wide CM program.

The CM process includes both *strategic* and *programmatic* activities. The strategic activities usually occur at the higher level within the organization where the overall organizational risk tolerance is defined. However, CM strategies can exist at individual tiers to address requirements specific to a mission or business process supported by the information system or information systems where stakeholders exist across more than one business unit or federal agency. To ensure that security-related information collected or resources required to support the tier-specific requirements are reusable, organizations should make sure that there is some consistency with higher-level tiers.

DEFINING A CM STRATEGY

The CM strategy reflects the organizational driver for CM within the organization. The execution of the CM program is facilitated through requirements and activities included in the strategy. The requirements and activities are defined in policies, procedures, and templates that support the CM strategy such as metrics, review/updates, assessment and status monitoring and reporting, risk assessments, and configuration management. These policies, procedures, and templates are supported through processes that addresses the requirements at the most appropriate level within the organization to ensure that risks can be managed at the organizational risk tolerance.

Strategies developed at the information system tier align more closely with the NIST Risk Management Framework (RMF).[41] CM within the NIST RMF will be discussed in more detail later in this chapter. For the purpose of this section, it is important to understand that security-related information produced through tier 3

---

[41]From Zients, J., Kundra, V., Schmidt, H. Office of Management and Budget (OMB) Memorandum 10—15, FY 2010 Reporting Instructions for the Federal Information System Management Act and Agency Privacy Management. Washington: Executive Office of the President, Office of Management and Budget; 2010. *"Agencies should develop an enterprise-wide strategy for selecting subsets of their security controls to be monitored on an ongoing basis to ensure all controls are assessed during the three-year authorization cycle."*

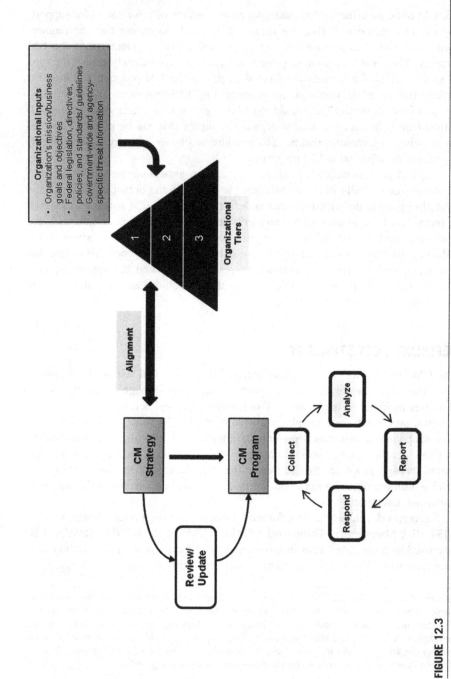

FIGURE 12.3

Integration of CM process with organization-wide risk management.

strategies and programs supports the organizational CM strategy and program at tiers 1 and 2. Management responsible and accountable for risk-based decisions at tier 1 or 2 are informed with regard to organizational risk based on information produced at the lower tiers so that appropriate mitigation strategies can be developed and implemented. In addition, the tier 3 CM strategy also supports ongoing authorizations [2].

NOTE

In August 2011, DHS released FISM 11-02, *FY 2011 Reporting Instructions for the Federal Information Security Management Act and Agency Privacy Management*. DHS was given the authority to provide direction on government-wide metrics and submit information according to the defined reporting activities and frequency. The activities [4] included:

- Data feeds
- Security question responses
- Cyberstat accountability sessions/agency interviews.

This government-wide CM strategy was developed through collaboration with the Federal Chief Information Officer (CIO) Council Information Security and Identity Management Committee (ISIMC) Continuous Monitoring Working Group (CMWG). The CMWG focused on the establishment of a government-wide CM and risk-scoring capability and the technology, people, and processes used to implement the capability to enhance the overall security posture of the federal government [8].

IMPLEMENTING A CM PROGRAM

The CM strategy is implemented through the CM program.[42] The scope of the program should address the requirements[43] defined in the strategy for the security-related information needed by the organization for making risk-based

---

[42]From Joint Task Force Transformation Initiative. NIST Special Publication (SP) 800-53 Revision 4, Security and Privacy Controls for Federal Information Systems and Organizations. Maryland: National Institute of Standards and Technology; 2013. *"Continuous monitoring programs facilitate ongoing awareness of threats, vulnerabilities, and information security to support organizational risk management decisions."*

[43]From Zients, J., Kundra, V., Schmidt, H. Office of Management and Budget (OMB) Memorandum 10−15, FY 2010 Reporting Instructions for the Federal Information System Management Act and Agency Privacy Management. Washington: Executive Office of the President, Office of Management and Budget; 2010. *"A robust and effective continuous monitoring program will ensure important procedures included in an agency's security authorization package (e.g. as described in system security plans, security assessment reports, and [Plans of Actions and Milestones] (POA&Ms)) are updated as appropriate and contain the necessary information for authorizing officials to make credible risk-based decisions regarding the security state of the information system on an ongoing basis."*

decisions. These requirements can be across all tiers, or specific to a tier, but should include at a minimum [9]:

- Monitoring metrics.
- Frequency of monitoring and assessments.
- Security status reporting.

The metrics defined by the organization can come from any tier across the organization and encompass different sources of security-related information. In addition, the information can be collected either through manual procedures and techniques[44] or automated tools and technologies.[45] The frequency can also vary based on the source of the requirements used as an input to the CM strategy. As an example, in February 2012, US DHS published the FISMA metrics[46] that were required by federal agencies to incorporate into their CM program for collection and reporting. Table 12.1 presents sample metrics related to CM published by DHS.

NOTE

The US Department of State established the iPost Risk Scoring Program to provide summary and detailed information on the current status of hosts[47] at a particular site.[48] In 2010, DHS released the Continuous Asset Evaluation, Situational Awareness, and Risk Scoring (CAESARS) Reference Architecture Report.[49] CAESARS was based in part on iPost.[50] DHS indicated that analyzing security-related information, defining and calculating risk, and assigning scores is a key part of the CM process [11]. However, it is important to note that some management and operational controls cannot be effectively scored and some aspect of risk management cannot be automated. The Federal CIO Information Security and Identity Management Committee (ISIMC) established an initiative that would extend the DHS CAESARS. The goal of the CAESARS

(Continued)

---

[44]For manual CM processes to be effective, they must be repeatable.

[45]Automation can ensure process consistency and efficiency.

[46]Metrics to support FISMA reporting may be an aggregate of information that is from various levels and sources from across the organization (i.e., governance, operations, and information system).

[47]Computer connected to a network.

[48]From Williams-Bridgers, J. State Has Taken Steps to Implement a Continuous Monitoring Application, but Key Challenges Remain. Washington: US Government Accountability Office; 2011. *"Sites, or operational units, within iPost are either identified based on physical location, such as an overseas embassy or domestic facility within the United States, or can be grouped by administrative responsibility or function, such as all hosts within a particular bureau."*

[49]NIST extended the CAESARS framework to address enterprise continuous monitoring. Available from: http://csrc.nist.gov/publications/PubsDrafts.html#NIST-IR-7756.

[50]From Department of Homeland Security, Federal Network Security Branch. Continuous Asset Evaluation, Situational Awareness, and Risk Scoring (CAESARS) Reference Architecture Report, Version 1.8. Washington, DC: US Department of Homeland Security; 2010. *"A target-state reference architecture is proposed for security posture monitoring and risk scoring, based on the work of three leading federal agencies: the Department of State (DOS) Security Risk Scoring System, the Department of Treasury, Internal Revenue Service (IRS) Security Compliance Posture Monitoring and Reporting (SCPMaR) System, and the Department of Justice (DOJ) use of BigFix and the Cyber Security Assessment and Management (CSAM) tool along with related security posture monitoring tools for asset discovery and management of configuration, vulnerabilities, and patches."*

Table 12.1 Continuous Monitoring Performance Metrics [10]

Asset Management (*Hardware*)	• Total number of organization hardware assets connected to the organization's network • Number of assets where an automated capability (device discovery process) provides visibility at the organization's enterprise level into asset inventory information for all hardware assets • Frequency (in days) at which automated capabilities are conducted on all assets • Time (in days) it takes to complete the device discovery process • Number of assets where identifying information is collected: *network IP address, hostname,* and *MAC address* • Number of assets where an automated capability exists to determine whether the asset is authorized and who manages the asset • Number of assets where an automated capability exists to identify and remove (manually or automated techniques such as through network access controls) unauthorized assets • Time (in days) it takes to assign management for the asset (i.e., authorize) or remove (i.e., unauthorize) the asset once identified • Number of assets where automated capabilities exist to detect and mitigate routes (including those across air-gapped networks)
Asset Management (*Software*)	• Number of installed operating systems (i.e., vendor, product, version number, and patch level) • Number of hardware assets where the operating system are installed to assess vulnerabilities without conducting a scan • Number of enterprise-wide commercial-off-the-shelf (COTS) applications installed on assets • Number of hardware assets where an automated capability exists to detect and block unauthorized software from executing
Configuration Management (*Operating Systems*)	• Number of installed operating systems (i.e., vendor, product, version number, and patch level) where a secure configuration baseline has been defined • Number of hardware assets where installed operating systems (i.e., vendor, product, version number, and patch level) have a secure configuration baseline

(Continued)

Table 12.1 Continuous Monitoring Performance Metrics [10] *Continued*

	• Percentage of hardware assets where the operating system software has an automated capability to identify deviations from approved secure configuration baselines and provide visibility to through enterprise-level reporting • Frequency (in days) the automated capability to identify operating system software deviations from approved secure configuration baselines is conducted
Configuration Management (*Applications*)	• Number of enterprise-wide COTS applications installed on assets where a secure configuration baseline has been defined • Number of hardware assets where installed applications have a secure configuration baseline • Percentage of hardware assets where the application has an automated capability to identify deviations from approved secure configuration baselines and provide visibility to through enterprise-level reporting • Frequency (in days) the automated capability to identify application deviations from approved secure configuration baselines is conducted
Configuration Management (*Configuration Baselines*)	• Number of hardware assets that the FDCC[a]/USGCB[b] baseline application has • Number of FDCC/USGCB baselines (in CCE[c]) where approved deviations exists from the FDCC/USGCB standards • CCE and number of hardware assets where the FDCC/USGCB standard applies but has approved deviations
Vulnerability Management	• Number of hardware assets where an automated capability exists to identify CVEs[d] from the National Vulnerability Database[e] and provide visibility to through enterprise-level reporting • Number of hardware assets identified that are evaluated using tools to assess the security of the systems and generate output compliant with CVE, CVSS,[f] and OVAL[g]

[a]*Federal Desktop Core Configuration*. Available from: http://nvd.nist.gov/fdcc/index.cfm.
[b]*United States Government Configuration Baseline*. Available from: http://usgcb.nist.gov.
[c]*Common Configuration Enumeration*. Available from: http://cce.mitre.org.
[d]*Common Vulnerability and Exposure*. Available from: http://cve.mitre.org.
[e]*National Vulnerability Database*. Available from: http://nvd.nist.gov.
[f]*Common Vulnerability and Scoring System*. Available from: http://www.first.org/cvss/cvss-guide.
[g]*Open Vulnerability and Assessment Language*. Available from: http://oval.mitre.org.

> **NOTE (CONTINUED)**
> Framework Extension (FE)[51] was to present a technical reference model to allow organizations to aggregate collected data from across a diverse set of security tools, analyze that data, perform scoring, enable user questions, and provide overall situational awareness [12].

Metrics used for measuring the organization's security posture may also be determined to be different depending on the organizational tier (see Fig. 12.2) where they are defined. For example, tier 1 metrics may be defined by the department/agency CIO and/or Chief Information Security Officer (CISO) based on a CM strategy that focuses on providing an organizational-wide view of the security posture at tiers 2 and 3, and to support security governance decisions. Whereas tier 3 metrics may be defined by the System Owner and/or Information System Security Officers (ISSOs) based on information collected for determining the security posture associated with the security control effectiveness in a specific information system and to support ongoing authorization decisions.

Defining the frequency of monitoring and assessment activities is essential for the implementation of an effective CM program. Establishing the frequency requires understanding the organization's objectives for monitoring and assessments. For example, the following criteria [2] can assist an organization in determining the frequency:

- Security control volatility.
- System categorization/impact level.
- Security controls or specific assessment objectives providing critical functions.
- Security control with identified weaknesses.
- Organizational risk tolerance.
- Threat/vulnerability information.
- Risk assessment results.
- Output of monitoring strategy reviews.
- Reporting requirements.

The collection and reporting of security-related information is supported by the CM architecture. Security automation[52] facilitates CM through an increase in the coverage and efficiency of information collection. To make the information useful and reusable, consideration should be given to ensure that the data supporting

---

[51]The CAESARS FE builds upon the DHS CAESARS to address requirements that would make it applicable to the US Department of Defense (DoD), Intelligence Community (IC), and the Civilian Agencies.
[52]Security automation is discussed in detail in Chapter 13, Cost-Effective Compliance Using Security Automation.

the CM strategy and program is interoperable[53] across the organization. Since accountability for the security posture may exist with different roles/functions within or between different organizations, the data needs to be portable when supporting different metrics or different monitoring and assessment frequencies [2]. Although briefly mentioned in this section, the next chapter discusses security automation in more detail as it relates to supporting CM requirements.

The implementation of the CM program involves operationalizing the organizational policies and procedures defined at tiers 2 and 3. The policies and procedures include identifying the types of reports,[54] the recipients of the reports, the frequency of reporting, and any tools and methodologies. In addition, processes and capabilities[55] at tiers 2 and 3 should be designed to enable the effective collection, analysis, reporting, and response. The collection of security-related information can be manual or automated, with emphasis placed on the assembly of the information to ensure it is in a format that makes it meaningful to stakeholders and provides the necessary visibility for making risk-based decisions.

The analysis and reporting of security-related information is conducted at tiers 1 and 2 as an aggregate view of the security status of operational and system-level security controls from across the organization. Tier 3 analysis and reporting primarily supports ongoing authorizations and system-level mitigations. The processes and capabilities support the analysis and reporting by enabling organizations to consistently and efficiently measure security, determine the effectiveness of security controls, and prioritize remediation actions.

A response to findings from CM analysis may require coordination with other stakeholders across the organization. Responses can occur at each organization tier (e.g., tier 1 responses focus on those aspects that mitigate risk[56] through governance and policies and tier 3 responses mitigate risk associated with system-level security policies, procedures, processes, and security controls). Responses could also include changes to the CM strategy and program discussed in the next section.

---

[53]From Dempsey, K., Nirali, C., Johnson, A., Johnston, R., Jones, A., Orebaugh, A., et al. NIST Special Publication (SP) 800-137, Information Security Continuous Monitoring (ISCM) for Federal Information Systems and Organizations. Maryland: National Institute of Standards and Technology; 2011. *"Interoperable data specifications (e.g. SCAP, XML) enable data to be collected once and reused many times."*

[54]From Dempsey, K., Nirali, C., Johnson, A., Johnston, R., Jones, A., Orebaugh, A., et al. NIST Special Publication (SP) 800-137, Information Security Continuous Monitoring (ISCM) for Federal Information Systems and Organizations. Maryland: National Institute of Standards and Technology; 2011. *"Examples include reoccurring reports, automated reports, ad hoc reports, data feeds and database views."*

[55]Continuous monitoring capabilities are enabled through technologies and techniques that provide the organization with the most accurate picture of the security and risk posture, visibility into, and near or real-time data through manual or automated data feeds.

[56]Risk responses are discussed in detail in Chapter 6, Risk Management.

REVIEW AND UPDATE CM STRATEGY AND PROGRAM

As previously discussed, the CM strategy and program evolves and must continue to be applicable to the organization's mission/objectives and operation/threat environment. CM is a recursive process in which the monitoring strategy is continually refined [2]. As changes occur to the strategy, the program may need to be reviewed and updated to support the organization's risk tolerance and to ensure the security-related information continues to be relevant and accurate.

NOTE

Changes to the CM strategy could occur due to the following factors [2]:

- Mission/business processes
- Enterprise architecture
- Organizational risk tolerance
- Threat/vulnerability information
- Plan of action and milestones (POA&Ms)
- Security trends
- Federal laws or regulations
- Reporting requirements.

The tier 1 and 2 policies and procedures should address the process for reviewing and updating the strategy. The process should consider potential aspects [2] of the strategy that ensure sufficiency of the information to support the organization risk management decisions[57] such as:

- Measurements
- Metrics
- Monitoring frequencies
- Reporting requirements.

CONTINUOUS MONITORING WITHIN FEDRAMP

The Federal Risk and Authorization Management Program (FedRAMP) Program Management Office (PMO) established a Concept of Operations (CONOPS), which later became the Security Assessment Framework (SAF)[58] that included the framework for CM within FedRAMP.[59] In addition, the FedRAMP PMO published a CM Strategy[60] for use once the Cloud Service Provider (CSP) receives a

---

[57]Risk management decisions include: *risk response*, *ongoing authorization*, and *resource/prioritization*.

[58]The Security Assessment Framework is discussed in detail in Chapter 8, FedRAMP Primer.

[59]Referred to as ongoing assessment and authorization.

[60]FedRAMP Program Management Office (PMO). Continuous Monitoring Strategy & Guide, Version 2.0. Available from: https://www.fedramp.gov/files/2015/03/FedRAMP-Continuous-Monitoring-Strategy-Guide-v2.0-3.docx.

Table 12.2 FedRAMP CM Roles and Responsibilities [13]

Authoring Official	FedRAMP PMO	DHS	3PAO
• Works in coordination with CSP to receive security control artifacts at various points in time.	• Acts as the liaison for the Joint Authorization Board for ensuring that CSPs with a JAB P-ATO strictly adhere to their established Continuous Monitoring Plan.	• Works in coordination with FedRAMP PMO to incorporate DHS's guidance into the FedRAMP program guidance and documents.	Responsible for independently verifying and validating the control implementation and test results for CSPs in the continuous monitoring phase of the FedRAMP process.

Provisional Authorization.[61] Although the specific aspects of CM implemented within FedRAMP are primarily limited to tier 3 CM activities, it is important to discuss how the organization-wide CM discussed earlier in this chapter supports the implementation of the FedRAMP CM process. Within the context of FedRAMP, the goal of CM is to enable visibility into the security posture of cloud services to support continuous risk management decisions. This visibility is achieved through reporting from the CSP in three areas: *operational visibility*, *change control*, and *incident response*.

The FedRAMP PMO, Third Party Assessment Organization (3PAO), and federal agency each have organizational CM roles and responsibilities when executing CM activities within the context of FedRAMP. Table 12.2 outlines the FedRAMP CM roles and responsibilities.

Each operates as an essential stakeholder that supports the effective integration of organization-wide CM into the FedRAMP process. For the effective management of risk CM needs to be applied consistently across the organizational tiers through common CM policies, procedures, processes, and templates.

In addition, FedRAMP established a methodology that enables the federal government to leverage security-related information that can be applied over more than one cloud service, effectively improving government-wide security. However, it is important to note that the CSP's role in CM is not a substitute for the federal government's responsibility and accountability for the use of cloud services.

Once a CSP receives a FedRAMP Authorization (JAB or Agency), it must implement a CM capability to ensure the cloud system maintains an

---

[61]FedRAMP Program Management Office (PMO). Continuous Monitoring Strategy & Guide, Version 1.1. Washington, DC: US General Services Administration; 2012. *"To receive reauthorization of a FedRAMP Provisional Authorization from year to year, CSPs must monitor their security controls, assess them on a regular basis, and demonstrate that the security posture of their service offering is continuously acceptable."*

acceptable risk posture. This process determines whether the set of deployed security controls in an information system remain effective in light of planned and unplanned changes that occur in the system and its environment over time. [13].

Through the three-tiered approach, illustrated in Fig. 12.4, the FedRAMP PMO, CSP, and federal agency can ensure that the CM strategy and program can be used to maintain the cloud service's authorization to operate. The tasks outlined in Fig. 12.5 support the three CM areas within the FedRAMP CM process by ensuring that system information is kept up-to-date while also facilitating risk-based decisions on an ongoing basis through the assessment and monitoring of security controls (*common, hybrid, or system-level*) using security management and reporting tools.[62] This transforms the security controls assessment and risk determination process into a dynamic process[63] that is supported by timely risk response actions and a cost-effective, ongoing authorization [2].

The FedRAMP security authorization process[64] focuses on integrating information security and risk management into the SDLC through the application of the NIST RMF. After the initial authorization, evidence of security control effectiveness will need to be obtained continuously to support the changes[65] within the cloud service and operating environment. The monitoring steps (*Step 6*) of the NIST RMF,[66] when aligned with the organization's CM and risk management activities, support the determination of risk at the organizational and mission/business tiers through system-level information.

The operational visibility provides the transparency required by the FedRAMP PMO and federal agencies through evidence that demonstrate the effectiveness of the CSPs CM program.[67] As we discussed earlier in this chapter, federal agencies are required to submit quarterly reporting on government-wide metrics to DHS. Evidence produced by the CSP should be integrated into existing capabilities within

---

[62]Security automation is discussed in detail in Chapter 12, Cost-Effective Compliance Using Security Automation.

[63]From Dempsey, K., Nirali, C., Johnson, A., Johnston, R., Jones, A., Orebaugh, A., et al. NIST Special Publication (SP) 800-137, Information Security Continuous Monitoring (ISCM) for Federal Information Systems and Organizations. Maryland: National Institute of Standards and Technology; 2011. "*Continuous monitoring of threats, vulnerabilities, and security control effectiveness provides situational awareness for risk-based support of ongoing authorization decisions.*"

[64]The FedRAMP process is discussed in detail in Chapter 8, FedRAMP Primer.

[65]From Dempsey, K., Nirali, C., Johnson, A., Johnston, R., Jones, A., Orebaugh, A., et al. NIST Special Publication (SP) 800-137, Information Security Continuous Monitoring (ISCM) for Federal Information Systems and Organizations. Maryland: National Institute of Standards and Technology; 2011. "*Ongoing assessment of security control effectiveness supports a system's security authorization over time in highly dynamic environments of operation with changing threats, vulnerabilities, technologies, and missions/business processes.*"

[66]The monitoring step is discussed in detail in Chapter 5, Applying the Risk Management Framework.

[67]FedRAMP Program Management Office (PMO). Continuous Monitoring Strategy & Guide, Version 2. Washington, DC: US General Services Administration; 2014. "*CSPs and its independent assessors are required to provide evidentiary information to AOs at a minimum of a monthly, annually, every 3 years, and on an as-needed frequency after authorization is granted. The submission of these deliverables allow AOs to evaluate the risk posture of the CSP's service offering.*"

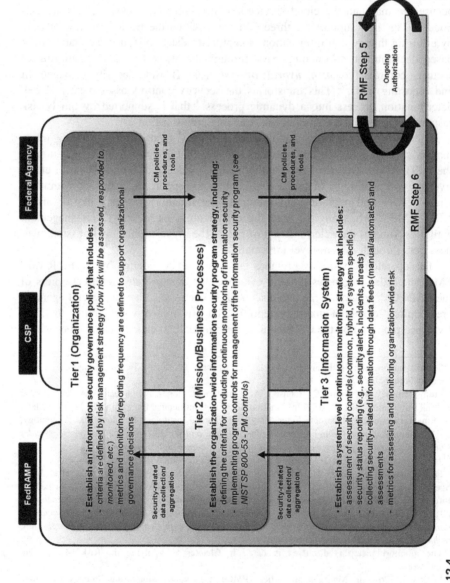

FIGURE 12.4

Organization-wide and FedRAMP continuous monitoring activities.

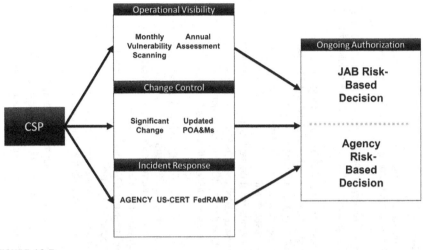

FIGURE 12.5

FedRAMP continuous monitoring [13].

the CSP's monitoring environment to align with the federal agency's reporting requirements. In addition to the CSP's CM activities, Table 12.3 identifies an example list of artifacts that must be submitted to the FedRAMP PMO.

The change control process is enabled by monitoring and reporting activities. CM provides insight into the implementation of organizational- and information system–level policies, procedures, and secure configuration baselines. Monitoring[68] also identifies undiscovered/undocumented system components, misconfigurations, vulnerabilities, and unauthorized changes [15]. The CSP's Configuration Management Plan (CMP) is an essential tool for identifying and communicating changes to the cloud service and any potential impacts to the security and risk posture. Through a security impact analysis,[69] changes can be analyzed (or assessed through the annual assessment activities) to determine if the existing security controls would impact the federal agencies' risk tolerance.

Incident response is a critical component of the FedRAMP CM process. A security incident[70] should be anticipated and response planned. The Incident Response Plan (IRP) documents the CSP's implementation of the incident response life cycle[71] that includes activities for the detection and analysis of and

---

[68]Security-focused configuration management includes four phases: *planning, identifying and implementing configurations, controlling configuration changes,* and *monitoring.*

[69]NIST Special Publication (SP) 800-128, Appendix I, *Guide for Security-Focused Configuration Management of Information Systems,* contains a sample security impact worksheet.

[70]NIST Special Publication (SP) 800-61 Revision 2, "*A computer security incident is a violation or imminent threat of violation1 of computer security policies, acceptable use policies, or standard security practices.*"

[71]NIST Special Publication (SP) 800-61 Revision 2, *Computer Security Incident Handling,* describes the incident response life cycle to support *containment, eradication,* and *recovery.*

Table 12.3 FedRAMP Continuous Monitoring Deliverables [14]

Security Control	Frequency	Deliverable	Description
IR-6—Incident Reporting	Continuous and Ongoing	• Security Incident Reports	• CSPs must report incidents in accordance with the FedRAMP Incident Communications Procedures. [a]
RA-5a— Vulnerability Scanning	Monthly	• Vulnerability Mitigation	• CSPs must mitigate all discovered high-risk vulnerabilities within 30 days and mitigate moderate vulnerability risks in 90 days. • CSPs must send their ISSO updated artifacts every 30 days to show evidence that outstanding high-risk vulnerabilities have been mitigated.
RA-5d— Vulnerability Scanning	Monthly	• Vulnerability Scan Results	• CSPs must scan operating systems, web applications, and databases monthly. • All scan reports must be sent to the ISSO monthly.
CA-5b—Plan of Action and Milestones	Monthly	• Updates to POA&Ms	• CSPs must update[b] the POA&M at least monthly and must submit it to the ISSO at least monthly.
XX-1—Information Security Policies	Annual	• Security Plan and Attached Information Security Policies and Procedures	• CSPs must review Information Security Policies and Procedures annually. • Insert the updated policy document as an attachment to the System Security Plan and submit the updated plan to the ISSO one year from the Provisional Authorization date and each year thereafter.
CA-2b—Security Assessments	Annually	• Security Assessment Report	• CSPs must have a 3PAO assess a subset of their security controls annually. • Submit the assessment report to the ISSO one year from the Provisional Authorization date and each year thereafter.
CA-2—Security Assessments	Annually	• Security Assessment Plan and Procedures	• The 3PAO develops a security assessment plan. • The 3PAO assesses the security controls annually. • The 3PAO produces a security assessment report and results.

Control	Frequency	Deliverable	Requirements
CA-2 (2) — Security assessments — Specialized Assessments	Annually	• Vulnerability Scan Results	• The 3PAO includes as part of security control assessments, annually, announced vulnerability scanning.
CA-8, CA-8 (1) — Penetration Testing	Annually	• Penetration Testing Reports	• CSPs must conduct penetration testing at least annually or when there is a major significant change to ensure compliance with all vulnerability mitigation procedures. • Penetration testing must be performed by a 3PAO. • All penetration testing reports must be sent to the ISSO.
CM-9 — Configuration Management Plan	Annual	• Configuration Management Plan	• CSPs must review and update the Configuration Management Plan annually. • Submit the new plan to the ISSO one year from the Provisional Authorization date (and each year thereafter).
CP-2d — Contingency Plan	Annual	• IT Contingency Plan	• CSPs must review and update the *IT Contingency Plan* annually. • Submit the new plan to the ISSO one year from the Provisional Authorization date (and each year thereafter).
CP-4a — Contingency Plan Testing (*Moderate and High Systems Only*)	Annual	• IT Contingency Plan Test Plan and Report	• CSPs must test and exercise[c] the *IT Contingency Plan* (for moderate and impact systems) at least annually using functional exercises. • CSPs must insert a new IT Contingency Plan Test Report into the proper Appendix F of the IT Contingency Plan.
IR-3 — Incident Response Testing	Annual	• Incident Response Plan and Test Report	• CSPs must perform incident response testing[d] annually. • When the *System Security Plan* is updated annually, record the results of the incident response testing directly in the control description box indicating when testing took place, testing materials, who participated, and who conducted the testing. • CSPs should test all contact information in the Appendices of the *Incident Response Plan* to make sure they are accurate.

(Continued)

Table 12.3 FedRAMP Continuous Monitoring Deliverables [14] *Continued*

Security Control	Frequency	Deliverable	Description
IR-8c—Incident Response Plan	Annual	• Incident Response Plan	• CSPs must review the *Incident Response Plan* annually and update it if necessary. • CSPs should insert the updated Incident Response Plan as an attachment to the *System Security Plan.*
PL-2b,c—System Security Plan	Annual	• System Security Plan	• CSPs must review and update their System Security Plan (SSP) annually. • Submit the new plan to the ISSO one year from the Provisional Authorization date (and each year thereafter).
RA-5a - Security Assessments	Annually	• Vulnerability Scan Results	• CSPs must have an accredited 3PAO scan operating systems/infrastructure, web applications, and databases annually. • All scan reports must be sent to the ISSO.
CP-4a—Contingency Plan Testing	Every three years	• IT Contingency Plan and Test Report	• CSPs should test and exercise[e] the *IT Contingency Plan* (for low-impact systems) every three years using tabletop written tests. • Record the testing date in the *System Security Plan.*

[a]*FedRAMP Incident Communications Procedures, Version 1.0.* Available from: https://www.fedramp.gov/files/2015/03/Incident-Comm-Procedure_040813_1. docx.

[b]From FedRAMP Program Management Office (OMB). FedRAMP continuous monitoring strategy and guide, version 2.0. Washington, DC: US General Services Administration; 2014. *"Updates must be based on the findings from security assessments, security impact analyses, CSP risk assessments, continuous monitoring activities and any other indications of a security weakness."*

[c]From FedRAMP Program Management Office (OMB). FedRAMP continuous monitoring strategy and guide, version 2.0. Washington, DC: US General Services Administration; 2014. *"Plans for tests and exercises must be submitted, at least 30 days, prior to the test to the ISSO. The test plans must be developed in accordance with NIST Special Publication 800-34 (as amended) and receive approval by Risk-executive/Authoring Official prior to initiating testing."*

[d]From FedRAMP Program Management Office (OMB). FedRAMP continuous monitoring strategy and guide, version 2.0. Washington, DC: US General Services Administration; 2014. *"Plans for tests and exercises must be submitted, at least 30 days, prior to the test to the ISSO. The test plans must be developed in accordance with NIST Special Publication 800-61 (as amended) and receive approval by Risk-executive/Authoring Official prior to initiating testing."*

[e]From FedRAMP Program Management Office (OMB). FedRAMP continuous monitoring strategy and guide, version 2.0. Washington, DC: US General Services Administration; 2014. *"Plans for tests and exercises must be submitted, at least 30 days, prior to the test to the ISSO. The test plans must be developed in accordance with NIST Special Publication 800-34 (as amended) and receive approval by Risk-executive/Authoring Official prior to initiating testing."*

response to a security incident[72] as follows for a single affected federal agency and multiple affected federal agencies:

- **One agency affected:**
  - "If a CSP detects an incident that has the potential to cause an agency service availability disruption, a compromise of data confidentiality, or a compromise of federal data integrity, the CSP should proceed with notification to stakeholders in accordance with its incident response plan. CSP's should first notify the agency customer who has the potential to be affected by the incident. All agencies that receive CSP incident reports should ask the CSP if they would like assistance from US-CERT. If the CSP opts to request assistance from US-CERT, the agency should notify US-CERT and provide US-CERT with information on the CSP point of contact." [14]
- **Multiple federal agencies affected:**
  - "After agency notification is completed, CSPs should notify their FedRAMP ISSO. FedRAMP ISSOs will engage in a dialogue with CSPs to obtain all relevant information. The FedRAMP ISSO will make note of whether or not the CSP requested assistance from US-CERT. The CSP's FedRAMP ISSO will confirm that all affected agency POCs are notified of the incident. After communications with the CSP takes place, the FedRAMP ISSO will contact US-CERT to confirm that US-CERT has been made aware of the incident. FedRAMP ISSOs will engage in a dialogue with US-CERT to obtain all relevant information." [14]

SUMMARY

In this chapter, CM was discussed from the perspective of the organization supporting the monitoring and assessment activities. CM includes both strategic and tactical components that enable it to be implemented cost-effectively. Beginning with a comprehensive and robust CM strategy, the organization can ensure alignment with the organization's overall risk management strategy. The design and implementation of the CM program is supported through the definition of metrics, frequencies, and formats for assembling and distributing security-related information. Within the context of FedRAMP, CM can be a complex activity that requires the appropriate coordination between multiple stakeholders. The interaction between the CSP, FedRAMP PMO, and federal agency relies upon the consistent implementation of policies, procedures, processes, and templates that support activities that enable operational visibility, change control, and incident response.

---

[72]FedRAMP Program Management Office (OMB) Office. FedRAMP continuous monitoring strategy and guide, version 2.0. Washington, DC: US General Services Administration; 2014. For incidents that are detected by the federal agency, *the CSP should work with the agency to determine if the incident is local to the agency host (or hosts), or is part of a larger incident that affects the CSP's underlying cloud infrastructure—affecting multiple cloud tenants."*

REFERENCES

[1] Guttman B, Rockback E. NIST Special Publication (SP) 800-12, an introduction to computer security: The NIST handbook. Maryland: National Institute of Standards and Technology; 1995.

[2] Dempsey K, Nirali C, Johnson A, Johnston R, Jones A, Orebaugh A, et al. NIST Special Publication (SP) 800-137, Information security continuous monitoring (ISCM) for federal information systems and organizations. Maryland: National Institute of Standards and Technology; 2011.

[3] GPRA Modernization Act of 2010 [Internet]. Washington, DC: US Government Publishing Office; [cited April 28, 2012]. <http://www.gpo.gov/fdsys/pkg/PLAW-111publ352/pdf/PLAW-111publ352.pdf>.

[4] Lew J. Office of Management and Budget (OMB) Memorandum 11-33, FY 2011 reporting instructions for the federal information system management act and agency privacy management. Washington, DC: Executive Office of the President, Office of Management and Budget; 2011.

[5] Lew J. Office of Management and Budget (OMB) Memorandum 10-28, Clarifying cybersecurity responsibilities and activities of the executive office of the president and the department of homeland security (DHS). Washington, DC: Executive Office of the President, Office of Management and Budget; 2010.

[6] Office of Management and Budget (OMB). Fiscal Year 2011 Report to Congress on the Implementation of the Federal Information Security Management Act of 2002. Washington, DC: Executive Office of the President, Office of Management and Budget; 2012.

[7] Federal Information Security Modernization Act (FISMA) [Internet]. Washington, DC: US Department of Homeland Security; [cited July 17, 2016]. <https://www.dhs.gov/fisma>.

[8] Coose M. Federal Continuous Monitoring Working Group (Draft) Presentation. Washington, DC: US Department of Homeland Security; 2011.

[9] Joint task force transformation initiative. NIST Special Publication (SP) 800-53 Revision 4, Security and privacy controls for federal information systems and organizations. Maryland: National Institute of Standards and Technology; 2012.

[10] US Department of Homeland Security. Federal Network Security Branch. FY 2012 Chief Information Officer, Federal Information Security Management Act reporting metrics. Washington, DC: US Department of Homeland Security; 2012.

[11] Williams-Bridgers J. State has taken steps to implement a continuous monitoring application, but key challenges remain. Washington, DC: US Government Accountability Office; 2011.

[12] US Department of Homeland Security. Federal Network Security Branch. Continuous Asset Evaluation, Situational Awareness, and Risk Scoring (CAESARS) reference architecture report, version 1.8. Washington, DC: US Department of Homeland Security; 2010.

[13] FedRAMP Program Management Office (PMO). FedRAMP Security Assessment Framework, version 2.1. Washington: US General Services Administration; 2015.

[14] FedRAMP Program Management Office (OMB) Office. FedRAMP continuous monitoring strategy and guide, version 2.0. Washington, DC: US General Services Administration; 2014.

[15] Johnson A, Dempsey K, Ross R, Gupta S, Bailey D. NIST Special Publication (SP) 800-128, Guide for security-focused configuration management of information systems. Maryland: National Institute of Standards and Technology; 2011.

Continuous monitoring through security automation

13

INFORMATION IN THIS CHAPTER:

- Introduction
- CM Reference Architectures
- Security Automation Standards and Specifications
- Operational Visibility and Continuous Monitoring

INTRODUCTION

Security automation is an essential part of an information security program, enabling organizations to achieve more efficiency in monitoring activities. Not all continuous monitoring (CM) can be accomplished through automation. However, where automation is applied, an organization can more cost-effectively monitor and continually assess security controls. The result of using security automation enhances the security-related information produced from monitoring activities, offering a more accurate measure of the state of the organization's security posture. Security automation is supported by the metrics established by the organization for the collection and analysis of the needed security-related information. This information becomes a valuable input into the organization's risk management function, thereby enabling the organization's management to realize "*near real-time*," risk-based decision-making.

Tools and technologies used in CM provide the organization with insight into the security controls that can be automated. However, in some circumstances manual monitoring may still be required in the organization's security program. This is important to note, because manual monitoring can still serve as a viable option, specifically in cases where the organization's CM strategy is still maturing and metrics required for the collection of information are largely undefined.

The CM strategy should address the *people*, *processes*, *technologies* and the *environment*. In addition, the CM strategy does not focus solely on the security-related information that is easy for an organization to collect or easy to automate [1]. Therefore, where automation is used, the organization will also need to ensure that the strategy reflects its role to ensure that it achieves the desired efficiency in

Federal Cloud Computing. DOI: http://dx.doi.org/10.1016/B978-0-12-809710-6.00013-5

obtaining outcome-oriented results. For example, where large volumes of security-related information are collected, automation augments existing processes by reducing the burden and potential errors associated with the human aspects[1] of conducting analysis. Automation also supports the organization by interpreting[2] the collected data to enable stakeholders to make more informed, risk-based decisions.

Automation is not a replacement for the human element in an information security program. The application of automation within an organization's CM strategy should be linked to the existing processes (or new processes[3] where gaps exist) to ensure that the organization understands the associated impact in the potential loss of visibility and efficiency due to a compromise in the tools and technologies relied upon when making risk-based decisions. This will also guide the organization in ensuring any automation that is used to supplement monitoring capabilities[4] within the information security program is appropriately protected.

As illustrated in Fig. 13.1, CM plays a critical role in the organization's risk management strategy. The use of automated tools facilitates the collection of "a larger and more diverse pool of technologies, people, processes, and environments" [1]. However, the selection of the tools and technologies should be considered only after the organization has thoroughly defined the metrics that the organization will use as a basis for analyzing and responding[5] to findings through the organization's risk management processes.

---

[1]From Dempsey, K., Nirali, C., Johnson, A., Johnston, R., Jones, A., Orebaugh, A., et al. NIST Special Publication (SP) 800-137, Information Security Continuous Monitoring (ISCM) for Federal Information Systems and Organizations. Maryland: National Institute of Standards and Technology; 2011. "*Automation serves to augment the security processes conducted by security professionals within an organization and may reduce the amount of time a security professional must spend on doing redundant tasks, thereby increasing the amount of time the trained professional may spend on tasks requiring human cognition.*"

[2]From Dempsey, K., Nirali, C., Johnson, A., Johnston, R., Jones, A., Orebaugh, A., et al. NIST Special Publication (SP) 800-137, Information Security Continuous Monitoring (ISCM) for Federal Information Systems and Organizations. Maryland: National Institute of Standards and Technology; 2011. "*Automated tools are often able to recognize patterns and relationships that may escape the notice of human analysts, especially when the analysis is performed on large volumes of data.*"

[3]From Dempsey, K., Nirali, C., Johnson, A., Johnston, R., Jones, A., Orebaugh, A., et al. NIST Special Publication (SP) 800-137, Information Security Continuous Monitoring (ISCM) for Federal Information Systems and Organizations. Maryland: National Institute of Standards and Technology; 2011. "*Tools operate within the context of processes designed, run, and maintained by humans.*"

[4]From Dempsey, K., Nirali, C., Johnson, A., Johnston, R., Jones, A., Orebaugh, A., et al. NIST Special Publication (SP) 800-137, Information Security Continuous Monitoring (ISCM) for Federal Information Systems and Organizations. Maryland: National Institute of Standards and Technology; 2011. "*During security control implementation (RMF Step 3), consideration is given to the capabilities inherent in available technology to support ISCM as part of the criteria in determining how best to implement a given control.*"

[5]From Dempsey, K., Nirali, C., Johnson, A., Johnston, R., Jones, A., Orebaugh, A., et al. NIST Special Publication (SP) 800-137, Information Security Continuous Monitoring (ISCM) for Federal Information Systems and Organizations. Maryland: National Institute of Standards and Technology; 2011. "*Response to findings at all tiers may include risk mitigation, risk acceptance, risk avoidance/rejection, or risk sharing/transfer, in accordance with organizational risk tolerance.*"

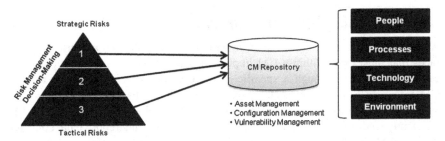

FIGURE 13.1

Automating CM activities that support risk management.

Through the development of metrics, the organization can identify the tools and technologies that present the necessary information at a frequency consistent with those defined in the strategy.

TIP

Tools and technologies enhance CM activities. Several considerations [1] when selecting tools and technologies to support automation capabilities include:

- Collection sources.[6]
- Open specification support (e.g., SCAP[7]).
- Interoperability.
- Reporting.
- Data aggregation.

This chapter will focus on CM reference architectures developed to support the identification of tools and technologies that enable organizations to automate different aspects of CM (i.e., gathering, aggregating, analyzing, and reporting). Additionally, existing and emerging security automation standards and specifications will be briefly discussed as a means of addressing the importance of standardization in the reporting and the exchange of data when organizations implement security automation in CM-related activities.

---

[6]From Dempsey, K., Nirali C., Johnson, A., Johnston, R., Jones, A., Orebaugh, A., et al. NIST Special Publication (SP) 800-137, Information Security Continuous Monitoring (ISCM) for Federal Information Systems and Organizations. Maryland: National Institute of Standards and Technology; 2011. *"Automation supports collecting more data more frequently and from a larger and more diverse pool of technologies, people, processes, and environments."*

[7]*Security Content Automation Protocol (SCAP).* Available from: http://scap.nist.gov/.

CM REFERENCE ARCHITECTURES

A CM reference architecture is an abstract depiction of the components and interfaces that must exist within a CM implementation. It operates as a template that can be customized through a specific set of CM solutions. In addition, using a CM reference architecture, such as those that will be discussed in this section, assists organizations in selecting the tools and technologies that can be used to efficiently and effectively gather, aggregate, analyze, and report data collected through CM activities.

CONTINUOUS ASSET EVALUATION, SITUATIONAL AWARENESS, AND RISK SCORING REFERENCE ARCHITECTURE

The US Department of Homeland Security (DHS), developed a reference architecture that provided an abstraction of a security posture monitoring and risk scoring system, that is informed by computing and network assets that can be used by other federal agencies seeking to apply risk scoring principles to their information security program [2]. The DHS Continuous Asset Evaluation, Situational Awareness, and Risk Scoring (CAESARS) reference architecture report provided the initial framework for implementing monitoring process and for establishing requirements for automated tool selection and integration. For completeness and for illustration purposes, Fig. 13.2 provides a view of the CAESAR subsystems. In the next section, the follow-on reference architecture CAESARS Framework Extension (FE) developed by National Institute of Standards and Technology (NIST), an enterprise continuously monitoring technical reference model, will be discussed with additional detail as it relates to supporting automation in a CM program.

CAESARS FRAMEWORK EXTENSION REFERENCE ARCHITECTURE

The CAESARS FE is an enhanced version of the CM reference architecture that was developed by DHS. The specific differences will not be discussed in this chapter, but it is important to note that the essential characteristics have remained the same, with differences focused on adding additional functionality, granularity within subsystem specifications, and to further leverage existing and emerging security automation standards [3]. The CAESARS FE is a conceptual model used to enable the real-time capabilities of the NIST Risk Management Framework (RMF)[8] with specific emphasis placed on automating CM *(RMF Step)* functions. Through an elaboration of a technical architecture using the model presented in the CAESARS FE, tools and technologies can be developed that facilitate CM within an enterprise and make information available to support risk-based decision-making.

---

[8]NIST RMF is discussed in detail in Chapter 5, Applying the Risk Management Framework.

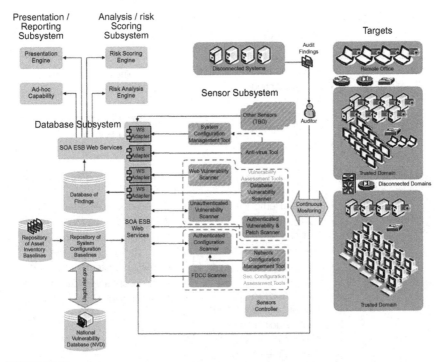

FIGURE 13.2

Continuous Asset Evaluation, Situational Awareness, and Risk Scoring (CAESARS)
Reference Architecture [2].

In this section, the subsystems and components, and specifications will be
briefly discussed, followed by a description of how the application of the
CAESAR FE technical reference model supports each of the data domains.[9]
Although a specific discussion of security automation domains[10] is beyond the
scope of this book, it is important to list those domains identified [1] that require
support by the CM reference technical model[11] as shown in Table 13.1.

---

[9]From Waltermire, D., Halbardier, A., Humenansky, A., Mell, P. NIST Interagency Report (IR)
7800 (Draft), Applying the Continuous Monitoring Technical Reference Model to the Asset,
Configuration, and Vulnerability Management Domains. Maryland: National Institute of Standards
and Technology; 2012. *"A specific class of cyber security data, methodologies, and procedures."*

[10]From Dempsey, K., Nirali C., Johnson, A., Johnston, R., Jones, A., Orebaugh, A., et al. NIST Special
Publication (SP) 800-137, Information Security Continuous Monitoring (ISCM) for Federal
Information Systems and Organizations. Maryland: National Institute of Standards and Technology;
2011. *"A security automation domain is an information security area that includes a grouping of tools,
technologies, and data. Data within the domains is captured, correlated, analyzed, and reported to
present the security status of the organization that is represented by the domains monitored."*

[11]From Dempsey, K., Nirali C., Johnson, A., Johnston, R., Jones, A., Orebaugh, A., et al. NIST
Special Publication (SP) 800-137, Information Security Continuous Monitoring (ISCM) for Federal
Information Systems and Organizations. Maryland: National Institute of Standards and Technology;
2011. *The tools support these VI need to be instrumented to interface with CM solutions (i.e. external systems instrumented for CM integration).*

Table 13.1 Security Automation Domains [1]

Domain	Security Controls[a]	
Vulnerability and Patch Management	• CA-2—Security Assessments • CA-7—Continuous Monitoring • CM-3—Configuration Change Control • IR-4—Incident Handling • IR-5—Incident Monitoring	• MA-2—Controlled Maintenance • RA-5—Vulnerability Scanning • SA-11—Developer Security Testing • SI-2—Flaw Remediation • SI-11—Error Handling
Event and Incident Management ([1]*Logging Only*, [2]*IDPS Only*, **Both*)	• AC-4—Information Flow Enforcement[2] • AC-17—Remote Access[2] • AC-18—Wireless Access[2] • AU-2—Auditable Events* • AU-3—Content of Audit Records[1] • AU-6—Audit Review, Analysis, and Reporting* • AU-7—Audit Reduction and Report Generation[1] • AU-8—Time Stamps[1] • AU-12—Audit Generation*	• AU-13—Monitoring for Information Disclosure[2] • CA-2—Security Assessments* • CA-7—Continuous Monitoring* • IR-5—Incident Monitoring[1] • RA-3—Risk Assessment*SI-4—Information System Monitoring* • SC-7—Boundary Protection[2] • SI-3—Malicious Code Protection[2] • SI-7—Software and Information Integrity[2]
Malware Detection	• CA-2—Security Assessments • CA-7—Continuous Monitoring • IR-5—Incident Monitoring • RA-3—Risk Assessment • SA-12—Supply Chain Protection • SA-13—Trustworthiness	• SI-3—Malicious Code Protection • SI-4—Information System Monitoring • SI-7—Software and Information Integrity • SI-8—Spam Protection
Asset Management	• CA-7—Continuous Monitoring • CM-2—Baseline Configuration • CM-3—Configuration Change Control	• CM-8—Information System Component Inventory • SA-10—Developer Configuration Management
Configuration Management	• AC-2—Account Management • AC-3—Access Enforcement • AC-5—Separation of Duties	• CM-6—Configuration Settings • CM-7—Least Functionality • IA-2—Identification and Authentication (Organizational Users)

(Continued)

Table 13.1 Security Automation Domains [1] *Continued*

Domain	Security Controls[a]	
	• AC-7—Unsuccessful Login Attempts • AC-9—Previous Logon (Access) Notification • AC-10—Concurrent Session Control • AC-11—Session Lock • AC-19—Access Control for Mobile Devices • AC-20—Use of External Information Systems • AC-22—Flaw Remediation • CA-2—Security Assessments • CA-7—Continuous Monitoring • CM-2—Baseline Configuration • CM-3—Configuration Change Control • CM-5—Access Restrictions for Change	• IA-3—Device Identification and Authentication • IA-4—Identifier Management • IA-5—Authenticator Management • IA-8—Identification and Authentication (Nonorganizational Users) • IR-5—Incident Monitoring • MA-5—Maintenance Personnel • PE-3—Physical Access Control • RA-3—Risk Assessment • SA-7—User-Installed Software • SA-10—Developer Configuration Management • SI-2—Flaw Remediation
Network Management	• AC-4—Information Flow Enforcement • AC-17—Remote Access • AC-18—Wireless Access • CA-7—Continuous Monitoring • CM-2—Baseline Configuration • CM-3—Configuration Change Control • CM-4—Security Impact Analysis • CM-6—Configuration Settings	• CM-8—Information System Component Inventory • SC-2—Application Partitioning • SC-5—Denial of Service Protection • SC-7—Boundary Protection • SC-10—Network Disconnect • SC-32—Information System Partitioning • SI-4—Information System Monitoring
License Management	• CA-7—Continuous Monitoring • CM-8—Information System Component Inventory • CM-10—Software Usage Restrictions	

(Continued)

Table 13.1 Security Automation Domains [1] *Continued*

Domain	Security Controls[a]	
Information Management	• AC-4—Information Flow Enforcement • AC-17—Remote Access • CA-3—Information System Connections • CA-7—Continuous Monitoring	• SC-9—Transmission Confidentiality • SI-12—Information Output Handling and Retention
Software Assurance	• CA-7—Continuous Monitoring • SA-4—Acquisition • SA-8—Security Engineering Principles • SA-11—Developer Security Testing	• SA-12—Supply Chain Protection

[a]*Security automation domains cover 60 of the total 171 available controls in NIST SP 800-53 Revision 4 (inclusive of* low, moderate, *and* high *baselines).*

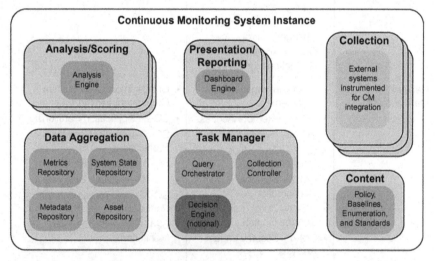

FIGURE 13.3

CAESARS FE subsystems and components [3].

Subsystems and components

The CAESARS FE reference architecture consists of six subsystems. Each subsystem, as depicted in Fig. 13.3, contains one or more components that provide a specific function or capability (e.g., analysis and scoring, collection, content

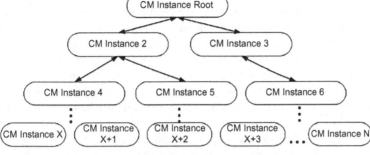

Hierarchical Federated CM Multiinstance Model

FIGURE 13.4

Multitiered, hierarchical CM implementation [3].

management, etc.). The subsystems and components are meant to be independent and security tool and technology agnostic.

Therefore, it is important to understand the intent of the subsystems and components to enable organizations to apply the technical reference model in a way that will assist in identifying and implementing CM capabilities that result in a solution that cost-effectively supports the CM requirements. Below is an overview of each of the subsystems and components:

- The *presentation/reporting* subsystem, consisting of the *dashboard engine*, is the source for user input/outputs. Within the CM system instance, this subsystem would primarily interface with the task manager subsystem using queries designed to fulfill user requests for security-related information.
- The *task manager* subsystem performs the orchestration in the CM system instance between the analysis/scoring, data aggregation, presentation/reporting, and collection subsystems. This subsystem performs the orchestration through use of several components, such as the *query orchestration*, *collection controller*, and *decision engine*.
- The *collection* subsystem collects data based on a user query (task manager), using content that describes the organization's policies (content), and stores the results (data aggregation). When a multitiered[12] CM capability is used, as illustrated in Fig. 13.4, a collection subsystem may not exist within all of the CM instances.[13] It is also important to highlight that a collection subsystem is

---

[12]From Mell, P., Waltermire, D., Feldman, L., Booth, H., Regland, Z., Ouyang, A., et al. NIST Interagency Report (IR) 7756 (Second Draft), CAESARS Framework Extension: An Enterprise Continuous Monitoring Technical Reference Model. Maryland: National Institute of Standards and Technology; 2012. *In a multitiered CM situation, a CM instance higher in the hierarchy may not have any assets to monitor, but instead rely upon data feeds from lower tier CM instances.*

[13]More than one CM instance can be used in organizations that have a need to structure the CM implementation organization-wide to support the different tiers of decision-makers within the CM program (e.g., tier 1—governance, tier 2—mission/business processes, and tier 3—information system).

not a core component of the CM implementation and could be an external system that interfaces with a CM instance.

- The *data aggregation* subsystem is the central repository for data (e.g., raw, analyzed, etc.). This subsystem consists of multiple repositories: *system state*, *asset*, *metrics*, and *metadata*. The data aggregation subsystem interfaces with other subsystems such as input from the collection subsystem for storage of raw collected data, raw data retrieval, and analyzed data storage from the analysis/scoring subsystem, and query result storage from task managers that exist in lower-tiers in a multitiered hierarchical model [3] (see Fig. 13.3).
- The *analysis/scoring* subsystem provides the analysis and scoring function within the CM implementation, potentially supporting multiple scoring methodologies *analysis engine* components. This subsystem is a critical component of the CM implementation. It receives queries from the task manager subsystem, retrieves and stores data in the data aggregation subsystem, and obtains scoring algorithms, parameters, and associated scoring data from the content subsystem [3].
- The *content* subsystem maintains the organizational policies that are used to compare system state. The primary purpose of this subsystem is to maintain the policies (e.g., security baselines configurations) and supporting data (e.g., enumeration of products being evaluated, or vulnerabilities being identified) that are used by the collection subsystem(s) or the analysis/risk scoring subsystem(s). Since an organization may have a single source for storing organizational policies, only one content subsystem would be required for an entire CM implementation to enable sharing among the different CM instances.

Specifications: Workflows, subsystems, and interfaces

The CAESARS FE technical specification consists of the workflows, subsystems, and interfaces that enable the implementation of the CM reference model. The *workflows* specifications define the "coordinated operations of all the subsystems and components within the model" [4]. The *subsystem* specifications enable subsystems to operate as independent and tool agnostic, "plug-in-play" modules that are interoperable between CM implementations. Since subsystems perform an independent role within the CM implementation, clearly defining the required functionality at a "generic" level enables easier integration of different products/services. The last specification, the *interfaces*, plays an essential role in bridging the communication between the individual subsystems and facilitating workflow interactions.

This section is not intended to provide a detailed description of these specifications, but instead to provide a general overview to expand the discussion of the CAESARS FE as a technical reference model for identifying tools and technologies that can be integrated into CM solutions to assist Cloud Service Providers (CSPs) in addressing the Federal Risk and Authorization Management Program (FedRAMP) operational visibility and other CM requirements. Through the selection of CSPs that implement the specifications, federal agencies can focus on

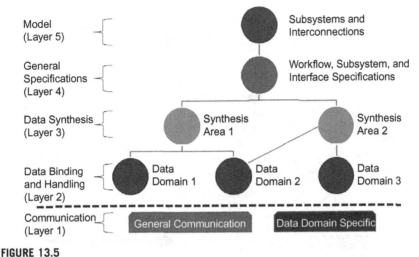

Model (Layer 5) — Subsystems and Interconnections

General Specifications (Layer 4) — Workflow, Subsystem, and Interface Specifications

Data Synthesis (Layer 3) — Synthesis Area 1, Synthesis Area 2

Data Binding and Handling (Layer 2) — Data Domain 1, Data Domain 2, Data Domain 3

Communication (Layer 1) — General Communication, Data Domain Specific

FIGURE 13.5

CAESAR FE specification layers [4].

continuously monitoring security-related information across the enterprise (i.e., hardware, software, and services) under a single governance structure to include those mission/business processes that have been extended to the cloud service environment.[14]

Specification layers

The CAESARS FE consists of multiple layers that extend from a high-level reference model description to a technical specification that links the CM implementation to a specific data domain (e.g., asset management, configuration management, and vulnerability management). As illustrated in Fig. 13.5, the layers of the CM specifications extend from layer 5 where the subsystem and interconnections[15] are defined, to layer 4 that addresses specifications for describing the workflows, subsystems, and interfaces,[16] to the actual binding of the

[14]Department of Homeland Security/Federal Network Security (DHS/FNS) is in the process of establishing technical requirements for the Continuous Diagnostic and Mitigation (CDM) Program that will provide federal agencies and state and local governments with the ability to enhance and automate their existing continuous network monitoring capabilities, correlate and analyze critical security-related information, and strengthen risk-based decision making at the agency and federal enterprise level. Available from: https://www.fbo.gov/utils/view?id = ae650dd0661deab13c6805f94a542a25.

[15]NIST Interagency Report (IR) 7756 (Second Draft), *"CAESARS Framework Extension: An Enterprise Continuous Monitoring Technical Reference Model."* Available from: http://csrc.nist.gov/publications/drafts/nistir-7756/Draft-NISTIR-7756_second-public-draft.pdf.

[16]NIST Interagency Report (IR) 7799 (Draft), *Continuous Monitoring Reference Model Workflow, Subsystem, and Interface Specifications.* Available from: http://csrc.nist.gov/publications/drafts/nistir-7799/Draft-NISTIR-7799.pdf.

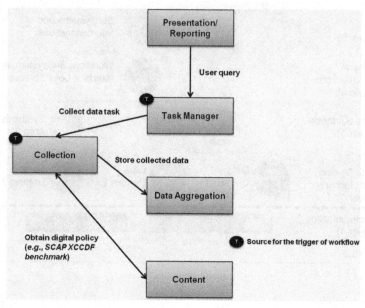

FIGURE 13.6

Example data acquisition workflow.

technical reference model to data domains in layer 2.[17] Layers 3 and 1 are beyond the scope of this book.

Workflows

As described earlier, workflows provide coordinated operations for moving data within the CM technical reference model. Workflows describe specific use cases that are driven by the necessity for different subsystems and components to interoperate to perform a specific function (e.g., acquiring data through collection and reporting, fulfilling queries requests). For example, a workflow for the data acquisition involves the collection subsystem interacting with other subsystems to support the acquisition of data. Fig. 13.6 provides an illustration for how this workflow would be executed in a CM implementation. Omitted from the diagram is specific component interaction within the workflow. Since components within a subsystem collectively support the subsystem's implementation of a specific requirement within a workflow (e.g., collection controller initiating a task to the collection subsystem to collect data would be sent by the task manager), the actions of components have been abstracted to the subsystem level.

---

[17]NIST Interagency Report (IR) 7800 (Draft), *Applying the Continuous Monitoring Technical Reference Model to the Asset, Configuration, and Vulnerability Management Domains.* Available from: http://csrc.nist.gov/publications/drafts/nistir-7800/Draft-NISTIR-7800.pdf.

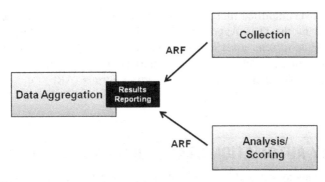

FIGURE 13.7

Results reporting interface.

Subsystems

The subsystem specifications provide a detailed description of the requirements that must be supported by a specific subsystem to effectively implement the CM technical reference model. Since the specifications are data domain agnostic, they are not specifically linked with a specific monitoring domain (i.e., asset management, configuration management, vulnerability management). Instead, the specifications describe the capabilities that must be supported by individual components. For example, the collection controller within the task manager subsystem provides the capability to process tasks (*task processing*[18]) and initiate data collection tasks (*subtask propagation*[19]) [4]. For the task manager to support the ability to initiate a task to request the collection of data from a user query, the task manager needs to be able to support multiple capabilities offered through these discrete services that interact within the CM implementation to support workflows.

Interfaces

Interface specifications provide the standardized mechanism in which subsystems can effectively communicate with each other and enable them to operate as independent modules that, when collectively implemented, support the entire CM technical reference model. Interfaces are exposed through Web Services Definition Language (WSDL)[20] that describes the web services implemented within the subsystem(s) where the interface exists. For example, Fig. 13.7

---

[18]From Mell, P., Waltermire, D., Halbardier, A., Feldman, L. NIST Interagency Report (IR) 7799 (Draft), Continuous Monitoring Reference Model Workflow, and Specifications. Maryland: National Institute of Standards and Technology; 2012. *"The Collection Controller can receive incoming tasks, manage data collection fulfillment, and respond with completion status."*

[19]From Mell, P., Waltermire, D., Halbardier, A., Feldman, L. NIST Interagency Report (IR) 7799 (Draft), Continuous Monitoring Reference Model Workflow, and Specifications. Maryland: National Institute of Standards and Technology; 2012. *"The Collection Controller can propagate data collection tasking to the appropriate Collection subsystems and keep track of their completion."*

[20]*Web Services Description Language (WSDL)*. Available from: http://www.w3.org/TR/wsdl.

provides an oversimplified illustration of the "Results Reporting" interface that is implemented by the Data Aggregation subsystem that enables other subsystems and components to send asset information for storage [4]. The WSDL describes the services(s) that are supported by the interface and the requirements for sending the asset[21] information (e.g., Asset Reporting Format (ARF)[22]).

SECURITY AUTOMATION STANDARDS AND SPECIFICATIONS

The implementation of CM requires using tools and technologies that are based on standards and specifications that are open and industry-supported. Standards and specifications provide a foundation for implementing automation that promotes portability and interoperability across tool sets and domain boundaries. As discussed earlier, the layer 2 in the CAESARS FE technical reference model binds the reference model to data domains (e.g., asset management,[23] configuration management,[24] and vulnerability management[25]). This section is not intended to be a comprehensive review of all security automation standards and specifications, but instead will provide a high-level overview that furthers investigation.

---

[21]From Halbardier, A., Waltermire, D., Johnson, M. NIST Interagency Report (IR) 7694, Specification for the Asset Reporting Format 1.1. Maryland: National Institute of Standards and Technology; 2011. "*Anything that has value to an organization, including, but not limited to, another organization, person, computing device, information technology (IT) system, IT network, IT circuit, software (both an installed instance and a physical instance), virtual computing platform (common in cloud and virtualized computing), and related hardware (e.g. locks, cabinets, keyboards).*"

[22]From Halbardier, A., Waltermire, D., Johnson, M. NIST Interagency Report (IR) 7694, Specification for the Asset Reporting Format 1.1. Maryland: National Institute of Standards and Technology; 2011. "*A data model to express the transport format of information about assets and the relationships between assets and reports.*"

[23]From Waltermire, D., Halbardier, A., Humenansky, A., Mell, P. NIST Interagency Report (IR) 7800 (Draft), Applying the Continuous Monitoring Technical Reference Model to the Asset, Configuration, and Vulnerability Management Domains. Maryland: National Institute of Standards and Technology; 2012. *Activities associated with understanding the relationship of assets across an enterprise.*

[24]From Waltermire, D., Halbardier, A., Humenansky, A., Mell, P. NIST Interagency Report (IR) 7800 (Draft), Applying the Continuous Monitoring Technical Reference Model to the Asset, Configuration, and Vulnerability Management Domains. Maryland: National Institute of Standards and Technology; 2012. *Activities associated with verifying the status of configuration of computing devices across an enterprise.*

[25]From Waltermire, D., Halbardier, A., Humenansky, A., Mell, P. NIST Interagency Report (IR) 7800 (Draft), Applying the Continuous Monitoring Technical Reference Model to the Asset, Configuration, and Vulnerability Management Domains. Maryland: National Institute of Standards and Technology; 2012. *Activities associated with understanding the security posture through the identification of known vulnerabilities across an enterprise.*

Table 13.2 SCAP Specification Categories [5]

Category	Description
Languages	Provide standard vocabularies and conventions for expressing security policy, technical check mechanisms, and assessment results
Reporting Formats	Provide the necessary constructs to express collected information in standardized formats
Enumerations	Define a standard nomenclature (naming format) and an official dictionary or list of items expressed using that nomenclature
Measurement and Scoring Systems	Evaluate specific characteristics of a security weakness (e.g., software vulnerabilities and security configuration issues) and, based on those characteristics, generating a score that reflects their relative severity
Integrity	Helps to preserve the integrity of SCAP content and results

SECURITY CONTENT AUTOMATION PROTOCOL

The Security Content Automation Protocol (SCAP)[26] provides the bindings for supporting the layer 2 data domains through a series of specifications. SCAP provides a "suite of specifications that standardize the format and nomenclature by which software flaw and security configuration information is communicated, both to machines and humans" [5] that includes: languages (XCCDF,[27] OVAL,[28] OCIL[29]), reporting formats (ARF[30]), enumerations (CPE,[31] CCE,[32] and CVE[33]), measurement and scoring systems (CVSS,[34] CCSS[35]), and supports the preservation of integrity (TMSAF[36]) of content and results. Table 13.2 provides a description of the five categories that cover the component specifications included within SCAP.

---

[26]*Security Content Automation Protocol (SCAP).* Available from: http://scap.nist.gov/index.html.

[27]*Extensible Configuration Checklist Description Format.* Available from: http://scap.nist.gov/specifications/xccdf/index.html.

[28]*Open Vulnerability and Assessment Language.* Available from: http://oval.mitre.org/.

[29]*Open Checklist Interactive Language.* Available from: http://scap.nist.gov/specifications/ocil/.

[30]*Asset Reporting Format.* Available from: http://scap.nist.gov/specifications/arf/.

[31]*Common Platform Enumeration.* Available from: http://scap.nist.gov/specifications/cpe/.

[32]*Common Configuration Enumeration.* Available from: http://cce.mitre.org/.

[33]*Common Vulnerabilities and Exposures.* Available from: http://cve.mitre.org/.

[34]*Common Vulnerability Scoring System.* Available from: http://www.first.org/cvss.

[35]*Common Configuration Scoring System.* Available from: http://csrc.nist.gov/publications/nistir/ir7502/nistir-7502_CCSS.pdf.

[36]*Trust Model for Security Automation Data.* Available from: http://scap.nist.gov/specifications/tmsad/.

CYBERSECURITY INFORMATION EXCHANGE FRAMEWORK

Cybersecurity Information Exchange (CYBEX)[37] was originally produced in 2011 and later amended in 2016 by the International Telecommunication Union (ITU) Study Group (SG) 17.[38] CYBEX provides a model and technique for exchanging cybersecurity information (e.g., vulnerability and incident). It focuses on providing the means to support a trusted bi-directional exchange, but does not extend to the acquisition or use of the cybersecurity information that is contained within the organization's boundary. Although CYBEX is an international specification, it is briefly mentioned here as it relates to supporting the CAESARS FE where CM implementations within different organizational security boundaries are required to support the exchange of security-related information.

OPERATIONAL VISIBILITY AND CONTINUOUS MONITORING

The FedRAMP's ongoing assessment and authorization process includes a requirement for operational visibility and CM requirements. In Fig. 13.8, the CAESARS FE (discussed earlier in this chapter) is shown alongside the Cloud Security Alliance (CSA) Governance, Risk Management, and Compliance (GRC) Stack.

The purpose of this diagram is to illustrate how the GRC Stack can support many of the aspects of the operational visibility and CM requirements. In this section, the focus will be on providing an introduction to the components of the GRC Stack and a description of how they collectively can be used by CSPs, Third Party Assessment Organizations (3PAOs), and the federal government to achieve cost-effective compliance, and obtain security-related information to support CM activities.

Operational visibility focuses on demonstrating compliance on an ongoing basis through automated and manual processes. CSPs are required to provide data feeds (automated/manual), periodically assess security controls to determine continued effectiveness, and a report (annually) through a self-attestation certification. The data feeds should be in a compatible format that can be consumed by the CyberScope.[39] CyberScope is an application that enables the federal government to support an "on-demand" view of the government-wide security posture. To enable the ability to achieve near "real-time" risk management, the CyberScope application must handle manual and automated inputs from federal agencies based on data feeds produced using SCAP for Federal information

---

[37]Recommendation X.1500, *Overview of cybersecurity information exchange.* Available from: http://www.itu.int/rec/T-REC-X.1500/en.

[38]*Cybersecurity Information Exchange techniques (CYBEX).* Available from: http://www.itu.int/en/ITU-T/studygroups/com17/Pages/cybex.aspx.

[39]*CyberScope.* Available from: http://scap.nist.gov/use-case/cyberscope/.

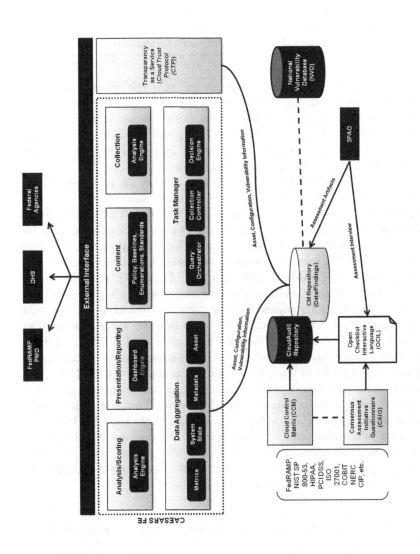

FIGURE 13.8

Integrating tools and technologies into FedRAMP.

Table 13.3 Cloud Trust Protocol Configuration and Vulnerability EoTs [10]

EoT	Description
3	Current configuration
4	Differential comparison of current configuration and organizational policy
5	Results of last vulnerability assessment (scan)
6	Data of last vulnerability assessment (scan)
7	Request "on-demand" vulnerability assessment (scan)

Security Modernization Act (FISMA) reporting [6]. The annual assessment requires a 3PAO to conduct an assessment and the CSP's cloud service environment to certify the accuracy of the results before being submitted to the FedRAMP Program Management Office (PMO) and the leveraging federal agency to assist in integrating the cloud service into the enterprise-wide risk management process when making risk-based decisions.

The GRC Stack, depicted in Figure 13.8, comprises of four components: *Cloud Control Matrix (CCM)*, *Consensus Assessment Initiative Questionnaire (CAIQ)*, *CloudAudit*, and *Cloud Trust Protocol (CTP)*. The CCM "is specifically designed to provide fundamental security principles to guide cloud vendors and to assist prospective cloud customers in assessing the overall security risk of a cloud provider" [7]. The CCM provides a mapping between multiple compliance frameworks to include the FedRAMP security controls.[40] The CAIQ "provides a set of questions a cloud consumer and cloud auditor may wish to ask of a cloud provider" [8]. The questions are aligned with the control requirements defined in the CCM. The next component is CloudAudit, which provides a common interface and namespace that enables streamlining the audit processes [9]. The last component, the CTP, is a mechanism by which consumers request for and receive information about the elements of transparency (EoT)[41] as applied to CSPs [10].

The data feeds focus on obtaining information to enable federal agencies to report on the level of performance of FISMA metrics[42] for asset management, configuration management, and vulnerability management. The CTP EoTs 3–4 (configuration information) and 5–7 (vulnerability information) focus on collecting and returning information, in a SCAP-consistent format, about the assets being used by the federal agency within the cloud service environment. Table 13.3 provides a description of EoTs 3–7.

---

[40]*FedRAMP Security Control Requirements*. Available from: https://www.fedramp.gov/resources/documents-2016/.

[41]From Cloud Trust Protocol (CTP) [Internet]. Washington, DC: Cloud Security Alliance; [cited 2012 June 22]. Available from: https://cloudsecurityalliance.org/group/cloudtrust-protocol/. *23 elements of information that provide characteristics of the compliance, security, privacy, integrity, and operational security.*

[42]*FY 2012 Chief Information Officer, Federal Information Security Management Act Reporting Metrics*. Available from: http://www.dhs.gov/xlibrary/assets/nppd/ciofismametricsfinal.pdf.

The periodic assessment of security controls may be performed by a CSP to support other obligations of compliance or to support contractual requirements (or service-level agreements). The CCM, CAIQ, and CloudAudit collectively enable CSPs to perform internal assessment and third-party assessors (i.e., 3PAOs) to obtain evidence of security control implementation and continued effectiveness. As illustrated in Figure 13.8, the CCM includes mappings to multiple frameworks that address those requirements defined by FedRAMP. The CAIQ can be converted into an OCIL-compliant automated checklist (questionnaire) that can be used to collect information through the assessment of security controls related to people and processes. This is specifically useful when assessing security controls that cannot be completely or fully monitored through security automation tools and technologies. CloudAudit provides a specification for a common namespace which aligns with the CCM to reduce the complexity of 3PAOs in collecting and storing evidentiary artifacts that support a CSPs' expression of its ability to meet compliance obligations.

SUMMARY

The use of security automation within information security programs focuses on achieving efficiency in the monitoring of security controls implemented within information systems. Automating CM activities requires understanding the processes that will be used by the organization, including the tools and technologies to provide a more frequent collection and analysis of security-related information. Therefore, the organization will need to ensure the CM strategy includes both a defined set of metrics and processes that will be used to monitor and respond to findings. Within FedRAMP the CSP's CM capability supports the ongoing authorization and reauthorization decisions. Through the implementation of security automation, the CSP can more cost-effectively provide assurance of the security controls implemented and the confidence in their effectiveness. The CSA GRC Stack addresses many of the aspects of the operational visibility and CM requirements of FedRAMP and supports federal agencies in reclaiming the transparency into the security posture of cloud services, enabling them to make more informed, risk-based decisions.

REFERENCES

[1] Dempsey K, Nirali C, Johnson A, Johnston R, Jones A, Orebaugh A. NIST Special Publication (SP) 800-137, Information security continuous monitoring (ISCM) for federal information systems and organizations. Maryland: National Institute of Standards and Technology; 2011.
[2] Department of Homeland Security, Federal Network Security Branch. Continuous asset evaluation, situational awareness, and risk scoring (CAESARS) reference architecture report version 1.8. Washington, DC: US Department of Homeland, Security; 2010.

[3] Mell P, Waltermire D, Feldman L, Booth H, Regland Z, Ouyang A. NIST Interagency Report (IR) 7756 (Second Draft), CAESARS framework extension: an enterprise continuous monitoring technical reference model. Maryland: National Institute of Standards and Technology; 2012.

[4] Mell P, Waltermire D, Halbardier A, Feldman L. NIST Interagency Report (IR) 7799 (Draft), continuous monitoring reference model workflow, and specifications. Maryland: National Institute of Standards and Technology; 2012.

[5] Waltermire D, Quinn S, Sarfone K, Halbardier A. NIST Special Publication (SP) 800-126 Revision 2, The technical specification for the security content automation protocol (SCAP): SCAP version 1.2. Maryland: National Institute of Standards and Technology; 2011.

[6] CyberScope [Internet]. Maryland: National Institute of Standards and Technology [cited June 16, 2012]. <http://scap.nist.gov/use-case/cyberscope>.

[7] Cloud Control Matrix (CCM) [Internet]. Washington, DC: Cloud Security Alliance [cited June 22, 2012]. <https://cloudsecurityalliance.org/group/cloud-controls-matrix/>.

[8] Consensus Assessment Initiative [Internet]. Washington, DC: Cloud Security Alliance [cited June 22, 2012]. <https://cloudsecurityalliance.org/group/consensus-assessments/>.

[9] CloudAudit [Internet]. Washington, DC: Cloud Security Alliance [cited June 22, 2012]. <https://cloudsecurityalliance.org/group/cloudaudit/>.

[10] Cloud Trust Protocol (CTP) [Internet]. Washington, DC: Cloud Security Alliance [cited June 22, 2012]. <https://cloudsecurityalliance.org/group/cloudtrust-protocol/>.

A case study for cloud service providers

14

INFORMATION IN THIS CHAPTER:

- Case Study Scenario: "Healthcare Exchange"
- Applying the Risk Management Framework within FedRAMP

CASE STUDY SCENARIO: "HEALTHCARE EXCHANGE"

The *Patient Privacy and Protection Act*,[1] recently signed into law, creates a new requirement for patient healthcare exchanges to be built, herein referred to as "Healthcare Exchanges." The "Federal Agency" responsible for implementing the requirements of the law chose to use an operating expense model instead of a capital expense model; usage-based pricing for processing, storage, bandwidth, and license management; and support for elasticity as demand for computing resources may change over time.

Since the "Federal Agency" will require collaboration with external partners to support the development of State Healthcare Exchanges, the "Federal Agency" chose to acquire Infrastructure as a Service (IaaS) and Platform as a Service (PaaS) environments from one provider to support the delivery of a computing platform and an application platform (similar to the cloud configuration use case included in Fig. 14.1). This allows the States to build, test, deploy, and run portable, interoperable, and secure State "Healthcare Exchanges." This also enables the Federal Agency to quickly meet its requirements under the new law. In addition, the IaaS/PaaS environments will be used by other federal agencies to support the development of a federal "Healthcare Exchange" and other functions required to share information between State and federal government entities.

The cloud computing environment will also be used to support the "Federal Agency" mission and will contain federal information and information systems. Therefore, the infrastructure and platform environment of the cloud computing stack will be required to address federal cloud computing security standards. To reduce the complexity, the scenario will be limited to a discussion of only the federal "Healthcare Exchange." The cloud computing infrastructure (IaaS/PaaS)

---

[1]This Act is fictitious and does not exist.

Federal Cloud Computing. DOI: http://dx.doi.org/10.1016/B978-0-12-809710-6.00014-7

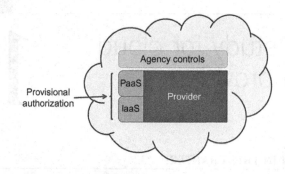

FIGURE 14.1

IaaS/PaaS cloud configuration use case [1].

will be required to address not only federal information security requirements under Federal Risk and Authorization Management Program (FedRAMP), but also to meet all data management safeguard requirements required for the protection of Personally Identifiable Information (PII), Personal Health Information (PHI), and Federal Tax Information (FTI) data.

In this chapter, we will discuss the application of the FedRAMP deliverable documents from the FedRAMP Security Assessment Framework (SAF). The case study in this section will be used to support the discussion.

APPLYING THE RISK MANAGEMENT FRAMEWORK WITHIN FEDRAMP

This section will focus on the application of Steps 1−4 of the National Institute of Standards and Technology (NIST) Risk Management Framework (RMF), which corresponds to document, assess, and authorize phases of the FedRAMP SAF (see Fig. 14.2). The case study provided in the last section will be used as a basis for discussing how to approach using the FedRAMP deliverables to support a FedRAMP Provisional Authorization.

TIP

At this point, the most critical step in the process is for the Cloud Service Provider (CSP) to conduct an in-depth analysis of their security authorization boundary. The CSP will need to be very clear where the security authorization boundary starts and ends. The CSP will need to develop a system description and inventory that can be clearly understood by the "Federal Agency" and the Third Party Assessment Organization (3PAO). The system description will need to be both a physical and logical inventory of what components, assets, and data will be part of the security authorization boundary. As a rule of thumb, the CSP should develop a system description that clearly describes the data-flow (showing the flow of ports, protocols, and services of all system assets) and network diagrams included in their security authorization boundary.

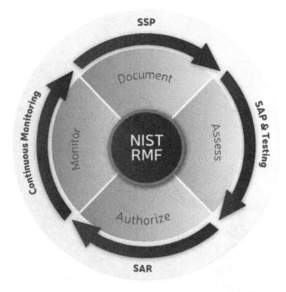

FIGURE 14.2

FedRAMP risk management framework [2].

CATEGORIZE INFORMATION SYSTEM

The CSP must identify the applicable information types and conduct a security categorization[2] of the cloud service to determine the impact level. As depicted in Fig. 14.3, the CSP can use available federal governmental standards, guidelines, and regulations, and industry-specific "best practices" to assist in establishing a characterization of types of information currently stored, processed, or transmitted in the cloud service environment. The Federal Information Processing Standard (FIPS) 199 analysis represents the information type and sensitivity levels of the CSP's cloud service offering and is not intended to include sensitivity levels for federal agency customer data, because they will be expected to perform a separate FIPS 199 analysis for federal information hosted on the CSP's cloud environment [3]. Once the CSP has identified all the potential information types, the CSP will need to document this information in the FIPS 199.[3]

---

[2]Security categorization is discussed in detail in Chapter 5, Applying the Risk Management Framework.

[3]From FedRAMP Program Management Office (PMO). FedRAMP Template and Process Quick Guide. Washington, DC: US General Services Administration; 2012. *"The Federal Information Processing Standard 199 (FIPS 199) Categorization (Security Categorization) report is a key document in the security authorization package developed for submission to the Federal Risk and Authorization Management Program (FedRAMP) authorizing officials. The FIPS 199 Categorization report includes the determination of the security impact level for the cloud environment that may host any or all of the service models [Information as a Service (IaaS), Platform as a Service (PaaS), and Software as a Service (SaaS)]. The ultimate goal of the security categorization is for the cloud service provider (CSP) to be able to select and implement the FedRAMP security controls applicable to its environment."*

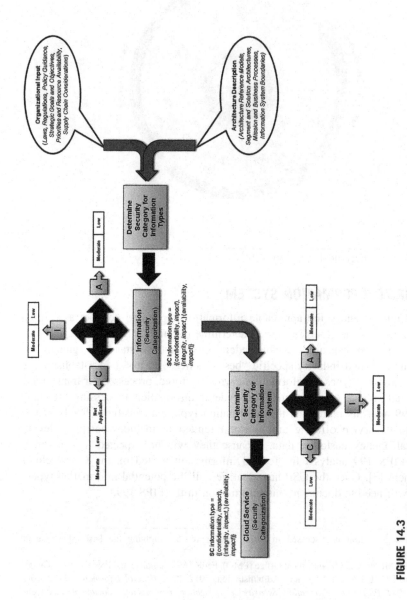

FIGURE 14.3

Role of cloud service provider in the security categorization process.

In documenting the FIPS 199, the CSP will need to provide an overview of the cloud service (i.e., high-level system description). Cloud services generally operate through the concept of a shared responsibility model, where both the CSP and the "Federal Agency" consumer will share the responsibility[4] for specific aspects of securing the cloud environment. Therefore, the FIPS 199 completed by the CSP will need to address only[5] the information types and sensitivity levels of the cloud service for which the CSP is responsible. For example, Table 14.1 provides the information types that may be applicable to the IaaS and PaaS provider.

However, if the CSP operated a Software as a Service (SaaS) cloud service, all applicable information types will need to be examined. This may require the CSP to become familiar with the specific business use cases[6] and the types of information that the "Federal Agency" customer would process, store, or transmit in the cloud environment as a basis for determining the security categorization of the cloud service. This activity would be accomplished by using publicly available information from government-wide or agency-specific Federal Enterprise Architecture (FEA)[7] or Federal Segment Architecture (FSA) documentation. A segment architecture is a "detailed results-oriented architecture (baseline and target) and a transition strategy for a portion or segment[8] of the enterprise" [5]. Tables 14.2−14.4 provide a list of potential information types and the recommended (provisional[9]) impact levels for the confidentiality, integrity, and availability security objective of *Low*, *Moderate*, or *High Baselines*.

---

[4]From FedRAMP Program Management Office (PMO). FedRAMP Concept of Operations (CONOPS) Version 1.1. Washington, DC: US General Services Administration; 2012. *"The Control Implementation Summary (CIS) document is used to enable the CSP to delineate where both the CSP and a federal agency may have a shared responsibility."*

[5]From FedRAMP Program Management Office (PMO). Guide to Understanding FedRAMP Version 1.1. Washington, DC: US General Services Administration; 2012. *"Customer agencies will be performing a separate FIPS 199 analysis for their customer owned data hosted on the system."*

[6]NIST Cloud Computing Business Use Cases Working Group. Available from: http://collaborate.nist.gov/twiki-cloud-computing/bin/view/CloudComputing/BusinessUseCases.

[7]Federal Enterprise Architecture (FEA). Available from: http://www.whitehouse.gov/omb/e-gov/fea.

[8]From Architecture and Infrastructure Committee. Federal Segment Architecture Methodology Version 1.0. Washington, DC: CIO Council; 2008. *"A business service segment includes common or shared business services supporting the core mission areas."*

[9]From Stine, K., Kissel, R., Barker, W., Fahlsing, J., Gulick J. NIST Special Publication (SP) 800-60 Revision 1, Volume I: Guide for Mapping Types of Information and Information Systems to Security Categories. Maryland: National Institute of Standards and Technology; 2008. *"Provisional security impact levels are the initial or conditional impact determinations made until all considerations are fully reviewed, analyzed, and accepted in the subsequent categorization steps by appropriate officials."*

Table 14.1 IaaS and PaaS Information Types [4]

Information Type	Description
C.3.5.1 System Development Information Type	System Development supports all activities associated with the in-house design and development of software applications.
C.3.5.2 Lifecycle/Change Management Information Type	Lifecycle/Change Management involves the processes that facilitate a smooth evolution, composition, and workforce transition of the design and implementation of changes to agency resources such as assets, methodologies, systems, or procedures.
C.3.5.3 System Maintenance Information Type	System Maintenance supports all activities associated with the maintenance of in-house designed software applications.
C.3.5.4 IT Infrastructure Maintenance Information Type	IT infrastructure maintenance involves the planning, design, implementation, and maintenance of an IT infrastructure to effectively support automated needs (i.e., operating systems, applications software, platforms, networks, servers, printers, etc.). IT infrastructure maintenance also includes information systems configuration and security policy enforcement information. This information includes password files, network access rules and implementing files and/or switch setting, hardware and software configuration settings, and documentation that may affect access to the information system's data, programs, and/or processes.
C.3.5.5 Information Security Information Type	IT Security involves all functions pertaining to the securing of federal data and systems through the creation and definition of security policies, procedures, and controls covering such services as identification, authentication, and nonrepudiation.
C.3.5.6 Record Retention Information Type	Records Retention involves the operations surrounding the management of the official documents and records for an agency.
C.3.5.7 Information Management Information Type	Information Management involves the coordination of information collection, storage, and dissemination, and destruction as well as managing the policies, guidelines, and standards regarding information management.
C.3.5.8 System and Network Monitoring Information Type	System and Network Monitoring supports all activities related to the real-time monitoring of systems and networks for optimal performance.
C.3.5.9 Information Sharing Information Type	The Business Reference Model (BRM) provided in the *FEA Consolidated Reference Model Document, Version 2.3*, October 2007 specifies Information Sharing as relating to any method or function, for a given business area, facilitating: data being received in a usable medium by one or more departments or agencies as provided by a separate department or agency or other entity; and data being provided, disseminated, or otherwise made available or accessible by one department or agency for use by one or more separate departments or agencies, or other entities, as appropriate.

Table 14.2 Service Delivery Support Information Types [4]

Information Type	Confidentiality	Integrity	Availability
Controls and Oversight			
Corrective Action (Policy/Regulation)	Low	Low	Low
Program Evaluation	Low	Low	Low
Program Monitoring	Low	Low	Low
Regulatory Development			
Policy and Guidance Development	Low	Low	Low
Public Comment Tracking	Low	Low	Low
Regulatory Creation	Low	Low	Low
Rule Publication	Low	Low	Low
Planning and Budgeting			
Budget Formulation	Low	Low	Low
Capital Planning	Low	Low	Low
Enterprise Architecture	Low	Low	Low
Strategic Planning	Low	Low	Low
Budget Execution	Low	Low	Low
Workforce Planning	Low	Low	Low
Management Improvement	Low	Low	Low
Budgeting and Performance Integration	Low	Low	Low
Tax and Fiscal Policy	Low	Low	Low
Internal Risk Management and Mitigation			
Contingency Planning	Moderate	Moderate	Moderate
Continuity of Operations	Moderate	Moderate	Moderate
Service Recovery	Low	Low	Low
Revenue Collection			
Debt Collection	Moderate	Low	Low
User Fee Collection	Low	Low	Moderate
Federal Asset Sales	Low	Moderate	Low
Public Affairs			
Customer Services	Low	Low	Low
Official Information Dissemination	Low	Low	Low
Product Outreach	Low	Low	Low
Public Relations	Low	Low	Low
Legislative Relations			
Legislation Tracking	Low	Low	Low
Legislation Testimony	Low	Low	Low
Proposal Development	Moderate	Low	Low
Congressional Liaison Operations	Moderate	Low	Low

(Continued)

Table 14.2 Service Delivery Support Information Types [4] *Continued*

Information Type	Confidentiality	Integrity	Availability
General Government			
Central Fiscal Operations	Moderate	Low	Low
Legislative Functions	Low	Low	Low
Executive Functions	Low	Low	Low
Central Property Management	Low	Low	Low
Central Personnel Management	Low	Low	Low
Taxation Management	Moderate	Low	Low
Central Records and Statistics Management	Moderate	Low	Low
Income Information	Moderate	Moderate	Moderate
Personal Identity and Authentication	Moderate	Moderate	Moderate
Entitlement Event Information	Moderate	Moderate	Moderate
Representative Payee Information	Moderate	Moderate	Moderate
General Information	Low	Low	Low

Table 14.3 Resource Management Information Types [4]

Information Type	Confidentiality	Integrity	Availability
Administrative Management			
Facilities, Fleet, and Equipment Management	Low	Low	Low
Help Desk Services	Low	Low	Low
Security Management	Moderate	Moderate	Low
Travel	Low	Low	Low
Workplace Policy Development and Management	Low	Low	Low
Financial Management			
Asset and Liability Management	Low	Low	Low
Reporting and Information	Low	Moderate	Low
Funds Control	Moderate	Moderate	Low
Accounting	Low	Moderate	Low
Payments	Low	Moderate	Low
Collections and Receivables	Low	Moderate	Low
Cost Accounting/Performance Measurement	Low	Moderate	Low
Human Resource Management			
HR Strategy	Low	Low	Low
Staff Acquisition	Low	Low	Low
Organization and Position Management	Low	Low	Low
Compensation Management	Low	Low	Low
Benefits Management	Low	Low	Low

(Continued)

Table 14.3 Resource Management Information Types [4] *Continued*

Information Type	Confidentiality	Integrity	Availability
Employee Performance Management	Low	Low	Low
Employee Relations	Low	Low	Low
Labor Relations	Low	Low	Low
Separation Management	Low	Low	Low
Human Resources Development	Low	Low	Low
Supply Chain Management			
Goods Acquisition	Low	Low	Low
Inventory Control	Low	Low	Low
Logistics Management	Low	Low	Low
Services Acquisition	Low	Low	Low
Information and Technology Management			
System Development	Low	Moderate	Low
Lifecycle/Change Management	Low	Moderate	Low
System Maintenance	Low	Moderate	Low
IT Infrastructure Maintenance	Low	Low	Low
Information System Security	Low	Moderate	Low
Record Retention	Low	Low	Low
Information Management	Low	Moderate	Low
System and Network Monitoring	Moderate	Moderate	Low
Information Sharing	N/A	N/A	N/A

> **TIP**
>
> If the CSP determines, through a review of the recommended impact levels, that there are differences in the selected impact levels, the CSP will need to provide justification (rationale) for any changes. During the review, the following factors [6] can be used to assist the CSP in determining if the impact levels should be adjusted based on the applicable security objectives:
>
> - Sensitivity of change of information when aggregated.
> - Compromise in critical system functionality.
> - Elevation based on extenuating circumstances.
> - Integrity of public information, loss of system availability, privacy information, and so on.

The role of the "Federal Agency" in the security categorization process is the characterization of the information that it plans to store, process, or transmit in the cloud service. The application of the security categorization process by the "Federal Agency" will require an evaluation of multiple sources of information[10]

---

[10]It is important to understand that not all information might be available; however, since the security categorization effects the other steps of the NIST RMF, a regular review may be required to identify any changes that would have impact.

Table 14.4 Mission-Based Information Types [4]

Information Type	Confidentiality	Integrity	Availability
Defense and National Security	Nat'l Security	Nat'l Security	Nat'l Security
Homeland Security			
Border Control and Transportation Security	Moderate	Moderate	Moderate
Key Asset and Critical Infrastructure Protection	High	High	High
Catastrophic Defense	High	High	High
Executive Functions of the Executive Office of the President (EOP)	High	Moderate	High
Intelligence Operations	High	High	High
Disaster Management			
Disaster Monitoring and Prediction	Low	High	High
Disaster Preparedness and Planning	Low	Low	Low
Disaster Repair and Restoration	Low	Low	Low
Emergency Response	Low	High	High
International Affairs and Commerce			
Foreign Affairs	High	High	Moderate
International Development and Humanitarian Aid	Moderate	Low	Low
Global Trade	High	High	High
Natural Resources			
Water Resource Management	Low	Low	Low
Conservation, Marine, and Land Management	Low	Low	Low
Recreational Resource Management and Tourism	Low	Low	Low
Agricultural Innovation and Services	Low	Low	Low
Energy			
Energy Supply	Low	Moderate	Moderate
Energy Conservation and Preparedness	Low	Low	Low
Energy Resource Management	Moderate	Low	Low
Energy Production	Low	Low	Low
Environmental Management			
Environmental Monitoring/Forecasting	Low	Moderate	Low
Environmental Remediation	Moderate	Low	Low
Pollution Prevention and Control	Low	Low	Low
Economic Development			
Business and Industry Development	Low	Low	Low
Intellectual Property Protection	Low	Low	Low
Financial Sector Oversight	Moderate	Low	Low
Industry Sector Income Stabilization	Moderate	Low	Low

(Continued)

Table 14.4 Mission-Based Information Types [4] *Continued*

Information Type	Confidentiality	Integrity	Availability
Community and Social Services			
Homeownership Promotion	Low	Low	Low
Community and Regional Development	Low	Low	Low
Social Services	Low	Low	Low
Postal Services	Low	Moderate	Moderate
Transportation			
Ground Transportation	Low	Low	Low
Water Transportation	Low	Low	Low
Air Transportation	Low	Low	Low
Space Operations	Low	High	High
Education			
Elementary, Secondary, and Vocational Education	Low	Low	Low
Higher Education	Low	Low	Low
Cultural and Historic Preservation	Low	Low	Low
Cultural and Historic Exhibition	Low	Low	Low
Workforce Management			
Training and Employment	Low	Low	Low
Labor Rights Management	Low	Low	Low
Worker Safety	Low	Low	Low
Health			
Access to Care	Low	Moderate	Low
Population Health Management and Consumer Safety	Low	Moderate	Low
Health Care Administration	Low	Moderate	Low
Health Care Delivery Services	Low	High	Low
Health Care Research and Practitioner Education	Low	Moderate	Low
Income Security			
General Retirement and Disability	Moderate	Moderate	Moderate
Unemployment Compensation	Low	Low	Low
Housing Assistance	Low	Low	Low
Food and Nutrition Assistance	Low	Low	Low
Survivor Compensation	Low	Low	Low
Law Enforcement			
Criminal Apprehension	Low	Low	Moderate
Criminal Investigation and Surveillance	Moderate	Moderate	Moderate
Citizen Protection	Moderate	Moderate	Moderate
Leadership Protection	Moderate	Low	Low
Property Protection	Low	Low	Low
Substance Control	Moderate	Moderate	Moderate

(Continued)

Table 14.4 Mission-Based Information Types [4] *Continued*

Information Type	Confidentiality	Integrity	Availability
Crime Prevention	Low	Low	Low
Trade Law Enforcement	Moderate	Moderate	Moderate
Litigation and Judicial Activities			
Judicial Hearings	Moderate	Low	Low
Legal Defense	Moderate	High	Low
Legal Investigation	Moderate	Moderate	Moderate
Legal Prosecution and Litigation	Low	Moderate	Low
Resolution Facilitation	Moderate	Low	Low
Federal Correctional Activities			
Criminal Incarceration	Low	Moderate	Low
Criminal Rehabilitation	Low	Low	Low
General Science and Innovation			
Scientific and Technological Research and Innovation	Low	Moderate	Low
Space Exploration and Innovation	Low	Moderate	Low
Knowledge Creation and Management			
Research and Development	Low	Moderate	Low
General Purpose Data and Statistics	Low	Low	Low
Advising and Consulting	Low	Low	Low
Knowledge Dissemination	Low	Low	Low
Regulatory Compliance and Enforcement			
Inspections and Auditing	Moderate	Moderate	Low
Standards Setting/Reporting Guideline Development	Low	Low	Low
Permits and Licensing	Low	Low	Low
Public Goods Creation and Management			
Manufacturing	Low	Low	Low
Construction	Low	Low	Low
Public Resources, Facility, and Infrastructure Management	Low	Low	Low
Information Infrastructure Management	Low	Low	Low
Federal Financial Assistance			
Federal Grants (NonState)	Low	Low	Low
Direct Transfers to Individuals	Low	Low	Low
Subsidies	Low	Low	Low
Tax Credits	Moderate	Low	Low
Credits and Insurance			
Direct Loans	Low	Low	Low
Loan Guarantees	Low	Low	Low
General Insurance	Low	Low	Low

(Continued)

Table 14.4 Mission-Based Information Types [4] *Continued*

Information Type	Confidentiality	Integrity	Availability
Transfers to State/Local Governments			
Formula Grants	Low	Low	Low
Project/Competitive Grants	Low	Low	Low
Earmarked Grants	Low	Low	Low
State Loans	Low	Low	Low
Direct Services for Citizens			
Military Operations	N/A	N/A	N/A
Civilian Operations	N/A	N/A	N/A

as the basis for determining the security objectives for the types of information that will be processed, transmitted, or stored in the cloud service. The sources of information include, but not limited to, the organizational input from key stakeholders (e.g., other federal agencies and State partners), the architectural descriptions of the "Healthcare Exchange," and EA reference models used to establish a business case.[11]

The "Federal Agency" established a business case[12] for the "Healthcare Exchange" information technology (IT) investment. The "Healthcare Exchange" provides a platform for organizing health information. The "Federal Agency" identified two mission-essential functions supported by the IT investment: *Exchange Systems* and *Data Services*. Through an evaluation of the architectural descriptions (e.g., architecture reference models, mission, and business processes, etc.), organizational inputs (laws, directives, policy guidance, etc.), and specific mission-based information,[13] management and support information[14] can be identified and categorized using information associated with the "Healthcare Exchange" as a point of reference to understand the potential impact due to a compromise in the confidentiality (C), integrity (I), and availability (A).

---

[11]From Office of Management and Budget (OMB). FY13 Guidance on Exhibit 300—Planning, Budgeting, Acquisition, and Management of IT Capital Assets. Washington, DC: Executive Office of the President, Office of Management and Budget; 2011. *"The business case must demonstrate the relationship between the investment and the business, performance, data, services, application and technology layers of the agency's EA."*

[12]A business case assists stakeholders in making decisions regarding the viability of a proposed project effort. The Office of Management and Budget (OMB) requires a business case as part of Part 7, Section 300. Additionally, business cases are considered standard practice throughout private and public industry in addition to specific laws and regulations that mandate business cases for certain project types.

[13]Information that is specific to individual departments and agencies or sets of departments and agencies.

[14]Information that supports the delivery of services or the management of resources.

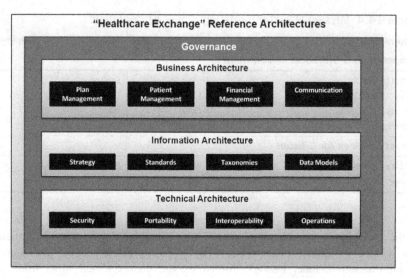

FIGURE 14.4

Exchange reference architecture framework.

The "Federal Agency" established an Exchange Reference Architecture,[15] as illustrated in Fig. 14.4, that defines the key business information and technical areas and also provides a high-level view of the business architecture,[16] information architecture (DRM),[17] and technical reference architecture (TRM).[18] The Exchange Reference Architecture[19] provides the description of the core business areas and

[15]From Office of Management and Budget (OMB). The Common Approach to Federal Enterprise Architecture. Washington, DC: Executive Office of the President, Office of Management and Budget; 2012. *"A 'Reference Architecture' is an authoritative source of information about a specific subject area that guides and constrains the instantiations of multiple architectures and solutions."*

[16]From Office of Management and Budget (OMB). FY2014 Guide on Exhibit 53 and 300— Information Technology and E-Government. Washington, DC: Executive Office of the President, Office of Management and Budget; 2012. *"Business Reference Model (BRM) a classification taxonomy used to describe mission sectors, business functions, and services that are performed within and between Federal agencies and with external partners."*

[17]From Office of Management and Budget (OMB). Consolidated Reference Model Version 2.3. Washington, DC: Executive Office of the President, Office of Management and Budget; 2007. *Data Reference Model (DRM) is "a flexible and standards-based framework to enable information sharing and reuse across the federal government via the standard description and discovery of common data and the promotion of uniform data management practices."*

[18]From Office of Management and Budget (OMB). Consolidated Reference Model Version 2.3. Washington, DC: Executive Office of the President, Office of Management and Budget; 2007. *Technical Reference Model (TRM) is a "technical framework categorizing the standards and technologies to support and enable the delivery of Service Components and capabilities."*

[19]Similar to the role of the enterprise architecture discussed in detail in Chapter 5, Applying the NIST Risk Management Framework.

Table 14.5 Key Data Definitions

Term	Definition
PII	As defined in OMB Memorandum M-07-16, PII refers to any "information which can be used to distinguish or trace an individual's identity, such as their name, social security number, biometric records, etc. alone, or when combined with other personal or identifying information which is linked or linkable to a specific individual, such as date and place of birth, mother's maiden name, etc." [7]
PHI	The HIPAA Privacy Rule defines PHI as individually identifiable health information that is held or transmitted in any form or medium by a covered entity [8]
IIHI	HIPAA defines IIHI as any information, including demographic information, collected from an individual that is created or received by a health care provider, health plan, employer or health care clearinghouse, and relates to the past, present, or future physical or mental health or condition of an individual; the provision of health care to an individual; or the past, present, or future payment for the provision of health care to an individual, and identifies the individual or where there is a reasonable basis to believe that the information can be used to identify the individual [9]
FTI	Federal Tax Returns and return information are confidential, as required by IRC Section 6103. The IRS uses the IRC to ensure that agencies, bodies, and commissions maintain appropriate safeguards to protect the information confidentiality [10]

processes in the Business Architecture that will be used to exchange information defined in the Information Architecture and supported through the implementation of the business and information requirements in the Technical Reference Architecture.

The "Federal Agency" also identified key data types in Table 14.5 to use as a basis for characterizing the types of information that will require the highest level of protection when conducting security categorization. In addition, a list of related laws, standards, guidelines, and organizational agreements for consideration was developed and mapped against the "Healthcare Exchange" participants as organizational inputs into the security categorization process.

Based on the case study used in this section, several potential information types may be selected by the "Federal Agency" such as:

- $SC_{\text{Access to Care Information Type}}{}^{20}$ = {(confidentiality, Low), (integrity, Moderate), (availability, Low)}.

---

[20]From Stine, K., Kissel, R., Barker, W., Lee, A., Fahlsing, J. NIST Special Publication (SP) 800-60 Revision 1, Volume II: Appendices to Guide for Mapping Types of Information and Information Systems to Security Categories. Maryland: National Institute of Standards and Technology; 2008. *This information includes streamlining efforts to receive care; ensuring care is appropriate in terms of type, care, intensity, location, and availability; providing seamless access to health knowledge, enrolling providers; performing eligibility determination, and managing patient movement.*

- $SC_{\text{Health Care Delivery Services Information Type}}{}^{21}$ = {(confidentiality, Low), (integrity, High), (availability, Low)}.
- $SC_{\text{Taxation Management Information Type}}{}^{22}$ = {(confidentiality, Moderate), (integrity, Low), (availability, Low)}.

TIP

Before categorizing the cloud service, the CSP conducts a comprehensive system inventory and creates a system description. This allowed the CSP to create two major architecture drawings that may or may not have been part of the Enterprise Architecture (EA). Most CSP's should have at least created a mission statement, data-flow, and network diagram of their security authorization boundary.

The process of identifying all of the information types stored, processed, or transmitted is not as straight forward as it may seem for the cloud service. Information types have been identified at a high-level based on the cloud service description. However, the CSP may need to gather additional information (developer, system administration, back-up guides) about every component in the authorization boundary, requiring the CSP to take additional time in reviewing the database schemas to understand all of the information types that will be used in their cloud service.

The FedRAMP FIPS 199 Categorization Template requires the CSP to provide the system description. For each information type they will have identified, NIST SP 800-60 provides a recommendation for confidentiality, integrity, and availability. Although NIST has made recommendations, the CSP may need to adjust the CIA (Confidentiality, Integrity, and Availability) provisional impact level for the cloud service to ensure the impact levels more closely align with how the information types used to meet our cloud services' specific requirements. Pay special attention to "Special Factors Affecting Confidentiality Impact Determination" in NIST SP 800-60 Volume 2 when selecting a higher or lower CIA. Whether the CSP adjusts the CIA up or down, the CSP will need to explain their rationale.

It is essential that the CSP understand all of the components that reside in their cloud service authorization boundary, including all corporate components outside the IaaS or PaaS boundary drawings and inventory. For example, the CSP may have an HR database that creates and feeds credentials to their user shares after a new employee is processed for their position. This component is important to the IaaS and may also be required to comply with the FedRAMP security control requirements.

SELECT SECURITY CONTROLS

The security control selection process relies on the definition of the security control boundary and a clear delineation of the security controls responsibility across service and deployment models. It also requires an understanding of any

---

[21]From Stine, K., Kissel, R., Barker, W., Lee, A., Fahlsing, J. NIST Special Publication (SP) 800-60 Revision 1, Volume II: Appendices to Guide for Mapping Types of Information and Information Systems to Security Categories. Maryland: National Institute of Standards and Technology; 2008. *This information includes assessing health status; planning health services; ensuring quality of services and continuity of care; and managing clinical information and documentation.*

[22]From Stine, K., Kissel, R., Barker, W., Lee, A., Fahlsing, J. NIST Special Publication (SP) 800-60 Revision 1, Volume II: Appendices to Guide for Mapping Types of Information and Information Systems to Security Categories. Maryland: National Institute of Standards and Technology; 2008. *This information includes activities associated with the implementation of the Internal Revenue Code and the collection of taxes in the United States and abroad.*

decomposition of cloud services into associated subsystems and the mapping of data flows to ensure that adequate protective measures are applied cost-effectively to sensitive data throughout the cloud service lifecycle.

The implementation of the "Healthcare Exchange" includes a complicated set of security and privacy requirements. Fig. 14.5 illustrates the different requirements derived from various laws, requirements, standards, guidelines, and control frameworks, in addition to any organization-specific requirements established by the information sharing agreement.[23] For example, under the Health Insurance Portability and Accountability Act of 1996 (HIPAA) Privacy and Security Rule, covered entities "must comply with the Rules' requirements to protect the privacy and security of health information and must provide individuals with certain rights with respect to their health information" [11]. These requirements could include the additional administrative, physical, and technical safeguards that exceed the security control requirements defined in the FedRAMP baseline security controls.[24]

Defining the boundary

The first step in the security control selection process is to define the boundary.[25] We have already covered this process earlier and cannot highlight the importance of doing this right the first time and keeping it up-to-date as the boundary changes. This provides the scope of protection for the system components and interfaces for interconnections and is critical for understanding and clarifying the shared responsibilities for implementing, monitoring, and assessing security controls allocated[26] across the various cloud service and deployment models. Although only conceptual, Fig. 14.6 provides a high-level illustration of the

[23]From Grance, T., Hash, J., Peck, S., Smith, J., Korow-Diks, K. NIST Special Publication (SP) 800-47, Security Guide for Interconnecting Information Technology Systems. Maryland: National Institute of Standards and Technology; 2002. *"Organizations should examine privacy issues related to data that will be exchanged or passed over the interconnection and determine whether such use is restricted under current statutes, regulations, or policies."*

[24]NIST Special Publication (SP) 800-66 Revision 1, *Introductory Resource Guide for Implementing the HIPAA Security Rule*, discusses security considerations and resources for use when implementing the requirements of the Security Rule.

[25]From Joint Task Force Transformation Initiative, NIST Special Publication (SP) 800-53 Revision 3, Recommended Security Controls for Federal Information System and Organizations. Maryland: National Institute of Standards and Technology; 2010. *"Well-defined boundaries establish the scope of protection for organizational information systems (i.e. what the organization agrees to protect under its direct management control or within the scope of its responsibilities) and include the people, processes, and information technologies that are part of the systems supporting the organization's missions and business processes."*

[26]From Joint Task Force Transformation Initiative, NIST Special Publication (SP) 800-53 Revision 3, Recommended Security Controls for Federal Information System and Organizations. Maryland: National Institute of Standards and Technology; 2010. *"Allocation is a term used to describe the process an organization employs: (i) to determine whether security controls are defined as system-specific, hybrid, or common; and (ii) to assign security controls to specific information system components responsible for providing a particular security capability (e.g. router, server, remote sensor)."*

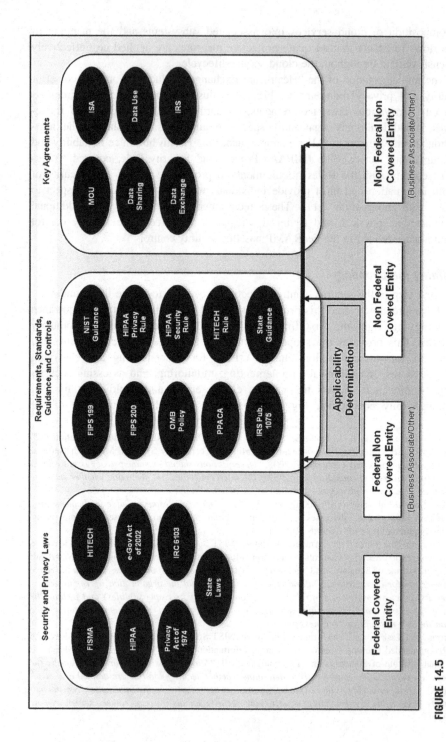

FIGURE 14.5

Laws, required standards, and guidance.

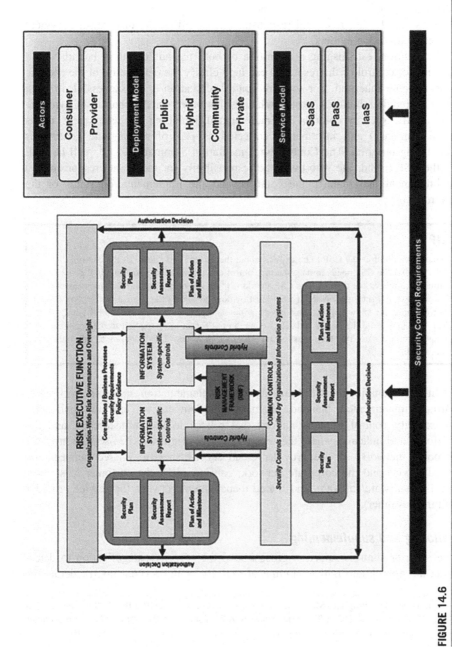

FIGURE 14.6

Security control allocation.

factors that might be considered when allocating security controls and assigning ownership between the CSP and the "Federal Agency." For example, identifying those controls that are inherited from one or more organizations (*common controls*) or are shared between one or more organizations (*hybrid controls*), requires establishing roles and responsibilities based on the different deployment models and service models.

In addition, establishing a definition of both the authorization boundary and the level of control of the resources can help clarify the delineation of the specific aspects being inherited. For security control allocation to be successful, in most cases, it requires building trusted relationships based on the sharing of evidence that specific security controls are implemented, including any assessment results (or a summary) and information collected as part of an ongoing continuous monitoring program. The Control Implementation Summary (CIS)[27] will be used by the CSP to indicate who owns the responsibility (or the shared responsibility) to implement and manage the controls, and the implementation status of the controls [12].

TIP

Inheritance requires the CSP to be explicit about the "what" and "how" of the control. Specifically, the CSP needs to describe the control and all of the specific details that are required to inherit the control. The CSP should explain not only the control implementation but also explicit information about what must be done to inherit the control or the "how." For example, we know that we must have a policy and procedure for each control family. The CSP may write the policy and select common but forget to be explicit to the organization inheriting the control that they must create their own procedure for the policy to fully inherit the control.

In this scenario, the CSP provides the implementation status (i.e., in-place, partially implemented, planned, alternative implementation, and not applicable) for security control implementations that relates to the infrastructure and the platform, and indicates where the security control originates (i.e., service provider corporate network, service provider cloud service-specific, shared between the cloud service and the corporate network, configured by the customer, customer-specific hardware/software, and shared management between the service provider and the customer).

Tailoring and supplementing

The security controls selection process uses the security categorization to determine the appropriate initial baseline of security controls (i.e., low, moderate, or

---

[27]From FedRAMP Program Management Office (PMO). FedRAMP FIPS 199 Categorization Template. Washington, DC: US General Services Administration; 2012. *"The CIS report includes control implementation responsibility and implementation status of the FedRAMP security controls."*

high) that will provide adequate protection for the information and information systems that reside within the cloud service environment. A cloud service may require the implementation of alternative or compensating security controls not included in the initial baseline, or adding additional security controls or enhancements to address unique organizational needs based on a risk assessment or organization-specific security requirements.

Tailoring and supplementing the baseline is important in our scenario as the FedRAMP baseline requirements will not only need to be met, but a gap analysis[28] will need to be performed against specific protection requirements based on the type of information being stored, processed, or transmitted (e.g., PII, PHI, FTI), but also regulatory requirements (e.g., HIPAA) or Agency-specific requirements. Although many of these controls can be mapped to the security and privacy requirements in NIST SP 800-53, some are very specific to the type of data (PII, PHI) and the additional control requirements (HIPAA and Agency Controls).

IMPLEMENT AND DOCUMENT SECURITY CONTROLS

Documenting security controls within the cloud service requires the CSP to describe how the security controls were implemented in the System Security Plan (SSP). In the previous section, security controls were allocated based on specific responsibilities (i.e., inherited by another organization, shared between organizations, or implemented by an organization). In the SSP, information system components will need to be described based on the authorization boundary. The SSP details how the implementations address each required security control and enhancement in the selected, tailored, and supplemented security control baseline, descriptions of roles and responsibilities, and expected behavior of individuals with system access [12].

In addition, some security controls may require developing supporting documentation. For example, Table 14.6 identifies some of the documents that will be implemented by the CSP for FedRAMP.

---

[28]FedRAMP Program Management Office (PMO). Guide to Understanding FedRAMP. Washington, DC: US General Services Administration; 2014. *"For each cloud system, agencies should review the implemented security controls, and perform a gap analysis using the FedRAMP security control baseline to identify which security controls are missing. A gap analysis identifies which new security controls must be implemented on the respective cloud system. The gap analysis can serve as an agenda item for meetings with the cloud service provider. Agencies will need to work in concert with their CSPs to implement missing security controls required by the FedRAMP baseline."*

Table 14.6 SSP Supporting Documents

Document Name	Security Control Requirement

IT Contingency Plan[a] (including Business Impact Analysis[b])	*CP-2—Contingency Plan* [13]
	
	The Cloud Service Provider (CSP):
	
	a. Develops a contingency plan for the information system that:
	  1. Identifies essential missions and business functions and associated contingency requirements;
	  2. Provides recovery objectives, restoration priorities, and metrics;
	  3. Addresses contingency roles, responsibilities, assigned individuals with contact information;
	  4. Addresses maintaining essential missions and business functions despite an information system disruption, compromise, or failure;
	  5. Addresses eventual, full information system restoration without deterioration of the security safeguards originally planned and implemented; and
	  6. Is reviewed and approved by *CSP-defined personnel or roles;*
	b. Distributes copies of the contingency plan to *CSP-defined key contingency personnel (identified by name and/or by role) and organizational elements;*
	c. Coordinates contingency planning activities with incident handling activities;
	d. Reviews the contingency plan for the information system *at least annually,*
	e. Updates the contingency plan to address changes to the organization, information system, or environment of operation and problems encountered during contingency plan implementation, execution, or testing;
	f. Communicates contingency plan changes to *CSP-defined key contingency personnel (identified by name and/or by role) and organizational elements;* and
	g. Protects the contingency plan from unauthorized disclosure and modification.
	
	Additional FedRAMP Requirements
	
	• For JAB authorizations the contingency lists include designated FedRAMP personnel.

Configuration Management Plan[c]	*CM-9—Configuration Management Plan* [13] The Cloud Service Provider (CSP) develops, documents, and implements a configuration management plan for the information system that: a. Addresses roles, responsibilities, and configuration management processes and procedures; b. Establishes a process for identifying configuration items throughout the system development life cycle and for managing the configuration of the configuration items; c. Defines the configuration items for the information system and places the configuration items under configuration management; and d. Protects the configuration management plan for unauthorized disclosure and modification.

Incident Response Plan[d]	*IR-9 – Incident Response Plan* [13] The Cloud Service Provider (CSP) responds to information spills by: a. Identifying the specific information involved in the information system contamination; b. Alerting *CSP-defined personnel or roles* of the information spill using a method of communication not associated with the spill; c. Isolating the contaminated information system or system component; d. Eradicating the information from the contaminated information system or component; e. Identifying other information systems or system components that may have been subsequently contaminated; and f. Performing other *CSP-defined actions.*
E-Authentication[e]	*IA-2 – Identification and Authentication (Organizational Users)* The information system uniquely identifies and authenticates organizational users (or processes acting on behalf of organizational users). *IA-8 – Identification and Authentication (Nonorganizational Users)* The information system uniquely identifies and authenticates nonorganizational users (or processes acting on behalf of nonorganizational users).
Privacy Threshold Analysis and Privacy Impact Assessment[f,g]	An analysis of how information is handled: (i) to ensure handling conforms to applicable legal, regulatory, and policy requirements regarding privacy; (ii) to determine the risks and effects of collecting, maintaining, and disseminating information in identifiable form in an electronic information system; and (iii) to examine and evaluate protections and alternative processes for handling information to mitigate potential privacy risks. [14]

[a]*NIST Special Publication (SP) 800-34 Revision 1, Contingency Planning Guide for Federal Information Systems contains sample Information System Contingency Plans for Low-Impact (A.1), Moderate-Impact (A.2), and High-Impact (A.3) systems. Available from: http://csrc.nist.gov/publications/nistpubs/800-34-rev1/sp800-34-rev1_errata-Nov11-2010.pdf.*

[b]*NIST Special Publication (SP) 800-34 Revision 1, Contingency Planning Guide for Federal Information Systems contains sample Business Impact Analysis Template (Appendix B). Available from: http://csrc.nist.gov/publications/nistpubs/800-34-rev1/sp800-34-rev1_errata-Nov11-2010.pdf.*

[c]*NIST Special Publication (SP) 800-128, Guide for Security-Focused Configuration Management of Information Systems contains sample outline for a Security Configuration Management Plan (Appendix D). Available from: http://csrc.nist.gov/publications/nistpubs/800-128/sp800-128.pdf.*

[d]*NIST Special Publication (SP) 800-61 Revision 2, Computer Security Incident Handling Guide contains a description of elements of the Incident Response Plan (Section 2.3.2—Plan Elements). Available from: http://csrc.nist.gov/publications/nistpubs/800-61rev2/SP800-61rev2.pdf.*

[e]*NIST Special Publication (SP) 800-63-2, Electronic Authentication Guide contains information on e-authentication. Available from: http://nvlpubs.nist.gov/nistpubs/SpecialPublications/NIST.SP.800-63-2.pdf. Additional information can be found at IDManagement.gov.*

[f]*Office of Management and Budget (OMB) Memorandum 03-22, OMB Guidance for Implementing the Privacy Provisions of the E-Government Act of 2002 provides guidance on conducting a privacy impact assessment (PIA). Available from: http://www.whitehouse.gov/omb/memoranda_m03-22.*

[g]*Joint Task Force Transformation Initiative. NIST Special Publication (SP) 800-53 Revision 4, Security and Privacy Controls for Information Systems and Organizations. Available from: http://nvlpubs.nist.gov/nistpubs/SpecialPublications/NIST.SP.800-53r4.pdf.*

> **TIP**
>
> When implementing security controls, one of the most important things the CSP can do is ensure that they have adopted and documented a security baseline for their system boundary. Poor implementation of a baseline will become very apparent when the CSP or the 3PAO conducts authenticated scans of the environment. Therefore, the CSP needs to decide how they are going to lock-down each type of technology deployed (facilities, hardware, firmware, software, and applications). The 3PAO is required to use the same type of scanners (static code, vulnerability, database, web, and application) the CSP uses to conduct ongoing assessments, therefore the CSP should be able to validate the baseline before engaging the 3PAO to conduct the test.
>
> Below are the pros and cons of the three most common baseline option referred to in NIST SP 800-70[29]:
>
> 1. DoD Security Technical Implementation Guides (STIGs)
>   a. Pros:
>   i. Provide extensive guidance on how to lock-down just about every type of technology
>   ii. Supported by the Security Content Automation Protocol (SCAP)
>   iii. Available from http://iase.disa.mil/ (some require PKI DoD Certificate for access)
>   b. Cons:
>   i. Very difficult and time-consuming if the CSP has never implemented STIGs Automation tools are very critical in the successful implementation
>   ii. The CSP must test each setting to ensure that it does not adversely affect the operation of their system – then write a deviation or risk acceptance of why the CSP is not implementing the setting.
> 2. Center for Internet Security (CIS) Baseline
>   a. Pros:
>   i. Strong commercial support and documentation
>   ii. Supported by the SCAP
>   b. Cons:
>   i. Can be very expensive to implement
>   ii. Some of the settings may not be acceptable and require the CSP to supplement with similar settings from DoD STIGs
> 3. CSP-Specific Baseline
>   a. Pros
>   i. Allows the CSP to select their security settings and map them to NIST SP 800-53 and other compliance requirements such as Payment Card Industry Data Security Standards (PCI DSS) or Health Insurance Portability and Accountability Act (HIPAA)
>   ii. Allows the CSP to tailor their baseline to their mission and compliance requirements
>   b. Cons:
>   i. Very time-consuming to create and maintain
>   ii. May cost more to get accessed by the 3PAO
>   iii. Not usually supported by the SCAP
>   iv. Some of the settings may not be acceptable and require the CSP to supplement with similar settings from DoD STIGs

---

[29]*National Checklist Program for IT Products—Guidelines for Checklist Users and Developers.* Available from: http://nvlpubs.nist.gov/nistpubs/SpecialPublications/NIST.SP.800-70r3.pdf.

ASSESSING SECURITY CONTROLS

The assessment of security controls is primarily driven by the security control assessor. Within FedRAMP, an accredited 3PAO performs and independently tests the CSP's cloud service to determine the effectiveness of security control implementation [15]. A discussion of the 3PAO's responsibilities is beyond the scope of this section. The CSP will need to be prepared for the assessment. Before the 3PAO conducts any security testing, the CSP may want to perform the entire test according to the FedRAMP templates, and collect and organize all of the evidence supporting the security control implementations as documented in the SSP. The CSP will also need to focus on fixing any critical or high risk security vulnerabilities and develop a Plan of Action and Milestones (POA&Ms).[30]

Once the 3PAO has completed conducting an assessment of the security controls, the Security Assessment Report (SAR)[31] is developed, which is used by the CSP as a source for identifying, documenting, and managing the mitigation[32] of "medium"[33] and "high"[34] risk security vulnerabilities.[35] The POA&M is a tool used by the CSP, FedRAMP, and the "Federal Agency" when tracking and reporting on the progress of remediating security weaknesses and deficiencies. The POA&M[36] addresses the specific tasks and resources, including a schedule for completing the remediation activities.

SUMMARY

This chapter presented a short case study to illustrate how the NIST RMF can be applied within the context of FedRAMP. In addition, some of the various FedRAMP deliverables were discussed as they relate to the security categorization, security control selection, and the implementation of the security controls (including supporting documentation) and documenting corrective actions resulting from the security controls assessment. Since the NIST RMF is a continuous process, documents will require regular reviews and updates on a continuous basis to address changes to the cloud service information system and the operating environment.

---

[30]Office of Management and Budget (OMB) Memorandum 02-01, Guidance for Preparing and Submitting Security Plans of Action and Milestones, preparing the plan of action and milestones (POA&Ms). Available from: http://www.whitehouse.gov/omb/memoranda_m02-01.
[31]From FedRAMP Program Management Office (PMO). Plan of Action and Milestones (Template). Washington, DC: US General Services Administration; 2012. *POA&Ms are based on the findings and recommendations of the SAR excluding any remediation actions taken.*
[32]FedRAMP specifies 90 days for "medium" and 30 days for "high."
[33]Vulnerabilities are labeled "medium" if they have a CVSS base score of 4.0−6.9.
[34]Vulnerabilities are labeled "high" if they have a CVSS base score of 7.0−10.0.
[35]The Common Vulnerability Scoring System (CVSS) standard provides guidance on scoring vulnerabilities. Available from: https://www.first.org/cvss/specification-document.
[36]The POA&M document is one of three key documents (*SSP, SAR,* and *POA&M*) used by the JAB to make a determination of a provisional authorization and the federal agency in making a determination for leveraging the cloud service.

REFERENCES

[1] FedRAMP Program Management Office (PMO). Guide to Understanding FedRAMP, V2.0. Washington, DC: US General Services Administration; 2014.

[2] FedRAMP Program Management Office (PMO). FedRAMP Security Assessment Framework Version 2.1. Washington, DC: US General Services Administration; 2015.

[3] FedRAMP Program Management Office (PMO). FedRAMP FIPS 199 Categorization Template. Washington, DC: US General Services Administration; 2012.

[4] Stine K, Kissel R, Barker W, Lee A, Fahlsing J. NIST Special Publication (SP) 800-60 Revision 1, Volume II: Guide for mapping types of information and information systems to security categories. Maryland: National Institute of Standards and Technology; 2008.

[5] Architecture and Infrastructure Committee. Federal segment architecture methodology version 10. Washington, DC: CIO Council; 2008.

[6] Stine K, Kissel R, Barker W, Fahlsing J, Gulick J. NIST Special Publication (SP) 800-60 Revision 1, Volume I: Guide for mapping types of information and information systems to security categories. Maryland: National Institute of Standards and Technology; 2008.

[7] Johnson C. Office of Management and Budget (OMB) memorandum 07-16, safeguarding against and responding to the breach of personally identifiable information. Washington, DC: Executive Office of the President, Office of Management and Budget; 2007.

[8] HIPAA Privacy Rule [Internet]. Washington, DC: US Government printing office [cited June 18, 2012]. <http://www.gpo.gov/fdsys/pkg/CFR-2010-title45-vol1/pdf/CFR-2010-title45-vol1-sec160-103.pdf>.

[9] Health Insurance Portability and Accountability Act of 1996 [Internet]. Washington, DC: US Government printing office [cited December 15, 2011]. <http://www.gpo.gov/fdsys/pkg/PLAW-104publ191/html/PLAW-104publ191.htm>.

[10] IRC Section 6103, Confidentiality and disclosure of returns and return information [Internet]. Washington, DC: US Government printing office [cited December 17, 2011]. <http://www.gpo.gov/fdsys/pkg/PLAW-104publ191/html/PLAW-104publ191.htm>.

[11] For Covered Entities [Internet]. Washington, DC: US Department of Health & Human Services [cited December 15, 2011]. <http://www.hhs.gov/ocr/privacy/hipaa/understanding/coveredentities/index.html>.

[12] FedRAMP Program Management Office (PMO). Guide to understanding FedRAMP version 1.1. Washington, DC: US General Services Administration; 2012.

[13] FedRAMP Program Management Office (PMO). FedRAMP High System Security Plan (SSP) Template [Internet]. Washington, DC: US General Services Administration [cited September 8, 2016]. <https://www.fedramp.gov/files/2016/07/FedRAMP-SSP-Template-High-2016-06-20-v01-00.docx>.

[14] Joint Task Force Transformation Initiative. NIST Special Publication (SP) 800-53 Revision 4, Security and Privacy Controls for Information Systems and Organizations. Maryland: National Institute of Standards and Technology; 2013.

[15] FedRAMP Program Management Office (PMO). FedRAMP Concept of Operations (CONOPS) version 1.0. Washington, DC: US General Services Administration; 2012.

Index

Note: Page numbers followed by "*f*," "*t*," and "*b*" refer to figures, tables, and boxes, respectively.

Printed in the United States
By Bookmasters